Official
Microsoft®
Internet
Explorer 4
Site Builder
Toolkit

Alan Simpson

Microsoft Press

PUBLISHED BY
Microsoft Press
A Division of Microsoft Corporation
One Microsoft Way
Redmond, Washington 98052-6399

Library of Congress Cataloging-in-Publication Data
Simpson, Alan, 1953-
    Official Microsoft Internet Explorer 4 Site Builder Toolkit
  Alan Simpson.
        p.   cm.
    Includes index.
    ISBN 1-57231-572-5
    1. Microsoft Internet Explorer.   2. Web sites--Design.   3. Web
publishing.   I. Title.
  TK5105.883.M53S56   1997
  005.2'76--dc21   97-26385
                                                                CIP

Printed and bound in the United States of America.

1 2 3 4 5 6 7 8 9 MLML 3 2 1 0 9 8

Distributed to the book trade in Canada by Macmillan of Canada, a division of Canada Publishing
Corporation.

A CIP catalogue record for this book is available from the British Library.

Microsoft Press books are available through booksellers and distributors worldwide. For further
information about international editions, contact your local Microsoft Corporation office. Or
contact Microsoft Press International directly at fax (425) 936-7329. Visit our Web site at
mspress.microsoft.com.

Acquisitions Editor: David Clark
Project Editors: Erin O'Connor, Ina Chang, Anne Taussig
Technical Editors: Kurt Meyer, Robert Lyon

To Susan, Ashley, Alec, Clifford, Lana, Tracker, Tigger,
FluffyFluffyBunBun, and all those fish
whose names I can't remember.

Contents
at a Glance

Table of Contents

Acknowledgments

Many thanks are due all the people at Microsoft Press who contributed to this project. Editor support from Erin O'Connor and Ina Chang. Technical editing by Kurt Meyer and Robert Lyon. Acquisitions by David Clark and Steve Guty. Thanks also to Anne Taussig, Bill Teel, Kim Eggleston, Devon Musgrave, Abby Hall, Steven Hopster, and Joel Panchot. And to everyone around that conference table at the meeting I was unprepared for.

Thanks to everyone at Waterside Productions, my literary agency, for making this opportunity happen.

And, of course, many thanks to Susan, Ashley, and Alec for putting up with yet another Daddy project and the long hours that go along with that.

Introduction

The lengthy title of this book is probably enough to get you wondering what this book is about and who it's written for. So I'll get right into that. In a nutshell, this book is for experienced HTML authors who want to add the many new tools and techniques that Microsoft Internet Explorer 4 brings to their world of creativity. The major authoring tools and techniques covered in this book include:

- Dynamic HTML
- Cascading Style Sheets
- VBScript
- Special effects with filters and transitions
- ActiveX
- Data binding
- Channels

That's a lot of stuff. And chances are you could write an entire book dedicated to each one of those topics. So why try to cover so much in a single book? Well, because these technologies are all interrelated. In fact, any web page that you create can use any combination of all these technologies. A broad understanding of what each of them is about will increase your creative potential.

WHO THIS BOOK IS FOR

If you're thinking, "I don't know what *any* of those technologies is about," that's OK. I'll tell you what they are and how to use them to build bigger, better, and more exciting web pages. However, I will assume that you're *not* new to authoring web pages. To use this book, you should already know:

- How to create a basic web page
- What HTML is about (basically)
- How to publish web pages

This book is for those who are already familiar with traditional HTML and are ready to expand on that knowledge. If you're a web-authoring newbie with no HTML experience, this book is sure to be over your head and will leave you feeling bewildered (and not too fond of me).

ANY SERVER WILL DO...

I'll bet that at least 90 percent of the web sites out there are published on "rented" web server space rather than on private web servers. For that reason, this book focuses heavily on authoring techniques that will work with *any* web server. I won't assume that you're using Microsoft Windows NT Server, Internet Information Server, Site Server, or any other particular server software. Nothing presented in this book requires that you own your own web server.

...BUT NOT JUST ANY BROWSER

Of course, on the client side of things, you *do* need to have Internet Explorer 4. Most of the new cutting-edge technologies described in this book will work only in Internet Explorer 4. However, Microsoft regularly submits specifications to the World Wide Web Consortium for future standards. So, if we're lucky, all of these emerging technologies might become the standard capabilities of all of tomorrow's web browsers. I sure hope so, because authoring in Dynamic HTML is a lot of fun. And there is *so* much you can do!

PART I

GETTING STARTED WITH DYNAMIC HTML

In these first five chapters, I'll introduce you to the tools and technologies that Internet Explorer 4 offers web authors and developers. All of these technologies share a similar goal—to give you, the web designer, a lot more creative freedom. The technologies I'll introduce are the "big four" that you'll use for all your web page creations: Dynamic HTML, Cascading Style Sheets (CSS), scripting (with VBScript), and the Dynamic HTML Object Model.

All of these technologies build on current-day HTML tags and techniques. As an experienced web author, you already have a leg up on learning all that's new. But there's a whole lot that's new, and there's a whole lot to learn. So let's get started....

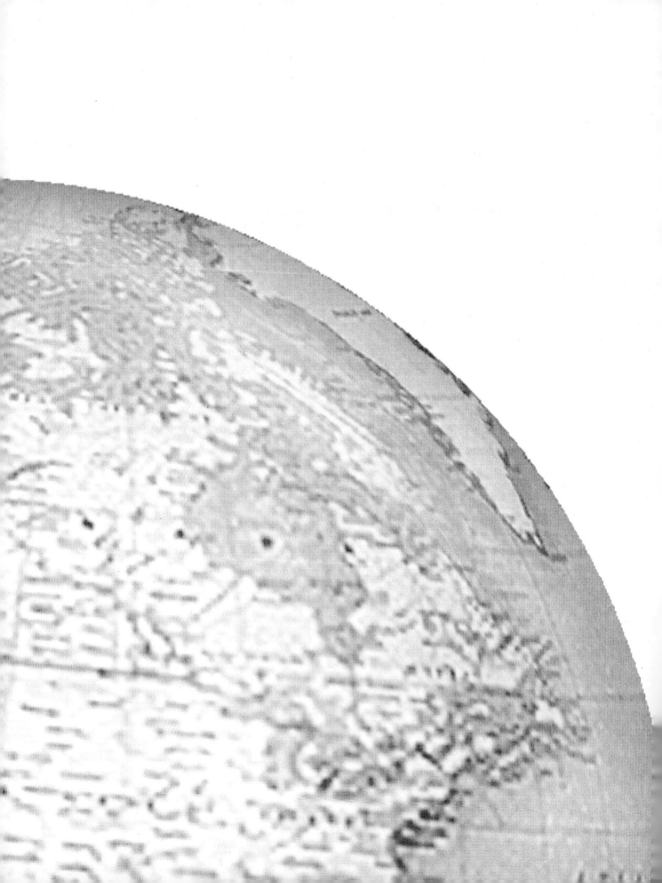

Chapter 1

Dynamic HTML Prerequisites

Dynamic HTML, which is new with Microsoft Internet Explorer 4, is a set of features that extends HTML and allows you, the web page author, to create more interactive web sites. For example, Dynamic HTML gives you the ability to control virtually anything in a web page. Dynamic HTML's foundation is HTML. So before we get deep into the nitty-gritty of Dynamic HTML and all the things that go into making rich, dazzling web sites, I'd like to "review" some of the basics of HTML. I'm hoping that this material is "review" to you because, as I mentioned in the introduction to this book, I'm assuming you already have some experience in building web sites. I won't be discussing the basics of "How to Create Your First Web Page" in this book.

Also in this chapter, I'd like to show you some tips for setting up your Microsoft Windows 95 Send To menu to simplify the task of editing your HTML files. So all in all, this chapter will cover:

■ What HTML documents are made of

■ Some common HTML tags and terminology

■ Wysiwyg tools for creating HTML documents

■ Using text editors to edit a web page's document source

■ Customizing your Send To menu to streamline your work

■ Using absolute and relative referencing to create links to other files

WHAT IS A WEB PAGE?

Hopefully you already know that the thing we call a web page is actually an HTML file. An HTML file, in turn, is a simple text file that contains text and markup tags. The markup tags are unique in that they are surrounded by angle brackets (<>), as in *<H1>*, *<B>*, *<BODY>*, and so forth. A relatively simple HTML file might look something like the example shown in Figure 1-1.

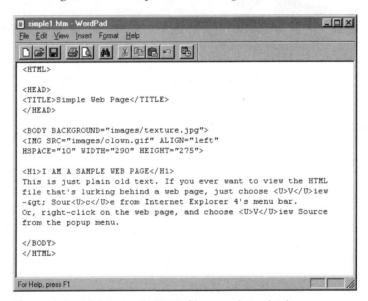

Figure 1-1. *A fairly simple HTML file named simple1.htm.*

Of course, Figure 1-1 is a view of the file through a simple text editor—WordPad in this example. A web browser such as Internet Explorer 4 will interpret the HTML tags to figure out how to present the page. It will also hide those tags from view. So if you were to view that sample page with Internet Explorer 4, the page would look more like Figure 1-2.

Figure 1-2. *The simple1.htm file viewed through Internet Explorer.*

Common HTML Tags

The tags in the simple1.htm file are pretty typical of web pages. The entire document is enclosed in a pair of *<HTML>...</HTML>* tags, which tell the web browser that this page is written in HTML.

The *<HEAD>...</HEAD>* tags identify the head of the document, where more information about the page might be stored. The title between the *<TITLE>...</TITLE>* tags appears in the web browser's title bar.

The *<BODY>...</BODY>* tags mark the body of the document. The body is the part that actually shows up in the web browser. In the simple1.htm file, the body tag contains one attribute, *BACKGROUND="images/texture.jpg"*. The *BACKGROUND* attribute tells the web browser to use a picture as the page's background. In this example, the name of that picture is texture.jpg. And texture.jpg is in a separate directory, named *images,* that's under the directory that the page itself is in. The *images/texture.jpg* part is what we call a *relative reference*. I'll talk more about relative references a little later in this chapter.

Below the body tag is an *<IMG...>* tag, which displays a graphic image. In this example, the image is a file named clown.gif. That file is in a directory named *images* beneath the directory that the page itself is on. This tag contains several attributes:

- *SRC* specifies the image file that's to be displayed in the page.

- *ALIGN* specifies how the image should be aligned with the surrounding text.

- *HSPACE* specifies the horizontal blank space next to the image so neighboring text doesn't touch the image.

- *WIDTH* specifies the width of the image in pixels.

- *HEIGHT* specifies the height of the image in pixels.

The *<H1>I AM A SAMPLE WEB PAGE</H1>* part displays text in the Heading1 style, which is larger than regular body text. The text that follows the closing *</H1>* tag appears as regular body text—not particularly large or particularly small, but just right for reading.

The *<U>...</U>* tags underline single characters in the words <u>V</u>iew and Sou<u>rc</u>e. The *</BODY>* tag marks the end of the body of the document, and the *</HTML>* tag marks the end of the document.

I hope that nothing I've told you so far qualifies as "news," because this is the kind of stuff I'm assuming you already know. Now let's talk about some of the different ways that you can create HTML documents.

CREATING HTML DOCUMENTS

In the olden days (a couple of years ago), people had to create web pages by actually typing all those little HTML tags manually. There are some major disadvantages to that approach. For one thing, it's really hard to tell what the page is going to look like when you're typing up a document that looks like simple1.htm back in Figure 1-1. For another, it's way too easy to make mistakes, because it's difficult to remember the exact name and spelling of every single HTML tag and attribute.

Fortunately, we now have wysiwyg (what-you-see-is-what-you-get) HTML editors that let you put together a web page in much the same way that you put together a word processing document. You just type your text, apply formatting with point-and-click ease, and insert pictures. What you see on the screen as you're typing closely resembles what the page will look like in a web browser. As you type the document, the wysiwyg editor automatically puts in all the appropriate tags for you. So you don't have to memorize every single tag and attribute.

You'll find dozens of wysiwyg HTML editors on the market today. A few that come to mind right off the bat are Microsoft's FrontPage Express (which is a freebie that comes with Internet Explorer 4), Microsoft FrontPage (which isn't a freebie), and Netscape Composer (which is part of the Netscape Communicator package). Actually, Microsoft Word 97 is another darn good wysiwyg HTML editor!

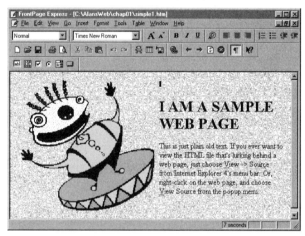

Figure 1-3. *The simple1.htm file viewed through Microsoft's FrontPage Express editor.*

If you already have a favorite wysiwyg HTML editor, you can continue to use it for your Dynamic HTML pages because Dynamic HTML builds on HTML. So any editor that can help you create HTML documents can also help you create Dynamic HTML.

If you don't already have a favorite wysiwyg HTML editor, you'd do well to pick one and learn to use it before you go any further in this book. It doesn't matter much which editor you use, because you'll use it only to design the basic layout of the page. The more advanced topics discussed in this book require "tweaking" the static HTML that most wysiwyg editors create for you. You use a simple text editor to do the tweaking.

CHOOSING YOUR TEXT EDITOR(S)

For the Dynamic HTML jockey, a simple text editor is just as important as a wysiwyg HTML editor. That's because many situations require getting right to the document source—the raw HTML and text—to make changes. Most people use Notepad, which comes with Windows 95, as their text editor. And in fact, Notepad is the default text editor that Internet Explorer uses when you ask to view the document's source.

Let's suppose you're viewing your web page in Internet Explorer 4. You have a sudden urge to tweak the source document. When you choose Source from the View menu, the source appears in Notepad, as in the example shown in Figure 1-4.

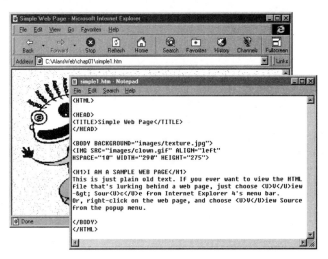

Figure 1-4. *The source document is ready for editing in Notepad.*

You can do your editing right in Notepad and then choose Exit from the File menu when you're done. Be sure to choose Yes when you're asked about saving your changes.

Initially, Internet Explorer 4 *won't* show the effects of your changes, because it's still displaying the copy it loaded before you made your changes. However, if you click the Refresh button, Internet Explorer will reload the page from the disk and your changes will be visible.

If you happen to be editing your page in FrontPage Express or FrontPage 97, and you want to get to the source, just choose HTML from the View menu. The document source will appear in a special editing window, as in the example shown in Figure 1-5. Type your changes and choose OK. FrontPage Express or FrontPage 97 will display your changes automatically. To view the source in FrontPage 98, just click the HTML tab at the bottom of the FrontPage Editor window.

TIP You can also get to a text editor from the FrontPage Explorer. Just right-click on the page you want to edit, choose Open With, select a text editor, and click OK.

Figure 1-5. *The FrontPage Express built-in text editor.*

In Microsoft Word 97, you just choose HTML Source from the View menu to get to your underlying source. Make your changes, and then click the Exit HTML Source button. When asked about saving your changes, choose Yes, and Word will automatically show you the updated page.

CREATING A GREAT AUTHORING ENVIRONMENT

If you plan to use many different tools to create and edit web pages, web page graphics, and so forth, you can make life simpler by customizing your Windows 95 Send To menu. Doing so allows you to right-click any file and then send it to the program of your choice. For example, you might want to right-click an .htm or .html file and send it to a web browser for viewing or send it to a text editor for editing. This is much more efficient than opening a program such as WordPad and then using File-Open within that program to find the file you want to edit.

TIP If you use FrontPage to create and edit web pages, you might want to customize the FrontPage Explorer's Open With Editor dialog box rather than your Send To menu. See "Customizing the FrontPage Explorer's Open With Editor Dialog Box" on page 14.

Customizing your Send To menu is pretty easy. Here are the exact steps:

1. Using My Computer, open your C: drive, open your Windows folder, and then open the Send To folder.

2. Size and position the Send To window so it's off to one corner of the screen. If necessary, you can close all open windows except the Send To window. In Figure 1-6, I've positioned the Send To window near the upper-right corner of the screen.

3. Right-click the Start button and choose Open.

4. Open the Programs folder, and then size and position its window so you can easily see its contents as well. In Figure 1-6, I've positioned the Programs window down near the lower-left corner of the screen.

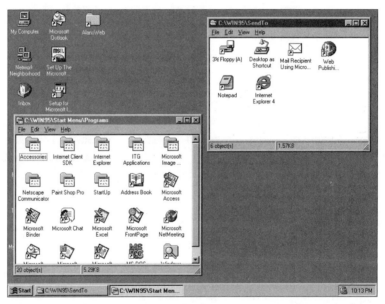

Figure 1-6. *Folder windows for the Programs group and the Send To menu.*

5. The Programs window now shows you the same programs and program groups that are available on the Start-Programs menu. In this view, however, you can easily drag-and-drop the shortcut icons for the various programs.

6. To add a program to your Send To menu, just copy that program's shortcut icon from the Programs window over to the Send To window, as discussed in the next section, "Copying Program Shortcuts."

7. You can repeat Step 6 as necessary to copy as many shortcut icons as you want over to the Send To window. When you finish, just close all open windows.

The next time you right-click any document icon and choose Send To, all the program shortcuts you copied to the Send To window will be available for selection, as in Figure 1-7.

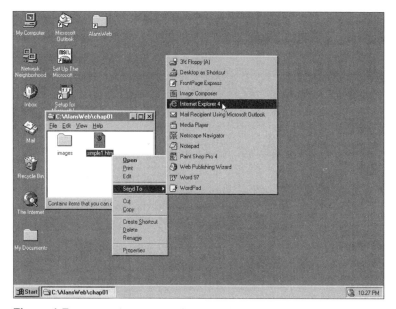

Figure 1-7. *My Send To menu after I added several programs to it.*

Copying Program Shortcuts

When adding programs to your Send To menu, you want to simply create a shortcut icon to the program. You don't want to actually copy the program to the Send To window. You can identify a shortcut icon by the little curved arrow at the lower-left corner of the icon. When you copy icons from the Programs window, many of the icons will already be shortcut icons. So you just need to right-drag (drag using the right mouse button) the icon from the Programs window, drop it into the Send To window, and then choose Copy Here. Don't just drag-and-drop with the left mouse button, or you'll *move* the shortcut icon to the Send To window, which means it will no longer be available from the Start-Programs menu!

Feel free to explore all the folders in the Programs window to see which programs have shortcut icons. When you come across a program that you might want to send a file to, just copy that program's shortcut icon over to the Send To window. It's easy! For example, my Send To menu gives me quick access to my text editors (Notepad and WordPad), graphics editors (Image Composer and Paint Shop Pro), Internet Explorer, FrontPage Express, and other programs that I often use to create documents. If you follow suit, you'll find it very easy to open a document in the program of your choice right from the Windows 95 My Computer, Explorer, or Find windows.

Customizing the FrontPage Explorer's Open With Editor Dialog Box

If you use the FrontPage Explorer to manage your web site, you can customize its Open With Editor dialog box to give yourself access to multiple tools on your PC. The process is different from that used in the Windows 95 desktop, but it's still pretty easy:

> **NOTE** In this book, I am not assuming that you own FrontPage. If you don't have FrontPage, don't worry about it. I offer this tidbit of advice only as a convenience for those readers who do have FrontPage.

1. Open the FrontPage Explorer.

2. Choose Options from the Tools menu, and then click the Configure Editors tab.

3. To add a new program, click the Add button and fill in the blanks in the dialog box that appears. Note that it's not necessary to define a full extension for every program, so you can avoid conflicts with existing editors. For example, you can use .h* and .ht* to define text editors for HTML files. Use g*, .gi*, j*, .jp* to define graphics editors for GIF and JPEG files.

4. Repeat Step 3 to add as many programs as you want. Figure 1-8 shows an example in which I've added WordPad and Paint Shop Pro as external editors.

5. Click the OK button when you're done.

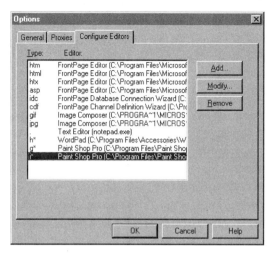

Figure 1-8. *WordPad and Paint Shop Pro have been added to the FrontPage Explorer as external editors.*

In the future, you can right-click on any file name in the FrontPage Explorer and choose Open With. Then select your editor from the list in the Open With Editor dialog box. Figure 1-9 shows an example.

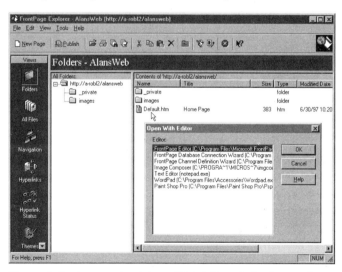

Figure 1-9. *A customized Open With Editor dialog box in the FrontPage 98 Explorer.*

Now onto an altogether different, yet vitally important, topic for web authors—absolute and relative referencing within, and between, your web pages.

ABSOLUTE VS. RELATIVE REFERENCING

In this book, I'll often use the terms "absolute reference" and "relative reference." I'm sure that many of you veteran web authors are quite familiar with these concepts. However, if you've been using wysiwyg HTML editors—which take care of all your pages' references automatically—you might not be familiar with these terms. Since we'll be tweaking the HTML manually in this book, it's important for you to understand how absolute and relative references work. So I'd like to take a moment now to discuss those terms.

Web pages contain lots of references to other files on the Internet. For example, take a look at the following hyperlink:

```
<A HREF="http://www.coolnerds.com">Go to Coolnerds</A>
```

When viewed through a web browser, the text between the tags appears as a hyperlink, usually blue and underlined—something like this:

Go to Coolnerds

Any visitor who clicks on that underlined text will be taken to the home page at http://www.coolnerds.com.

In this example, the URL http://www.coolnerds.com is an *absolute reference*. It's absolute in that it takes the visitor to a very specific place on the Internet.

When you're authoring pages on your own PC, in many instances you'll want to use a *relative reference* rather than an absolute reference. In fact, any time you're making a link to a file within your own web site (as opposed to someone else's web site), you'll probably want to use a relative reference. Doing so is the only way to be sure that the link will work on your local PC as well as after the pages are uploaded to the web server.

A relative reference doesn't contain a full URL. Rather, it just points to a local file. For example, the following hyperlink, when clicked, will send the reader to a page called page2.htm. However, it will work only if page2.htm is in the same directory as the page that contains the hyperlink.

```
<A HREF="page2.htm">Go to Page 2</A>
```

The concept of relative referencing isn't limited to *<A HREF=...>* tags. For example, here's an *<IMG>* (image) tag that uses a relative reference to display a picture named mygif.gif. The reference assumes that mygif.gif is in the same directory as the page that contains the tag.

```
<IMG SRC="mygif.gif" HEIGHT=100 WIDTH=50>
```

Below are a couple of tags used to play a midi file as the background sound track for the current page. The *<BGSOUND>* tag is supported only by Internet Explorer; the *<EMBED>* tag is supported by Netscape Navigator and Internet Explorer. Both tags use a relative reference to play a midi file named mymidi.mid, which is, presumably, in the same directory as the page that contains the tag.

```
<BGSOUND SRC="mymidi.mid">
<EMBED SRC="mymidi.mid" AUTOSTART=TRUE HIDDEN=TRUE>
```

All of the sample tags and relative references will work just fine in a web site in which all the files are in one directory on the web server. Problems can arise, however, when you start adding subdirectories to your web server home directory, because the relative links must point to the correct subdirectory as well as the correct file name. Let me give you an example of what I mean.

> **WARNING** Many UNIX web servers are case-sensitive to directory and file names. This means the link won't work if all the uppercase and lowercase letters don't match. To play it safe, you can make up a simple rule, such as using only lowercase letters in directory and file names.

Suppose you decide to store your home page and perhaps some other pages in your web server home directory (or root directory, as it's also called). You decide to put all your image files in a subdirectory named *images,* and your sound and music files in another subdirectory named *sounds*. And, just for the sake of example, you create a subdirectory named misc1 and, within misc1, another subdirectory named misc2. So your directory tree ends up looking like Figure 1-10.

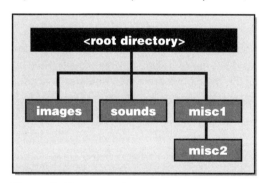

Figure 1-10. *A hypothetical directory tree. The site's home page is in the <root directory>.*

The relationships between the directories can be expressed as follows. The root directory is the *parent* to the images, sounds, and misc1 directories. The images, sounds, and misc1 directories are *siblings,* because they're at the same level. (They all share the same parent.) You could also say that images, sounds, and misc1 are all *children* of the root directory. The misc2 directory is a child of the misc1 directory. And misc1 is the immediate parent of misc2, because it's right above misc2.

When typing your relative references, you need to keep in mind some basic rules. The first rule is that when you type just a file name as a reference, as in SRC="myfile.gif", the link will work *only* if myfile.gif is in the current directory. By "current directory" I mean "the directory that stores the page that contains this link." (In other words, a relative reference is always relative to the page that contains the HTML tag that specifies the link.)

If the file you're referring to is not in the current directory, you need to use a particular syntax to specify the path to the correct directory. In a nutshell, that syntax consists of three things: a directory name, two dots (..) to refer to the parent directory, and forward slashes to separate directory and file names. The basic rules of the syntax are as follows:

■ *directoryName/* refers to the directory named *directoryName* but works only if that directory is immediately beneath the current directory.

■ *../* refers to the parent directory—the directory above the current directory.

WARNING Even though MS-DOS and Windows use backslashes (\) to separate directory and file name, HTML always uses forward slashes (/). Also, in Windows 95, directories are called "folders."

Let's take a look at some specific examples. Suppose you're authoring a web page that's in the root directory. In that page, you want to display an image named mygif.gif, and it just so happens that mygif.gif is in the images directory. Since the current directory (the one that contains the page you're writing) is directly above the images directory, the correct tag would be:

```
<IMG SRC="images/mygif.gif">
```

Likewise, let's say you want to embed a sound file named mymidi.mid in that page. The sound files are in the sounds directory, which again is directly below the current directory. So the correct tags are:

```
<BGSOUND SRC="sounds/mymidi.mid">
<EMBED SRC="sounds/mymidi.mid" AUTOSTART=TRUE HIDDEN=TRUE>
```

Now, let's say you're authoring a page that will be stored in the misc1 directory, and within that page, you want to add a hyperlink back to your home page. Your home page, named index.htm, is in the root directory. Since the root directory is directly above the misc1 directory, the correct hyperlink will look something like this:

```
<A HREF="../index.htm">Go Home</A>
```

What if you want to show an image named mygif.gif from the images directory in this page that's in the misc1 directory? You can't refer to that image file as images/mygif.gif because the images directory is not directly below the misc1 directory. The images directory is "next to" (at the same level as) the misc1 directory. So you have to define a path that tells the browser how to get to the images directory. The path is, in English, "Up one level, and then down to the *images* directory from there." The syntax for expressing that will look like

```
<IMG SRC="../images/mygif.gif">
```

where ../ points up from the current directory to the root, and images/ points down from there into the images directory.

If you want to embed a sound file in a page that's in the misc1 directory, again the path needs to point up to the parent directory and then down to the sounds directory. For example, to play mymidi.mid from the sounds directory in a page that's stored in the misc1 directory, you use the following tags:

```
<BGSOUND SRC="../sounds/mymidi.mid">
<EMBED SRC="../sounds/mymidi.mid" AUTOSTART=TRUE HIDDEN=TRUE>
```

And what if you're creating a page in the misc2 directory? Well, if you want to create a hyperlink to the home page, index.htm, which is up in the parent directory, you need to point upward two levels, like this:

```
<A HREF="../../index.htm">Go Home</A>
```

How about if a page in the misc2 directory needs to show the mygif.gif file from the images directory? Well, the path is two levels up to the root and then down to the images directory. So the correct tag here is:

```
<IMG SRC="../../images/mygif.gif">
```

Table 1-1 on the next page presents a summary of the syntax used to express absolute and relative references. Most wysiwyg HTML editors do a pretty good job of creating, automatically, the correct relative references to other files in your site. However, when you go in and start writing your own tags or tweaking existing tags, it's your responsibility to get them right. Remember, too, that the relative reference is always relative to the directory that contains the current page (the page you're working on that contains the reference).

Table 1-1

EXAMPLES OF ABSOLUTE AND RELATIVE REFERENCES

Example	Type	Points to
SRC="http://www.coolnerds.com"	Absolute	A specific URL on the Web
SRC="myfile.ext"	Relative	Same directory
SRC="subdir/myfile.ext"	Relative	Child—a subdirectory immediately below the current directory
SRC="../myfile.ext"	Relative	Parent directory
SRC="../direc/myfile.ext"	Relative	Sibling directory—same level as current directory

ELECTRONIC HTML RESOURCES

If, after reading this chapter, you think that maybe you've gotten in over your head, you can look at some additional resources to get caught up on HTML basics. If you already have a favorite HTML editor, its documentation and built-in help can also be valuable sources of information.

If you need more information on creating web pages, a trip to your local bookstore will probably yield dozens of books on HTML basics and creating your first web site. Electronic documents and sites that can offer assistance with HTML are listed below.

■ *Dynamic HTML Reference* is an easy-to-use Windows help file that acts as a good "pop-up" reference on your screen. It's available as HTMLRef.zip from www.microsoft.com/workshop/author/dynhtml/.

■ *A Beginner's Guide to HTML* at www.ncsa.uiuc.edu/General/Internet/ WWW/HTMLPrimer.html is a good place to brush up on basic HTML.

■ *HTML Goodies* lets you learn about specific aspects of HTML, such as forms and frames. Stop by www.htmlgoodies.com.

If you have any problems getting on any of these sites, or if you want to check out my current and complete selection of HTML-related web sites, stop by www.coolnerds.com and check out my Links section.

SUMMARY

I'd like to sum up this chapter by saying that basic, "static" HTML is an important part of Dynamic HTML. In this book, I'm assuming that you're already familiar with HTML basics and ready to move on to those features that make Dynamic HTML newer, bigger, and better. In this chapter, I did briefly review some HTML basics, just to make sure we're on the same wavelength. The main points are as follows:

■ All web pages contain text as well as HTML tags that format the text, provide hyperlinks, display pictures and multimedia files, and so forth.

■ All HTML tags are enclosed in angle brackets, as in *<H1>* and *<BODY>*.

■ Many HTML tags include attributes. For example, the tag *<BODY BACKGROUND="myimage.gif">* specifies a value for the *BACKGROUND* attribute of that tag.

■ Many modern HTML editors are available for creating HTML files in a wysiwyg manner.

■ When dealing with more advanced features of Dynamic HTML, you'll probably need to go beyond your wysiwyg editor's capabilities and edit the HTML source directly using a text editor such as Notepad or WordPad.

■ Adding frequently used programs to your Windows 95 Send To menu is easy and can speed up your work flow considerably.

■ FrontPage users can gain easy access to external editing programs by customizing the Open With Editors dialog box in the FrontPage Explorer.

■ When you're editing HTML pages manually, be sure that any references to files outside the current page obey the rules of absolute and relative referencing.

Chapter 2

Introducing Cascading Style Sheets

HTML lets you define the *structure* of a web page. But it really doesn't let you define the exact appearance of the page. For instance, you can mark a chunk of text as a Heading 1 using the *<H1>* tag, but you can't really say exactly how you want all your Heading 1 tags to look. So, for example, you can't make up a rule that says, "Show all my H1 tags in Arial 18-point bold italic blue text." You can, however, do that sort of thing using *CSS*—cascading style sheets.

CSS is a very important element in the overall Dynamic HTML picture because you can do a lot to change the appearance of text, interactively, just by altering the style of the text. You can also use CSS to exactly position certain elements, such as pictures, on the page and even move those elements around to create animations. So in this chapter, I'll teach you what CSS is all about and show you how to incorporate CSS into your web designs. Specifically, I'll cover:

■ What CSS brings to web authoring

■ How to create styles

■ When to use external, embedded, and inline style sheets

- Why they're called "cascading" style sheets
- How to define "custom tags" with class names and the *<DIV>* and *<SPAN>* tags
- CSS shortcuts
- A quick reference to all the CSS attributes

WHY BOTHER WITH CASCADING STYLE SHEETS?

Just about every written document, including books, magazine articles, and web pages, uses certain *design elements* to format sections of text to look alike. For example, a Heading 1 design element is usually some large font that identifies all the main topic sections in a chapter, article, or web page. A Heading 2 design element identifies all the subtopic headings. HTML includes a tag for virtually all the commonly used design elements, including headings (*<H1>*, *<H2>*, ...*<H6>* tags), lists (the *<OL>* tag for ordered lists, the *<UL>* tag for unordered lists), and so forth.

In the past, the *<H1>* tag in nearly everyone's web site looked the same— black text that was considerably larger than normal body text. If you wanted to make your own headings unique, you had to format each heading tag individually, using *<FONT>* or similar tags. If you later changed your mind about the appearance of those headings, you had to go back and change every single heading individually. A slow and laborious process!

Cascading style sheets change all that. With a style sheet, you can make a "global statement," such as "I want all my *<H1>* headings to be green." You have to say that only once, and every *<H1>* head in your web site will be green. Should you later decide that blue would be a better color, you don't have to go back and individually change each *<H1>* tag to the color blue. Instead, you just have to change the style—the "rule"—to "I want all my *<H1>* headings to be blue," and bingo, all the *<H1>* heads are blue.

You're certainly not limited to headings, nor to the color blue. You can define a custom style for virtually every design element in your web site, including headings, lists, tables, and graphic images, to name a few. And, in addition to defining a color, you can define the font, size, alignment, border thickness, and so forth. This is really cool because you can still use all the basic HTML tags you're already familiar with, such as *<H1>*, *<TABLE>*, and so forth. But you can give your web site a totally unique appearance simply by defining your own style for each of those tags. And you can get the kind of precise control over appearance that was formerly available only in desktop publishing and sophisticated word processing programs.

HOW TO CREATE STYLES

Every style you create will be defined as a CSS *rule*. Each rule must use the following syntax:

```
element {attribute: value[; attribute: value...]}
```

Here's an explanation of the syntax:

- *element*—describes the design element to which the style is to be applied. Same as the HTML tag but without the angle brackets. This part of the rule is sometimes called the *selector*.

- *attribute*—the specific aspect of the element that you want to stylize. Must be a valid CSS attribute name, such as *font-size* or *color*.

- *value*—the setting applied to the attribute. Must be a valid setting for the attribute in question, such as *20pt* (20 points) for font-size, or *blue* or *#0000FF* for color.

- *attribute: value*—the *declaration* portion of the rule. You can assign multiple declarations if you separate them with semicolons (;). Do not put a semicolon after the last declaration.

Now for some examples. Here's a CSS rule that specifies that all level-1 headings (*<H1>* tags) be displayed with a 36-point font:

```
H1 {font-size: 36pt}
```

Here's a sample rule that says all level-2 headings (*<H2>* tags) must be in 24-point size and colored blue. Note the semicolon between the two declarations.

```
H2 {font-size: 24pt; color: blue}
```

> **NOTE** Color names and RGB color values such as *#C0C0C0* are discussed in Appendix C.

You can put line breaks and blank spaces within the rule if you like. Doing so can make it easier to see all the declarations and make sure you've put all the semicolons and curly braces in the correct place. For example, here's a rule that says paragraphs will be in Times font, 12-point, blue, and indented one-half inch from the left edge of the page:

```
P {font-family: Times;
   font-size: 12pt;
   color: blue;
   margin-left: 0.5in}
```

Notice how easy it is to see all the declarations applied to the paragraph (P) element, and to verify that every declaration except the last one is followed by the required semicolon character. A little later in this chapter, I'll list all the valid CSS attributes that you can use in defining your own rules. But first, let's see where you put these CSS rule thingies.

WHERE THE STYLES GO

You can define CSS rules in three possible places. And as a matter of fact, you can use any combination of the three methods in your web sites. How the rules interact with one another is where the "cascading" part comes in, as I'll discuss in a moment. But the three places are: 1) in a separate document outside all HTML documents, 2) in the head of a document, and 3) right inside the HTML tag. Each of these methods has a name and affects the HTML pages in your web site in different ways, as discussed here:

■   *External*—External means you put the CSS rules in a separate file, and then your HTML page can link to this file. This approach lets you define rules in one or more files that can be applied to any page in your web site.

■   *Embedded*—Embedded means you specify the CSS rules in the document head. Embedded rules affect the current web page only.

■   *Inline*—Inline means you specify the CSS rules right inside the HTML tag. These affect only the current tag.

Now let's discuss how you go about setting up the external, embedded, and inline CSS rules.

External Styles

To define a set of style rules that you can easily apply to any page in your web site, you need to put the rules into a text file. You can create that file with any simple text editor, such as Notepad or WordPad, and give its file name the .css extension. Save the .css file in the same directory as your home page.

Whenever you want to use those styles in a new web page you're creating, just put a *<LINK>* tag in the head that refers to that .css file. Let me give you an example so you can see exactly how it's done.

Figure 2-1 shows a text file named mystyles.css typed up in Notepad. Notice that the .css file does not contain any HTML tags and has the following structure:

css rules

That simple format will work for any number of styles you want to create. In the example shown in the figure, notice that I've created CSS rules for the H1, H2, and P elements.

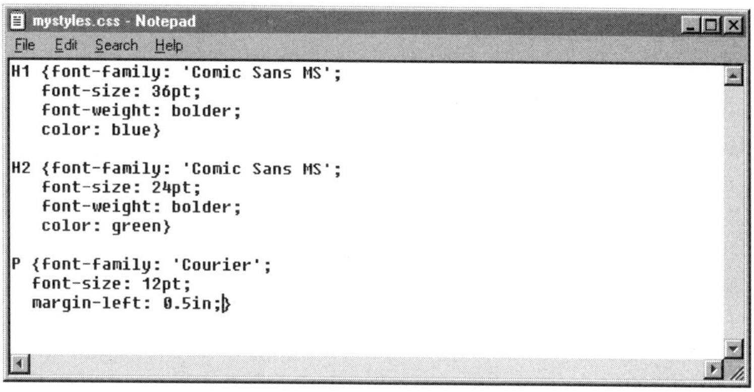

Figure 2-1. *A sample .css text file in Notepad.*

To use the styles defined in your .css file in any web page, you need to add the following tag to the head of the page, where *filename* is an absolute or relative reference to the .css file.

```
<LINK REL="STYLESHEET" HREF="filename" TYPE="text/css">
```

For example, assuming that I saved my .css file in the same directory as my home page and that I wanted to apply those styles to my home page, I would need to put this tag somewhere between the *<HEAD>...</HEAD>* tags of my home page:

```
<LINK REL="STYLESHEET" HREF="mystyles.css" TYPE="text/css">
```

Figure 2-2 on the next page shows an example in which the entire document is visible. Notice that other than the *<LINK...>* tag in the head, the rest of the tags look like standard HTML.

Figure 2-3, also on the next page, shows how the extsty.htm file looks when opened up in Microsoft Internet Explorer. Although you can't tell in the figure, the first heading is indeed blue and the second is green. Both headings use the Comic Sans MS font. The body text between the *<P>...</P>* tags is indented one-half inch from the left margin and displayed in Courier font, as the external style sheet dictates.

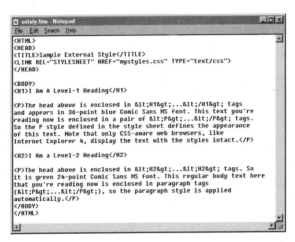

Figure 2-2. *A sample HTML document named extsty.htm that includes a link to mystyles.css.*

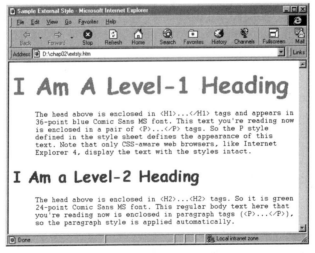

Figure 2-3. *The extsty.htm page as it looks in Internet Explorer.*

NOTE Fonts in a web page work only if the client PC has them installed. If a specified font is not installed, the default font for the element is shown instead. For example, text appears in Comic Sans MS font only on computers that have that font installed. It is possible to have the font downloaded to the user's computer. For more information, see *Typography on the Web* at www.microsoft.com/truetype/web/ and Chapter 10.

Now let me illustrate one of the great beauties of an external style sheet. Suppose I've created a whole bunch of pages for this web site and put that *<LINK REL="STYLESHEET" HREF="mystyles.css"...>* tag in the head section of all those pages. Every one of those pages will, of course, show its headings and text according to the rules defined in mystyles.css. But let's say I decide that I don't like the big gap between the headings and body text in those pages. I want to reduce that gap in all the pages. Simple! I just open up mystyles.css in my trusty text editor and take out some pixels from the top margin of the paragraph style. I can use the CSS margin-top attribute with a setting of –20px (minus 20 pixels) to do that. Here's how the CSS rule for the P element looks in mystyles.css after I make that change:

```
P {font-family: 'Courier';
   font-size: 12pt;
   margin-left: 0.5in;
   margin-top: -20px}
```

I then just close and save that file, and I'm done. Any page that links to mystyles.css will automatically inherit the new style when opened in Internet Explorer. Figure 2-4 shows how the extsty.htm page looks after making the change to mystyles.css.

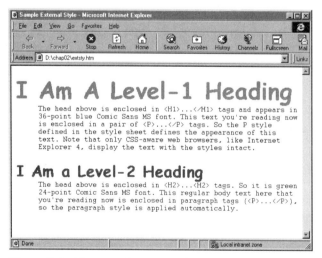

Figure 2-4. *The extsty.htm page after I removed 20 pixels from the top margin of the P style.*

As an experienced HTML author, you can probably see a couple of major advantages to style sheets just from this first example. For one, you can control something that wasn't even possible to control in HTML—the amount of white space between a heading and the text that follows it. And you can make a simple change in one document that automatically carries over to any number of pages in your site. You don't need to go in and mess with the individual pages at all. (I'll bet quite a few of you are thinking, "Boy, I could have used *that* feature a few months ago....") But we've just scratched the tip of the proverbial iceberg here. There's more, as you'll see.

USING YOUR WYSIWYG HTML EDITOR

Cascading style sheets need not discourage you from using your favorite wysiwyg HTML editor. You can still use that editor to create the web page and let the editor put in all the *<H1>*, *<H2>*, *<P>*, and other HTML tags automatically. Those elements will be shown in their default formats. But that's OK because you can still see the basic layout of the page.

After the page is done, you can use your basic text editor to create an external style sheet for the page or several pages. Then you can also use your text editor to add the *<LINK REL="STYLESHEET"...>* tag to the web page. Doing so will apply the styles to all the corresponding tags that your wysiwyg editor created for you. However, you'll see the styles applied only when viewing the page in your web browser.

Microsoft FrontPage 98 does allow you to preview HTML documents that use external style sheets, but you must create the .css file and enter the *<LINK...>* tag manually. FrontPage 98 also provides support for creating embedded and inline styles, which I'll discuss next. Since CSS is such a powerful tool, I expect that an increasing number of wysiwyg HTML editors will provide support for them.

Embedded Styles

If you want to create a set of styles that apply to one page only, you can set up the styles just as we did for the external styles example—but rather than putting the *<STYLE>...</STYLE>* tags and the rules in a separate document, you put those tags right into the web page itself. The basic structure of a web page that uses embedded styles looks something like the following code.

```
<HTML>
<HEAD>
head tags
<STYLE TYPE="text/css">
<!--
    css rules
-->
</STYLE>
</HEAD>

<BODY>
    body text and tags
</BODY>
</HTML>
```

The comment tags <!-- and --> prevent web browsers that don't support style sheets from interpreting and displaying the CSS rules as text on the screen. Figure 2-5 shows a sample HTML file with an embedded style sheet. In this example, I've created two rules, one styling the *<P>* (paragraph) tag, the other styling the *<H1>* tag.

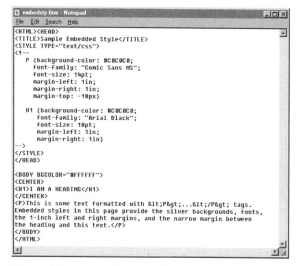

Figure 2-5. *A sample HTML file with an embedded style sheet in its head section.*

Figure 2-6 on the next page shows how this file looks when opened in Internet Explorer. The styles apply to the *<H1>* and *<P>* tags within this page. The styles in this page, however, won't affect any other styles in the web site.

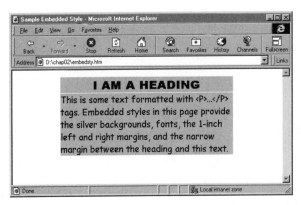

Figure 2-6. *The file from Figure 2-5 as viewed in a web browser.*

Inline Styles

Inline styles have the smallest range of effect of any style. They affect only the current tag—not any other tags in the page and certainly not any other documents. The syntax for defining an inline style is:

```
<TAG STYLE="css rules">
```

Note that instead of *<STYLE>...</STYLE>* tags, you just use a *STYLE* attribute within the tag to define a style. And rather than enclosing the CSS rules in curly braces, you enclose them in quotation marks. You can still use multiple declarations within those quotation marks, though, separating them with semicolons as usual.

Here's an example in which we use an inline style to add a twist to one instance of the *<B>* (boldface) tag. We make the text between the *<B>* and *</B>* tags green. (It will still be boldfaced as well, since adding a color style doesn't take away the existing effect of the tag, which is to make the text bold.)

```
Here is some <B STYLE="color: green">bold green text</B> for you.
```

Figure 2-7 shows an entire HTML document with an inline style used to format one hyperlink. Note the inline style:

```
<A STYLE="color: green; font-style: italic" HREF=...>
```

Figure 2-8 shows how the page looks in Internet Explorer. As you can see, the hyperlink text *Go to Coolnerds* is italicized. But I guess you'll have to take my word for it that the text is also green. The underline comes from the fact that hyperlinks are underlined by default. The color and italics are simply added to that existing attribute.

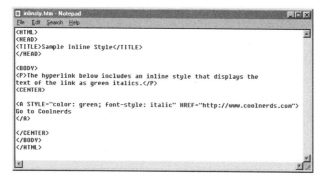

Figure 2-7. *A sample HTML document with an inline style applied to the <A> tag.*

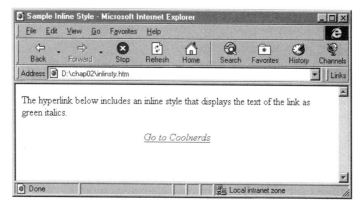

Figure 2-8. *The document from Figure 2-7 viewed in Internet Explorer.*

WHY "CASCADING"?

So now you might be wondering why they're called *cascading* style sheets. The reason is that they are "additive." Let me explain what I mean by that. Suppose you create an external style sheet for the *<BIG>* tag, as shown below. You save that file as mystyle2.css.

```
BIG {font-family: 'Arial';
     font-size: 36pt;
     font-weight: bold;
     color: blue}
```

Let's say that you then design a web page that includes a link to that style sheet. But also in that web page there's an embedded style that styles the *<BIG>* tag, as well as an inline style that styles the *<BIG>* tag, as in Figure 2-9 on the next page.

Figure 2-10 shows how the styles cascade. The first style sheet to be applied to this page is the external style sheet, which defines BIG text as blue 36-point Arial bold text. The next style, which is embedded, defines BIG as italic. However, since the styles are additive, the italics are simply added to the existing style. So the first *<BIG>* tag shows its text as blue 36-point Arial bold italic.

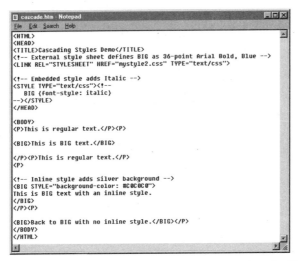

Figure 2-9. *This HTML document uses external, embedded, and inline styles.*

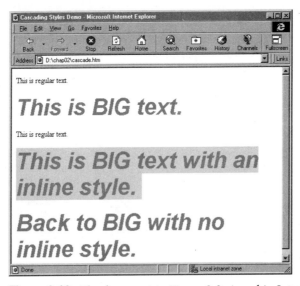

Figure 2-10. *The document in Figure 2-9 viewed in Internet Explorer.*

The inline style adds a silver background (*background-color: #C0C0C0*). The preceding styles still apply, however, so the second chunk of big text is identical to the first chunk of big text except that the text has a silver background.

The last chunk of big text uses the *<BIG>* tag as well, with no inline style. Since an inline style affects only the tag it's placed in, the third chunk of text looks just like first one—blue, bold, and italic with no special background color.

All of this is good because it means you can define a set of styles for your entire web site, using an external style sheet. If need be, you can tweak any one of those styles for just a certain page (using an embedded style) or even just a certain chunk of text (using an inline style) without compromising the initial style definition outside the current page or chunk of text.

Conflicting Styles

In our previous example, the effects of the various styles were additive because there were no conflicts among the styles. The external style defined the font face, size, weight, and color. The embedded style *added* the italic style. The inline style *added* a silver background. But what happens if the styles conflict? For example, what if the external style says the font is blue, the embedded style says it's green, and the inline style says it's red?

The answer is pretty simple: The most recent definition wins. Thus, if the *<LINK REL...>* tag comes first, the big text will initially be blue. If the embedded style that says the big text is green comes next, the big text in that page will actually be green. If an inline style says the big text is red, it will be red, but just for that one *<BIG>...</BIG>* pair of tags.

CREATING AND USING STYLE CLASSES

With *style classes,* you can define several variations of a single tag. For example, you might make a "right-aligned text" paragraph style, a "centered-text" paragraph style, and so forth by creating multiple stylistic themes centered around the paragraph (*<P>*) tag.

You can define style classes in either external or embedded style sheets. (It wouldn't make sense to define a class in an inline style, because inline styles affect only the tag they're in at the moment.) The syntax is virtually identical to the normal syntax for external and embedded styles, with the addition of a dot and class name after the selector, as in the example below, in which the new *classname* attribute is any name you want to give the style.

```
<STYLE TYPE="text/css"><!--
    element.classname {attribute: value[; attribute: value...]}
--></STYLE>
```

Here's an example in which I've created three renditions of the paragraph style named p.centered, p.rightaligned, and p.pullquote:

```
<STYLE TYPE="text/css"><!--
    P.centered      {text-align: center}
    P.rightaligned {text-align: right}
    P.pullquote     {background-color: yellow;
                     font: bold 18pt 'Comic Sans MS';
                     margin-left: 1in;
                     margin-right: 1in}
--></STYLE>
```

To use one of these defined style classes in your document, add the *CLASS="classname"* attribute to the tag. For example, here's the centered paragraph style applied to a little chunk of text:

```
<P CLASS="centered">I am centered text</P>
```

Here's an example of the right-aligned paragraph style applied to a couple of lines of text:

```
<P CLASS="rightaligned">Alan Simpson<BR>
http://www.coolnerds.com</P>
```

And here's an example of the pullquote style applied to a passage of text:

```
<P CLASS="pullquote">It's almost like creating your own custom tags
</P>
```

Figure 2-11 shows an example in which the styles are embedded in an HTML document. Figure 2-12 shows how that document looks when opened in Internet Explorer.

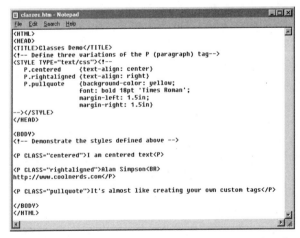

Figure 2-11. *Three classes of paragraph (<P> tag) styles are defined in this HTML document.*

Tip Technically, quotation marks around font names are required only when the font name contains a space. You can use either single (') or double (") quotation marks.

Figure 2-12. *The document from Figure 2-11 as viewed in Internet Explorer.*

Using the *<DIV>* Tag to Define Styles

The HTML *<DIV>...</DIV>* tags can be used to format a large chunk of text—a division—spanning several paragraphs and other elements. This makes them a good choice for defining styles that affect large sections of text in a page. Figure 2-13 shows an example in which I've used DIV to define a style that will affect a whole division of text.

```
<HTML><HEAD>
<TITLE>Style Based on DIV Tag</TITLE>

<!-- Define a style named sidebar that can affect a whole division of text -->
<STYLE TYPE="text/css"><!--
    DIV.sidebar {font-family: 'Comic Sans MS';
                 font-size: 12pt;
                 text-align: right;
                 background-color: #C0C0C0;
                 margin-left: 1in;
                 margin-right: 1in}
--></STYLE>

</HEAD>
<BODY>
<P>This is regular body text, above the DIV tag.</P>

<DIV CLASS="sidebar">
<!-- Apply the DIV style to a heading, paragraph, and image below-->

<H1>Sidebar with 3 Elements</H1>
<P>The heading above, this text here, and the graphic image below are all
enclosed in a style that's defined by a DIV tag. So all three elements --
the head, text, and graphic -- are influenced by the style.<BR></P>
<IMG SRC="beany.gif">

</DIV>

<P>Text outside the division is not affected by the sidebar style.</P>
</BODY>
</HTML>
```

Figure 2-13. *An HTML document that uses a custom sidebar style based on the <DIV> tag.*

As you can see in the figure, and below, the style will display text in 12-point Comic Sans MS font with a silver background, along with right-alignment between one-inch left and right margins. Note the use of the class name to give the division style a name—*sidebar* in this example.

```
<STYLE TYPE="text/css"><!--
    DIV.sidebar {font-family: 'Comic Sans MS';
                 font-size: 12pt;
                 text-align: right;
                 background-color: #C0C0C0;
                 margin-left: 1in;
                 margin-right: 1in}
--></STYLE>
```

Down in the body of the document, three separate elements are enclosed in the *<DIV CLASS="sidebar">...</DIV>* tags, some H1 text, some paragraph (*<P>*) text, and a graphic image (*<IMG>* tag). Figure 2-14 shows how the file looks in Internet Explorer. All the text between the *<DIV CLASS="sidebar">* and *</DIV>* tags is right-aligned and displayed in the 12-point Comic Sans MS font with the silver background and narrowed margins. The graphic is also right-aligned within the narrow margins because the background, alignment, and margins are relevant to the figure. The font, of course, isn't relevant to the figure, so that aspect of the style is just ignored.

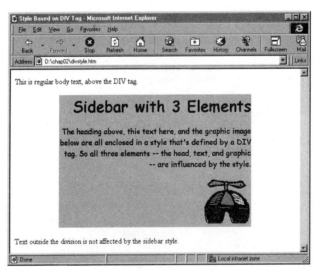

Figure 2-14. *The web browser view of the file in Figure 2-13, illustrating the* DIV CLASS="sidebar" *style.*

The *<SPAN>...</SPAN>* Tags

The *<SPAN>...</SPAN>* tags are like the *<DIV>...</DIV>* tags in that you can use them to define styles that format a chunk of text. Unlike *<DIV>*, however, which is used for large divisions of text, the *<SPAN>* tag is specialized for smaller chunks of text—chunks of text as small as a single character! Here's an example in which we create a style called hot (SPAN.hot, actually) to identify shortcut keys in a menu sequence. Here is the style that colors the text green and underlines it:

```
<STYLE TYPE="text/css"><!--
   SPAN.hot {color: green;
           text-decoration: underline}
--></STYLE>
```

Wherever you want to show green underlined text, just enclose the text in the *<SPAN CLASS="hot">...</SPAN>* tags. In the example below, a few individual characters in a numbered list are formatted as green underlined text:

```
<BODY>
To exit the program:
<OL>
<LI>Choose <SPAN CLASS="hot">F</SPAN>ile ->
   E<SPAN CLASS="hot">x</SPAN> it from the menu bar.
<LI>Choose <SPAN CLASS="hot">Y</SPAN>es if asked about saving your work.
</OL>
</BODY>
```

Figure 2-15 shows how the green underlined letters look in Internet Explorer:

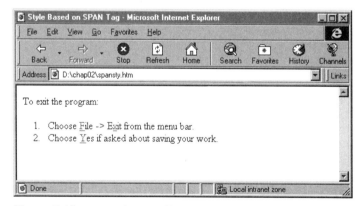

Figure 2-15. *A sample page illustrating the* SPAN CLASS="hot" *style.*

CSS SHORTCUTS

A few CSS attributes let you make a number of settings in one statement. For example, suppose you want to define several aspects of the font used for H1 tags, as follows:

```
H1 {font-style: italic;
    font-weight: bold;
    font-size: 18pt;
    font-family: 'Times Roman'}
```

As an alternative to specifying all those font items individually, you can use the *font:* attribute to define them all in one fell swoop, like this:

```
H1 {font: italic bold 18pt 'Times Roman'}
```

Notice how the various values—italic, bold, 18pt, and Times Roman—are separated only by blank spaces. These abbreviated rules certainly save some space and typing. However, they can be a bit tricky to use. So be sure to refer to the Internet Client SDK, described in Appendix A, for the exact syntax of any CSS attribute you plan to use.

Here's another shortcut. If you're planning to assign the same style to several elements, you can group the selectors next to each other, separated by commas, rather than repeating the rules for each element. For example, suppose you want to assign the font family Arial Black and boldface to the H1, H2, and H3 elements. Without using the shortcut method, you'd have to type them like this:

```
H1 {font-family: 'Arial Black';
    font-weight: bold}
H2 {font-family: 'Arial Black';
    font-weight: bold}
H3 {font-family: 'Arial Black';
    font-weight: bold}
```

Using the shortcut technique of putting multiple selectors on a line, you can type the same set of rules as follows:

```
H1, H2, H3 {font-family: 'Arial Black'; font-weight: bold}
```

INTERNET EXPLORER 4 CSS ATTRIBUTES

Now that you have some idea of what styles can do for you and how to define them, it's time to get a feel for just what kinds of things you can style. In Table 2-1, I've listed all the CSS attributes that Internet Explorer 4 supports. Use the table as a quick reference. For details on a particular attribute, see *CSS Attributes* in the Internet Client SDK.

Table 2-1

CSS ATTRIBUTES SUPPORTED BY INTERNET EXPLORER 4

CSS Attribute	*What It Styles*
background:	Background color, image, transparency, position, tiling
background-attachment:	Background scrolling/watermark
background-color:	Background color or transparency
background-image:	Background image
background-position:	Placement of background image
background-repeat:	Tiling of background image
border:	All four borders' width, style, and color
border-bottom:	Bottom border's width, style, and color
border-bottom-color:	Bottom border's color
border-bottom-style:	Bottom border's style
border-bottom-width:	Bottom border's width
border-color:	Color of all four borders
border-left:	Left border's width, style, and color
border-left-color:	Left border's color
border-left-style:	Left border's style
border-left-width:	Left border's width
border-right:	Right border's width, style, and color
border-right-color:	Right border's color
border-right-style:	Right border's style
border-right-width:	Right border's width
border-style:	All four borders' style
border-top:	Top border's width, style, and color
border-top-color:	Top border's color
border-top-style:	Top border's style
border-top-width:	Top border's width
border-width:	All four borders' width
clear:	Floating elements to the left or right of an element
clip:	Visible portion of an element
color:	Foreground color
cursor:	Type of mouse pointer

(continued)

CSS ATTRIBUTES SUPPORTED BY INTERNET EXPLORER 4 *continued*

CSS Attribute	What It Styles
display:	Whether element is rendered and space for it is reserved
filter:	Type of filter applied to element
float:	Whether element floats
font:	Font style, variant, weight, size, line height, typeface
@font-face:	Font to embed into HTML file
font-family:	Font typeface
font-size:	Font size
font-style:	Font italics
font-variant:	Font small caps
font-weight:	Font weight from light to bold
height:	Element's display height
@import:	Style sheet to import
left:	Position of element relative to the left edge of the page
letter-spacing:	Distance between letters
line-height:	Distance between baselines
list-style:	List style type, image, position
list-style-image:	List item marker
list-style-position:	List item marker position
list-style-type:	Alternative list item marker
margin:	All four margin sizes
margin-bottom:	Size of bottom margin
margin-left:	Size of left margin
margin-right:	Size of right margin
margin-top:	Size of top margin
overflow:	Display of graphics that are larger than their frames
padding:	Space around an element on all sides
padding-bottom:	Space on bottom of element
padding-left:	Space on left of element
padding-right:	Space on right of element
padding-top:	Space on top of element
page-break-after:	Position page break after element

CSS Attribute	What It Styles
page-break-before:	Position page break before element
position:	How element is placed on the page
text-align:	Left, center, right, justified text alignment
text-decoration:	Underline, overline, line-through
text-indent:	Indentation on first line of paragraph
text-transform:	Transformation to uppercase, lowercase, initial cap
top:	Position of element relative to top of page
vertical-align:	Element's vertical alignment
visibility:	Whether element is visible or invisible
width:	Width of element
z-index:	Stacking position of element

ELECTRONIC CSS RESOURCES

You have plenty of electronic online resources to support your efforts to become a CSS guru. Here are some good candidates to get you started:

- For electronic documentation, see *Dynamic Styles* and *CSS Attributes* in the Internet Client SDK, which is described in Appendix A.

- You can also see my current collection of CSS resources in the Links section of my web site at www.coolnerds.com.

- *CSS Windows 95 Help* by the Web Design Group offers CSS documentation in Windows Help format at www.htmlhelp.com.

- Microsoft's Style Sheets Gallery presents sample style sheets. See www.microsoft.com/gallery/files/styles/default.htm.

- *A User's Guide to Style Sheets* by Handan Selamoglu covers CSS basics at www.microsoft.com/workshop/author/css/css-f.htm.

- *Cascading Style Sheets, Level 1,* by the W3C discusses the style sheets specification at www.w3.org/pub/WWW/TR/WD-css1.

- *Typography on the Web* discusses web fonts and Microsoft's plans for using fonts on the web. Go to www.microsoft.com/truetype/web/.

SUMMARY

Whereas HTML (which we discussed in Chapter 1) lets you define the basic elements of a document, such as headings, lists, and body text, cascading style sheets (CSS) let you define the *appearance* of those elements. For instance, with a style sheet you can define the exact font and color of all the *<H1>* elements in your web site. The main points to remember about CSS at this juncture are as follows:

- The basic structure of most CSS rules is *element {attribute: value}*, where *element* is the HTML tag (without the angle brackets) that you want to style, *attribute* is any valid CSS attribute, and *value* is the setting to assign to the attribute.

- External style sheets are great for styles that you want to use in multiple pages. To create external style sheets, store the CSS rules in one or more text files and then use a *<LINK>* tag in the head of any page that will use those styles.

- Embedded style sheets are defined in the head of a web page and are best used to define styles that are relevant to the current page only.

- Inline styles are defined right inside the HTML tag, using the *STYLE* attribute, and are best used in cases where you want to style only that particular instance of the tag.

- Styles cascade if a CSS rule defines some new aspect of an existing rule. That new aspect of the rule is added to the existing rule as an embellishment. The new rule doesn't necessarily replace the existing rule.

- In cases where a new rule redefines or conflicts with some aspect of an existing rule, the most recent rule takes precedence over the older rule.

- You can, in a sense, create your own custom HTML tags by defining CSS *style classes*.

- The CSS attributes are summarized in Table 2-1 in this chapter. Each attribute is further documented in the Internet Client SDK.

Now that we've covered the basic techniques for controlling the structure and appearance of an HTML document, we're ready to move on to the third element of Dynamic HTML: controlling the *behavior* of a web page.

Chapter 3

Scripting with VBScript

HTML and CSS (cascading style sheets) let you define the structure and appearance of a web page. In this chapter, we'll look at a third major component of Dynamic HTML—scripting. In a nutshell, scripting lets you control how your page behaves on the visitor's computer. Scripting allows you to do all sorts of things, but it is primarily used to define some action that takes place in response to some event. For example, perhaps you want some element on your page to light up when the visitor moves the mouse pointer over that element. Scripting allows you to do that.

There are actually two components to scripting—the scripting language and the object model. In this chapter, we'll focus mainly on the scripting language. The language I've chosen to cover in this book is VBScript. (I'll discuss why, and what the alternatives are, shortly). In this chapter, we'll cover the "absolute basics" and the "underlying assumptions"—what VBScript is all about:

■   What VBScript is and why you'd want to use it

■   How to add a VBScript script to a web page

■   The various components that make up a script—variables, literals, expressions, statements, comments, subs, and functions

■   Controlling when a script runs

■   How to debug (fix the errors in) a faulty script

WHAT IS VBSCRIPT?

VBScript is a *scripting language* designed to give people who aren't necessarily programmers a means of activating and extending the capabilities of their web pages. The idea is to give nonprogrammers a programming language they can learn relatively quickly and put to use in practical ways. The *VB* part of the name stands for Visual Basic. The *Basic* part of the name has evolved from an old acronym for Beginners All-purpose Symbolic Instruction Code. The original BASIC language was designed to teach programming to rookie computer science students.

Microsoft's Visual Basic is a 1990s version of that original BASIC language, and Microsoft offers several "flavors" of Visual Basic. Visual Basic for Applications lets you customize the capabilities of programs in the Microsoft Office suite. Visual Basic Enterprise Edition helps professional programmers create custom programs for large corporate networks. Visual Basic Scripting Edition (VBScript) helps you create active content for the Internet.

Of all the flavors of Visual Basic, VBScript is clearly the one best suited to our needs. It's the only one specifically designed to help web authors and programmers activate and extend the capabilities of pages published on the World Wide Web or on corporate intranets.

WHY VBSCRIPT?

I must confess that there's a downside to using VBScript as your scripting language: Only Microsoft Internet Explorer 4 supports the version of VBScript that we'll be discussing in this chapter. Other browsers, such as Netscape Navigator, cannot interpret VBScript at all.

There is another scripting language for web pages, called JavaScript (also called JScript in its Microsoft incarnation), that is supported by multiple browsers, including Internet Explorer and Netscape Navigator. So why not talk about JavaScript rather than VBScript in this book?

Well, for one thing, Netscape's JavaScript and Microsoft's equivalent JScript are not entirely compatible. Nor are the object models that allow the scripting languages to do their thing. So even if I were to go with JavaScript/JScript as the scripting language in this book, there would still be plenty of web pages that would work only in Internet Explorer 4.

Another reason for choosing VBScript is that if you're new to scripting, VBScript is a much easier language to learn. And if you're an experienced programmer, you'll probably find that VBScript is a lot easier to use. For example, whereas JavaScript is case-sensitive (meaning that if you use a lowercase letter where an uppercase letter belongs, the whole script bombs!), VBScript is not case-sensitive. Also, whereas JavaScript offers only 2 built-in functions, VBScript offers more than 80. And those built-in functions really make a difference in defining how easy a language is to learn and use.

There is hope for VBScript programmers. Even though Netscape has opted not to build VBScript support into its web browser, you can easily add a plug-in named ScriptActive to Navigator to make it VBScript-aware. I can't say for certain that a version capable of handling Internet Explorer 4's rendition of VBScript will be ready as you're reading this chapter, but you can easily find out what is available by visiting NCompass Labs' Web site at www.ncompasslabs.com.

The unpleasant fact of life is that the once semi–platform-independent World Wide Web is becoming more and more platform-dependent as time goes by. The reason is that as big companies such as Netscape and Microsoft come up with bigger and better tools and technologies for exploiting the Internet, they do so outside the scope of any predefined standards. And perhaps rightly so, because innovation requires, by definition, some freedom of creativity in developing solutions to problems.

Hopefully, the committees who define just what is "standard" on the Web will be able to catch up with all the recent innovations and agree on tools and technologies that will make all web browsers compatible. However, until that happens, we're all sort of stuck with the fact that the more innovative you are in your web authoring, the less likely you are to get your pages to work in multiple web browsers. Bummer, I know. Personally, I think VBScript will eventually be a standardized language on the Web, so I don't worry (too much) about all the time I've invested in learning to become fluent in that language.

And finally, on perhaps a more personal note, I've discovered that the whole Internet Explorer 4/CSS/VBScript/Dynamic HTML Object Model/ActiveX "thing" is an incredibly rich set of tools for creativity. I can hardly resist exploring its seemingly infinite possibilities. And in fact, I find those explorations and countless discoveries to be just plain fun. (My wife thinks this response is caused by some genetic defect. And she worries that I may have passed it on to our kids.)

WHAT YOU CAN DO WITH VBSCRIPT

Learning a first programming language—be it VBScript or any other—is generally not a whole lotta fun for most people. How do you justify all the time and brain energy that goes into getting up to speed? Before we go into any VBScript details, I'd better persuade you that it's worthwhile by giving you some idea of what you can do with VBScript.

You can:

- Move, size, hide, and display objects interactively on the screen to create more compelling web pages

- Change the appearance of text, pictures, and styles as the visitor moves the mouse around the screen and clicks on objects

- Control the behavior of ActiveX controls and other external components

- Add a new level of interactivity to your pages by displaying custom messages to your reader

- Have your pages ask questions of your reader and respond based on the answers

- Extend the capabilities of your forms to include immediate validation and feedback

…and a whole lot more, as you'll see.

What You'll Need

Even though VBScript is a Microsoft product, you don't need to buy anything. VBScript is automatically installed with Internet Explorer versions 3 and 4. You can write VBScript code using any text editor—Notepad or WordPad, for instance—and with many of the wysiwyg editors such as Microsoft FrontPage Express and Microsoft FrontPage. Some VBScript and Dynamic HTML Object Model documentation is also required. The Internet Client SDK, described in Appendix A, should do the trick.

What VBScript Looks Like

VBScript code goes right into your web page code along with your text and your regular HTML tags. Every VBScript script is enclosed within a pair of HTML *<SCRIPT LANGUAGE="VBScript">* and *</SCRIPT>* tags. A pair of comment tags, *<!--* and *-->*, hide VBScript code from browsers that can't interpret VBScript. When you're looking at the HTML source code for a page, any VBScript in the source will take this form:

```
<SCRIPT LANGUAGE="VBScript"><!--
    VBScript code
--></SCRIPT>
```

The *VBScript code* placeholder is where the actual VBScript code goes. It's important, right off the bat, for you to understand that *only* valid VBScript code can be placed between those tags. If you put any HTML tags or regular text in there, the script won't work. The *VBScript code* that I refer to is "stuff" that's written in the VBScript language. Here's a somewhat simple example. (Don't worry if you have no idea what this script does—I just want to show you an example at this point.)

```
<SCRIPT LANGUAGE="VBScript"><!--
    MsgBox "Hello World"
--></SCRIPT>
```

You can add plain-English programmer comments to your VBScript code, but they must be preceded by a single quotation mark (') and extend to the end of the line. The comment appears only in the document source and has no effect on how the code behaves. As an example, the little script below contains a comment that describes what the *MsgBox* statement does.

```
<SCRIPT LANGUAGE="VBScript"><!--
    'Show a simple Hello World message in a custom message box.
    MsgBox "Hello World"
--></SCRIPT>
```

Figure 3-1 shows how that script might look within the context of an HTML document. As you can see, most of the document is your standard HTML and text. The VBScript code—a comment and one VBScript statement—is correctly snuggled between a pair of *<SCRIPT LANGUAGE="VBScript"><!--* and *--></SCRIPT>* tags.

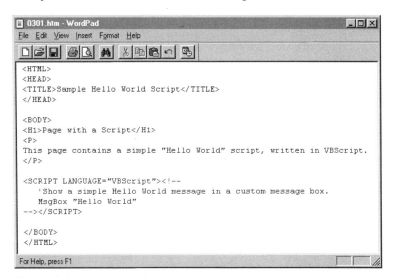

Figure 3-1. *A sample HTML document that contains a simple VBScript script.*

ADDING SCRIPTS TO YOUR PAGES

As the example in Figure 3-1 illustrates, VBScript code goes right into your web page. There are several ways to get the code into the page. One simple technique is to open the HTML file using a text editor such as Notepad or WordPad. Then you type the *<SCRIPT LANGUAGE="VBScript"><!-- and --></SCRIPT>* tags and the VBScript code between those tags. That's how I did it in Figure 3-1. I just opened an existing web page using WordPad and then typed in the script as shown. To edit a script that you created with a text editor, just reopen the page with any text editor and make your changes.

If your wysiwyg HTML editor offers the ability to edit the document source, you can use that editor as well. For example, if you use FrontPage or FrontPage Express to create and edit web pages, you can view the document source. You can then move the cursor to where you want to insert a script and type in the script.

Some wysiwyg HTML editors provide special tools for adding scripts to a page. For instance, if you're using FrontPage Express, you can follow these steps to add a script to whatever page you're editing at the moment:

1. Position the insertion point at about where you want the script to be placed in the web page.

    NOTE   Where you place a script can be important, as we'll discuss later. You might not be able to get the exact placement you want when typing a script in a wysiwyg HTML editor. But that's no biggie because you can always reopen the page in some standard text editor and then move the script using standard cut-and-paste techniques.

2. Choose Insert-Script from the menu bar.

3. In the dialog box that appears, select VBScript and leave the other options deselected.

4. Type in the VBScript code, but *don't* type in the *<SCRIPT LANGUAGE="VBScript"><!-- and --></SCRIPT>* tags, as in the example shown in Figure 3-2.

5. Click the OK button.

Only a small icon representing the script appears in the document, as in the example shown in Figure 3-3.

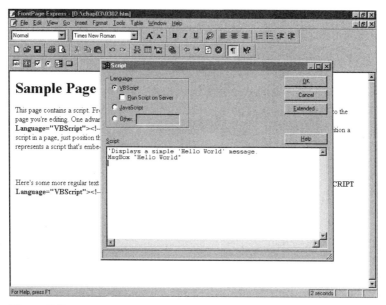

Figure 3-2. *Inserting a script in FrontPage Express.*

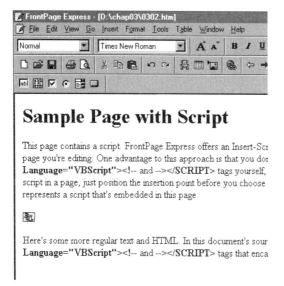

Figure 3-3. *In FrontPage Express (and also in FrontPage), small icons represent the locations of scripts in a page.*

If you need to change the script, you can just double-click that little icon to return to the same dialog box in which you created the script. There you can simply type your changes and then click the OK button to save those changes.

If you want, you can choose View-HTML from the menu bar to get to the entire document source. You'll see the script, including the *<SCRIPT...>* and *</SCRIPT>* tags, as in Figure 3-4. You can then make your changes and click OK.

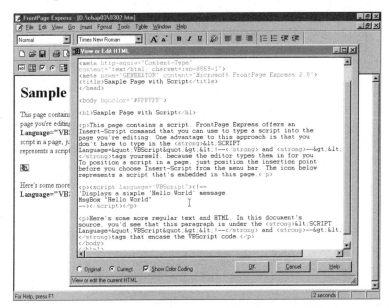

Figure 3-4. *A script that I inserted in FrontPage Express by choosing Insert-Script.*

You might have noticed that the HTML tags in Figure 3-4 are in lowercase letters. That's just the way FrontPage Express renders them. When typing these things manually, I tend to use uppercase letters for HTML tags. Not that it matters— HTML, CSS, and VBScript are all case-insensitive. So uppercase and lowercase letters are treated as equivalent. I mention this only because you might wonder why these discrepancies exist. And the truth of the matter is, it just depends on which editor I happened to use to create the page.

I should point out that the ActiveX Control Pad, which I'll be discussing in Part III, is another good tool for adding VBScript code to a page. It has the big advantage of offering a Script Wizard, which can automatically write quite a bit of error-free code for you!

So really, the bottom line on typing scripts is simply that any editing technique you use to type and edit HTML tags in an HTML document will also let you type and edit VBScript scripts. The real trick in programming, however, isn't typing the script. The trick is figuring out how to write a script that does whatever it is you want your page to do. Most people learn this more esoteric aspect of scripting by looking at examples of other people's scripts and seeing how more experienced programmers get their scripts to do what they do. But looking at other people's scripts can be overwhelming unless you understand some of the basic tenets of the scripting language.

I'm going to devote the rest of this chapter to an overview of the VBScript language elements. Being able to recognize the VBScript elements will take a lot of the mystery out of all those VBScript scripts you're likely to come across as you go peeking at the document source behind other people's web pages.

THE VBSCRIPT LANGUAGE

Let's take a look at some of the various elements that make up the VBScript language. If you're new to programming, you'll probably wonder what purpose any of these elements could possibly serve—and the answer is, individually not much. But once you start seeing examples of VBScript in action, you'll see that every little piece of the puzzle has its own contribution to make.

VBScript Data Types

VBScript can store "data" (pieces of information) of various kinds, or "types." Officially, VBScript has only one data type, called a *variant*. A variant is a special data type for a variable that can contain different types of information depending on how the variable is being used. Typically, you'll use the following four general types of data in a variant:

- number: a number, such as *123.45*

- string: text, such as *"Hello There"*

- date: a point in time, such as *#12/31/97#* for December 31, 1997

- Boolean: only two possible values—*True* or *False*

That's the simple side of things, and most of the time, you'll work only with numbers and strings—and perhaps a few dates and Booleans. The variant types can be further distinguished, though. In some situations, you may want to categorize, or "define," a chunk of data as one of the "subtypes" shown in Table 3-1 on the next page.

Table 3-1

VARIANT DATA SUBTYPES

Subtype	Meaning
Empty	Variant is uninitialized—contains *0* for number or null string ("") for string.
Null	Variant intentionally contains no data.
Boolean	Variant contains either *True* or *False*.
Byte	Variant contains an integer in the range *0* through *255*.
Integer	Variant contains an integer in the range *−32,768* through *32,767*.
Currency	Variant in the range *−922,337,203,685,477.5808* through *922,337,203,685,477.5807*.
Long	Variant contains an integer in the range *−2,147,483,648* through *2,147,483,647*.
Single	Variant contains a single-precision, floating-point decimal number roughly in the range *−3.403E^{38}* through *−1.401E^{-45}* for negative numbers and *1.401E^{-45}* through *3.403E^{38}* for positive numbers. It can also contain *0*.
Double	Variant contains a double-precision, floating-point decimal number roughly in the range *−1.780E^{308}* through *−4.941E^{-324}* for negative numbers and *4.941E^{-324}* through *1.780E^{308}* for positive numbers. It can also contain *0*.
Date (Time)	Variant contains a number that represents a date from *1/1/100* through *12/31/9999*, enclosed in # characters, as in *#12/31/97#*.
String	Variant contains a string—which can be as many as approximately 2 billion characters in length—enclosed in single or double quotation marks, as in *'Hello There'* or *"Hello There"*.
Object	Variant contains a "pointer" to an object such as an ActiveX control or one of the Dynamic HTML objects described in Chapter 4. (A pointer specifies the memory location the computer uses to get at the object itself.)
Error	Variant contains a number that refers to a specific error message.

VBScript includes many built-in *functions* that allow you to be very specific about how you want to handle a particular piece of data. We'll look at some of those functions later in this chapter. Right now, we'll focus on VBScript *operators*, which are used to manipulate data.

VBScript Operators

VBScript operators let you manipulate and compare numbers and strings. Most of us mere mortals will use the standard operators such as + for addition, − for subtraction, and so forth. But there are plenty of other VBScript operators you can learn about as you go along. For future reference, Table 3-2 shows all of the VBScript operators.

Table 3-2
VBSCRIPT OPERATORS

Symbol	*Description*
Arithmetic operators (in order of precedence)	
^	Exponentiation
−	Unary negation
*	Multiplication
/	Division
\	Integer division
Mod	Modulo division
+	Addition
−	Subtraction
&	String/variant concatenation
Comparison operators	
=	Equals (a comparison operator in an expression and an assignment operator in a statement)
<>	Does not equal
<	Is less than
>	Is greater than
<=	Is less than or equal to
>=	Is greater than or equal to
Is	Is equivalent object
Logical operators	
Not	Logical negation
And	Logical conjunction
Or	Logical disjunction
Xor	Logical exclusion
Eqv	Logical equivalence
Imp	Logical implication

VBScript Variables, Literals, and Expressions

A *variable* is the name of a place in which you can store a data value, such as a number or a name (a string), that can change. To store data in a variable, you use a small assignment statement with the general format

```
variableName = value
```

In this statement format, *variableName* is some name you make up yourself. (So we'll use an initial lowercase letter and an internal capital letter.) The name must start with a letter, cannot contain spaces or periods, and cannot exceed 255 characters. The *value* is the data you want to store in the variable. Here are some examples of assigning values to (storing data in) variables:

```
myFirstName = "Alan"
myLastName = "Simpson"
ashleyAge = 8
alecAge = 4
```

Notice that the names *Alan* and *Simpson* are enclosed in quotation marks. The quotation marks indicate that those data items are *literal strings* so that VBScript won't go looking around for a variable named *Alan* or a variable named *Simpson*.

Now let's look at some statements that can manipulate those variables:

```
fullName = myFirstName & " " & myLastName
sumOfKidsAges = ashleyAge + alecAge
```

After the two lines above are executed, a new variable named *fullName* exists, and it contains the result of the expression

```
myFirstName & " " & myLastName
```

The contents of the *myFirstName* variable and a blank space and the contents of the *myLastName* variable result in the value *Alan Simpson*.

The new *sumOfKidsAges* variable contains the value *12* because the expression *ashleyAge + alecAge* adds the number *8* (*ashleyAge*) and the number *4* (*alecAge*), producing the result, *12*.

You can also do arithmetic with date values, which follow these rules:

■ When you add a date to or subtract a date from a date, you get back a value expressing a number of days.

■ When you add a number to or subtract a number from a date, you get back a date value representing the date falling that number of days after or before the original date.

Let's look at an example of subtracting one date from another:

```
<SCRIPT LANGUAGE="VBScript"><!--
   Christmas = #12/25/97#
   today = #11/1/97#
   shoppingDays = Christmas - today
   document.write shoppingDays
   document.write " shopping days until Christmas."
--></SCRIPT>
```

If you put this script between the *<BODY>...</BODY>* tags in an HTML document and then open the page with your browser, the screen shows this:

54 shopping days until Christmas.

because 12/25/97 minus 11/1/97 equals 54 (days).

> TIP In this case, the *document.write* statement tells VBScript to write the contents of the *shoppingDays* variable and the literal text *shopping days until Christmas.* onto the screen. We'll look at *document.write* in more detail in Chapter 4 when we take up the Dynamic HTML Object Model. You can also look up *document* object and *write* method in the Internet Client SDK, described in Appendix A, for more information about the elements of this VBScript statement.

Now let's look at an example of adding a number to a date:

```
<SCRIPT LANGUAGE="VBScript"><!--
   today = #1/1/97#
   dueDate = today + 30
   document.write "Payment due on " & dueDate
--></SCRIPT>
```

If you view the result of this script through your web browser, you see the sentence

Payment due on 1/31/97

because 1/1/97 plus 30 (days) equals 1/31/97.

> TIP VBScript's built-in *Date()* function returns the today's date stored on the web page reader's PC.

You'll see many more examples of variables, literals, and expressions as we progress through the chapter. Right now, I'd like to introduce you to some other important elements of the VBScript language.

VBScript Comments

As I mentioned briefly earlier, a *programmer comment* is a little passage of text within a script that has no effect on what the script does. The comment simply acts as a note to oneself or to other programmers, usually to explain the purpose of some chunk of code.

The apostrophe comment delimiter (') starts a VBScript comment line. The comment extends to the end of the line. You don't need to type a closing delimiter. In the script below, the first line inside the script is a VBScript comment describing what the next line does:

```
<SCRIPT LANGUAGE="VBScript"><!--
    'Ask reader if it's OK to continue.
    answer = MsgBox("OK to continue", 6, "Question")
--></SCRIPT>
```

Remember, the comments have no effect on how the script behaves.

It's also common practice to put the HTML comment tags (<!-- and -->) just inside the *<SCRIPT...>...</SCRIPT>* tags to hide the script from browsers that don't interpret VBScript. Even though non-VBScript browsers will ignore the *<SCRIPT...>...</SCRIPT>* tags, they will interpret the stuff between those tags as plain text and show it on the visitor's screen as such. The <!-- and --> comment tags hide the code inside the script from those non-VBScript browsers so they never see it at all.

Don't forget that the apostrophe (') comment delimiter works only when placed inside the *<SCRIPT LANGUAGE="VBScript"><!--* and *-->/SCRIPT>* tags. If you want to put a comment outside a script, use the HTML comment tags *<!--...-->* as in the comment in the example below that tells what the upcoming script does:

```
<!--This an HTML comment, as is the one below-->
<!--Ask reader if it's OK to continue.-->
<SCRIPT LANGUAGE="VBScript"><!--
    'This VBScript comment is inside the script.
    answer = MsgBox("OK to continue", 6, "Question")
--></SCRIPT>
```

VBScript Built-in Functions

VBScript contains over 80 built-in *function procedures,* often called *functions* for short. The functions provide a wide variety of services, including getting information from your reader's PC, changing and manipulating the contents of variables, testing the contents of variables, and more.

I won't bog you down with descriptions of all the VBScript function procedures right here. They're all documented in the Internet Client SDK, and you can look them up as you need to. However, I'd like you to be able to recognize a function when you see one in somebody else's script. Built-in functions take the form

`FunctionName(arguments)`

FunctionName is the name of the function and *arguments* is either nothing or one or more expressions that will pass data to the function. In code, the name of a function that has no parameters—that accepts no arguments—should still be followed by a pair of empty parentheses. For example, the built-in *Date( )* function, which accepts no arguments, should have empty parentheses.

All function procedures "return" some data. The *Date( )* function returns the current system date from the reader's PC. Thus, this tiny script

```
<SCRIPT LANGUAGE="VBScript"><!--
   document.write "According to your PC, today is "
   document.write Date()
--></SCRIPT>
```

writes something like this on the browser screen, where *12/31/97* is replaced by whatever date the reader's PC has in its system clock:

According to your PC, today is 12/31/97

Let's look at an example of a built-in function procedure that does accept an argument. The *UCase( )* function takes any string that's passed to it and returns that same string with all the lowercase letters converted to uppercase. Take a look at this small script:

```
<SCRIPT LANGUAGE="VBScript"><!--
   myName = "alan simpson"
   document.write UCase(myName)
--></SCRIPT>
```

Opening the page that contains this little script displays

ALAN SIMPSON

on the screen. All the letters are in uppercase because the script doesn't just say to write *myName*. The script says to write *UCase* of *myName*. The expression *myName* (which is just a simple variable) passes the string *"alan simpson"* as an argument to the *UCase( )* function.

Here's an example of a built-in function procedure that accepts multiple arguments:

```
variable = MsgBox(message, buttonCode, title)
```

MsgBox() displays a custom message on the screen in a dialog box. The *message* argument specifies a message to appear in the dialog box. The *buttonCode* argument specifies a code that defines which buttons are to be displayed. (If the *buttonCode* argument is *0*, for example, the dialog box displays an OK button.) The argument passed to the *title* parameter is the text to be displayed in the dialog box's title bar. The *variable* component of the statement is the name of some variable that will hold the reader's response to the dialog box message—although the variable is useful only when the dialog box contains multiple buttons, as we'll see in Chapter 5.

Figure 3-5 shows a sample HTML document in which I've typed a script between the *<BODY>...</BODY>* tags. The script uses the *MsgBox()* function to display a custom dialog box on the screen.

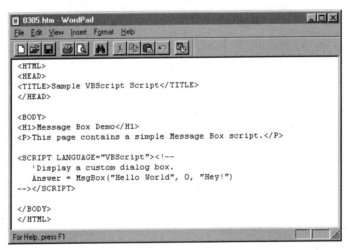

Figure 3-5. *An HTML document containing a script that uses the* MsgBox() *function.*

If I save and close the HTML document and then open the page in Internet Explorer, the message box will appear as soon as the page is opened, as shown in Figure 3-6.

The built-in *Date()*, *UCase()*, and *MsgBox()* function procedures are just a few examples I picked out of a hat. I think it's fair to say that most people will use only one or two dozen of the more than 80 available built-in functions in their work. You don't need to know about all of the functions right off the bat. A lot of the functions are for doing trigonometry, for instance, and if, like most people, your work doesn't require doing trigonometric calculations, you don't really need to know about those functions. Let's look at some other, more pressing, features of VBScript.

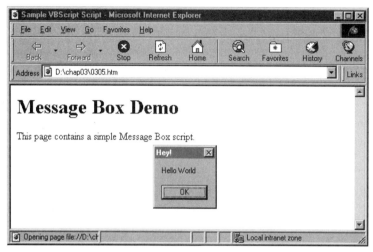

Figure 3-6. *The custom message box viewed in Internet Explorer.*

CONTROLLING WHEN A SCRIPT RUNS

A script is never executed (that is, "run," or "played") until the page or the HTML file that contains the script is opened in a web browser—that is to say, scripts are executed only at run time (in the browser) and never at design time (in the program you're using to write the script).

Once a page is opened in a VBScript-enabled web browser, the browser reads the page from top to bottom, left to right, in the same way you read a page. When the browser encounters a script in the page, it *compiles* the script—which means that it changes the script into a language the web browser can quickly execute. Whether or not the script is run immediately after it is compiled depends on how the script is written, as we'll see in the sections that follow. Basically, you can design a script so that it runs

■ Immediately after it's compiled, or

■ Only when some event occurs, or

■ Only when it's called in a tag or by some other script

Scripts That Run Immediately

Let's start with the simplest possible script—one that's executed as soon as the reader opens the web page. Such code can be anywhere in the HTML source, just as long as it falls between the *<SCRIPT...>...<SCRIPT>* tags but *not*·inside the *Function...End Function* statements or inside the *Sub...End Sub* statements. These scripts are generally placed between the *<BODY>...</BODY>* tags of the HTML document and are written in this basic syntax:

```
<SCRIPT LANGUAGE="VBScript"><!--
    code
--></SCRIPT>
```

The sample script shown back in Figure 3-5 on page 62 is a perfect example of a script that's run as soon as it's compiled. When a reader browses the page whose HTML code is shown in that figure, the script is immediately executed, displaying the message box shown in Figure 3-6 on the previous page.

Scripts That Run When Some Event Occurs

A sub procedure is one type of script—a function procedure is another—whose execution is deferred. Like all scripts, a sub procedure is compiled as soon as the browser encounters it in the HTML code for a page. But it isn't executed until either some event sends the procedure into action or a tag or some other script in the page calls the sub procedure to do its thing.

The name of the sub procedure can actually determine when the script is executed. A sub procedure's name can refer to an object and to an event that starts the execution of the procedure. To name a sub procedure so that it is automatically attached to some object and some event that happens to that object, use the syntax

```
Sub objectName_event()
    code
End Sub
```

objectName is the name of some object within the page and *event* is the event that sends the script into action. The *code* is the VBScript code that's executed when the script is played. A sub procedure that uses this type of syntax is said to be *bound to* the object and event for which it's named. Let's look at an example.

The document shown in Figure 3-7 contains some regular HTML and text, as well as a script. Notice that within the head of the document and between the *<SCRIPT...>...</SCRIPT>* tags, is a sub procedure named *myHeading_onmouseover*, also shown on the next page.

```
<SCRIPT LANGUAGE="VBScript"><!--
    'Here's a sub procedure that's bound to the
    'onmouseover event of an object named myHeading.
    Sub myHeading_onmouseover()
        answer = MsgBox("Hello World", 0, "Hey!")
    End Sub
--></SCRIPT>
```

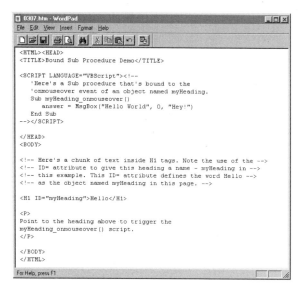

Figure 3-7. *This HTML document contains an object named* myHeading *and a sub procedure that's bound to the* onmouseover *event of that object.*

When triggered, this sub procedure executes the VBScript statement *answer = MsgBox("Hello World", 0, "Hey!")*, which in turn displays a simple Hello World message box on the screen. But simply opening this page in a web browser isn't enough to trigger the sub procedure because the sub procedure is bound to the *onmouseover* event of some object named *myHeading*. So the question becomes what—and where—is this object named *myHeading*?

Looking into the body of the document, we see a chunk of level-1 heading text that contains just the word *Hello*. That text is formatted with the usual *<H1>...</H1>* tags. But there's something unique about this heading. The opening *<H1>* tag also contains an *ID="myHeading"* attribute, as you can see below:

```
<H1 ID="myHeading">Hello</H1>
```

Opening this sample page displays the usual HTML and text, as in Figure 3-8 on the next page. Initially the script does nothing. As soon as the mouse pointer touches the Hello heading, however, the script is triggered and the Hello World message box appears on the screen, as in Figure 3-9, also on the next page.

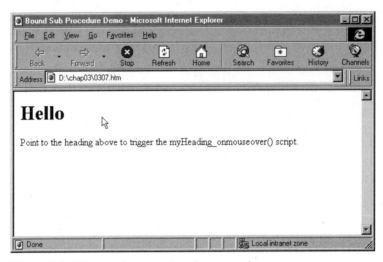

Figure 3-8. *The sample page when first opened.*

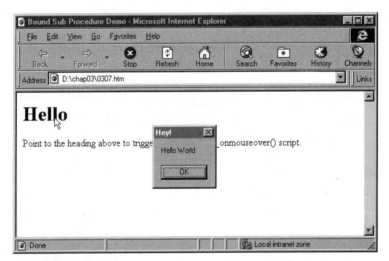

Figure 3-9. *The sample page after the mouse pointer is moved to the Hello heading.*

Perhaps this example brings up the question, "What kinds of things can be considered objects in a web page, and what kinds of events can trigger scripts into actions?" Well, one of the beauties of Dynamic HTML is that virtually *anything* in a web page can be treated as an object! A heading, a graphic image, a list—virtually *anything*. Quite a few events can trigger scripts as well. I'll get into the details of these later (and they're all referenced in the Internet Client SDK). But just to give you a sneak peek at things to come, the events that Internet Explorer 4 can detect and respond to are listed on the next page.

onabort	*onkeydown*
onafterupdate	*onkeypress*
onbeforeunload	*onkeyup*
onbeforeupdate	*onload*
onblur	*onmousedown*
onbounce	*onmousemove*
onchange	*onmouseout*
onclick	*onmouseover*
ondataavailable	*onmouseup*
ondatasetchanged	*onreadystatechange*
ondatasetcomplete	*onreset*
ondblclick	*onresize*
ondragstart	*onrowenter*
onerror	*onrowexit*
onerrorupdate	*onscroll*
onfilterchange	*onselect*
onfinish	*onstart*
onfocus	*onsubmit*
onhelp	*onunload*

Using the *Sub objectName_event()* naming convention is just one way to bind a script to an object and an event. You can also bind a script to an object and an event by using the *FOR* and *EVENT* attributes inside the opening *<SCRIPT>* tag, as discussed next.

Using *<SCRIPT FOR=...EVENT=...>*

Another way to defer script execution until some event sends the script into action doesn't require either a sub or a function procedure. Instead, you just specify right in the *<SCRIPT...>* tag the name of the object and event that will launch the script, using this syntax:

```
<SCRIPT FOR="objectName" EVENT="event" LANGUAGE="VBScript"><!--
    code
--></SCRIPT>
```

objectName is the name of an object in the page and *event* is a valid event for that object.

This approach is a good way to put a script close to the object it's bound to so that it's easy to see the object and its related script at a glance. For example,

Figure 3-10 shows an HTML document that contains a form. The form contains two controls—a text box named *myTextBox* and a button named *myButton*:

```
<!--Define a form with a text box and button-->
<FORM NAME="myForm">
  <P>
  Type something using lowercase letters:
  <INPUT NAME="myTextBox">
  ...
  <INPUT TYPE="Button" VALUE="Then Click Me" NAME="myButton">
  ...
</FORM>
```

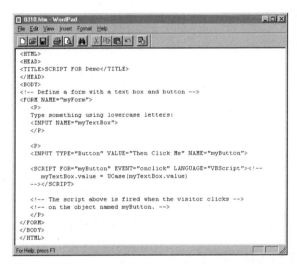

Figure 3-10. *An example of using* <SCRIPT FOR=…> *to bind a script to an object and an event.*

Inside the form there's also a script. That script is bound to the *onclick* event of the *myButton* object using this syntax:

```
<SCRIPT FOR="myButton" EVENT="onclick" LANGUAGE="VBScript"><!--
  myTextBox.value = UCase(myTextBox.value)
--></SCRIPT>
```

When the script is executed, it takes whatever is in the *myTextBox* textbox (expressed as *myTextBox.value* in the Dynamic HTML Object Model) and converts that to all uppercase letters using the *UCase()* function. That new uppercase text replaces the current contents of the text box. Figure 3-11 shows how the page looks when first opened in Internet Explorer. In that figure, I've already typed some text, *willie wonka,* into the text box. After I click the button, the contents of the text box change to all uppercase letters, *WILLIE WONKA.*

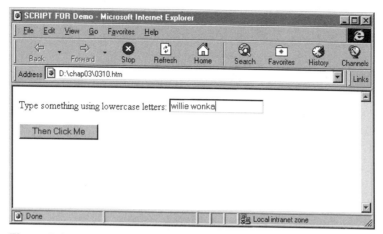

Figure 3-11. *The sample page from Figure 3-10 in Internet Explorer after I typed* willie wonka.

Scripts That Run When They're Called: Stand-Alone Sub and Function Procedures

You can write sub and function procedures that don't run until they're called and aren't bound to any particular object or event. For example, here's a custom sub procedure named *showMessage* that isn't associated with any particular control or event:

```
<SCRIPT LANGUAGE="VBScript"><!--
   Sub showMessage()
      answer = MsgBox("Hey There", 0, "Look at me")
   End Sub
--></SCRIPT>
```

This sub procedure is just a stand-alone procedure with its own unique name. Because it's a procedure, it won't run automatically when the page is open. And because it isn't associated with an event, it will run only when some other script or an HTML tag calls upon it to run.

Figure 3-12 on the next page shows an example of the *showMessage* sub procedure inserted into an HTML document, along with HTML tags that can send the procedure into action. In this case, the HTML tags are the *<BUTTON...>...</BUTTON>* tags. These tags show a button on the screen, and the text between the tags appears on the face of a button. The *onclick="showMessage"* attribute in the opening tag says that when the button is clicked, the procedure named *showMessage* is to be fired.

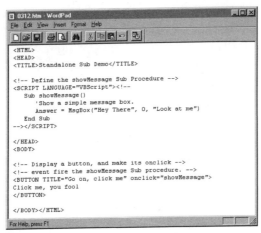

Figure 3-12. *The* showMessage *sub procedure inserted into the HTML code for a web page.*

Figure 3-13 shows how the page looks after opening it in Internet Explorer and clicking the button. The *showMessage* sub procedure has already been executed, and the message box it defines is visible on the screen.

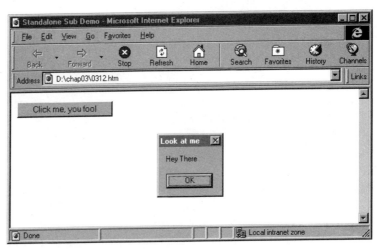

Figure 3-13. *Clicking the "Click me, you fool" button causes the* showMessage() *procedure to execute.*

TIP   The *TITLE* attribute inside the *<BUTTON>* tag defines the tooltip that will appear on the screen when a visitor points to the button.

Passing Arguments to Sub Procedures

A sub or function procedure can be designed so that it accepts one or more *arguments,* which are just items of data—values—passed into the procedure's *parameters.* The procedure then uses those argument values when it runs. To define a sub procedure that accepts arguments, use the following syntax, where *parameter1, parameter2,* and so on are variables that will receive a value:

```
<SCRIPT LANGUAGE="VBScript"><!--
    Sub name(parameter1, parameter2, etc.)
       code
    End Sub
--></SCRIPT>
```

To call a sub procedure that accepts one or more arguments, follow the name of the procedure with the values you want to pass to it. For example, here's a version of our custom *showMessage* sub procedure that's able to accept one argument value, in an *anyText* parameter:

```
<SCRIPT LANGUAGE="VBScript"><!--
    Sub showMessage(anyText)
       answer = MsgBox(anyText, 0, "Hey")
    End Sub
--></SCRIPT>
```

Notice that in the *MsgBox()* function, *anyText* is *not* enclosed in quotation marks. We don't want the message box to display the literal string *"anyText"*. We want the message box to display whatever text has been passed to the procedure in the *anyText* argument.

The idea behind parameters is to let you create a procedure that can perform some action with different data values. For example, one part of the page can call *showMessage* with this syntax:

```
showMessage "Hello There"
```

and the message box will appear with the words *Hello There* as the message text inside the box. Another can call can call the procedure with this syntax:

```
showMessage "Click OK to continue"
```

and the message box will appear with the words *Click OK to continue* in the box.

Note that the syntax rules require that when defining the sub procedure, the parameter name is enclosed in parentheses, like this:

```
Sub showMessage(anyText)
```

But when *calling* the sub procedure and passing values to it, you typically omit the parentheses, like this:

```
showMessage "Howdy World"
```

Some sub procedures can be passed more than one argument value when called. In this situation, you must omit the parentheses; otherwise, an error will occur.

It's not necessary to pass the entire message to *showMessage*. If most of the messages would be the same, you need only pass the part that's unique about each message. For instance, the version of *showMessage* shown below accepts one parameter, named *anyText*. It then tacks the value of that parameter onto the end of the string *"You are entering"* and displays the entire message, stored in a variable named *msg*, in the message box:

```
<SCRIPT LANGUAGE="VBScript"><!--
   Sub showMessage(anyText)
      msg = "You are entering " & anyText
      answer = MsgBox(msg, 0, "Bye Bye")
   End Sub
--></SCRIPT>
```

Thus, if you call the procedure using the syntax *showMessage "The Twilight Zone"*, the variable named *msg* becomes *You are entering the Twilight Zone*, and that message appears in the message box because the *MsgBox()* function uses *msg* as its message text: *answer = MsgBox(msg, 0, "Bye Bye")*.

Figure 3-14 shows a more complete example. That document contains HTML *<BUTTON>* tags that display two buttons. As you can see, the code also contains the modified *showMessage* sub procedure we've just seen, which can accept one argument for its *anyText* parameter.

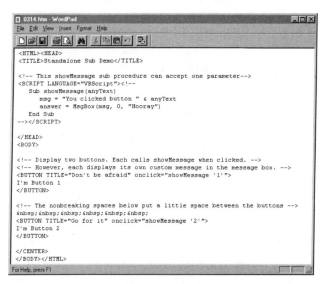

Figure 3-14. *The modified version of the* showMessage *sub procedure, which is able to accept one argument.*

Opening the page in Internet Explorer displays the two buttons on the screen, as shown in Figure 3-15. But of course the *showMessage* procedure isn't executed until one of the buttons is clicked.

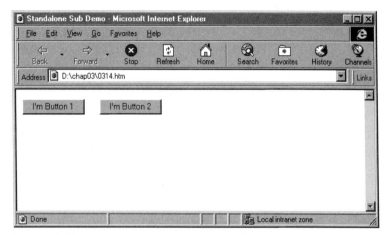

Figure 3-15. *The file from Figure 3-14 as it first looks when opened in Internet Explorer.*

Clicking the button on the left displays the message *You clicked button 1* because the *onclick* event of that button's HTML tag calls the *showMessage* procedure with this syntax:

```
showMessage "1"
```

Clicking the button on the right also calls the *showMessage* sub procedure. But that button's *onclick* event calls *showMessage* with this syntax:

```
showMessage "2"
```

Thus, the message box that appears after this button is clicked contains the message *You clicked button 2.*

A sub procedure can accept any number of arguments. Just be sure to separate the arguments with a comma. Do so both when defining the procedure and when calling it. For example, here's a version of *showMessage* that has two parameters, named *msgText* and *titleText*:

```
<SCRIPT LANGUAGE="VBScript"><!--
   Sub showMessage(msgText, titleText)
      answer = MsgBox(msgText, 0, titleText)
   End Sub
--></SCRIPT>
```

Calling that version of *showMessage* with the following syntax displays the little message box shown in Figure 3-16.

```
showMessage "I am the message", "I'm the Title"
```

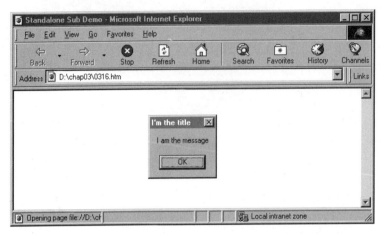

Figure 3-16. *A message box showing its message text and title text.*

Passing Arguments to Function Procedures

Like a sub procedure, a function procedure can be designed to accept one or more arguments. The procedure then uses those arguments when it runs. To define a function procedure that accepts arguments, use this syntax:

```
<SCRIPT LANGUAGE="VBScript"><!--
   Function functionName(parameter1, parameter2, etc.)
      code
      functionName = returnValue
   End Function
--></SCRIPT>
```

functionName is a name you make up and assign to the function; *parameter1, parameter2,* and so forth are zero or more variables separated by commas that receive values passed to the function as arguments; *code* is any valid VBScript code; and *returnValue* is an expression representing the value the function will return.

Let's use an example. The custom function procedure at the top of the next page is named *salesTax()*. It has one parameter, named *anyNumber*. This particular function contains only one line of code, which sets the function name, *salesTax*, equal to the passed value (the value in *anyNumber*) multiplied by 8.25 percent (*0.0825*):

```
<SCRIPT LANGUAGE="VBScript"><!--
   Function salesTax(anyNumber)
      salesTax = 0.0825 * anyNumber
   End Function
--></SCRIPT>
```

To call any function—whether built-in or user-defined—from within a script, you use the function in an expression, as in the syntax below for calling a user-defined function:

```
value = functionName(argument1, argument2, etc.)
```

value can be any variable name or any object that can contain some value. *functionName* is the name of the function as defined next to the *Function* keyword. (Note the lowercase *f*.) *argument1, argument2,* and so forth are the expressions that will pass data to the function. In the HTML document shown in Figure 3-17, the *salesTax()* function calculates the sales tax on some number typed into a form text box.

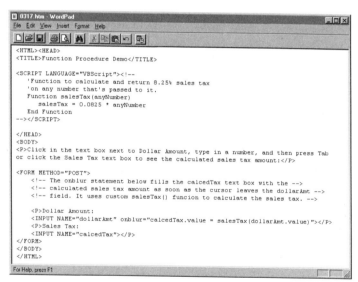

Figure 3-17. *The HTML document containing the custom* salesTax() *function.*

The code contains a standard HTML form with *<INPUT...>* tags that define two text boxes. The top text box is named *dollarAmt*, and the bottom text box is named *calcedTax*. Notice the *onblur* attribute assignment in the first *<INPUT...>* tag:

```
onblur="calcedTax.value = salesTax(dollarAmt.value)"
```

That attribute assignment says, "When the blinking cursor or focus leaves this control—*onblur*—make the value of the *calcedTax* text box—*calcedTax.value*—equal to *salesTax()* of the *dollarAmt*—*salesTax(dollarAmt.value)*."

When I initially open the page in a web browser, I see its text and the two text boxes. If I then type some number, say *100*, into the first text box and press the Tab key, the second text box is automatically filled with 8.25 percent of whatever number I typed into the first text box—8.25 in the example shown in Figure 3-18.

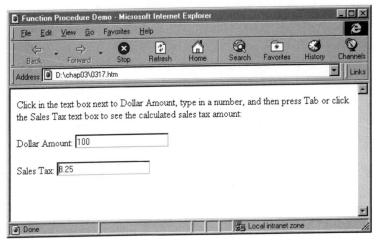

Figure 3-18. *The results of typing* 100 *into the first text box and pressing Tab.*

I realize that if you're not already familiar with HTML *<FORM>* and *<INPUT...>* tags, this example might be a real dome-scratcher. And all that *.value* stuff might be confusing if you've never been exposed to the Dynamic HTML Object Model before. I apologize if that's the case, but I don't want that to discourage you. We'll get into those topics shortly. For now, the main purpose of this example is just to show you how to set up a function procedure using the *Function...End Function* statements and how to call the function using *value = functionName(argument1, argument2, etc.)* syntax.

Sub and Function Procedure Differences

Here are the differences between function procedures and sub procedures:

■ A function procedure is defined using *Function...End Function* statements, whereas a sub procedure is defined using *Sub...End Sub* statements.

■ A function procedure generally "figures something out" and then returns some value based on what it figured out. A sub procedure usually "does something" but does not return a value.

■ When calling a function, use the syntax *value = functionName-(argument1, argument2, etc.)*, where *value* is any variable that will hold the value returned by the function. The parentheses are required.

■ The syntax for calling a sub procedure is *subName argument1, argument2*, etc. If you pass multiple arguments to a sub procedure when calling it, be sure not to include parentheses around the passed arguments.

■ A function always contains a statement in the form *functionName = returnValue*, where *functionName* is the same as the *functionName* as defined in the *Function* statement (but without the parentheses) and *returnValue* is the value that the function returns.

■ Functions that accept arguments always use parentheses. If a function does not accept any arguments, you still should include parentheses. For example, the built-in *Date()* function returns the system date but accepts no arguments. So to put the system date into a variable named *Today*, you use the syntax *Today = Date()*.

The main thing to remember at this point is that you can control when a script does its thing in a variety of ways: by naming a script after the object and event it's bound to, by using *<SCRIPT FOR=... EVENT=...>* to say which object and event the script is bound to, or by defining a custom sub procedure or function procedure that's called upon. You'll see plenty of examples of all these methods put to good use as you progress through this book.

DEALING WITH BUGS IN YOUR SCRIPTS

The one thing about programming that drives people batty is that everything needs to be exact. The slightest typographical error, including one too many or one too few parentheses, commas, or quotation marks, will cause a script to "bomb." A slight misspelling in a statement or a function name will also cause a script to bomb. And since it's human nature to commit little typos here and there, much of your programming time can be spent just debugging your scripts.

Basic typographical errors, also called *syntax errors,* are common when someone first learns a new language, because it's hard to remember the exact spelling of every statement and function name and it's hard to always put in every comma, quotation mark, parenthesis, and so forth. When Internet Explorer comes across something in a script that it can't interpret, it displays an Internet Explorer Script Error dialog box, similar to the one shown in Figure 3-19 on the next page.

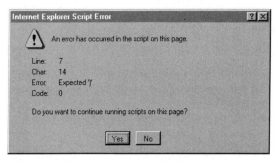

Figure 3-19. *The Internet Explorer Script Error dialog box indicating a problem in a script.*

Before you close such an error message dialog box, always take a moment to absorb what it's telling you. The first three items are the most important. For example, in Figure 3-19 the first three lines tell you the following:

- *Line: 7*—the exact line (counting from the top of the HTML source document) in which the error occurred.

- *Char: 14*—the exact character (counting from the left) in that line that caused the error message to appear.

- *Error: Expected ')'*—a brief explanation of why script processing stopped where it did. This message might not always be a good indication of how to fix the problem, but it can provide a clue to what went wrong.

To correct the script, you need to get to the HTML source code in a text editor or through the HTML editor in your wysiwyg editor. Then you need to edit the code to correct the error and save the document. Then once again you need to open the page in the web browser and check to see whether the script will compile and run correctly.

It isn't always easy to debug a script. You might need to refer to the Internet Client SDK, described in Appendix A, for details about the exact syntax of a statement and to carefully check several lines above the line the error message homes in on.

> **TIP** One big advantage of using an electronic rather than a printed VBScript reference is that you can copy-and-paste code from the electronic reference into your script. That helps to minimize the pesky little syntax errors caused by improperly placed quotation marks, missing parentheses, and simple misspellings.

You should try to prevent bugs. If you're using an electronic reference, you might want to copy-and-paste example code from the document right into your script and then modify the code to do what you want it to do in your page. And don't forget basic assumptions, such as the fact that variable names should *never* be enclosed in quotation marks, whereas literal text must *always* be enclosed in quotation marks.

ELECTRONIC VBSCRIPT RESOURCES

The VBScript tutorials and examples in upcoming chapters will give you much more background on VBScript. But it never hurts to back that up with some good electronic resources. Here are a couple good ones that every VBScript programmer should be aware of:

■   The sections titled *VBScript Tutorial* and *VBScript Language* in the Internet Client SDK, described in Appendix A, offer lots of detailed information on VBScript.

■   *The VBScript Start Page* at www.microsoft.com/vbscript/ offers answers to frequently asked questions, documentation, samples, links to other sites, and more.

SUMMARY

This chapter has been a real whirlwind tour of the basic "how to's" of scripting with VBScript. There's much more to the language than what you've seen here, but if this chapter has done its job, you'll recognize a script when you see one in somebody else's web page source code and some of the mystery will be gone. You'll also be able to type scripts into your own web pages. Here's a recap of the major points we covered in this chapter:

■   A VBScript script is always enclosed in a pair of *<SCRIPT LANGUAGE="VBScript"><!--* and *--></SCRIPT>* tags.

■   You can type and edit scripts right in any text editor or HTML source editor.

- Each of the various data subtypes—which can be broadly categorized as numbers, strings (text), dates, and Booleans (True/False)—contains a unique kind of data.

- A variable is a name that acts as a placeholder for data that's likely to change.

- Operators, such as + (addition), <> (does not equal), and & (concatenation) enable your scripts to manipulate and compare items of data.

- VBScript's 80-plus built-in functions provide more options for acting on data. You can also create your own custom functions (a.k.a. "user-defined functions") that provide even more capabilities for dealing with data.

- You can write a script that is executed as soon as the web page is opened in a web browser, when some "event" occurs in the page, or only when the script is called.

- To run (or test) a script, open the page that contains the script in your web browser.

- Scripts are very fussy about spelling and syntax. Use the electronic resources described in this chapter as your guides to minimize errors and the time you have to spend debugging.

In the next chapter, we'll greatly expand your VBScript programming prowess as we focus on the objects, properties, methods, and events in Internet Explorer 4's Dynamic HTML Object Model.

Chapter 4

The Dynamic HTML Object Model

When it comes to scripting in web pages, there are really two sides of the coin. There's the *scripting language* (VBScript, for example), which you use to write instructions that define what the script will do. We introduced that side of the coin in the preceding chapter. On the other side of the coin are the *objects* that the scripts work upon and the objects that trigger the scripts into action. Each of these objects has a unique name so that scripts can refer to specific objects within the current web page. The system for naming all the objects is called the *object model,* and that's what this chapter is about. The topics include:

- What the Dynamic HTML Object Model is all about

- Understanding the Dynamic HTML Object Hierarchy

- Getting to know window objects, document objects, and collections

- Finding HTML Element Objects in the *all* collection

- Creating your own object names

- Object properties, methods, and events

- Understanding event bubbling

WHAT IS THE DYNAMIC HTML OBJECT MODEL?

When you're sitting at your computer looking at a web page in Internet Explorer 4, just about everything you see is an object. But to be more specific, an object is something that *exposes* itself to VBScript (or any other scripting language). What do we as web authors gain when an object exposes itself? A peek at the object's underwear? Not exactly. We gain the ability to write scripts that make the object behave in new ways. And we gain the ability to trigger scripts in response to some event that happens to an object, such as when a visitor points to, clicks on, or double-clicks on an object.

While an object is something that can interact with VBScript (or any other scripting language), the object model is the total group of all those objects. Although it might be more accurate to say that the object model is a system for naming all those things. The naming system is based on the *object hierarchy*. Figure 4-1 shows the object hierarchy of the objects and collections commonly used in Internet Explorer 4.

At the top of the object hierarchy is the *window* object. That's the broadest, most general object because all other objects are contained within the *window* object. (The collections within the *window* object are just groups of related objects.) Some of the objects in the *window* object are plainly visible on the screen, as Figure 4-2 on page 82 illustrates. Some objects have no visual counterpart on the screen, but as you'll see, they're useful for scripting nonetheless.

While I don't want to bog you down with too much detail right now, I do want to give you some idea of just what the objects and collections within the *window* object offer us as web authors and VBScript programmers. So here's a summary of the objects and the one collection immediately below the *window* object:

- *location* object: Contains information about the URL of the current page. VBScript can use this object to navigate to new web sites or pages.

- *frames* collection: A collection of all the frames in a framed site. VBScript can use this collection to alter the appearance of frames, control the contents of each frame, and more.

- *history* object: Keeps track of recently visited pages. VBScript can use the information in this object to navigate to previously visited pages.

- *navigator* object: Contains information about a visitor's web browser. VBScript can use this information to make decisions about how to behave based on the brand name and version number of the visitor's web browser.

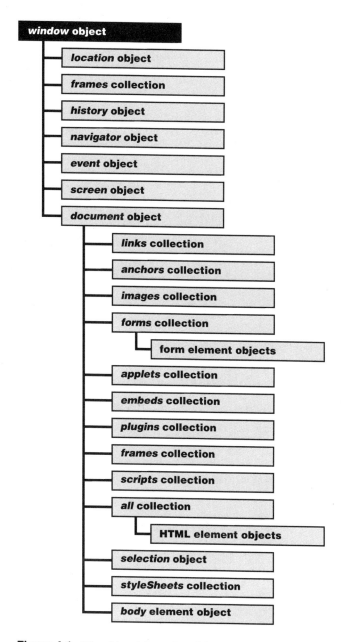

Figure 4-1. *The object hierarchy of the objects and collections commonly used in Internet Explorer 4.*

- *event* object: Keeps track of the state of an event. VBScript can use this object to determine what element caused the event, whether the left or the right mouse button was clicked, the position of the mouse, whether the Alt, Ctrl, or Shift key was held down during a keypress, and more.

- *screen* object: Contains information about the visitor's screen settings. VBScript can use this object to decide how best to display information on the screen.

- *document* object: The HTML document currently displayed by the web browser.

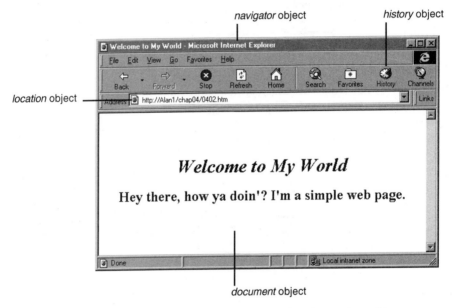

Figure 4-2. *Some of the objects contained within the* window *object.*

If you take a look at the object hierarchy, you'll notice that the *document* object is the last object directly under the *window* object. The *document* object, however, contains a whole bunch of objects and collections of its own. We'll take a look at some of those next.

Objects in the *document* Object

The web page currently being viewed in the web browser is an object, called the *document* object. The *document* object, in turn, contains all the objects that make up the current web page. Figure 4-3 shows three examples of *document* objects—some *document.links* objects, a *document.images* object, and a *document.forms* object.

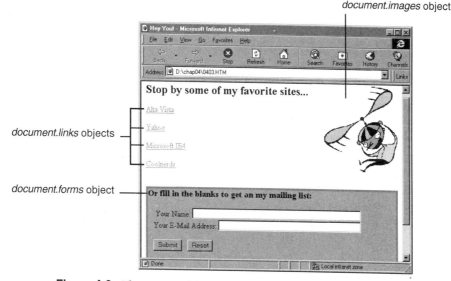

Figure 4-3. *Three examples of objects contained within the* document *object.*

Right off the bat you'll probably notice something unique about the objects contained within the document—they all start with *document.* (the word *document* followed by a period). This is because in the object hierarchy it's necessary to refer to the parent object (the object that contains the current object) whenever you refer to an object.

The *window* object is typically an exception to this rule because when you omit *window.* in an object name, the script assumes that you mean "the current window that we're in right now." So it's not necessary to refer to the *location* object as *window.location* or the *history* object as *window.history.*

But since the objects in Figure 4-3 are contained within the *document* object (which itself is contained within the *window* object), it is necessary to use the *document.* prefix.

You might also notice that the object names in Figure 4-3 are plural—*document.links* and *document.images*, for example. This is because the *document* object poses a unique problem. Any web page might contain one link, a dozen links, or hundreds of links. For that matter, it might contain many images and many forms. So there needs to be some way of referring to all the links, or all the images, or all the forms in the current document. And the object model does that by offering collections of objects within the *document* object.

Collections

A *collection* is a group of similar objects. For example, the *links* collection includes all the hyperlinks (*<A HREF=...>* tags) within the document. When Internet Explorer loads a new web page, it gathers information about all the links in the page and puts that information in the *links* collection. That way, all of the links in the web page can be exposed to VBScript.

The way Internet Explorer creates the *links* collection is fairly straightforward. The first *<A HREF=...>* tag becomes item number 0 in the list—that is, *document.links(0)*. The next *<A HREF=...>* tag it encounters in the page becomes *document.links(1)*, and so forth. So if we were to peek behind the scenes and see how the object model identifies each of the links in Figure 4-3, we'd see that they're named as in Figure 4-4.

> **NOTE** It's a bummer that they use zero-based lists in these collections, because it means the first item in the list is number 0, the second item is number 1, and so forth. Really helps confuse an already complicated thing, ya know? But lots of programming languages work that way, so it's just something we all have to get used to.

All of the collections in the Dynamic HTML Object Model—the *images* collection, the *anchors* collection, and so forth—are created in the same manner. The web browser just "adds them to the lists" as it encounters them during the loading of the document.

So, then, what do you think the object name for the picture in Figure 4-3 would be? If you guessed *document.images(0)*, you're right. Because that's the first (and only) image in that document. Likewise for the form. Since there's only one form, it's official name is *document.forms(0)*.

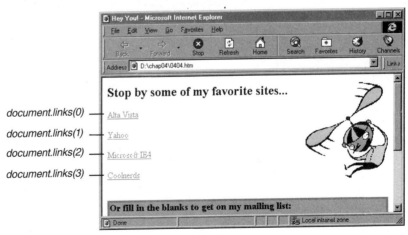

Figure 4-4. *This* links *collection contains four items, numbered 0 through 4.*

TIP The names we're discussing here are object names assigned automatically by Internet Explorer 4. You can, as an alternative, make up your own names for objects, using the *ID* attribute or *NAME* attribute in the object's HTML tag. More on this a little later in the chapter.

So now if you were to peek back at the object hierarchy shown in Figure 4-1, you'd see that the *document* object exposes more than just the *links*, *images*, and *forms* collections. Here is a brief description of the objects and collections exposed by the *document* object. All of these are referenced in more detail in the Internet Client SDK, described in Appendix A. But for now, I think you'd do well just to stick with the big picture. Because there's more coming!

- *links* collection (*document.links*): Exposes all the hyperlinks and client-side image maps in the document (*<A HREF=...>...</A>* tags and *<AREA>* tags).

- *anchors* collection (*document.anchors*): Exposes all the named targets in the document (*<A NAME=...>...</A>* and *<A ID=...>...</A>* tags).

- *images* collection (*document.images*): Exposes all the graphic images in the document (*<IMG>* tags).

- *forms* collection (*document.forms*): Exposes all the forms in the document (*<FORM>...</FORM>* tags). Each form has its own collection of form element objects, as discussed a little later in this chapter.

- *applets* collection (*document.applets*): Exposes all the Java applets in the document (*<APPLET>...</APPLET>* tags).

- *embeds* collection (*document.embeds*): Exposes all the embedded objects in the document (*<EMBED>...</EMBED>* tags).

- *plugins* collection (*document.plugins*): Same as the *embeds* collection—exposes all the embedded objects in the document (*<EMBED>...</EMBED>* tags).

- *frames* collection (*document.frames*): Exposes all the floating frames in the document (*<IFRAME>...</IFRAME>* tags).

- *scripts* collection (*document.scripts*): Exposes information about all the scripts in the document (*<SCRIPT>...</SCRIPT>* tags).

- *all* collection (*document.all*): Exposes all of the HTML element objects in the document, as discussed a little later in this chapter.

- *selection* object (*document.selection*): Exposes any text and/or other elements that the visitor has selected (by dragging the mouse pointer through them).

- *styleSheets* collection (*document.styleSheets*): Exposes style sheet information for elements in a document.

- *body* element object (*document.body*): Exposes information from the *<BODY>...</BODY>* tags such as the background color (*bgColor*).

Whew! A lot of exposure going on here. Two items in the list, the *forms* collection and the *all* collection, deserve some additional explanation here. They're unique in that even though they are contained within the document object, they themselves act as containers to still more objects.

The *forms* Collection

An HTML form is enclosed in *<FORM>...</FORM>* tags. Some of the elements that you can use to define fields in a form include the *<INPUT>*, *<BUTTON>...</BUTTON>*, *<SELECT>...</SELECT>* and *<OPTION>*, and *<TEXTAREA>...</TEXTAREA>* tags. For example, Figure 4-5 shows the HTML source for a sample form. Note the use of the *NAME* attribute in the various tags.

Figure 4-6 shows how the web page that contains the form looks when opened in Internet Explorer. Let's look at how the object model assigns names to all the objects on the screen.

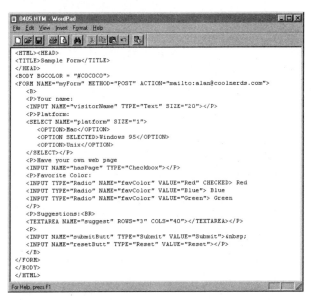

```
<HTML><HEAD>
<TITLE>Sample Form</TITLE>
</HEAD>
<BODY BGCOLOR = "#COCOCO">
<FORM NAME="myForm" METHOD="POST" ACTION="mailto:alan@coolnerds.com">
   <B>
   <P>Your name:
   <INPUT NAME="visitorName" TYPE="Text" SIZE="20"></P>
   <P>Platform:
   <SELECT NAME="platform" SIZE="1">
      <OPTION>Mac</OPTION>
      <OPTION SELECTED>Windows 95</OPTION>
      <OPTION>Unix</OPTION>
   </SELECT></P>
   <P>Have your own web page
   <INPUT NAME="hasPage" TYPE="Checkbox"></P>
   <P>Favorite Color:
   <INPUT TYPE="Radio" NAME="favColor" VALUE="Red" CHECKED> Red
   <INPUT TYPE="Radio" NAME="favColor" VALUE="Blue"> Blue
   <INPUT TYPE="Radio" NAME="favColor" VALUE="Green"> Green
   </P>
   <P>Suggestions:<BR>
   <TEXTAREA NAME="suggest" ROWS="3" COLS="40"></TEXTAREA></P>
   <P>
   <INPUT NAME="submitButt" TYPE="Submit" VALUE="Submit"> 
   <INPUT NAME="resetButt" TYPE="Reset" VALUE="Reset"></P>
   </B>
</FORM>
</BODY>
</HTML>
```

Figure 4-5. *The document source for a web page containing a form.*

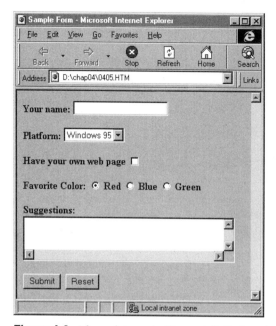

Figure 4-6. *The web page in Figure 4-5 displayed in Internet Explorer.*

As you might recall, all the forms in a page are collected in the *forms* collection. The first form encountered in the document is form number 0. The page in Figure 4-6 only contains one form, so that form is named *document.forms(0)*. Again, the *document.* prefix is required because the *form* object is contained within the larger *document* object.

Each form has its own collection of form fields or form elements. Those elements are also put into a collection by the object model. The first field in a form becomes *elements(0)*, the next field becomes *elements(1)*, and so forth. But because the form elements are contained within the *form* object, the entire prefix becomes *document.forms(0)*. Thus, the complete name of the first field in the form shown in Figure 4-6 is actually *document.forms(0).elements(0)*. The second field in that form is named *document.forms(0).elements(1)*, and so forth, down to the last field in the form (which in this example is a Reset button), whose name is *document.forms(0).elements(8)*. Figure 4-7 on the next page shows the complete Dynamic HTML Object Model names for all the fields in the form.

If you look back at the original source code for the form back in Figure 4-5, you'll see that I used a *NAME* attribute in every HTML tag that defines the form and its fields. For example, the form itself is named *myForm (<FORM NAME="myForm"...>)*. The first field in the form is named *visitorName (<INPUT NAME="visitorName"...>)*, and so forth. The question then becomes: Can you use those names rather than the subscripts—the little numbers in parentheses? The answer is Yes.

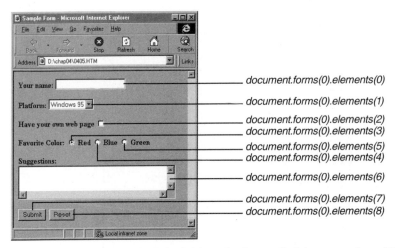

Figure 4-7. *The names of all the fields in the form called* document.forms(0).

To use the name rather than the subscript, you remove the subscript and replace it with a dot (period) followed by that name. For example, the entire form can also be referred to as *document.forms.myForm*. The name of the first field in that form can be referred to as *document.forms.myForm.visitorName,* and so forth, as illustrated in Figure 4-8. (Note that because the radio buttons form a group of objects all named *favColor*, it's still necessary to add the subscripts to their names.)

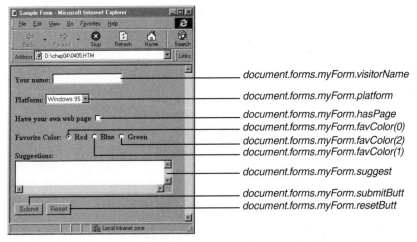

Figure 4-8. *Using names defined by* NAME *attributes rather than subscripts to identify form fields.*

As you can see, the deeper you get into the object hierarchy, the longer the names of objects become. When you tack on a method or a property (as we'll discuss in a moment), it gets even longer. For example, the name of the first field in our form is *document.forms.myForm.visitorName*, but the contents (whatever is typed into that field at the moment) of the form are defined by the *.value* property of that object. Thus, for a line of VBScript code to fetch or change the contents of that *visitorName* field, this rather lengthy reference is required:

```
document.forms.myForm.visitorName.value
```

Or, if you want to use subscripts rather than names, the reference is:

```
document.forms(0).elements(0).value
```

Sheesh! Whatever happened to the good old days when creating a web page required you to simply type some simple text and HTML tags into a document?

The *all* Collection

The *all* collection is new to Internet Explorer 4 and the Dynamic HTML Object Model. This collection consists of every HTML tag in the page. As with other collections, items in the collection are added as they are encountered while the page is being loaded into the web browser. The first item in the collection is number 0.

WHAT AM I POINTING TO?

Here's a neat trick that lets you see which object the mouse pointer is resting on at the moment. Type this script somewhere between the *<HEAD>…</HEAD>* tags in any web page:

```
<SCRIPT LANGUAGE="VBScript"><!--
   Sub document_onmousemove()
      subscript = window.event.srcElement.sourceIndex
      tagType = window.event.srcElement.tagName
      msg= "document.all(" & subscript & ") - "
      msg = msg & "Tag = <" & tagType & ">"
      window.status = msg
   End Sub
--></SCRIPT>
```

Close and save the page as you normally would. Open the page in Internet Explorer 4. Then, as you move the mouse pointer around the web page, the status bar will show you exactly which object in the *document.all* collection you're pointing to at the moment, and the HTML tag you used to define that object. (Keep in mind that when you include this script in your web page, a *SCRIPT* element is added to the *all* collection. Therefore, the *document.all* subscript for the elements after the *<SCRIPT>…</SCRIPT>* tags is incremented by one.)

The items that the *all* collection references are sometimes called *HTML Element Objects* or *HTML elements*. Rather than summarize all those elements here, which would take a few pages, I've simply listed their names below. It's easy to figure out what each element object represents—you just put a pair of angle brackets around the name, and you have the HTML tag that defines the object. For example, an *IMG* element is something in the document that's defined by an *<IMG>* tag. An *ADDRESS* element is some chunk of text that's enclosed in *<ADDRESS>...</ADDRESS>* tags. All of the HTML elements are referenced, in detail, in the Internet Client SDK.

!-- --	DFN	INS	SCRIPT
!DOCTYPE	DIR	ISINDEX	SELECT
A	DIV	KBD	SMALL
ACRONYM	DL	LABEL	SPAN
ADDRESS	DT	LEGEND	STRIKE
APPLET	EM	LI	STRONG
AREA	EMBED	LINK	STYLE
B	FIELDSET	LISTING	SUB
BASE	FONT	MAP	SUP
BASEFONT	FORM	MARQUEE	TABLE
BGSOUND	FRAME	MENU	TBODY
BIG	FRAMESET	META	TD
BLOCKQUOTE	H1	NOBR	TEXTAREA
BODY	H2	NOFRAMES	TFOOT
BR	H3	NOSCRIPT	TH
BUTTON	H4	OBJECT	THEAD
CAPTION	H5	OL	TITLE
CENTER	H6	OPTION	TR
CITE	HEAD	P	TT
CODE	HR	PARAM	U
COL	HTML	PLAINTEXT	UL
COLGROUP	I	PRE	VAR
COMMENT	IFRAME	Q	WBR
DD	IMG	S	XMP
DEL	INPUT	SAMP	

Let me show you an example of how the *all* collection would look for a sample page. Figure 4-9 shows a fairly simple web page. Figure 4-10 shows the document source for that web page.

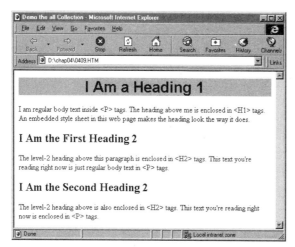

Figure 4-9. *A simple web page with some headings and text.*

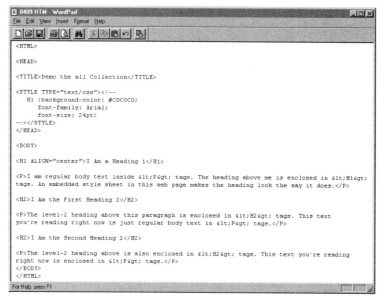

Figure 4-10. *The document source for the page shown in Figure 4-9.*

Figure 4-11 shows how Internet Explorer 4 would organize the *all* collection for that page. Notice that the structure of the *all* collection is pretty straightforward. The item *document.all(0)* (pronounced "document dot all sub zero") is the *HTML* element, which represents both the opening *<HTML>* tag and closing *</HTML>* tag. Then *document.all(1)* is the next element in the page, *HEAD*, and so forth, down to the last opening tag in the page.

This is good because it means that literally everything in a web page can be identified and thus exposed to VBScript and all scripting languages. And that, in turn, means you can write code that responds to just about anything a visitor does while viewing your page. And you can write code that changes just about anything on the page, right in front of the visitor's eyes.

But perhaps you're thinking, "Yeah, well, suppose I want to write some code that interacts with the second *<H2>* tag in a page. How do I know that the second *H2* element is *document.all(9)*, or whatever the case might be?" That's certainly a valid question. And the answer is, "You probably don't know that the second *H2* element is *document.all(9)*. But fortunately, you don't have to." The reason is that the *all* collection also provides an easy way to create sort of "mini-collections" of specific elements in the page.

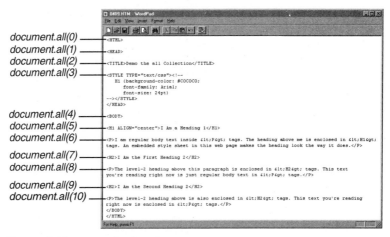

Figure 4-11. *A sample* all *collection.*

Two special versions of the *all* collection's syntax go like this:

```
document.all.tags("elementName")
```

and

```
document.all.tags("elementName").item(position)
```

elementName is the name inside the angle brackets of the corresponding HTML tag and *position* is the specific item you want based on its position in the page. For example, the following is a collection of all the *H2* elements in the current document.

```
document.all.tags("H2")
```

The first *H2* element in the document is

```
document.all.tags("H2").item(0)
```

and the second *H2* element in the document is

```
document.all.tags("H2").item(1)
```

as illustrated in Figure 4-12. The syntax is a little weird, but I often think of something like *document.all.tags("H2").item(1)* as saying, "Out of *all* the *<H2> tags* in the *document,* I want the second *item.*" (Intuitively, the second *H2* element in the document should be *item(2)*. But unfortunately, due to the zero-based lists, *item(0)* is the first item and *item(1)* is the second item. Ugh!)

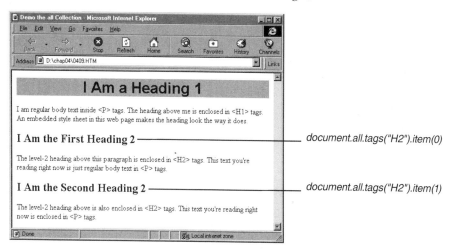

Figure 4-12. *How the* all *collection identifies text formatted with* <H2> *tags.*

All the names of objects that we've discussed so far in this chapter are ones that the object model provides automatically. You can also assign your own custom names to objects, as we'll discuss next.

NAMING YOUR OWN OBJECTS

The object model provides names for every object in the web page so that you can refer to those things in your code. But you're not limited to the names that the object model provides. Thanks to the HTML *ID* attribute, you can also make up names for objects in your page. To assign a name to an object, just put the *ID* attribute followed by any name of your choosing into the object's HTML tag. For example, in the line below, I've named the Heading 1 title *mainTitle*:

```
<H1 ID="mainTitle" ALIGN="center">I Am a Heading 1</H1>
```

Figure 4-13 shows our trusty sample document with three of the objects named using the *ID* attribute—the first heading named *mainTitle* and the two subheadings named *subTitle1* and *subTitle2*.

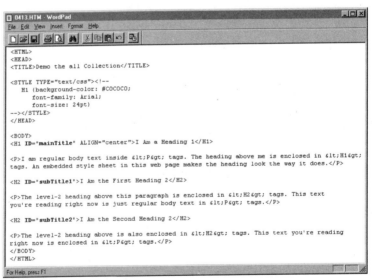

```
<HTML>
<HEAD>
<TITLE>Demo the all Collection</TITLE>

<STYLE TYPE="text/css"><!--
    H1 {background-color: #C0C0C0;
        font-family: Arial;
        font-size: 24pt}
--></STYLE>
</HEAD>

<BODY>
<H1 ID="mainTitle" ALIGN="center">I Am a Heading 1</H1>

<P>I am regular body text inside &lt;P&gt; tags. The heading above me is enclosed in &lt;H1&gt;
tags. An embedded style sheet in this web page makes the heading look the way it does.</P>

<H2 ID="subTitle1">I Am the First Heading 2</H2>

<P>The level-2 heading above this paragraph is enclosed in &lt;H2&gt; tags. This text
you're reading right now is just regular body text in &lt;P&gt; tags.</P>

<H2 ID="subTitle2">I Am the Second Heading 2</H2>

<P>The level-2 heading above is also enclosed in &lt;H2&gt; tags. This text you're reading
right now is enclosed in &lt;P&gt; tags.</P>
</BODY>
</HTML>
```

Figure 4-13. *Headings all have custom names defined by the* ID *attribute.*

All of these objects are still in the *all* collection. But to get to them you can now use this simple syntax:

```
document.all("id")
```

id is the name you've specifed in the *ID* attribute. Hence the "official" object model names for the three headings become *document.all("mainTitle")*, *document.all("subTitle1")*, and *document.all("subTitle2")*, as illustrated in Figure 4-14.

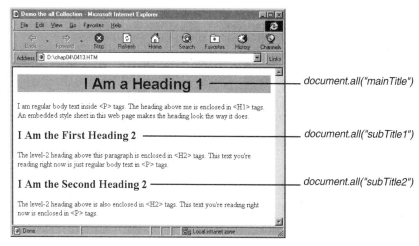

Figure 4-14. *Object model names for tags that contain* ID *attributes.*

Be aware that the new names do not replace the names that the object model applies automatically. Both names still apply. For instance, you can refer to the second heading in Figure 4-14 as either *document.all("subTitle2")* or *document.all.tags("H2").item(1)*. Use whichever name is most convenient at the moment.

If two or more HTML tags in the page contain the same name, as defined in the *ID* attribute, those items will be put into a collection and numbered. For example, look at the tags below, each of which is named *subHead*:

```
<H2 ID="subHead" ALIGN="left">First SubHead</H2>
<H2 ID="subHead" ALIGN="center">Second SubHead</H2>
<H2 ID="subHead" ALIGN="right">Third SubHead</H2>
```

Using the syntax *document.all("subHead")* in this example would actually refer to the collection of elements named *subHead*. To refer to a specific subhead, you need to tack on *item(position)* where *position* is a number referring to a specific object. The first object would be *item(0)*, the second one *item(1)*, and so forth. Thus, the names of the three objects above would be:

```
document.all("subHead").item(0)
document.all("subHead").item(1)
document.all("subHead").item(2)
```

WHO AM I POINTING TO?

If you use *ID* attributes in your HTML tags, you might want to modify the script that I presented in the previous sidebar so that it displays that tag's ID. Place this script between the *<HEAD>…</HEAD>* tags of any page. (If you already have the other script in that page, remove it and put in the following one):

```
<SCRIPT LANGUAGE="VBScript"><!--
    Sub document_onmousemove()
        subscript = window.event.srcElement.sourceIndex
        tagType = window.event.srcElement.tagName
        tagID = window.event.srcElement.id
        msg = "document.all(" & subscript & ") - "
        msg = msg & "Tag = <" & tagType & "> - "
        msg = msg & "ID = " & tagID
        window.status = msg
    End Sub
--></SCRIPT>
```

When you're browsing the document, the status bar will display the *document.all* subscript, the tag, and the *ID* (if any) of whatever object you're pointing to at the moment.

Now you might be thinking, "Let's say I'm somehow able to remember all this and actually refer to objects by name. What good will it do me?" Well, the truth is, the object name in and of itself isn't so valuable. The real power comes when you use an object name in conjunction with one of the properties, methods, or events that the object exposes.

PROPERTIES, METHODS, AND EVENTS

All of the objects we've discussed so far expose some combination of properties, methods, and events. These are defined as follows:

■ Property: Some characteristic of the object, such as its color, size, or *ID*.

■ Method: Something the object can do, such as open or close.

■ Event: Something that happens to the object, such as when the visitor clicks on it or changes its contents.

Every object exposes its own unique combination of properties, methods, and events. The Internet Client SDK, described in Appendix A, provides a reference to the properties, methods, and events of each object in the Dynamic HTML Object Model, as do the electronic references discussed in the section titled "Electronic Resources" near the end of this chapter. In the next three sections, I'll discuss what these items are and how you use them.

Object Properties

As mentioned above, an object property is some characteristic of the object. For example, the *navigator* object exposes the *appName* property, which contains the name of the web browsing program in use. The *location* object exposes the *href* property, which contains the URL of the current page. The *document* object exposes the *bgColor* property, which contains the background color of the page (as defined by the *BGCOLOR* attribute in the *<BODY>* tag.

To refer to an object's property, you use the following syntax:

```
objectName.property
```

objectName is any valid object name (as discussed earlier in this chapter) and *property* is the name of any property that the object exposes. You can use properties to get information about an object, and in many cases you can change the value of the property. To get information about a property, use the following syntax:

```
variableName = objectName.property
```

For example, let's say the current web page has a silver background, defined by this tag:

```
<BODY BGCOLOR="#C0C0C0">
```

The page also contains a button named *bgColorButton* and the following script:

```
<SCRIPT LANGUAGE="VBScript"><!--
   Sub bgColorButton_onclick()
      currentColor = document.bgColor
      msg = "Current background color is " & currentColor
      temp = MsgBox(msg, 0, "Hey")
   End Sub
--></SCRIPT>
```

When you click the button, a message box is displayed indicating the background color, as shown in Figure 4-15 on the following page.

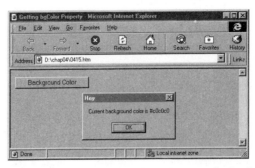

Figure 4-15. *A message box indicating the background color by using the* document.bgColor *property.*

Suppose a web page contains a form named *myForm*. The form contains a text box named *readerName* and a button named *nameButton*, as in the example below:

```
<FORM NAME="myForm">
    <P>Enter your name: <INPUT NAME="readerName"></P>
    <P><INPUT NAME="nameButton" TYPE="Button" VALUE="Your Name"></P>
</FORM>
```

The *.value* property of a text box field is the property that holds whatever is in the text box at the moment. The following script shows how to get the name entered in the text box field:

```
<SCRIPT LANGUAGE="VBScript"><!--
    Sub nameButton_onclick()
        personName = document.myForm.readerName.value
        msg = "Hello " & personName
        temp = MsgBox(msg, 0, "Yoo Hoo")
    End Sub
--></SCRIPT>
```

As shown in Figure 4-16, when the reader clicks the *nameButton* button, a message box is displayed with the text *Hello* followed by whatever name was in the *readerName* field at the moment the button was clicked.

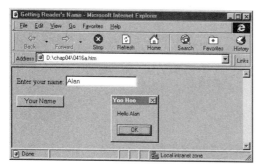

Figure 4-16. *A message box that displays the reader's name by using the* value *property of the text box.*

Incidentally, you can use the *ID* attribute to get a property as well. Here's a different version of the sample form, which uses the *ID* attribute and no *NAME* attributes:

```
<FORM NAME="myForm">
    <P>Enter your name: <INPUT ID="readerName"></P>
    <P><INPUT ID="nameButton" TYPE="Button" VALUE="Your Name"></P>
</FORM>
```

This version of the script uses the *document.all* approach to get the value of the field named *readerName*:

```
<SCRIPT LANGUAGE="VBScript"><!--
    Sub nameButton_onclick()
        personName = document.all("readerName").value
        msg = "Hello " & personName
        temp = MsgBox(msg, 0, "Yoo Hoo")
    End Sub
--></SCRIPT>
```

Some object properties are read-only (r/o), which means that VBScript can get, but not change, the value of the property. Many properties—including the ones we just used in the preceding examples, are read-write (r/w), which means you can get, and optionally change, the value of the property by using VBScript code. The syntax for changing a property is as follows:

```
objectName.property = newValue
```

objectName is, once again, a valid object name, *property* is a valid property for that particular object, and *newValue* is a new value you want to assign to the property. For example, this little script changes the background color of the current web page to silver:

```
<SCRIPT LANGUAGE="VBScript"><!--
    document.bgColor = "#C0C0C0"
--></SCRIPT>
```

Let's look at this example from a larger perspective. Figure 4-17 shows an HTML file that contains two buttons. One button is labeled *Make Background Red*. Clicking that button executes the sub procedure named *makeRed*. That sub procedure contains the following statement, which, when executed, does indeed change the background color to red.

```
document.bgColor = "#FF0000"
```

The other button is labeled *Make Background Blue*. When clicked, that button executes the sub procedure named *makeBlue*. It contains the following statement, which changes the background color to blue.

```
document.bgcolor = "#0000FF"
```

Figure 4-18 shows this page after the Make Background Red button is clicked.

Figure 4-17. *An HTML file containing scripts that change the* bgColor *property.*

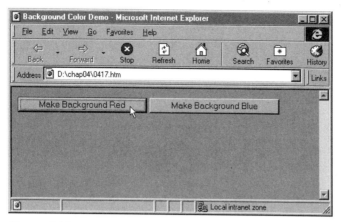

Figure 4-18. *A sample web page that can change its own background color.*

The Dynamic HTML Object Model exposes over 250 properties to VBScript! That's quite a few, and to discuss them all here would take a whole lot of pages. So, to whet your whistle, I've just listed the properties below. To learn more about a property, you can look it up in the Internet Client SDK, described in Appendix A. Furthermore, when you look up an object in the Internet Client SDK, you'll find a list of the properties that that particular object exposes.

accessKey	*backgroundRepeat*	*borderRightColor*
action	*balance*	*borderRightStyle*
activeElement	*behavior*	*borderRightWidth*
align	*bgColor*	*borderStyle*
alinkColor	*bgProperties*	*borderTop*
alt	*border*	*borderTopColor*
altHTML	*borderBottom*	*borderTopStyle*
altKey	*borderBottomColor*	*borderTopWidth*
appCodeName	*borderBottomStyle*	*borderWidth*
appName	*borderBottomWidth*	*bottomMargin*
appVersion	*borderColor*	*bufferDepth*
background	*borderColorDark*	*button*
backgroundAttachment	*borderColorLight*	*cancelBubble*
backgroundColor	*borderLeft*	*cellPadding*
backgroundImage	*borderLeftColor*	*cellSpacing*
backgroundPosition	*borderLeftStyle*	*charset*
backgroundPositionX	*borderLeftWidth*	*checked*
backgroundPositionY	*borderRight*	*classid*

(continued)

className	dialogTop	isTextEdit
clear	dialogWidth	keyCode
clientInformation	direction	lang
clientHeight	disabled	language
clientLeft	display	lastModified
clientTop	domain	left
clientWidth	dynsrc	leftMargin
clientX	encoding	length
clientY	event	letterSpacing
clip	expando	lineHeight
closed	face	linkColor
code	fgColor	listStyle
codeBase	filter	listStyleImage
codeType	font	listStylePosition
color	fontFamily	listStyleType
colorDepth	fontSize	location
cols	fontStyle	loop
colSpan	fontVariant	lowsrc
compact	fontWeight	map
complete	form	margin
content	frame	marginBottom
cookie	frameBorder	marginHeight
cookieEnabled	frameSpacing	marginLeft
coords	fromElement	marginRight
cssText	hash	marginTop
ctrlKey	height	marginWidth
cursor	Hidden	maxLength
data	host	media
dataFld	hostname	method
dataFormatAs	href	Methods
dataPageSize	hspace	mimeTypes
dataSrc	htmlFor	multiple
defaultCharset	htmlText	name
defaultChecked	httpEquiv	noHref
defaultSelected	id	noResize
defaultStatus	indeterminate	noShade
defaultValue	index	noWrap
dialogArguments	innerHTML	object
dialogHeight	innerText	offscreenBuffering
dialogLeft	isMap	offsetHeight

offsetLeft	*reason*	*text*
offsetParent	*recordNumber*	*textAlign*
offsetTop	*recordset*	*textDecoration*
offsetWidth	*referrer*	*textDecorationBlink*
offsetX	*rel*	*textDecorationLineThrough*
offsetY	*returnValue*	*textDecorationNone*
opener	*rev*	*textDecorationOverline*
outerHTML	*rightMargin*	*textDecorationUnderline*
outerText	*rows*	*textIndent*
overflow	*rowSpan*	*textTransform*
owningElement	*rules*	*title*
padding	*screenX*	*toElement*
paddingBottom	*screenY*	*top*
paddingLeft	*scroll*	*topMargin*
paddingRight	*scrollAmount*	*trueSpeed*
paddingTop	*scrollDelay*	*type*
pageBreakAfter	*scrollHeight*	*units*
pageBreakBefore	*scrolling*	*updateInterval*
palette	*scrollLeft*	*URL*
parent	*scrollTop*	*url*
parentElement	*scrollWidth*	*urn*
parentStyleSheet	*search*	*useMap*
parentTextEdit	*selected*	*userAgent*
parentWindow	*selectedIndex*	*vAlign*
pathname	*self*	*value*
pixelHeight	*shape*	*verticalAlign*
pixelLeft	*shiftKey*	*visibility*
pixelTop	*size*	*vlinkColor*
pixelWidth	*sourceIndex*	*volume*
plugins	*span*	*vspace*
pluginspage	*src*	*width*
port	*srcElement*	*wrap*
posHeight	*srcFilter*	*x*
position	*start*	*y*
posLeft	*status*	*zIndex*
posTop	*style*	
posWidth	*styleFloat*	
protocol	*tabIndex*	
readOnly	*tagName*	
readyState	*target*	

Object Methods

Many of the objects in a web page expose *methods* to VBScript. A method is something the object can do or some behavior it can perform all on its own. To trigger a method into action, from a script, use this general syntax:

```
objectName.method()
```

objectName is any valid object name from the object model and *method()* is any valid method for the object being referenced. Some, but not all, methods accept arguments inside the parentheses.

For example, the *window* object is capable of showing an *alert box*—a special dialog box that displays a warning (exclamation point) icon and a message of your choosing. That method has one parameter—a message to show inside the dialog box. So the syntax is actually as follows, where *message* is either a literal string (text enclosed in quotation marks) or the name of a variable that contains a string.

```
alert(message)
```

> **NOTE**   The *alert()* method is a method of the *window* object. While *window.alert(message)* works, it's not necessary to add the *window.object* prefix because when it's omitted, the current window is assumed.

Here's a script that displays the alert message shown in Figure 4-19:

```
<SCRIPT LANGUAGE="VBScript"><!--
   alert("Scary web site ahead!")
--></SCRIPT>
```

Figure 4-19. *A sample alert dialog box.*

The script below displays exactly the same message:

```
<SCRIPT LANGUAGE="VBScript"><!--
   myMsg = "Scary web site ahead!"
   alert(myMsg)
--></SCRIPT>
```

The document object supports a *write()* method. This method uses the following syntax, where *text* is the text to write into the document.

```
document.write(text)
```

The text can contain HTML tags. Use either a literal string enclosed in quotation marks, or use a variable that contains a string as the parameter.

For example, this script displays the text *HOWDY* in *<H1>* format in the current document:

```
<SCRIPT LANGUAGE="VBScript"><!--
   document.write("<H1>HOWDY</H1>")
--></SCRIPT>
```

The script below performs exactly the same task:

```
<SCRIPT LANGUAGE="VBScript"><!--
   myMsg = "<H1>HOWDY</H1>"
   document.write(myMsg)
--></SCRIPT>
```

> **NOTE** In VBScript, it's not always necessary to include the parentheses. For example, *document.write "<H1>HOWDY</H1>"* also works. Typically, it is a good idea to include parentheses. However, when calling a sub procedure with multiple arguments, you must omit the parentheses around the passed arguments. Otherwise, you will receive an error.

So now we come to the question, What kinds of methods are exposed to VBScript? Once again, I won't attempt to give any detail, because there are more than 80 of them. You can look up any one of them in the Internet Client SDK. But to give you a feel for what's available, here's a quick list of all the methods provided by Internet Explorer 4's objects:

add()	*confirm()*	*getAttribute()*
addImport()	*contains()*	*getBookmark()*
addReadRequest()	*createElement()*	*go()*
addRule()	*createRange()*	*inRange()*
alert()	*createStyleSheet()*	*insertAdjacentHTML()*
assign()	*createTextRange()*	*insertAdjacentText()*
back()	*doReadRequest()*	*isEqual()*
blur()	*duplicate()*	*item()*
clear()	*elementFromPoint()*	*javaEnabled()*
clearInterval()	*empty()*	*move()*
clearRequest()	*execCommand()*	*moveBy()*
clearTimeout()	*execScript()*	*moveEnd()*
click()	*expand()*	*moveStart()*
close()	*findText()*	*moveTo()*
collapse()	*focus()*	*moveToBookmark()*
compareEndPoints()	*forward()*	*moveToElementText()*

(continued)

moveToPoint()	*reload()*	*setInterval()*
navigate()	*remove()*	*setTimeout()*
nextPage()	*removeAttribute()*	*showHelp()*
open()	*replace()*	*showModalDialog()*
parentElement()	*reset()*	*start()*
pasteHTML()	*resizeBy()*	*stop()*
prevPage()	*resizeTo()*	*submit()*
prompt()	*scroll()*	*tags()*
queryCommandEnabled()	*scrollBy()*	*taintEnabled()*
queryCommandIndeterm()	*scrollIntoView()*	*write()*
queryCommandState()	*scrollTo()*	*writeln()*
queryCommandSupported()	*select()*	*zOrder()*
queryCommandValue()	*setAttribute()*	
refresh()	*setEndPoint()*	

Object Events

Events are things that happen to an object that VBScript can detect. For example, VBScript can detect when a reader has clicked on most objects. It can even detect when the reader is pointing to an object or has stopped pointing to an object. As discussed in Chapter 3, there are three ways to attach a script to a particular event that happens to a particular object. One technique is to use the *Sub objectName_event()* syntax to create a sub procedure. For example, Figure 4-20 shows an HTML file that contains a sub procedure named *myButton_onclick()*. In the body of the file, you can see the object named *myButton*. Opening the file in Internet Explorer and clicking the button that appears on the page displays the message *You clicked my button* in an alert box.

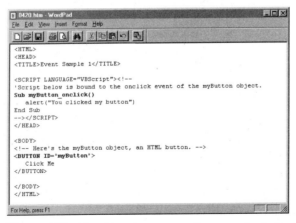

Figure 4-20. *The* objectName_event() *approach of attaching a script to an event that happens to an object.*

A second way to bind a script to an event that happens to an object is to use the *<SCRIPT FOR=…>* syntax to define the script. The approach is handy for keeping scripts near the objects that call them—making it easier for you to see both the object and the script at a glance. Figure 4-21 shows an example in which the script defined under the *<BUTTON>* tag is bound to the *onclick* event of that button.

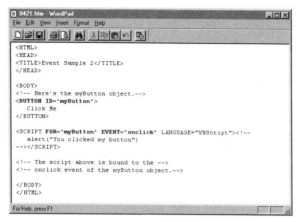

Figure 4-21. *Using <SCRIPT FOR=…> to bind a script to an object and an event.*

The third approach is to not bind the script to anything at all, but rather to call the script right from an HTML tag. This approach is useful when you want to create a general-purpose sub procedure or function procedure that's accessible to two or more objects in your page. Figure 4-22 shows an example of an HTML file using a sub procedure named *showAlert*. The *onclick* event of the *<BUTTON>* tag calls that procedure when the reader clicks the button.

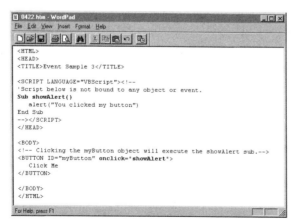

Figure 4-22. *Using an event inside an HTML tag to call a general-purpose procedure.*

Here's a quick list, once again, of all the events that Dynamic HTML supports. Notice that the event names all start with the letters *on*. For more information on any event, or to see which objects it can be used with, look up the event name in the Internet Client SDK.

onabort	*onerror*	*onmouseover*
onafterupdate	*onerrorupdate*	*onmouseup*
onbeforeunload	*onfilterchange*	*onreadystatechange*
onbeforeupdate	*onfinish*	*onreset*
onblur	*onfocus*	*onresize*
onbounce	*onhelp*	*onrowenter*
onchange	*onkeydown*	*onrowexit*
onclick	*onkeypress*	*onscroll*
ondataavailable	*onkeyup*	*onselect*
ondatasetchanged	*onload*	*onstart*
ondatasetcomplete	*onmousedown*	*onsubmit*
ondblclick	*onmousemove*	*onunload*
ondragstart	*onmouseout*	

EVENT BUBBLING

There's one more issue about the object hierarchy that deserves some mention at this point. And that's a concept known as *event bubbling*. When a visitor clicks on some object, that causes an event that rises up through the object hierarchy to the document object. For example, suppose we have the following tags in a page:

```
<BODY>
    <A HREF="http://www.coolnerds.com">
        <IMG SRC="buttnpic.gif">
    </A>
</BODY>
```

Let's say the reader then clicks on the picture defined by the *<IMG>* tag. What did the reader click on—the image, the hyperlink, or the document? The answer is all three. Why so? Because the image is contained within the hyperlink, and the hyperlink is contained within the document. We can envision this containership as shown in Figure 4-23. Event bubbling causes *all* events to bubble up from wherever they start until the event gets to the *document* object.

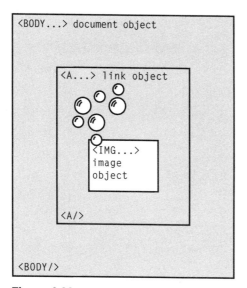

Figure 4-23. *The image is contained within the hyperlink, and the hyperlink is contained within the document.*

Most of the time, this event bubbling is trivial and unimportant. Ignore it, and it does no harm. But there may be occasions where you don't want an event to reach all the way to the document object. For instance, you want the document object to handle *some* mouse clicks, but not *all* mouse clicks. To prevent an event from making it all the way up to the document, you can "pop the bubble"—cancel bubbling at any point in the hierarchy.

Popping the Bubble

To prevent an event from bubbling up beyond a particular object, you need to execute the following statement in a script that's attached to the object that needs to get, but not pass on the event.

```
window.event.cancelBubble = True
```

> **NOTE** The event object is one of those objects that has no visual counterpart on the screen.

Let me show you an example, starting with an HTML file that *doesn't* cancel event bubbling. Figure 4-24 on the next page shows such a file.

Figure 4-24. *An HTML document with no bubble cancellation.*

This file contains three sub procedures, one bound to the *onclick* event of the *document* object (*document_onclick( )*), one bound to the *onclick* event of an object named *myLink* (*myLink_onclick( )*), and one bound to the *onclick* event of an object named *myPic* (*myPic_onclick( )*). The <BODY>...</BODY> tags always define the *document* object. You can see the *myLink* and *myPic* objects, which get their names from *ID* attributes, in the body of the page.

When we open this page in a web browser, it displays an image and the text *Go to Coolnerds*. Both the image and the text are "hot" because they're within the <A>...</A> tags, and clicking either one takes the reader to a page named page2.htm (assuming such a page exists). However, because of the way we've set up this page, we can see what *really* happens when the reader clicks on the picture.

In this sample page, clicking the picture first displays the message *You clicked myPic* in an alert box, as shown in Figure 4-25.

Clicking OK in the alert box then causes the following message to appear in an alert box:

`You clicked myLink`

Clicking that box's OK button causes the following message to appear:

`You clicked the document`

Clicking the OK button in that last alert box causes the current page to disappear and the page named page2.htm to appear within the browser.

Figure 4-25. *A sample page with no bubble cancellation.*

Notice the chain of events. The image gets the click, the hyperlink gets the click, and then the document gets the click. After the event has bubbled up to the highest element, the document, the *<A>* tag's natural response to a mouse click takes place. That natural, built-in response, of course, is to navigate the reader to the URL specified in the *HREF* attribute of the tag.

So now, let's say we *don't* want the event to bubble up all the way to the document. We want the event to stop at the hyperlink. All we need to do is add the *window.event.cancelBubble = True* statement to the script that's attached to the hyperlink, as shown below:

```
'Fired when the object named myLink gets an onclick event.
Sub myLink_onclick()
    alert("You clicked myLink")
    'Prevent the onclick event from bubbling up to the
    'document object.
    window.event.cancelBubble = True
End Sub
```

Opening this modified version of the page and clicking on the picture displays the *You clicked myPic* and *You clicked myLink* messages. But the *You clicked the document* message will never appear because the event bubbling was cancelled before the click got that far up the hierarchy.

Incidentally, the reader will still be taken to page2.htm. That's because event bubbling and canceling events doesn't impair the natural, built-in response.

This little fact can be confusing. For example, suppose you cancel the event at the image level rather than at the hyperlink level, like this:

```
'Fired when the object named myLink gets an onclick event.
Sub myLink_onclick()
    alert("You clicked myLink")
End Sub
```

```
'Fired when the object named myPic gets an onclick event.
Sub myPic_onclick()
    alert("You clicked myPic")
    'Prevent the onclick event from bubbling up beyond the picture.
    window.event.cancelBubble = True
End Sub
```

In this case, clicking the picture displays the *You clicked myPic* message. But that's the only message that gets displayed because the event doesn't bubble up to either the *hyperlink* or *document* objects. The natural behavior of clicking a hot image, however, still takes place. This means that after seeing the *You clicked myPic* message, the reader is still taken to page2.htm—unless, for some reason, you decide you don't *want* that click to trigger the natural response of the *<A>* tag, as discussed next.

Disabling the Natural Response

In addition to being able to keep an event from bubbling up to through objects in the hierarchy, you can also disable an object's natural response to a click. The statement for doing so is:

```
window.event.returnValue = False
```

Figure 4-26 shows a sample page that's similar to our previous sample pages. However, there is no event canceling in this page. Rather, there's a *window.event.returnValue = False* statement in this page.

Figure 4-26. *An HTML document with a* window.event.returnValue = False *statement.*

Opening this page in a web browser and clicking the picture causes all three messages, *You clicked myPic*, *You clicked myLink*, and *You clicked the document*, to appear in that order, just as in the original document shown earlier in Figure 4-24. However, the reader never leaves this page—is never taken to page2.htm—because the natural ability of the *<A>* tag to take the reader to a new page has been wiped out by the *window.event.returnValue = False* in the *myLink_onclick()* sub procedure.

What all of this buys you is extremely precise control over everything that happens as a visitor interacts with your web page. And there's more to the event object than *cancelBubble* and *returnValue*. That object also supports a *srcElement* property, which returns the object that initiated the event, various properties that can detect which mouse button was clicked or which key was pressed, and the exact position of the mouse pointer when the event was fired.

> **NOTE**   The *event* object is one of the few that require the *window.* prefix. Like all objects, the *event* object is referenced in detail in the Internet Client SDK as well as in some of the electronic resources listed below.

You can write scripts that make decisions about what to do next based on information from the event object. We'll take a look at decision-making and other more advanced features of VBScript in the next chapter. Then we'll see some practical examples in Chapter 7.

ELECTRONIC RESOURCES

As you've seen, there are a whole lot of objects in the new Dynamic HTML. And those objects expose a pretty substantial selection of properties, methods, and events to VBScript. A good reference where all these things are cross-referenced, such as the Internet Client SDK, is a must. Here are some helpful electronic resources:

- The Internet Client SDK, described in Appendix A. See *Objects*, *Properties*, *Methods*, *Events*, *Collections*, and *HTML Elements*.

- The Dynamic HTML discussions in the SiteBuilder Network at www.microsoft.com/workshop/author/dhtml/.

- The Internet Explorer 4.0 Demos at www.microsoft.com/ie/ie40/demos/.

- The Dynamic HTML Gallery at www.microsoft.com/gallery/files/html/.

- *An Introduction to the Dynamic HTML Object Model* by Michael Wallent at www.microsoft.com/sitebuilder/features/dynamicom.asp.

SUMMARY

In this chapter, you learned about the Dynamic HTML Object Model, which is a naming system of sorts that exposes objects in the web browser, and your web page, to VBScript (and to JavaScript as well). The key points to remember are:

- An object that can be accessed or modified by a scripting language is said to be *exposed* to that language.

- The object model provides a hierarchical naming system for referring to objects in a web page.

- Several collections of objects are also made available through the object model. For example, all the graphic images in a document make up the *images* collection.

- Objects in a collection can be referenced by subscript—a number that indicates the object's position in the page. For example, *document.images(0)* is the first graphic image in the page, *document.images(1)* is the second image in the page, and so forth.

- The *document.all* collection is a collection of every HTML tag in the page.

- To refer to a particular tag in a document, you can use the syntax *document.all.tags("tagName").item(position)*, where *tagName* is the HTML tag of interest and *position* is the zero-based position in the page. For example, *document.all.tags("H2").item(0)* refers to the first H2 head in the page.

- You can provide your own names by using an *ID* attribute in the HTML tag. For example, *<A ID="firstLink" HREF="http://www.coolnerds.com">* names this hyperlink *firstLink*.

- To access a named object, use the syntax *document.all("id")*, where *id* is the name as defined in the HTML tag. For example, *document.all("firstLink")* refers to the object named *firstLink*.

- Typically, an object name alone doesn't do you any good. The power of an object lies in the properties, methods, and events it exposes.

- Object properties are characteristics of an object. To get information about an object property, use the syntax *variable = objectName.property*, where *variable* is the name of the variable that will hold the information, *objectName* is any valid object name, and *property* is any valid property for that object.

■ To change an object's property, use the syntax *objectName.property = newValue,* where *objectName* is any valid object name, *property* is any valid read/write property for that object, and *newValue* is the new value you want to assign to the property.

■ Many objects expose methods—things they can do. The general syntax for accessing a method is *objectName.method()*, where *objectName* is any valid object name and *method* is any valid method for that particular object.

■ An event is something that happens to an object. Event names all start with the letters *on* and can be used to bind scripts to events that happen to objects.

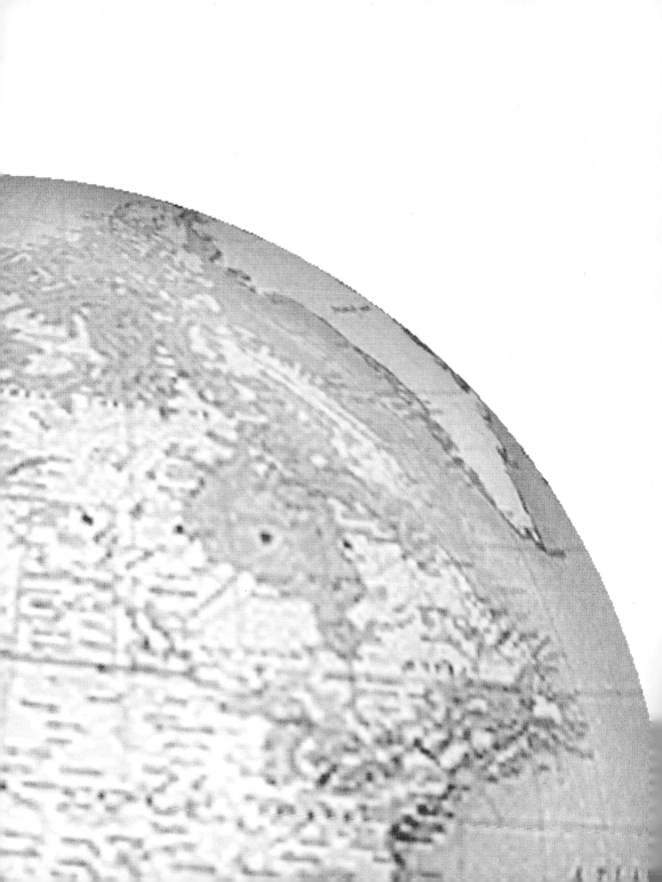

Chapter 5

Deeper into VBScript

Now that you have some VBScript and Dynamic HTML Object Model basics under your belt, let's move on to some of the more advanced features of the VBScript language. In particular, we'll look at:

■ VBScript functions and Dynamic HTML methods for custom dialog boxes

■ VBScript decision-making statements

■ VBScript arrays

■ VBScript loops

■ Variable lifetime

■ Quotation marks

■ Where JavaScript fits in

CUSTOM DIALOG BOXES

One of the more enjoyable things you can do with VBScript is to present custom messages in small dialog boxes to readers of your web pages. You can even ask questions and reply to readers' answers.

The *MsgBox()* Function

You already saw *MsgBox()* in Chapter 3. It's a built-in VBScript function that can display a custom message (or question). Let's look at that function in more depth. The syntax for *MsgBox()*—minus two of its optional parameters for simplicity's sake—is as follows:

```
variableName = MsgBox(prompt[, buttons][, title])
```

variableName is a variable name of your own choosing in which the reader's response will be stored. *prompt* is the message that appears in the dialog box. *buttons* is a sum of numbers or a sum of *constants* indicating which buttons you want the dialog box to contain, which icon is to be displayed in the dialog box, which button is to be the default button, and what modality the dialog box is to have. The numbers and constants are shown in Table 5-1. *title* is the text that appears in the title bar of the dialog box. If the *title* parameter is omitted, the title *Visual Basic* appears in the title bar.

> **NOTE** A constant is like a variable that's been preassigned a value in the language. The purpose of a constant is to give some numeric value a more meaningful name. You can use either a number or its equivalent constant in your code. Almost all of VBScript's constants begin with the letters *vb* and are referenced in the Internet Client SDK (described in Appendix A).

You can create a sum for the *buttons* argument of the *MsgBox()* function by adding one number from each of two or more of the four groups: 1 + 32 + 256 + 0 = 289, for example. A message box defined in the following way

```
answer = MsgBox("Are you sure?", 289, "Careful")
```

displays the OK and Cancel buttons (1) and the Warning Query icon (32). The second button, Cancel, is the default button (256), and the user must answer the query before doing more work in that application (0).

You can also use an expression to sum the constants for the *buttons* arguments, as in these two lines:

```
buttons = vbOKCancel + vbQuestion + vbDefaultButton2
answer = MsgBox("Are you sure?", buttons, "Careful")
```

Either way, the resulting message box will look like the one shown in Figure 5-1.

Figure 5-1. *A sample custom message box.*

NOTE The default button is the one that's selected if the reader just presses Enter in response to the message box query without clicking a button with the mouse. The default button has a darker frame around it and a dotted line along its edge.

Table 5-1

NUMBERS AND CONSTANTS
USED TO DEFINE A CUSTOM DIALOG BOX

Number	Constant	Meaning
Buttons		
0	*vbOKOnly*	Display OK button only (the default if *buttons* is omitted).
1	*vbOKCancel*	Display OK and Cancel buttons.
2	*vbAbortRetryIgnore*	Display Abort, Retry, and Ignore buttons.
3	*vbYesNoCancel*	Display Yes, No, and Cancel buttons.
4	*vbYesNo*	Display Yes and No buttons.
5	*vbRetryCancel*	Display Retry and Cancel buttons.
Icon		
16	*vbCritical*	Display Critical Message icon.
32	*vbQuestion*	Display Warning Query icon.
48	*vbExclamation*	Display Warning Message icon.
64	*vbInformation*	Display Information Message icon.
Default Button		
0	*vbDefaultButton1*	First button is default.
256	*vbDefaultButton2*	Second button is default.
512	*vbDefaultButton3*	Third button is default.
768	*vbDefaultButton4*	Fourth button is default.
Modality		
0	*vbApplicationModal*	Application modal: The user must respond to the message in the dialog box before continuing work in the current application.
4096	*vbSystemModal*	System modal: All applications are suspended until the user responds to the message in the dialog box.

The *variableName* component of the *MsgBox( )* function is set to a numeric value when the reader clicks a button. The number and the constant you can use to represent each of the buttons a reader can click in response to a message are shown in Table 5-2. If the reader clicks the OK button in response to our sample dialog box message, the variable named *answer* is set to the value *1*. If the reader clicks the Cancel button, the *answer* variable is set to the value *2*. You can use the constants shown in Table 5-2 to check which button the reader clicked.

Table 5-2

BUTTON VALUES
RETURNED BY THE *MSGBOX()* FUNCTION

Button Clicked	Value Returned	Constant
OK	1	*vbOK*
Cancel	2	*vbCancel*
Abort	3	*vbAbort*
Retry	4	*vbRetry*
Ignore	5	*vbIgnore*
Yes	6	*vbYes*
No	7	*vbNo*

Suppose you want a custom message box to display a question, Yes and No buttons (4, or *vbYesNo*), and a warning message icon (48, or *vbExclamation*), with the second button, No, as the default button (256, or *vbDefaultButton2*). After the reader makes a selection by clicking either the Yes or the No button, you want to display either a page named spooky.htm (if the reader clicked Yes) or an Alert box (if the reader clicked No). Here's how the script looks if you use numbers rather than constants for the *buttons* argument and the return value:

```
<SCRIPT LANGUAGE="VBScript"><!--
    msg = "Eeks! Are you sure you want to go there?"
    title = "Spooky!"
    buttons = 308
    answer = MsgBox(msg, buttons, title)
    'Respond to button click.
    If answer = 6 Then
        location.href = "spooky.htm"
    Else
        alert("I don't blame ya!")
    End If
--></SCRIPT>
```

If you prefer to use the constants rather than the numbers, the script looks like this:

```
<SCRIPT LANGUAGE="VBScript"><!--
   msg = "Eeks! Are you sure you want to go there?"
   title = "Spooky!"
   buttons = vbYesNo + vbDefaultButton2 + vbExclamation
   answer = MsgBox(msg, buttons, title)
   'Respond to button click.
   If answer = vbYes Then
      location.href = "spooky.htm"
   Else
      alert("I don't blame ya!")
   End If
--></SCRIPT>
```

Whether you use numbers or constants is entirely a matter of personal preference. The numbers have the advantage of being a bit more compact. The constants have the advantage of being more descriptive and probably easier to remember. But the end result from the reader's perspective is the same. Either of the two scripts above will display the message box shown in Figure 5-2. And either will respond to the reader's selection by either displaying the spooky.htm page or displaying the *I don't blame ya!* message in an Alert box.

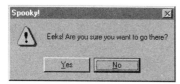

Figure 5-2. *Another sample custom message box.*

I'll discuss *If...Then...Else* and other decision-making statements in more detail a little later in this chapter. For now, let's look at another type of custom dialog box you can display.

The *InputBox()* Function

You can display a dialog box that accepts a string of text typed by the reader rather than just a button click. You use VBScript's *InputBox()* function with the following syntax (again, minus a few optional parameters for simplicity's sake):

```
variableName = InputBox(prompt[, title][, default])
```

Here's a sample script that displays an Input box:

```
<SCRIPT LANGUAGE="VBScript"><!--
   promptText = "Please type in your name"
   title = "What is your name?"
```

(continued)

```
        defaultText = "Type name here"
        readerName = InputBox(promptText, title, defaultText)
        'The statements below show a message
        'containing the reader's name.
        msg = "Well hello there " & readerName
        alert(msg)
--></SCRIPT>
```

When a web page containing this script is opened, the Input dialog box shown in Figure 5-3 is displayed. (The Input dialog box comes with OK and Cancel buttons.) If the reader types in *Alan* and clicks the OK button, the Alert dialog box shown in Figure 5-4 appears. If the user clicks the Cancel button, *variableName* is set to an empty string ("").

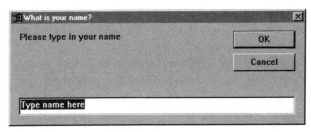

Figure 5-3. *A sample Input dialog box.*

Figure 5-4. *A sample Alert dialog box.*

The *alert* Method

Dynamic HTML has some custom dialog box methods built into it. In object model parlance, each is considered "a method of the window object." The *alert* method, which we've already seen in the preceding example, uses this syntax:

```
window.alert(message)
```

window. refers to an open window. (You can omit *window.* if you're referring to the current window.) *message* is the message to be displayed. We've already seen, in Figure 5-4, what an Alert box looks like.

The *confirm* Method

The Dynamic HTML *confirm* method displays a message box containing OK and Cancel buttons. The syntax is:

```
variableName = window.confirm(message)
```

variableName is the name of a variable that will hold the reader's entry, and the optional *window.* object specifies an open window—if omitted, the current web browser window is assumed. If the reader clicks the OK button, *variableName* contains *True*. If the reader clicks the Cancel button, *variableName* contains *False*.

The script below displays the Confirm dialog box shown in Figure 5-5. After the reader clicks a button, an Alert box displays a message indicating the current value of the *answer* variable:

```
<SCRIPT LANGUAGE="VBScript"><!--
   msg = "Do you want to continue?"
   answer = confirm(msg)
   'Display answer in an Alert box.
   msg2 = "You picked " & answer
   alert(msg2)
--></SCRIPT>
```

Figure 5-5. *A sample Confirm dialog box.*

The *prompt* Method

The *prompt* method displays a dialog box much like the dialog box displayed by VBScript's *InputBox()* function. The syntax for the *prompt* method is:

```
variableName = window.prompt(message, default)
```

variableName is the name of a variable that will hold the reader's entry. The optional *window.* object specifies an open window—if omitted, the current web browser window is assumed. The *message* parameter is the message to be displayed in the box, and the *default* parameter is text to be displayed where the reader is to type.

The script below displays the Prompt dialog box shown in Figure 5-6. After the reader types in an entry and clicks the OK button, the entry is displayed in an Alert box.

```
<SCRIPT LANGUAGE="VBScript"><!--
    msg = "Please type in your name:"
    defaultText = "Your Name Here"
    readerName = prompt(msg, defaultText)
    'Display reader's entry in an Alert box.
    alert("Welcome " & readerName)
--></SCRIPT>
```

Figure 5-6. *A sample Prompt dialog box.*

VBSCRIPT DECISION MAKING

A VBScript script can make a decision about which course of action to take based on some fact or on the contents of some variable. Decision making is one of the best features of any programming language because it enables a program to behave "intelligently."

The *If...Then* Statements

You can use the VBScript *If...Then* statement or one of its variants to have your script make decisions. The simplest *If...Then* statement is:

```
If expression Then do this
```

expression is an expression that results in a true or false result, and *do this* is a VBScript statement. If *expression* proves to be true, *do this* is executed. If *expression* proves to be false, *do this* is ignored.

To make several statements dependent on the outcome of an expression, use this syntax:

```
If expression Then
    do this
    and do this
    and do this
    ...
End If
```

In this kind of *If...Then* statement, if *expression* proves to be true, all statements up to the matching *End If* statement are executed. If *expression* proves to be false, the statements up to the matching *End If* are all ignored.

A third variety of *If...Then* statement, one that we saw earlier in this chapter, enables you to have your program do one thing (or one set of things) if *expression* proves to be true, and to do an alternative thing (or set of things) if *expression* proves to be false. The syntax for such an *If...Then...Else* statement is:

```
If expression Then
    do this
    and do this
    and do this
    ...
Else
    do this
    and do this
    and do this
    ...
End If
```

For an example that uses an *If...Then...Else* statement, let's suppose that you want your web page to present a simple dialog box containing Yes and No buttons. If the reader of your web page clicks the Yes button, you want to display a particular custom message. If the reader clicks the No button, you want to display some other message. Figure 5-7 shows exactly how such a script can be written.

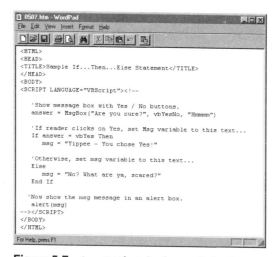

Figure 5-7. *A script that displays a dialog box with Yes and No buttons and then displays different messages depending on the reader's choice.*

Let's take a moment to analyze the script to see how it works. First, the statement displays the message box shown in Figure 5-8.

```
answer = MsgBox("Are you sure?", vbYesNo, "Hmmmm")
```

Notice the Yes and No buttons displayed in the box as a result of our passing the constant *vbYesNo* as the *buttons* argument to the *MsgBox()* function.

Figure 5-8. *The message box displayed by* answer = MsgBox("Are you sure?", vbYesNo, "Hmmmm").

When VBScript sees the *answer = MsgBox...* line, it displays the dialog box and waits for the reader to click a button. When the reader clicks a button, the statements below the *answer = MsgBox...* line are executed. The

```
If answer = vbYes Then
```

and

```
msg = "Yippee - You chose Yes!"
```

lines say, "If the reader clicked the Yes button, store the text *Yippee - You chose Yes!* in a new variable named *msg*." (Recall from Table 5-2 that *vbYes* is the constant used to represent Yes.) If the reader clicks the No button, the *Else* part of the *If...Then...Else* statement is executed and the variable named *msg* receives the text *No? What are ya, scared?*

The *End If* statement marks the end of the *If...Then...Else* statement. The last line, *alert(msg)*, is executed regardless of whether the reader clicks Yes or No. The simple *alert(msg)* statement displays only the text shown in the *msg* variable, along with an OK button. If the reader clicks Yes, the resulting message looks like the one shown in Figure 5-9. If the reader clicks No, a similar dialog box appears but the message inside the box reads, *No? What are ya, scared?*

Figure 5-9. *The resulting message if the reader clicks the Yes button in the Hmmmm dialog box shown in Figure 5-8.*

The *Select Case* Statement

VBScript also features a *Select Case* statement that you can use to have your code run any one of several mutually exclusive chunks of code. The syntax for the *Select Case* statement looks like this:

```
Select Case testValue
   Case value1
      statements1
   Case value2
      statements2
   ...
   Case valuen
      statementsn
   Case Else
      else statements
End Select
```

testValue is generally either a number or an expression that results in a number or a string. *value1* is a number or a string that is compared to the *testValue* value. *statements1* is VBScript code that's executed if (and only if) *value1* in the first *Case* statement matches the value in *testValue*. You can put any number of *Case value*n statements between the *Select Case* and *End Select* statements. *Case Else* and *else statements* are optional. The *else statements* are only executed if there are no *value*n values that match *testValue*.

A classic example of using a *Select Case* statement is to have a program act on a selection the reader has made from a drop-down list—a.k.a. a *select* element object in object model jargon. Suppose you want your web page to show a drop-down list like the one shown in Figure 5-10. As soon as the reader makes a selection, you want his web browser to take him to the appropriate web site.

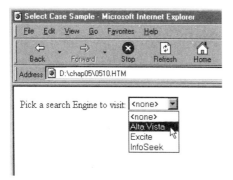

Figure 5-10. *A drop-down list that enables the reader to navigate to a site.*

Figure 5-11 shows the HTML source code for a web page that will present the drop-down list to the reader and then take the reader to the selected site. Let's see how the source code works this little magical feat.

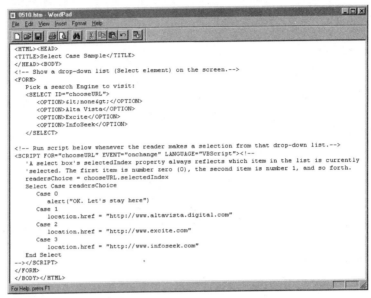

```
0510.htm - WordPad
File  Edit  View  Insert  Format  Help

<HTML><HEAD>
<TITLE>Select Case Sample</TITLE>
</HEAD><BODY>
<!-- Show a drop-down list (Select element) on the screen.-->
<FORM>
    Pick a search Engine to visit:
    <SELECT ID="chooseURL">
        <OPTION>&lt;none&gt;</OPTION>
        <OPTION>Alta Vista</OPTION>
        <OPTION>Excite</OPTION>
        <OPTION>InfoSeek</OPTION>
    </SELECT>

<!-- Run script below whenever the reader makes a selection from that drop-down list.-->
<SCRIPT FOR="chooseURL" EVENT="onchange" LANGUAGE="VBScript"><!--
    'A select box's selectedIndex property always reflects which item in the list is currently
    'selected. The first item is number zero (0), the second item is number 1, and so forth.
    readersChoice = chooseURL.selectedIndex
    Select Case readersChoice
        Case 0
            alert("OK. Let's stay here")
        Case 1
            location.href = "http://www.altavista.digital.com"
        Case 2
            location.href = "http://www.excite.com"
        Case 3
            location.href = "http://www.infoseek.com"
    End Select
--></SCRIPT>
</FORM>
</BODY></HTML>
For Help, press F1
```

Figure 5-11. *An example of using a* Select Case *statement to respond to a change in a* select *element's current value.*

First, the standard HTML *<FORM...>* and *<SELECT...>* tags define a form and the drop-down list. Notice that I've assigned the ID property of the *select* element object to *chooseURL*. You'll see that name used again for referring to that drop-down list.

Below the closing select tag is a script that's bound to the *onchange* event of the select object. Thus, that script is launched whenever the reader makes a selection from the drop-down list. The first executable line in the script is:

```
readersChoice = chooseURL.selectedIndex
```

selectedIndex is a property of the *select* object that contains a number indicating the element's current selection. If the first option in the drop-down list is selected, the *selectedIndex* property contains *0*. If the second option is selected, the *selectedIndex* property contains *1;* if the third option is selected, the *selectedIndex* property contains *2;* and if the fourth option is selected, the *selectedIndex* contains *3*. The value of the *selectedIndex* property is assigned to a variable named *readersChoice*. Then a *Select Case* statement decides what to do based on the value in the *readersChoice* variable:

```
Select Case readersChoice
```

If *readersChoice* contains *0*, only a simple message appears on the screen:

```
Case 0
    alert("OK. Let's stay here")
```

If *readersChoice* contains *1*, the reader is sent to www.altavista.digital.com. This is accomplished by changing the *href* property of the *location* object to that URL:

```
Case 1
    location.href = "http://www.altavista.digital.com"
```

If *readersChoice* contains *2*, the reader is sent to www.excite.com:

```
Case 2
    location.href = "http://www.excite.com"
```

If *readersChoice* contains *3*, the reader is sent to www.infoseek.com:

```
Case 3
    location.href = "http://www.infoseek.com"
End Select
```

The *End Select* statement says, "There are no more cases to check for."

There you have it—at least three ways to have your scripts make decisions: the *If...Then statement,* the *If...Then...Else* statement, and the *Select Case* statement. Now let's turn our attention to a couple of features of VBScript that have a useful relationship to each other: arrays and loops.

VBSCRIPT ARRAYS

Most programming languages, including VBScript, support *arrays*. An array is a list of variables, each of which has the same name but a different subscript. For example, the tiny array shown in the code below contains eight elements. The first element of the *color* array, *color(0)*—pronounced "color sub zero"— contains the string *silver.* The second element, *color(1)*—"color sub one"— contains the string *red,* and so forth down to the eighth element, *color(7)*, which contains the string *black.*

```
Dim color(7)
color(0) = "silver"
color(1) = "red"
color(2) = "orange"
color(3) = "yellow"
color(4) = "green"
color(5) = "blue"
color(6) = "violet"
color(7) = "black"
```

To set up an array or to dimension an array, you first use a *Dim* statement followed by a variable name and a value in parentheses. The *Dim* statement sets aside memory for storing the array—in this case, enough memory to store eight elements. The value in the parentheses specifies the upper subscript of the array. In VBScript, the lower subscript is always zero. VBScript stores all the elements in an array together in memory for quick performance as your script accesses the array elements.

NOTE   Programmers often use the term *declare* rather than *dimension*. To declare an array means the same thing as to dimension an array.

The beauty of an array is that you can refer to any variable in the array by its subscript—its *index number*—rather than by some particular name. As you'll see in the next section, you can set up a simple "loop" in a script to process each item in an array, one at a time.

NOTE   An array is the same as a collection in the object model—a "list" of similar things, each with a unique subscript. Unlike a collection, however, a VBScript array is a collection that you create yourself. Since you create the array yourself, you can ignore the zero element and leave it empty. This means you can start your array lists with subscript number one if you want to!

VBSCRIPT LOOPS

A *loop* is a little chunk of VBScript code that's executed over and over again until some condition arises that terminates the loop. In this section, we'll look primarily at *For…Next* loops—*For* loops for short.

The *For…Next* Loop Statement

One of the more common looping statements you'll see is the *For…Next* loop, which uses this syntax:

```
For counter = start To end
   code to execute
Next
```

counter is some variable that automatically receives the integer value specified by *start* when the loop is first executed. With each pass through the loop, the *code to execute* is executed. Then the *counter* variable is automatically incremented by 1 and the loop repeats until the *counter* variable's value is greater than the value specified by *end*. At that point, the loop stops and execution resumes at the first command under the *Next* statement.

Here's an example of a script that counts from 1 through 5 as the instructions in the loop iterate. With each pass through the loop, the script writes the current value of the *counter* variable followed by a period and a line break (the *
* tag) into the current web page:

```
<SCRIPT LANGUAGE="VBScript"><!--
   For counter = 1 To 5
      document.write counter
      document.write ".<BR>"
   Next
--></SCRIPT>
```

Opening the web page whose HTML code contains this script displays the following on a (otherwise empty) page:

1.
2.
3.
4.
5.

Let's see why this script does what it does. The statement below sets up a loop that will count from 1 through 5.

```
For counter = 1 To 5
```

At the start of each pass through the instructions that follow, the variable named *counter* receives an incremented numeric value. Thus, on the first pass through the instruction loop, *counter* contains *1*. On the second pass through the loop, *counter* contains *2*, and so forth.

Within the instruction loop, the *document.write counter* statement inserts the current value of the *counter* variable into the web page. The *document.write ".
"* statement inserts a period and a *
* tag right after that number. Since the loop is repeated from 1 through 5, the loop generates the following output:

```
1.<BR>2.<BR>3.<BR>4.<BR>5.<BR>
```

The web browser correctly interprets the *
* tags as line breaks, so instead of displaying those tags, it breaks the line just after the period. We end up with the numbered list format in which each number and its period appear on a separate line.

If you change the script so that the loop goes to *100* rather than *5*, as shown below, the next time you open the page, you'll see the numbers from 1 through 100 listed on separate lines.

```
<SCRIPT LANGUAGE="VBScript"><!--
   For counter = 1 To 100
      document.write counter
```

(continued)

```
      document.write ".<BR>"
   Next
--></SCRIPT>
```

Now let's take a look at how we might use a loop to step through all the items in an array. In the example shown in Figure 5-12, you can see the source for a web page containing a script that features both an array and a loop.

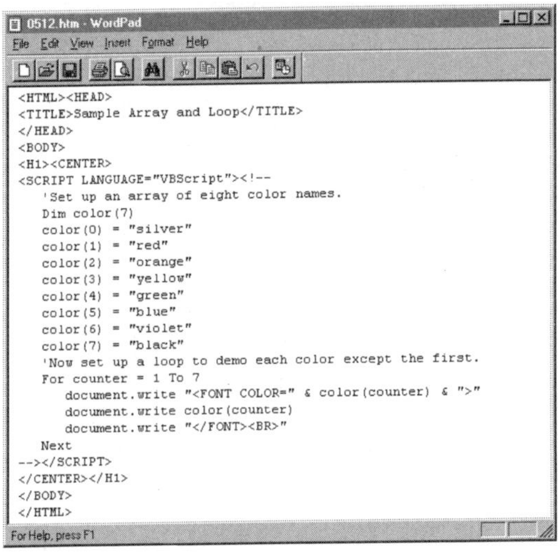


```
<HTML><HEAD>
<TITLE>Sample Array and Loop</TITLE>
</HEAD>
<BODY>
<H1><CENTER>
<SCRIPT LANGUAGE="VBScript"><!--
   'Set up an array of eight color names.
   Dim color(7)
   color(0) = "silver"
   color(1) = "red"
   color(2) = "orange"
   color(3) = "yellow"
   color(4) = "green"
   color(5) = "blue"
   color(6) = "violet"
   color(7) = "black"
   'Now set up a loop to demo each color except the first.
   For counter = 1 To 7
      document.write "<FONT COLOR=" & color(counter) & ">"
      document.write color(counter)
      document.write "</FONT><BR>"
   Next
--></SCRIPT>
</CENTER></H1>
</BODY>
</HTML>
```

Figure 5-12. *A sample script containing an array and a loop.*

Note that within the script, a *Dim* statement declares an array named *color*, with eight elements. The series of statements starting with the ones below then "populate," or fill, that array with some strings, which in this example happen to be color names.

```
color(0) = "silver"
color(1) = "red"
color(2) = "orange"
```

Following the declaring and populating of the array is a *For...Next* loop that counts from 1 through 7. With each pass through that loop, the following statements are executed:

```
document.write "<FONT COLOR=" & color(counter) & ">"
document.write color(counter)
document.write "</FONT><BR>"
```

When a reader opens the page whose source contains this script, the script is executed. With the first pass through the loop, the following code is generated because *counter* contains *1* on that first pass and *color(1)* is the string *red*.

```
<FONT COLOR=red>red</FONT><BR>
```

On the second pass through the loop, the *document.write* statements produce the following because *counter* contains *2* and *color(2)* is the string *orange*.

```
<FONT COLOR=orange>orange</FONT><BR>
```

The loop is repeated seven times, so the web page ends up displaying the equivalent of these tags:

```
<FONT COLOR=red>red</FONT><BR>
<FONT COLOR=orange>orange</FONT><BR>
<FONT COLOR=yellow>yellow</FONT><BR>
<FONT COLOR=green>green</FONT><BR>
<FONT COLOR=blue>blue</FONT><BR>
<FONT COLOR=violet>violet</FONT><BR>
<FONT COLOR=black>black</FONT><BR>
```

Remember, though, that that's not what the reader sees on the screen. What is visible on the screen is the browser's interpretation of those tags. Thus, the result of running this script, when viewed in a web browser, looks like the screen shown in Figure 5-13, where each word is actually displayed in its color—that is, *red* is in red letters, *orange* is in orange letters, and so forth.

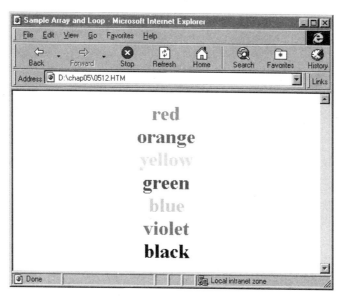

Figure 5-13. *The result of running the script shown in Figure 5-12.*

Even though the color array does have a zero element, the string *silver* in this case, it was not accessed in the *For…Next* loop. If you want to include the *silver* string in the results, you can just change the loop counter to go from 0 to 7 instead of from 1 to 7.

Looping Through Collections

Since collections are arrays, you can use a loop to step through and observe, or change, some property of each item in the collection. All collections have a built-in *.length* property, which defines how many items are in the collection. So a loop that accesses each item in the collection needs to count from zero (because built-in collections are always zero-based), to the length minus one. Here is the general structure of such a loop:

```
<SCRIPT LANGUAGE="VBScript"><!--
    For counter = 0 to collection.length-1
      action collection(counter).property
    Next
--></SCRIPT>
```

collection is the name of the collection you're interested in, *action* is code describing what to do with each item in the collection, and *property* is some property that's appropriate for the type of object in the collection.

Here's an example. Suppose you have a page with a lot of graphic images in it. At the bottom of that page you want to see a list of all the image file names. In that case, you're interested in the images (*document.images*) collection. And you're interested in the *src* property of each image. So, down at the bottom of the web page (perhaps just above the closing *</BODY>* tag), you can type in this script:

```
<SCRIPT LANGUAGE="VBScript"><!--
    For counter = 0 to document.images.length-1
      document.write "Image(" & counter & ") source is: "
      document.write document.images(counter).src
      document.write "<BR>"
    Next
--></SCRIPT>
```

After opening the page in a web browser, you can scroll down to the bottom of the page, where you'll see a list of all the image sources in the document. There will be one line for each *<IMG SRC=...>* tag in the page, and it will look something like Figure 5-14.

If you want to see a list of all the hyperlinks in the page, change the collection to *document.links* and change the property to some property that the links collection supports, such as *href.* The script below Figure 5-14 lists the *HREF* attribute from every *<A HREF=...>* tag in the current page.

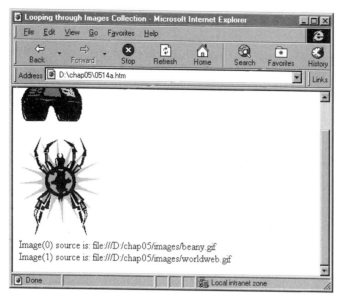

Figure 5-14. *Listing the images in the* images *collection.*

```
<SCRIPT LANGUAGE="VBScript"><!--
   For counter = 0 to document.links.length-1
      document.write "Hyperlink(" & counter & ") points to: "
      document.write document.links(counter).href
      document.write "<BR>"
   Next
--></SCRIPT>
```

The output from this script is a list at the bottom of the page that looks
something like this (and so forth), one line for each *<A HREF=...>* tag in the page.

```
Hyperlink(0) points to: http://www.coolnerds.com/
Hyperlink(1) points to: http://www.microsoft.com/
```

If you're curious about what tags are in the *document.all* collection for a
given page, you can put this script down at the bottom of that page, again just
above the closing *</BODY>* tag:

```
<SCRIPT LANGUAGE="VBScript"><!--
   For counter = 0 to document.all.length-1
      document.write "document.all(" & counter & ") tag is: "
      document.write document.all(counter).tagName
      document.write "<BR>"
   Next
--></SCRIPT>
```

The resulting list down at the bottom of the page will look something like Figure 5-15.

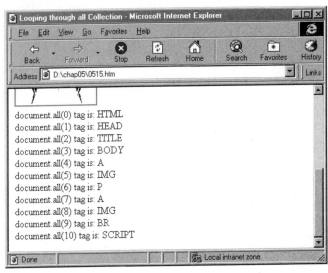

Figure 5-15. *Listing the tags in the* all *collection.*

Here's a funky little number that presents a button on the screen. Clicking that button colors all the H1 headings in the current document green. Figure 5-16 shows an example of this script in a web page.

```
<P>
<BUTTON ID="Button1">
Click Me
</BUTTON>
</P>
<SCRIPT FOR="Button1" EVENT="onclick" LANGUAGE="VBScript"><!--
   For counter = 0 to document.all.tags("H1").length-1
      document.all.tags("H1").item(counter).style.color = "green"
   Next
--></SCRIPT>
```

This last example doesn't display information *about* the items in the collection. Rather, it actually colors each H1 heading by setting its *style.color* property to green.

I admit that these scripts have limited value in terms of what they present to anyone visiting your web page. However, to the novice programmer, they reveal a lot about loops and collections. It might be worthwhile to type some of these scripts into copies of your current web pages. Seeing the output of such scripts can help you build a clearer mental picture of what's in all those invisible collections that the object model creates.

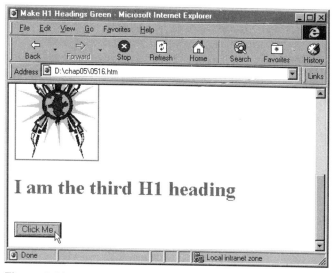

Figure 5-16. *Clicking the Click Me button turns the H1 headings green.*

Other Kinds of Loop Statements

You'll see more examples of arrays and loops in upcoming chapters. For now, it's sufficient for you to understand that arrays and loops exist in VBScript (and other languages) and are used in many of the active web pages you'll come across on the Web.

For...Next is not the only "looping pair" of statements in VBScript. There is also a *Do...Loop* statement, a *While...Wend* statement, and a *For Each...Next* statement. And an *Exit* statement can force a loop to stop dead in its tracks. All of these statements are documented in the Internet Client SDK.

THE LIFETIME OF A VARIABLE

Nothing lives forever, including a VBScript variable. Three basic rules govern how long a variable "lives" (holds its value):

- A "public," or "global," variable is declared at the script level and is accessible by default to all scripts and procedures in a page. A global variable exists only while the page is open, and it becomes a property of the window object.

- A "private," or "local," variable is declared inside a sub or function procedure and is accessible by default to only that sub or function. A local variable exists only while that procedure is running.

- You can use two VBScript statements, *Public* and *Private*, to change the default lifetime of a variable.

Take a look at the source code below, which we'll say is named page1.htm. The source creates two variables named x and y. The x variable is defined at the script level (not inside a procedure) and is thus accessible throughout the scripts for the page. The y variable is defined inside a sub procedure named *makeY()* and is thus local to that procedure. Its value can't be known outside that procedure. Some VBScript statements at the bottom of the page source print the contents of the x and y variables on the screen.

```
<HTML><HEAD>
<TITLE>Test Variables - page1.htm</TITLE></HEAD>
<BODY>
<SCRIPT LANGUAGE="VBScript"><!--
    'Global variable x is defined at the script level,
    'meaning that it's not declared inside a procedure.
    x = 100
    Sub makeY()
        'Local variable y is created inside a sub procedure.
        y = 200
    End Sub
    'Run the makeY() procedure.
    makeY()
    'Print the contents of variables x and y.
    document.write "x = " & x
    document.write "<P>"
    document.write "y = " & y
--></SCRIPT>
<P>
<A HREF="page2.htm">Go to Page 2</A>
</P>
</BODY>
</HTML>
```

Suppose that I open the page1.htm page in Microsoft Internet Explorer. The screen will show just this:

x = 100

y =

Go to Page 2

Notice that no value is displayed for variable y. That's because the *document.write* statement that prints the contents of the y variable is outside the *makeY()* procedure in which the y variable is defined. The value of y is not known outside that procedure, so the value of y is printed as nothing.

I've also added a link to a page named page2.htm. Let's suppose that page2.htm contains the following source:

```
<HTML><HEAD>
<TITLE>Test Variables - page2.htm</TITLE></HEAD>
<BODY>
<SCRIPT LANGUAGE="VBScript"><!--
    'Try to print the variables that were defined in Page 1.
    document.write "x = " & x
    document.write "<P>"
    document.write "y = " & y
--></SCRIPT>
</BODY>
</HTML>
```

If I click the link that takes me to Page 2, that page displays the following on the screen:

```
x =
y =
```

Here, neither x nor y seems to contain any data. Why is that? Because even a public variable such as x exists only when the page in which it was defined is open. When Page 2 took over the screen, it essentially threw Page 1 and all of its variables right into the big cyber-trashcan. The variables x and y used in Page 2 are new variables that are empty. If you go back to Page 1, the scripting code in Page 1 is executed again and the variables x and y are recreated and their values are modified as before.

Getting back to page1.htm: What do you think might happen if there are several scripts rather than one big script in that file set? Let's rewrite it this way:

```
<HTML><HEAD>
<TITLE>Test Variables - page1b.htm</TITLE></HEAD>
<BODY>

<SCRIPT LANGUAGE="VBScript"><!--
    'Global variable x is defined at the script level,
    'meaning that it's not declared inside a procedure.
    x = 100
--></SCRIPT>

I am regular HTML and text, outside any script.<P>

<SCRIPT LANGUAGE="VBScript"><!--
    Sub makeY()
        'Local variable y is defined inside a sub procedure.
        y = 200
    End Sub
--></SCRIPT>
```

(continued)

```
I, too, am regular HTML and text, outside any script.<P>

<SCRIPT LANGUAGE="VBScript"><!--
    'Run the makeY() procedure.
    makeY()
    'Print the contents of variables x and y.
    document.write "x = " & x
    document.write "<P>"
    document.write "y = " & y
--></SCRIPT>
<P>
<A HREF="page2.htm">Go to Page 2</A>
</P>
</BODY>
</HTML>
```

Here, the code from page1b.htm is divided into three scripts, each with its own enclosing *<SCRIPT...>...</SCRIPT>* tags. The effect of this division on the *x* and *y* variables, however, is...nothing. A public variable such as *x* is accessible to all of the scripts in the page, regardless of how many *<SCRIPT...>...</SCRIPT>* tags that page contains. And as you might imagine, a private variable such as *y* is still accessible only to the procedure in which it was created.

When I open the page1b.htm page in Internet Explorer, the screen shows the following:

I am regular HTML and text, outside any script.

I, too, am regular HTML and text, outside any script.

x = 100

y =

Go to Page 2

A Procedure Can Change a Public Variable

Remember that a variable is private to a procedure only if the variable is initially declared in that procedure. If a variable is declared at the script level, it's public, even if a sub procedure changes its value. Take a look at the script below. As in the first example, we define a variable named *x* at the script level and define a variable named *y* at the procedure level. However, we've added a twist in which the procedure named *fudgeVars()* alters the contents of the *x* variable ($x = x + 1$):

```
<SCRIPT LANGUAGE="VBScript"><!--
    'Global variable x is defined at the script level.
    x = 100
    Sub fudgeVars()
        x = x + 1
        y = x + 2
    End Sub
```

```
      'Run the fudgeVars() procedure.
      fudgeVars()
      'Print the contents of variables x and y.
      document.write "x = " & x
      document.write "<P>"
      'Local variable y is defined at the procedure level.
      document.write "y = " & y
--></SCRIPT>
```

Opening this page in a web browser displays the following on the screen:

x = 101

y =

As before, the variable *y* has no value outside the procedure in which it was defined. The variable *x* was defined at the script level, so execution of the statement *x = x + 1* added 1 to the value of the public variable named *x*.

Why Bother with All This?

Now, you might wonder, why all this business of public and private variables? Why not just make all variables public so we don't have to think about all this stuff? The rationale stems from the creation of large, complicated programs such as Microsoft Word and Microsoft Excel. Programs like these contain millions of lines of code and are usually created by teams of programmers. If all the hundreds and even thousands of variables these programmers created constantly intermingled with one another, it would be difficult for the programmers to keep from stepping on each other's toes.

It's much easier for the programmers if they can just come up with a list of public variables that have meaning throughout the program. That way, when a programmer is creating her own unique procedures for her contribution to the project, she can avoid messing up somebody else's variables by simply avoiding variable names on the "public" list. Even if just one programmer is working on a project, using private variables allows the programmer to reuse the same variable name in different contexts.

It's fairly common now for a professional programmer to explicitly declare variables as either public or private so that other programmers viewing the code can see at a glance which variables are public and which are private. In VBScript, you use the statements *Public* and *Private* to declare variables this way. Take a look at the code below:

```
<HTML><HEAD>
<TITLE>Test Variables - page1d.htm</TITLE></HEAD>
<BODY>
```

(continued)

```
<SCRIPT LANGUAGE="VBScript"><!--
    'Declare the public variables for this page.
    Public x, readerName, readerAddress
    'Create a sub procedure named fillVars().
    Sub fillVars()
        x = 100
        readerName = "Alan"
        readerAddress = "alan@coolnerds.com"
        z = 99
    End Sub
--></SCRIPT>
```

This page contains some public and private variables.<P>

```
<SCRIPT LANGUAGE="VBScript"><!--
    'Run the fillVars() procedure.
    fillVars()
    'Print the contents of all variables.
    document.write "x = " & x
    document.write "<BR>"
    document.write "readerName = " & readerName
    document.write "<BR>"   document.write "readerAddress = " & readerAddress
    document.write "<BR>"
    document.write "z = " & z
--></SCRIPT>
```

```
</BODY>
</HTML>
```

THE *OPTION EXPLICIT* STATEMENT

As a general rule, VBScript lets you create variables on the fly, which can be both a kiss and a curse. A kiss because you can just make up variables spontaneously on an as-needed basis. A curse because if you unwittingly misspell one of your variable names in a script and the script bombs, it might not be so easy to find the problem.

VBScript offers an *Option Explicit* statement that you can use to reverse the rules. If you simply add the two words *Option Explicit* on their own line, near the top of a script, you make a rule that says, "Only variables that have be declared using *Public* or *Dim* are acceptable in this script." When you run the script, an error message appears whenever an undeclared variable name is accessed by the script. This helps you find misspellings and other errors that are causing your script to bomb.

Right off the bat, the programmer (you or I) can tell which variables in this code will be treated as public variables—that is, which variables retain their values all the time the page is open and are accessible to all the scripts in the page. In this example, the variables named *x*, *readerName*, and *readerAddress* are all public variables.

The page1d.htm source also contains a script with a sub procedure named *fillVars()* that puts data into four variables named *x*, *readerName*, *readerAddress*, and *z*:

```
Sub fillVars()
    x = 100
    readerName = "Alan"
    readerAddress = "alan@coolnerds.com"
    z = 99
End Sub
```

In a later script, this statement runs that procedure:

```
'Run the fillVars() procedure.
fillVars()
```

When the page is opened, these statements display the contents of the four variables on the screen:

```
'Print the contents of all variables.
document.write "x = " & x
document.write "<BR>"
document.write "readerName = " & readerName
document.write "<BR>"
document.write "readerAddress = " & readerAddress
document.write "<BR>"
document.write "z = " & z
```

If I open the page in a web browser, this is what I see on the screen:

This page contains some public and private variables.

x = 100

readerName = Alan

readerAddress = alan@coolnerds.com

z =

Only the variable *z* has no value to display. It was created inside the *fillVars()* sub procedure and was never declared a public variable.

To summarize: All variables declared at the script level (outside a sub or function procedure) are public—they are accessible to all the scripts in a web page, including procedures. Likewise, any variable that's declared public by means of the *Public* statement is accessible throughout a web page—even if that variable gets its initial value inside a sub or function procedure.

THE *PRIVATE* AND *DIM* STATEMENTS

At the risk of confusing things, I need to mention a couple of tidbits. The *Public* statement did not exist before version 2.0 of VBScript, so programmers often used *Dim* (which has the same basic effect) rather than *Public* to declare variables global within a page. If you see something like *Dim x, y, z* in VBScript code near the top of someone's page, that means the same thing as *Public x, y, z*.

VBScript also has a *Private* statement that is supposed to make a variable local to the script in which it was declared so that you don't have to declare such a variable within a sub or a function. However, it doesn't seem to work in the current version of Internet Explorer. In fact, variables declared *Private* appear to behave exactly as variables declared *Public*! Until that problem is fixed, there's no point in even using the *Private* statement.

Variables created within procedures are already private by default, so there's no need to explicitly declare them private.

A variable defined inside a sub or function procedure that has never been declared public is accessible only to that procedure. It exists only within the procedure that contains it.

Here's one more wrinkle: Public variables exist *only* when the web page in which they are declared is open. When the reader jumps to another web page in the same browser window, all variable names and their contents are not accessible in the new page. If you need to carry the contents of a VBScript variable from one page to the next, you can use a cookie—a topic we'll discuss in depth in Chapter 10.

WATCH THOSE QUOTATION MARKS!

When you're writing code, dealing with punctuation marks and other special characters can get complicated—especially when you're working with characters that have one meaning in ordinary English, another meaning in HTML, and yet another meaning in VBScript. Quotation marks and apostrophes definitely fall into that category of special characters with multiple frames of reference.

The URL in an HTML *<A HREF...>* tag should be enclosed in quotation marks, as in this example:

```
<A HREF="http://www.coolnerds.com">coolnerds</A>
```

Most values being assigned to an attribute should be enclosed in quotation marks. If the value contains spaces, you must enclose it in quotation marks.

In VBScript, string literals must be enclosed in quotation marks. Sometimes, though, you'll want to put a string that requires quotation marks itself into a string literal. The general rule in that case is to use double quotation marks to delimit the larger, outermost string. Then use single quotation marks to delimit the smaller, embedded string.

For example, suppose you want to use *document.write* in a script to put a hyperlink *<A HREF="http://www.coolnerds.com">coolnerds</A>* into your web page. You have to replace those internal double quotation marks with single quotation marks and then delimit the larger string with double quotation marks, like this:

```
document.write "<A HREF='http://www.coolnerds.com'>coolnerds</A>"
```

That's not *too* hard to remember. But things can get more complicated when you want a *document.write* statement to display English text that contains both single and double quotation marks. Suppose you want your *document.write* statement to put this little chunk of text into your page:

Mary said, "Let's play!"

Yikes! Here we're faced with a string that has two double quotation marks and one single quotation mark (the apostrophe) embedded in it. How do we delimit that whole thing in quotation marks?

When things get this complicated, you can just revert to using ASCII codes in place of the English text quotation marks. Rather than type the character into the code, you insert a VBScript *Chr(number)* function where *number* is the ASCII code for the character you want. There are over 200 ASCII codes, but the ones you're most likely to need are the ones that have special meaning in HTML and VBScript and the ones you can't type from the keyboard at all. Some of those characters and their ASCII codes are shown in Table 5-3 on the next page.

Using *Chr()* function codes, we can build strings containing any characters and put those strings into variables. Then we can use *document.write* statements to print the contents of the variables. Here's an example:

```
<BODY>
<SCRIPT LANGUAGE="VBScript"><!--
    msg1 = "Mary said, " & Chr(34)
    msg1 = msg1 & "Let" & Chr(39) & "s play!"
    msg1 = msg1 & Chr(34)
    msg2 = "<P>This idea " & Chr(169) & " nobody."
    document.write msg1
    document.write msg2
--></SCRIPT>
</BODY>
```

Table 5-3

THE *CHR()* FUNCTION CODES YOU'LL NEED MOST

Character	*Code*
"	*Chr(34)*
'	*Chr(39)*
<	*Chr(60)*
>	*Chr(62)*
, (comma)	*Chr(44)*
(blank space)	*Chr(32)*
. (period)	*Chr(46)*
;	*Chr(59)*
&	*Chr(38)*
©	*Chr(169)*
®	*Chr(174)*
™	*Chr(153)*

In the reader's web browser, the output of this little script looks something like this:

Mary said, "Let's play!"
This idea © nobody.

If you don't like the idea of having all those *Chr()* function codes making your scripts more mysterious, you can define your own constants early in your source code to represent the characters you need to use. Then use the constant names in place of *Chr()* in other scripts, as in the example below:

```
<HTML><HEAD>
<TITLE>Home Grown Constants</TITLE>
<SCRIPT LANGUAGE="VBScript"><!--
    'Declare and define special character constants.
    Public myDblQuote, myApostrophe, myCopyright
    myDblQuote = Chr(34)
    myApostrophe = Chr(39)
    myCopyright = Chr(169)
--></SCRIPT>
</HEAD>
<BODY>

<!-- Make up some fancy text strings using the constants
     defined above. -->

<SCRIPT LANGUAGE="VBScript"><!--
    msg1 = "Mary said, " & myDblQuote
```

```
    msg1 = msg1 & "Let" & myApostrophe & "s play!"
    msg1 = msg1 & myDblQuote
    msg2 = "<P>This idea " & myCopyright & " nobody."
    document.write msg1
    document.write msg2
--></SCRIPT>
</BODY>
</HTML>
```

The output of this page, shown below, is identical to the output of the previous script. But you might find the code in the second script a little more palatable since names like *myDblQuote* and *myApostrophe* are more descriptive than codes like *Chr(34)* and *Chr(39)*.

Mary said, "Let's play!"
This idea © nobody.

NOTE The *vbConstants* referenced in the Internet Client SDK are accessible to all pages you create. However, any constants that you create yourself within a web page will work only in that page.

WHERE JAVASCRIPT FITS IN

Like VBScript, JavaScript (Microsoft's implementation is known as JScript) is a web author's scripting language. The main difference between JavaScript and VBScript is that VBScript's roots come from the Basic programming language while JavaScript's roots are in the C language.

Braces and Parentheses in JavaScript

Basic is a "wordy" language in that it uses English-like words where more abstract languages such as JavaScript might use symbols. For example, here's how a *For...Next* loop that contains an *If...Then...Else* statements looks when written in VBScript:

```
<SCRIPT LANGUAGE="VBScript"><!--
    For counter = 1 To 10
        document.write counter
        document.write " is "
        If counter/2 = Int(counter/2) Then
            document.write "even"
        Else
            document.write "odd"
        End If
        document.write "<P>"
    Next
    document.write "<P>All Done!"
--></SCRIPT>
```

JavaScript, being a less wordy language, uses curly braces ({}) rather than words to encapsulate the code inside a loop and an *if...then* statement. It uses more operators such as <= and ++, too. When the little script above is translated into JavaScript, it looks like this:

```
<SCRIPT LANGUAGE="JavaScript"><!--
    for (var counter=1; counter<=10; counter++) {
        document.write(counter)
        document.write(" is ")
        if (counter/2 == parseInt(counter/2)) {
            document.write("even")
        }
        else {
            document.write("odd")
        }
        document.write("<BR>")
    }
    document.write("<P>All Done!")
//--></SCRIPT>
```

Both chunks of code do exactly the same thing—they display the numbers 1 through 10 on the screen, with the word *even* next to even numbers and the word *odd* next to odd numbers. Both languages use the same object model. And in these examples, both scripts use the *write* method of the *document* object (*document.write*) to display information in the web page. Figure 5-17 shows the results of the JavaScript example.

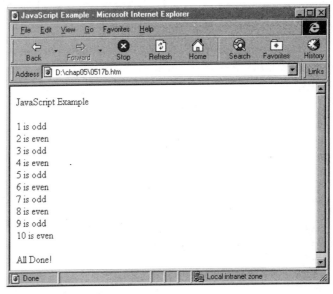

Figure 5-17. *The results of the JavaScript example.*

In addition to being less wordy, JavaScript is much fussier than VBScript. For example, JavaScript requires that text to the rig2ht in a *document.write* statement always be enclosed in parentheses, whereas VBScript doesn't care whether the parentheses are there or not.

Case Sensitivity in JavaScript

JavaScript is also case-sensitive—and that can really drive you nuts! The following statement in JavaScript, for example, generates a syntax error message because of the capital F at the beginning of the keyword *For*.

```
For (var counter=1; counter<=10; counter++)
```

References to object model elements are also case-sensitive in JavaScript. While the following statement works fine in VBScript, it bombs in a JavaScript script because of the capital *W* of the *write* method.

```
document.Write("even")
```

Case Sensitivity for VBScript Programmers

VBScript programmers generally don't have to worry much about case sensitivity. Once you're writing code inside a pair of *<SCRIPT LANGUAGE="VBScript">... </SCRIPT>* tags, you don't have to worry about uppercase and lowercase letters in VBScript code elements.

However, *outside* those tags, JavaScript is the default language and case sensitivity can rear its ugly head. (JavaScript is the default scripting language probably because it was the *first* scripting language for Web authors.) When you use object names outside of *<SCRIPT LANGUAGE="VBScript">...</SCRIPT>* tags, case sensitivity can become an issue again. For example, the tag below creates a button that, when clicked, displays an Alert box containing the words *Hello You*.

```
<INPUT TYPE="Button" VALUE="Click Me" onclick="alert('Hello You')">
```

The tag below, which looks as if it would do the same thing, actually bombs and displays an error message because in JavaScript the *alert* method name must be in lowercase.

```
<INPUT TYPE="Button" VALUE="Click Me" onclick="Alert('Hello You')">
```

The simple solution to this problem is to be aware of uppercase and lowercase letters whenever you're putting code into an HTML tag.

Whenever you have a problem with a little piece of code embedded in an HTML tag, you'd do well to look up the troublesome word in the Internet Client SDK to make sure you're using uppercase and lowercase letters correctly.

ELECTRONIC VBSCRIPT RESOURCES

Here are some electronic resources you might want to use to reinforce what you've learned in this chapter:

- *VBScript Tutorial* and *VBScript Language Reference* in the Internet Client SDK, described in Appendix A.

- Microsoft VBScript Start Page at www.microsoft.com/vbscript/.

- The VBScript section of my own web site at www.coolnerds.com.

- VBScript Gallery at www.inquiry.com/thevbpro/.

SUMMARY

VBScript offers the same kinds of tools and lends itself to the same techniques that other programming languages do. Here's a recap of our deeper delving into VBScript:

- Procedures in VBScript and methods in the Dynamic HTML Object Model both give you ways to put a variety of custom message boxes and dialog boxes into your web pages.

- For decision making, VBScript offers the *If...Then* statement, the *If...Then...Else* statement, as well as the *Select Case* statement.

- VBScript arrays—lists of variables with the same name but different subscripts—enable you to refer to any variable in an array by its subscript. Before populating an array, you must declare it, or dimension it, with a *Dim* statement.

- VBScript offers several statements for setting up a loop in a script, including *For...Next, Do...Loop, While...Wend,* and *For Each...Next.* Exit gives you a quick way out of a loop.

- By nature, a variable declared at the script level is "global"—accessible to all the scripts in the current page. A variable declared inside a sub or function procedure is "local"—accessible to only that procedure.

- The *Chr()* function can be helpful when working with quotation marks and other special characters.

- Since JavaScript is the default scripting language and is case-sensitive, correct usage of uppercase and lowercase letters outside of the *<SCRIPT LANGUAGE="VBScript">...</SCRIPT>* tags is important.

This concludes Part I of the book. The purpose of these past five chapters has been to expose you to general Dynamic HTML concepts and technologies, including HTML, Cascading Style Sheets, the Dynamic HTML Object Model, and the VBScript scripting language. In Part II, we'll actually apply these concepts to the task of creating more awe-inspiring web pages that engage your site's visitors and keep them coming back for more. Hopefully, the information you've learned so far will take some of the mystery (and intimidation) out of the many scripts you'll encounter in those chapters. And hopefully, all of this will make it easier to start creating your own custom scripts and more dazzling, interactive web pages.

PART II

DEEPER INTO DYNAMIC HTML

These next six chapters expound on the basics presented in Part I and show you how to do lots of *really* cool things with Dynamic HTML and VBScript. Chapter 6 covers some general tips and techniques, such as detecting which web browser a visitor is using, creating custom hotspots and tooltips, using drop-down lists, and more. Then, in Chapter 7, you'll learn how to change the appearance of a web page, right in front of the visitor's eyes and without reloading the page, by using VBScript to change CSS attributes.

In Chapters 8 and 9, you'll learn about positioning, one of the absolute hottest new features of Microsoft Internet Explorer 4. More specifically, you'll learn how to position, stack, hide, display, move, and animate objects. In Chapters 10 and 11, we'll discuss other great new features such as dynamic text, embedded fonts, and how to use filters for special effects and more. What fun!

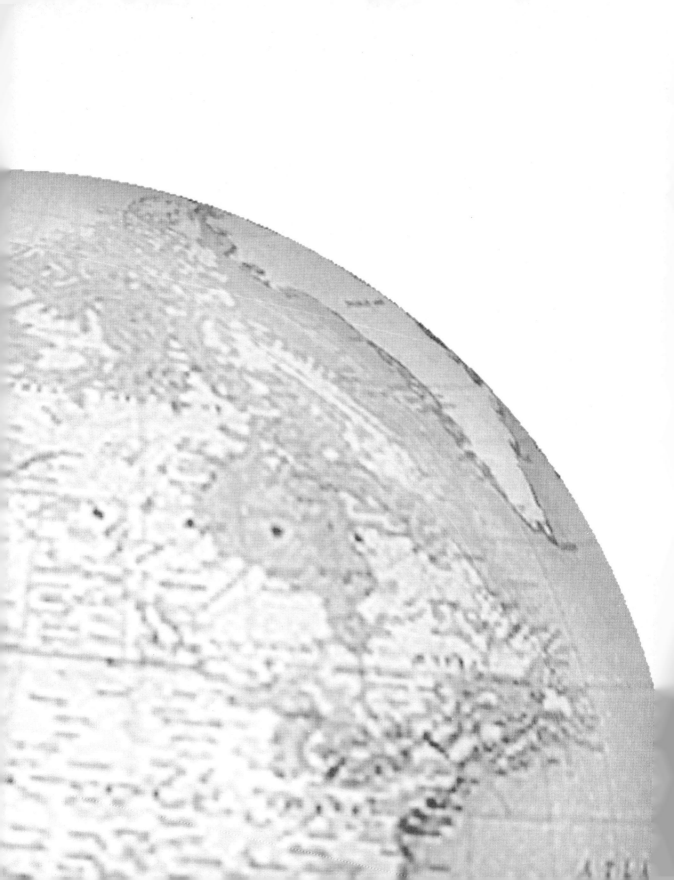

Chapter 6

Cool Tips and Generic Scripts

In Part I, we talked about Dynamic HTML, cascading style sheets, the Dynamic HTML Object Model, and scripting as if they were separate entities. And in some ways they are. But developing interactive web sites in the real world involves mixing all these technologies together. In this chapter, I'll show you examples of all this stuff mixed together in real web pages. While we're at it, though, I'll also give you some specific techniques and scripts that you can start using in your own web site right now. The examples in this chapter demonstrate how to:

- Detect which web browser a visitor is using

- Create your own hotspots

- Create custom tooltips in your pages

- Make text appear and disappear

- Use drop-down lists to present options

You'll also learn about lots of handy HTML attributes, events, properties, and so forth along the way. So without any further ado, let's get into it.

DETECTING THE VISITOR'S WEB BROWSER

Let's take care of some unpleasant business first, just to get it out of the way. Unless you're developing pages for a corporate intranet and can dictate that everyone use Microsoft Internet Explorer 4, you have a compatibility problem right off the bat. On the public World Wide Web, there's no telling *what* browser a given visitor will be using when she first comes to your web site.

The concept of *graceful degradation* helps somewhat with this problem. Graceful degradation allows older browsers to access at least some of the capabilities of pages built for Internet Explorer 4. At the very least, the page won't just "bomb" in most cases. However, graceful degradation doesn't solve all the problems. The unpleasant fact is that if you want to use cutting-edge technologies in your web pages, you're best off knowing which browser your visitor is using and then steering her to whichever home page is best for that web browser.

For example, Internet Explorer versions 3 and 4 support JavaScript, VBScript, ActiveX, and Java applets, while Netscape Navigator versions 3 and 4 support only JavaScript and Java applets. And while both Netscape Navigator 4 and Internet Explorer 4 support positioning of objects, they support different and incompatible tools. Netscape supports its own *<LAYER>* tag. Internet Explorer builds positioning into CSS. And that's just for starters. The list of incompatibilities between browser brands and browser versions goes on and on.

Does this mean you need to develop half a dozen different web sites to support different browsers? No, not exactly. Not *all* of the pages in your site have to offer cutting-edge technologies. But if you want to make a good first impression, you'd do well to design different home pages for different browsers. You can then link from those home pages to whatever pages you want, including more technologically tame pages that work in a wide range of browsers.

To offer multiple home pages, your default home page (the one that's named index.htm or index.html on most web servers) has to detect which browser the reader is using and then send the reader directly to whichever opening page is best for that browser. For example, if you're feeling very generous about supporting multiple browsers, you might create five different home pages, as follows:

- homeie4.htm—home page for visitors using Internet Explorer 4
- homeie3.htm—home page for visitors using Internet Explorer 3
- homens4.htm—home page for visitors using Netscape Navigator 4

- homens3.htm—home page for visitors using Netscape Navigator 3

- homegen.htm—home page for visitors using a browser other than the four listed above

So now the question is: How do you create a default home page—index.htm or index.html—so that all it does is steer the reader to some other opening page? You write a JavaScript script to do the job. JavaScript is preferred in this case because it's supported by the widest range of browsers, including those from Microsoft and Netscape. Figure 6-1 on the next page shows the top half of that script. The bottom half of that page is shown in Figure 6-2. (Sorry, the page is too big to be shown in a single WordPad screen!)

> **TIP** The file named 0601.htm on this book's companion CD contains the complete browser-detection script shown in Figures 6-1 and 6-2. Feel free to copy it to your own home page and/or modify it to suit your needs.

As I've mentioned, I won't discuss JavaScript very much in this book, because we're focusing on Internet Explorer 4. And even though Internet Explorer does support JavaScript, I think you'll find VBScript to be an easier scripting language to use with Internet Explorer 4. I will, however, discuss the browser-detection script because, despite the fact that it's written in JavaScript, you can learn some things about the object model from this script. The object model is part of the web browser and is separate from the scripting language; but you can manipulate objects in the object model using either JavaScript or VBScript. (Internet Explorer versions 3 and 4 and Netscape Navigator versions 3 and 4 were designed based on an object model.)

First, the browser-detection script creates some variables and assigns some initial values to them. The variable I named *ua* (for *user agent*) accesses the *userAgent* property of the *navigator* object to get information about the current web browser:

```
<SCRIPT LANGUAGE="JavaScript"><!--
    //Set up some variables and get ua (user agent) info.
    var browser = "unknown"
    var version = 0
    var detected = false
    var ua = window.navigator.userAgent
```

Figure 6-1. *The top half of an index.htm or index.html page that steers the reader to a specific opening page.*

Figure 6-2. *The bottom half of an index.htm or index.html page that steers the reader to a specific opening page.*

At this point the *ua* variable contains information about the browser. That information is stored as a string (a chunk of text) that looks something like this in Internet Explorer 4:

```
Mozilla/4.0 (compatible; MSIE 4.0; Windows 95)
```

Netscape Navigator 4 would provide that information in a string that looks something like this:

```
Mozilla/4.0 [en] (Win95; I)
```

To determine which browser the visitor is using, the script uses *if* statements and string methods (JavaScript methods that work with strings of text) to ferret out specific parts of the string. The first *if...else* statement determines whether the first seven characters of the *ua* string are *Mozilla*. If so, it checks to see whether the string also contains *MSIE*. If so, the browser must be Internet Explorer. If not, the browser is Netscape Navigator:

```
//Are we in Microsoft Internet Explorer or Netscape Navigator?
if (ua.substring(0,7) == "Mozilla") {
    if (ua.indexOf("MSIE") > 0) {
        browser = "Microsoft"
    }
    else {
        browser = "Netscape"
    }
```

At this point, the variable named *browser* contains either the string *Microsoft*, *Netscape*, or perhaps *unknown* (if the first seven characters aren't *Mozilla*).

The next two *if* statements determine the version of the browser. If the *ua* string contains *4.* (as in 4.0), the version number must be 4. Perhaps it's 4.0 or 4.01 or 4.1. But here we won't worry about the decimal portion of the version number.

If the *ua* string contains *3.*, as in 3.0, the browser version must be 3-dot-something. If neither of those cases is true, the *version* variable hasn't changed and still contains its original value of zero:

```
//Now check the browser version number.
    if (ua.indexOf("4.") > 0) {
        version = 4
    }
    if (ua.indexOf("3.") > 0) {
        version = 3
    }
}
```

Now that the variables named *browser* and *version* contain information about the visitor's web browser, we can use another series of *if* statements to send the reader to a particular page. For example, if *browser* equals *"Microsoft"* and *version* equals *4*, we'll use the *href* property of the *location* object to send the reader to a page named homeie4.htm. We'll also set the variable named *detected* to true to indicate that we've detected which browser the visitor is using. We'll use that variable again in a moment:

```
//If Microsoft Internet Explorer 4 is in use, go to homeie4.htm.
if (browser == "Microsoft" && version == 4) {
    detected = true
    location.href="homeie4.htm"
}
```

The next series of *if* statements perform a similar function—they send the reader to some page based on the contents of the *browser* and *version* variables:

```
//If Microsoft Internet Explorer 3 is in use, go to homeie3.htm.
if (browser == "Microsoft" && version == 3) {
    detected = true
    location.href="homeie3.htm"
}
//If Netscape Navigator 4 is in use, go to page homens4.htm.
if (browser == "Netscape" && version == 4) {
    detected = true
    location.href="homens4.htm"
}
//If Netscape Navigator 3 is in use, go to page homens3.htm.
if (browser == "Netscape" && version == 3) {
    detected = true
    location.href="homens3.htm"
}
```

If we get through all those *if* statements and the variable named *detected* still contains false, the visitor is using some browser other than what we've looked for. That visitor is sent to a page named homegen.htm:

```
//If still not detected, some other JavaScript-enabled
//browser is in use.
//Go to page homegen.htm
if (detected == false) {
    detected = true
    location.href = "homegen.htm"
}
//--></SCRIPT>
```

USING THE *LOCATION* OBJECT IN FRAMED SITES

If your site uses frames, you should be aware that the *location* object isn't sensitive to the *<BASE TARGET...>* tag. If you want to use VBScript or JavaScript to show a page in a particular frame, use the syntax *parent.frameName.location.href="url"*, where *frameName* is the name of the frame to use (as defined by the *<FRAME NAME=...>* tag that defines the frame) and *url* is an absolute or relative reference to the page you want to show. For example,

```
parent.mainFrame.location.href="homeie4.htm"
```

displays the page named homeie4.htm in the frame named *mainFrame*.

NOTE The Internet Client SDK, described in Appendix A, has a tutorial and a language reference for JScript, which is Microsoft's implementation of JavaScript. There you can find information on JavaScript statements and methods, such as *var*, *substring*, and *indexOf*.

Figure 6-3 shows a visitor who is using Netscape Navigator 4. After a page containing the browser-detection script is opened, the visitor is taken to the appropriate home page, which in this case is homens4.htm.

Figure 6-3. *A visitor's browser is detected, and the appropriate home page is displayed.*

The unfortunate bottom line here is that only visitors who are steered to the page named homeie4.htm by the browser-detection script can enjoy all the features that Internet Explorer 4 offers. It would be nice if there were some magic tag that made everyone's web browser compatible with Internet Explorer 4, but no such tag exists. Such is life in the web-authoring fast lane.

With that unpleasantness out of the way, let's look at some tips and techniques that you can use to make your own Internet Explorer 4 pages dazzle.

MAKE ANYTHING HOT

With early web browsers and pages based on previous versions of HTML, about the only things that were *hot* (that responded to a mouse click) were items defined with the *<A...>* tag. Later, the *<AREA>* tag extended that capability to image maps. Next, support for an *onclick* event handler was added, which allowed for a few other page elements to be made hot.

Internet Explorer 4 offers *onclick* and *ondblclick* events that work with many different tags in a web page. Figure 6-4 shows an example in which just a little chunk of boldfaced text is made hot. Clicking on the boldfaced text causes a VBScript sub procedure specified right in the opening *<B>* tag to be called.

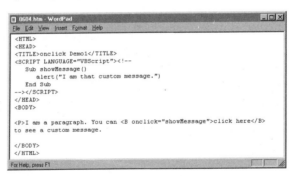

Figure 6-4. *A simple chunk of boldfaced text is made hot using an* onclick *event.*

Opening the page shows this simple paragraph:

I am a paragraph. You can **click here** to see a custom message.

Clicking anywhere on the boldfaced text causes the custom message to pop up, as shown in Figure 6-5.

You can use the *ondblclick* event in a similar manner, as shown in Figure 6-6, using an italicized (*<I>* tag) chunk of text rather than boldfaced text. Opening that page in a web browser displays this paragraph:

I am a paragraph. You can *double-click here* to see a custom message.

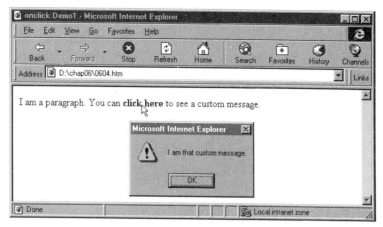

Figure 6-5. *Clicking on the boldfaced text displays an alert dialog box.*

```
0606.htm - WordPad
File  Edit  View  Insert  Format  Help
<HTML>
<HEAD>
<TITLE>ondblclick Demo1</TITLE>
<SCRIPT LANGUAGE="VBScript"><!--
    Sub showMessage()
        alert("I am that custom message.")
    End Sub
--></SCRIPT>
</HEAD>
<BODY>

<P>I am a paragraph. You can <I ondblclick="showMessage">double-click here</I>
to see a custom message.

</BODY>
</HTML>
For Help, press F1
```

Figure 6-6. *An example of using the* ondblclick *event inside a simple <I> tag.*

Double-clicking anywhere on the italicized text displays the custom message.

The upshot here is that you have tremendous freedom in defining what's hot, and what's not, in your page. Even a simple colored chunk of text can be made hot, like this:

```
<P>I am regular text. Part of me is <FONT COLOR="red"
onclick="showMessage">hot hot hot<FONT>. Click on the red text to see
for yourself</P>
```

If you don't like cluttering up your HTML tags with event handlers, you can use the alternative script-binding methods discussed in Chapter 3. Just use an *ID* attribute inside almost any tag, as in the example below:

```
<P>Hey there. You can <B ID="hot1">click here</B> to launch a
script!</P>
```

Then name a sub procedure with the syntax

```
Sub hot1_onclick()
```

or

```
Sub hot1_ondblclick()
```

to attach that procedure to the hot text. Figure 6-7 shows a complete example.

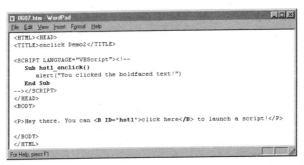

Figure 6-7. *A sub procedure bound to the* onclick *event of a chunk of boldfaced text.*

The *<SCRIPT FOR=...>* approach discussed in Chapter 3 works equally well. Figure 6-8 shows an example of this approach, where *FOR* is set to the name of the object and *EVENT* is set to the event that should trigger the script. In this example, double-clicking the picture named alanbw.gif launches the script defined below the *<IMG>* tag.

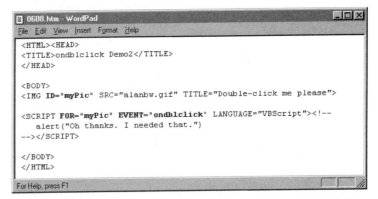

Figure 6-8. *A script bound to an <IMG> tag using the <SCRIPT FOR=...> approach.*

Now you might be thinking, "Yikes, but how do I know when to use *onclick* inside a tag vs. *Sub objectName_event()* vs. *<SCRIPT FOR=...>*?" Actually, you don't need to know. You just use whichever approach you're most comfortable with or whatever is convenient at the moment. Likewise, you might be thinking,

"How do I know which tags support *onclick, ondblclick,* and *ID?*" Well, that one's pretty easy, too. Most tags support *ID, onclick,* and *ondblclick.* If in doubt, just try it out. If you're not comfortable with that, you can always look up any event name in the Internet Client SDK to see exactly which tags support that event.

To top it all off, *onclick* and *ondblclick* aren't the only events VBScript can detect. It also detects *onmousemove, onmouseover, onmouseout, onkeypress, onkeydown, onkeyup,* and a whole slew of others. These other events aren't quite as universal as *onclick* and *ondblclick.* But as you'll learn, quite a few tags do support them. And that boils down to even greater control over how your page responds to whatever your visitor does while viewing your page.

CUSTOM TOOLTIPS

With all these different kinds of hotspots available to us, how are we supposed to let visitors know exactly what is and isn't hot? How do we tell them what will happen if they click or double-click some hot object? A simple solution is to provide a tooltip—a small piece of advisory information that appears after the visitor rests the mouse pointer on an object for a couple of seconds.

Creating tooltips in Dynamic HTML is simple. You just add a *TITLE* attribute, followed by the tooltip text, to virtually any tag. I already snuck an example by you back in Figure 6-8, in the *<IMG>* tag shown below:

```
<IMG ID="myPic" SRC="alanbw.gif" TITLE="Double-click me please">
```

Opening that page in Internet Explorer 4 and resting the mouse pointer on the picture for a second or two displays the tooltip *Double-click me please,* as shown in Figure 6-9.

Figure 6-9. *The tooltip displayed by* TITLE="Double-click me please".

Just about every HTML tag supports the *TITLE* attribute. So feel free to add a tooltip to any chunk of text that's enclosed in a pair of HTML tags. For example, pointing to the little chunk of italicized text in the example below displays a tooltip. Clicking on that text displays a definition:

```
<P>You can click on any italicized term to see its definition. So now
let's talk about the <I onclick="showDef('Word Wide Web Consortium')"
TITLE="Click for definition">W3C</I> and see what those folks are up
to.</P>
```

Figure 6-10 shows a more complete example, in which the page contains two italicized, clickable terms. Figure 6-11 shows how the reader might experience the page. Pointing to *IETF* displays the tooltip *Click for definition*. The figure also shows the message box that appears after the reader clicks on the term. (In real life, the reader sees either the tooltip or the message box; I "fudged" the figure to show both.)

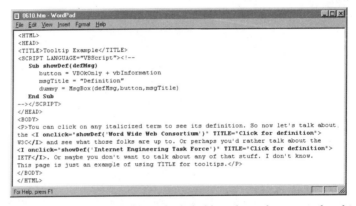

Figure 6-10. *A sample file with clickable italicized terms and tooltips.*

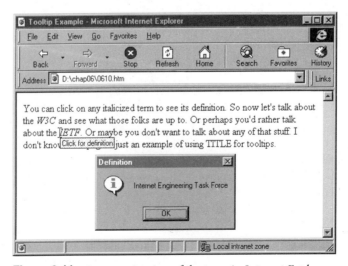

Figure 6-11. *A composite view of the page in Internet Explorer.*

MAKING TEXT APPEAR AND DISAPPEAR

Another fairly easy technique that Internet Explorer 4 offers is the ability to make text appear and disappear on the screen. For example, Figure 6-12 shows how a small part of a page looks when first displayed on the screen. Figure 6-13 shows how that same page looks when the mouse pointer is touching the button titled *I Am A Button.* The text to the right of the button is invisible except when the mouse pointer is actually touching the button.

To make this happen, you want to create a chunk of text that's initially invisible. To do so, set the CSS visible property to *hidden*, using this general syntax within the opening HTML tag for the text to be hidden:

```
STYLE="visibility: hidden"
```

One way to make the text visible is to use the general syntax below in an appropriate tag, where *event* is the event that will make the object visible (such as *onmouseover* or *onclick*) and *objectName* is the name of the hidden object.

```
event="document.all.objectName.style.visibility='visible'"
```

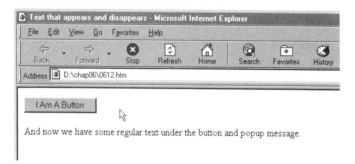

Figure 6-12. *A sample button and some text.*

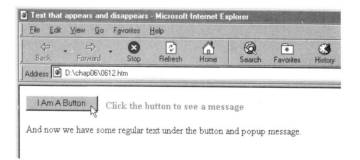

Figure 6-13. *A help message becomes visible when the mouse pointer touches the button.*

To make an object invisible, you can use this general syntax in an appropriate tag:

```
event="document.all.objectName.style.visibility='hidden'"
```

Let me show you how I set up the button and the popup message in Figures 6-12 and 6-13. The button is defined by the *<BUTTON>…</BUTTON>* tags shown below:

```
<BUTTON ID="button1"
onmouseover="document.all.button1Help.style.visibility='visible'"
onmouseout="document.all.button1Help.style.visibility='hidden'">
I Am A Button
</BUTTON>
```

Note the *onmouseover* event, which says, "When the mouse pointer is resting on the button, make the object named *button1Help* visible." The *onmouseout* event handler says, "When the mouse pointer leaves the button, make the object named *button1Help* invisible."

So where is this chunk of text named *button1Help* that is being made visible and invisible? It's right near the button in a pair of *<B>…</B>* (boldface) tags. To ensure that it is initially invisible, its visibility style setting is set to hidden:

```
<B ID="button1Help" STYLE="color: blue; visibility: hidden">
       Click the button to see a message
</B>
```

Figure 6-14 shows the complete document source for this sample page.

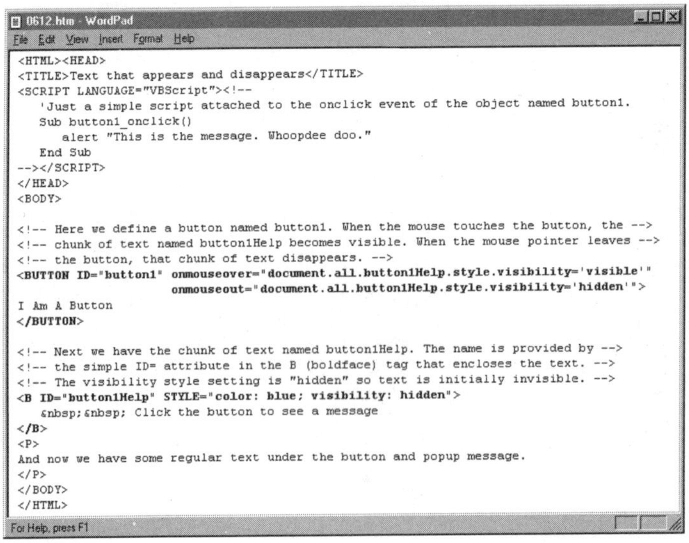

Figure 6-14. *The source code for a page with text that appears and disappears.*

In the next chapter, we'll get much deeper into the *onmouseover* and *onmouseout* events as well as techniques for changing the appearance of text. For now, I want to introduce you to another good general-purpose technique for your Internet Explorer 4 web pages.

PROVIDING DROP-DOWN LISTS

I'm sure you're very familiar with drop-down lists—called *select element objects* in Dynamic HTML argot. These are a great way to present a list of options to your readers without taking up a lot of screen space. Initially, the list is closed. But when you click the little down arrow to the right of the drop-down list, a list of options appears under it, as in the example shown in Figure 6-15 on the next page.

It's pretty easy to add a select element to your web page, especially if you want to use it to display a list of sites to navigate to or a list of files to download. For example, Figure 6-16 on the next page shows the document source for the example in Figure 6-15. Let's take a moment to pick it apart and see how it works.

The select element itself is defined by the *<SELECT>…</SELECT>* tags, which are between the *<FORM>…</FORM>* tags. Notice that in this example I used the *ID* attribute to give the select element object the name *gotoURL*. Note also the syntax of the *<OPTION>* tags. Each tag contains a *VALUE* attribute, which is the URL of a search engine. Just after the opening *<OPTION VALUE=…>* tag is the actual text that appears in the drop-down list:

```
<!-- Display the drop-down list. -->
<FORM>
<SELECT ID="gotoURL">
    <OPTION VALUE="nowhere">Choose a Search Engine</OPTION>
    <OPTION VALUE="http://www.altavista.com">Alta Vista</OPTION>
    <OPTION VALUE="http://www.excite.com">Excite</OPTION>
    <OPTION VALUE="http://www.hotbot.com">Hot Bot</OPTION>
    <OPTION VALUE="http://www.infoseek.com">InfoSeek</OPTION>
    <OPTION VALUE="http://www.lycos.com">Lycos</OPTION>
    <OPTION VALUE="http://www.webcrawler.com">Web Crawler</OPTION>
    <OPTION VALUE="http://www.yahoo.com">Yahoo</OPTION>
</SELECT>
```

To breathe some life into the select element, we bind a script to its *onchange* event in the following way:

```
<SCRIPT FOR="gotoURL" EVENT="onchange" LANGUAGE="VBScript"><!--
```

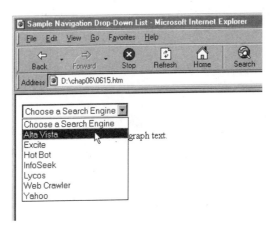

Figure 6-15. *A sample drop-down list that offers a choice of search engines.*

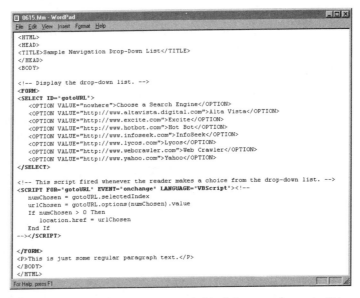

Figure 6-16. *The document source behind the page shown in Figure 6-15.*

Within that script we use the *selectedIndex* property of the *select* object to determine which item the reader selected. As with all collections, the object model considers the first item number 0, the second item number 1, and so forth. Thus, if the reader selected the first item in the select box, the variable named *numChosen* contains 0. If the reader selected the second item in the select element, Alta Vista, *numChosen* contains 1, and so forth:

```
numChosen = gotoURL.selectedIndex
```

Next, the script uses the *options* collection to get the value of the selected item. The value, in this case, is whatever is defined by the *VALUE* attribute of the *<OPTION>* tag. Thus, if the reader selected the first item, number 0, *gotoURL.options(numChosen).value* returns the string *nowhere*. If the reader selected the second item, Alta Vista, *gotoURL.options(numChosen).value* returns the string *http://www.altavista.com*, and so forth. So after this next statement is executed, the variable named *urlChosen* contains the string *nowhere* or some actual URL:

```
urlChosen = gotoURL.options(numChosen).value
```

The *If...Then* statement that follows determines whether the reader selected something other than option *0*. If so, the reader is taken to that site. The script uses the *href* property of the *location* object to perform that task:

```
If numChosen > 0 Then
   location.href = urlChosen
End If
--></SCRIPT>

</FORM>
```

One of the best things about this particular algorithm is that you can adapt it pretty easily to just about any file type. For example, let's say you have a bunch of MIDI files and you'd like to give your reader a simple drop-down list of possible files to save or open and listen to. You just need to replace the *VALUE* attributes of the option tags with the file names of the MIDI files and replace the text between the *<OPTION>...</OPTION>* tags with the appropriate descriptions, and you're (probably) done. Figure 6-17 on the next page shows how such a list looks in the document source.

The reason I say you're *probably* done after making those changes is that you need to be sure that the references in the *VALUE* attributes are valid. In Figure 6-17, relative references (just file names) are used rather than absolute references. This assumes that the MIDI files are in the same directory as the page itself.

If the MIDI files are in some other directory, an appropriate path to those files is required. For example, if all the MIDI files listed are in a directory named *midis* that's under the page's directory, you need to tack *midis/* to the front of each file name. You can do that right in the code, like this:

```
<SCRIPT FOR="gotoURL" EVENT="onchange" LANGUAGE="VBScript"><!--
   numChosen = gotoURL.selectedIndex
   urlChosen = "midis/" & gotoURL.options(numChosen).value
   If numChosen > 0 Then
      location.href = urlChosen
   End If
--></SCRIPT>
```

NOTE If your site contains frames and you want to specify a frame in which to display the new page, replace the *location.href = urlChosen* statement with *parent.frameName.location.href = urlChosen*, where *frameName* is the name of the frame that should display the new page.

Exactly how a visitor experiences a downloaded MIDI file (or any other multimedia file, for that matter) is largely dependent on that visitor's web browser and current preferences within that browser. However, as I'll discuss in Chapter 13, you can do things to influence how every reader experiences a multimedia file.

If you want to use the select element to let the reader download .zip, .exe, or whatever files, all you need to do is (once again) change the *VALUE* attributes and item text, as in this example:

```
<SELECT ID="gotoURL">
    <OPTION VALUE="nowhere">Choose a file to download</OPTION>
    <OPTION VALUE="coolstuf.zip">Cool Stuff</OPTION>
    <OPTION VALUE="coolprog.exe">Cool Program</OPTION>
    <OPTION VALUE="somedoc.zip">Documentation/OPTION>
    <OPTION VALUE="somehlp.zip">Help Files</OPTION>
</SELECT>
```

Again, if the files to be downloaded are not in the same directory as the page itself, make sure you modify the code so that the final file name (*urlChosen*) is a complete and accurate relative reference to the requested file.

```
<HTML>
<HEAD>
<TITLE>Sample Midi File Drop-Down List</TITLE>
</HEAD>
<BODY>

<!-- Display the drop-down list. -->
<FORM>
<SELECT ID="gotoURL">
    <OPTION VALUE="nowhere">Choose a MIDI file to listen to</OPTION>
    <OPTION VALUE="1812over.mid">1812 Overture</OPTION>
    <OPTION VALUE="amazing.mid">Amazing Grace</OPTION>
    <OPTION VALUE="5thsymth.mid">Beethoven's Fifth</OPTION>
    <OPTION VALUE="nutcrack.mid">Nutcracker Suite</OPTION>
    <OPTION VALUE="requiem.mid">Requiem for the Masses</OPTION>
    <OPTION VALUE="tellover.mid">William Tell Overture</OPTION>
</SELECT>

<!-- This script fired whenever the reader makes a choice from the drop-down list. -->
<SCRIPT FOR="gotoURL" EVENT="onchange" LANGUAGE="VBScript"><!--
    numChosen = gotoURL.selectedIndex
    urlChosen = gotoURL.options(numChosen).value
    If numChosen > 0 Then
        location.href = urlChosen
    End If
--></SCRIPT>

</FORM>
<P>This is just some regular paragraph text.</P>
</BODY>
</HTML>
```

Figure 6-17. *This drop-down list lets the reader select a MIDI file to save or open and listen to.*

WARNING VISITORS WHO ARE USING OTHER BROWSERS

At the beginning of this chapter, I showed you a script that pointed a visitor to a specific page in your web site, based on the visitor's particular web browser. I also whined about having to do that, and I mentioned graceful degradation as an alternative. Graceful degradation is actually built right into web browsers and HTML. It allows the web browser to ignore any HTML tags or attributes that it doesn't understand, as opposed to "blowing up" when it encounters something unexpected.

If you're not up for creating umpteen different versions of your web site for umpteen different browsers, you should at least inform non–Internet Explorer 4 browsers that they won't get all the bells and whistles your site has to offer. You'd do well to write the necessary code in JavaScript, since that scripting language is supported by a wider variety of web browsers. Figure 6-18 shows some code that will do the trick. You can put the code anywhere in your home page.

```
0618.htm - WordPad
File   Edit   View   Insert   Format   Help
<HTML><HEAD><TITLE>Warning Demo</TITLE></HEAD>
<BODY>
<SCRIPT LANGUAGE="JavaScript"><!--
    //Get browser brand and version, and display message if necessary.
    var ua = window.navigator.userAgent
    var browser = "unknown"; var version = 0
    if (ua.substring(0,7) == "Mozilla") {
        if (ua.indexOf("MSIE ") > 0) {
            browser = "Microsoft Internet Explorer"
        }
        else {
            browser = "Netscape Navigator"
        }
        if (ua.indexOf("4.") > 0) {
            version = 4
        }
        if (ua.indexOf("3.") > 0) {
            version = 3
        }
    }
    //Display warning if visitor is not using IE4.
    if (browser != "Microsoft Internet Explorer" || version != 4) {
        document.write("<P><CENTER><BLINK><FONT COLOR='red'>")
        document.write("This site is best experienced with Microsoft Internet Explorer version 4.")
        document.write("</FONT></BLINK><BR>")
        document.write("You are using " + browser + " version " + version + ".")
        document.write("<BR>You can download IE4 from ")
        document.write("<A HREF='http://www.microsoft.com/ie/ie40/'>")
        document.write("Microsoft</A>.</CENTER></P>")
    }
//--></SCRIPT>
<!-- Web authors - Proceed with home page HTML and text below... -->
</BODY></HTML>
For Help, press F1
```

Figure 6-18. *This JavaScript code warns non–Internet Explorer 4 users that they won't get all that your site has to offer.*

173

Opening the page shown in Figure 6-18 in Internet Explorer 4 does absolutely nothing. The script is written so that its message is presented only to non–Internet Explorer 4 browsers. As in the first example presented in this chapter, this script obtains user agent information and puts it into a variable named *ua*. Then some *if* statements determine the browser brand name and version number and store that information in two variables—one named *browser* and the other named *version*:

```
<SCRIPT LANGUAGE="JavaScript"><!--
    //Get browser brand and version, and display message if necessary
    var ua = window.navigator.userAgent
    var browser = "unknown"
    var version = 0
    if (ua.substring(0,7) == "Mozilla") {
        if (ua.indexOf("MSIE ") > 0) {
            browser = "Microsoft Internet Explorer"
        }
        else {
            browser = "Netscape Navigator"
        }
        if (ua.indexOf("4.") > 0) {
            version = 4
        }
        if (ua.indexOf("3.") > 0) {
            version = 3
        }
    }
```

Next, some *document.write* statements within an *if* statement write HTML tags and text into the current document, but only if the *browser* variable does not equal the string *Microsoft Internet Explorer* or the *version* variable does not equal *4*:

```
    //Display warning if visitor is not using IE4.
    if (browser != "Microsoft Internet Explorer" || version != 4) {
        document.write("<P><CENTER><BLINK><FONT COLOR='red'>")
        document.write("This site is best experienced with Microsoft " +
            "Internet Explorer version 4.")
        document.write("</FONT></BLINK><BR>")
        document.write("You are using " + browser + " version " +
            version + ".")
        document.write("<BR>You can download IE4 from ")
        document.write("<A HREF='http://www.microsoft.com/ie/ie40/'>")
        document.write("Microsoft</A>.</CENTER></P>")
    }
//--></SCRIPT>
```

The exact HTML tags and text written into the document are shown below. *browser* and *version* get their values from the script. The *<BLINK>* tag works only in Netscape Navigator; it's ignored in Internet Explorer. Figure 6-19 shows a sample of a page containing this script when viewed in Netscape Navigator 4.

```
<P><CENTER><BLINK><FONT COLOR='red'>
This site is best experienced with Microsoft Internet Explorer version 4.
</FONT></BLINK><BR>
You are using browser version version.
<BR>You can download IE4 from
<A HREF='http://www.microsoft.com/ie/ie40/'>
Microsoft</A>.</CENTER></P>
```

While this approach to handling non–Internet Explorer 4 browsers isn't quite as magnanimous as our original approach of offering multiple web pages, it does give the visitor some useful information. It's also a good example of using the *document.write* method to add text and tags into the web page, based on some condition.

Let me point out that the link to www.microsoft.com/ie/ie40/ might not be the best possible link. By the time you read this book, Microsoft might be suggesting a different URL to use in your web pages. You might also be able to pick up a small Internet Explorer graphic and some prewritten code that you can plop right into your page to direct visitors to the proper location. I suggest that you stop by Microsoft's Internet Explorer home page at www.microsoft.com/ie/. When you get there, look for the latest information on giving your visitors an easy way to download Internet Explorer 4 to their PCs.

Figure 6-19. *A page warning a visitor that it contains content best viewed with Internet Explorer 4.*

SUMMARY

In this chapter, my main goal was to provide you with some examples of how the object model, style sheets, and scripting are used together in the real world. I provided some practical examples of scripts that you can start putting to work in your web site right away. The chapters that follow will focus more closely on particular aspects of web development. But before we move on, let's take a moment to review some of the main points and techniques presented in this chapter.

- The *navigator.userAgent* property provides information about the visitor's web browser.

- The *location.href* property lets you specify the URL to another page from within a script. You can also use it to specify files to download to the reader's PC.

- You can use the *onclick* and *ondblclick* events to make many objects hot—even text in simple boldface, italic, or heading tags.

- The *onmouseover* event fires when the mouse pointer touches an object, and the *onmouseout* event fires when the mouse pointer leaves an object.

- The *TITLE* attribute, which you can use in most HTML tags, lets you define a custom tooltip for the object.

- You can use *document.all.objectName.style.visibility = "hidden"* to hide an object, and you can use *document.all.objectName.style.visibility = "visible"* to bring an object out of hiding. In Chapter 7, you'll learn a lot more about using scripts to manipulate styles.

- The *<FORM><SELECT>...</SELECT></FORM>* tags, along with a little VBScript code, provide a cool way to present a drop-down list of options to visitors without taking up a lot of screen space.

- The *document.write* method lets a script add text and HTML tags right into a web page.

Chapter 7

Changing Styles on the Fly

In this chapter, I'll show you some general techniques for changing the appearance of text and other objects in a web page via styles and VBScript code. These techniques will help you create more compelling and interactive web pages. The specific techniques we'll cover include:

- How to change an object's appearance using VBScript code
- Using *onmouseover* and *onmouseout* to make pages more interactive
- Standardizing style changes in a web page
- Changing the style of an individual object
- Changing the style of all objects defined with the same type of tag
- Changing the style of all objects with the same *ID*

We have quite a bit of ground to cover; we'll start with the most basic techniques you'll need to change the appearance of an object in a web page.

USING VBSCRIPT CODE TO CHANGE AN OBJECT'S APPEARANCE

You can use VBScript code to change an object's style or appearance in a few different ways. For starters, many of the attributes that an HTML tag supports are "stylistic." For instance, the heading tags (*<H1>* through *<H6>*) and paragraph tag (*<P>*) all support an *ALIGN* attribute that determines how the text in the tags is aligned relative to the margins. For example, the following tags display the word *Welcome* as a level-1 heading centered between the left and right margins:

```
<H1 ALIGN="center">Welcome</H1>
```

These tags display text with the beginning of each line aligned to the left margin of the page:

```
<P ALIGN="left">This is a paragraph.</P>
```

These tags display *About This Site* as a level-2 heading aligned with the right margin:

```
<H2 ALIGN="right">About This Site</H2>
```

Most of the time, the attributes for an HTML tag are also properties for the corresponding HTML element object. So from a scripting and object model perspective, we can say that *align* is a property of the heading element object or that the heading element object exposes an *align* property.

Because attributes are typically exposed as properties, we can use the following standard syntax in a script to change a property for an object:

```
objectName.property = newValue
```

objectName can be any name that the object model provides automatically, such as *document.all.tags("H1").item(0)* to represent the first *<H1>* tag in the page. Thus, this statement, if enclosed in *<SCRIPT>…</SCRIPT>* tags, changes the alignment of the first heading in the page to *right*, overriding the original *ALIGN* attribute used within the tag:

```
document.all.tags("H1").item(0).align = "right"
```

As we discussed in Part I, you can also make up your own names for objects by using the *ID* attribute within the HTML tag. Thus, if you create a heading named *mainTitle* using these tags

```
<H1 ID="mainTitle" ALIGN="center">Welcome</H1>
```

you can use the following simpler sytax to change that heading's alignment to *left*:

```
mainTitle.align = "left"
```

Figure 7-1 illustrates these concepts within the context of a complete HTML document. The document has four named objects, two paragraphs named *bodyText* and *buttonHolder*, and two headings named *mainTitle* and *subHeading*. One script in the document uses the standard *objectName.property* = *newValue* syntax to alter the alignment of each of those elements in response to a button click.

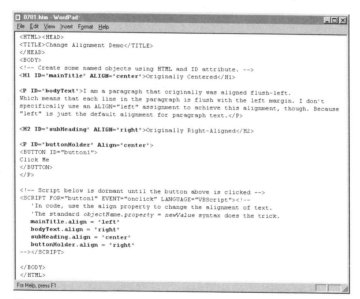

Figure 7-1. *An HTML document with a script that changes the alignment of several objects.*

Figure 7-2 shows how the page looks when first opened in Internet Explorer (before the Click Me button is clicked). Clicking the button fires the script, which in turn changes the alignment of the objects. After the button is clicked, the page looks like Figure 7-3.

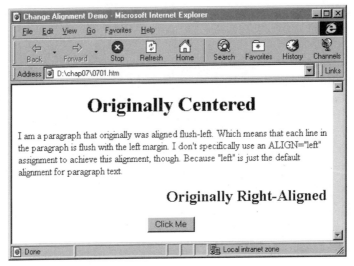

Figure 7-2. *The page whose source is shown in Figure 7-1 before the Click Me button is clicked.*

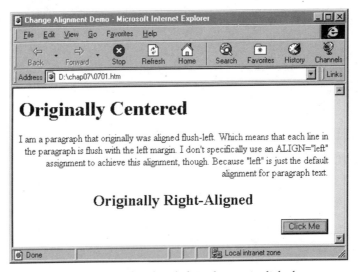

Figure 7-3. *The page after the Click Me button is clicked.*

Using Code to Change Styles

As you learned in Chapter 2, CSS (cascading style sheets) allows you to stylize many objects. As a general rule, CSS offers more flexibility than the attributes provided by HTML. For example, the heading tags and paragraph tag don't offer any built-in attribute for defining the color of text within the tag. However, CSS offers a color attribute that lets you define the text color. As we discussed in Chapter 2, there are several ways to assign styles to objects. You can define styles "in line" using a *STYLE* attribute, as follows:

```
<H1 ID="mainTitle" STYLE="color:blue">
```

You can also define styles separately and then embed or link them into the current page. I'll review the embed approach in a moment. For now, I'll focus on changing an inline style using scripting code. The general syntax for doing so is virtually identical to the syntax for changing a property. However, you need to interject a reference to the *style* object, as shown here:

```
objectName.style.CSSProperty = newValue
```

objectName is once again any valid object name, *CSSProperty* is some CSS property, and *newValue* is a valid setting for that CSS property.

NOTE CSS properties and CSS attributes are not exactly the same, even though some CSS properties are spelled the same as their corresponding CSS attributes. CSS properties do not have any dashes in their names and are internally capitalized. CSS properties are properties of the *style* object and are used for manipulating styles in scripting code. CSS attributes are used for defining styles. Table 7-1 later in this chapter lists both the CSS properties and the corresponding CSS attributes.

Here's an example in which a little chunk of code turns the color style attribute for the first heading in a page to red:

```
document.all.tags("H1").item(0).style.color = "red"
```

Once again, if you used an *ID* attribute to give that particular object its own name, as shown here

```
<H1 ID="mainTitle" ALIGN="center">Welcome</H1>
```

you can use that *ID* as the object name:

```
mainTitle.style.color = "red"
```

The result of either statement is to change the text color of the heading from its current value (black, if not specified) to red.

Figure 7-4 shows a sample document that's similar to the one shown earlier in Figure 7-1. However, rather than changing the built-in *ALIGN* attributes of the text, the script in this page changes the CSS color and visibility properties of several objects in the page.

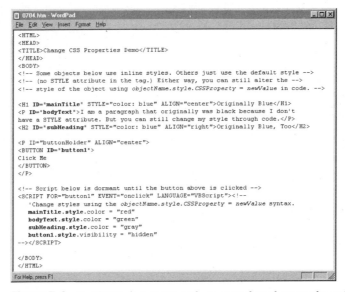

Figure 7-4. *An HTML document with a script that changes the style properties of several objects.*

Figure 7-5 shows the document in Internet Explorer. Although you can't really tell from the figure, take my word for it that the two headings are both colored blue. The paragraph text is black, and the Click Me button is (obviously) visible.

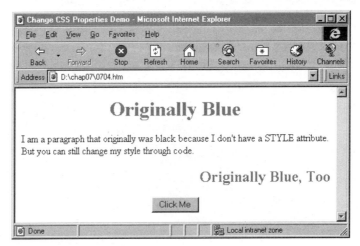

Figure 7-5. *The page whose source is shown in Figure 7-4 before the Click Me button is clicked.*

Figure 7-6 shows how the page looks after the button is clicked. Once again, you'll have to take my word for it. But the first heading is now red, the paragraph text is green, and the second heading is gray. The button is invisible.

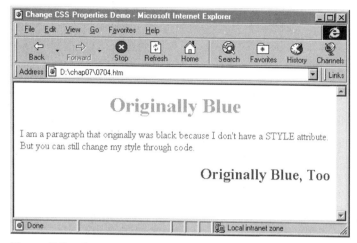

Figure 7-6. *The page after the Click Me button is clicked.*

Table 7-1 shows all the CSS properties along with the corresponding CSS attributes that were introduced in Chapter 2. The properties and attributes are discussed in greater detail in the Internet Client SDK, described in Appendix A. You can change any of these style properties using the syntax *object-Name.style.CSSProperty = newValue*, where *CSSProperty* is any CSS property listed in the table.

Table 7-1
CSS PROPERTIES AND CORRESPONDING CSS ATTRIBUTES

CSS Property	CSS Attribute
background	*background*
backgroundAttachment	*background-attachment*
backgroundColor	*background-color*
backgroundImage	*background-image*
backgroundPosition	*background-position*
backgroundPositionX	*background-position*
backgroundPositionY	*background-position*
backgroundRepeat	*background-repeat*
border	*border*
borderBottom	*border-bottom*
borderBottomColor	*border-bottom-color*

(continued)

CSS PROPERTIES AND CORRESPONDING CSS ATTRIBUTES *continued*

CSS Property	CSS Attribute
borderBottomStyle	*border-bottom-style*
borderBottomWidth	*border-bottom-width*
borderColor	*border-color*
borderLeft	*border-left*
borderLeftColor	*border-left-color*
borderLeftStyle	*border-left-style*
borderLeftWidth	*border-left-width*
borderRight	*border-right*
borderRightColor	*border-right-color*
borderRightStyle	*border-right-style*
borderRightWidth	*border-right-width*
borderStyle	*border-style*
borderTop	*border-top*
borderTopColor	*border-top-color*
borderTopStyle	*border-top-style*
borderTopWidth	*border-top-width*
borderWidth	*border-width*
clear	*clear*
clip	*clip*
color	*color*
cursor	*cursor*
display	*display*
filter	*filter*
styleFloat	*float*
font	*font*
fontFamily	*font-family*
fontSize	*font-size*
fontStyle	*font-style*
fontVariant	*font-variant*
fontWeight	*font-weight*
height	*height*
pixelHeight	*height*
posHeight	*height*
left	*left*
pixelLeft	*left*
posLeft	*left*

CSS Property	*CSS Attribute*
letterSpacing	*letter-spacing*
lineHeight	*line-height*
listStyle	*list-style*
listStyleImage	*list-style-image*
listStylePosition	*list-style-position*
listStyleType	*list-style-type*
margin	*margin*
marginBottom	*margin-bottom*
marginLeft	*margin-left*
marginRight	*margin-right*
marginTop	*margin-top*
overflow	*overflow*
padding	*padding*
paddingBottom	*padding-bottom*
paddingLeft	*padding-left*
paddingRight	*padding-right*
paddingTop	*padding-top*
pageBreakAfter	*page-break-after*
pageBreakBefore	*page-break-before*
position	*position*
textAlign	*text-align*
textDecoration	*text-decoration*
textDecorationLineThrough	*text-decoration*
textDecorationOverline	*text-decoration*
textDecorationUnderline	*text-decoration*
textIndent	*text-indent*
textTransform	*text-transform*
top	*top*
pixelTop	*top*
posTop	*top*
verticalAlign	*vertical-align*
visibility	*visibility*
width	*width*
pixelWidth	*width*
posWidth	*width*
zIndex	*z-index*

Changing an Object's Style Using Style Classes

A *style class,* as you might recall from Chapter 2, lets you give several style attributes a single name. A style class is defined within a pair of *<STYLE>...</STYLE>* tags. The name you want to assign to the class should be preceded by a period. Here's an example in which I've defined two style classes—one named *slanted,* which goes with the *<H1>* tag, and another named *blueOnYellow,* which isn't associated with any tag:

```
<STYLE TYPE="text/css"><!--
   H1 {font-family: Arial;
       font-weight: bold;
       font-size: 24pt}

   H1.slanted {font-style: italic}

   .blueOnYellow {color: blue;
                  background-color: yellow}
--></STYLE>
```

The *blueOnYellow* style class offers a new technique that I haven't mentioned yet in this book—defining a class without an associated HTML tag such as *<H1>* or *<P>*. This approach is useful because you can apply such a class to any object in your page. For example, you can apply the *blueOnYellow* class to a paragraph (*<P>* tag), an item in a list (*<LI>* tag), a heading (*<H1>* through *</H6>* tags), or just about any other chunk of text.

After you define one or more classes, you can apply a style class to an object using the following syntax, where *objectName* is any valid object name and *newClass* is the name of any style class that has already been defined between *<STYLE>...</STYLE>* tags:

```
objectName.className = newClass
```

Figure 7-7 shows an example. Let's look at the document in some detail. First, I set up a style that, by default, displays all level-1 headings in a 24-point Arial bold font:

```
<STYLE TYPE="text/css"><!--
   H1 {font-family: Arial;
       font-weight: bold;
       font-size: 24pt}
```

In addition, I created a style class for the *<H1>* tag, named *slanted,* that italicizes the text:

```
   H1.slanted {font-style: italic}
```

Figure 7-7. *An HTML document containing style classes and code for assigning classes to objects.*

I also set up the "free-floating" *blueOnYellow* style class, which can be applied to any object in the document:

```
.blueOnYellow {color: blue;
               background-color: yellow}
--></STYLE>
```

The document contains an object named *mainTitle*, which is a chunk of text between *<H1>...</H1>* tags. In this document, that title will be shown in 24-point Arial bold by default because I already defined that font as the default for all *<H1>* tags in the document:

```
<H1 ID="mainTitle">Originally just Arial bold 24 pt.</H1>
```

I also added three scripts to the document, each bound to its own button. The first script uses the basic *objectName.className = newClass* syntax to assign the slanted style class to the object named *mainTitle*:

```
<BUTTON ID="slantText">Apply slanted Style Class</BUTTON>
<SCRIPT FOR="slantText" EVENT="onclick" LANGUAGE="VBScript"><!--
   mainTitle.className = "slanted"
--></SCRIPT>
```

The second sample script uses the same syntax to apply the *blueOnYellow* style class to the object named *mainTitle*:

```
<BUTTON ID="colorText">Apply blueOnYellow Style Class</BUTTON>
<SCRIPT FOR="colorText" EVENT="onclick" LANGUAGE="VBScript"><!--
   mainTitle.className = "blueOnYellow"
--></SCRIPT>
```

The last sample script replaces any style class that happens to be assigned to the *mainTitle* object at the moment with a null string (*""*). The effect is to remove the style class, thereby returning it to its default appearance:

```
<BUTTON ID="removeClass">Remove Style Class</BUTTON>
<SCRIPT FOR="removeClass" EVENT="onclick" LANGUAGE="VBScript"><!--
   'Remove any style class (return to default style).
   mainTitle.className = ""
--></SCRIPT>
```

Opening the document in Internet Explorer initially displays the page shown in Figure 7-8.

Clicking the first button applies the *slanted* style class, thereby italicizing the existing text, as shown in Figure 7-9. Note that the style class is *added* to the default style. That is, the heading is still in 24-point Arial bold font but now it's also italicized.

Clicking the second button applies the *blueOnYellow* style class. Note that this button would *remove* the *slanted* style class if it were already applied. That's because only one style class at a time can be assigned to an object. However, the default style, 24-point Arial bold font, would remain intact because it is the default style, not a separate style class.

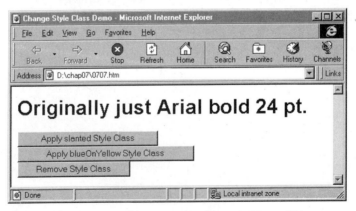

Figure 7-8. *The page whose source is shown in Figure 7-7.*

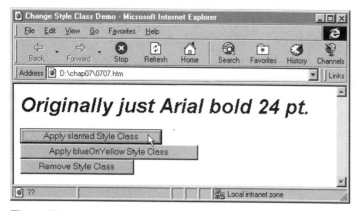

Figure 7-9. *The page after the Apply slanted Style Class button is clicked.*

Clicking the third button makes the text look just as it did originally (see Figure 7-7 on page 187) because no style class is attributed to the *mainTitle* object anymore.

By the way, if you want the *blueOnYellow* style class to show italicized text as well, you simply add the attribute and value to the original definition of the *blueOnYellow* style class, as shown below:

```
.blueOnYellow {color: blue;
          background-color: yellow;
          font-style: italic}
```

The important point to glean from everything that we've discussed so far is that there are basically three "syntaxes" you can use to change the appearance of any object in your web page. Those three syntaxes are summarized in Table 7-2.

Table 7-2

THREE WAYS TO CHANGE AN OBJECT'S APPEARANCE USING CODE

Syntax	Purpose
objectName.property = newValue	Assign some new value to a built-in property. The property is often defined by an attribute in the object's HTML tag.
objectName.style.CSSProperty = newValue	Assigns a new value to a single CSS property for the specified object.
objectName.className = newClass	Applies an existing style class to the object.

USING THE *ONMOUSEOVER* AND *ONMOUSEOUT* EVENTS

The technique of changing the appearance of text as the mouse pointer moves over it is commonly used in multimedia programs. For instance, you might have used programs in which a link or an option lights up when the mouse pointer touches it. You can easily add such effects to your Internet Explorer 4 web pages by using VBScript code to dynamically change the style of an object in response to *onmouseover* and *onmouseout* events.

One way to do this is to put all of the necessary code right into the HTML tag. Here's an example of that approach, in which the alignment of the text changes when the mouse pointer touches the text (*onmouseover*) in *<H1>…</H1>* tags. Moving the mouse pointer away from the text (*onmouseout*) returns the style of the heading to its previous, default setting:

```
<H1 ID="mainTitle"
onmouseover="mainTitle.align = 'right'"
onmouseout="mainTitle.align = ''">
I change alignment when you point to me
</H1>
```

The same idea applies to changing a style attribute. Here's a little chunk of HTML that displays a level-2 heading. When the mouse pointer touches the heading, the text color changes to green. When the mouse pointer moves away from the heading, the text returns to its previous style:

```
<H2 ID="subHead"
onmouseover="subHead.style.color = 'green'"
onmouseout="subHead.style.color = ''">
I change color when you point to me
</H2>
```

Likewise, if you've defined any style classes, you can use the *object.className = newValue* syntax to change, assign, or remove a style class in response to a mouse event. For example, let's say the current page has a style class named *blueOnYellow* defined within it, as shown below:

```
<STYLE TYPE="text/css"><!--
    .blueOnYellow {color: blue;
                    background-color: yellow}
--></STYLE>
```

WARNING HTML is very liberal when it comes to line breaks. You can break a line in most places within an HTML tag. VBScript is not nearly so liberal. You cannot arbitrarily break a VBScript line of code into two or more lines.

The paragraph below changes to blue text on a yellow background when the mouse pointer touches the paragraph. It reverts to its previous style when the mouse pointer leaves.

```
<P ID="graf"
onmouseover="graf.className = 'blueOnYellow'"
onmouseout="graf.className = ''">
This is a paragraph enclosed in &lt;P&gt; and &lt;/
P&gt; tags. Pointing to this paragraph changes its appearance
because the onmouseover event applies a style class named blueOnYellow.
Removing the mouse pointer changes it back to its previous appearance
because an onmouseout event sets the className value back to null ('').
</P>
```

Figure 7-10 shows an HTML document that uses all three techniques of changing a style. Figure 7-11 on the next page shows how this page looks when the user points to the paragraph.

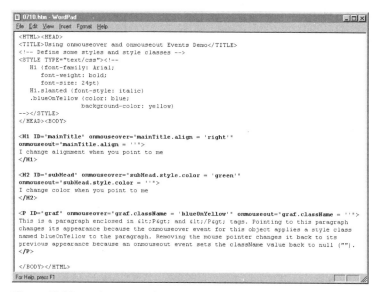

Figure 7-10. *A document that uses* onmouseover *and* onmouseout *events to trigger the change of styles.*

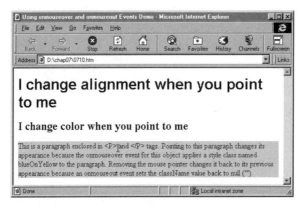

Figure 7-11. *The page whose source is shown in Figure 7-10. It contains three examples of using mouse events to change the appearance of text.*

Incidentally, the examples in this chapter show the style classes being defined as embedded styles. However, the technique works just as well if those styles are defined in an external file that's linked to the current page using the *<LINK REL="STYLESHEET"...>* tag that we discussed in Chapter 2.

STANDARDIZING A STYLE CHANGE

While *onmouseover* and *onmouseout* work fine within an HTML tag, that approach has a drawback: Your page can become so cluttered with stuff inside the HTML tags that you can't easily see the basic structure of the page. This is especially true if you want, say, all headings to change when the mouse pointer touches them. It is more efficient to make up a general rule that says, "Whenever the mouse pointer touches a level-1 heading, change that heading to green." Or a rule that says, "Whenever the mouse pointer touches an item in a list, italicize that item." That way, you can simply define the rule once and not have to put all that code inside the heading and list item HTML tags.

The "rule" you define in this type of situation is actually a script that fires whenever an *onmouseover* or *onmouseout* event occurs. That same script also determines whether the object that fired the event was a heading or a list item; if so, it applies the appropriate style to that item. Likewise, another script catches all *onmouseout* events and resets the object back to its original style. Let's create those scripts now.

Creating the Scripts

We need two scripts for starters—one that fires whenever an *onmouseover* event occurs in the current page, and one that fires whenever an *onmouseout* event occurs. The scripts can go into the document header and can be defined as sub procedures using this basic syntax:

```
<HTML><HEAD>
<TITLE>Standardized Style Change Demo</TITLE>
<SCRIPT LANGUAGE="VBScript"><!--

    'Sub procedure to detect whenever an onmouseover event occurs.
    Sub document_onmouseover()
        'More code will go in here.
    End Sub

    'Sub procedure to detect whenever an onmouseout event occurs.
    Sub document_onmouseout()
        'More code will go here.
    End Sub
--></SCRIPT>
</HEAD>
```

Because of the way it's named, the *document_onmouseover()* sub procedure fires whenever an *onmouseover* event occurs in the document. Likewise, the *document_onmouseout()* sub procedure fires whenever an *onmouseout* event occurs in the document. We don't necessarily want to respond to every single *onmouseover* and *onmouseout* event, however. Perhaps we simply want to respond to the mouse touching or leaving the text that's inside a pair of *<H1>* tags.

To limit which tags are actually affected by the scripts, we can add an *If...Then* statement that checks whether the tag that fired the current event is a certain tag, such as an *<H1>* tag. Here's that code added in:

```
<HTML><HEAD>
<TITLE>Standardized Style Change Demo</TITLE>
<SCRIPT LANGUAGE="VBScript"><!--

    'Sub procedure to detect whenever an onmouseover event occurs.
    Sub document_onmouseover()
        'If an H1 heading triggered this onmouseover event...
        If window.event.srcElement.tagName = "H1" Then
            'More code will go in here.
        End If
    End Sub

    'Sub procedure to detect whenever an onmouseout event occurs.
    Sub document_onmouseout()
```

(continued)

```
        'If an H1 heading triggered this onmouseout event...
        If window.event.srcElement.tagName = "H1" Then
           'More code will go in here.
        End If
   End Sub
--></SCRIPT>
</HEAD>
```

Within each of those *If...Then* statements, we need to determine exactly which H1 heading in the page triggered the event. We can do this by grabbing the object's subscript—its position in the *document.all* collection. So the code to determine exactly which object fired the most recent event is:

```
subscript = window.event.srcElement.sourceIndex
```

This little chunk of code grabs the *sourceIndex* (the position in the *document.all* collection) of whatever object (*srcElement*) triggered the event, and it stores that number in a variable named *subscript*.

So now we know that the object named *document.all(subscript)* fired the event. To change the appearance of that object, we use the following syntax:

```
document.all(subscript).property = newValue
```

or

```
document.all(subscript).style.CSSProperty = newValue
```

or

```
document.all(subscript).className = newClass
```

Let's say that whenever the mouse pointer touches an H1 heading, we want that heading's text to change to green. When the mouse pointer leaves an H1 heading, we want that heading to return to its previous appearance. The code ends up looking like this:

```
<HTML><HEAD>
<TITLE>Standardized Style Change Demo</TITLE>
<SCRIPT LANGUAGE="VBScript"><!--
   'Sub procedure to detect whenever an onmouseover event occurs.
   Sub document_onmouseover()
      'If an H1 heading triggered this onmouseover event...
      If window.event.srcElement.tagName = "H1" Then
         'make H1 heading green.
         subscript = window.event.srcElement.sourceIndex
         document.all(subscript).style.color = "green"
      End If
   End Sub
```

```
'Sub procedure to detect whenever an onmouseout event occurs.
Sub document_onmouseout()
    'If an H1 heading triggered this onmouseout event...
    If window.event.srcElement.tagName = "H1" Then
        'return H1 heading to default style.
        subscript = window.event.srcElement.sourceIndex
        document.all(subscript).style.color = ""
    End If
End Sub
--></SCRIPT>
</HEAD>
```

Figure 7-12 shows the scripts within the context of a complete HTML document. Even though the *<H1>* tags in the body of the page contain no excess code, the headings will still turn green when the mouse touches them. Figure 7-13 on the next page shows the page in action.

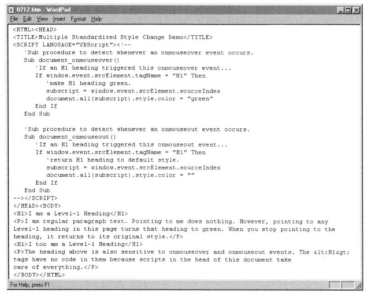

Figure 7-12. *An HTML document that uses a standardized approach to changing a style.*

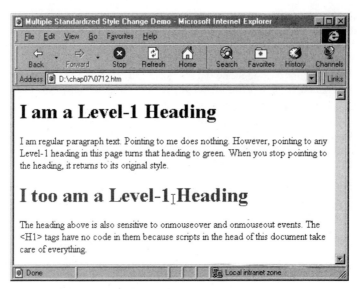

Figure 7-13. *The page whose source is shown in Figure 7-12. Both H1 headings turn green when the mouse touches them.*

Extending the Standardized Style Change

It's pretty easy to adapt the scripts shown in Figure 7-12 so that they apply to other objects. For example, let's say you want *all* levels of headings—H1, H2, and so forth to H6—to turn green when the mouse touches them. The following fairly simple change to the code will do the trick:

```
<SCRIPT LANGUAGE="VBScript"><!--
    'Sub procedure to detect whenever an onmouseover event occurs.
    Sub document_onmouseover()
        thisTag = window.event.srcElement.tagName
        'If an H1 - H6 heading triggered this onmouseover event...
        If thisTag >= "H1" And thisTag <= "H6" Then
            'make heading green.
            subscript = window.event.srcElement.sourceIndex
            document.all(subscript).style.color = "green"
        End If
    End Sub

    'Sub procedure to detect whenever an onmouseout event occurs.
    Sub document_onmouseout()
        thisTag = window.event.srcElement.tagName
        'If an H1 - H6 heading triggered this onmouseout event...
        If thisTag >= "H1" And thisTag <= "H6" Then
            'return heading to default style.
```

```
        subscript = window.event.srcElement.sourceIndex
        document.all(subscript).style.color = ""
    End If
  End Sub
--></SCRIPT>
```

Defining Multiple Standardized Style Changes

Suppose you want to define another "rule" for style changes in your web page—for example, a rule that says, "Whenever the reader points to an item in a list, italicize that item." First, you can create a default style for list items (*<LI>* tags) and an italicized style class, as shown below:

```
<STYLE TYPE="text/css"><!--
   LI {font: 14pt/16pt 'Times Roman'}
   .listItalic {font-style: italic}
--></STYLE>
```

> **TIP** When a script converts text to italics, the text might grow a little taller. If this occurs, neighboring text tends to shift accordingly. You can eliminate that shift by making the line height a couple of points greater than the font height. In the sample LI style, the *14pt/16pt* setting does just that—it makes the line height two points taller than the font height.

The code for displaying a list item in italics when the mouse pointer touches the list item looks like this:

```
'Sub procedure to detect whenever an onmouseover event occurs.
Sub document_onmouseover()
   'Get tag name of object that fired this sub procedure.
   thisTag = window.event.srcElement.tagName
   If thisTag = "LI" Then
      subscript = window.event.srcElement.sourceIndex
      document.all(subscript).className = "listItalic"
   End If
End Sub
```

The code to return the list item to its default state when the mouse pointer leaves looks like this:

```
Sub document_onmouseout()
   'Get tag name of object that fired this sub procedure.
   thisTag = window.event.srcElement.tagName
   If thisTag = "LI" Then
      subscript = window.event.srcElement.sourceIndex
      document.all(subscript).className = ""
   End If
End Sub
```

Figure 7-14 shows the styles and scripts in the context of a more complete HTML document. This document also retains the *If…Then* statments required to make headings green on mouse contact. Figure 7-15 shows the page in action.

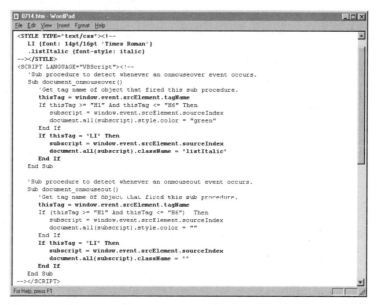

Figure 7-14. *An HTML document containing scripts that handle multiple mouse event style changes.*

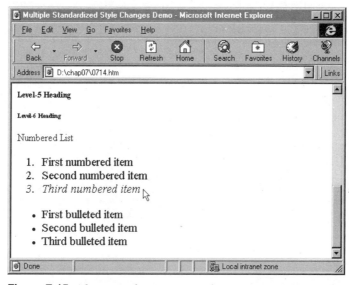

Figure 7-15. *The page whose source is shown in Figure 7-14. It has headings and list items that change on mouse contact.*

Refining a Standardized
Style Change with *parentElement*

The *parentElement* property of an HTML element object returns the parent or "container" element object. For example, take a look at the following bulleted (unordered) list as expressed in HTML:

```
<UL>
<LI>First bulleted item</LI>
<LI>Second bulleted item</LI>
<LI>Third bulleted item</LI>
</UL>
```

The parent element of each list item is the *UL* element because all the *<LI>* tags are contained within a pair of *<UL>...</UL>* tags.

You might find it handy to refer to the *parentElement* when deciding whether to apply a style. For example, suppose you want your style rule to state, "When the mouse pointer touches a list item in a bulleted list, make the list item italic." To create such a rule, we need to determine not only the specific element that fired the event but also the parent element of the object that fired the event. That code looks like this:

```
Sub document_onmouseover()
    'Get tag name and parent tag name of object that fired this
    'sub procedure.
    thisTag = window.event.srcElement.tagName
    parentTag = window.event.srcElement.parentElement.tagName
```

Figure 7-16 on the next page shows the "Only italicize items in a bulleted list on mouse contact" pair of scripts in the context of a more complete document. Figure 7-17, also on the next page, shows a sample.

Figure 7-16. *An HTML document containing scripts that use the* parentElement *property.*

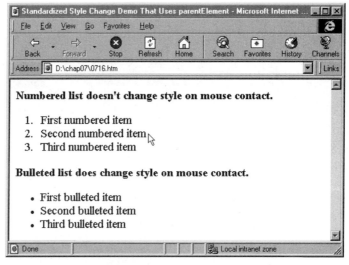

Figure 7-17. *The page whose source is shown in Figure 7-16. It only italicizes items in a bulleted (unordered) list on mouse contact.*

Styling Table Behavior

Even though I've used some simple tags such as *<H1>*, *<P>*, and *<LI>* in these examples, I don't want you to get the impression that you're limited to just styling text. You can easily style a table, an image, or any other object. For example, suppose you want to set up a "rule" that says, "Whenever the reader points to a table cell, make that cell's border blue and its background color yellow." Figure 7-18 shows the scripts that would enforce such a rule on every data cell (*<TD>* tag) in every table in the current web page. Figure 7-19 shows a sample.

```
0718.htm - WordPad
File Edit View Insert Format Help
<HTML><HEAD>
<TITLE>Styling Table Cells Demo</TITLE>
<SCRIPT LANGUAGE="VBScript"><!--
    'Sub procedure to detect whenever an onmouseover event occurs.
    Sub document_onmouseover()
        'Get tag name of object that fired this sub procedure.
        thisTag = window.event.srcElement.tagName
        If thisTag = "TD" Then
            subscript = window.event.srcElement.sourceIndex
            document.all(subscript).bgColor="yellow"
            document.all(subscript).borderColor="blue"
        End If
    End Sub

    'Sub procedure to detect whenever an onmouseout event occurs.
    Sub document_onmouseout()
        'Get tag name of object that fired this sub procedure.
        thisTag = window.event.srcElement.tagName
        If thisTag = "TD" Then
            subscript = window.event.srcElement.sourceIndex
            document.all(subscript).bgColor=""
            document.all(subscript).borderColor=""
        End If
    End Sub
--></SCRIPT>

</HEAD><BODY>
<TABLE BORDER="1">
    <TR>
        <TH>ColHead1</TH> <TH>ColHead2</TH> <TH>ColHead3</TH>
    </TR>
    <TR>
        <TD>cell A1</TD> <TD>cell A2</TD> <TD>cell A3</TD>
For Help, press F1
```

Figure 7-18. *An HTML document containing scripts that style table cells.*

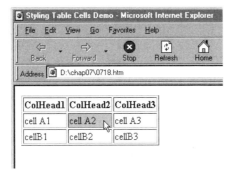

Figure 7-19. *The page whose source is shown in Figure 7-18. It changes a table cell's background color on mouse contact.*

Copy-and-Paste Standard Style Changes

Another handy thing about defining standard style changes "rules" through code is that you can easily copy-and-paste the code from one page to the next in your site. In this way, you can maintain a consistent look and consistent behavior across all of your pages without typing all those *onmouseover* and *onmouseout* expressions into each and every tag in each and every page.

onclick and *TITLE* Still Work!

Perhaps I should also mention that nothing we've discussed here precludes your using the *onclick* or *ondblclick* events with the object that change styles. Nor does it preclude your using the *TITLE* attribute to give the objects a tooltip. For instance, Figure 7-20 shows an HTML document that changes the heading style on mouse contact. But within the body of the document, a couple of headings also use an *onclick* event to navigate the reader to a new page when the headings are clicked on. Also, the headings use the *TITLE* attribute to display tooltips.

```
0720.htm - WordPad
File  Edit  View  Insert  Format  Help

<HTML><HEAD>
<TITLE>Style, TITLE, onclick Demo</TITLE>
<SCRIPT LANGUAGE="VBScript"><!--
    'Sub procedure to detect whenever an onmouseover event occurs.
    Sub document_onmouseover()
        'Get tag of object that fired this sub procedure.
        thisTag = window.event.srcElement.tagName
        If thisTag >= "H1" And thisTag <= "H6" Then
            subscript = window.event.srcElement.sourceIndex
            document.all(subscript).style.color = "green"
        End If
    End Sub

    'Sub procedure to detect whenever an onmouseout event occurs.
    Sub document_onmouseout()
        'Get tag of object that fired this sub procedure.
        thisTag = window.event.srcElement.tagName
        If (thisTag >= "H1" And thisTag <= "H6")  Then
            subscript = window.event.srcElement.sourceIndex
            document.all(subscript).style.color = ""
        End If
    End Sub
--></SCRIPT>

</HEAD><BODY>
<H1 onclick="location.href = 'pepe.htm'" TITLE="More about Pepe">Pepe Le Pew</H1>
<P>Pepe Le Pew is Warner Brothers' amorous skunk. To see more info, click the
heading above.</P>

<H1 onclick="location.href = 'daffy.htm'" TITLE="More about Daffy">Daffy Duck</H1>
<P>Daffy Duck is a slightly speech-impaired duck with an attitude. For more
information about Daffy, click the heading above this paragraph.</P>
</BODY></HTML>
For Help, press F1
```

Figure 7-20. *The <H1> tags in this document use the* onclick *event and the* TITLE *attribute.*

The headings in the sample document will still turn green on mouse contact. A moment later, the tooltip will appear near the mouse pointer, as shown in Figure 7-21. If the reader clicks on the heading, he will be taken to some new page. This is a good combination of visual cues for the reader because the immediate color change upon touching the heading hints that "something is special here." Holding the mouse pointer there for one or two seconds displays the tooltip, which provides more information about what's special. And of course, clicking on the heading takes the reader to a new page.

Figure 7-21. *A page with headings that change style on mouse contact, display tooltips, and navigate to a new page when clicked.*

Lighting Up Hyperlinks

The natural behavior of hyperlinks (*<A HREF=…>* tags) is also not impaired by the *document_onmouseover()* or *document_onmouseout()* sub procedures. So you can use these mouse events to spice up your regular hyperlinks. For example, Figure 7-22 shows an HTML document that changes the background color of any hyperlink to yellow on mouse contact.

```
0722.htm - WordPad
File Edit View Insert Format Help
<HTML><HEAD>
<TITLE>Light-Up Hyperlinks Demo 1</TITLE>
<STYLE TYPE="text/css"><!--
    .yellowBack {background-color: yellow}
--></STYLE>
<SCRIPT LANGUAGE="VBScript"><!--
    'Sub procedure to detect whenever an onmouseover event occurs.
    Sub document_onmouseover()
        'If an A tag fired this script, give it a yellow background.
        If window.event.srcElement.tagName = "A" Then
            subscript = window.event.srcElement.sourceIndex
            document.all(subscript).className = "yellowBack"
        End If
    End Sub

    'Sub procedure to detect whenever an onmouseout event occurs.
    Sub document_onmouseout()
        'Change A tag back to normal color when mouse pointer leaves.
        If window.event.srcElement.tagName = "A" Then
            subscript = window.event.srcElement.sourceIndex
            document.all(subscript).className = ""
        End If
    End Sub
--></SCRIPT>
</HEAD>
<BODY>
<P>A couple of my personal favorite web sites include
<A HREF="http://www.coolnerds.com" TITLE="Click to go there">Coolnerds</A>
and Microsoft's <A HREF="http://www.microsoft.com/workshop/" TITLE="Click to go there">
Site Builder's Workshop</A>. By the way, notice how the hyperlinks here "light up" when
you touch them with the mouse pointer.</P>
</BODY></HTML>
For Help, press F1
```

Figure 7-22. *A document that uses the mouse event to light up hyperlinks.*

Figure 7-23 shows how the page looks in Internet Explorer. Notice that the mouse pointer is touching one of the hyperlinks in the page. The background of that hyperlink is yellow, and you can also see the tooltip that appears near the mouse pointer.

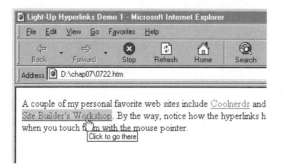

Figure 7-23. *The page whose source is shown in Figure 7-22. It contains hyperlinks that light up.*

Here's another example of lighting up hyperlinks. In this case, however, we'll use a framed site with hyperlinks in the left frame and pages showing up in the right frame. Also, we'll give the hyperlinks a unique appearance—a heavy font named Arial Black, which is initially gray in color. Touching a hyperlink lights it up by changing the text color from gray to blue. I know you can't see the exact colors here, but you can probably tell in Figure 7-24 that the hyperlink the mouse pointer is touching looks a little different from the other hyperlinks in that frame.

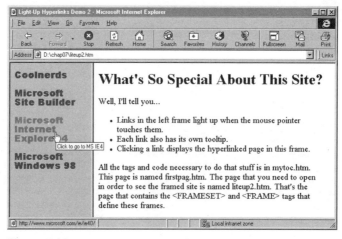

Figure 7-24. *Hyperlinks in the left frame that light up.*

To create this sample site, I first created a document named liteup2.htm that defines the left and right frames. That document contains the following tags:

```
<HTML>
<HEAD>
<TITLE>Light-Up Hyperlinks Demo 2</TITLE>
<!-- This page just defines the frames -->
<FRAMESET COLS = "180,*">
   <FRAME NAME="leftFrame" SRC="mytoc.htm">
   <FRAME NAME="rightFrame" SRC="firstpag.htm">
</FRAMESET>
</HTML>
```

The top half of the document named mytoc.htm is shown in Figure 7-25.

Let's pick apart mytoc.htm to get a better feel for how it works. Within the head of the document, I specified the base target frame. The *<BASE TARGET=...>* tag below ensures that any *<A HREF=...>* tag that doesn't have its *TARGET* attribute specified will display its referenced page in the frame named *rightFrame*.

```
<BASE TARGET="rightFrame">
```

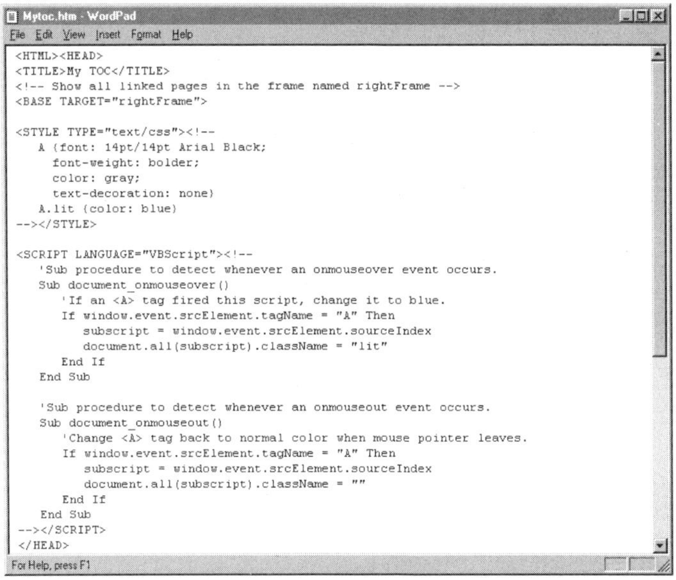

Figure 7-25. *The top portion of the document named mytoc.htm, which appears in the left frame.*

Also within the head of the document, I defined a default style for *<A>* tags and a style class named *lit*. The *lit* style class changes the color of the hyperlink text to blue.

```
<STYLE TYPE="text/css"><!--
   A {font: 14pt/14pt Arial Black;
      font-weight: bolder;
      color: gray;
      text-decoration: none}
   A.lit {color: blue}
--></STYLE>
```

> **Tip**   Arial Black is one of those freebie TrueType fonts that you can download from Microsoft's site at www.microsoft.com/truetype/fontpack/.

Next, I used my *document_onmouseover()* sub procedure to change the color of the current hyperlink (the one that that mouse pointer is resting on) to blue:

```
<SCRIPT LANGUAGE="VBScript"><!--
   'Sub procedure to detect whenever an onmouseover event occurs.
   Sub document_onmouseover()
      'If an <A> tag fired this script, then change it to blue.
      If window.event.srcElement.tagName = "A" Then
         subscript = window.event.srcElement.sourceIndex
         document.all(subscript).className = "lit"
      End If
   End Sub
```

The *document_onmouseout()* sub procedure in this example removes the *lit* style class when the mouse pointer leaves the hyperlink:

```
   'Sub procedure to detect whenever an onmouseout event occurs.
   Sub document_onmouseout()
      'Change <A> tag back to normal color when mouse pointer leaves.
      If window.event.srcElement.tagName = "A" Then
         subscript = window.event.srcElement.sourceIndex
         document.all(subscript).className = ""
      End If
   End Sub
--></SCRIPT>
```

Down in the body of the document (see Figure 7-26), the various hyperlinks are expressed with the basic *HREF* and *TITLE* attributes to define the destination of the hyperlink and its tooltip. There's no need to do anything fancier than that because the *<BASE>* and *<STYLE>* tags and the two sub procedures take care of sending the referenced page to the correct frame and take care of the visual appearance and behavior of each hyperlink.

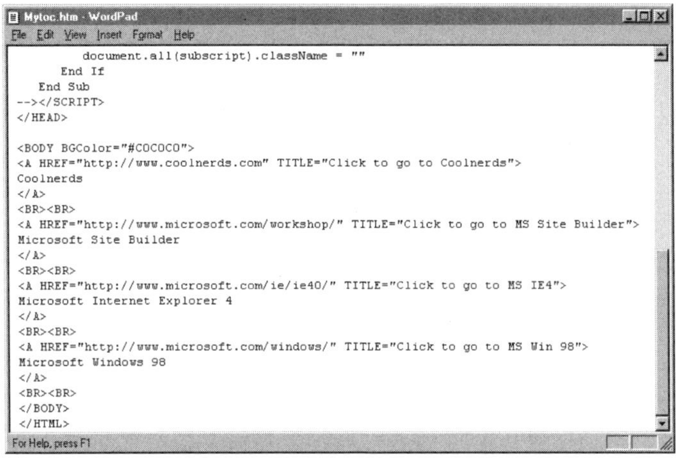

```
        document.all(subscript).className = ""
      End If
   End Sub
--></SCRIPT>
</HEAD>

<BODY BGColor="#COCOCO">
<A HREF="http://www.coolnerds.com" TITLE="Click to go to Coolnerds">
Coolnerds
</A>
<BR><BR>
<A HREF="http://www.microsoft.com/workshop/" TITLE="Click to go to MS Site Builder">
Microsoft Site Builder
</A>
<BR><BR>
<A HREF="http://www.microsoft.com/ie/ie40/" TITLE="Click to go to MS IE4">
Microsoft Internet Explorer 4
</A>
<BR><BR>
<A HREF="http://www.microsoft.com/windows/" TITLE="Click to go to MS Win 98">
Microsoft Windows 98
</A>
<BR><BR>
</BODY>
</HTML>
```

Figure 7-26. *The remaining portion of the mytoc.htm file.*

Changing the Style of Individual Objects

Well, I think we've discussed the custom *document_onmouseover()* and *document_onmouseout()* procedures in enough depth. In this section, I'd like to turn our attention away from that and talk about different ways of styling individual tags on mouse contact. One of my main motivations for doing so centers around some inconsistencies (perhaps bugs) in the beta version of Internet Explorer 4. Whether these items will still be an issue when the final product is released remains to be seen. Let's take it from the top.

Theoretically, if you want to change the appearance of a single object in response to *onmouseover* and *onmouseout* events, you can use this syntax:

```
<tag onmouseover="this.style.attribute = 'newValue'"
onmouseout="this.style.attribute = ''">
```

tag is any HTML tag that supports *onmouseover* and *onmouseout*. For example, here's an *<H1>* tag that turns the color of the enclosed text to blue on mouse contact:

```
<H1 onmouseover="this.style.color = 'blue'"
onmouseout="this.style.color = ''">
I Am a Level-1 Heading
</H1>
```

The keyword *this*, which is part of the JavaScript language, is a shortcut way of referring to the current object. Now here's the rub: That tag works fine as long as there is no *<SCRIPT LANGUAGE="VBScript">* tag in the head or body of the page! The failure of this tag might be due to the fact that VBScript uses the keyword *me* rather than the keyword *this* to refer to the current object. However, if this is the case, the following tag should work fine in a page that contains the *<SCRIPT LANGUAGE="VBScript">* tag:

```
<H1 onmouseover="me.style.color = 'blue'"
onmouseout="me.style.color = ''">
I Am a Level-1 Heading
</H1>
```

But oddly enough, that doesn't work either. (Again, I'm working with the beta copy of Internet Explorer 4 as I write this chapter. These problems might have been resolved by the time you read this.)

A solution that works, regardless of whether your page contains a *<SCRIPT LANGUAGE="VBScript">* tag, is to give the object its own unique name, using *ID*. You then use that name in place of *this* or *me*. For example, the following tag and text work fine regardless of whether the current page contains a *<SCRIPT LANGUAGE="VBScript">* tag.

```
<H1 ID="FirstH1" onmouseover="FirstH1.style.color = 'blue'"
onmouseout="FirstH1.style.color = ''">
I Am a Level-1 Heading
</H1>
```

This approach has one small drawback. Mainly, it requires assigning unique names to the objects in your web page. This can become tedious. And, as we'll discuss in the next section, you might encounter situations in which you want to assign the same name to several objects within a page.

I have a couple of strategies you can use to avoid the *this* and *me* keywords and the *ID* attribute if you like. One is a custom sub procedure named *reColor* that just changes the color of the current object to whatever color you specify. For example, this changes the color of the current object to green:

```
onmouseover="reColor('green')"
```

Another custom sub procedure, which I've named *reClass*, lets you apply a style class to the current object. For example, if the current page includes a style class named *greenOnYellow*, this chunk of code applies that style class to the current object:

```
onmouseover="reClass('greenOnYellow')"
```

The two custom sub procedures, *reClass* and *reColor*, are shown between the *<SCRIPT>…</SCRIPT>* tags in Figure 7-27. Note that if you want to use these scripts in a page, you should put them into the heading of that page between the *<HEAD>…</HEAD>* tags.

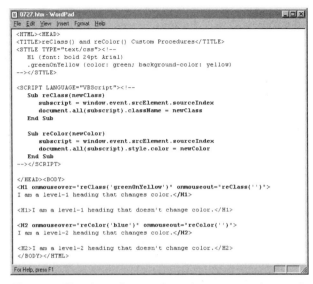

Figure 7-27. *The* reClass *and* reColor *custom sub procedures.*

The scripts both use the *subscript = window.event.srcElement.sourceIndex* syntax to get the position of the object that called the script. The *reClass* sub procedure looks like this:

```
Sub reClass(newClass)
   subscript = window.event.srcElement.sourceIndex
   document.all(subscript).className = newClass
End Sub
```

The statement *document.all(subscript).className = newClass* assigns whatever class name was passed by the calling code to the current object. Thus, this call applies the *greenOnYellow* style class to the calling object:

```
onmouseover="reClass('greenOnYellow')"
```

This call removes the style class, returning the object to its previous appearance:

```
onmouseout="reClass('')"
```

The *reColor* custom sub procedure looks like this:

```
Sub reColor(newColor)
   subscript = window.event.srcElement.sourceIndex
   document.all(subscript).style.color = newColor
End Sub
```

The statement *document.all(subscript).style.color = newColor* assigns whatever value was passed to the procedure as the new color of the calling object. For example, this call turns the current object to blue:

```
onmouseover="reColor('blue')"
```

This call turns the object back to its previous color:

```
onmouseout="reColor('')"
```

If you look down into the body of the document, you can see the *reClass* sub procedure being called up to recolor one H1 heading on mouse contact. The *greenOnYellow* style class is defined between the *<STYLE>...</STYLE>* tags near the top of the page. That same tag also calls *reClass* to restore the previous color when the mouse pointer leaves the heading, as shown here:

```
<H1 onmouseover="reClass('greenOnYellow')" onmouseout="reClass('')">
I am a level-1 heading that changes color.</H1>
```

An H2 heading in the body of the same page calls on the *reColor* custom sub procedure to change the heading to blue on mouse contact and to return the heading to its previous color when the mouse leaves the object, as shown here:

```
<H2 onmouseover="reColor('blue')" onmouseout="reColor('')">
I am a level-2 heading that changes color.</H2>
```

STYLING SEVERAL OBJECTS AT ONCE

You might come across a situation in which you want to light up or, in some other way, change the appearance of several objects on a page, all at the same time. For example, maybe your page is a tutorial of some sort, and you want to give the reader a button that lights up all the hyperlinks in a page so that they are easier to spot at a glance.

I have two custom sub procedures that can make this job easy for you. One lights up all the objects defined with the same type of tag, such as all the *<P>* tags or all the *<H1>* tags or all the *<A>* tags. I've named this sub procedure *reClassTags*. The second procedure changes the appearance of all objects with a certain name, such as all the objects with *ID="liteup"* in their opening tags. This procedure doesn't care what kind of tag is used to format the text. The name of this second sub procedure is *reClassIDs*. I'll discuss both sub procedures in the next two sections.

The *reClassTags* Sub Procedure

The custom *reClassTags* sub procedure is shown below:

```
<SCRIPT LANGUAGE="VBScript"><!--
    'Changes all tags of the same type to some style class.
    Sub reClassTags(tagType, newClass)
        Dim changeIt
        Set changeIt = document.all.tags(tagType)
        For counter = 0 to changeIt.length - 1
            changeIt(counter).className = newClass
        Next
    End Sub
--></SCRIPT>
```

Let me explain how it manages to do its thing. The *reClassTags* sub procedure has two parameters, one named *tagType* and the other named *newClass*:

```
Sub reClassTags(tagType, newClass)
```

When calling the procedure, you pass it the type of tag that you want to restyle and you pass the style class name you want to apply to the tags. For example, if your document includes a style class named *blueBold*, the following call applies the *blueBold* class to all text between <P>...</P> tags in the current document:

```
onclick="reClassTags 'P', 'blueBold'"
```

ABOUT *DIM* AND *SET*

When you want to assign a simple value to a variable, you can use a simple expression such as *x = 10* or *myName = "Alan"*. However, when you want to assign an object or a collection to a variable, it is a good idea to first use a *Dim* statement to declare the variable. Next, you must use the *Set* statement to assign the object or collection to the variable.

The main reason for this is that Internet Explorer doesn't actually "put" the object or collection into the variable. Instead, it uses the variable name as a *pointer*—a shortcut name, if you will—that refers to the object or collection. The *Set* keyword gives Internet Explorer the clue it needs to treat the name as a pointer to an object or a collection rather than as a simple variable.

Within the procedure, a *Dim* statement declares a variable named *changeIt*. Then a *Set* statement assigns a collection name that contains all of the tags of the type specified in the *tagType* parameter to the *changeIt* variable:

```
Dim changeIt
Set changeIt = document.all.tags(tagType)
```

All collections support a *length* property, which returns a number indicating how many items are in the collection. All collections also start with item zero. The *reClassTags* sub procedure uses a *For...Next* loop that steps through each item in the collection and applies a new style class to each object within that collection.

```
For counter = 0 to changeIt.length - 1
    changeIt(counter).className = newClass
Next
```

Figure 7-28 shows an example of the *reClassTags* sub procedure within the context of a complete HTML document. Notice that, near the top of the document, I defined a style class named *blueBold*. The body of the document contains some text in *<P>...</P>* tags. A button near the bottom of the document executes the following command when clicked:

```
onclick="reClassTags 'P', 'blueBold'"
```

Figure 7-28. *An HTML document that uses* reClassTags *to apply the* blueBold *class to all paragraphs (<P> tags).*

That command applies the *blueBold* style class to all the text between *<P>* and *</P>* tags in the document.

A second button executes this command when clicked:

```
onclick="reClassTags 'P', ''"
```

This command removes the style class from all the *<P>* tags, thereby changing all paragraphs to their previous appearance.

Figure 7-29 shows how the sample page looks when first opened. Figure 7-30 on the next page shows how the page looks after the button is clicked. I realize that you can't see the blue color applied to the two paragraphs. However, you can probably see how those two paragraphs are bolder than the originals shown in Figure 7-29.

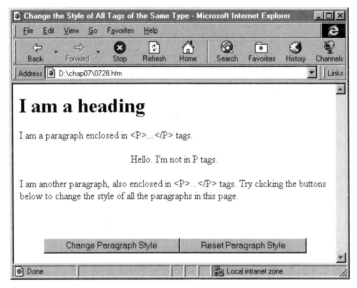

Figure 7-29. *The page whose source is shown in Figure 7-28, before the Change Paragraph Style button is clicked.*

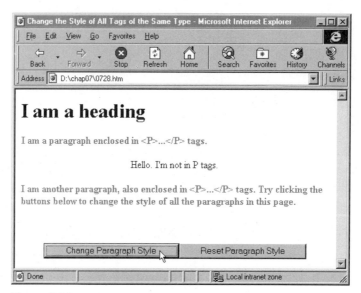

Figure 7-30. *The page after the Change Paragraph Style button is clicked.*

So now you might wonder, "How can I use this same procedure to light up all the hyperlinks in my web page?" Well, you really don't need to change the sub procedure per se. Rather, you need to define a style class that will make the hyperlinks look the way you want when lit up. Let's say you name that style class *litLink*, as shown below:

```
<STYLE TYPE="text/css"><!--
    .litLink {color: blue; background-color: yellow}
--></STYLE>
```

You then use this statement to apply the *litLink* style to all the *<A>* tags in the page:

```
onevent="reClassTags 'A', 'litLink'"
```

To change all the hyperlinks back to their previous appearance, use this statement:

```
onevent="reClassTags 'A', ''"
```

Figure 7-31 shows these changes made in a sample web page.

```
 0731.htm - WordPad                                              _ □ ×
File  Edit  View  Insert  Format  Help
<HTML><HEAD><TITLE>Change the Style of All Tags of the Same Type</TITLE>
<STYLE TYPE="text/css"><!--
    .litLink {color: blue; background-color: yellow}
--></STYLE>
<SCRIPT LANGUAGE="VBScript"><!--
    'Changes all tags of the same type to some style class.
    Sub reClassTags(tagType, newClass)
        Dim changeIt
        Set changeIt = document.all.tags(tagType)
        For counter = 0 to changeIt.length - 1
            changeIt(counter).className = newClass
        Next
    End Sub
--></SCRIPT>

</HEAD><BODY>
<H1>I am a heading</H1>
<P>I am a paragraph enclosed in &lt;P&gt;...&lt;/P&gt; tags. And
<A HREF="http://www.coolnerds.com"></P>I am a hyperlink</A> enclosed in &lt;A&gt;
tags.<BR><A HREF="http://www.microsoft.com">I am another hyperlink</A>
<P>I am another paragraph, also enclosed in &lt;P&gt;...&lt;/P&gt; tags.
Try clicking the buttons below to change the style of all the links
in this page.</P>
<BR><BR><CENTER>
<!-- These buttons test the custom reClassTags sub procedure. -->
<BUTTON onclick="reClassTags 'A', 'litLink'">
Change Hyperlink Style
</BUTTON>
<BUTTON onclick="reClassTags 'A', ''">
Reset Hyperlink Style
</BUTTON>
</CENTER></BODY></HTML>
For Help, press F1
```

Figure 7-31. *An HTML document that uses* reClassTags *to change the style of all hyperlinks (<A> tags).*

The *reClassIDs* Sub Procedure

As mentioned, the *reClassIDs* sub procedure lets you apply a new style class to all the tags in a page with some common *ID*. For example, you can name a whole bunch of objects *lightMe* and then use *reClassIDs* to apply some style to all those objects at the same time. Here's what the *reClassIDs* sub procedure looks like:

```
<SCRIPT LANGUAGE="VBScript"><!--
    Sub reClassIDs(IDName, newClass)
        Dim IDCollection
        Set IDCollection = document.all.item(IDName)
        For counter = 0 to IDCollection.length - 1
            IDCollection(counter).className = newClass
        Next
    End Sub
--></SCRIPT>
```

The script is similar to the *reClassTags* sub procedure. However, the *Set* statement uses the value passed in the *IDName* parameter to obtain a pointer to a collection of all objects that have that *ID*. So for instance, if you call *reClassTags* with the syntax

```
onevent="reClassIDs 'lightMe', 'blueOnYellow'"
```

the procedure obtains a pointer to a collection of all the objects that have *ID="lightMe"* in their opening HTML tags (regardless of whether that tag is *<P>*, *<H1>*, *<LI>*, *<IMG>*, or whatever). The second argument, the *blueOnYellow* style class in this example, is then applied to each item in that collection via a *For...Next* loop.

Figure 7-32 shows the *reClassIDs* sub procedure within the context of a complete HTML document. Note that a style class named *blueOnYellow* is defined near the top of that document. The first button defined close to the bottom of the document executes the following statement, which applies the *blueOnYellow* style class to every object named *lightMe* in the document.

```
onclick="reClassIDs 'lightMe', 'blueOnYellow'"
```

```
0732.htm - WordPad
File  Edit  View  Insert  Format  Help
<HTML><HEAD><TITLE>Change All Tags with the Same ID to Some New Style Class</TITLE>
<STYLE TYPE="text/css"><!--
   .blueOnYellow {color: blue; background-color: yellow}
--></STYLE>

<SCRIPT LANGUAGE="VBScript"><!--
   Sub reClassIDs(IDname, newClass)
      Dim IDCollection
      Set IDCollection = document.all.item(IDname)
      For counter = 0 to IDCollection.length - 1
         IDCollection(counter).className = newClass
      Next
   End Sub
--></SCRIPT>

</HEAD>
<BODY>
<P ID="lightMe">I am a paragraph named lightMe. I will change when you click the button.</P>
<P>I am a paragraph, too. But I'm not named lightMe, so I won't change.</P>
<P>I contain some <B ID="lightMe">boldfaced text</B> named lightMe that will change, too.</P>
<!-- Test the reStyleIDs sub procedure -->
<CENTER>

<BUTTON onclick="reClassIDs 'lightMe', 'blueOnYellow'">
Change Style
</BUTTON>
  

<BUTTON onclick="reClassIDs 'lightMe', ''">
Reset Original Style
</BUTTON>
</CENTER>
</BODY></HTML>
For Help, press F1
```

Figure 7-32. *The* reClassIDs *sub procedure used in a sample HTML document.*

Figure 7-33 shows how the sample web page looks when first opened in Internet Explorer. Figure 7-34 shows how the page looks after the first button is clicked, which applies the *blueOnYellow* style class to the two objects named *lightMe* in that page.

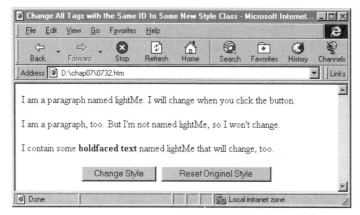

Figure 7-33. *The page whose source is shown in Figure 7-32, before the Change Style button is clicked.*

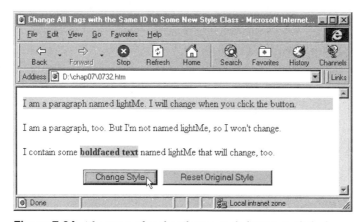

Figure 7-34. *The page after the Change Style button is clicked.*

SUMMARY

We've discussed quite a few ways that you can go about changing the appearance of objects in your web page. Many modern multimedia programs use—and in the near future many web pages will also use—these techniques to present a more interactive and compelling interface. Let's review some of the really important "elemental" facts and techniques introduced in this chapter:

- Most HTML attributes are included as properties of the corresponding HTML element object.

- To change a property of an object, use the syntax *objectName.property = newValue*, where *objectName* is the name of the specific object, *property* is some property of that object, and *newValue* is some new setting for that property.

- CSS properties are used to change styles in scripting code, and CSS attributes are used to define styles.

- To change a CSS property, use the syntax *objectName.style.CSSProperty = newValue*.

- To apply some new style class to an object, use the syntax *objectName.className = newClass*.

- When the mouse pointer touches an object, that object's *onmouseover* event occurs.

- When the mouse pointer leaves an object, that object's *onmouseout* event occurs.

- You can use the *onmouseover* and *onmouseout* events to create more interactive pages that respond when the reader simply points to an object.

- To set up a routine that fires every time a particular event occurs in a page, use the syntax *Sub document_event()*, where *event()* is some valid event for the document object. For example, a sub procedure named *document_onmouseover()* fires every time an *onmouseover* event occurs within the current document.

- To assign an object or a collection to a variable, use the VBScript *Set* statement.

- The length of any collection is provided by the *length* property.

- To set up a loop that steps through each item in a collection, use the syntax *For variable = 0 to collection.length - 1*.

Chapter 8

Positioning, Stacking Order, and Visibility

Microsoft Internet Explorer 4 offers many new techniques for controlling the exact size and position of objects in a web page. These techniques are based on CSS attributes, which are easy to apply to a wide range of HTML tags and objects. In this chapter, we'll look at these CSS attributes and explore how to:

■ Place objects precisely in a web page

■ Size objects in a page

■ Stack objects

■ Hide and display objects

■ Use relative positioning

■ Write VBScript code to change an object's visibility properties

PLAIN OLD HTML OBJECT POSITIONING

Let's start off by taking a look at how HTML normally positions things. In regular HTML, text and tags come into the web browser window as a stream (actually called a *text stream*) and fill the window from the top-left corner, breaking lines between words near the right margin of the page if necessary. Some tags, such as *<P>*, *
*, *<H1>*, and *<DIV>*, cause text to start on a new line. But in general, the flow is top to bottom, left to right.

Take a look at the HTML document in Figure 8-1. It contains some HTML tags and text—nothing too spectacular. Figure 8-2 shows how the text flows top to bottom, left to right, when the page is viewed in Internet Explorer.

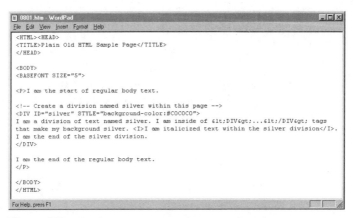

Figure 8-1. *The document source for a sample web page.*

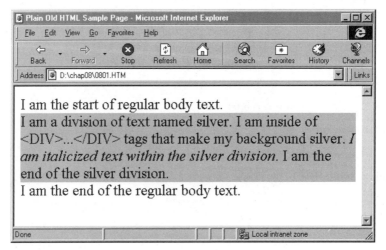

Figure 8-2. *The page whose source is shown in Figure 8-1, viewed in Internet Explorer.*

NOTE The casual name of the color defined by the RGB triplet *#C0C0C0* is silver. That's why I refer to the color as silver in Figure 8-2 and through-out this chapter. In truth, I suppose the color is more like a light gray, especially as printed in this book!

Positioning gives you more control over where text and other objects appear on your page. The positioning options are actually CSS attributes.

CSS ATTRIBUTES FOR POSITIONING AND SIZING

Several CSS attributes are specifically for positioning and sizing objects on a page. They're summarized in Table 8-1. You'll see examples of most of these CSS attributes as we progress through the chapter. For more details on any CSS attribute, see the Internet Client SDK, described in Appendix A.

Table 8-1

CSS ATTRIBUTES FOR POSITIONING AND SIZING OBJECTS

CSS Attribute	*What It Defines*
position: absolute | relative | static	How the object is positioned and whether it can be moved.
top: *size* | *percentage* | auto	The distance from the top of the parent element to the top of the object.
left: *size* | *percentage* | auto	The distance from the left edge of the parent element to the left edge of the object.
width: *size* | *percentage* | auto	The width of the object.
height: *size* | *percentage* | auto	The height of the object.
clip: *shape* | auto	What portion of an object is visible.
overflow: scroll | hidden | visible | auto	How to treat an object that doesn't fit within the specified size.
z-index: *number* | auto	Where the object appears in the stack of objects.
visibility: visible | hidden | inherit	Whether the object is visible. An invisible object still occupies space in the page.
display: none	Visibility and space usage. An object with its display set to *none* is invisible and doesn't take up any space in the page.
float: left | right | none	Whether neighboring text wraps around the object and on which side of the text the object appears.

The *top* and *left* CSS attributes both refer to the *parent element*. If the object is not contained within some other object, that parent element is the web page itself. The *size* measurement in each example can be expressed using any of the units of measurement shown in Table 8-2. If no unit of measurement is specified, pixels (px) are used by default.

Table 8-2

UNITS OF MEASUREMENT FOR CSS *SIZE* ATTRIBUTES

Units	Abbreviation	Example
Pixels (the default)	px (or nothing)	100px or just 100
Points	pt	10pt
Proportional	em	-0.5em
Inches	in	2in
Centimeters	cm	1.5cm
Percentage	%	20%

A pixel, as you probably know, is one "dot" on the screen. For example, a screen set to a resolution of 800 x 600 is actually 800 dots (pixels) wide and 600 dots (pixels) tall. Points are a unit of measurement generally used in typography, where 1 point equals about $1/72$ inch. The proportional measurement, em, is often used in typography as well, where 1 em refers to the size of an uppercase letter *M*. The exact size, of course, depends on the size of the font in use at the moment. For example, in a large font of, say, 72 points (1 inch), 1 em is about 1 inch. In a small font of, say, 10 points, 1 em is about 10 points.

Although inches and centimeters are offered as units, their meaning is ambiguous when something is displayed on a computer screen. What you refer to as an inch or a centimeter will actually vary based on the size and resolution of the monitor. So, as a general rule, we don't use inches and centimeters as units of measurement on computer screens.

The percentage unit allows you to size and position objects based on a percentage of the parent object. I think some examples will best illustrate these concepts, so I'll discuss this topic in more detail in the sections titled "Percentage Measurements" and "Relative Positioning" later in this chapter.

ABSOLUTE POSITIONING

To give an object an absolute position on the page, you need to add (at least) the following CSS attributes to the object's HTML tag, where *value* is some number expressed in one of the discussed units of measurement:

```
STYLE="position:absolute; top:value; left:value"
```

For example, Figure 8-3 shows the first sample document from this chapter, with some settings added to the *STYLE* attribute inside the *<DIV>* tag:

```
STYLE="position:absolute; top:100; left:200;
```

Figure 8-4 shows how that document looks when opened in Internet Explorer. Hmmmm. Looks like there are a few issues we need to discuss.

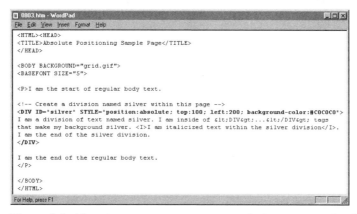

Figure 8-3. *The <DIV> tag now contains a style that positions the object.*

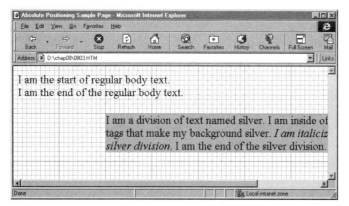

Figure 8-4. *The page whose source is shown in Figure 8-3, viewed in Internet Explorer.*

ABOUT THE GRAPH-PAPER BACKGROUND

You'll probably notice that many of the sample pages in this chapter show a peculiar background that looks something like graph paper. The dark lines in the graph paper are 100 pixels apart. The lighter lines are 10 pixels apart. My main purpose for using the graph-paper background image is to give you the clearest possible idea of where an absolute position, such as *top:100; left:200*, appears on the screen.

In real life, you probably want to eliminate that graph-paper background because it's not all that aesthetically pleasing (to put it mildly). But it might come in handy when you start developing your own pages that contain positioned objects. Near the end of Chapter 9, I'll discuss how you can use the graph-paper background image, and some other tools, in your own page-building efforts.

First of all, everything between the *<DIV>...</DIV>* tags (the stuff with the silver background) is now off to the side of the page and lower on the page. In fact, if you look closely at the underlying grid lines, you'll see that, indeed, the upper-left corner of that object is exactly 100 pixels from the top of the document window and 200 pixels from the left margin of the document window. This corresponds to the *top:100; left:200* portion of our *STYLE* attribute. So far, so good.

If you compare Figure 8-4 to Figure 8-2 on page 220, you'll notice that the *silver* object is missing some text. Actually, that text is scrolled off into never-never land off the right edge of the window. We can fix that problem by sizing the object, as I'll discuss later in the section titled "Sizing an Object."

Also notice that the last sentence in the page, *I am the end of the regular body text,* is now above the *silver* object rather than below it. In fact, the two sentences *I am the start of regular body text* and *I am the end of the regular body text* are now laid out as if the *silver* object doesn't even exist! Let me explain why. Any object that is positioned absolutely on the page is essentially non-existent to everything outside that object. Absolutely positioned objects never "wrap" around neighboring objects. And neighboring objects never "wrap" around absolutely positioned objects. The two just ignore each other and, in fact, can overlap.

This last fact is probably the hardest for most people to get accustomed to. Looking at the document source in Figure 8-3 on the previous page, you might think that the sentence *I am the end of the regular body text* would appear below the *silver* object. But you have to remember that the text outside the *silver* object is "unaware" that the positioned object exists. And thus, everything outside of a positioned object flows just as it would if the positioned object didn't exist at all.

PERCENTAGE MEASUREMENTS

When used to define the *top* and *left* positioning attributes, the percentage unit of measurement is an interesting one because it varies with the size of the document window. For example, suppose we change the *<DIV>* tag used in the previous example so that it places the *silver* object at 50 percent of the distance from the top of the document window to the bottom and 25 percent of the distance from the left edge of the document window to the right:

```
STYLE="position:absolute; top:50%; left:25%; ..."
```

Exactly how the page looks at any given moment depends on the size of the document window. For example, Figure 8-5 shows how our sample page looks with the *top:50%; left:25%* settings and with Internet Explorer open full-screen.

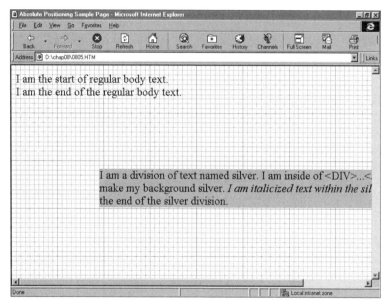

Figure 8-5. *A full-screen view of the sample page with the* silver *object positioned at* top:50%; left:25%.

Just eyeballing Figure 8-5 lets you see that the upper edge of the *silver* object starts at about half (50 percent) of the document window height. Likewise, the left edge of the *silver* object starts at about 25 percent of the document window width.

Now, suppose I shrink the entire Internet Explorer window, as in Figure 8-6. What happens to the *silver* object? Well, it moves closer to the upper-left corner of the page. Why? Because the document window is smaller now—50 percent of the document window height is a smaller distance, as is 25 percent of the document window width. The document window is so small, in fact, that the *silver* object actually covers some of the regular text in the document.

Keep in mind that the only reason the *silver* object shifted its position in Figure 8-6 is because we defined the *top* and *left* attributes as percents: *top:50%; left:25%*. If we use numbers, such as *top:200; left:400*, the object won't budge, no matter how you size the Internet Explorer window. If the Internet Explorer window is tiny enough, say 100 pixels tall and 100 pixels wide, the object position at *top:200; left:400* won't be visible in the window!

> TIP   If you feel like experimenting, use the standard *<IMG SRC=...>* tag to add a graphic image to a web page. Then add a *STYLE="position:absolute; left:50%; top:50%"* attribute to that *<IMG>* tag. Then view the page in Internet Explorer, and try resizing the Internet Explorer window. As you do this, the image will move about the web page. The upper-left corner of the image will attempt to stay centered within the current document window dimensions.

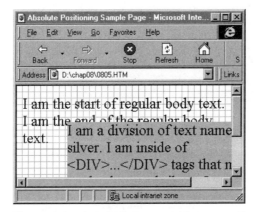

Figure 8-6. *The* silver *object is still positioned at* top:50%; left:25%, *but the window is now smaller.*

SIZING AN OBJECT

We had a little problem in our previous example when some text in the *silver* object was out of view off the right edge of the document window. You can easily rectify that problem by tailoring the size of the object to fit its content. The *height* and *width* CSS attributes let you define the size of an object in pixels (px), points (pt), percentage of the document window size (%), inches (in), or centimeters (cm).

If you specify only the width, the object is automatically sized, vertically, to whatever height is required to display the full contents of the object. For example, suppose we change the *<DIV>* tag in our sample page to this:

```
<DIV ID="silver" STYLE="position:absolute; top:100; left:200; width:400;
background-color:#C0C0C0">
```

The new *width:400* attribute forces the *silver* object to be exactly 400 pixels wide, as in Figure 8-7. The height of the object is just large enough to show all the text between the *<DIV>...</DIV>* tags.

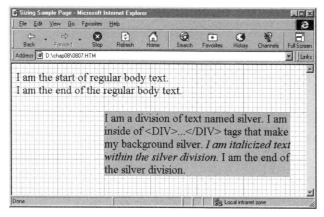

Figure 8-7. *The* silver *object with a specified width of 400 pixels.*

If we specify both a height and a width for the *silver* object, as shown below, the object will be sized accordingly:

```
<DIV ID="silver" STYLE="position:absolute; top:100; left:200;
width:400; height:200; background-color:#C0C0C0">
```

In Figure 8-8 on the next page, you can see that the *silver* object is indeed 400 pixels wide and 200 pixels tall.

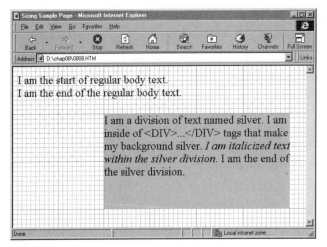

Figure 8-8. *The* silver *object is 400 pixels wide and 200 pixels tall.*

TIP Here's another little experiment you can try. Add the attribute *STYLE="position:absolute; height:50%; width:50%"* to an *<IMG...>* tag in a web page. When you view the page in Internet Explorer, the image will take up half the height and half the width of the page. As you change the size of the Internet Explorer window, the image will change size as well, always trying to be half the available width and half the available height.

Perhaps this brings up the question, "What happens if you make the size of the object too small to show all the contents?" The answer is, "It depends on how you set the overflow option."

HANDLING OVERFLOW

The *overflow* CSS attribute lets you specify how to handle content within an object if the content is too large for the object. Your options are:

- *overflow:hidden*—extra content is clipped off and inaccessible.
- *overflow:scroll*—extra content is clipped off but can be accessed by adjacent scroll bars.
- *overflow:visible*—overflow is not allowed. The object size is automatically increased to accommodate all content.
- *overflow:auto*—browser determines how to display content. For example, if the object is too small to display content, scroll bars are added.

Figure 8-9 shows the *silver* object set to a width of 170 pixels and a height of 170 pixels, which is way too small to show all of the object's content. But as the figure demonstrates, you have four ways to deal with the problem.

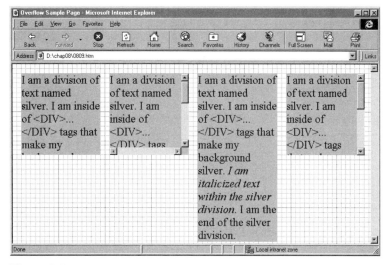

Figure 8-9. *The* overflow *attribute set to* hidden, scroll, visible, *and* auto.

The *silver* object on the left has its *overflow* CSS attribute set to *hidden*, as shown below:

```
<DIV ID="silver" STYLE="position:absolute; top:20; left:20;
width:170; height:170; overflow:hidden; background-color:#C0C0C0">
```

As you can see in the figure, excess content in the first *silver* object is simply clipped off. It's not accessible to the reader in any way. The second version of the *silver* object has its *overflow* attribute set to *scroll*, like this:

```
<DIV ID="silver2" STYLE="position:absolute; top:20; left:210;
width:170; height:170; overflow:scroll; background-color:#C0C0C0">
```

Its content is also clipped off. But scroll bars appear automatically so the reader can scroll down to view the content that's out of view. The third version of the *silver* object has its *overflow* attribute set to *visible*, like this:

```
<DIV ID="silver3" STYLE="position:absolute; top:20; left:400;
width:170; height:170; overflow:visible; background-color:#C0C0C0">
```

The result is the same as if no height is defined or no *overflow* attribute is defined—the object is just automatically resized to whatever height will show all of its content.

The last version of the *silver* object, on the right, has its overflow property set to *auto*, as shown below. Its content is clipped off, but a scroll bar appears automatically at the right edge of the object so the reader can scroll down to view the content that's out of view.

```
<DIV ID="silver4" STYLE="position:absolute; top:20; left:590;
width:170; height:170; overflow:auto; background-color:#C0C0C0">
```

PADDING AND BORDERS

The CSS *padding* and *border* attributes can be applied to numerous objects—
not just to positioned objects. But they can certainly be applied to positioned
objects to improve their appearance. For instance, if you look at the examples of
the *silver* object in previous sections, you'll see that the text inside the object
actually touches the edges of the objects—especially the left and top edges. You
can add a little space between the edge of the object and its contents using the
padding attribute. For example, take a look at the *<DIV>* tag used here to format
a new version of our *silver* object:

```
<DIV ID="silver" STYLE="position:absolute; top:100; left:200; width:400;
padding:15; background-color:#C0C0C0">
```

Notice that I didn't define a height for the object, so it will be automatically
sized to whatever height is required to display the content. A 15-pixel space will
also be placed all the way around the inside of the object, as shown in Figure 8-10.

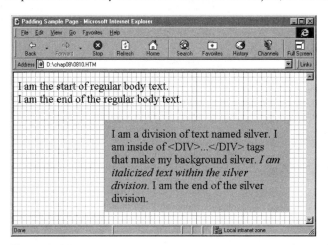

Figure 8-10. *The* silver *object with a 15-pixel space all the way around
the inside.*

If you don't want the space on all four sides to be the same size, you can
use the *padding-bottom*, *padding-left*, *padding-top*, and *padding-right* attributes
to size each space independently. For example, the tag below sets the left space
to 20 pixels, the top space to 15 pixels, the right space to 5 pixels, and the bottom
space to 5 pixels:

```
<DIV ID="silver" STYLE="position:absolute; top:100; left:200; width:400;
padding-left:20; padding-top:15; padding-right:5; padding-bottom:5;
background-color:#C0C0C0">
```

If you want to give an object a border, you can use this syntax:

```
border:size style color
```

size is the width of the border in pixels, points, or whatever; *style* is a valid border style, such as *solid*, *dotted*, *dashed*, etc.; and *color* is a valid color name or color RGB triplet. For example, this slightly modified version of our sample *<DIV>* tag displays a thin, solid (2-pixel) border around the *silver* object, as shown in Figure 8-11. (I removed the grid background so you can see the border better.)

```
<DIV ID="silver" STYLE="position:absolute; top:100; left:200; width:400;
padding:15; border:2 solid black; background-color:#C0C0C0">
```

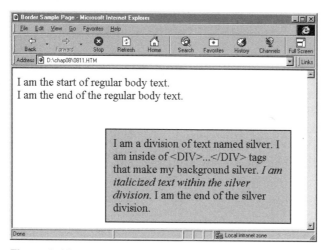

Figure 8-11. *A border is added to our* silver *object.*

As with *padding*, you can design each border side independently by using the many *border* attributes (which are all referenced in the Internet Client SDK).

STACKING OBJECTS

When objects are positioned absolutely on the page, they can overlap the text of the page (if any). Any object can also overlap or even completely obscure some other object. As you might have guessed, however, there is a style attribute that helps you determine what overlaps what. It's the *z-index* attribute.

Before I show you how overlapping and the *z-index* attribute work, let me show you a couple of graphic images that I plan to use in these examples. One, named saucer.jpg, is a flying saucer art piece with a gray background. The other, named saucer.gif, is exactly the same image but with a transparent background. Figure 8-12 on the next page shows the two images.

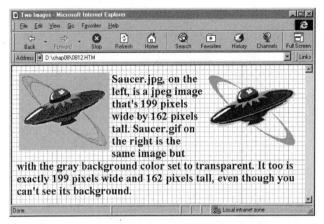

Figure 8-12. *The images named saucer.jpg and saucer.gif.*

Now that you've had a sneak peak at saucer.gif and saucer.jpg, let's talk about how objects positioned on a page might overlap. First, you need to understand that the HTML text and graphics you're familiar with are all part of just one layer. That layer is number 0.

You can control how objects overlap by putting them on different layers. Objects on the higher-numbered layers can cover or overlap objects on lower-numbered layers. One small exception to this is the transparent background GIF image. Any layer that's behind such an image is visible through the transparent portion of the image.

Let's look at an example of these concepts in action. Figure 8-13 shows an HTML document that contains some regular body text in *<P>...</P>* tags. That text will make up layer 0.

TRANSPARENT BACKGROUND GIFs

Several graphics packages on the market allow you to define a transparent color for GIF files. Two that come to mind are Microsoft Image Composer, which comes with the Microsoft FrontPage 98 package, and Microsoft Visual InterDev. For more information about Image Composer, point your web browser to www.microsoft.com/imagecomposer/.

Another product that can create GIF transparencies is JASC's Paint Shop Pro. That product also provides good tools for converting non-GIF and non-JPEG files to GIF or JPEG for use on the web. You can download a shareware evaluation copy of Paint Shop Pro, free of charge, from www.jasc.com.

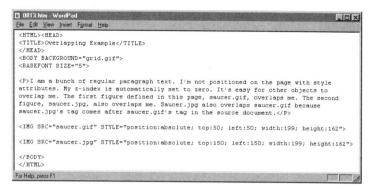

Figure 8-13. *The images in this document use absolute positioning.*

The document also contains the saucer.gif image, positioned absolutely on the page using the standard CSS attributes. Here is the exact tag:

```
<IMG SRC="saucer.gif" STYLE="position:absolute; top:50; left:50;
width:199; height:162">
```

The document also contains the saucer.jpg image, which is defined by this tag:

```
<IMG SRC="saucer.jpg" STYLE="position:absolute; top:150; left:150;
width:199; height:162">
```

So how does all of this look in Internet Explorer? A bit messy, as Figure 8-14 shows.

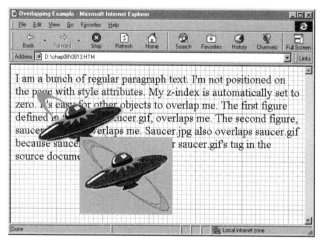

Figure 8-14. *The page whose source is shown in Figure 8-13, viewed in Internet Explorer.*

Even though it's messy, Figure 8-14 shows exactly how the objects stack up. The regular body text is on layer 0 and is beneath both positioned graphic images in the "stack." Saucer.gif is on top of the body text. The underlying text is visible through the transparent portions of saucer.gif. But you can plainly see that the nontransparent portions of saucer.gif cover the text.

The saucer.jpg image is at the top of the stack because its tag was the last one in the page to employ a *position:absolute* attribute. Since that image is on top of the stack, it partially covers both saucer.gif and the underlying body text.

The *z-index* attribute lets you change the default "rules" for how objects stack up. Basically, you can put any positioned object on any layer, thereby making it appear in front of or behind some other object. For example, suppose I use the *z-index* attribute to put the saucer.gif image on layer 2 and the saucer.jpg image on layer 1 using these tags:

```
<IMG SRC="saucer.gif" STYLE="position:absolute; top:50; left:50;
z-index:2; width:199; height:162">

<IMG SRC="saucer.jpg" STYLE="position:absolute; top:150; left:150;
zindex:1; width:199; height:162">
```

Viewing this rendition of the page shows that saucer.gif with its transparent background is at the top of the stack and is no longer obscured by saucer.jpg, as you can see in Figure 8-15.

You can even give an object a negative layer value. This places the layer behind the body text and graphics that naturally reside on layer 0. For example, using negative *z-index* values in our flying saucers example, as shown in the following code, puts saucer.jpg on the bottommost layer in this example, layer −2.

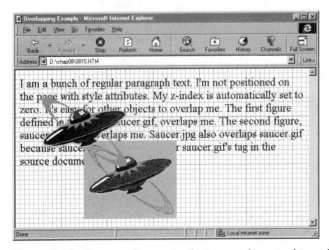

Figure 8-15. *Saucer.gif is now in the topmost layer and is no longer obscured by saucer.jpg.*

```
<IMG SRC="saucer.gif" STYLE="position:absolute; top:50; left:50;
z-index:-1; width:199; height:162">
```

```
<IMG SRC="saucer.jpg" STYLE="position:absolute; top:150; left:150;
z-index:-2; width:199; height:162">
```

Saucer.gif goes to layer −1, above saucer.jpg but still below the text in the document. When viewed in Internet Explorer, the text and objects (though still a bit messy) end up as shown in Figure 8-16.

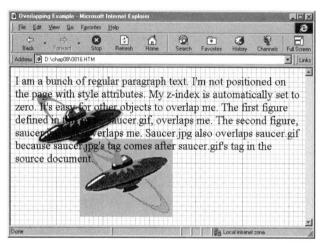

Figure 8-16. *Both saucers are now beneath layer 0.*

HIDING AND DISPLAYING OBJECTS

Two CSS attributes let you determine whether an object is visible on the screen. The *visibility* attribute allows an object to be visible or invisible. You can also specify that an object inherit its *visibility* attribute from its parent element. Your options are:

- *visibility:hidden*—The object is not visible on the screen.

- *visibility:visible*—The object is visible on the screen.

- *visibility:inherit*—The visibility setting is the same as the parent object's visibility setting.

An object that isn't visible still takes up space on the screen. It leaves a blank area where it would otherwise appear. The *display* attribute also lets you hide or display an object. However, an object that is not displayed takes up no space on the screen. The syntax for the *display* attribute is simply *display:none.*

To make sure an object is displayed, you omit the *display* attribute altogether. For example, Figure 8-17 shows a sample page with three instances of the same image. At the top, the image is displayed by a normal *<IMG SRC=...>* tag. The image, a fancy letter *A,* is clearly visible. And it takes up space as shown by the way the neighboring text wraps around it.

The second example has a *STYLE="visibility:hidden"* attribute setting in the *<IMG SRC=...>* tag. The image is invisible, but it still takes up space. The neighboring text still aligns next to the image even though the image isn't visible.

The third example has a *STYLE="display:none"* attribute setting in the *<IMG SRC=...>* tag. The image is invisible and doesn't take up any space. That's why the neighboring text aligns with the left edge of the page. Figure 8-18 shows the document source behind that sample page.

It might seem odd to put something invisible in your web page. After all, why put it there if the reader can't even see it? The reason is that you can control the visibility with code. Therefore, you can make objects appear and disappear in response to some event. We'll look at some practical examples of hiding and showing objects in just a moment.

Figure 8-17. *A regular image, a hidden image, and an image with the* display *attribute set to* none.

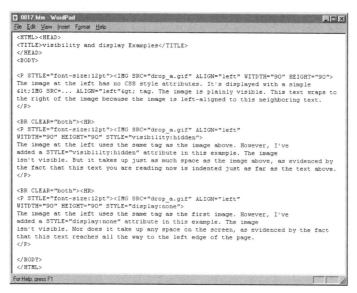

Figure 8-18. *The document source for the page shown in Figure 8-17.*

RELATIVE POSITIONING

We probably all have a few relatives that we'd like to reposition, either closer to or farther from where we live. But the relative positioning we'll discuss here has nothing to do with relocating kin. It has to do with positioning objects *relative to* other objects in the page. As you might recall, absolutely positioned objects are virtually ignorant of one another and make no attempt to wrap around one another. The exact opposite is true with relative positioning. Relatively positioned objects are very aware of neighboring objects.

You can use this to your advantage in several ways. For example, you can position an object relative to the left margin but make sure that it never covers text above or below it. Or you can make a tiny percentage adjustment to an object to improve its position in the page. Figure 8-19 on the next page shows an HTML document that uses relatively positioned *DIV* and *IMG* objects to create a floating sidebar.

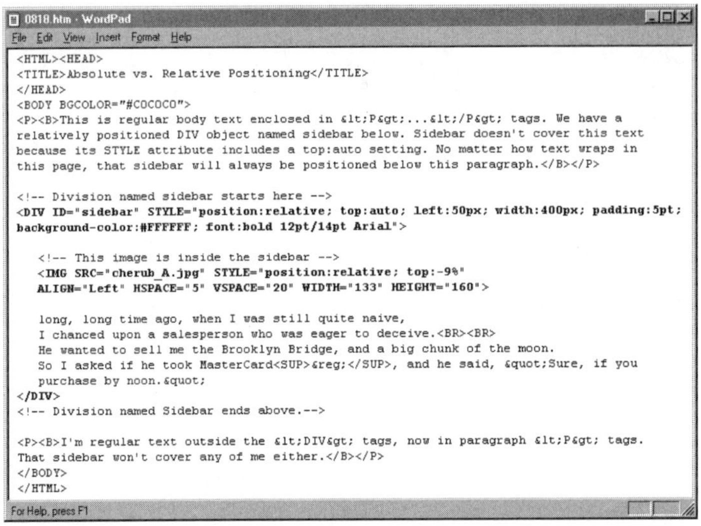

```
<HTML><HEAD>
<TITLE>Absolute vs. Relative Positioning</TITLE>
</HEAD>
<BODY BGCOLOR="#COCOCO">
<P><B>This is regular body text enclosed in &lt;P&gt;...&lt;/P&gt; tags. We have a
relatively positioned DIV object named sidebar below. Sidebar doesn't cover this text
because its STYLE attribute includes a top:auto setting. No matter how text wraps in
this page, that sidebar will always be positioned below this paragraph.</B></P>

<!-- Division named sidebar starts here -->
<DIV ID="sidebar" STYLE="position:relative; top:auto; left:50px; width:400px; padding:5pt;
background-color:#FFFFFF; font:bold 12pt/14pt Arial">

   <!-- This image is inside the sidebar -->
   <IMG SRC="cherub_A.jpg" STYLE="position:relative; top:-9%"
   ALIGN="Left" HSPACE="5" VSPACE="20" WIDTH="133" HEIGHT="160">

   long, long time ago, when I was still quite naive,
   I chanced upon a salesperson who was eager to deceive.<BR><BR>
   He wanted to sell me the Brooklyn Bridge, and a big chunk of the moon.
   So I asked if he took MasterCard<SUP>&reg;</SUP>, and he said, &quot;Sure, if you
   purchase by noon.&quot;
</DIV>
<!-- Division named Sidebar ends above.-->

<P><B>I'm regular text outside the &lt;DIV&gt; tags, now in paragraph &lt;P&gt; tags.
That sidebar won't cover any of me either.</B></P>
</BODY>
</HTML>
```

Figure 8-19. *An HTML document with relatively positioned* DIV *and* IMG *objects.*

If you look at the *STYLE* attribute for the *<DIV>* tag, you'll see that it includes the following:

```
position:relative; top:auto; left:50px; width:400px;
```

The *position:relative* setting ensures that all positioning takes place relative to where the *DIV* object would have fallen "naturally" in the text flow if it weren't a positioned object. The *top:auto* setting makes sure the object isn't placed any higher or lower than it would naturally fall in regular HTML. This ensures that the *DIV* object won't obscure any regular text above or below it. The *left:50px* setting indents the *DIV* object 50 pixels from the left margin, and *width:400px* gives it an exact width of 400 pixels.

The image (*<IMG>* tag) also uses a little relative positioning. Its *STYLE* attribute looks like this:

```
STYLE="position:relative; top:-9%"
```

Essentially, this says that the image should appear where it would naturally fall in the regular HTML text flow, but I want to raise it up just a tad—9 percent, to be exact. A negative number for the *top* attribute moves the object up, while a positive number moves it down.

Figure 8-20 shows how the page looks in Internet Explorer. As you can see, the entire sidebar is placed between the paragraphs. It's indented 50 pixels and has a specific width of 400 pixels. It's a little harder to tell how the image has been influenced by relative positioning. If you view this page without the *STYLE="position:relative; top:-9%"* attribute in the *<IMG>* tag, the letter *A* is vertically centered in the sidebar. Scooting the image up 9 percent moves the whole letter up just a tad in the sidebar. A minor adjustment, indeed. But that's one of the things that relative positioning is good for.

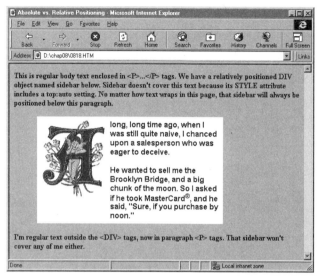

Figure 8-20. *The page whose source is shown in Figure 8-19, with a relatively positioned sidebar.*

USING VBSCRIPT CODE TO CONTROL VISIBILITY

Now that you've seen examples of the various CSS attributes that let you control positioning of objects, stacking order, and visibility, let's look at some examples of using VBScript code to manipulate the corresponding CSS properties to produce some interesting visual effects. The basic VBScript syntax for changing an object's CSS property is as follows:

```
objectName.style.CSSProperty = newValue
```

objectName is a valid object model name for an existing object, *CSSProperty* is any valid CSS property, and *newValue* is the new setting for that property. For example, this line of code makes the object named *myPicture* invisible:

```
myPicture.style.visibility = "hidden"
```

Select-an-Image Example

Here's an example that uses several graphic images stacked one on top of another, with only one image visible at a time. Figure 8-21 shows the page with one of the images—a sample from the Aridi Drop Caps III product—visible on the page.

NOTE   The images in Figure 8-21 are from Aridi's Drop Caps III collection. That product can be purchased via Aridi's web site at www.aridi.com. It's also available at Image Club's web site at www.imageclub.com.

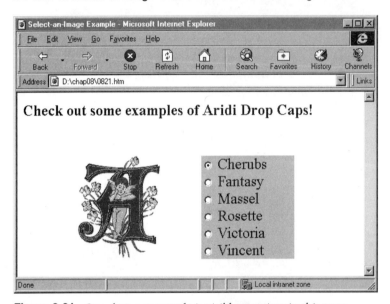

Figure 8-21. *One drop-cap sample is visible at a time in this page.*

Selecting one of the other radio buttons replaces the current image with a sample image from another category in that same product. Figure 8-22 shows how the page looks after the reader selects the Vincent category.

This example gives us the opportunity to explore several aspects of positioning and visibility. So let's take it from the top. Figure 8-23 shows the complete document source behind the Aridi Drop Caps page.

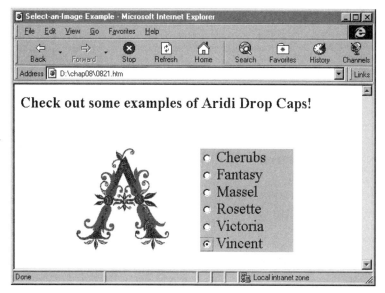

Figure 8-22. *A drop-cap sample from the Vincent collection.*

```
0821.htm - WordPad
File Edit View Insert Format Help

<HTML><HEAD><TITLE>Select-an-Image Example</TITLE>
<!-- All images use the same absolutely positioned style. -->
<STYLE TYPE="text/css"><!--
    IMG {position:absolute; top:100; left:100; height:160}
--></STYLE>
</HEAD><BODY><H2>Check out some examples of Aridi Drop Caps!</H2>
<IMG SRC="cherub_A.jpg" WIDTH="133" HEIGHT="160" STYLE="visibility:visible">
<IMG SRC="fantas_b.jpg" WIDTH="145" HEIGHT="160" STYLE="visibility:hidden">
<IMG SRC="massel_a.jpg" WIDTH="165" HEIGHT="160" STYLE="visibility:hidden">
<IMG SRC="rosett_a.jpg" WIDTH="155" HEIGHT="160" STYLE="visibility:hidden">
<IMG SRC="victor_a.jpg" WIDTH="100" HEIGHT="160" STYLE="visibility:hidden">
<IMG SRC="vince_a.jpg" WIDTH="150" HEIGHT="160" STYLE="visibility:hidden">

<!-- Radio buttons are all together in an absolutely positioned DIV object. -->
<DIV ID="choices" STYLE="position:absolute; top:100; left:300; width:150;
background-color:#C0C0C0; font-size:18pt">
    <INPUT TYPE="radio" NAME="rad" CHECKED> Cherubs<BR>
    <INPUT TYPE="radio" NAME="rad"> Fantasy<BR>
    <INPUT TYPE="radio" NAME="rad"> Massel<BR>
    <INPUT TYPE="radio" NAME="rad"> Rosette<BR>
    <INPUT TYPE="radio" NAME="rad"> Victoria<BR>
    <INPUT TYPE="radio" NAME="rad"> Vincent<BR>
</DIV>
<!-- Script fires whenever visitor clicks in the choices object. -->
<SCRIPT FOR="choices" EVENT="onclick" LANGUAGE="VBScript"><!--
    For counter = 0 To document.images.length - 1
        document.images(counter).style.visibility = "hidden"    'Make invisible.
        If rad(counter).checked Then
            document.images(counter).style.visibility = "visible"    'Make this one visible.
        End If
    Next
--></SCRIPT>
</BODY></HTML>

For Help, press F1
```

Figure 8-23. *The document source for the Aridi Drop Caps page.*

First, the page uses the embedded style below to set all the images in the page at the same absolute position and height. This is an easy way to ensure that all of the images overlap one another:

```
<!-- All images use the same absolutely positioned style. -->
<STYLE TYPE="text/css"><!--
    IMG {position:absolute; top:100; left:100; height:160}
--></STYLE>
```

Next, the page loads the images. Initially, only the first image is visible. All the rest of the images are invisible:

```
<IMG SRC="cherub_A.jpg" WIDTH="133" HEIGHT="160"
    STYLE="visibility:visible">
<IMG SRC="fantas_b.jpg" WIDTH="145" HEIGHT="160"
    STYLE="visibility:hidden">
<IMG SRC="massel_a.jpg" WIDTH="165" HEIGHT="160"
    STYLE="visibility:hidden">
<IMG SRC="rosett_a.jpg" WIDTH="155" HEIGHT="160"
    STYLE="visibility:hidden">
<IMG SRC="victor_a.jpg" WIDTH="100" HEIGHT="160"
    STYLE="visibility:hidden">
<IMG SRC="vince_a.jpg" WIDTH="150" HEIGHT="160"
    STYLE="visibility:hidden">
```

The radio buttons come next, placed within a <DIV> tag that I've named *choices*. This approach makes it easy to position the radio buttons precisely on the screen. Notice that the first radio button is the one that's selected initially. That radio button corresponds to the first image in this page, which, as you might recall, is the only one that's visible initially:

```
<DIV ID="choices" STYLE="position:absolute; top:100; left:300;
width:150; background-color:#C0C0C0; font-size:18pt">
    <INPUT TYPE="radio" NAME="rad" CHECKED> Cherubs<BR>
    <INPUT TYPE="radio" NAME="rad"> Fantasy<BR>
    <INPUT TYPE="radio" NAME="rad"> Massel<BR>
    <INPUT TYPE="radio" NAME="rad"> Rosette<BR>
    <INPUT TYPE="radio" NAME="rad"> Victoria<BR>
    <INPUT TYPE="radio" NAME="rad"> Vincent<BR>
</DIV>
```

That's all we need to give the page its initial visual appearance. Next, we need a script that responds to the reader selecting a radio button. In this example, I bound a script to the *onclick* event of the *choices* object, which houses all the radio buttons.

```
<!-- Script fires whenever visitor clicks in the choices object. -->
<SCRIPT FOR="choices" EVENT="onclick" LANGUAGE="VBScript"><!--
```

Within that script, a loop counts from zero to the number of images in the document minus one. As you might recall, the *length* property always contains a number indicating how many items are in a collection. To step through each item in the collection, we need to set up a loop that counts from zero to one less than the value that the *length* property provides:

```
For counter = 0 To document.images.length - 1
```

> **NOTE** Although you can access the images using the *document.all* collection, it is easier to use the *document.images* collection.

Within the loop, this statement makes the current image invisible:

```
document.images(counter).style.visibility = "hidden"
```

An *If...Then* statement then checks to see if the corresponding radio button is selected. If the radio button is indeed selected, that one corresponding image is made visible:

```
    If rad(counter).checked Then
        document.images(counter).style.visibility = "visible"
    End If
  Next
--></SCRIPT>
```

By the time this script has finished running, all of the images—except the one that corresponds to the reader's radio button selection—are invisible. And that's all there is to it!

A Collapsible Outline Example

Here's an example of using the *display* attribute to create a collapsible outline. I'll keep it short so I don't bog you down with too much text, tags, and code. But let's say the reader opens the page and is presented with the two "main topics" shown in Figure 8-24 on the next page.

Clicking on any of the main topic headings reveals a list of subheadings, which are actually hyperlinks to other pages, right under the main heading. For example, Figure 8-25 on the next page shows how this page looks after the reader clicks the first main topic heading. Clicking the heading a second time hides the list of subtopics. This popular approach to presenting information makes it easy for the reader to select the level of detail that he or she prefers.

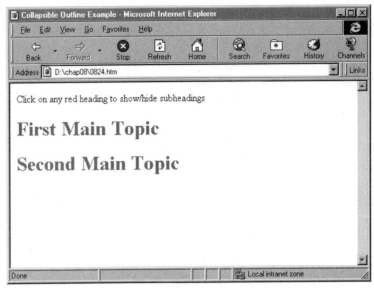

Figure 8-24. *A collapsible outline before a main topic is clicked.*

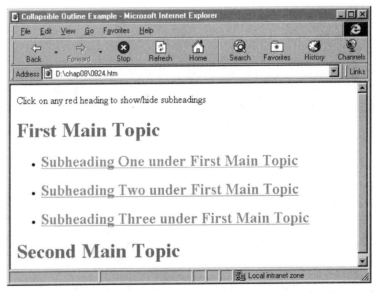

Figure 8-25. *The page from Figure 8-24 after the first topic heading is clicked.*

Let's look at the collapsible outline page to see what makes it tick. Figure 8-26 shows the complete document source for the page. Let's skip over the stuff in the head section for the moment and look at the body of the document.

```
0824.htm - WordPad                                                    _ □ ×
File  Edit  View  Insert  Format  Help

<HTML><HEAD><TITLE>Collapsible Outline Example</TITLE>
<SCRIPT LANGUAGE="VBScript"><!--
    'Shows or hides subheadings based on list's position in the page.
    Function showHide(listNum)
        Dim whichList
        Set whichList = document.all.tags("UL").item(listNum)
        If whichList.style.display = "none" Then
            whichList.style.display = ""
        Else
            whichList.style.display = "none"
        End If
    End Function
    'Hides lists when page first opens.
    Sub window_onload()
        document.all.tags("UL").item(0).style.display = "none"
        document.all.tags("UL").item(1).style.display = "none"
    End Sub
--></SCRIPT>
</HEAD><BODY>
<P>Click on any red heading to show/hide subheadings</P>
<H1 onclick="showHide(0)" STYLE="color:red">First Main Topic</H1>
<UL>
    <LI><H2><A HREF="s1.htm">Subheading One under First Main Topic</A></H2></LI>
    <LI><H2><A HREF="s2.htm">Subheading Two under First Main Topic</A></H2></LI>
    <LI><H2><A HREF="s3.htm">Subheading Three under First Main Topic</A></H2></LI>
</UL>
<H1 onclick="showHide(1)" STYLE="color:red">Second Main Topic</H1>
<UL>
    <LI><H2><A HREF="s4.htm">Subheading One under Second Main Topic</A></H2></LI>
    <LI><H2><A HREF="s5.htm">Subheading Two under Second Main Topic</A></H2></LI>
    <LI><H2><A HREF="s6.htm">Subheading Three under Second Main Topic</A></H2></LI>
</UL>
</BODY></HTML>

For Help, press F1
```

Figure 8-26. *The document source for the page shown in Figures 8-24 and 8-25.*

The body starts off with some basic paragraph text and then a level-1 heading that, when clicked, calls a function named *showHide()* and passes to that function the number 0:

```
<BODY>
<P>Click on any red heading to show/hide subheadings</P>
<H1 onclick="showHide(0)" STYLE="color:red">First Main Topic</H1>
```

Below that level-1 heading is a list formatted using *<UL>...</UL>* tags. These tags define a bulleted list (an unordered list). Each item in the list is enclosed in *<LI>...</LI>* tags, as is typical of HTML lists. In this case, I made the text of each item fairly large, using *<H2>...</H2>* tags. Furthermore, each item in the list is actually a hyperlink to some other page. I named those pages s1.htm, s2.htm, and so forth. But of course *HREF* attributes can be any valid URLs on the Internet:

```
<UL>
    <LI><H2><A HREF="s1.htm">Subheading One under First
        Main Topic</A></H2></LI>
    <LI><H2><A HREF="s2.htm">Subheading Two under First
        Main Topic</A></H2></LI>
    <LI><H2><A HREF="s3.htm">Subheading Three under First
        Main Topic</A></H2></LI>
</UL>
```

The second main topic heading looks much like the first. Clicking this heading, however, passes the number 1 to the *showHide()* function. But other than that, the basic structure of the heading and its list of subtopics is pretty much the same as the first heading and its list of subtopics:

```
<H1 onclick="showHide(1)" STYLE="color:red">Second Main Topic</H1>
<UL>
    <LI><H2><A HREF="s4.htm">Subheading One under Second
        Main Topic</A></H2></LI>
    <LI><H2><A HREF="s5.htm">Subheading Two under Second
        Main Topic</A></H2></LI>
    <LI><H2><A HREF="s6.htm">Subheading Three under Second
        Main Topic</A></H2></LI>
</UL>
```

You can add as many topics and subtopics as you want, following the same pattern. A third main heading would use the event *onclick="showHide(2)"*, a fourth would use *onclick="showhide(3)"*, and so forth. So now let's take a look at the *showHide()* function, which, as you might have guessed, is what makes the sub-topic lists appear and disappear. That function is up in the head of the sample page, and looks like this:

```
'Shows or hides subheadings based on list's position in the page.
Function showHide(listNum)
    Dim whichList
    Set whichList = document.all.tags("UL").item(listNum)
    If whichList.style.display = "none" Then
      whichList.style.display = ""
    Else
      whichList.style.display = "none"
    End If
End Function
```

Here's how the function works. Some number (either 0 or 1 in our current example) gets passed to the function. That number is stored in a local variable named *listNum*. Next, *Dim* and *Set* statements isolate the specific list of subtopics to be worked upon by the function. For example, if 0 is passed to the function, the *Set* statement becomes *Set whichList = document.all.tags("UL").item(0)*, which makes the *whichList* variable point to the first subtopic list in the page. If 1 gets passed to the function, the *Set* statement becomes *set whichList = document.all.tags("UL").item(1)*, which makes *whichList* point to the second subtopic list in the page. And so forth. This same routine can handle any number of subtopic lists.

Next, an *If...Then...Else* statement decides whether to make the current subtopic list visible or invisible, based on the current *display* setting of the subtopic list. If the subtopic list's *display* property is set to *none*, it is changed to *""*, which makes the list visible. If the subtopic list's *display* property isn't already set to *none*, the *Else* clause kicks in and sets *display* to *none*, making the list invisible.

That's all the *showHide()* function needs to do. One last little routine is fired only once, when the page is first loaded into the web browser—*Sub window_onload()*. That procedure makes sure that all subtopic lists are initially invisible by setting their *display* properties to *none*:

```
'Hides lists when page first opens.
Sub window_onload()
    document.all.tags("UL").item(0).style.display = "none"
    document.all.tags("UL").item(1).style.display = "none"
End Sub
```

And that's how the whole page works. Perhaps I should point out that if the current page contains, say, 10 main topics and 10 subtopic lists, the *window_onload()* sub procedure can use a *For...Next* loop rather than a lengthy series of statements to hide all the subtopic lists. In that case, the *window_onload()* sub procedure looks like this:

```
'Hides lists when page first opens.
Sub window_onload()
    For counter = 0 to 9
        document.all.tags("UL").item(counter).style.display = "none"
    Next
End Sub
```

Another point worth mentioning is that when visitors click a hyperlink, they are, of course, taken to some new page. When they use the Back button to get back to the outline page, all the subtopic lists are closed, because when the page is reloaded, the subtopic lists are all returned to their initial hidden state. In actual practice, these sort of collapsible outlines are more often used in framed sites, where the topic list never gets reloaded and hence remains unchanged as the reader explores the site. Figure 8-27 on the next page shows an example. The collapsible outline is in the left frame. The subtopic lists are visible under the first two main topics. But the reader can, of course, hide and display subtopic lists just by clicking on any main topic.

I'll assume that you already know the basics of defining a framed site. But let me show you the specifics of this particular example. The page that first gets opened by the reader is the one that defines the frames. In this example, that page contains the code shown on the next page.

```
<HTML>
<HEAD>
<TITLE>Sample Framed Site</TITLE>
</HEAD>
<FRAMESET COLS="175,*">
    <FRAME NAME="myTOC" SRC="outline.htm">
    <FRAME NAME="mainFrame" SRC="s0.htm">
</FRAMESET>
</HTML>
```

I've opted to name the narrow left frame (the one that will display the collapsible outline) *myTOC*. The actual page containing the collapsible outline is named outline.htm in this example. Note, too, that the frame on the right that will display actual web pages is named *mainFrame* in this example.

The page named outline.htm can be structured like our original example. However, to reduce the size of the text in the outline, you might want to remove all the *<H1>...</H1>* and *<H2>...</H2>* tags. Also, to make each hyperlink display its content in the frame named *mainFrame*, you should add the *<BASE TARGET="mainFrame">* tag to the head of the document.

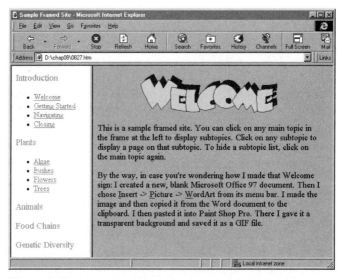

Figure 8-27. *The collapsible outline in the left frame aids navigation.*

Figure 8-28 gives you an idea of how the document source for the collapsible outline might look. Some of the main topics and subtopics, as well as the closing *</BODY>* and *</HTML>* tags, are scrolled off the bottom of the screen. But the topics follow the same basic pattern of the main topics (*<P>*...*</P>* tags) and subtopics (*<UL>*...*</UL>* tags) closer to the top of the page.

The significant changes are in the head section of the page. The new *<BASE TARGET = "mainFrame">* tag ensures that each hyperlink that follows it displays its referenced page in the right frame, named *mainFrame*. The *Sub window_onload()* procedure has also been modified to handle all five main topics used in this example.

Other than those changes, the basic structure and logic of the page stays the same as in the smaller example shown earlier in this section.

```
Outline.htm - WordPad                                             _ □ ×
File  Edit  View  Insert  Format  Help
<HTML><HEAD><TITLE>Collapsible Outline</TITLE>
<SCRIPT LANGUAGE="VBScript"><!--
    'Shows or hides subheadings based on list's position in the page.
    Function showHide(listNum)
        Dim whichList
        Set whichList = document.all.tags("UL").item(listNum)
        If whichList.style.display = "none" Then
            whichList.style.display = ""
        Else
            whichList.style.display = "none"
        End If
    End Function
    'Hides lists when page first opens. There are five main topics in this sample page.
    Sub window_onload()
        For counter = 0 to 4
            document.all.tags("UL").item(counter).style.display = "none"
        Next
    End Sub
-->/SCRIPT>
<BASE TARGET="mainFrame">
</HEAD><BODY>
<P onclick="showHide(0)" STYLE="font-size:14pt; color:red">Introduction</P>
<UL>
    <LI><A HREF="s1.htm">Welcome</A></LI>
    <LI><A HREF="s2.htm">Getting Started</A></LI>
    <LI><A HREF="s3.htm">Navigating</A></LI>
    <LI><A HREF="s4.htm">Closing</A></LI>
</UL>
<P onclick="showHide(1)" STYLE="font-size:14pt; color:red">Plants</P>
<UL>
    <LI><A HREF="s5.htm">Algae</A></LI>
    <LI><A HREF="s6.htm">Bushes</A></LI>
    <LI><A HREF="s7.htm">Flowers</A></LI>
For Help, press F1
```

Figure 8-28. *The source for a collapsible outline applied to a framed site.*

SUMMARY

We've covered quite a lot of territory here, discussing some of the CSS attributes that let you position, stack, and hide objects on the screen. We've also looked at some coding examples that change an object's CSS properties to make it visible and invisible. To summarize the main points:

- Historically, text in an HTML document has flowed into the web browser from left to right and top to bottom.

- The positioning CSS attributes let you place an object at a specific position in the document window.

- The general syntax for positioning an object is to add a *STYLE* attribute to the object's tag, followed by CSS attributes and values enclosed in quotation marks.

- The *position* CSS attribute lets you define the type of positioning an object uses as *absolute* (without regard to other objects on the page), *relative* (with regard to other objects on the page), or *static* (using standard HTML text flow formatting).

- The *top* and *left* CSS attributes let you define where the upper-left corner of an object will be placed. For example, *STYLE= "position:absolute; top:50; left:100"* puts the upper-left corner of the object 50 pixels below the top of the document window and 100 pixels in from the left edge of the document window.

- The *width* and *height* CSS attributes let you specify an exact width, height, or both for an object.

- You can control how objects overlap in a web page by using the *z-index* CSS attribute.

- You can hide an object by using the *visibility:hidden* CSS attribute setting or the *display:none* CSS attribute setting.

- An object hidden using *visibility:hidden* still takes up space on the page. An object hidden using *display:none* takes up no space on the page.

- In VBScript, you can use the general syntax *objectName.style.CSSProperty = newValue* to change an object's CSS property.

In the next chapter, we'll look at some more sophisticated scripting techniques for manipulating positioned objects.

Chapter 9

Simple Animation and Drag-and-Drop

In this chapter, I'll show you some fun techniques for moving and sizing objects in your web pages, right in front of your readers' eyes. In particular, we'll look at how to:

- Move an object from one place to another using code

- Make objects glide across the screen

- Make objects move continuously

- Size an object right in front of the visitor's eyes

- Add drag-and-drop capability to a web page

- Use a tool to position objects

Let's start off easy by discussing the most rudimentary code required to make an object change its position on the screen.

REPOSITIONING OBJECTS

Moving an absolutely positioned object to a new location on the page can be as simple as changing its *top* and *left* CSS properties. Figure 9-1 shows a simple example of a page with an image and a button.

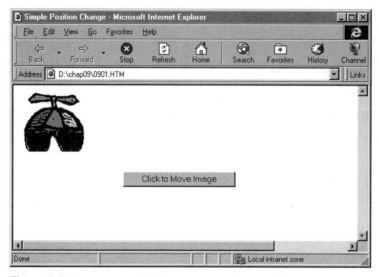

Figure 9-1. *An image and a button in a web page.*

Figure 9-2 shows what happens after the reader clicks the button. The image is repositioned in a new location on the page (behind the button in this example). And the button gets disabled (grayed out) as an added little feature.

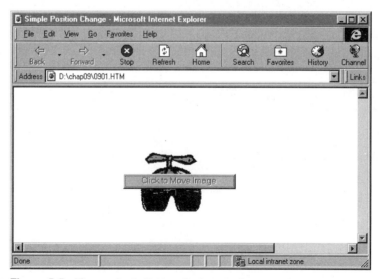

Figure 9-2. *The result of clicking the button shown in Figure 9-1.*

Figure 9-3 shows the document source for the web page. Let's take a look at how it works.

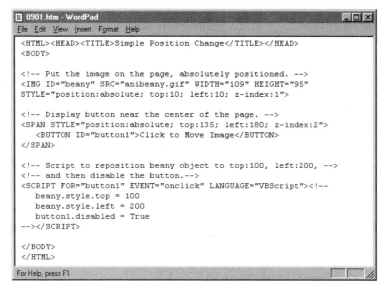

Figure 9-3. *The source code for the position change page.*

The first tag in the body of the document uses an *<IMG>* tag to place the image named anibeany.gif into the web page, at 10 pixels from the top and left edges of the page. (It just so happens that this image is an animated GIF, hence the name anibeany.gif. This same technique will work, however, with any image—or any object, for that matter!). Note that the object is named *beany*, using the *ID* attribute within the *<IMG>* tag:

```
<!-- Put the image on the page, absolutely positioned. -->
<IMG ID="beany" SRC="anibeany.gif" WIDTH="109" HEIGHT="95"
STYLE="position:absolute; top:10; left:10; z-index:1">
```

Next comes the button. The button is also positioned absolutely on the page:

```
<!-- Display button near center the of the page. -->
<SPAN STYLE="position:absolute; top:135; left:180; z-index:2">
   <BUTTON ID="button1">Click to Move Image</BUTTON>
</SPAN>
```

Next the script in this page, shown on the next page, is executed when the reader clicks the button. The script is pretty simple—it changes the image's *top* CSS property to 100 and its *left* CSS property to 200, thereby moving the image to that new position on the page. Because clicking the button again would have no effect in this particular example, I also added the statement *button1.disabled = True* to give the button the grayed-out look.

```
<!-- Script to reposition beany object to top:100, left:200, -->
<!-- and then disable the button.-->
<SCRIPT FOR="button1" EVENT="onclick" LANGUAGE="VBScript"><!--
    beany.style.top = 100
    beany.style.left = 200
    button1.disabled = True
--></SCRIPT>

</BODY>
</HTML>
```

Incidentally, the image is behind the button in Figure 9-2 because I set the z-index of the *beany* object to 1 and the z-index of the button object to 2. Had I reversed that—setting the *beany* object's z-index to 2 and the button's z-index to 1—the *beany* object would appear to cover the button in Figure 9-2.

ANIMATING OBJECTS

More often than not, you'll want to write scripts that do more than just reposition an object from point A to point B. You might want to have an image actually glide across the page in an animated manner. You can do this in a couple of ways. One way is to use the Microsoft DirectAnimation Path control. The other is to simply write some code that alters the position of the object on the screen. In this chapter, I'll discuss the latter method. I'll talk about the Path control in Chapter 14 after we cover some of the basics of ActiveX controls.

There's one major trick to writing scripts to make an object glide smoothly across the page. Every time your code changes the position of the object on the page, the code needs to pause, for just a moment, to allow the screen to repaint the object in its new location. The pause can be ever so slight—one millisecond ($1/1000$ second) is usually sufficient. But without some kind of pause, the approach simply won't work. The pausing capability is actually provided by methods available in the object model.

Understanding Simple Animations

When animating objects, you should define a pause that occurs at regular intervals. The pause can be as short as one millisecond or as long as you want. Microsoft Internet Explorer takes advantage of that pause to bring the screen up to date, if necessary. In code, a pause translates to temporarily stopping a script from running for some length of time.

The *window* object provides methods for working with timed actions. These methods include the *setTimout()* and *clearTimeout()* methods. The *setTimeout()* method has the following syntax:

```
variable = window.setTimeout(expression, milliseconds, language)
```

variable is an arbitrary name that you assign to the timed action and is used only to stop the timed action using the *clearTimeout()* method. *expression* is code that's executed after the pause and is usually the name of some procedure in the page. *milliseconds* is the duration of the pause in thousandths of a second. *language* is the language the code is written in.

For example, the statement below indicates to execute a VBScript procedure named *moveRight* after pausing for one millisecond:

```
myTimer = window.setTimeout("moveRight", 1, "VBScript")
```

The *clearTimeout()* method cancels a timed action. The *clearTimeout()* method has the following syntax, where *variable* is the identifier initially assigned to the timed action in the *variable = window-.setTimeout(…)* statement:

```
window.clearTimeout(variable)
```

For example, the statement below stops the timed action named *myTimer*:

```
window.clearTimeout(myTimer)
```

As a general rule, the code to animate an absolutely positioned object is structured like this:

```
<SCRIPT LANGUAGE="VBSCRIPT"><!--
   'Initialize positioning variables.
   Public position
   'Initially set to starting position.
   position = startValue

   Sub subName
      'Calculate new position.
      position = position +/- increment
      object.style.coordinate = position
      'Move some more, if appropriate.
      If stillWantToMove Then
         myTimer = window.setTimeout("subName", 1, "VBScript")
      Else
         'Stop all activity when stillWantToMove
         'is False.
         window.clearTimeout(myTimer)
      End If
   End Sub
--></SCRIPT>
```

In this code:

- *position* is the current position of the object.

- *startValue* is the position of the object before the motion begins.

- *subName* is the name of the animation sub procedure. (This can be any name you like.)

- *coordinate* is the *top* or *left* CSS property.

- *increment* is some value to add to, or subtract from, the current position.

- *object* is the name (ID) of the object being moved.

- *stillWantToMove* is some expression that determines whether to keep moving the object.

I realize that's all pretty vague. There are, in fact, countless ways to fill in the blanks to achieve all kinds of different motion effects. So we'd do well to explore some further examples.

Gliding up the Screen

Figure 9-4 shows a sample web page with an image and a button. When the reader first opens that page, however, only the button is visible. Clicking the button causes the rocket to appear out of nowhere at the bottom of the page and then glide up across the button and off the top of the page. In the figure, the rocket is partway through its journey.

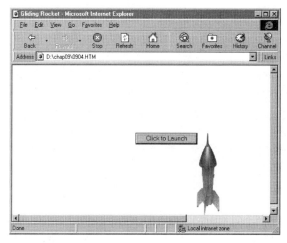

Figure 9-4. *Clicking the button causes the rocket to glide up and off the top of the page.*

Figure 9-5 shows the document source for the sample page.

```
0904.htm - WordPad
File  Edit  View  Insert  Format  Help
<HTML><HEAD><TITLE>Gliding Rocket</TITLE>
<SCRIPT LANGUAGE="VBScript"><!--
    'Initialize topPos variable.
    Public topPos
    'Set to same as style top attribute.
    topPos = 500

    Sub glideUp()
        'Decrease topPos by 5 pixels.
        topPos = topPos - 5
        rocket.style.top = topPos
        'Move some more, but only if topPos is greater than -177.
        If topPos > -177 Then
            myTimer = window.setTimeout("glideUp", 2, "VBScript")
        Else
            'Stop all activity when topPos is less than or equal to -177.
            window.clearTimeout(myTimer)
            'Reset topPos in case reader wants to try again.
            topPos = 500
        End If
    End Sub
--></SCRIPT>
</HEAD>
<BODY>
<IMG SRC="rocket.gif" WIDTH="50" HEIGHT="177" ID="rocket"
STYLE="position:absolute; left:400; top:500; z-index=2">

<!-- Show the button that launches the rocket -->
<SPAN STYLE="position:absolute; top:50%; left:50%; z-index:1">
    <BUTTON onclick="glideUp">Click to Launch</BUTTON>
</SPAN>
</BODY></HTML>
For Help, press F1
```

Figure 9-5. *The document source for the page shown in Figure 9-4.*

The script first creates a public variable named *topPos* and then gives that variable an initial value of 500. Five hundred pixels down from the top of the document window is pretty far. In fact, the rocket probably wouldn't even be visible at 800 x 600 resolution. (The title bar, menu bar, and toolbars take up quite a few pixels, so the actual height of the document window is usually less than 500 pixels.)

```
<SCRIPT LANGUAGE="VBScript"><!--
    'Initialize topPos variable.
    Public topPos
    'Set to same as style top attribute.
    topPos = 500
```

Next comes a sub procedure named *glideUp*. The *glideUp* procedure first subtracts 5 (pixels) from the current *topPos* value and then assigns the resulting value to the *top* CSS property of the rocket:

```
Sub glideUp()
    'Decrease topPos by 5 pixels.
    topPos = topPos - 5
    rocket.style.top = topPos
```

NOTE When you use just numbers with the *top* and *left* properties, the default unit of measurement, pixels, is assumed. For instance, rocket.style.top = 25 sets the *top* property to 25 pixels.

Next, the procedure makes a decision. If the current value of *topPos* is greater than −177, it pauses a brief 2 milliseconds and "calls itself" again. In case you're wondering, I chose −177 because the height of the rocket is 177 pixels. So moving the top of the rocket image to −177 pixels is just enough to make the whole rocket disappear from the page:

```
'Move some more, but only if topPos is greater
'than -177.
If topPos > -177 Then
    myTimer = window.setTimeout("glideUp", 2, "VBScript")
```

When the *topPos* variable contains a value that's less than or equal to −177, the timed action is cancelled, which stops all motion. In this example, I also reset the *topPos* variable to 500. Doing so allows the whole thing to work again if the reader clicks the button again:

```
Else
    'Stop all activity when topPos is less
    'than or equal to -177.
    window.clearTimeout(myTimer)
    'Reset topPos in case reader wants to
    'try again.
    topPos = 500
End If
End Sub
--></SCRIPT>
</HEAD>
```

That ends the script and the head of the document. In the body of the document, the *<IMG>* tag positions, absolutely, the image named rocket.gif. Here you can see that the rocket image is, indeed, 177 pixels tall, and I initially placed its top point 500 pixels from the top of the document window. Here, too, I named the object *rocket* using the *ID* attribute:

```
<BODY>
<IMG SRC="rocket.gif" WIDTH="50" HEIGHT="177" ID="rocket"
STYLE="position:absolute; left:400; top:500; z-index=2">
```

Next comes the button, which is also positioned on the screen. Clicking the button calls the *glideUp* sub procedure, which gets the motion started:

```
<!-- Show the button that launches the rocket. -->
<SPAN STYLE="position:absolute; top:50%; left:50%; z-index:1">
   <BUTTON onclick="glideUp">Click to Launch</BUTTON>
</SPAN>
</BODY>
</HTML>
```

Gliding Diagonally Using Percentages

Let's look at another example in which an image glides from the upper-left corner of the document window down to the lower-right corner. As an added twist, we'll specify where to position the image using the percentage unit of measurement rather than pixels. That is, we'll move the image from 1 percent of the distance from the top-left corner of the page to 100 percent of the distance from the top-left corner of the page—the latter being the lower-right corner of the page.

Using percentages rather than pixels allows the page to behave identically on different browser window sizes. Also, it doesn't matter if the reader is viewing the page at 640 x 480, 800 x 600, or any other screen resolution, because the object will move from 1 percent to 100 percent of the distance down and across the page.

Figure 9-6 shows the page I'll use in this example. The reader has clicked the button and the beanyboy image is gliding down from the top-left corner to the lower-right corner. Figure 9-7 on the next page shows the document source for the page.

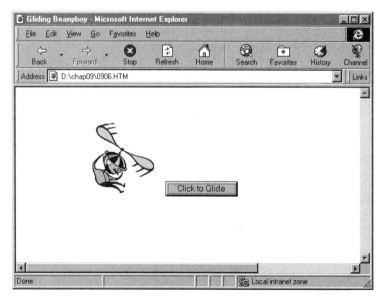

Figure 9-6. *The beanyboy image is gliding from the top-left to the lower-right corner.*

```
0906.htm - WordPad
File  Edit  View  Insert  Format  Help

<HTML><HEAD><TITLE>Gliding Beanyboy</TITLE>
<SCRIPT LANGUAGE="VBScript"><!--
    'Initialize topPos and leftPos variables.
    Public topPos, leftPos
    topPos = 1 : leftPos = 1

    Sub glideDown()
        topPos = topPos + 1       'Increase topPos by 1%.
        leftPos = leftPos + 1     'Increase leftPos by 1%.
        beanyboy.style.top = topPos & "%"
        beanyboy.style.left = leftPos & "%"
        'Move some more, but only if topPos is less than 100%.
        If topPos < 100 Then
            myTimer = window.setTimeout("glideDown", 2, "VBScript")
        Else
            window.clearTimeout(myTimer)
            'Put beanyboy back in upper left corner.
            beanyboy.style.top = 1 : topPos = 1
            beanyboy.style.left = 1 : leftPos = 1
        End If
    End Sub
--></SCRIPT>
</HEAD>

<BODY>
<IMG ID="beanyboy" SRC="beanyboy.gif" WIDTH="100" HEIGHT="110"
STYLE="position:absolute; top:1%; left:1%">
<!-- Show the button that gets the motion going -->
<SPAN STYLE="position:absolute; top:60%; left:45%; z-index:1">
    <BUTTON onclick="glideDown">Click to Glide</BUTTON>
</SPAN>
</BODY></HTML>

For Help, press F1
```

Figure 9-7. *The document source for the page shown in Figure 9-6.*

For this example, the script needs to manipulate two position variables—the top position and the left position. The script defines two public variables named *topPos* and *leftPos*, and it gives them each an initial value of 1 (for one percent):

```
<SCRIPT LANGUAGE="VBScript"><!--
    'Initialize topPos and leftPos variables.
    Public topPos, leftPos
    topPos = 1 : leftPos = 1
```

NOTE   In the code above, I used a colon (:) to separate the two assignment statements. I did this so I could put both statements on the same line.

Next comes the *glideDown* sub procedure, which makes the object glide from corner to corner. The procedure starts by increasing the *topPos* and *leftPos* variables by one:

```
Sub glideDown()
    topPos = topPos + 1       'Increase topPos by 1%.
    leftPos = leftPos + 1     'Increase leftPos by 1%.
```

The next lines assign the new *topPos* and *leftPos* values to the *top* and *left* properties of the *beanboy* object. Notice that a percent sign (%) is tacked on when doing the assignment. This means that the *beanyboy top* and *left* properties actually become something like 2%, 3%, or some other percentage. That's all that's required to use percentages rather than pixels:

```
beanyboy.style.top = topPos & "%"
beanyboy.style.left = leftPos & "%"
```

The *If...Then...Else* statement that decides whether to keep the object moving determines whether *topPos* is less than 100 (as in 100%). If so, the procedure pauses for a moment (2 milliseconds) to let the screen refresh. Then it calls itself to keep the object moving:

```
'Move some more, but only if topPos is less
'than 100%.
If topPos < 100 Then
    myTimer = window.setTimeout("glideDown", 2, "VBScript")
```

When *topPos* reaches 100, the next lines cancel the timed action, which stops the motion. In this example, I also added some code that puts *beanyboy* back into the upper-left corner of the page and resets the *topPos* and *leftPos* variables back to 1:

```
Else
    window.clearTimeout(myTimer)
    'Put beanyboy back in upper left corner.
    beanyboy.style.top = 1 : topPos = 1
    beanyboy.style.left = 1 : leftPos = 1
    End If
End Sub
--></SCRIPT>
</HEAD>
```

That ends the script and the head section of the page. The rest of the page is the body starting with the *<IMG>* tag that places the image near the top left corner of the screen:

```
<BODY>
<IMG ID="beanyboy" SRC="beanyboy.gif" WIDTH="100" HEIGHT="110"
STYLE="position:absolute; top:1%; left:1%">
```

Next, the button is defined. When clicked, the button calls the *glideDown* procedure, which gets the motion going:

```
<!-- Show the button that gets the motion going -->
<SPAN STYLE="position:absolute; top:60%; left:45%; z-index:1">
    <BUTTON onclick="glideDown">Click to Glide</BUTTON>
</SPAN>
</BODY></HTML>
```

ANIMATING OBJECTS CONTINUOUSLY

The object on your page needn't simply go from one position to another. You can set up your scripts to have the object move continuously. Figure 9-8 shows an example of such a page. Clicking the Start Motion button gets the little car moving from left to right. When the car gets to the right edge of the screen, it does a quick U-turn and heads the other direction, as shown in Figure 9-9. The car keeps moving back and forth like this until the reader clicks the Stop Motion button. As an added effect, it passes in front of the poles in one direction and behind them in the other direction.

Figure 9-8. *The car moves left to right, in front of the poles.*

To create this page, I first created the graphic images. I needed two cars—one pointing left and the other pointing right. The car is actually a piece of commercial clip art. To make one car point in the opposite direction, I just used the Image-Mirror command in Paint Shop Pro. To make the car background and windows transparent, I colored them blue and then made blue the transparent color when saving each image as a GIF. The poles are also clip art images. Figure 9-10 shows all the images in Paint Shop Pro.

Figure 9-9. *The car moves right to left, behind the poles.*

NOTE The car image is a piece of commercial clip art from the Art Parts collection, which is available at many computer stores as well as online at www.imageclub.com/artparts/. Paint Shop Pro is also a commercial product. A shareware evaluation version is available at www.jasc.com.

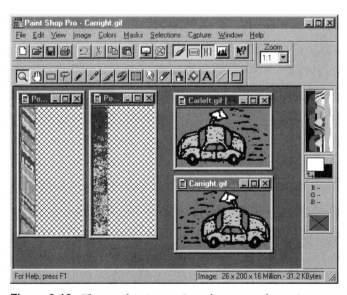

Figure 9-10. *The graphic images I used to create the roving car sample page.*

Next comes the actual HTML document. As you might imagine, there's a fair amount of VBScript code in this page. It's all in the head section in this example. Figure 9-11 shows roughly the top third of the document source.

Figure 9-11. *The top third of the document source for the roving car example.*

The script starts out by creating five public variables named *myTimer*, *startPixel*, *endPixel*, *curPixel*, and *howManyPixels*. The roles that these variables play are summarized below:

■   *myTimer*—used to stop the car motion.

■   *startPixel*—the starting pixel position of the car that travels left to right, and also the leftmost pixel position to which the right-to-left car is allowed to travel.

■   *endPixel*—the rightmost pixel position to which the left-to-right car is allowed to travel, and also the starting pixel position of the car that travels right to left.

■   *curPixel*—the current pixel position of the current car. This is the variable we change in order to make the car move.

■   *howManyPixels*—how far the car travels in pixels with each timeout.

The last variable, *howManyPixels*, holds a number that indicates how far the car travels with each timeout. The larger the number assigned to this variable, the faster the car moves. The beginning of the script is shown here:

```
'Public variables accessible to all code in this page.
Public myTimer, startPixel, endPixel, curPixel
Public howManyPixels
startPixel = 33 : endPixel = 620 : howManyPixels = 3
```

The first sub procedure in the document makes sure that the cars are in their proper starting positions. The car that travels left to right is initially visible, and the car that travels right to left is initially invisible. This sub procedure also gives the *curPixel* variable an initial value equal to the starting value of the car that travels left to right, and then it gets the car moving by calling the *moveRight* sub procedure:

```
'Gets cars in starting position, then gets carRight moving.
Sub initializeCars()
   document.all.carRight.style.left = startPixel
   document.all.carRight.style.visibility = "visible"
   document.all.carLeft.style.left = endPixel
   document.all.carLeft.style.visibility = "hidden"
   curPixel = startPixel
   moveRight
End Sub
```

The *moveRight* sub procedure moves the car named *carRight* (the car that faces right) from left to right across the screen. When that car reaches the *endPixel* position, however, the sub procedure then makes *carRight* invisible, moves it back to its starting position, brings *carLeft* (the car that points to the left) out of hiding, and then gets *carLeft* moving by calling the procedure named *moveLeft*:

```
'Moves the carRight object right until endPixel is reached.
Sub moveRight()
   curPixel = curPixel + howManyPixels
   'If haven't reached farthest right limit, move
   'farther right.
   If curPixel < endPixel Then
      document.all.carRight.style.left = curPixel
      myTimer = window.setTimeout("moveRight", 1, "VBScript")
   'If endPixel reached, switch to carLeft object
   'and move it to the left.
   Else
      document.all.carRight.style.visibility = "hidden"
      document.all.carRight.style.left = startPixel
      document.all.carLeft.style.visibility = "visible"
      moveLeft
   End If
End Sub
```

Figure 9-12 on the next page shows roughly the second third of the roving car page's document source.

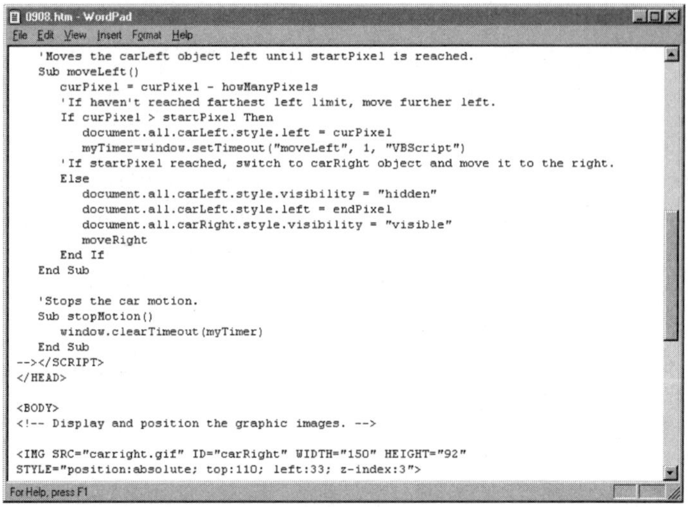

Figure 9-12. *The second third of the roving car page's document source.*

The first sub procedure in this section of the page is *moveLeft*. It moves the car named *carLeft* across the screen until that car reaches the *startPixel* position. When *carLeft* reaches the *startPixel* position, the procedure makes the car invisible, moves it back to its original position, makes the other car (*carRight*) visible once again, and gets that car moving left to right across the screen:

```
'Moves the carLeft object left until startPixel is reached.
Sub moveLeft()
   curPixel = curPixel - howManyPixels
   'If haven't reached farthest left limit, move
   'further left.
   If curPixel > startPixel Then
      document.all.carLeft.style.left = curPixel
      myTimer = window.setTimeout("moveLeft", 1, "VBScript")
   'If startPixel reached, switch to carRight object
   'and move it to the right.
   Else
      document.all.carLeft.style.visibility = "hidden"
      document.all.carLeft.style.left = endPixel
      document.all.carRight.style.visibility = "visible"
      moveRight
   End If
End Sub
```

The cars could just travel indefinitely back and forth across the screen until the reader closes the current page. However, in this example I also added a button that allows the reader to stop the car. That button, which I'll discuss in a moment, calls on the *stopMotion* sub procedure shown on the next page to stop the car motion. As you can see, this sub procedure calls the *clearTimeout()* method with *myTimer* as the argument to stop the car motion:

```
'Stops the car motion.
Sub stopMotion()
   window.clearTimeout(myTimer)
End Sub
```

Part of the body of the document is also visible in Figure 9-12. There you can see the *<IMG>* tag that puts the carright.gif image on the page and gives it the object name *carRight*. The car is positioned absolutely on the page—as all movable objects should be—and it has a z-index value of 3:

```
<BODY>
<!-- Display and position the graphic images. -->

<IMG SRC="carright.gif" ID="carRight" WIDTH="150" HEIGHT="92"
STYLE="position:absolute; top:110; left:33; z-index:3">
```

Figure 9-13 shows the rest of the document source for the roving car page. The first three *<IMG>* tags place the poles on the page. Each pole has a z-index of 2 so that *carRight*, which has a z-index of 3, will pass in front of all the poles.

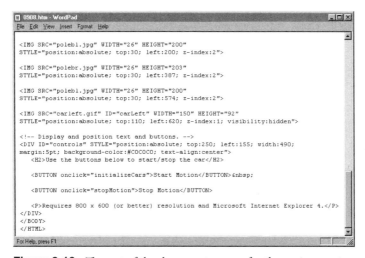

Figure 9-13. *The rest of the document source for the roving car page.*

```
<IMG SRC="polebl.jpg" WIDTH="26" HEIGHT="200"
STYLE="position:absolute; top:30; left:200; z-index:2">

<IMG SRC="polebr.jpg" WIDTH="26" HEIGHT="203"
STYLE="position:absolute; top:30; left:387; z-index:2">

<IMG SRC="polebl.jpg" WIDTH="26" HEIGHT="200"
STYLE="position:absolute; top:30; left:574; z-index:2">
```

The last *<IMG>* tag places the carleft.gif image on the page, gives it the object name *carLeft*, makes it invisible initially, and gives it a z-index of 1. The z-index setting ensures that this car passes behind the poles, which all have a z-index of 2:

```
<IMG SRC="carleft.gif" ID="carLeft" WIDTH="150" HEIGHT="92"
STYLE="position:absolute; top:110; left:620; z-index:1;
visibility:hidden">
```

The text and buttons beneath the cars are within the *<DIV>...</DIV>* tags, which have a silver background. The button labeled Start Motion calls the *initializeCars* sub procedure when clicked, which gets the first car moving:

```
<!-- Display and position text and buttons. -->
<DIV ID="controls" STYLE="position:absolute; top:250; left:155;
width:490; margin:5pt; background-color:#C0C0C0; text-align:center">
    <H2>Use the buttons below to start/stop the car</H2>

    <BUTTON onclick="initializeCars">Start Motion</BUTTON> 
```

The button labeled Stop Motion calls the *stopMotion* sub procedure when clicked, which makes all car motion stop:

```
    <BUTTON onclick="stopMotion">Stop Motion</BUTTON>

    <P>Requires 800 x 600 (or better) resolution and Microsoft
    Internet Explorer 4.</P>
</DIV>
</BODY>
</HTML>
```

And that, my friends, is what makes the roving cars page do its thing.

SIZING OBJECTS

Just as you can change the position of an object by altering its *top* and *left* CSS properties, you can change the size of an object by altering its *width* and *height* CSS properties. Figure 9-14 shows a funky example in which the reader initially sees just a page with a button and some text. Clicking the button makes a tiny balloon appear out of nowhere. The balloon grows, as shown in Figure 9-15, until it fills the screen, and then it pops and disappears. As an added twist, the button disappears as well.

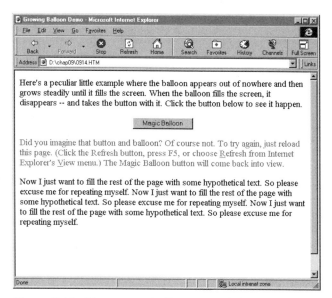

Figure 9-14. *The growing balloon example before the button is clicked.*

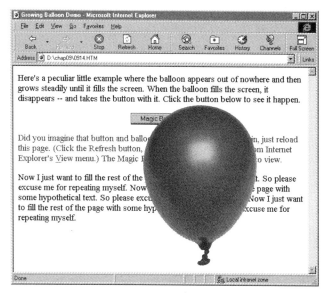

Figure 9-15. *The balloon starts growing after the button is clicked.*

Figure 9-16 shows the top half of the document source for the growing balloon page, which includes everything in the head section. The script initially creates some public variables named *newWidth*, *newHeight*, *newTop*, and *newLeft*. These variables are used to calculate the size and position of the balloon with each timeout.

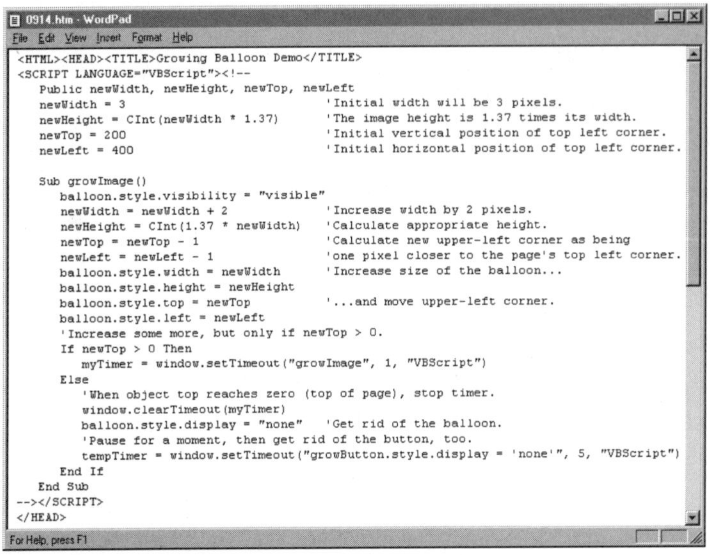

Figure 9-16. *The top half of the document source for the growing balloon page.*

```
<HTML><HEAD><TITLE>Growing Balloon Demo</TITLE>
<SCRIPT LANGUAGE="VBScript"><!--
    Public newWidth, newHeight, newTop, newLeft
    'Initial width will be 3 pixels.
    newWidth = 3
    'Image height is 1.37 times width.
    newHeight = CInt(newWidth * 1.37)
    'Initial vertical position of top left corner.
    newTop = 200
    'Initial horizontal position of top left corner.
    newLeft = 400
```

You might wonder about that *newHeight = CInt(newWidth * 1.37)* statement. Its purpose is to ensure that as the image grows, it maintains the same *aspect ratio*—the same relationship between height and width. This prevents the image from getting distorted as it grows.

How do I know that the ratio of the width to the height in the balloon.gif image is 1.37? Well, I opened balloon.gif in Paint Shop Pro and rested the mouse pointer on that image. Paint Shop Pro's status bar told me the size of the image: .

333 pixels wide and 455 pixels tall. I divided 455 by 333 and ended up with 1.366366..., which I rounded to 1.37 for simplicity. Thus, 1.37 is the aspect ratio of this particular image.

When assigning a size to an image, you must use a whole number. An image can't be part of a pixel wide. The *CInt()* VBScript function does that for you—it rounds the result of multiplying the *newWidth* value by 1.37 to the nearest integer.

Next in the page comes the sub procedure named *growImage*. When called, this procedure makes the balloon visible, increases its width by two pixels, and calculates a new height based on the new width. It also calculates a new upper-left corner position for the object by subtracting 1 from the *newTop* and *newLeft* variables:

```
Sub growImage()
    balloon.style.visibility = "visible"
    'Increase width by 2 pixels.
    newWidth = newWidth + 2
    'Calculate appropriate height.
    newHeight = CInt(1.37 * newWidth)
    'Calculate new upper-left corner position.
    newTop = newTop - 1
    newLeft = newLeft - 1
```

The newly calculated values are then applied to the CSS properties that size and position the balloon:

```
    'Increase size of the balloon...
    balloon.style.width = newWidth
    balloon.style.height = newHeight
    '...and move upper-left corner.
    balloon.style.top = newTop
    balloon.style.left = newLeft
```

Next comes the decision-making part of the procedure. If the *newTop* value is greater than 0, the top of the object hasn't reached the top of the page yet. Hence the procedure pauses for a moment to give the screen a chance to refresh. Then the procedure calls itself to further expand and reposition the balloon:

```
    'Increase some more, but only if newTop > 0.
    If newTop > 0 Then
        myTimer = window.setTimeout("growImage", 1, "VBScript")
```

When the *newTop* value reaches 0, the show is over. The timeout is cleared to stop the growth of the object. Then the *display* property of both the balloon and the button is set to *none*, which makes both objects disappear. The timeout used in this part of the script (shown on the next page) is there simply to give the balloon a moment to completely disappear before the button disappears.

```
    Else
        'When object top reaches zero (top of page), stop timer.
        window.clearTimeout(myTimer)
        'Get rid of the balloon.
        balloon.style.display = "none"
        'Pause for a moment, then get rid of the button, too.
        tempTimer = window.setTimeout _
            ("growButton.style.display = 'none'", 5, "VBScript")
    End If
End Sub
--></SCRIPT>
</HEAD>
```

The body of this document is shown in Figure 9-17. An *<IMG>* tag places the balloon on the page as an absolutely positioned object and initially makes it invisible. I didn't bother to give it an initial size or position because it's invisible; the balloon gets its subsequent size and position values from the *growImage* sub procedure after that procedure makes it visible. The *<IMG>* tag also contains the *ID* attribute that assigns the name *balloon* to the object:

```
<BODY>
<!-- Size, position, and hide the balloon. -->
<IMG ID="balloon" SRC="balloon.gif" STYLE="position:absolute;
visibility:hidden">
```

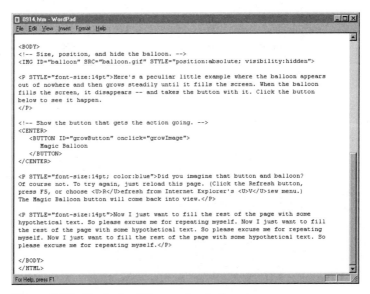

Figure 9-17. *The body of the growing balloon page.*

The rest of the document body is just the text that appears in the page and the button that launches the *growImage* sub procedure:

```
<P STYLE="font-size:14pt">Here's a peculiar little example where the
balloon appears out of nowhere and then grows steadily until it
fills the screen. When the balloon fills the screen, it disappears --
and takes the button with it. Click the button below to see it happen.
</P>

<!-- Show the button that gets the action going. -->
<CENTER>
    <BUTTON ID="growButton" onclick="growImage">
        Magic Balloon
    </BUTTON>
</CENTER>

<P STYLE="font-size:14pt; color:blue">Did you imagine that button
and balloon? Of course not. To try again, just reload this page.
(Click the Refresh button, press F5, or choose <U>R</U>efresh from
Internet Explorer's <U>V</U>iew menu.) The Magic Balloon button will
come back into view.</P>

<P STYLE="font-size:14pt">Now I just want to fill the rest of the
page with some hypothetical text. So please excuse me for repeating
myself. Now I just want to fill the rest of the page with some
hypothetical text. So please excuse me for repeating myself. Now I
just want to fill the rest of the page with some hypothetical text.
So please excuse me for repeating myself.</P>

</BODY>
</HTML>
```

DRAG-AND-DROP OBJECTS

As an Internet Explorer 4 web author, you can give your visitors the ability to drag-and-drop objects on a web page. Figure 9-18 on the next page shows a sample web page with a bunch of little graphic images. The smaller images to the left of the face can all be dragged around the page and dropped wherever. The reader can drag objects onto and off of the oval to make up faces, as in the example in Figure 9-19, also on the next page.

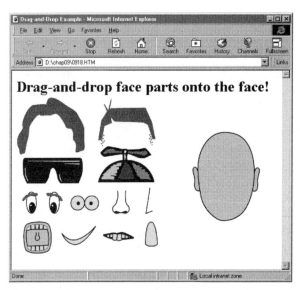

Figure 9-18. *A page with drag-and-drop capability at first glance.*

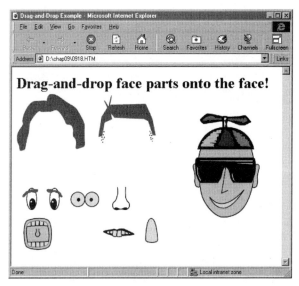

Figure 9-19. *The drag-and-drop page after some shapes have been dragged onto the oval.*

Figure 9-20 shows the graphic images used in the drag-and-drop page. Each is a GIF file with a transparent background. My very first step in creating this was to create and save all those images.

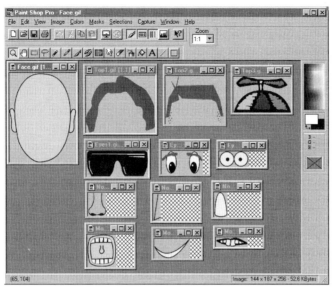

Figure 9-20. *Little graphic images used in the drag-and-drop page.*

Let's look behind the scenes to see what this page does to enable drag-and-drop objects. Figure 9-21 on the next page shows some of the head section of the page's document source. The *<STYLE>…</STYLE>* tags define an embedded style for images. The style sets the *position* CSS attribute of all images (*<IMG>* tags) in the page to *absolute*. This saves me from having to put *STYLE= "position:absolute;…"* into every *<IMG>* tag later in the page:

```
<!-- Make all images in the page absolutely positioned. -->
<STYLE TYPE="text/css"><!--
   IMG {position:absolute}
--></STYLE>
```

Next, the scripts are created. First the page declares four public variables named *thisObject*, *dragOK*, *xOffset*, and *yOffset*. The *dragOK* variable is initially assigned a value of False:

```
<SCRIPT LANGUAGE="VBScript"><!--
   Public thisObject, dragOK, xOffset, yOffset
   dragOK = False
```

```
0918.htm - WordPad
File  Edit  View  Insert  Format  Help
<HTML><HEAD><TITLE>Drag-and-Drop Example</TITLE>
<!-- Make all images in the page absolutely positioned. -->
<STYLE TYPE="text/css"><!--
   IMG {position:absolute}
--></STYLE>
<SCRIPT LANGUAGE="VBScript"><!--
   Public thisObject, dragOK, xOffset, yOffset
   dragOK = False
   'On mouse down, see if object is draggable and, if it is, set up variables.
   Sub document_onmousedown()
      If window.event.button = 1 Then
         If window.event.srcElement.tagName="IMG" and window.event.srcElement.id <> "face" Then
            Set thisObject = window.event.srcElement
            dragOK = True
            xOffset = window.event.offsetX
            yOffset = window.event.offsetY
            thisObject.style.zindex = 3
         End If
      End If
   End Sub

   'Keep the upper-left corner of the object near the mouse pointer as
   'the reader drags the object around on the page.
   Sub document_onmousemove()
      If window.event.button = 1 And dragOK Then
         newLeft = window.event.x - xOffset
         newTop = window.event.y - yOffset
         thisObject.style.left = newLeft
         thisObject.style.top = newTop
         window.event.returnValue = False
         window.event.cancelBubble = True
      End If
   End Sub
For Help, press F1
```

Figure 9-21. *The top of the document source for the drag-and-drop page.*

The roles played by these variables in later scripts are summarized below:

- *thisObject*—the object that the reader is dragging or attempting to drag

- *dragOK*—set to True for objects that the reader is allowed to drag, and set to False otherwise

- *xOffset*—the distance from the mouse pointer to the top of the object being dragged

- *yOffset*—the distance from the mouse pointer to the left edge of the object being dragged

The first sub procedure in the page, *document_onmousedown()*, is triggered whenever the mouse pointer is hovering over the document and the reader presses one of the mouse buttons. The procedure first determines whether the reader pressed the main mouse button (typically the left one). (The main mouse button is number 1.)

```
'On mouse down, see if object is draggable and, if it is,
'set up variables.
Sub document_onmousedown()
   If window.event.button = 1 Then
```

If, indeed, the main mouse button is being held down, the script also has to determine whether the object under the mouse pointer is draggable. In my sample page, I need a "rule" that says, "Any image except the one named *face* is draggable," because the image named *face* is the gray oval-shaped face outline, and I prefer that the reader drag things to the face rather than drag the face around. Here is the *If…Then* statement that allows all images—except the one named *face*—to be dragged around the page:

```
If window.event.srcElement.tagName = "IMG" and _
window.event.srcElement.id <> "face" Then
```

WARNING In this book, the lengthy lines of code wrap to a second line so they'll fit within the margins of the printed page. When you're typing actual code in a web page, you can break most code statements into two or more lines. With HTML code, this can easily be done by just breaking a long line in the appropriate spot. With VBScript code, you break a long line in the appropriate spot, but you must also add a space and the line continuation character (_), as shown above. The character is an underscore and must be preceded by a space. Also, you cannot add a comment after a line continuation character on the same line.

By the time the code below is executed, the mouse pointer is definitely resting on a draggable image with the main mouse button held down. So this procedure sets the global variable named *dragOK* to True. Then the script determines the distance from the left edge of the object to the mouse pointer, using the *window.event.offsetX* property, and it stores that number in the variable named *xOffset*. The distance between the mouse pointer and the top of the object is calculated and stored in the variable named *yOffset*. (As you'll see in the *document_onmousemove()* sub procedure, the *xOffset* and *yOffset* values let us keep the upper-left corner of the object in sync with the mouse pointer position—hence the "dragging" effect.) In this example, *thisObject.style.zindex = 3* puts the object at a higher level than the other objects in the page. That way, as the reader drags the object across the page, it passes over, rather than under, the other objects.

```
            Set thisObject = window.event.srcElement
            dragOK = True
            xOffset = window.event.offsetX
            yOffset = window.event.offsetY
            thisObject.style.zindex = 3
        End If
    End If
End Sub
```

The next sub procedure, *document_onmousemove()*, is executed whenever the mouse button moves across the page. This procedure first checks to see whether the *dragOK* variable is set to True (indicating that the mouse pointer is over a draggable image), and it checks to see that that the main (left) mouse button is still being held down (*window.event.button = 1*):

```
'Keep the upper-left corner of the object near the mouse pointer
'as the reader drags the object around on the page.
Sub document_onmousemove()
   If window.event.button = 1 And dragOK Then
```

Since the reader is trying to drag an image, the next step is to reposition the upper-left corner of the object as the mouse moves so that the object follows the mouse pointer around. Here's the code that does it all:

```
newLeft = window.event.x - xOffset
newTop = window.event.y - yOffset
thisObject.style.left = newLeft
thisObject.style.top = newTop
```

Just to make sure that no higher-level event handlers are influenced by any of this, we send back a "false" result to prevent the object from responding to the button activity, and we cancel event bubbling:

```
window.event.returnValue = False
window.event.cancelBubble = True
   End If
End Sub
```

At some point, the reader will drop the object (by releasing the mouse button). The procedure below executes whenever the mouse button is released. The procedure sets the *dragOK* variable back to False (since we can assume that the reader isn't dragging any more.) In this example, the image is placed back at layer 2 because that's where it was before the dragging started:

```
'Once the reader releases the mouse button, the item has been
'dropped.
Sub document_onmouseup()
   dragOK = False
   thisObject.style.zindex = 2
End Sub
--></SCRIPT>

</HEAD>
```

Figure 9-22 shows the *document_onmouseup()* sub procedure and the rest of the drag-and-drop page—the body of the document that contains the text and the image (*<IMG>* tags) that display the pictures. Note that one image is named *face* using the *ID* attribute. That's the only image in this page that I *don't* want dragged around. And as you might recall, I set up the *document_onmousedown()* sub procedure to accept any image except the one named *face*.

Don't forget that for this example to work, all the images must be positioned absolutely on the page. You don't see the *STYLE="position:absolute..."* business in the *<IMG>* tag, however. But that's only because I already made absolute positioning the default style for all the images in the page. I did that using the *<STYLE>...</STYLE>* tags near the top of the document.

The drag-and-drop procedures presented here are fairly portable. By that I mean you can generally copy all three scripts into any page to bring drag-and-drop capabilities to that page. The only adjustment you need to make is in the *If...Then* statement for the first procedure, which determines whether the item under the mouse pointer is draggable.

In my example, the rule is, "If it's an image but not the image named *face*, it's draggable." The *If window.event.srcElement.tagName = "IMG" and window.event.srcElement.id <> "face" Then* statement in the *document_onmousedown()* procedure makes that decision in our example.

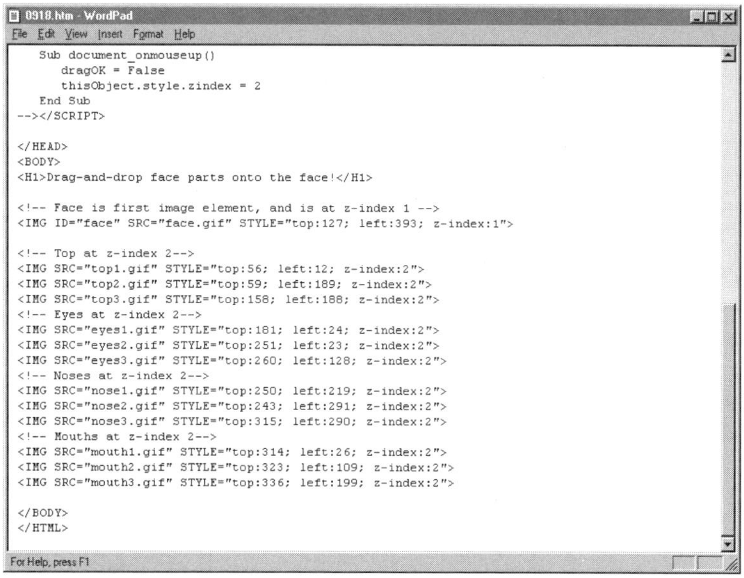

```
    Sub document_onmouseup()
        dragOK = False
        thisObject.style.zindex = 2
    End Sub
--></SCRIPT>

</HEAD>
<BODY>
<H1>Drag-and-drop face parts onto the face!</H1>

<!-- Face is first image element, and is at z-index 1 -->
<IMG ID="face" SRC="face.gif" STYLE="top:127; left:393; z-index:1">

<!-- Top at z-index 2-->
<IMG SRC="top1.gif" STYLE="top:56; left:12; z-index:2">
<IMG SRC="top2.gif" STYLE="top:59; left:189; z-index:2">
<IMG SRC="top3.gif" STYLE="top:158; left:188; z-index:2">
<!-- Eyes at z-index 2-->
<IMG SRC="eyes1.gif" STYLE="top:181; left:24; z-index:2">
<IMG SRC="eyes2.gif" STYLE="top:251; left:23; z-index:2">
<IMG SRC="eyes3.gif" STYLE="top:260; left:128; z-index:2">
<!-- Noses at z-index 2-->
<IMG SRC="nose1.gif" STYLE="top:250; left:219; z-index:2">
<IMG SRC="nose2.gif" STYLE="top:243; left:291; z-index:2">
<IMG SRC="nose3.gif" STYLE="top:315; left:290; z-index:2">
<!-- Mouths at z-index 2-->
<IMG SRC="mouth1.gif" STYLE="top:314; left:26; z-index:2">
<IMG SRC="mouth2.gif" STYLE="top:323; left:109; z-index:2">
<IMG SRC="mouth3.gif" STYLE="top:336; left:199; z-index:2">

</BODY>
</HTML>
```

Figure 9-22. *The* document_onmouseup() *sub procedure and the body for the drag-and-drop page.*

If you want all absolutely positioned elements in a web page to be draggable, you can change that procedure to something like this:

```
'On mouse down, see if object is draggable and, if it is,
'set up variables.
Sub document_onmousedown()
   If window.event.button = 1 and _
   window.event.srcElement.style.position = "absolute" Then
     Set thisObject = window.event.srcElement
     dragOK = True
     xOffset = window.event.offsetX
     yOffset = window.event.offsetY
     thisObject.style.zindex = 3
   End If
End Sub
```

> **NOTE**   Be aware that the above procedure might not work with objects that have their position attribute defined in an external or embedded style sheet. You might need to specify *position:absolute* in an inline style.

Another approach might be to assign the same *ID*, say *dragMe*, to every draggable item in the web page, like this:

```
<BODY>
<!-- Non-draggable object below -->
<IMG ID="face" SRC="face.gif"
STYLE="position:absolute; top:127; left:393; z-index:1">

<!-- Draggable objects below -->
<IMG ID="dragMe" SRC="top1.gif"
STYLE="position:absolute; top:56; left:12; z-index:2">

<IMG ID="dragMe" SRC="top2.gif"
STYLE="position:absolute; top:59; left:189; z-index:2">
```

Then you can use the *document_onmousedown()* sub procedure shown below to limit dragging to objects that contain an *ID="dragMe"* attribute:

```
Sub document_onmousedown()
   If window.event.button = 1 and _
   window.event.srcElement.id = "dragMe" Then
     Set thisObject = window.event.srcElement
     dragOK = True
     xOffset = window.event.offsetX
     yOffset = window.event.offsetY
     thisObject.style.zindex = 3
   End If
End Sub
```

However you go about it, you should make sure that any item that is to be draggable is positioned absolutely in the page using *STYLE= "position:absolute..."*. And you should ensure that you have some means of identifying objects that the reader is allowed to move, so you can set up the appropriate *If* condition in the *document_onmousedown()* sub procedure.

A HANDY TOOL FOR POSITIONING

As I write this chapter, I have yet to come across a wysiwyg HTML editor that lets you design your web page by dragging objects into position on the page. Figuring out the *top* and *left* CSS attributes is often something of a guessing game. I do have a little tool that can help, however. The "tool" is actually two files, one named 2Dhelp.htm and the other named grid.gif, which is the graph-paper background you saw back in Chapter 8.

Bear in mind that these "tools" are actually a couple of files I created for my own personal use and are not fancy at all. Neither one is an HTML editor or a "product" that comes with documentation and technical support. I only include them here because I've found them useful in my own work and I think that you might also find them useful.

> **TIP** A must-have tool for web designers and authors is a shareware product called Screen Ruler. As the name implies, it's a ruler that you can actually use on your screen. You must try it! You can pick up a shareware evaluation version from www.infinet.com/~microfox/.

Anyway, let me explain what the two files are about and how I use them. The grid.gif background acts as a piece of graph paper to help you position and align objects on the page. When you see the grid in color, be aware that the blue lines are 100 pixels apart. The lighter gray lines are 10 pixels apart. The sole purpose of grid.gif is to give you visual reference points for the pixel position of any area on the page.

The 2Dhelp.htm page automatically displays grid.gif when you open it. That page also contains a script that shows, in the status bar, exactly where the mouse pointer is resting. So you can simply point to some place on the page and then look at the status bar for the top and left settings to use to position the upper-left corner of an object.

The status bar also displays some additional information. For example, when the mouse pointer is resting on an object, the status bar shows you a name to identify the object, the tag name that defines the object, and the *top, left, zIndex*, and *position* property settings.

Furthermore, if the object you're pointing to contains a *STYLE= "position:absolute..."* setting in its HTML tag, you can drag that object around the grid while viewing your page in Internet Explorer 4. The status bar will always show you where the upper-left corner of the object is. So when you get the object to a position on the page that you like, you can look at the T: and L: values on the status bar. You can use these values to set the object's *top* and *left* CSS attributes in the document source if you want the object to always appear at its current location in the page. That information takes a lot of the guesswork out of figuring out the correct top and left settings for an object's upper-left corner.

You might need to fool around with 2Dhelp.htm for a while to really get the hang of it. As I said, it's not really a full-blown, user-friendly software product. It might help, however, if I give you an example of how I use it when positioning an object absolutely in a web page.

Let's say I've copied 2Dhelp.htm and grid.gif from the companion CD or from my web site to the folder where I initially create new web pages. When I'm ready to create a new web page that will use positioning, I don't start with a blank page. Instead, I open 2Dhelp.htm. To get started, I right-click on my 2Dhelp.htm file and send it to FrontPage Express. (In Figure 9-23, I'm about to create a new web page in FrontPage Express.) Right off the bat you can see the grid.gif background. The little icon in the page indicates that this page contains scripting code. You should never place anything *below* that icon in the page.

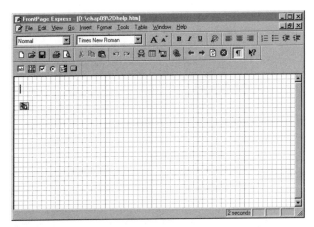

Figure 9-23. *2Dhelp.htm is opened in FrontPage Express to help create a new web page.*

To use the capabilities of 2Dhelp.htm without changing it, I choose Save As from the File menu and then save the document as a file with a new name. For example, I can name the page 2Dtest.htm.

Next I begin developing my page in FrontPage Express as I normally do. (The 2Dhelp.htm page doesn't really offer any help while I edit a document.)

For example, I might type in some text and plop in an image. I can specify that the image is positioned absolutely while in FrontPage Express by using the Image Properties dialog box as shown here:

1. Right-click on the image and choose Image Properties.

2. In the Image Properties dialog box, click the Extended button.

3. In the Extended Attributes dialog box, click the Add button.

4. In the Name/Value Pair dialog box, type *STYLE* in the Name text box. In Value text box, type the style setting that will absolutely position the image.

5. Click OK in each of the dialog boxes.

Figure 9-24 shows how I absolutely positioned the beanboy.gif image 10 pixels from the top and 10 pixels from the left. Even though adding the position setting does not change the appearance of the image in FrontPage Express, in a moment I'll show you the benefit of doing this.

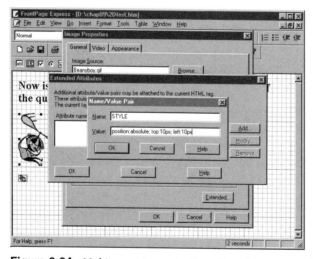

Figure 9-24. *Making an image in FrontPage Express an absolutely-positioned object.*

Now let's say I'm finished with this page for the moment. In FrontPage Express, I choose Exit from the File menu, save the changes, and then open it in Internet Explorer 4. This is when 2Dhelp.htm starts showing its stuff. For one thing, as I move the mouse pointer around on the screen, the status bar always shows exactly where the mouse pointer is, using a message like this one:

```
Top=100 Left=200
```

That little feature is pretty handy because it lets you point to any position on the page and see immediately what *top* and *left* settings are needed to put the upper-left corner of the object at that exact mouse position.

If I move the mouse pointer to an object in the page, the status bar gives me some brief information about the object. For instance, if the mouse pointer is resting on an object named *myObj* (via an *ID* attribute), the status bar shows something like this:

```
Top=100 Left=200 myObj <tag> T:y L:x Z:z P:absolute
```

If the mouse pointer is resting on an object that doesn't have an *ID* attribute in its HTML tag, the information in the status bar might look something like this:

```
Top=100 Left=200 all(i) <tag> T:y L:x Z:z P:absolute
```

Everything is abbreviated because there isn't much room in the status bar. So let me tell you what the information means. The Top and Left items show the current mouse position in pixels, as usual. Then the part that shows *myObj* or *all(i)* shows the name of the object that's under the mouse pointer. The "English" name you provided via the *ID* attribute (*myObj* in this example) appears only if the current object has such a name. If the current object doesn't have a name, the status bar shows the *all* collection's name for the object. For example, if you see *all(11)*, you can refer to this object as *document.all(11)* from within your scripting code.

The *tag* item refers to the name of the HTML tag that defines the object— for example, *IMG* for an image. The T: value (*y*) shows the *top* property of the current object, and the L: value (*x*) shows the *left* property of the current object. The Z: value (*z*) shows the object's *zIndex* property, and P shows the *position* property, such as absolute or relative.

Now let's say I'm pointing to the beanyboy image. Remember that in FrontPage Express I gave that object an absolute position in the page by adding a *STYLE* attribute to its *<IMG>* tag (via the Extended button in the Image Properties dialog box). Because I made that change in FrontPage Express, I can now drag that image around in Internet Explorer. The status bar will keep me informed of the object's current upper-left position. For instance, in Figure 9-25, I dragged the image down and to the right.

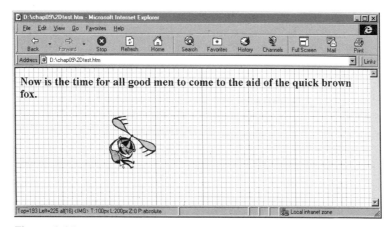

Figure 9-25. *2Dtest.htm after the beanyboy image has been dragged.*

The status bar tells me quite a few things about the beanyboy image in its current position:

```
all(16) <IMG> T:100px L:200px Z:0 P:absolute
```

The *all(16)* tells me that I didn't name this object. But I can refer to it as *document.all(16)* in an y code I write, if I want. The T: and L: positions are the current upper-left corner of the object in the web browser. If I want to place the image at that position when the reader first opens the page, I know that in my document source I need to set the image's *top* attribute to 100px and its *left* attribute to 200px. Actually, I can make that change right in Internet Explorer. I just choose Source from the View menu to get to the document source. I then find the tag for the image and adjust the image's attributes, as shown in Figure 9-26, down near the bottom of the window where the *<img src...>* tag starts.

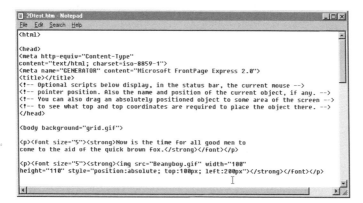

Figure 9-26. *Setting up a new starting position for the beanyboy image.*

I can then close and save the document source and click the Refresh button in Internet Explorer to bring the browser's view of the document up to date with the document's current source content.

To summarize, if I create a web page starting with 2Dhelp.htm rather than with a blank page, and then I add an absolutely positioned object to that page, I can drag that object around when viewing the page in Internet Explorer. As I do that, the status bar will show me the current *top* and *left* properties of the object in pixels. When I find the position I want for the object, I jot down the object's current position as defined by the T: and L: indicators on the status bar. To make the image *always* appear at that position when the reader first opens the page, I simply take that information presented by T: and L: and copy it into the *top* and *left* CSS attributes in the document source. It's not as easy as falling off a log, but it does reduce the guesswork and trial and error involved in determining the exact pixel coordinates for a certain place in the page.

Of course, before you go public with your page, you'll probably want to remove the 2Dhelp scripts and the grid.gif background. To get rid of the background grid, delete the *BACKGROUND="grid.gif"* setting in the *<BODY>* tag of the document. To get rid of the 2Dhelp scripts, you can delete the *<SCRIPT>* …*</SCRIPT>* tags, and everything between them, at the bottom of the document. The status bar will return to its normal state, which is what you'll want your visitors to see.

> **WARNING** Be sure to remove 2Dhelp's *document_onmouse...* sub procedures before creating any procedures of your own with the same names. Otherwise, your scripts might conflict with the scripts built into 2Dhelp.htm, which will really confuse things!

I won't bother to describe all the code in 2Dhelp.htm. If you get curious and decide to take a look, you'll see that it's basically the same code that's in the drag-and-drop sample page you saw in the previous section. I simply added some *window.status* statements to ensure that the status bar always shows useful information.

SUMMARY

Well, we've certainly covered lots of ground here in showing what you can do with CSS positioning and some VBScript code. In a nutshell, all the stylistic information about an object's position on the page is exposed to VBScript, and in most cases, VBScript can alter CSS positioning properties to move and resize objects right before the reader's eyes. With a little more fancy scripting footwork, you can also add drag-and-drop capability to your pages. To summarize the important points:

- VBScript code can move an absolutely positioned object in a web page by changing the object's *top, left,* and *zIndex* CSS properties.

- To make an object glide across the screen, you need to set up a sub procedure that pauses between repositioning to allow the screen to catch up with the code as it's running.

- Use can use the *setTimeout()* method of the *window* object to define a pause or a timeout between object repositioning. Use the *clearTimeout()* method to stop the timeout.

- To size an image, use code to alter its *height* and *width* CSS properties.

- To give your readers the ability to drag-and-drop objects on your page, you can use the *document_onmousedown()*, *document_on-mousemove()*, and *document_onmouseup()* procedures shown in this chapter. But...

- You might need to modify *document_onmousedown()* to make sure it accepts only objects that you've designated as "draggable" in your own web page.

In the next chapter, we'll look at some more fancy stuff you can do with dynamic text and fonts in your web pages.

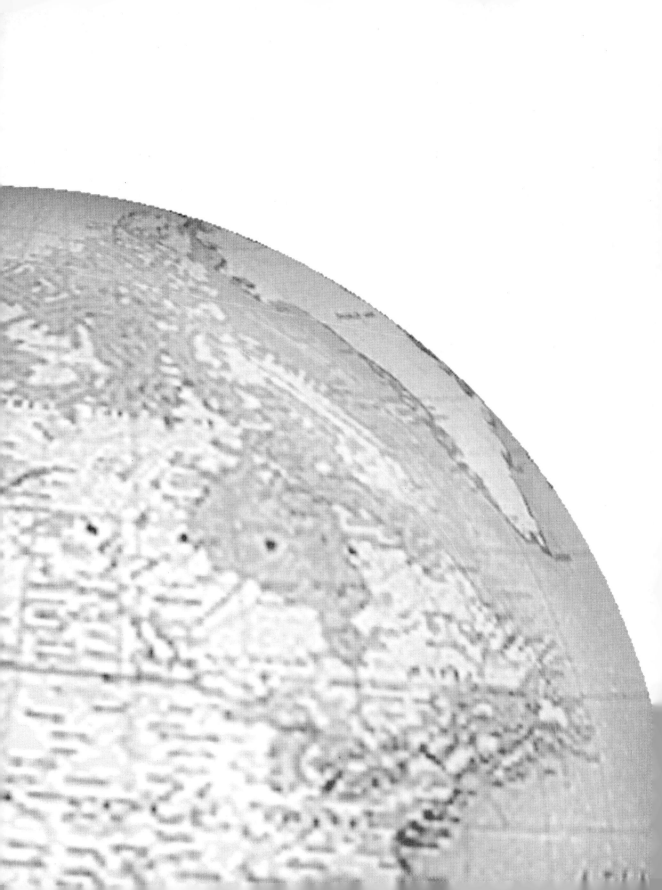

Chapter 10

Dynamic Text, Embedded Fonts

In this chapter, I'll discuss techniques that focus on text and, to some extent, on HTML tags. For starters, we'll look at *dynamic content,* a feature of Microsoft Internet Explorer 4 that lets you programmatically change text and HTML tags on the fly, as a visitor is viewing your page. Then we'll look at passing data from one page to another and using passwords. And finally, we'll cover fonts, particularly the new embedded fonts technology. Here are the topics we'll cover:

- Replacing and deleting text and HTML tags using VBScript code
- Using VBScript code to insert text and HTML tags
- Using cookies to pass data from one page to another
- Simple password protection
- Specifying fonts
- Embedding fonts

DYNAMIC CONTENT

In previous chapters, we saw some examples of using VBScript code to change the appearance (style) of objects, the size and position of objects, and so forth—even though we haven't yet discussed how to change the actual *content* of a web page. In Internet Explorer 4, all the content (the text and tags that define the page) is *dynamic,* which means it can be changed at any time using VBScript code.

The Internet Explorer 4 Dynamic HTML Object Model offers four properties that make it easy to programmatically change virtually any content in a web page:

- *objectName.innerText*—gets or sets the text (only) between the object's opening and closing tags.

- *objectName.innerHTML*—gets or sets the text and tags between the object's opening and closing tags.

- *objectName.outerText*—gets or sets the text (only) of the entire object, including the opening and closing tags that define the object.

- *objectName.outerHTML*—gets or sets the text and tags of the entire object, including the opening and closing tags that define the object.

To help you envision the difference between "inner" and "outer" in these four properties, Figure 10-1 shows a sample object named *myHeading*. The "inner" stuff, as you can see, refers only to what's *between* the *<H1>* and *</H1>* tags that define the object. The "outer" stuff refers to the entire object, including the tags that define the object.

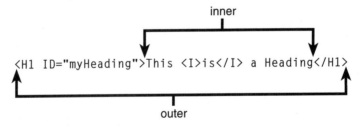

Figure 10-1. *The difference between "inner" and "outer" properties.*

The difference between *Text* and *HTML* in the properties is that *innerText* and *outerText* always return just the raw text, without any HTML tags. The *innerHTML* and *outerHTML* properties return the text and the tags. Thus, since the name of the object in Figure 10-1 is *myHeading*, Table 10-1 shows what the four different properties—*innerText*, *innerHTML*, *outerText*, and *outerHTML*—return when you refer specifically to that *myHeading* object.

Table 10-1

THE *INNERTEXT*, *INNERHTML*, *OUTERTEXT*, AND *OUTERHTML* PROPERTIES

Property	*What It Returns*
document.all.myHeading.innerText	This is a Heading
document.all.myHeading.innerHTML	This <I>is</I> a Heading
document.all.myHeading.outerText	This is a Heading
document.all.myHeading.outerHTML	<H1 id=myHeading>This <I>is</I> a Heading</H1>

A couple of important points to remember: Even though I used an object defined by *<H1>...</H1>* tags in the example, you're not limited to those tags. All four "inner" and "outer" properties are available with many HTML tags, including *<P>...</P>* tags, *<SPAN>...</SPAN>* tags, *<BUTTON>...</BUTTON>* tags, and *<MARQUEE>...</MARQUEE>* tags, just to name a few. Furthermore, all four properties share the read-write distinction, which means you can get, and also change, the value of the property. Let's look at some examples.

Replacing Text and Tags

To replace the text or the tags of an object, you set the appropriate property to some new value. For instance, to change only the internal text of an object, you replace the *innerText* property with some new value. Or, if the new text will be formatted with HTML, you set the *innerHTML* property to some new value. To change an object altogether, you set its *outerText* or *outerHTML* property to some new value.

Figure 10-2 on the next page shows a sample HTML document that contains four objects named *myHeading*, *banner1*, *banner2*, and *button1*. That document also contains a script that uses the various "inner" and "outer" properties to change those objects.

```
1002.htm - WordPad

File  Edit  View  Insert  Format  Help

<HTML><HEAD><TITLE>Inner/Outer Demo</TITLE>

<SCRIPT LANGUAGE="VBScript"><!--
    Sub button1_onclick()
        'Change inner and outer properties of sample objects.
        document.all.myHeading.innerText = "Everything Has Changed!"
        document.all.banner1.innerHTML = "<FONT SIZE='+5'>Banner1 here has changed</FONT>"
        document.all.banner2.outerText = "This banner isn't even a banner any more."
        document.all.button1.innerText = "You've already clicked me"
    End Sub
--></SCRIPT>

</HEAD>
<BODY><CENTER>
<!-- The myHeading object -->
<H1 ID="myHeading" ALIGN="center">Sample Inner/Outer Properties</H1>

<!-- The banner1 object --><P>
<MARQUEE ID="banner1" ALIGN="middle" BGCOLOR="#FFFF00" HEIGHT="50" WIDTH="80%">
    <FONT SIZE="+5">I am a scrolling marquee message</FONT>
</MARQUEE></P>

<!-- The banner2 object --><P>
<MARQUEE ID="banner2" ALIGN="middle" BGCOLOR="#FFFF00" HEIGHT="50" WIDTH="80%">
    <FONT SIZE="+5">I am also a scrolling marquee message</FONT>
</MARQUEE></P>

<!-- The button1 object --><P>
<BUTTON ID="button1">
    Click to See Changes
</BUTTON></P>
</CENTER></BODY></HTML>

For Help, press F1
```

Figure 10-2. *An HTML document that uses "inner" and "outer" properties.*

Figure 10-3 shows how that page looks when it's first opened in Internet Explorer. Figure 10-4 shows how it looks after the button is clicked. As you can see, the text of the *myHeading* and *banner1* objects has changed. The entire *banner2* object has been replaced by plain text (because we changed the *outerText* of that tag). And even the text on the label of the button has changed.

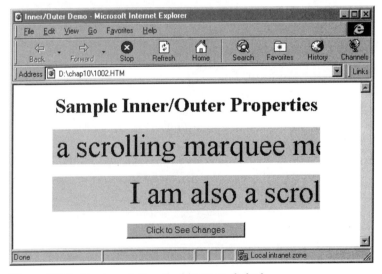

Figure 10-3. *The page before the button is clicked.*

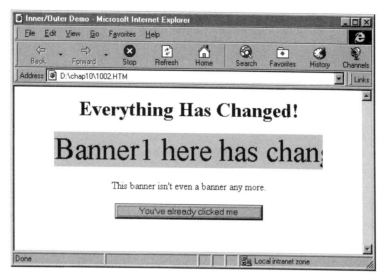

Figure 10-4. *The page after the button is clicked.*

Note that in this example, the object named *banner2* ceases to exist altogether because I've replaced the entire object, which includes the *<MARQUEE ID="banner2"...>...</MARQUEE>* tags with some plain text. Therefore, clicking the button a second time actually causes the following error message to appear:

```
Object doesn't support this property or method:
'document.all.banner2'.
```

The error message here is a little misleading. The real problem is that when the button is clicked a second time, the script attempts to alter the *banner2* object, which at that point no longer exists in the document.

CODING IS NOT EDITING

Don't confuse editing a document with using code to programmatically change the appearance of a document. When you edit the document source directly using a program such as FrontPage Express or WordPad and then save those changes, you permanently change the web page. When VBScript code changes the content of a page, only the copy of the page that's currently visible on the screen is altered. The original, underlying document source is not altered in any way.

To prevent the reader from trying to click the button a second time, you can have the script disable the button. To disable a button, you set its *disabled* property to True. Here's how the script looks if I add the appropriate statement to that script:

```
Sub button1_onclick()
   'Change inner and outer properties of sample objects.
   document.all.myHeading.innerText = "Everything Has Changed!"
   document.all.banner1.innerHTML = _
      "<FONT SIZE='+5'>Banner1 here has changed</FONT>"
   document.all.banner2.outerText = _
      "This banner isn't even a banner any more."
   document.all.button1.innerText = "You've already clicked me"
   document.all.button1.disabled = True
End Sub
```

Another approach is to keep the *banner2* object even after radically changing its appearance. You can do that by putting the marquee within a paragraph and naming the paragraph *banner2*, like this:

```
<!-- The banner2 object -->
<P ID="banner2">
<MARQUEE ALIGN="middle" BGCOLOR="#FFFF00" HEIGHT="50" WIDTH="80%">
   <FONT SIZE="+5">I am also a scrolling marquee message</FONT>
</MARQUEE></P>
```

The script can be rewritten to change only the stuff inside the *<P ID= "banner2">…</P>* tags, like this:

```
document.all.banner2.innerHTML = "This banner isn't even a banner
any more."
```

The *banner2* object still exists in this example because only the *<MARQUEE…>…</MARQUEE>* tags and text in the *banner2* object have been replaced. Now, clicking the button a second time does not generate an error message.

Let's look at another example in which a scrolling marquee changes appearance. Touching the marquee makes the message stop scrolling and appear as regular text on the page. Moving the mouse pointer away from the text changes it back to a marquee. Figure 10-5 shows a web page that has that capability, and Figure 10-6 shows the document source for that page.

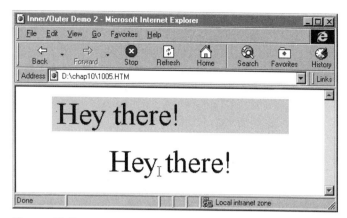

Figure 10-5. *A page with a marquee that changes to static text on mouse contact.*

```
<HTML><HEAD><TITLE>Inner/Outer Demo 2</TITLE>

<SCRIPT LANGUAGE="VBScript"><!--
    'Change banner1 to static text when mouse pointer is touching it.
    Sub banner1_onmouseover()
        newInnerTag = "Hey there!"
        document.all.banner1.innerHTML = newInnerTag
    End Sub
    'Change banner1 back to a marquee when the mouse pointer leaves.
    Sub banner1_onmouseout()
        newInnerTag = "<MARQUEE ALIGN='middle' BGCOLOR='#FFFF00' "
        newInnerTag = newInnerTag & "HEIGHT='50' WIDTH='80%'>"
        newInnerTag = newInnerTag & "Hey there!"
        newInnerTag = newInnerTag & "</MARQUEE>"
        document.all.banner1.innerHTML = newInnerTag
    End Sub
--></SCRIPT>

</HEAD>
<BODY><CENTER><FONT SIZE="+5">
<!-- The banner0 object -->
<P ID="banner0">
<MARQUEE ALIGN="middle" BGCOLOR="#FFFF00" HEIGHT="50" WIDTH="80%">
    Hey there!
</MARQUEE>
</P>
<!-- The banner1 object -->
<P ID="banner1">
<MARQUEE ALIGN="Middle" BGCOLOR="#FFFF00" HEIGHT="50" WIDTH="80%">
    Hey there!
</MARQUEE>
</P>
</FONT></CENTER></BODY></HTML>
```

Figure 10-6. *The document source for the page shown in Figure 10-5.*

Now let me explain how it works. The *banner1* object is actually a paragraph defined by *<P ID="banner1">...</P>* tags. Initially, that object contains a marquee that's defined by the *<MARQUEE>...</MARQUEE>* tags:

```
<!-- The banner1 object -->
<P ID="banner1">
<MARQUEE ALIGN="middle" BGCOLOR="#FFFF00" HEIGHT="50" WIDTH="80%">
    Hey there!
</MARQUEE>
</P>
```

The first procedure in the page, shown below, is fired whenever the mouse pointer touches the *banner1* object:

```
'Change banner1 to static text when mouse pointer is touching it.
Sub banner1_onmouseover()
    newInnerTag = "Hey there!"
    document.all.banner1.innerHTML = newInnerTag
End Sub
```

So after that procedure is executed, the inner HTML of the *banner1* object is replaced with some plain text. The tags for the *banner1* object now actually look like this:

```
<!-- The banner1 object -->
<P ID="banner1">
Hey There!
</P>
```

Removing the mouse pointer from the *banner1* object fires the second procedure in the page, as shown below:

```
'Change banner1 back to a marquee when the mouse pointer leaves.
Sub banner1_onmouseout()
    newInnerTag = "<MARQUEE ALIGN='middle' BGCOLOR='#FFFF00'"
    newInnerTag = newInnerTag & "HEIGHT='50' WIDTH='80%'>"
    newInnerTag = newInnerTag & "Hey there!"
    newInnerTag = newInnerTag & "</MARQUEE>"
    document.all.banner1.innerHTML = newInnerTag
End Sub
```

I broke this procedure into several lines to make it fit within WordPad's margins. But basically what it does is create a new string of text, in a variable named *newInnerTag*, that contains *<MARQUEE ALIGN='middle' BGCOLOR= '#FFFF00' HEIGHT='50' WIDTH='80%'>Hey there!</MARQUEE>*. That gets substituted for the inner HTML of *banner1*, so behind the scenes the underlying tags for the *banner1* object look like this again:

```
<!-- The banner1 object -->
<P ID="banner1">
<MARQUEE ALIGN='middle' BGCOLOR='#FFFF00' HEIGHT='50' WIDTH='80%'>
   Hey there!
</MARQUEE>
</P>
```

Thus, the *banner1* object looks like a scrolling banner once again.

Figure 10-7 shows an example in which a script changes the label that appears on a button face each time the reader clicks the button. The HTML that defines the button is quite simple, as shown below. Here you can see that the button label (also the *innerText* for the button object) is initially *Click Me*:

```
<!-- The button1 object -->
<BUTTON ID="button1">
   Click Me
</BUTTON>
```

```
1007.htm - WordPad
File Edit View Insert Format Help

<HTML><HEAD><TITLE>Inner/Outer Demo 3</TITLE></HEAD>
<BODY><CENTER>
<P>Click the button below a few times, and watch its label change.</P>

<!-- The button1 object -->
<BUTTON ID="button1">
   Click Me
</BUTTON>

<!-- Script to change button1 label with each mouse click -->
<SCRIPT FOR="button1" EVENT="onclick" LANGUAGE="VBScript"><!--
    currentLabel = document.all.button1.innerText
    If currentLabel = "Click Me" Then
       currentLabel = "<B>Do it Again</B>"
    Else
       currentLabel = "Click Me"
    End If
    document.all.button1.innerHTML = currentLabel
--></SCRIPT>

</CENTER>
</BODY></HTML>

For Help, press F1
```

Figure 10-7. *An HTML document containing a simple script to change a button label every time the reader clicks the button.*

EFFECTS ON THE *ALL* COLLECTION

When a script alters an *innerHTML* or *outerHTML* property, the document's entire object model changes instantly to reflect the new page. Thus, objects in the various collections, including the *all* collection, might not be numbered in the same way they were before the script was executed. To avoid potential problems, use the *ID* attribute to name objects in your page rather than using the built-in *collection.item(index)* syntax to refer to objects by their position in the page.

The script, which fires every time the reader clicks the button, uses the *innerText* property to determine what label is currently shown on the button. It stores that text in a variable named *currentLabel*:

```
<!-- Script to change button1 label with each mouse click -->
<SCRIPT FOR="button1" EVENT="onclick" LANGUAGE="VBScript"><!--
    currentLabel = document.all.button1.innerText
```

The *If...Then...Else* statement then decides how to change the label. If the button label is *Click Me*, the *currentLabel* variable is set to *<B>Do it Again</B>*. Otherwise, *currentLabel* is set to *Click Me*. The last statement then replaces the *innerHTML* of the button label with whatever is in the *currentLabel* variable. Using *innerHTML* rather than *innerText* in that line ensures that the *<B>...</B>* tags in the alternative label are interpreted as tags rather than as text and hence makes the button display its label in boldface:

```
    If currentLabel = "Click Me" Then
        currentLabel = "<B>Do it Again</B>"
    Else
        currentLabel = "Click Me"
    End If
    document.all.button1.innerHTML = currentLabel
--></SCRIPT>
```

Figure 10-8 shows the page after the button is clicked once.

Now let's look at how you might use the inner and outer properties to delete text and tags in a document.

Figure 10-8. *The page whose source is shown in Figure 10-7, after the button is clicked.*

Deleting Text and Tags

In Chapter 8, you learned how to make an object visible or invisible by altering the *display* or *visibility* property of the object. You can also delete some text or delete an object altogether. To delete text within an object, you change its *innerText* or *innerHTML* property to a zero-length string. To delete an object, you replace its *outerText* or *outerHTML* with a zero-length string (*""*).

Figure 10-9 shows a simple HTML document that contains four "named" objects (objects with *ID* attributes): a heading object named *mainTitle*, a paragraph object named *firstPara*, and two button objects named *button1* and *button2*. I'll show you how the page behaves and how the scripts make it behave that way.

When the reader first opens the page, the page title, first paragraph, and two buttons are plainly visible. Clicking the first button executes a little script that shows the names of all the named objects in that page—*mainTitle*, *firstPara*, *button1*, and *button2*, as you can see in Figure 10-10 on the next page.

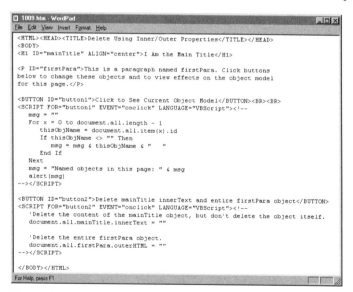

```
1009.htm - WordPad
File  Edit  View  Insert  Format  Help
<HTML><HEAD><TITLE>Delete Using Inner/Outer Properties</TITLE></HEAD>
<BODY>
<H1 ID="mainTitle" ALIGN="center">I Am the Main Title</H1>

<P ID="firstPara">This is a paragraph named firstPara. Click buttons
below to change these objects and to view effects on the object model
for this page.</P>

<BUTTON ID="button1">Click to See Current Object Model</BUTTON><BR><BR>
<SCRIPT FOR="button1" EVENT="onclick" LANGUAGE="VBScript"><!--
    msg = ""
    For x = 0 to document.all.length - 1
        thisObjName = document.all.item(x).id
        If thisObjName <> "" Then
            msg = msg & thisObjName & "   "
        End If
    Next
    msg = "Named objects in this page: " & msg
    alert(msg)
--></SCRIPT>
<BUTTON ID="button2">Delete mainTitle innerText and entire firstPara object</BUTTON>
<SCRIPT FOR="button2" EVENT="onclick" LANGUAGE="VBScript"><!--
    'Delete the content of the mainTitle object, but don't delete the object itself.
    document.all.mainTitle.innerText = ""

    'Delete the entire firstPara object.
    document.all.firstPara.outerHTML = ""
--></SCRIPT>

</BODY></HTML>
For Help, press F1
```

Figure 10-9. *An HTML document with a script to replace the* innerText *and* outerHTML *properties with zero-length strings.*

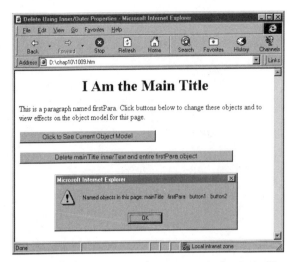

Figure 10-10. *The page whose source is shown in Figure 10-9, after the first button is clicked.*

Clicking the second button replaces the *innerText* of the *mainTitle* object with a zero-length string and replaces the entire *outerHTML* of the *firstPara* object with a zero-length string. The effect, of course, is to delete the *mainTitle* text and to delete the *firstPara* object. Clicking the first button again redisplays the names of all named objects in the page. As you can see in the alert box, the page no longer contains an object named *firstPara*.

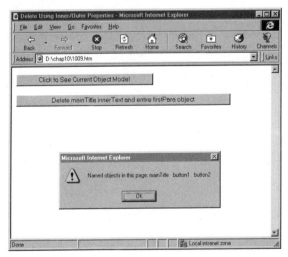

Figure 10-11. *The result of clicking the second button and then the first button in the sample page.*

Inserting Text and Tags

You can add new text and tags to a document or an object in your web page using the *insertAdjacentHTML()* method. The syntax for this method is:

```
objectName.insertAdjacentHTML where, string
```

objectName is the complete name of the object into which you want to insert text or tags. *where* is one of the keywords *BeforeBegin*, *AfterBegin*, *BeforeEnd*, or *AfterEnd*. *string* is the new text or HTML to be inserted.

Figure 10-12 shows where the keywords position the insertion, using a heading named *myHeading* as the object. Figure 10-13 shows an HTML document that uses *insertAdjacentHTML()* to insert sample text and tags into a page when the reader clicks a button.

Figure 10-12. insertAdjacentHTML() *keywords indicating where text and tags will be inserted.*

```
1013.htm - WordPad
File Edit View Insert Format Help

<HTML><HEAD>
<TITLE>Demo insertAdjacentHTML Method</TITLE>
</HEAD>

<!-- Entire web page is named wholePage -->
<BODY ID="wholePage">

<!-- A few sample objects -->
<H1 ID="first">Hello There</H1>
<H1 ID="second">Hello There</H1>
<H1 ID="third">Hello There</H1>
<H1 ID="fourth">Hello There</H1>

<BUTTON ID="myButton">
Click to Insert Stuff
</BUTTON>

<SCRIPT FOR="myButton" EVENT="onclick" LANGUAGE="VBScript"><!--
   'Insert some HTML tags and text at the top of the page.
   document.all.wholePage.insertAdjacentHTML "AfterBegin", "<H2>Tippy Top</H2>"

   'Insert HTML text in the first, second, third, and fourth objects.
   document.all.first.insertAdjacentHTML "BeforeBegin", "<I>Yowsa</I>"
   document.all.second.insertAdjacentHTML "AfterBegin", "<I>Yowsa</I>"
   document.all.third.insertAdjacentHTML "BeforeEnd", "<I>Yowsa</I>"
   document.all.fourth.insertAdjacentHTML "AfterEnd", "<I>Yowsa</I>"

   'Insert some HTML text at the bottom of the page.
   document.all.wholePage.insertAdjacentHTML "BeforeEnd", "<H2>The End</H2>"
--></SCRIPT>

</BODY></HTML>

For Help, press F1
```

Figure 10-13. *An HTML document that uses* insertAdjacentHTML() *to insert text and HTML into a page.*

Notice in Figure 10-13 that the body of the document is actually an object named *wholePage*. The page also contains several smaller objects named *first*, *second*, *third*, and *fourth*, each defined by the *<H1>...</H1>* tags. Figure 10-14 shows how the page in Figure 10-13 looks when first opened in Internet Explorer.

Figure 10-15 shows how the page looks after the button is clicked. As you can see, lots of text is inserted into the page.

Figure 10-14. *The page from Figure 10-13 when first opened in Internet Explorer.*

Figure 10-15. *The page from Figure 10-14 after the button is clicked.*

First, the text *Tippy Top*, formatted as a level-2 heading, is inserted at the top of the document because of the statement *document.all.wholePage. insertAdjacentHTML "AfterBegin", "<H2>Tippy Top</H2>"*.

The *first* heading has the italicized word *Yowsa* inserted before it. The *document.all.first.insertAdjacentHTML "BeforeBegin", "<I>Yowsa</I>"* does the insertion. *Yowsa* is on a separate line because the text that follows is in an *<H1>* tag, and an *<H1>* tag always starts its text on a new line.

The italicized word *Yowsa* is also inserted into the *second* heading. Since this text is placed in the *AfterBegin* position, the new text is inside the *<H1>...* *</H1>* tags and therefore is formatted as a level-1 heading.

The *third* heading has the word *Yowsa* inserted within the heading because the string is placed using the *BeforeEnd* position. The word *Yowsa* is also inserted after the *fourth* heading. Again, this one is on a separate line because any text following an *</H1>* tag is always placed on a new line.

At the very bottom of the document is a new line of text reading *The End*, formatted as a level-2 heading and placed just before the end of document body using the statement *document.all.wholePage.insertAdjacentHTML "BeforeEnd", "<H2>The End</H2>"*.

The bottom line here is that the *innerText*, *innerHTML*, *outerText*, and *outerHTML* properties allow you to replace or even delete text and HTML in many places throughout a document. The *insertAdjacentHTML()* method lets you insert text and HTML tags almost anywhere in a document.

> **NOTE** Be aware that there is an *insertAdjacentText()* method, which works about the same way as the matching *insertAdjacentHTML() method* but only allows you to insert text. I typically just use *insertAdjacentHTML()* because it will handle both HTML and text.

Some Caveats

There are a few little caveats to keep in mind when using these properties and the *insertAdjacentHTML()* method. For one, the *innerText*, *outerText*, *inner-HTML*, and *outerHTML* properties don't work until the document is fully loaded. Therefore, it's important to use these properties only in scripts that are bound to some specific event. If you want to execute such scripts as soon as a page is opened, put them in a sub procedure named *window_onload()*.

The *innerHTML* and *outerHTML* properties will fail if you attempt to insert a tag that makes no sense in the current context. For example, take a look at the text, tags, and script on the next page.

```
<BODY>
<P ID="firstGraf">
This is a paragraph. It is also an object named firstGraf.
</P>
<BUTTON ID="myButton">
   Click Me
</BUTTON>
<SCRIPT FOR="myButton" EVENT="onclick" LANGUAGE="VBScript">
   document.all.firstGraf.innerHTML = "<P>Try to put this in.</P>"
</SCRIPT>
</BODY>
```

Opening this page and clicking its button causes an error message to pop up on the screen because the statement *document.all.firstGraf.innerHTML = "<P>Try to put this in.</P>"* tries to put a paragraph within a paragraph. That is, the script attempts to make the underlying source code look like this:

```
<P ID="firstGraf">
<P>
Try to put this in.
</P></P>
```

But you're not allowed to nest the *<P>...</P>* tags within another set of *<P>...</P>* tags. Doing so makes no sense and confuses the web browser, which in turn displays an error message. If you change the script to something like this

```
<SCRIPT FOR="myButton" EVENT="onclick" LANGUAGE="VBScript">
   document.all.firstGraf.innerText = "Try to put this in."
</SCRIPT>
```

the script will work fine because it's just replacing the text inside the *firstGraf* object, like this:

```
<P ID="firstGraf">
Try to put this in.
</P>
```

As I mentioned earlier, inserting HTML into your document changes the underlying object model for that document. For instance, let's say your document initially contains 15 objects, *document.all.item(0)* through *document.all-.item(14)*. Then a script inserts a new object near the middle. The document now contains 16 objects, *document.all.item(0)* through *document.all.item(15)*. Any objects that are *below* the newly inserted object will also have their subscripts (*sourceIndex* properties) incremented by 1.

Finally, as I also mentioned earlier, when you replace, insert, or delete text or tags using code, you alter only the appearance of the document on the screen. The original, underlying document source is not altered in any way. The only way to permanently alter the underlying document source for a page is to edit the page directly using an editor such as FrontPage Express or WordPad.

Global Replacements

Replacing, deleting, or inserting something *globally* means making that change through the entire document. For example, let's say you want to personalize a web page by sprinkling the reader's name throughout the page. When a visitor first comes to the page, he or she is greeted with an input box like the one shown in Figure 10-16. After typing in a first name and clicking the OK button, the reader is then taken to the actual page. There, the reader's name (Bob, in our example) appears in boldface several times in the page, as shown in Figure 10-17.

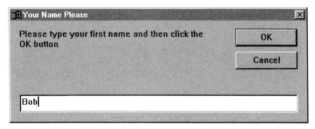

Figure 10-16. *An input box that asks for the visitor's first name.*

Figure 10-17. *The visitor's first name, Bob, is sprinkled throughout the page.*

Figure 10-18 on the next page shows the document source for the page. Let's see what makes it tick. The only line of code that's executed immediately is the *Public visitorName* statement, which simply defines a global variable that will be used to store the visitor's name:

```
<HTML><HEAD><TITLE>Global Replace Demo</TITLE>
<SCRIPT LANGUAGE="VBScript">
    Public visitorName
```

```
1016.htm - WordPad                                              _ □ X
File  Edit  View  Insert  Format  Help

<HTML><HEAD><TITLE>Global Replace Demo</TITLE>
<SCRIPT LANGUAGE="VBScript">
    Public visitorName
    Sub window_onload()
        'After page loads, get the reader's name.
        prmpt="Please type your first name and then click the OK button"
        title="Your Name Please"
        visitorName = inputBox(prmpt, title)
        'Add boldface tags to visitorName
        visitorName = "<B>" & visitorName & "</B>"

        'Globally fill in reader's name between all <SPAN ID="visitorName">...</SPAN> tags.
        'First define the collection, and set up a loop to step through it.
        Dim nameCollection
        Set nameCollection = document.all("visitorName")
        For x = 0 to nameCollection.length - 1
            nameCollection.item(x).innerHTML = visitorName
        Next
    End Sub
</SCRIPT>
</HEAD>
<BODY>
<!-- In this page the <SPAN ID="visitorName"></SPAN> tags act as a placeholder -->
<!-- which gets filled in with the visitorName value after the visitor enters -->
<!-- his or her name into the inputBox presented by the opening script. -->
<H1>Welcome <SPAN ID="visitorName"></SPAN></H1>
<P>So glad you came by, <SPAN ID="visitorName"></SPAN>. As you may
already know, <SPAN ID="visitorName"></SPAN>, this page is just a simple
demo of inserting text globally throughout a document.</P>
<P>Well, <SPAN ID="visitorName"></SPAN>, that's all for now. Bye!</P>
</BODY></HTML>

For Help, press F1
```

Figure 10-18. *The document source for the page shown in Figure 10-17.*

The *window_onload* procedure is executed after the page is fully loaded. Delaying this script in this manner ensures that the *innerHTML* property used a little later in the script will work properly. The script initially displays the input box asking for the visitor's name. After the visitor types a name and clicks OK, that name is stored in the *visitorName* variable. As a little bonus, this example also adds the boldface (*<B>…</B>*) tags around that name variable:

```
Sub window_onload()
    'After page loads, get the reader's name.
    prmpt = "Please type your first name then click the OK button"
    title = "Your Name Please"
    visitorName = inputBox(prmpt, title)
    'Add boldface tags to visitorName
    visitorName = "<B>" & visitorName & "</B>"
```

At this point, the *visitorName* variable contains something like *<B>Bob</B>* or *<B>Sally</B>* or whatever name the visitor typed in, with boldface tags added. Next comes the job of putting the reader's name into the document. To simplify that task, I set up little placeholders in the body of the document where I want the name to appear. Wherever the *<SPAN ID="visitorName"></SPAN>* tags appear is where I want to insert the name. The next chunk of code does the job. The first two lines define a pointer to an object (a collection, actually) of all the objects named *visitorName*:

```
Dim nameCollection
Set nameCollection = document.all("visitorName")
```

By default, all collections support a *length* property that indicates how many items are in the collection. To step through each item in the collection, we need to have the loop count from 0 (zero) to the length of the collection minus 1. The loop shown below will step through the collection of *<SPAN ID="visitorName"> </SPAN>* tags and put *visitorName* right in between those tags:

```
    For x = 0 to nameCollection.length - 1
        nameCollection.item(x).innerHTML = visitorName
    Next
  End Sub
</SCRIPT>
</HEAD>
```

That's all the code you need to get the job done. The rest of the page is the body of the document, including the *<SPAN ID="visitorName"></SPAN>* tags that act as placeholders for the visitor's name:

```
<H1>Welcome <SPAN ID="visitorName"></SPAN></H1>
<P>So glad you came by, <SPAN ID="visitorName"></SPAN>. As you may
already know, <SPAN ID="visitorName"></SPAN>, this page is just a
simple demo of inserting text globally throughout a document.</P>
<P>Well, <SPAN ID="visitorName"></SPAN>, that's all for now.
Bye!</P>
</BODY></HTML>
```

As is always the case when using code to change a web page, the changes are never permanent in global replacements. That is, the visitor sees his or her name sprinkled throughout the page, but the underlying document source still contains the *<SPAN ID="visitorName"></SPAN>* tags where the visitor is seeing the name.

PASSING VARIABLE TEXT USING COOKIES

The previous example brings up a sticky question: "What if I want to insert the visitor's name throughout *several* pages in my web site?" This question is sticky because HTML is generally *stateless*—that is, your web browser makes no attempt to "remember" data from one page to the next. When a reader leaves a page, all VBScript variables that were created within that page—even the *Public* variables— cease to exist.

You can get around this problem by using a *cookie*. A cookie is actually a little chunk of text stored on the visitor's PC. The *document.cookie* property provides the basic ability to read and store data in cookies. To do the job right, you need some custom cookie-making procedures, but you don't have to write those procedures yourself because some programmer at Microsoft already has. I've included the necessary procedures on the book's companion CD and in the

Chapter 10 examples for this book at my web site (www.coolnerds.com). To use the procedures, just copy the file named cookies.vbs to the folder that the rest of your web pages are stored in.

Within any page that needs to access cookies, add these two tags:

```
<SCRIPT SRC="cookies.vbs" LANGUAGE="VBScript"></SCRIPT>
```

After you add those tags, you can use the *setCookie* sub procedure, the *getCookie()* function procedure, and the *killCookie* sub procedure that are defined within that file. The next sections will show you how.

> **NOTE** The .vbs file name extension is completely arbitrary—I just made it up to stand for VBScript. You can use just about any file name extension you like.

The *setCookie* Sub Procedure

You call the *setCookie* sub procedure in cookies.vbs with the following syntax:

```
setCookie cookieName, cookieValue
```

cookieName is a name you want to assign to the cookie, similar to a variable name in VBScript code. *cookieValue* is the value that you want to store in cookie—either a number, a literal string enclosed in quotation marks, or the name of a VBScript variable that contains the data you want to store in the cookie.

For example, the following code stores the name *Alan* in a cookie named *visitorNameCookie*:

```
<SCRIPT LANGUAGE="VBScript"><!--
   myName="Alan"
   setCookie "visitorNameCoookie" myName
--></SCRIPT>
```

The *getCookie()* Function Procedure

The *getCookie()* function procedure in cookies.vbs pulls data out of a cookie and lets you put that information into a VBScript variable. The syntax for *get-Cookie()* is:

```
variableName = getCookie(cookieName)
```

variableName is the name of the VBScript variable that will hold the cookie data in the current web page. *cookieName* is the name of the cookie as initially defined in the *setCookie* call.

For example, the following code takes whatever is stored in the *visitor-NameCookie* cookie and puts that value into a public variable named *visitorName*:

```
<SCRIPT LANGUAGE="VBScript"><!--
   Public visitorName
   visitorName = getCookie("visitorNameCookie")
--></SCRIPT>
```

The *getCookie()* function returns *NOT_FOUND* if the requested cookie doesn't exist. If, for instance, the PC executing the above statement doesn't have a cookie named *visitorNameCookie*, the *visitorName* variable will contain the string *NOT_FOUND*. No error message is generated when you attempt to access a nonexistent cookie.

The *killCookie* Sub Procedure

The *killCookie* sub procedure lets you get rid of a cookie. At this point, the cookies.vbs procedures create cookies that last as long as the current session (until the visitor exits his or her web browser). But if you want to get rid of a cookie before that, you can use the following syntax, where *cookieName* is the name of the cookie that you want to get rid of:

```
killCookie(cookieName)
```

For example, this statement gets rid of the cookie named *visitorNameCookie*:

```
killCookie("visitorNameCookie")
```

A Cookies Example

To illustrate the use of cookies in a practical setting, here are some sample pages presented from the perspective of a visitor to a site. When the reader opens the page named cookie.htm, an input box appears asking for his or her name. In Figure 10-19, the reader has typed *Wanda*. After the reader clicks the OK button, that name is sprinkled throughout the current page, as in Figure 10-20 on the next page.

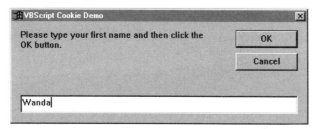

Figure 10-19. *The cookie.htm page asks for the visitor's name.*

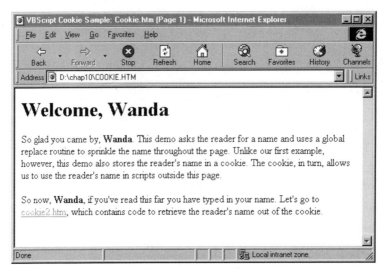

Figure 10-20. *The cookie.htm page after the reader types her name and clicks OK.*

Here's where the cookie comes in. Normally, it wouldn't be possible to carry the reader's name over to other pages in the web site because VBScript erases all the variables created by a page when that page is closed. But in this example, if the reader clicks the link to cookie2.htm—a new page—the visitor's name is carried over to that page, as shown in Figure 10-21. Code for managing cookies in both the cookie.htm and cookie2.htm pages makes this happen.

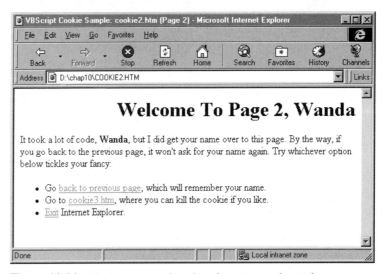

Figure 10-21. *The page named cookie2.htm "remembers" the visitor's name.*

Let me show you the document source for these two pages so you can see how I used the cookie procedures to make it all happen. Figures 10-22 and 10-23 show the document source for the cookie.htm file. Figure 10-24 on the next page shows the document source for the cookie2.htm page.

```
Cookie.htm - WordPad
File  Edit  View  Insert  Format  Help
<HTML><HEAD><TITLE>VBScript Cookie Sample: Cookie.htm (Page 1)</TITLE>

<SCRIPT LANGUAGE="VBScript"><!--
    'Let's just bail out if cookies aren't enabled.
    If Not navigator.cookieEnabled Then
        document.close()
        'Assumes page named nocookie.htm is in this same directory.
        location.href = "nocookie.htm"
    End If
--></SCRIPT>

<!-- setCookie, getCookie(), and killCookie are defined in cookies.vbs -->
<SCRIPT SRC="cookies.vbs" LANGUAGE="VBScript"></SCRIPT>
</HEAD>

<BODY>
<SCRIPT LANGUAGE="VBScript"><!--
    'Check to see if visitor name is already in cookie. If not, ask for that name now.
    Public visitorName
    visitorName = getCookie("visitorNameCookie")
    'If visitorNameCookie not found, get visitor name.
    If visitorName = NOT_FOUND Then
        msg = "Please type your first name and then click the OK button."
        visitorName = inputBox(msg, "VBScript Cookie Demo", "Your Name")
        While visitorName = ""
            visitorName = inputBox(msg, "VBScript Cookie Demo", "Your Name")
        Wend
    End If

    'One way or the other, the visitor's name is now in the visitorName variable.
For Help, press F1
```

Figure 10-22. *The top half of the document source for cookie.htm.*

```
Cookie.htm - WordPad
File  Edit  View  Insert  Format  Help
    'One way or the other, the visitor's name is now in the visitorName variable.
    'Put name into a cookie, under the name visitorNameCookie, for other pages to use.
    setCookie "visitorNameCookie", visitorName

    'This procedure is run after the page is loaded. Globally fill in the
    'visitor's name between <SPAN ID="visitorName">...</SPAN> tags.
    Sub window_onload()
        'First define the collection, and set up a loop to step through it.
        Dim nameCollection
        Set nameCollection = document.all("visitorName")
        For x = 0 to nameCollection.length - 1
            'Bold the visitor's name using the <B>...</B> tags.
            nameCollection.item(x).innerHTML = "<B>" & visitorName & "</B>"
        Next
    End Sub
--></SCRIPT>

<!-- And finally, onto the regular text, HTML, and placeholders of the document body.-->
<H1>Welcome, <SPAN ID="visitorName"></SPAN></H1>

<P>So glad you came by, <SPAN ID="visitorName"></SPAN>. This demo asks the reader for a
name and uses a global replace routine to sprinkle the name throughout the page.
Unlike our first example, however, this demo also stores the reader's name in a cookie.
The cookie, in turn, allows us to use the reader's name in scripts outside this page.</P>

So now, <SPAN ID="visitorName"></SPAN>, if you've read this far you have typed in your
name. Let's go to <A HREF="cookie2.htm">cookie2.htm</A>, which contains code to retrieve
the reader's name out of the cookie.</P>
</BODY></HTML>
For Help, press F1
```

Figure 10-23. *The bottom half of the document source for cookie.htm.*

```
Cookie2.htm - WordPad                                              _ □ X
File  Edit  View  Insert  Format  Help
<HTML><HEAD><TITLE>VBScript Cookie Sample: cookie2.htm (Page 2)</TITLE>
<!-- setCookie, getCookie(), and killCookie are defined in cookies.vbs -->
<SCRIPT SRC="cookies.vbs" LANGUAGE="VBScript"></SCRIPT>
</HEAD>
<BODY>
<SCRIPT LANGUAGE="VBScript"><!--
    'Get that visitor name value from the cookie.
    Public visitorName
    visitorName = getCookie("visitorNameCookie")
    'This procedure is run after the page is loaded. Globally fills in reader's name
    'between all <SPAN ID="visitorName">...</SPAN> tags.

    Sub window_onload()
       'First define the collection, and set up a loop to step through it.
       Dim nameCollection
       Set nameCollection = document.all("visitorName")
       For x = 0 to nameCollection.length - 1
          nameCollection.item(x).innerHTML = "<B>" & visitorName & "</B>"
       Next
    End Sub
--></SCRIPT>
<!-- And finally, onto the regular text, HTML, and placeholders of the document body.-->
<H1 ALIGN="right">Welcome To Page 2, <SPAN ID="visitorName"></SPAN></H1>
<P>It took a lot of code, <SPAN ID="visitorName"></SPAN>, but I did get your name over
to this page. By the way, if you go back to the previous page, it won't ask for your
name again. Try whichever option below tickles your fancy:
<UL>
<LI>Go <A HREF="cookie.htm">back to previous page</A>,
which will remember your name.</LI>
<LI>Go to <A HREF="cookie3.htm">cookie3.htm</A>,
where you can kill the cookie if you like.</LI>
<LI onclick="window.close()"><U STYLE="color:blue">Exit</U> Internet Explorer.</LI>
</UL></BODY></HTML>
For Help, press F1
```

Figure 10-24. *The document source for cookie2.htm.*

Source Code for the Cookies Example

Rather than nit-picking through every tag and line of code, I'd like to focus on the elements involved in managing the cookie in these examples. Starting with cookie.htm, the opening page, you can see the tags you need to make the procedures in cookies.vbs a part of this page:

```
<!-- setCookie, getCookie(), and killCookie -->
<!-- are defined in cookies.vbs -->
<SCRIPT SRC="cookies.vbs" LANGUAGE="VBScript"></SCRIPT>
```

Within the body of the document, this code attempts to pull a value out of a cookie named *visitorNameCookie*. That value gets stored in a public variable named *visitorName*:

```
<SCRIPT LANGUAGE="VBScript"><!--
   'Check to see if visitor name is already in cookie. If not, ask
   'for that name now.
   Public visitorName
   visitorName = getCookie("visitorNameCookie")
```

The next routine checks to see if the *visitorName* variable contains the string *NOT_FOUND*, which would indicate that the reader hasn't typed a name yet. If that's the case, the next routine displays an input box that asks for the reader's name:

```
'If visitorNameCookie not found, get visitor name.
If visitorName = NOT_FOUND Then
   msg = "Please type your first name and then click the OK button."
   visitorName = inputBox(msg, "VBScript Cookie Demo", "Your Name")
   While visitorName = ""
      visitorName = inputBox(msg, "VBScript Cookie Demo", "Your Name")
   Wend
End If
```

Finally, whatever name the reader typed into the input box is stored in a cookie named *visitorName*:

```
'Put name into a cookie, under the name visitorNameCookie, for
'other pages to use.
setCookie "visitorNameCookie", visitorName
```

The *visitorName* variable is then used to globally insert the reader's name within the *<SPAN ID="visitorName"></SPAN>* tags. To accomplish this task, I used the same code that I used in the "global replacement" example earlier in this chapter. The important point, however, is that at this juncture the cookie named *visitorNameCookie* definitely exists, and it contains whatever the reader typed in as a first name.

Now let's take a look at how cookie2.htm gets data out of the cookie. If you look at the cookie2.htm document source, you can see that it contains the tags needed to bring in the cookie procedures defined in cookies.vbs:

```
<!-- setCookie, getCookie(), and killCookie -->
<!-- are defined in cookies.vbs -->
<SCRIPT SRC="cookies.vbs" LANGUAGE="VBScript"></SCRIPT>
```

ARE COOKIES ENABLED?

Most web browsers give their users the option to disallow cookies on their PC. If your site relies on cookies, readers who have disabled their cookie acceptance won't be able to fully experience your site. You can use the *navigator.cookieEnabled* property to determine whether the reader's PC is willing to accept cookies.

If *navigator.cookieEnabled* returns True, you have nothing to worry about. Your cookies will work fine. But if *navigator.cookieEnabled* returns False, the visitor's PC will not accept the cookie. In that case, you might want to display some special instructions to that reader. The first script in the sample cookie.htm page shows an example of sending the reader to some other page (nocookies.htm) if the reader's browser is set to disable cookie use.

Within the body of the page, a script uses the *getCookie()* function to fish out the value of the cookie named *visitorName*. It stores that value in a public VBScript variable named *visitorName*:

```
<BODY>
<SCRIPT LANGUAGE="VBScript"><!--
    'Get that visitor name value from the cookie.
    Public visitorName
    visitorName = getCookie("visitorNameCookie")
```

That's really all the cookie-handling code this page needs. Once the *visitorName* variable has its value, remaining scripts can sprinkle the visitor's name throughout the page. The cookie2.htm file uses the same "global replacement" procedure that cookie.htm uses to accomplish that task.

This demo includes a third page, named cookie3.htm, that allows the visitor to kill the cookie. (In real life, it probably wouldn't be necessary to kill a cookie since the cookies are automatically killed off when the browser closes; I include this page only to illustrate the syntax of the *killCookie* procedure.) Figure 10-25 shows the cookie3.htm page from the visitor's perspective.

Figure 10-26 shows the document source for that page. Like the other two pages, cookie3.htm contains the tags needed to include the procedures of cookies.vbs in the current web page:

```
<!-- setCookie, getCookie(), and killCookie -->
<!-- are defined in cookies.vbs -->
<SCRIPT SRC="cookies.vbs" LANGUAGE="VBScript"></SCRIPT>
```

Within the body of the page is a button that, when clicked, checks whether the cookie named *visitorNameCookie* even exists. If it does exist, the statement *killCookie("visitorNameCookie")* is executed to get rid of it:

```
<CENTER><BUTTON ID="killer">Kill the Cookie</BUTTON></CENTER>

<SCRIPT FOR="killer" EVENT="onClick" LANGUAGE="VBScript"><!--
    'Get the cookie to make sure it exists.
    visitorName = getCookie("visitorNameCookie")
    If visitorName = NOT_FOUND then
       MsgBox("Cookie not found! Already deceased.")
    Else
       killCookie("visitorNameCookie")
       MsgBox("Cookie variable deceased.")
    End If
</SCRIPT>
```

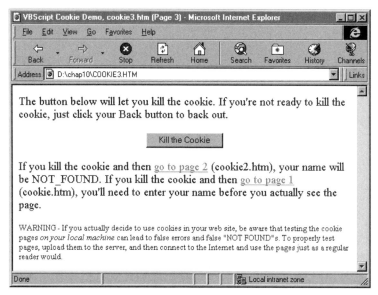

Figure 10-25. *A page named cookie3.htm lets the visitor kill the cookie.*

Figure 10-26. *The document source for cookie3.htm.*

If you decide to incorporate cookies into your own web site, remember that you don't need to reinvent the wheel and write a bunch of scripts to manage cookies. You can simply incorporate the cookies.vbs file into any web page that needs access to cookies. Within that page, you can use the *setCookie* sub procedure to create a cookie and use the *getCookie()* function procedure to read data out of a cookie and put it into a VBScript variable. If necessary, you can also use the *killCookie* sub procedure to delete a cookie when it's no longer needed.

SIMPLE PASSWORD PROTECTION

I occasionally get letters from readers asking if it's possible to set up simple password protection on rented web server space without the benefit of database connectivity. My reply is that, yes, you can set up a simple password system if every visitor that's allowed into the site uses the same password. Unfortunately, it's not possible to fully hide the underlying code, which exposes the password. So sophisticated visitors can get around the password protection just by examining the underlying code. But not many people would think to do that, so you do get some protection from this approach.

> NOTE   A secure web site with database connectivity allows you to build a database of visitor's names and the passwords they choose. Code in the home page can check the database to verify that a visitor has entered a valid name and password.

The approach I'm discussing involves creating a small script file like the one shown in Figure 10-27. I named my file password.vbs, but you might want to name yours something a little less obvious to probing eyes. When you create a similar page of your own, replace *SESAME* with whatever password you want to use for your site.

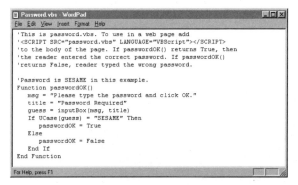

Figure 10-27. *The password.vbs file contains a function named* passwordOK() *that checks for a password.*

To put the password.vbs file to use, you need to include the script in a page using the *<SCRIPT SRC=…>* syntax. Then you set up an *If…Then…Else* statement that sends the reader to one page if she enters the correct password and sends her to some other page if she enters the wrong password. Figure 10-28 shows an HTML document that asks for the password. Visitors who enter the correct password are sent to page2.htm. Visitors who enter the wrong password are sent to nogo.htm.

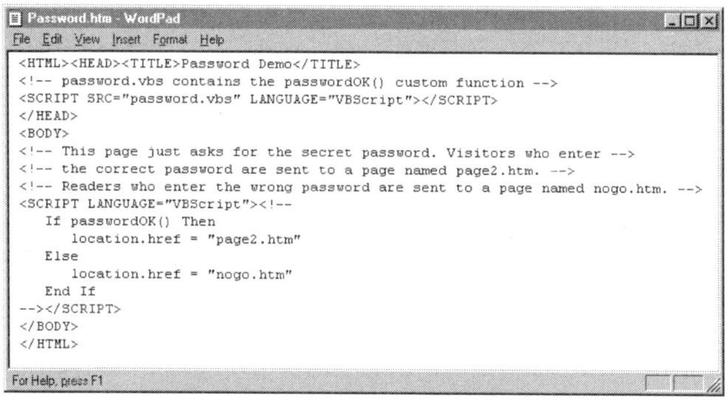

Figure 10-28. *A sample HTML document that uses password.vbs to screen visitors.*

I should add that any reader who views the document source will see only what you see in Figure 10-28. The password is not in plain view in the document source. Some sophisticated readers might be able to figure out that the password appears in password.vbs, and they might be able to download that file to determine what the password is. So this is no ironclad protection. But it's cheap—you don't need your own web server, database connectivity, and all that other stuff that sends the cost of publishing a web site into the tens of thousands of dollars!

ALL ABOUT FONTS

Since we've been discussing text-related issues in this chapter, this is probably a good place to get into some nitty-gritty details of using fonts in web pages. First, let's review the basics. As you probably know, there are two ways to specify a font in a web page. One way is via the HTML *<FONT>…</FONT>* tags. For example, the following tags try to display a heading in Comic Sans MS font at a large size (font sizes range from 1 to 7, where 7 is the largest) and in purple:

```
<FONT FACE="Comic Sans MS" SIZE="7" COLOR="purple">
I am a Heading
</FONT>
```

As an alternative to using the *<FONT>* tag, you can specify the font in a style. For example, the *<STYLE>...</STYLE>* tags below try to display all H1 headings in the page in Comic Sans MS font at 48 points in the color purple:

```
<HEAD>
<STYLE TYPE="text/css"><!--
H1 {font-family: "Comic Sans MS";
    font-size: 48pt;
    color: purple}
--></STYLE>
</HEAD>

<BODY>
<H1>I am a Heading</H1>
</BODY>
```

The reason I say that both approaches *try* to display their headings in the Comic Sans MS font is that they might not be able to! The Comic Sans MS font will appear only if the visitor happens to have the Comic Sans MS font already installed on his or her system. If the visitor does not have that font installed, the text will appear in the default typeface (Times Roman on most machines).

This creates something of a problem for web designers because it means you really cannot predict how your text will look on any given person's PC. But fortunately, there are a couple of solutions to this problem.

Specifying Multiple Fonts

You can specify multiple fonts in a *<FONT>* tag in order of preference. For instance, suppose you really want to use Comic Sans MS to display a heading. But if the visitor doesn't have that particular font, you'll settle for Helvetica (common on the Macintosh) or Arial (common on Windows-based PCs). You can specify this order or preference by including all three font names, separated by commas, in the *FACE* attribute of the *<FONT>* tag. Be sure to list the fonts in decreasing order of preference, with your preferred font listed first.

For example, the tags below display a heading in Comic Sans MS if it's available. If that font isn't available, the heading is displayed in Helvetica. If neither Comic Sans nor Helvetica is available on the visitor's PC, the heading is displayed in Arial. If none of those three fonts is available, the heading is displayed in the default font:

```
<FONT FACE="Comic Sans MS, Helvetica, Arial" SIZE="7" COLOR="purple">
I am a Heading
</FONT>
```

To accomplish the same thing using CSS attributes, you list the font names in order of preference, separated by commas, next to the font-face attribute, as shown below:

```
<STYLE TYPE="text/css"><!--
H1 {font-family: "Comic Sans MS, Helvetica, Arial";
    font-size: 48pt;
    color: purple}
--></STYLE>
</HEAD>

<BODY>
<H1>I am a Heading</H1>
</BODY>
```

Specifying multiple fonts gives you *some* increased control over how your page will look on a visitor's screen. But it still doesn't give you total control. There is, however, a new technology emerging that will allow you to embed specific fonts in your page to ensure that all readers see your page the same way. That newly emerging technology is called OpenType, and it is the topic of the rest of this chapter.

Embedding Fonts in a Web Page

As I write this section, embedded fonts and OpenType are still on the drawing board—they're not fully standardized technologies. The truth is, I'm guessing that all of this will be available by the time you read this book. And I'm also guessing that things will work the way I say they work here. But since I can't be 100 percent sure, I hope you'll supplement what I tell you with more current information (as discussed in the section titled "Current OpenType Information" later in this chapter)—especially if you have any problems with the techniques I describe. So with that megadisclaimer out of the way, here's the current game plan for how to embed fonts in your web pages.

You embed a font in a web page by using the *@font-face* CSS attribute and a URL that points to the font's location on the Internet. The font must be an OpenType font file with the .eot or .ote file name extension. When the reader opens a page that references an OpenType font file with the *@font-face* attribute, the browser first checks the reader's font download settings. Depending on these settings, the visitor might see the dialog box shown in Figure 10-29 on the next page. If the font is allowed to be used, the OpenType font file is automatically downloaded to the reader's PC, converted to a TrueType font, and temporarily installed. Internet Explorer 4 presently does not check to see if a version of the font is already installed on the reader's computer.

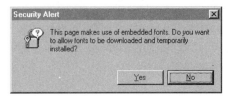

Figure 10-29. *A font about to be downloaded from the web.*

The syntax for embedding a font in your web pages is:

```
<STYLE TYPE="text/css"><!--
   @font-face {font-family: fontName;
               font-style: style;
               font-weight: weight;
               src: url(fontUrl)}
--></STYLE>
```

fontName is the name you will use to refer to this font throughout the current web page. *style* is any one of the valid words *normal*, *italic*, or *oblique*. *weight* is *normal*, *bold*, *bolder*, *lighter*, or a number of valid weight values. *fontURL* is a URL that points to the OpenType file.

Part of the trick, of course, is knowing where the OpenType files are located on the Internet. Unfortunately, I can't help you there because the technology isn't fully functional yet. I suspect, though, that you'll be able to buy OpenType fonts and store them on your own web server.

As a strictly hypothetical example, let's say I buy an OpenType font named Goofy and put it in a directory named fonts on my web server. The name of the file that contains the fonts is goofy.eot. Since the URL of my web site's home page is http://www.coolnerds.com, the exact location of that font would be http://www.coolnerds.com/fonts/goofy.eot.

CHANGING YOUR OWN FONT SECURITY

You can disable the warning message shown in Figure 10-29 on your own PC if you don't want to be prompted for permission every time a page wants to download a font. Just open Internet Explorer and choose Internet Options from the View menu. Click on the Security tab and select the appropriate zone from the Zone drop-down list. Select the Custom (for expert users) option, and then click the Settings button. In the Security Settings dialog box, scroll down to the Font Download options and change the setting from Prompt to Enable. Embedded fonts will be downloaded "behind the scenes" from this point on, without your having to respond to the dialog box.

To embed that font in a web page, I include the following embedded style in that page:

```
<HEAD>
<STYLE TYPE="text/css"><!--
   @font-face {font-family: goofy;
             font-style: normal;
             font-weight: normal;
             src: url(http://www.coolnerds.com/fonts/goofy.eot)}
--></STYLE>
</HEAD>
```

To use that font in a chunk of text later in the page, I use the regular *font-family* CSS attribute. For instance, if you want to use the Goofy font for all H1 headings, I can style H1 headings as follows:

```
<HEAD>
<STYLE TYPE="text/css"><!--
   @font-face {font-family: goofy;
             font-style: normal;
             font-weight: normal;
             src: url(http://www.coolnerds.com/fonts/goofy.eot)}

   H1 {font-family: goofy;
      font-size: 36pt}
--></STYLE>
</HEAD>
<BODY>
<H1>I am in 36 point Goofy font</H1>
...
</BODY>
```

I can also specify the embedded font in an inline style. For example, the tags below display a paragraph in the Goofy font at 18 points:

```
<P STYLE="font-family:goofy; font-size:18pt">Hi There</P>
```

Figure 10-30 on the next page shows the whole kit and caboodle within the context of a complete sample web page. Do keep in mind, however, that the example is strictly hypothetical. It won't work if you actually try it, because I really don't have a file named goofy.eot at http://www.coolnerds.com.

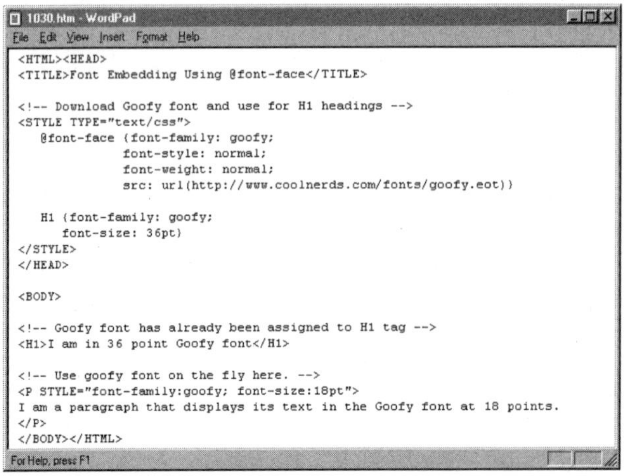

```
[ ] 1030.htm - WordPad                                        _ □ X
File  Edit  View  Insert  Format  Help
<HTML><HEAD>
<TITLE>Font Embedding Using @font-face</TITLE>

<!-- Download Goofy font and use for H1 headings -->
<STYLE TYPE="text/css">
    @font-face {font-family: goofy;
                font-style: normal;
                font-weight: normal;
                src: url(http://www.coolnerds.com/fonts/goofy.eot)}

    H1 {font-family: goofy;
        font-size: 36pt}
</STYLE>
</HEAD>

<BODY>

<!-- Goofy font has already been assigned to H1 tag -->
<H1>I am in 36 point Goofy font</H1>

<!-- Use goofy font on the fly here. -->
<P STYLE="font-family:goofy; font-size:18pt">
I am a paragraph that displays its text in the Goofy font at 18 points.
</P>
</BODY></HTML>
For Help, press F1
```

Figure 10-30. *A hypothetical web page that uses* @font-face *to embed a font.*

Current OpenType Information

As I said, I'm sticking my neck out a bit by writing about an emerging technology. I hope you'll supplement and verify everything I've said here by checking around for more information on OpenType. A good place to start is the *Font Embedding* section of the Internet Client SDK. Another good source is Microsoft's Typography site at www.microsoft.com/typography/. While you're there, you might want to look around for, and download, the free Font Properties Extension that provides more information (including licensing criteria) for the fonts that are already installed on your system.

Since OpenType is being developed jointly by Microsoft and Adobe, you might also want to check out Adobe's web site at www.adobe.com. And finally, you might want to check the World Wide Web consortium's site at www.w3.org for current information on OpenType and embedded fonts.

SUMMARY

Text and tags—they define the content and appearance of your web page. Internet Explorer 4 offers many ways to control and change text and tags dynamically—right on the screen, in front of your visitors' eyes. To review the main topics covered in this chapter:

- You can use the *innerText* and *innerHTML* properties to replace the text and tags between many opening and closing HTML tags in your web page.

- You can use the *outerText* and *outerHTML* properties to replace an entire object, including the outside tags that define the object.

- You can also use the *innerText*, *innerHTML*, *outerText*, and *outerHTML* properties to delete text and tags. Just replace the text or tags with a zero-length string (*""*).

- You can use the *insertAdjacentHTML()* method to insert new text or HTML into an object.

- Cookies allow you to pass data across multiple pages in your web site.

- The cookies.vbs file, available on this book's companion CD and at my web site, contains the *setCookie* sub procedure, the *getCookie()* function procedure, and the *killCookie* sub procedure, which allow you to easily manipulate cookies.

- OpenType, an emerging technology, will allow you to embed fonts in your web pages so that you know for sure how your page will look to all visitors.

Now, on to something fun—creating special effects with Internet Explorer's built-in Visual Filters and Transition Filters.

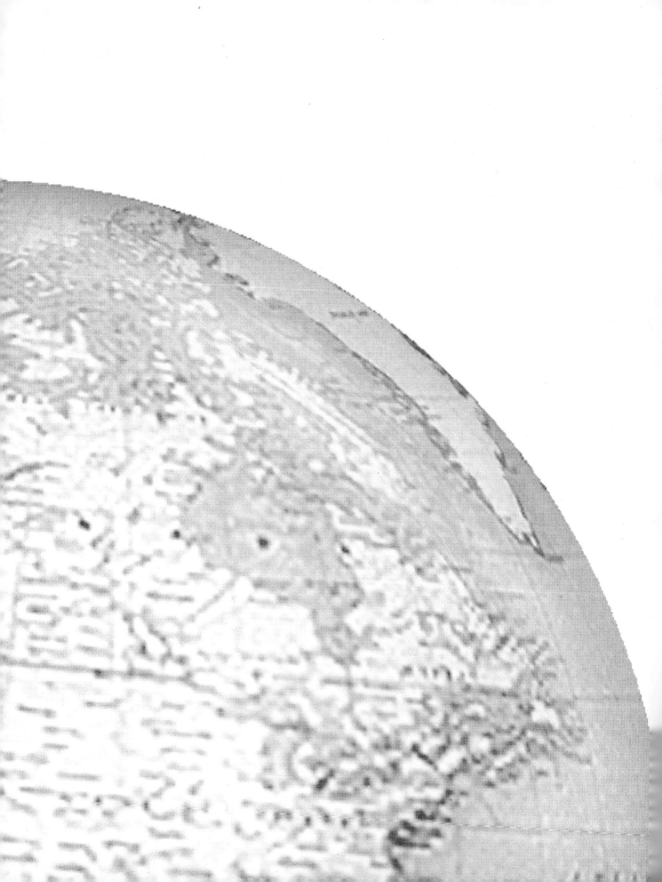

Chapter 11

Special Effects with Filters and Transitions

In this chapter, you'll learn how to add some wild and crazy special effects to your Microsoft Internet Explorer 4 web pages using the built-in visual filters and transition effects. Specifically, we'll cover:

■ Defining visual filters such as DropShadow and Glow

■ Controlling visual filters with VBScript code

■ Using VBScript code to animate visual filter special effects

■ Creating transitions such as wipes and dissolves

■ Defining interpage transitions to make navigation more interesting

As you'll see, all of the special effects tools described in this chapter are actually style sheet attributes, so you can apply special effects using syntax that's similar to the syntax for applying other kinds of styles. Let's start with the visual filters.

VISUAL FILTERS

Internet Explorer 4 comes with several visual filters that are part of the CSS (Cascading Style Sheets) technology. You can use these filters to apply interesting special effects to text and pictures. The visual filters are summarized in Table 11-1.

Table 11-1
VISUAL FILTERS FOR TEXT OR IMAGES

Filter	Description
Alpha	Sets the amount of opacity, which can be uniform or graded
Blur	Creates the impression of movement at high speed
Chroma	Makes a specific color transparent
DropShadow	Creates a background shadow that makes the object look like it's floating above the page
FlipH	Creates a horizontal mirror image
FlipV	Creates a vertical mirror image
Glow	Adds a radiant glow around the outside edges of the object
Gray	Displays image in grayscale by ignoring its color information
Invert	Reverses the hue, saturation, and brightness values
Light	Projects a light source onto an object (requires scripting)
Mask	Creates a transparent mask from an object
Shadow	Creates a shadow with feathered edges
Wave	Creates a sine wave distortion along the vertical axis
XRay	Makes an object look like a black and white X ray

Each visual filter is applied as a CSS style using this general syntax:

```
STYLE="filter:filterName(fparameter1, fparameter2,...)"
```

filterName is the name of the filter being applied, and *fparameter...* are any valid parameters for the filter in use. Different filters require different parameters. With the exception of the Light filter, all visual filters can be applied without having to use any scripting code. This means that the filter is applied once and doesn't change. All of the filters, however, can also be altered programmatically using VBScript or JavaScript code to produce more animated special effects.

In the sections that follow, we'll look at many examples of both static and animated visual filters. Many of the examples will show various filters applied to the text and image shown at the top of Figure 11-1. (That figure also shows examples of two filters already applied; I'll talk about these in a moment.)

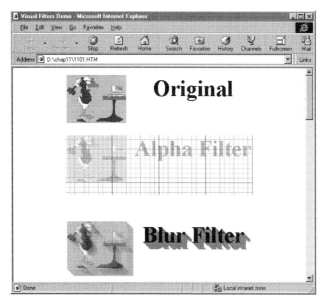

Figure 11-1. *The image and text at the top have no visual filters applied.*

The HTML used to display the graphic image and text is shown below:

```
<!-- Show original image and text with no filter applied. -->
<DIV STYLE="height:125; width:400">
  <SPAN STYLE="height:50; width:400">
  <IMG SRC="duck.jpg" WIDTH="127" HEIGHT="100" ALIGN="left">
   Original
  </SPAN>
</DIV>
```

Keep in mind that the examples in this chapter are by no means comprehensive. There are literally thousands of ways to apply and alter filters. I hope these examples will get you started in experimenting on your own.

Alpha Filter

The Alpha filter lets you control the opacity of an object in the range of 0 (completely transparent) to 100 (opaque). The first image and text under the original in Figure 11-1 shows an image and some text with a "graph paper" background. The Alpha filter has been applied using an opacity of 30. To make that happen, I first added a background-image style to the entire division. (That's what makes the "graph paper" visible.) Then, within the *<SPAN>...</SPAN>* tags, I applied the Alpha filter using the syntax *filter:Alpha(Opacity=30)*, as you can see in the HTML on the next page.

```
<!-- Create a background, then apply the Alpha filter. -->
<DIV STYLE="height:125; width:400;
background-image:url(grid.gif)">
   <SPAN STYLE="height:50; width:400; filter:Alpha(Opacity=30)">
   <IMG SRC="duck.jpg" WIDTH="127" HEIGHT="100" ALIGN="left">
    Alpha Filter
   </SPAN>
</DIV>
```

If you look closely at the Alpha filter example in Figure 11-1, you can see the background image showing right through the image and the text. That's exactly what the Alpha filter does—it makes its contents semitransparent so you can see whatever is behind the filtered object(s). (If I hadn't added the graph-paper background image, the filtered image and text would still look "faded," but you'd only see the plain white background behind the filtered objects.)

You can apply the Alpha filter uniformly, as in Figure 11-1, where all parts of the object have the same transparency, or you can apply the Alpha filter as a gradient, going from one level of opacity to another. The full syntax of the Alpha filter, shown below, includes parameters for opacity gradients:

```
filter:Alpha(Opacity=opacity, FinishOpacity=finishOpacity,
Style=style, StartX=startX, StartY=startY, FinishX=finishX,
FinishY=finishY)
```

opacity is the level of the opacity. 0, the default, is fully transparent, and 100 is fully opaque. This is the only required parameter; the rest that follow are optional.

finishOpacity is used to define the ending opacity in the range of 0 (fully transparent) to 100 (fully opaque). *style* is a number from 0 to 3 indicating the opacity gradient. Possible values are 0 (uniform), 1 (linear), 2 (radial), and 3 (rectangular). *startX* is the x coordinate for the opacity gradient to begin. *startY* is the y coordinate for the opacity gradient to begin. *finishX* is the x coordinate for the opacity gradient to end. *finishY* is the y coordinate for the opacity gradient to end.

Figure 11-2 shows an example in which a linear gradient (*Style=1*) starts with the opacity at 20 (*Opacity=20*) at the left side of the object (*StartX=0*) and ends at fully opaque (*FinishOpacity=100*) at the right side of the object (*FinishX=500*). Note that both the text and the button are affected by the filter. The HTML required to present that example is shown on the next page.

```
<HTML><HEAD><TITLE>Gradient Alpha Filter Demo</TITLE></HEAD>
<BODY BACKGROUND="marble.jpg">

<SPAN STYLE="width:500; height:100; font:Bold 36pt 'Arial Black';
color:#FFFFFF; filter:Alpha(Opacity=20, FinishOpacity=100,
Style=1, StartX=0, FinishX=500)">
    I AM WHITE TEXT
    <BUTTON>
        <B>I Am a Wide Button to Which the Alpha Filter is Applied</B>
    </BUTTON>
</SPAN>

</BODY></HTML>
```

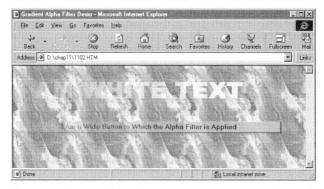

Figure 11-2. *An Alpha filter applied as a gradient from left to right.*

Blur Filter

The Blur filter streaks or blurs the object to give it the appearance of motion. The syntax for the Blur filter is:

```
filter:Blur(Add=add, Direction=direction, Strength=strength)
```

add specifies whether the original image is included in the filtered image. If *add* is set to False or 0 (zero), the original image is not included. If add is set to True or any nonzero number, the original image is included. By default, *add* is True. *strength* is the number of pixels the blur will extend.

direction specifies the direction of the motion blur in 45-degree increments. The default value is 0 (straight up). Positive increments rotate clockwise from the top center position. The possible values are shown in Table 11-2.

Table 11-2

NUMBERS THAT DEFINE THE DIRECTION OF A BLUR

Value	Description
0	Top edge
45	Top-right corner
90	Right edge
135	Bottom-right corner
180	Bottom edge
225	Bottom-left corner
270	Left edge
315	Top-left corner

Negative increments are rotated counter-clockwise. For example, −45 degrees is equivalent to 315 degrees. Increments larger than 360 degrees wrap around to their equivalent angle. Values that fall in between the 45-degree increments are rounded to the closest increment.

To create the Blur filter example at the bottom of Figure 11-1, I used these HTML tags:

```
<!-- Try the Blur filter. -->
<DIV STYLE="height:125; width:400;
filter:Blur(Direction=135, Strength=15)">
   <IMG SRC="duck.jpg" WIDTH="127" HEIGHT="100" ALIGN="left">
    Blur Filter
</DIV>
```

When using the Blur filter on text, it's best to omit the *Add=0* option (or use *Add=1*) because otherwise the text will probably be too blurry to read. With graphic images, you can go either way. However, the image must have enough empty space within it to handle the blur. For example, the left image in Figure 11-3 is a simple black and white GIF image with no transparency. A *BORDER="1"* attribute in the *<IMG...>* tag shows a border around the image. As you can see, there is a fair amount of white "margin" space around the symbol within the graphic image.

> TIP   If you use Paint Shop Pro as your graphics editor, you can use the Enlarge Canvas command on the Image menu to increase the size of the image background without altering the size of the actual image.

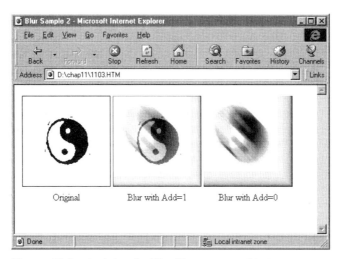

Figure 11-3. *Applying the Blur filter to a graphic image.*

Next to the original image is the same image with the Blur filter applied. Here the Blur filter is applied with the *Add=1* parameter. The original image is included with the blur, so there is a clear view of the image at the front of the blur lines. The rightmost image uses the Blur filter with *Add=0*. Without the original image added to the blur, the entire image is blurred. The tags used to create the page shown in Figure 11-3 are shown below:

```
<HTML><HEAD><TITLE>Blur Sample 2</TITLE></HEAD>
<BODY BGCOLOR="#FFFFFF">
<TABLE>
   <TR>
   <!-- Show the natural yinyang.gif file. -->
   <TD>
   <IMG SRC="yinyang.gif" HEIGHT="150" WIDTH="150" BORDER="1">
   </TD>

   <!-- Try the Blur filter with Add=1. -->
   <TD>
   <IMG SRC="yinyang.gif" BORDER="1" STYLE="height:150; width:150;
      filter:Blur(Add=1, Direction=315, Strength=25)">
   </TD>
```

(continued)

```
<!-- Try the Blur filter with Add=0. -->
<TD>
<IMG SRC="yinyang.gif" BORDER="1" STYLE="height:150; width:150;
    filter:Blur(Add=0, Direction=315, Strength=25)">
</TD>
</TR>
<TR>
<TD ALIGN="center">Original</TD>
<TD ALIGN="center">Blur with Add=1</TD>
<TD ALIGN="center">Blur with Add=0</TD>
</TR>
</TABLE>
</BODY></HTML>
```

> **NOTE** The *<TABLE>...</TABLE>*, *<TR>...</TR>* (table row) and *<TD>...</TD>* (table data cell) tags in the source code have nothing to do with the filter. They simply organize the images into an HTML table.

Chroma Filter

The Chroma filter lets you define a transparent color for any graphic image. The syntax for the Chroma filter is as follows, where *color* is an RGB triplet or a valid color name that specifies the transparent color:

```
filter:Chroma(Color=color)
```

This filter works best with simple line drawing images that contain relatively few colors. GIF files work well with the Chroma filter. Using the Chroma filter on a photograph (or any JPEG image) will likely cause uneven effects because there are so many colors in such images.

Anti-aliased images, in which sharp lines are smoothed by blending the colors of surrounding pixels, are also not good candidates for the Chroma filter because so many colors are used to smooth out the lines.

Figure 11-4 shows the Chroma filter applied to a several variations of the same image. Across the top row, the Chroma filter is applied to a GIF file that contains no transparency information. The original image in the top-left corner contains three basic colors—black, white, and pink. The pink color appears as gray in the figure. Applying a pink Chroma filter makes the pink areas transparent. Applying a black Chroma filter makes the black parts transparent, and applying a white Chroma filter makes the white parts transparent.

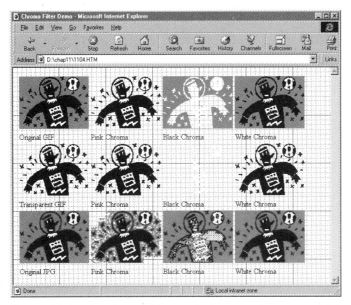

Figure 11-4. *The Chroma filter applied to several variations of the same image.*

The second row shows the same image. However, in that version of the image, pink is already defined as the transparent color (using a graphics program). With no filter, the pink background is, indeed, transparent. Applying a pink Chroma filter has no effect, which is expected. Applying a black or white Chroma filter makes those colors transparent in addition to the already transparent pink background.

The bottom row of Figure 11-4 shows the Chroma filter applied to a JPEG version of the same image. Because JPEG images contain a lot of colors, the results of the filter are somewhat uneven across the bottom row.

> TIP   When you use the Chroma filter to define a transparent color, you can programmatically change the Chroma filter with VBScript code. When you define a transparent color using a graphics program, such as Paint Shop Pro, you don't have that programmatic control over which color appears transparent.

To use the Chroma filter effectively, you should use it with a graphic image that contains relatively few colors. Also, you might need to experiment with the colors. I originally tried to make the pink background gray, but when I applied a gray Chroma filter, the gray unexpectedly turned black.

Incidentally, each of the images in Figure 11-4 uses virtually the same syntax to define a chroma key. All that varies is the actual color specified as the transparent color. Below are the basic tags used to display the graphic images across the top row of Figure 11-4. (The *<TABLE>*, *<TR>*, and *<TD>* tags are just for placing each picture in a table cell.)

```
<HTML><HEAD><TITLE>Chroma Filter Demo</TITLE></HEAD>
<BODY BACKGROUND="grid.gif">
<TABLE>
   <TR><TD>
   <IMG SRC="astroguy.gif" WIDTH="150" HEIGHT="109">
   </TD><TD>
   <IMG SRC="astroguy.gif" WIDTH="150" HEIGHT="109"
      STYLE="filter:Chroma(Color=#FF00FF)">
   </TD><TD>
   <IMG SRC="astroguy.gif" WIDTH="150" HEIGHT="109"
      STYLE="filter:Chroma(Color=#000000)">
   </TD><TD>
   <IMG SRC="astroguy.gif" WIDTH="150" HEIGHT="109"
      STYLE="filter:Chroma(Color=#FFFFFF)">
   </TD></TR>

   <!-- More of the same for the other two rows. -->

</TABLE>
</BODY></HTML>
```

DropShadow Filter

The DropShadow filter makes an object appear to float and cast a shadow onto the background. The syntax for the DropShadow filter is:

```
filter:DropShadow(Color=color, OffX=offX, OffY=offY,
Positive=positive)
```

color is the color of the shadow expressed as an RGB triplet or as a valid color name. *offX* is the number of pixels the drop shadow is offset from the object, along the *x* axis. A positive number moves the drop shadow to the right, and a negative number moves the drop shadow to the left. *offY* is the number of pixels the drop shadow is offset from the object along the *y* axis. A positive number moves the drop shadow down, and a negative number moves the drop shadow up. *positive* specifies whether the nontransparent pixels or the transparent pixels in the image file are used to create the shadow. If it is false or 0 (zero), drop shadows are created for any transparent pixel. If it is true or a non-zero number, which is the default, drop shadows are created for any nontransparent pixel.

At the top of Figure 11-5, you can see the DropShadow filter applied to the original image and text shown at the top of Figure 11-1. The exact HTML used to apply the filter is shown below. Note that to create the effect, I set the color of the shadow to a light gray (*Color=#C0C0C0*) and I offset the shadow 10 pixels to the right and 10 pixels down (*OffX=10, OffY=10*):

```
<!-- Try the DropShadow filter. -->
<DIV STYLE="height:125; width:400;
filter:DropShadow(Color=#C0C0C0, OffX=10, OffY=10)">
    <IMG SRC="duck.jpg" WIDTH="127" HEIGHT="100" ALIGN="left">
     DropShadow Filter
</DIV>
```

Figure 11-5. *The DropShadow, FlipH, and FlipV filters applied to the sample image and text.*

Figure 11-6 shows more examples of the DropShadow filter applied to text. Figure 11-7 shows the document source for that same page.

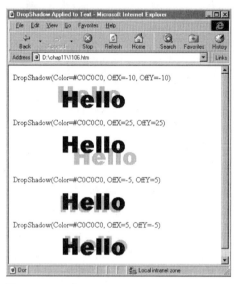

Figure 11-6. *More examples of the DropShadow filter applied to text.*

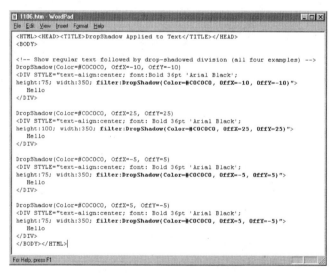

Figure 11-7. *The document source for the page shown in Figure 11-6.*

The optional *Positive* parameter of the DropShadow filter works only with objects containing transparent pixels. If you apply the DropShadow filter with *Positive=0* to an object containing transparency, you'll get the usual drop shadow effect. However, if you use *Positive=1* in applying the drop shadow to an object containing transparency, the drop shadow will be created from the transparent pixels and will appear only in the nontransparent regions.

FlipH and FlipV Filters

The FlipH and FlipV filters simply flip the object around either horizontally (FlipH) or vertically (FlipV). Neither filter accepts any parameters. The syntax for them is simply:

```
filter:FlipH
```

and

```
filter:FlipV
```

Figure 11-5 includes examples of our simple graphic image and text flipped horizontally and vertically. (It's kind of hard to read the text, since it's flipped). The tags used to flip the objects are shown below:

```
<!-- Try the FlipH filter. -->
<DIV STYLE="height:125; width:400; filter:FlipH">
   <IMG SRC="duck.jpg" WIDTH="127" HEIGHT="100" ALIGN="left">
    FlipH Filter
</DIV>

<!-- Try the FlipV filter. -->
<DIV STYLE="height:125; width:400; filter:FlipV">
   <IMG SRC="duck.jpg" WIDTH="127" HEIGHT="100" ALIGN="left">
    FlipV Filter
</DIV>
```

Glow Filter

The Glow filter makes the object appear to be glowing. The syntax for this filter is:

```
filter:Glow(Color=color, Strength=strength)
```

color is the color of the glowing pixels expressed as an RGB triplet or as a valid color name. *strength* is the intensity of the glow from 0 (lowest intensity) to 100 (highest intensity).

The top of Figure 11-8 shows the Glow filter applied to our sample image and text. The glow around the image might be difficult to see here, but there is a slight green glow. The glow around the text is much more obvious.

Figure 11-8. *The Glow, Gray, and Invert filters applied to the sample image and text.*

The HTML tags used to apply the Glow filter in that example are shown below:

```
<!-- Try the Glow filter. -->
<DIV STYLE="height:125; width:400;
filter:Glow(Color=#00FF00, Strength=10)">
    <IMG SRC="duck.jpg" WIDTH="127" HEIGHT="100" ALIGN="left">
     Glow Filter
</DIV>
```

Gray Filter

The Gray filter displays a color image in gray scale by ignoring the color information. This filter is applied to the middle example in Figure 11-8. When viewing that image on the screen, most of the duck images are in color but not the one to which the Gray filter is applied. That one is strictly black-and-white, with some shades of gray mixed in.

The Gray filter accepts no parameters, so it's syntax is simply:

```
filter:Gray
```

Here are the tags used to present the Gray filter example in Figure 11-8:

```
<!-- Try the Gray filter. -->
<DIV STYLE="height:125; width:400; filter:Gray">
   <IMG SRC="duck.jpg" WIDTH="127" HEIGHT="100" ALIGN="left">
    Gray Filter
</DIV>
```

Invert Filter

The Invert filter changes all colors to their opposite color. For example, black becomes white and green becomes magenta. The result is the equivalent of a color negative of a photo. The Invert filter does not have any parameters, and it has the following syntax:

```
filter:Invert
```

Here are the exact tags used to display the Invert filter example at the bottom of Figure 11-8. Notice that I changed the text color to green using the *<SPAN>...</SPAN>* tags. I did this because the inverted black text would display as white and thus would be invisible against the white background.

```
<!-- Try the Gray filter. -->
<DIV STYLE="height:125; width:400; filter:Invert">
   <IMG SRC="duck.jpg" WIDTH="127" HEIGHT="100" ALIGN="left">
   <SPAN STYLE="color:green"> Invert Filter</SPAN>
</DIV>
```

Light Filter

The Light filter projects light onto an object. This filter is unique among the visual filters because scripting code is required to activate it. There are three types of light you can shine on an object:

- ambient light—nondirectional light that shines uniformly on an object

- cone light—directional cone-shaped light

- point light—circular light that's brightest in the middle

Examples of the Light filter are shown in Figure 11-9 on the next page. With no light, the image object is completely dark. Ambient light lights up the entire image. The cone and point lights shine on only parts of the image.

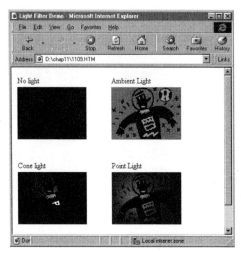

Figure 11-9. *Examples of no light, ambient light, cone light, and point light on an object.*

The syntax for adding a Light filter to an object is simply:

```
filter:Light
```

However, that only sets up a light that's initially turned off. (At this point, the lighted object will be completely dark, like the example in the upper-left corner of Figure 11-9.) To add an actual light, you need to use one or more of the following methods in a script:

- *addAmbient()* method—adds an ambient light source
- *addCone()* method—adds a cone light source
- *addPoint()* method—adds a point light source

Each of these methods is described in detail in the sections that follow.

addAmbient() Method

The *addAmbient()* method of the Light filter adds ambient light, which adds light uniformly to an object. The syntax of this method is:

```
call objectName.filters(n).addAmbient(R, G, B, strength)
```

objectName is the name of the object to which the Light filter is to be applied. *n* is the index number of the filter in the object's filters collection, which must be a Light filter. Each filter applied to an object has an index number, where 0 is the first filter and each additional applied filter has an index incremented by 1. *R* is the saturation of red in the light in the range of 0 (none) to 255 (total saturation). *G* is the saturation of green in the light in the range of 0 (none) to 255 (total saturation). *B* is the saturation of blue in the light in the range of 0 (none) to 255 (total saturation). *strength* is the intensity of the light, which ranges from 0 (lowest) to 100 (highest).

> TIP As we discussed in Chapter 3, if you pass multiple arguments to a sub procedure, you must omit the parentheses around the arguments. Otherwise, an error will be displayed. Since the Light filter methods *addAmbient()*, *addCone()*, and *addPoint()* are essentially sub procedures, you must omit the parentheses. However, you can get around this by using the *call* statement. This statement allows you to include parentheses when passing multiple parameters to a sub procedure.

In the ambient light example shown in Figure 11-9, the object and the Light filter are defined by these tags:

```
<DIV ID="picture2" STYLE="width:200; height:150; filter:Light">
   <IMG SRC="astroguy.gif" WIDTH="150" HEIGHT="109">
</DIV>
```

The following code is used to apply an ambient light to the object:

```
<SCRIPT LANGUAGE="VBScript">
   call picture2.filters(0).addAmbient(255, 255, 255, 100)
</SCRIPT>
```

The numbers 255, 255, 255 mixes all three colors at full saturation, resulting in white light. The intensity, 100, is full intensity.

> TIP As you've seen in other object model examples, there are usually a couple of different ways to accomplish the same thing. This is also the case when working with filters. For example, for a Light filter applied to an object named *picture2*, the following three statements are equivalent (where n is the index number of the Light filter in the *picture2* filters collection):
>
> call picture2.filters.Light.addAmbient(255, 255, 255, 100)
>
> call picture2.filters("Light").addAmbient(255, 255, 255, 100)
>
> call picture2.filters(n).addAmbient(255, 255, 255, 100)
>
> If you find one of those syntaxes easier to understand, you might want to use it when working with the Light filter.

addCone() **Method**

The *addCone()* method adds a cone light to the image. You can control the position of the virtual light source, as well as where the light hits the object. The syntax for the *addCone()* method is shown on the next page.

```
call objectName.filters(n).addCone(x1, y1, z1, x2, y2, R, G, B, _
    strength, spread)
```

objectName is the name of the object to which the light filter is to be applied. *n* is the index number of the filter in the object's filters collection, which must be a Light filter. *x1* is the horizontal pixel position of the source light. *y1* is the vertical pixel position of the source light. *z1* is the perpendicular distance, in pixels, between the position of light source and the object being lighted. *x2* is the horizontal pixel position at which the center of the cone of light hits the target object. *y2* is the vertical pixel position of that center point. Figure 11-10 shows a diagram of these parameters.

R is the red saturation from 0 (none) to 255 (full saturation). *G* is the green saturation from 0 (none) to 255 (full saturation). *B* is the blue saturation from 0 (none) to 255 (full saturation). *strength* is the intensity of the light, which ranges from 0 (lowest) to 100 (highest).

spread is the cone angle or light spread angle, as shown in Figure 11-10. *spread* ranges from 0 to 90 degrees. A low *spread* value produces a small shaped cone of light. A high *spread* value produces a large cone of light. The cone light fades with distance from the target *x2, y2* position. It displays a hard edge near the focus and gradually fades from there.

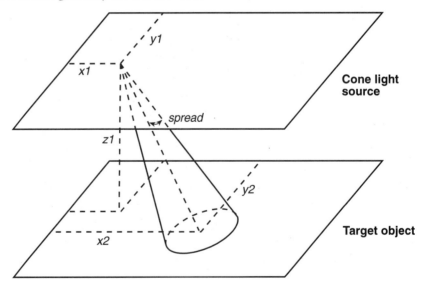

Figure 11-10. *A diagram of some of the* addCone() *method parameters.*

The tags that create the cone light example in Figure 11-9 are shown below. As with the other examples, the object simply has a *filter:Light* style applied to it:

```
<DIV ID="picture3" STYLE="width:200; height:150; filter:Light">
    <IMG SRC="astroguy.gif" WIDTH="150" HEIGHT="109">
</DIV>
```

The actual lighting of the object comes in a script. The code used to activate the cone light is shown below:

```
<SCRIPT LANGUAGE="VBScript">
   call picture3.filters(0).addCone(100, 75, 10, 75, 50, 255, 255, _
      255, 100, 25)
</SCRIPT>
```

The position of the light source is 100 pixels from the left, 75 pixels from the top, and 10 pixels away (back) from the lighted object. The light hits the object at 75 pixels from the left and 50 pixels from the top of the object. The light is bright white (255, 255, 255, 100) with a spread angle of 25 degrees.

addPoint() Method

The *addPoint()* method adds a point of light that's most intense in the center, then fades out from there. The syntax for the *addPoint()* method is:

```
call objectName.filters(n).addPoint(x, y, z, R, G, B, strength)
```

objectName is the name of the object to which the Light filter is applied. *n* is the index number of the filter in the object's filters collection, which must be a Light filter. *x* is the horizontal pixel position of the source light. *y* is the vertical pixel position of the source light. *z* is the distance, in pixels, between the light source and the object being lighted. *R* is the saturation of red from 0 (none) to 255 (fill saturation). *G* is the saturation of green from 0 (none) to 255 (fill saturation). *B* is the saturation of blue from 0 (none) to 255 (fill saturation). *strength* is the intensity of the light, which ranges from 0 (lowest) to 100 (highest).

The object to which the point light is applied in Figure 11-9 is defined by these tags:

```
<DIV ID="picture4" STYLE="width:200; height:150; filter:Light">
   <IMG SRC="astroguy.gif" WIDTH="150" HEIGHT="109">
</DIV>
```

The code that actually turns on the light is shown below:

```
<SCRIPT LANGUAGE="VBScript">
   call picture4.filters(0).addPoint(50, 50, 50, 255, 255, 255, 100)
</SCRIPT>
```

The source of the light is 50 pixels from the left, 50 pixels from the top, and 50 pixels back from the lighted object. White light is at full intensity (255, 255, 255, 100).

Other Light Methods

In addition to adding a light to an object, you can use the following methods to change the light:

- *changeColor()* method—changes the color of the light

- *changeStrength()* method—changes the strength of the light

- *clear()* method—removes all lights applied to an object

- *moveLight()* method—moves the light source

For example, the *changeColor()* method changes the color of the light cast on an object and uses this syntax:

```
call objectName.filters(n).changeColor(lightNumber, R, G, B, _
    fAbsolute)
```

objectName is the name of the object to which the light is being applied. *n* is the index number of the filter in the object's filters collection, which must be a Light filter. Each filter applied to an object has an index number, where 0 is the first filter and each additional applied filter has an index incremented by 1. *lightNumber* is the index number for the Light filter. The first Light filter applied has an index of 0 and each additional applied Light filter has an index that is incremented by 1. *R* is the saturation of red in the light from 0 (none) to 255 (full saturation). *G* is the saturation of green in the light from 0 (none) to 255 (full saturation). *B* is the saturation of blue in the light from 0 (none) to 255 (full saturation). *fAbsolute* is the absolute flag. If *fAbsolute* is True (any nonzero number), *changeColor()* sets the value to the new value. If *fAbsolute* is False (zero), *changeColor()* increments or decrements the color value by that amount.

For example, the following script changes the color of the first light (*lightNumber* 0) shining on an object named *picture4* to a purple color (255, 0, 255):

```
<SCRIPT LANGUAGE="VBScript">
   call picture4.filters(0).changeColor(0, 255, 0, 255, 1)
</SCRIPT>
```

The *changeStrength()* method changes the strength of the light being projected onto an object. The syntax for this method is:

```
call objectName.filters(n).changeStrength(lightNumber, _
    strength, fAbsolute)
```

objectName is the name of the object to which the Light filter is applied. *n* is the index number of the filter in the object's filters collection, which must be a Light filter. *lightNumber* is the index number for the Light filter. *strength* is the intensity.

fAbsolute is either True (some nonzero number) or False (zero). If *fAbsolute* is True (nonzero), *changeStrength()* sets the strength value to be the specified *strength* value. If *fAbsolute* is False (zero), *changeStrength()* increments or decrements the strength value by *strength* value.

For example, the script below changes the strength of the light shining on the object named *picture4* from its current value to 50:

```
<SCRIPT LANGUAGE="VBScript">
   call picture4.filters(0).changeStrength(0, 50, 1)
</SCRIPT>
```

The *clear()* method removes all lights applied to an object. Its syntax is:

```
call objectName.filters(n).clear
```

objectName is the name of the object to which the Light filter is applied. *n* is the index number of the filter in the object's *filters* collection, which must be a Light filter. For example, the script below removes all the lights applied to the object named *picture4*:

```
<SCRIPT LANGUAGE="VBScript">
   call picture4.filters(0).clear
</SCRIPT>
```

The *moveLight()* method moves the position of the light effect on the object. Its syntax is:

```
call objectName.filters(n).moveLight(lightNumber, x, y, z, _
   fAbsolute)
```

objectName is the name of the object to which the light is being projected. *n* is again the index number of the filter in the object's *filters* collection, which must be a Light filter. *lightNumber* is the index number for the Light filter. *x, y, z* are the new location to move the light to.

fAbsolute determines whether the movement is absolute or relative. If *fAbsolute* is True (a nonzero number), the new *x, y,* and *z* values replace existing values. If *fAbsolute* is False (zero), the new *x, y,* and *z* values are added to the existing values.

When used with a cone light, *moveLight()* changes the position of the light's focus (the *x2* and *y2* values on the target). With point lights, *moveLight()* changes the source location (the source *x, y,* and *z* values). *moveLight()* has no effect on ambient lights.

The script below moves the first light shining on an object named *picture4* from its current position to the coordinates 100, 100, 100:

```
<SCRIPT LANGUAGE="VBScript">
   call picture4.filters(0).moveLight(0, 100, 100, 100, 1)
</SCRIPT>
```

Mask Filter

The Mask filter creates a kind of "stencil" of the object that it is applied to. It turns all the transparent pixels into some opaque, solid color. It then makes a transparent mask from all of the image's nontransparent pixels. The syntax for the Mask filter is as follows, where *color* is the color of the mask expressed as an RGB triplet or as a valid color name:

```
filter:Mask(Color=color)
```

Figure 11-11 shows an example of applying the Mask filter using the graphic image and text shown at the top of Figure 11-1. The once-transparent background of the *DIV* object is now an opaque gray. The parts that were previously opaque—the graphic image and the text—are now transparent. (The white from the background is showing through.)

Figure 11-11. *The Mask, Shadow, Wave, and XRay filters applied to the sample image and text.*

The HTML used to create the Mask filter example in Figure 11-11 is shown below. The gray color is defined by the RGB triplet, *#C0C0C0*.

```
<!-- Try the Mask filter on the GIF image. -->
<DIV STYLE="height:125; width:400; filter:Mask(Color=#C0C0C0)">
   <IMG SRC="duck.gif" WIDTH="127" HEIGHT="100" ALIGN="left">
    Mask Filter
</DIV>
```

Shadow Filter

The Shadow filter adds a cast shadow that's similar to a Blur filter but is "feathered" at the edges. The syntax for applying this filter to an object is:

```
filter:Shadow(Color=color, Direction=direction)
```

color is the color of the shadow, expressed as an RGB triplet or as a valid color name. The *direction* parameter can be any number listed in the left column of Table 11-3.

Table 11-3

NUMBERS THAT DEFINE THE DIRECTION OF A SHADOW

Value	*Description*
0	Top edge
45	Top-right corner
90	Right edge
135	Bottom-right corner
180	Bottom edge
225	Bottom-left corner
270	Left edge
315	Top-left corner

Although you can't see the actual color here, the Shadow filter example in Figure 11-11 shows black text casting a green shadow. The HTML used to create that example is:

```
<!-- Try the Shadow filter. -->
<DIV STYLE="height:125; width:400;
filter:Shadow(Color=#00FF00, Direction=225)">
   <IMG SRC="duck.jpg" WIDTH="127" HEIGHT="100" ALIGN="left">
    Shadow Filter
</DIV>
```

Wave Filter

The Wave filter, as the name suggests, makes an object look wavy. (See the Wave filter example in Figure 11-11.) The syntax for applying a Wave filter to an object is:

```
filter:Wave(Add=add, Freq=freq, LightStrength=lightstrength,
Phase=phase, Strength=strength)
```

add is a True (any nonzero number) or False (zero) value that indicates whether to add the original image to the waved image. *freq* is the number of waves to appear in the visual distortion. *lightstrength* is the strength of the light on the wave effect expressed as a percentage, from 0 to 100. *phase* is the phase offset for the start of the sine wave effect, which is normally 0. Its value ranges from 0 to 100, which expresses the percentage of the wavelength at which the offset should start. For example, a value of 25 starts the wave effect at 90 degrees. A value of 100 is the equivalent of 0 or 360 degrees. *strength* is the intensity of the wave effect.

Here's the HTML used to create the Wave filter example shown in Figure 11-11:

```
<!-- Try the Wave filter. -->
<DIV STYLE="height:125; width:400;
filter:Wave(Add=True, Freq=2, LightStrength=25,
Phase=25, Strength=5)">
   <IMG SRC="duck.jpg" WIDTH="127" HEIGHT="100" ALIGN="left">
    Wave Filter
</DIV>
```

XRay Filter

The XRay filter makes an image look sort of like a black-and-white X ray. The syntax for applying this filter is simply:

```
filter:XRay
```

You can see the Xray filter applied to our sample text and image at the bottom of Figure 11-11. Here is the HTML used to apply the Xray filter in that example:

```
<!-- Try the XRay filter. -->
<DIV STYLE="height:125; width:400; filter:XRay">
   <IMG SRC="duck.jpg" WIDTH="127" HEIGHT="100" ALIGN="left">
    XRay Filter
</DIV>
```

Combining Visual Filters

You can combine two or more visual filters to get a new effect. Just separate each filter name and its parameters with a blank space, like this:

```
STYLE="filter:filterName(fparameters) filterName(fparameters)..."
```

For example, the *<DIV>* tag below applies both a Glow filter and a Drop-Shadow filter to the text between the *<DIV>...</DIV>* tags:

```
<!-- Apply the Glow and DropShadow filters to some text. -->
<DIV ALIGN="center" ID="sampleText" STYLE="height:70; width:500;
font:'Bold 24pt Arial';
filter:Glow(Color=#00FF00, Strength=10)
      DropShadow(Color=gray, OffX=10, OffY=10)">
  I Am a Chunk of Text
</DIV>
```

Figure 11-12 shows how the sample text looks in Internet Explorer 4. Although you can't really tell here, the glow is a bright green (*#00FF00*) and the drop shadow is gray.

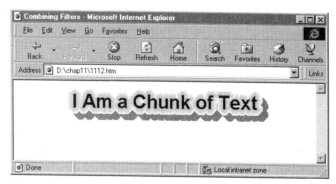

Figure 11-12. *A chunk of text with Glow and DropShadow filters applied.*

Scripting Visual Filters

You can use scripting code to apply a filter to any object, as well as to remove a filter. The basic VBScript syntax required is:

```
<SCRIPT LANGUAGE="VBScript"><!--
   'Apply a filter...
   objectName.style.filter = "filterName(fparameters, enabled=True)"
--></SCRIPT>
```

objectName is the name of the object to which you want to apply the filter. *filterName* is the name of the filter to apply, such as Glow or DropShadow. *fparameters* are valid parameters for the selected filter.

The same basic syntax lets you remove a filter as well. Just replace the *"filterName(fparameters, enabled=True)" part* of the syntax with a zero-length string (""). Figure 11-13 on the next page shows a sample web page that allows the user to apply or remove a filter by clicking the appropriate button. Figure 11-14 shows the document source for the page shown in Figure 11-13.

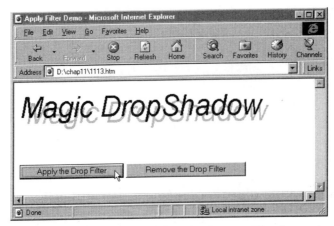

Figure 11-13. *A page after the Apply The Drop Filter button is clicked.*

```
<HTML><HEAD><TITLE>Apply Filter Demo</TITLE></HEAD>
<BODY>

<!-- Text with no filter applied initially -->
<SPAN ID="tryMe" STYLE="align:center; height:100; width:500; font:'Italic 36pt Arial'">
    Magic DropShadow
</SPAN>
<P> </P>

<!-- Button and script to apply DropShadow filter to the text above -->
<BUTTON ID="applyButton">
    Apply the Drop Filter
</BUTTON>

<SCRIPT FOR="applyButton" EVENT="onclick" LANGUAGE="VBScript"><!--
    tryMe.style.filter = "DropShadow(Color=#C0C0C0, OffX=10, OffY=10, enabled=True)"
--></SCRIPT>
 

<!-- Button and script to remove DropShadow filter to the text above -->
<BUTTON ID="removeButton">
    Remove the Drop Filter
</BUTTON>

<SCRIPT FOR="removeButton" EVENT="onclick" LANGUAGE="VBScript"><!--
    tryMe.style.filter = ""
--></SCRIPT>
</BODY></HTML>
```

Figure 11-14. *The document source for the page shown in Figure 11-13.*

As shown below, the text *Magic Drop Shadow* initially does not have a filter applied and has the name *tryMe*:

```
<!-- Text with no filter applied initially -->
<SPAN ID="tryMe" STYLE="align:center; height:100; width:500;
font:'Italic 36pt Arial'">
    Magic DropShadow
</SPAN>
```

Included on the page are two buttons—one that applies a DropShadow filter to that object when clicked and another that removes that filter when clicked. Here are the tags and code used to apply a DropShadow filter to the object:

```
<!-- Button and script to apply DropShadow filter to text above -->
<BUTTON ID="applyButton">
   Apply the Drop Filter
</BUTTON>

<SCRIPT FOR="applyButton" EVENT="onclick" LANGUAGE="VBScript"><!--
   tryMe.style.filter = _
      "DropShadow(Color=#C0C0C0, OffX=10,OffY=10, enabled=True)"
--></SCRIPT>
```

Here are the tags and script that present the button and remove the filter when the visitor clicks the button:

```
<BUTTON ID="removeButton">
   Remove the Drop Filter
</BUTTON>

<SCRIPT FOR="removeButton" EVENT="onclick" LANGUAGE="VBScript"><!--
   tryMe.style.filter = ""
--></SCRIPT>
```

Animating Visual Filters

The Internet Explorer 4 object model keeps track of filters applied to an object via the *filters* collection. Each object has its own *filters* collection. In the following example, two filters are applied to the object named *sampleText*:

```
<!-- Apply the Glow and DropShadow filters to some text. -->
<DIV ID="sampleText" STYLE="height:70; width:500;
font:'Bold 24pt Arial';
filter:Glow(Color=#00FF00, Strength=10)
      DropShadow(Color=gray, OffX=10, OffY=10)">
   I Am a Chunk of Text
</DIV>
```

From the object model's perspective, the Glow filter can be referenced in the following way:

```
sampleText.filters(0)
```

Similarly, the DropShadow filter can be referenced in the following way:

```
sampleText.filters(1)
```

To change a filter property or parameter, you can use this syntax:

```
objectName.filters(n).property = newValue
```

objectName is the name of the object to which the filter has already been applied. *n* is the index number of the filter you want to change. If the object has only one filter, that filter is filters(0). *property* is the property or parameter that you want to change. *newValue* is a new value to assign to the property or parameter.

TIP You can also reference a filter property or parameter as shown below, where *filterName* is the name of the filter, such as Glow or DropShadow.

objectName.filters.*filterName*.*property* = *newValue*

objectName.filters("*filterName*").*property* = *newValue*

So our *sampleText* object has two filters assigned to it, as shown below:

```
<!-- Apply the Glow and DropShadow filters to some text. -->
<DIV ID="sampleText" STYLE="height:70; width:500;
font:'Bold 24pt Arial';
filter:Glow(Color=#00FF00, Strength=10)
      DropShadow(Color=gray, OffX=10, OffY=10)">
   I Am a Chunk of Text
</DIV>
```

The following script changes the Glow filter's strength to 5 and the Drop-Shadow's *OffX* and *OffY* properties each to 20:

```
<SCRIPT LANGUAGE="VBScript"><!--
   'Change Glow filter's strength.
   sampleText.filters(0).strength = 5
   'Change DropShadow filter's offsets.
   sampleText.filters(1).OffX = 20
   sampleText.filters(1).OffY = 20
--></SCRIPT>
```

To produce some really interesting animated special effects, you can use a timer to repeatedly alter a filter's properties. We'll look at some examples in the sections that follow.

Rising Text Effect

As a first example of an animated filter, we'll create a chunk of text that seems to rise up off the page toward the reader. We'll use a DropShadow filter to have this rising text cast a shadow onto the page behind it, adding to the illusion that the text is rising up off the page. Although I obviously can't show the animation here in the book, Figure 11-15 shows basically how the page looks with the text "raised" pretty high off the page.

The HTML tags and code required to create the rising text are shown below. Notice that the name of the object to which the DropShadow filter is applied is *tryMe*:

```
<HTML><HEAD>
<TITLE>Animated DropShadow Filter Demo</TITLE>
</HEAD>
<BODY>
```

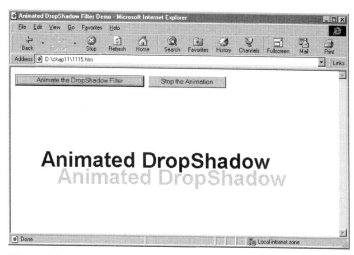

Figure 11-15. *Text rises up off the page in this animated DropShadow filter example.*

```
<!-- Text with DropShadow filter applied -->
<DIV ID="tryMe"
STYLE="position:absolute; top:200; left:100; height:100;
width:600; font:'Bold 0pt Arial';
filter:DropShadow(Color=#C0C0C0, OffX=0, OffY=0)">
   Animated DropShadow
</DIV>

<!-- Button to animate text and DropShadow filter -->
<BUTTON ID="animButton">
   Animate the DropShadow Filter
</BUTTON>
 

<!-- Button to stop animation -->
<BUTTON ID="stopButton">
   Stop the Animation
</BUTTON>

<!-- All scripts for this page -->
<SCRIPT LANGUAGE="VBScript"><!--
   'Initialize variables.
   Public offset, increment, timerID
   offset = 0
   increment = 1

   'This is the sub procedure that actually does the animation.
   Sub animateFilter()
```

(continued)

```
                 'Calculate new shadow offset and font size.
                 offset = offset + increment
                 tryMe.filters(0).OffX = offset
                 tryMe.filters(0).OffY = offset
                 tryMe.style.fontSize = offSet + 10
                 'Move top left corner of object up and to the left.
                 tryMe.style.pixelTop = tryMe.style.pixelTop - increment
                 tryMe.style.pixelLeft = tryMe.style.pixelLeft - increment
                 'When the offset value reaches 40, start decrementing.
                 If offset = 40 Then
                     increment = -1
                 End If
                 'When the offset value reaches 0, start incrementing.
                 If offset = 0 Then
                     increment = 1
                 End If
             End Sub

             'Script to start the animation (launches on button click)
             Sub animButton_onclick()
                 'Call the animateFilter procedure every 10 milliseconds.
                 timerID = window.setInterval("animateFilter", 10, "VBScript")
             End Sub

             'Script to stop the animation (launches on button click)
             Sub stopButton_onclick()
                 clearInterval(timerID)
             End Sub
         --></SCRIPT>

     </BODY></HTML>
```

The sub procedure named *animateFilter* does the actual animation by changing, just slightly, the *x* and *y* offsets of the drop shadow filter, the size of the font used to display the text, and the upper-left corner of the object. To get the animated effect, clicking the button named *animButton* calls the *animateFilter* sub procedure every 10 milliseconds using a *setInterval()* method.

Animated Wave Example

You can achieve interesting visual effects by animating a Wave filter. Figure 11-16 shows a page with some text with an animated Wave filter applied. Figure 11-17 shows the document source for this page.

Figure 11-16. *An animated Wave filter example.*

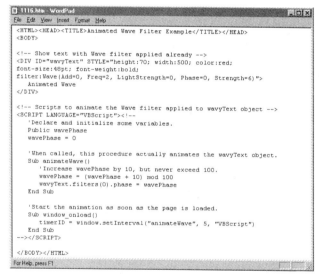

Figure 11-17. *The source document for the animated Wave filter example.*

Let's look at the document source more closely to see how it works. In the body of the page, we first create an object named *wavyText*, which is just a chunk of red text that says *Animated Wave* with a Wave filter applied:

```
<!-- Show text with Wave filter applied already -->
<DIV ID="wavyText" STYLE="height:70; width:500; color:red;
font-size:48pt; font-weight:bold;
filter:Wave(Add=0, Freq=2, LightStrength=0, Phase=0, Strength=6)">
   Animated Wave
</DIV>
```

The animation of the wave is handled by the code below. The sub procedure named *animateWave* increases the value of the phase property by 10 and then divides that value by 100 and takes the remainder (modulus) of that calculation (*wavePhase = (wavePhase + 10) mod 100*). This allows the *wavePhase* value to constantly increase by 10 but never exceed a value of 100.

NOTE The mod operator is part of VBScript and is short for modulo or modulus. It returns the remainder after one step of division. For example, 14 mod 10 returns 4 because 14 divided by 10 is 1, with a remainder of 4.

The real animation takes place using a *setInterval()* method to call the *animateWave* procedure every 5 milliseconds. The visitor has no buttons to push in this example. Instead, the animation kicks in automatically when the page is loaded because the sub procedure that starts the animation is bound to the *window_onload* event, which is triggered as soon as the page has been fully loaded into the visitor's web browser:

```
<!-- Scripts to animate wave filter applied to wavyText object -->
<SCRIPT LANGUAGE="VBScript"><!--
    'Declare and initialize wavePhase variable.
    Public wavePhase
    wavePhase = 0

    'When called, this procedure actually animates the
    'wavyText object.
    Sub animateWave()
        'Increase wavePhase by 10, but never exceed 100.
        wavePhase = (wavePhase + 10) mod 100
        wavyText.filters(0).phase = wavePhase
    End Sub

    'Start the animation as soon as the page is loaded.
    Sub window_onload()
        timerID = window.setInterval("animateWave", 5, "VBScript")
    End Sub
--></SCRIPT>
```

Pulsating, Color-Changing Glow Example

As a final example of animating a visual filter, let's assign the Glow filter to a chunk of text and then use code to vary the strength and color of the glow. Let's create an object named *glowText* that is just a chunk of text with a Glow filter applied, as shown on the next page.

```
<BODY>
<!-- Glow filter is applied to this object named glowText. -->
<DIV ID="glowText" STYLE="position:absolute; top:50; left:100;
width:400; height:300; font:Bold 36pt 'Comic Sans MS';
filter:Glow(Color=#0000FF, Strength=0)">
   Pulsating Glow
</DIV>
```

The scripts needed to animate the Glow filter can be placed anywhere in the same page. In my example, I start off by declaring some variables and assigning values to some of them:

```
<SCRIPT LANGUAGE="VBScript"><!--
   'Declare and initialize some variables.
   Public newStrength, strengthIncrement
   Public newColor, colorIncrement, timerID
   newStrength = 0
   strengthIncrement = 1
   newColor = 255
   colorIncrement = 1000000
```

Next comes a sub procedure named *animateGlow* that, when first called, changes the strength of the glow:

```
   'Sub procedure to change strength and color of glow
   Sub animateGlow()
      'Calculate new strength.
      newStrength = newStrength + strengthIncrement
      'Apply the newStrength value to the Glow filter.
      glowText.filters(0).Strength = newStrength
```

To keep the glow strength from growing indefinitely, the next routine sets the incrementing value to −1 as soon as the glow strength reaches 10. From that point on, the glow strength actually decreases by 1 each time the sub procedure is called:

```
      'Keep newStrength in the range of 0 to 10.
      If newStrength >= 10 Then
         strengthIncrement = -1
      End If
```

When the glow strength gets down to 0, the next *If...Then* statement changes the incrementing value back to 1 so the strength value gets incremented (rather than decremented) again for a while:

```
      If newStrength <= 0 Then
         strengthIncrement = 1
```

Here, too, we'll have the script change the color of the glow. First we increment the *newColor* value by the *colorIncrement* amount:

```
'Let's also change color here.
newColor = newColor + colorIncrement
```

We can't however, allow the new color to exceed FFFFFF hex (which is 16,777,215) because FFFFFF is the largest allowable number. So this next routine sets the color back to 255 (0000FF) when the current color gets too large:

```
'Don't let newColor value exceed FFFFFF (16.7 million).
If newColor >= 16777215 Then
    newColor = 255
End If
```

Here we apply the new color to the glow:

```
'Apply newColor value to the Glow filter.
glowText.filters(0).Color = newColor
End If
```

If you want to see the *newStrength* and *newColor* values in the status bar while the script is running, you can include these next lines in the *animateGlow* sub procedure:

```
'Show info in the status bar (optional).
'Feel free to delete next four lines if you like.
msg = "newStrength=" & newStrength & "  "
msg = msg & "newColor=" & newColor & "  "
msg = msg & "(#" & Hex(newColor) & ")"
window.status = msg
End Sub
```

To keep the animation moving, the next sub procedure calls the *animateGlow* procedure once every millisecond. The script is launched as soon as the page is loaded, so the animation starts as soon as the visitor sees the page:

```
Sub window_onload()
    timerID = setInterval("animateGlow", 1, "VBScript")
End Sub
--></SCRIPT>
</BODY></HTML>
```

Figure 11-18 shows a sample of the pulsating, color-changing glow text.

All of the filters we've discussed so far in this chapter are visual filters. Next we'll discuss another set of filters called reveal transition filters.

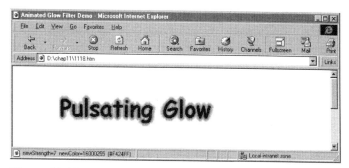

Figure 11-18. *Text with a Glow filter that pulsates and changes color.*

TIPS ON HEX

The hexadecimal numbers used for colors can be confusing. But you can easily convert between Hex and Decimal using the Microsoft Windows 95 (or Microsoft Windows 98) Calculator. Just open the Calculator. (From the Windows Start menu, choose Programs-Accessories-Calculator.) If the smaller standard calculator appears, choose View-Scientific from the Calculator's menu bar to switch to the larger scientific calculator.

From there, you can select the Hex option button to enter a number in hexadecimal or choose the Dec option button to enter a number in decimal. To convert the number, select the Hex or Dec option button. For example, if you select Hex, enter FFFFFF and then select Dec. The calculator will display 16777215, which is the decimal equivalent of FFFFFF.

The VBScript *Hex()* function can also convert a decimal number to a hexadecimal number for you. For example, a script containing *alert Hex(16777215)* displays FFFFFF, which is the hexadecimal equivalent of 16777215.

REVEAL TRANSITION FILTERS

You've probably heard of special transition effects called wipes, dissolves, and so forth. They're often used in videos to smooth out—or add a special effect to—the transition from one scene to another. To see some examples, open 1119.htm from the Chapter 11 examples on the companion CD (or at my web site). You'll come to a page that looks something like Figure 11-19 on the next page.

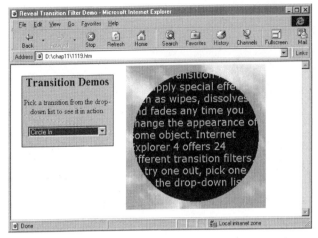

Figure 11-19. *The 1119.htm page demonstrates reveal transition filters.*

To experiment, select the name of a transition filter from the drop-down list. The text will dissolve and reveal a picture of some clouds. To try another one, select another transition filter.

Defining a Reveal Transition Filter

Like the visual filters, the reveal transition filters are CSS attributes. The syntax for defining a reveal transition filter within an HTML tag is:

```
filter:RevealTrans(Duration=duration, Transition=transition)
```

duration is how long it will take to complete the transition expressed in *seconds.milliseconds* format. (For example, 3.0 means 3 seconds). *transition* is a number from 0 to 23, which indicates the transition type. Table 11-4 lists all 24 available transition types.

To make the RevealTrans filter work, you must apply it to an object whose appearance will change. The most typical scenario is to apply it to a division (*<DIV>* tag) that contains two or more objects. Then you write a script that makes one of the objects in the division visible and the other object invisible. Within that script, you must use the *Apply()* and *Play()* methods of the RevealTrans filter to ensure that the filter does its thing when one object becomes invisible and the other becomes visible.

Let's take it from the top. Suppose we start with a blank web page and create the following division inside the *<BODY>...</BODY>* tags, like this:

```
<BODY>
<!-- Create a division named twoPix that contains two objects -->
<!-- and also has a reveal transition filter applied. -->
```

```
<DIV ID="twoPix" STYLE="position:absolute; left:50; top:50;
width:189; height:276; border:1 solid black;
background-color: silver;
filter:RevealTrans(Duration=4.0, Transition=23)">

</DIV>
</BODY>
```

Table 11-4

TRANSITION TYPES SUPPORTED BY THE REVEALTRANS FILTER

Transition Type	Value
Box in	0
Box out	1
Circle in	2
Circle out	3
Wipe up	4
Wipe down	5
Wipe right	6
Wipe left	7
Vertical blinds	8
Horizontal blinds	9
Checkerboard across	10
Checkerboard down	11
Random dissolve	12
Split vertical in	13
Split vertical out	14
Split horizontal in	15
Split horizontal out	16
Strips left down	17
Strips left up	18
Strips right down	19
Strips right up	20
Random bars horizontal	21
Random bars vertical	22
Random	23

Notice that I named this division object *twoPix*. I also assigned a reveal transition filter to the object using a *filter:RevealTrans(...)* CSS attribute. Within this division, we need at least two objects so we can hide one and reveal the other. For this example, we'll use graphic images, one named crayons.jpg, which is initially visible, and the other named clown.gif, which is initially invisible. We want these two image to overlap, so we'll give each the same size and position. Here are the appropriate *<IMG>* tags added to our *twoPix* division:

```
<BODY>
<!-- Create a division named twoPix that contains two objects -->
<!-- and also has a reveal transition filter applied. -->
<DIV ID="twoPix" STYLE="position:absolute; left:50; top:50;
width:189; height:276; border:1 solid black;
background-color: silver;
filter:RevealTrans(Duration=4.0, Transition=23)">

    <!-- Place two equal-sized, identically positioned objects, -->
    <!-- one visible and the other invisible, within this division. -->
    <IMG ID="firstImg" SRC="crayons.jpg" WIDTH="169" HEIGHT="256"
    STYLE="position:absolute; top:10; left:10; visibility:visible">

    <IMG ID="secondImg" SRC="clown.gif" WIDTH="169" HEIGHT="256"
    STYLE="position:absolute; top:10; left:10; visibility:hidden">
</DIV>

</BODY>
```

The next step is to create a script that applies (readies) the transition filter, defines the transition by making one object visible and the other invisible, and then plays the transition. The basic structure of such a script looks like this:

```
Sub whateverName()
    'Get that transition filter ready.
    objectName1.filters(n).Apply()

    'Make currently visible object invisible, then make
    'the other object visible.
    objectName2.style.visibility = "hidden"
    objectName3.style.visibility = "visible"

    'And now play the transition.
    objectName1.filters(n).Play()
End Sub
```

objectName1 is the name of the object that contains the reveal transition filter (*twoPix* in our example). The *n* value is the index of the reveal transition filter. For instance, if the object named *objectName1* has only one filter assigned to it or if the reveal transition filter is the first filter defined for the object, *n* will be zero.

The objects represented by the named *objectName2* and *objectName3* are objects within *objectName1* that can be made visible or invisible. As you might recall from the HTML tags, in this example I placed two objects, one named *firstImg* and the other named *secondImg*, within the *twoPix* object. Our sample page needs a script that follows the basic script structure discussed previously. The script named *doTrans*, added to our sample page below, will do the trick:

```
<BODY>
<!-- Create a division named twoPix that contains two objects -->
<!-- and also has a reveal transition filter applied. -->
<DIV ID="twoPix" STYLE="Position:absolute; Left:50; Top:50;
   Width:189; Height: 276; Border: 1 solid black;
   Background-color: silver;
   filter:RevealTrans(Duration=4.0, Transition=23)">

   <!-- Place two equal-sized, identically positioned objects, -->
   <!-- one visible and the other invisible, within this division. -->
   <IMG ID="firstImg" SRC="crayons.jpg" WIDTH="169" HEIGHT="256"
   STYLE="position:absolute; top:10; left:10; visibility:visible">

   <IMG ID="secondImg" SRC="clown.gif" WIDTH="169" HEIGHT="256"
   STYLE="position:absolute; top:10; left:10; visibility:hidden">
</DIV>

<SCRIPT LANGUAGE="VBScript"><!--
   Sub doTrans()
      'Get that transition filter ready.
      twoPix.filters(0).Apply()
      'Make currently visible image (firstImg) invisible, then make
      'the other image (secondImg) visible.
      firstImg.style.visibility = "hidden"
      secondImg.style.visibility = "visible"
      'And now play the transition.
      twoPix.filters(0).Play()
   End Sub
</SCRIPT>
```

We're almost done here. But we need some kind of event to trigger the *doTrans* sub procedure into action. We could bind this script to a button click or an *onmouseover* event or whatever. But for this example, let's say we want the transition to take place automatically, 5 seconds after the page is loaded. To make that happen, we need to add just one more procedure that, once the page is loaded, waits 5 seconds and then calls *doTrans* once. On the next page is the *window_onload()* procedure added to our page so far.

```
<BODY>
<!-- Create a division named twoPix that contains two objects -->
<!-- and also has a reveal transition filter applied. -->
<DIV ID="twoPix" STYLE="position:absolute; left:50; top:50;
width:189; height:276; border:1 solid black;
background-color: silver;
filter:RevealTrans(Duration=4.0, Transition=23)">

    <!-- Place two equal-sized, identically positioned objects, -->
    <!-- one visible and the other invisible, within this division -->
    <IMG ID="firstImg" SRC="crayons.jpg" WIDTH="169" HEIGHT="256"
    STYLE="Position:absolute; top:10; left:10; visibility:visible">

    <IMG ID="secondImg" SRC="clown.gif" WIDTH="169" HEIGHT="256"
    STYLE="position:absolute; top:10; left:10; visibility:hidden">
</DIV>

<SCRIPT LANGUAGE="VBScript"><!--
    Sub doTrans()
        'Get that transition filter ready.
        twoPix.filters(0).Apply()
        'Make currently visible image (firstImg) invisible, then make
        'the other image (secondImg) visible.
        firstImg.style.visibility = "hidden"
        secondImg.style.visibility = "visible"
        'And now play the transition.
        twoPix.filters(0).Play()
    End Sub

    Sub window_onload()
        'Call the doTrans sub 5 seconds after page is loaded.
        timeoutID = window.setTimeout("doTrans", 5000, "VBScript")
    End Sub
--></SCRIPT>
</BODY>
```

That's all it takes. To finish the job, you add the usual *<HTML>...</HTML>* and *<HEAD>...</HEAD>* tags and so forth. You then close the document and open it up in Internet Explorer. After a brief delay of about 5 seconds, the crayon image will automatically fade out, using some random transition filter (because I selected transition type 23), and reveal the picture of the clown. I can't really show a transition here, but Figure 11-20 gives you an idea how the effect would look to a visitor. The picture of the clown is gradually replacing the picture of the crayons using a box out transition.

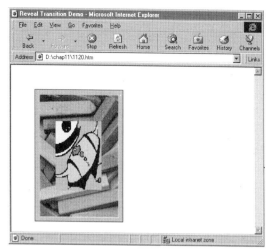

Figure 11-20. *A reveal transition filter slowly replacing the crayon picture with a clown picture using a box out type transition.*

BLEND TRANSITION FILTERS

The blend transition filters are similar to the reveal transition filters except that the transition from one object to the other is a smooth blending rather than a definite transition, and there are no multiple transition types. The syntax for defining a blend transition is almost identical to the syntax for a reveal transition. However, you use the word *BlendTrans* rather than *RevealTrans*, and you don't include a *Transition* parameter. Here is the actual syntax, where *duration* is the length of time the transition should take to complete, expressed in seconds.milliseconds (0.000).

```
filter:BlendTrans(Duration=duration)
```

The scripting syntax for making a blend transition happen is much the same as the syntax for starting a reveal transition. Once again, the basic syntax of the script is:

```
Sub whateverName()
   'Get that blend transition filter ready.
   objectName1.filters(n).Apply()

   'Make one object invisible, the other visible.
   objectName2.style.visibility = "hidden"
   objectName3.style.visibility = "visible"

   'And now play the blend transition.
   objectName1.filters(n).Play()
End Sub
```

Here's an example using a text object and an image object. These tags define a division object named *twoObjects* that has a blend transition applied to it. Within the *twoObject* division are two objects, *firstObject* (which is a yellow rectangle with some text) and *secondObject* (which is a picture of a clown). Initially, *firstObject* is visible and *secondObject* is invisible:

```
<BODY>
<!-- Create a division named twoObjects that contains two objects -->
<!-- and also has a blend transition filter applied. -->
<DIV ID="twoObjects" STYLE="position:absolute; left:50; top:50;
width:189; height:276; border:1 solid black;
background-color: silver;
filter:BlendTrans(Duration=10.0)">

    <!-- Place two equal-sized, identically positioned objects, -->
    <!-- one visible and the other invisible, within this division. -->
    <DIV ID="firstObject" WIDTH="169" HEIGHT="256"
    STYLE="position:absolute; top:10; left:10;
    width:169; height:256; background-color:yellow;
    visibility:visible; font-size:36pt">
      <CENTER>HI!</CENTER>
    </DIV>

    <IMG ID="secondObject" SRC="clown.gif" WIDTH="169" HEIGHT="256"
    STYLE="position:absolute; top:10; left:10; visibility:hidden">
</DIV>
```

Next we need a script to perform the transition and another script to trigger that first script into action based on some event. In the example below, the sub procedure named *doTrans* performs the transition. The *window_onload( )* procedure sees to it that the *doTrans* sub procedure is executed 3 seconds after the page has been loaded into the visitor's web browser:

```
<SCRIPT LANGUAGE="VBScript"><!--
   Sub doTrans()
      'Get that transition filter ready.
      twoObjects.filters(0).Apply()
      'Make currently visible object (firstObject) invisible, then
      'make the other object (secondObject) visible to cause
      'transition.
      firstObject.style.visibility = "hidden"
      secondObject.style.visibility = "visible"
      'And now play the transition.
      twoObjects.filters(0).Play()
   End Sub
```

```
Sub window_onload()
    'After loading page, wait 3 seconds then do the
    'transition.
    timeoutID = window.setTimeout("doTrans", 3000, "VBScript")
End Sub
--></SCRIPT>
</BODY>
```

Figure 11-21 shows the blend transition filter slowly replacing the yellow rectangle and text with a clown picture.

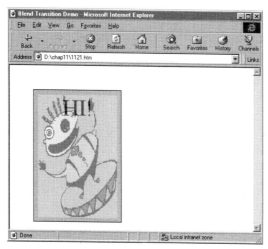

Figure 11-21. *A blend transition filter in progress.*

INTERPAGE TRANSITIONS

Last but not least is the type of transition that takes place just as the visitor is opening or exiting a particular page via a hyperlink or another navigation method. The interpage transition is applied to the entire page rather than to specific objects within the page. The code for interpage transitions is placed in a *<META>* tag in the head section of the page.

The syntax consists of three parts, which specify when the transition should be played, how long the transition should take, and the type of transition to use. All 24 transition types summarized earlier in Table 11-3 are acceptable. The basic structure of the *<META>* tag looks like this:

```
<META http-equiv="Page-when"
CONTENT="RevealTrans(Duration=duration, Transition=transition)>
```

when is the word *Enter* if you want the transition to take place when the page is first opened; it is the word *Exit* if you want the transition to take place when the visitor exits the page. *duration* is the how long it takes to complete the transition expressed in seconds.milliseconds (0.000), and *transition* is a number from 0 to 23 indicating which transition type to use. (See Table 11-4.)

Figure 11-22 shows the document source for a sample page with both Enter and Exit interpage transitions defined. The first *<META>* tag, shown below, defines a Random Dissolve (type 12) transition that will take 2 seconds when a visitor first opens the page.

```
<!-- Do a Random Dissolve transition on entry. -->
<META http-equiv="Page-Enter"
CONTENT="RevealTrans(Duration=2.0, Transition=12)">
```

The second *<META>* tag, shown below, defines a Circle Out (type 3) transition that will take 2 seconds and will be triggered when the visitor leaves this page.

```
<!-- Do a Circle Out transition on exit. -->
<META http-equiv="Page-Exit"
CONTENT="RevealTrans(Duration=2.0, Transition=3)">
```

Figure 11-23 shows the Circle Out transition in progress as the visitor leaves this page.

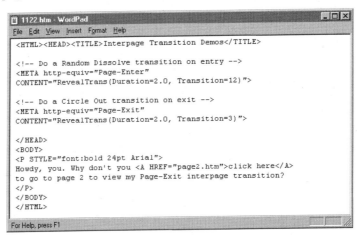

Figure 11-22. *The document source for the page with two interpage transitions defined.*

Figure 11-23. *A Circle Out interpage transition in progress.*

SUMMARY

I suppose I could have titled this chapter "Special Effects Mania" because there's so much you can do with all the visual filters and transition effects built into Internet Explorer 4. In true Dynamic HTML fashion, you can apply these filters and effects to virtually any object or group of objects that you place in a web page. Also in true Dynamic HTML fashion, you can write scripts to alter the appearance and behavior of the visual filters. To review the main points:

- A visual filter is a CSS attribute that applies some form of distortion or special effect to one or more objects in a page.

- Visual filters are defined using the general syntax STYLE="filter:*filterName*(*fparameters*)", where *filterName* is any valid visual filter (such as DropShadow, Glow, or Wave) and *fparameters* are parameters appropriate to that particular filter.

- The object model automatically creates a *filters* collection for every object that has one or more visual filters applied to it.

- To change a visual filter's parameters (properties) via VBScript code, use the general syntax *objectName*.filters(*n*).*property* = *newValue*.

- Reveal and blend transition filters let you define special effects that take place when displaying another object.

- Interpage transitions are transition filters that play when the reader enters or exits the page.

- Interpage transitions are defined by <*META*> tags in the head of the page.

Well, alright then. You've certainly learned a lot about Internet Explorer 4, Dynamic HTML, CSS, and VBScript by now. In the next chapter, which starts Part III, we'll look at yet another technology that offers web authors a cornucopia of creative possibilities—ActiveX controls.

PART III

USING ACTIVEX CONTROLS

So far, we've mainly focused on what's new in Microsoft Internet Explorer 4—particularly Dynamic HTML and the new object model. As you've seen, practically everything that you put into a web page can be treated as an object. And you can use VBScript (or JavaScript) code to programmatically control the appearance and behavior of any object. All of the objects we've discussed so far are "built in"—they're either a part of the web browser (for example, the *navigator* object) or part of the page being displayed (something you create by adding the appropriate HTML tags to a page).

In addition to the world of built-in objects, there's another entire world of "external" objects know as ActiveX controls. In Part III of this book, you'll learn, in general terms, what ActiveX controls are and how to add them to your web pages. We'll also look at some of the freebie ActiveX controls that come with Internet Explorer 4, including the DirectShow ActiveMovie control and the DirectAnimation Multimedia Path, Structured Graphics, Sequencer, and Sprite controls, all of which can help you jazz up your web pages!

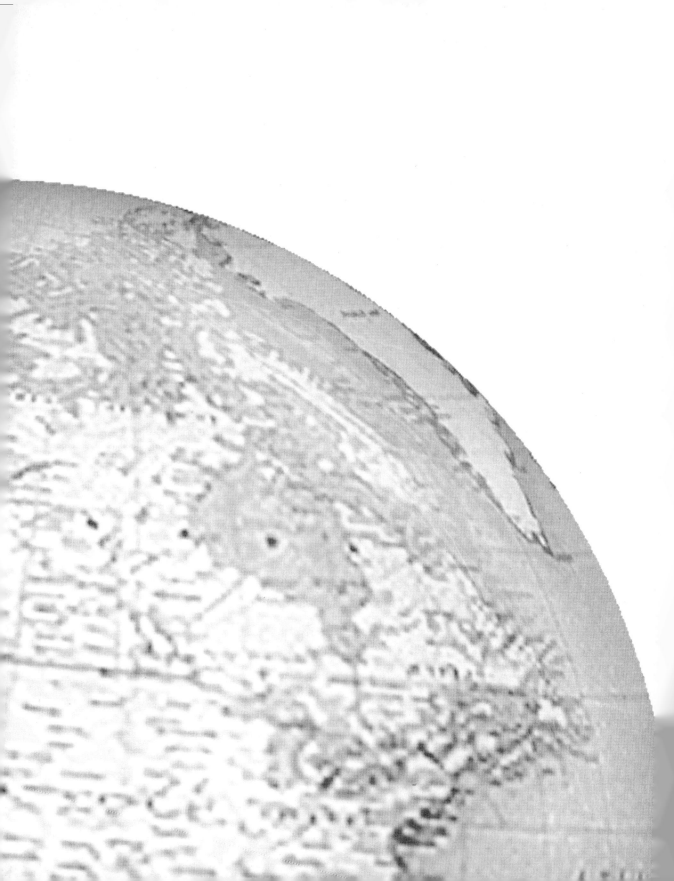

Chapter 12

Getting into ActiveX

As we've discussed in previous chapters, virtually everything that you put into a web page can be treated as an object and manipulated with code. The built-in object model provides the naming system for referring to the various objects in a page. Amazingly, though, you're not limited to using the many built-in objects. You can add external objects in the form of ActiveX controls (also called ActiveX objects) to bring even more capability to your web pages. In this chapter, you'll learn the basics of ActiveX controls, including:

■   What ActiveX is all about

■   Adjusting your security settings to accept ActiveX controls

■   How ActiveX controls look in a web page

■   The difference between run-time and developer versions of ActiveX controls

■   How to insert ActiveX controls into a web page

■   How to manipulate inserted ActiveX controls

■   ActiveX resources

Please keep in mind that this chapter is pretty general—I'm discussing issues that relate to all ActiveX controls. Dozens, perhaps hundreds, of ActiveX controls are available for Microsoft Internet Explorer. And many HTML editors are available, each with its own specific steps for inserting ActiveX controls into documents. I can't begin to cover the specifics of all those products. However, I think the general information presented here, followed by the more specific examples that follow in later chapters, will help you become an ActiveX guru in a fairly short time.

WHAT IS ACTIVEX?

ActiveX is a suite of technologies designed to make it easier to create applications and more interactive web sites. The idea behind ActiveX goes something like this: Most computer programs (including interactive web pages) use many of the same kinds of components—for example, a way for the reader to view videos, a simple scroll bar, or a way for the reader to get instant access to her Address Book in Microsoft Windows.

In the past, if you wanted to use such a component but didn't have one built into your programming language, you had to create it from scratch by writing code. This left a lot of programmers "reinventing the wheel"—writing their own code to do simple, common things. (It was an expensive and time-consuming process, I might add.)

ActiveX helps solve this problem by providing prewritten components, called ActiveX controls, that can easily be "dropped into" a web page (or a program). You don't need to write the code to create the control—you don't even have to know how to write code. All you have to do is get a licensed version of the control into your web page or program—a process we'll discuss as we proceed in this chapter. Figure 12-1 shows a sample of three ActiveX controls in a web page.

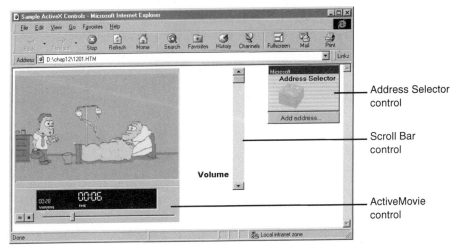

Figure 12-1. *A video viewer, a scroll bar, and an Address Book access ActiveX control.*

The ActiveX Controversy

You might be aware of the controversy about security risks that ActiveX controls pose to web browsers. Let me take a moment to discuss the issue and alleviate some of the anxiety it might cause. Every ActiveX control is actually a mini-program, and like any program, it is stored in a file. Before an ActiveX control can do its thing on someone's PC, a copy of that control's file must be downloaded to the PC if a copy has not been downloaded to that PC before. This downloading of files to PCs poses some risks to ActiveX "consumers." A cyber-vandal could easily create an ActiveX control that does harm to a visitor's computer. But the powers that be have taken measures to minimize the likelihood that bad ActiveX controls will get onto your PC.

When a reader accesses a web page containing ActiveX controls using an ActiveX-aware browser such as Internet Explorer, the browser checks certain security settings and behaves according to those settings. The browser might warn the reader and let him decide whether to proceed with the download or cancel the action, for instance. But how does the average web-browsing Joe (or Josephine) know which controls are safe to download and which aren't? This is where "digital signatures" come into play.

The Solution (So Far)

A digital signature makes the programmer or company who created the ActiveX control "findable." Anyone who is findable is obviously accountable. If a programmer were to plant something malicious in an ActiveX control, digitally signing that control would be a big mistake. Anyone who ended up with that bad control would know exactly who was to blame. But any software publisher who puts out clean ActiveX controls would be wise to digitally sign its controls to instill confidence in readers.

By default, when Internet Explorer detects a digital signature on an incoming ActiveX control, a dialog box asks the reader for permission to download the control. The dialog box also shows who certifies the control. For example, in Figure 12-2 on the next page, I'm asked if I'll allow an ActiveX control named "Smart Controls" from CNET to be downloaded to my PC. The warning shows me that the control is signed and verified by VeriSign Commercial Software Publishers.

If I don't trust this control, I can just click No to cancel the download, and no control will be downloaded to my PC. Or, I can click Yes to download the control. I can also click the *CNET, Inc.* link to learn more about CNET's certificate before making a decision. Notice the little check box labeled Always Trust Software From CNET, Inc. Selecting that check box grants CNET "trustworthy" status, which means that in the future, ActiveX controls from CNET will automatically be downloaded.

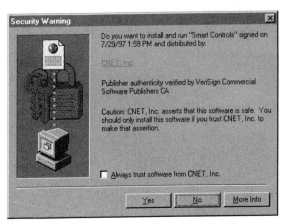

Figure 12-2. *A dialog box asking the visitor for permission to download a control digitally signed by CNET.*

So what happens if a web site tries to send me an unsigned control? By default, Internet Explorer will not allow the control to be downloaded and I won't even be given a choice. If my security settings are more liberal, I'll get a message that the current web site is trying to send an unsigned control to my PC—something like the one shown in Figure 12-3. Buttons let me choose whether I want to download this unsigned control.

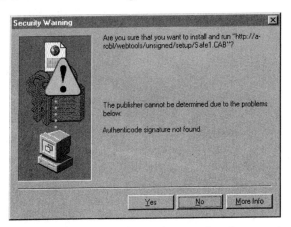

Figure 12-3. *A dialog box indicating that the control to be downloaded has not been digitally signed.*

So if you're planning to use ActiveX controls in your web site, the first thing you need to do is make sure that *your* web browser will allow—at the very least—signed controls to be downloaded to your PC. The next section shows you how to do that.

ADJUSTING YOUR BROWSER'S ACTIVEX SECURITY

You can decide how "liberal" you want your web browser to be in accepting ActiveX controls. If you plan to use ActiveX controls in your own web pages, the first thing you need to do is make sure that your web browser is capable of displaying those controls. You do this by adjusting the security level of the browser. Using Internet Explorer 4 as the browser, here are the exact steps:

1. Start Internet Explorer in the usual manner.

2. Choose Internet Options from the View menu to open the Internet Options dialog box.

3. Click on the Security tab (shown in Figure 12-4).

4. Select Internet Zone from the Zone drop-down list.

5. Select Medium from the Security Level options.

6. Click OK to save the changes.

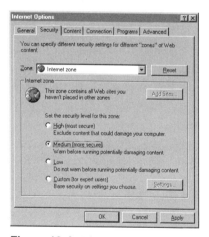

Figure 12-4. *The Internet Zone security level is set to Medium for this web browser.*

This setting will allow signed ActiveX controls to be downloaded to your PC and then run. However, it will not allow unsigned ActiveX controls onto your PC. If you want to experiment with unsigned ActiveX controls, you must repeat the steps above but set the Security Level to Low. Alternatively, you can also set the Security Level to Custom and adjust the security levels for signed and unsigned ActiveX controls individually.

WHAT AN ACTIVEX CONTROL LOOKS LIKE

Figure 12-1 showed some examples of ActiveX controls from a visitor's perspective. As a web author, you of course need to know what an ActiveX control looks like in the document source. Within the document source of a web page, an ActiveX control is represented by a pair of *<OBJECT>...</OBJECT>* tags, with typically some *<PARAM>* tags in between, as in the example shown in Figure 12-5.

```
1205.htm - WordPad
File  Edit  View  Insert  Format  Help
<HTML><HEAD><TITLE>Sample ActiveX Control</TITLE></HEAD>
<BODY>

<!-- Object below is for a Label Object control-->
<OBJECT ID="IeLabel1" WIDTH=189 HEIGHT=75
 CLASSID="CLSID:99B42120-6EC7-11CF-A6C7-00AA00A47DD2">
    <PARAM NAME="_ExtentX" VALUE="5001">
    <PARAM NAME="_ExtentY" VALUE="1958">
    <PARAM NAME="Caption" VALUE="SPINNY">
    <PARAM NAME="Angle" VALUE="0">
    <PARAM NAME="Alignment" VALUE="4">
    <PARAM NAME="Mode" VALUE="1">
    <PARAM NAME="FillStyle" VALUE="0">
    <PARAM NAME="FillStyle" VALUE="0">
    <PARAM NAME="ForeColor" VALUE="#000000">
    <PARAM NAME="BackColor" VALUE="#C0C0C0">
    <PARAM NAME="FontName" VALUE="Arial">
    <PARAM NAME="FontSize" VALUE="36">
    <PARAM NAME="FontItalic" VALUE="0">
    <PARAM NAME="FontBold" VALUE="1">
    <PARAM NAME="FontUnderline" VALUE="0">
    <PARAM NAME="FontStrikeout" VALUE="0">
    <PARAM NAME="TopPoints" VALUE="0">
    <PARAM NAME="BotPoints" VALUE="0">
</OBJECT>

</BODY></HTML>
For Help, press F1
```

Figure 12-5. *An ActiveX control in the document source of a web page.*

Let's look at some of the attributes specified in the opening *<OBJECT>* tag. The *ID* attribute specifies a name for the object. This is no different from the *ID* attribute used in any other HTML tag—you can use the name specified by the *ID* attribute to refer to the object from within scripting code.

The *CLASSID* attribute specifies the control's class ID value. Every ActiveX control has a unique class ID that was encoded into the control when the control was initially created. This value is very important because it's used by the web browser to determine which control should be loaded and possibly where to find the control. There's no way to guess the correct class ID for a control, and there's no margin for error when you type the class ID. If the class ID is incorrect, the control will not be loaded into the web page. Fortunately, as we'll discuss later, some tools are available for inserting an ActiveX control, including its proper class ID.

The *<OBJECT>* tag for some ActiveX controls will also contain a *CODEBASE* attribute. This attribute specifies the URL for where a copy of the control resides. When the web page containing an object tag is loaded into the visitor's web browser, the browser checks the Windows Registry to determine if the control is already installed on the reader's PC. If it has not already been installed, the browser automatically goes to the URL defined by the *CODEBASE* attribute and downloads the control from there.

Not all ActiveX controls require a *CODEBASE* attribute. The only way to know if you need to use a *CODEBASE* attribute is by referring to the documentation for the ActiveX control in use. I'll discuss that in more detail a little later in this chapter.

The *<PARAM NAME=... VALUE=...>* tags between the control's *<OBJECT>... </OBJECT>* tags are optional parameters that you can set to customize the control for your own purposes. Like properties in the object model, parameters are just the properties of the ActiveX control object. Every ActiveX control has its own unique set of customizable parameters. And again, the only way to know exactly which parameters a control supports is through the documentation that tells you about that control.

What the Object Tag Refers to

As I mentioned earlier, every ActiveX control is actually a "miniprogram" in its own file. That file generally has an .ocx file name extension. Most ActiveX controls are stored in the Windows\System folder on the visitor's hard disk. Controls downloaded with Internet Explorer 4 are typically installed in the special folder Windows\Downloaded Program Files. When a web browser encounters an *<OBJECT>* tag, it first checks to see if the control specified by the *CLASSID* attribute is indeed on the visitor's PC. If the control is there, the page just loads the control from the local hard drive.

If the control is not already on the reader's PC, the web browser uses information supplied by the *CLASSID* value (and perhaps the *CODEBASE* URL) to locate and download the control to the reader's PC. This is a clever approach because it means that any ActiveX control that a reader encounters need only be downloaded to that reader's PC once. Once the control has been downloaded, Internet Explorer 4 is smart enough to use the local copy of the control rather than making the visitor wait for the control to be downloaded again.

Developer vs. Run-Time Versions of Controls

There are web site "visitors" and there are web site authors. Likewise, there are two versions of most ActiveX controls available on the Web:

- Run-time version—used only by visitors and always free of charge
- Developer's version—used by web authors and usually not free of charge

Let me give you an example. Suppose you navigate to a web site and you see a message indicating that the current page wants to send you an ActiveX control named Rover (for lack of a better name). If you choose Yes, the run-time version of Rover is downloaded to your PC and does its thing (whatever that might be). However, this doesn't mean you can put Rover into your own pages as an ActiveX control for others to use.

If you want to use the Rover control in your own web page, you typically need to buy the developer's version of the control or at least a special license pack that allows you to distribute the control. I'll list some sites that sell developer's versions of ActiveX controls in the section titled "ActiveX Resources" near the end of this chapter.

Many publishers of ActiveX controls provide demonstration pages of their controls so you can try them out. If you try out a demo, you'll probably see the message asking whether it's OK to download the control to your PC. You have to choose Yes to actually see the demo. But keep in mind that the control being downloaded at that point is probably just the run-time version of the control. If you plan to use that control in the web pages you create yourself, you'll probably still need to purchase, and probably separately download, the developer's version, documentation, and licensing information for that control.

Finally, it's important to keep in mind that ActiveX technology is not just for the Internet. Some, but not all, ActiveX controls can be used with Internet Explorer. Other ActiveX controls can't be used on the Internet at all—they're designed for use with other Microsoft products such as Visual Basic or Access.

So before you purchase any ActiveX control, make sure that it will work with Internet Explorer 4. Also, be sure to tell the manufacturer that you plan to use the controls in your web site and therefore need the developer's version with the developer's documentation and license pack.

TIP   Internet Explorer 4 comes with the developer's version of some freebie ActiveX controls that you can put to use right away, even as a web author. We'll discuss the specifics in Chapter 13.

ADDING ACTIVEX CONTROLS TO A WEB PAGE

You can add an ActiveX control to a web page in several ways. The most basic way is to open the HTML document in a text editor such as Notepad or WordPad and manually type in the appropriate <OBJECT>...</OBJECT> tags with the <PARAM> tags in between. That method is prone to errors, however, so I don't recommend it. It's better to use a good HTML editor such as Microsoft FrontPage or the ActiveX Control Pad, which we'll discuss in the sections that follow.

Adding ActiveX Controls with FrontPage

FrontPage 97, FrontPage 98, and FrontPage Express all offer menu commands to simplify the task of adding an ActiveX control to a web page.

NOTE The example below is very general and is just meant to give you a feel for how you might go about inserting an ActiveX control into your web page. If you're looking for a more "hands-on" example, see Chapter 13.

Take the following steps to insert the control:

1. Create or open the page to which you want to add the ActiveX control.

2. In FrontPage, move the insertion point to about where you want to place the ActiveX control.

3. From the Insert menu, choose Other Components, and then choose ActiveX Control from the submenu. You'll see an ActiveX Control Properties dialog box like the one shown in Figure 12-6.

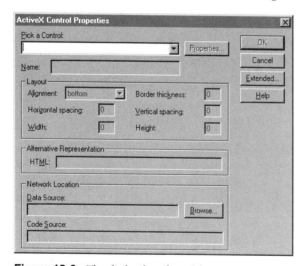

Figure 12-6. *The dialog box for adding an ActiveX Control in FrontPage Express.*

NOTE FrontPage 98 hadn't been released when I wrote this chapter. But from what I could see in the beta version, you might need to choose Insert-Advanced-ActiveX Control in step 3 if you're using FrontPage 98.

4. From the Pick A Control drop-down list, select the name of the ActiveX control you want to add to the current page. (The list shows the names of all ActiveX controls currently installed on your PC.)

5. In the Name text box, you can give this control a unique name for scripting purposes. You can also set the alignment, width, height, and so forth, just as you can with a graphic image. You can leave those options blank, though, and the defaults will be filled in automatically when you complete the next step.

6. To add or change the *<PARAM...>* tags that allow you to tailor the control to your needs, click the Properties button. Select or type in parameter values as described in the next section, "Specifying ActiveX Control Parameters."

7. Click OK after specifying your parameters.

8. Click OK to close the ActiveX Control Properties dialog box.

The ActiveX control appears in the page, usually represented by an icon showing how it looks or by an ActiveX icon (like the example near the upper-left corner of Figure 12-7). If you view the document source for the page (by choosing HTML from the View menu in FrontPage 97 and FrontPage Express or by clicking on the HTML tab in FrontPage 98), you can also see the *<OBJECT>...</OBJECT>* and *<PARAM>* tags inserted by FrontPage. FrontPage normally uses all lowercase letters for HTML tags, but I changed them to uppercase letters in Figure 12-7 to call attention to those tags.

To see the ActiveX control in action, you have to save the current web page and then open it up in Internet Explorer.

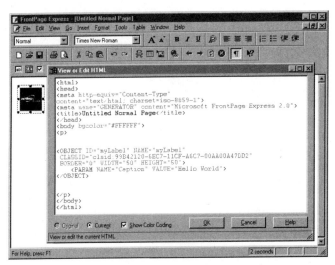

Figure 12-7. *The inserted ActiveX control is represented by an icon—and by* <OBJECT>...</OBJECT> *tags in the document source.*

Specifying ActiveX Control Parameters

When it comes time to specify parameters for an ActiveX control, you might be presented with an Edit ActiveX Control grid and Properties sheet, like that shown in Figure 12-8. Or you might see the Object Parameters dialog box shown in Figure 12-9. What you see depends on the control you are working with and the program you're using to add the control to your web page. The first situation, in which the Edit ActiveX Control grid and Properties sheet appear, is the easiest to work with, so I'll discuss it first.

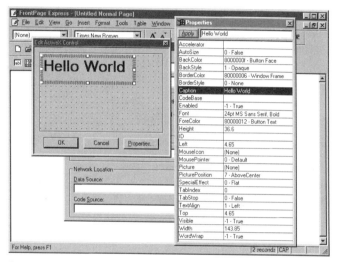

Figure 12-8. *The Edit ActiveX Control grid and Properties sheet for a sample control.*

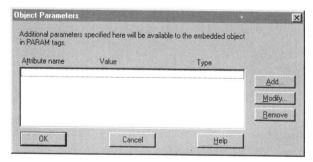

Figure 12-9. *The Object Parameters dialog box for a sample control.*

TIP If you're in FrontPage and want to change the parameters for a control that's already in your page, you can double-click on the icon that represents the control or right-click on the icon and choose ActiveX Control Properties from the popup menu.

Specifying Parameters Using the Edit ActiveX Control Grid and Properties Sheet

If you are fortunate enough to be using a control and an HTML editor that support the Edit ActiveX Control grid and Properties sheet, specifying parameters is fairly simple. You just click on the name of a parameter in the Properties sheet, click in the text box next to the Apply button near the top of the sheet, type in a new value for the parameter, and then click the Apply button or click on another parameter. For example, in Figure 12-8 I typed in *Hello World* as the new value for the *Caption* parameter and then clicked the Apply button.

The Edit ActiveX Control grid next to the Properties sheet lets you visually size the control, so you don't need to guess at the dimensions in pixels. To size the control displayed in the grid, rest the mouse pointer on any sizing handle until the mouse pointer turns into a two-headed arrow. Then drag that sizing handle in the direction you want to expand or shrink the control.

When you finish specifying parameters and sizing the control, close the Properties sheet by clicking its Close button. Then close the Edit ActiveX Control grid by clicking its Close button. When you view the document source, you'll see that the control's *<PARAM>* tags reflect the choices you made in the Properties sheet.

Specifying Parameters Using the Object Parameters Dialog Box

Unfortunately, not all ActiveX controls and HTML editors support the Edit ActiveX Control grid and Properties sheet approach to specifying parameters. In some cases, you'll get the less visually oriented Object Parameters dialog box. To fill that out, you need to know the exact spelling of every parameter that the control offers. And you need to know how to specify valid values for each parameter. In short, you *really* need the documentation that comes with the developer's version of the ActiveX control because there's no way to just "fool around" with parameters and values to see what happens.

The way you work the Object Parameters dialog box is pretty straight-forward. To add a parameter, you click the Add button. You'll see a dialog box like the one shown in Figure 12-10. In the Name text box, type the exact name of the parameter you want to assign a value to. In the Data text box, type the exact value you want to assign to the parameter. For instance, in Figure 12-10 I opted to assign the value *Hello World* to the *Caption* parameter for the control.

NOTE   The Page and Object text boxes let you type in URLs and ActiveX control object names. You must rely on the developer's documentation for your ActiveX control to determine whether either of these is appropriate for the current parameter.

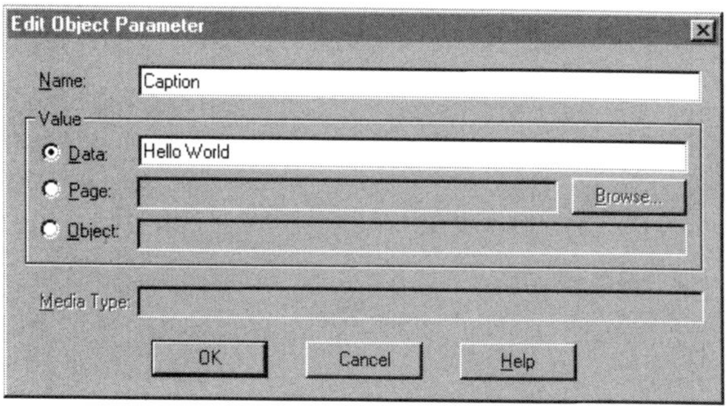

Figure 12-10. *I assigned the value* Hello World *to the* Caption *parameter.*

After typing the parameter name and value, click the OK button. Your new parameter name and value will be listed in the Object Parameters dialog box, as in Figure 12-11. If you want to change or delete an existing parameter definition, you can just click on it and then click the Modify button or the Remove button.

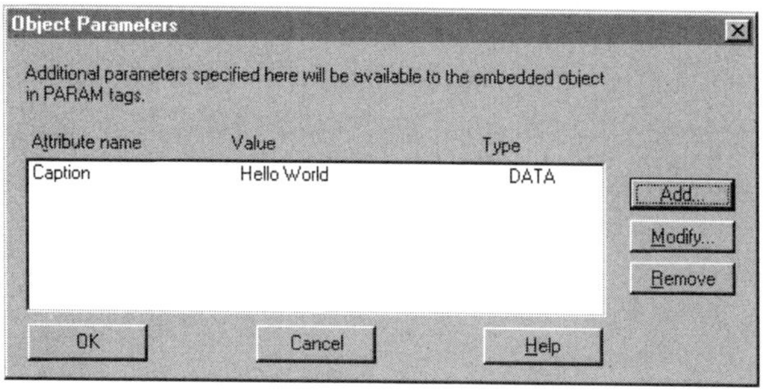

Figure 12-11. *One parameter and value added to the Object Parameters dialog box.*

When you finish adding all your parameters, you can click OK to close the Object Parameters dialog box.

Keep in mind that whether you use the Edit ActiveX Control grid and Properties sheet or the Object Parameters dialog box, all you're really doing is defining *<PARAM>* tags for the current ActiveX control. When you view the document source, you'll see the *<PARAM>* tags with the appropriate name and value, as in this example:

```
<OBJECT ID="myLabel"
 CLASSID="clsid:99B42120-6EC7-11CF-A6C7-00AA00A47DD2"
 BORDER="0" WIDTH="50" HEIGHT="50">
   <PARAM NAME="Caption" VALUE="Hello World">
</OBJECT>
```

If you like, you can also add, change, and delete parameters right in the document source. For example, to change the value of the *Caption* parameter from *Hello World* to *Howdy*, you can just type the change as shown below and then save the current version of the page:

```
<OBJECT ID="myLabel"
 CLASSID="clsid:99B42120-6EC7-11CF-A6C7-00AA00A47DD2"
 BORDER="0" WIDTH="50" HEIGHT="50">
    <PARAM NAME="Caption" VALUE="Howdy">
</OBJECT>
```

Adding Controls with the ActiveX Control Pad

Microsoft's ActiveX Control Pad is another tool for adding ActiveX controls to web pages. Unlike FrontPage and other wysiwyg editors, the Control Pad provides no wysiwyg view of your page. Instead, you work directly in the document source. Also unlike other HTML editors, which tend to be "general" in nature, the ActiveX Control Pad is specialized—its primary function is to help you place ActiveX controls in web pages.

In all fairness, I should say that the ActiveX Control Pad was designed as a tool for adding ActiveX controls to Internet Explorer 3 web pages, so adding newer controls in the Control Pad might produce unexpected results. Also, some of its features aren't really relevant to Internet Explorer 4. For example, the Control Pad contains a component called the HTML Layout control, which is used to position objects on the page. However, the *STYLE* attributes that the HTML Layout control inserts into *<OBJECT>...</OBJECT>* tags aren't quite up to modern CSS specifications for positioning objects. The Control Pad also includes a Script Wizard that's handy for piecing together scripts, but its scripts are based on the Internet Explorer 3 object model and don't take full advantage of the more extensive object model provided by Internet Explorer 4.

If you'd like to give the ActiveX Control Pad a whirl anyway, you can download a copy free of charge from www.microsoft.com/workshop/author/cpad/. That site also contains a white paper and information on using Control Pad, which you might want to print out. After you download the Control Pad, you must run the downloaded file—named setuppad.exe —to install the ActiveX Control Pad on your computer. You can then start the Control Pad from the Windows Start menu by choosing Programs-Microsoft ActiveX Control Pad-Microsoft ActiveX Control Pad. Once you're in the ActiveX Control Pad, you can use its Help menu to learn more about specific features of the program.

TIP   For quick access to the Control Pad, right-click on any .htm or .html document and choose Edit With ActiveX Control Pad from the popup menu. You can also drag copies of its shortcut startup icon to the desktop and to the C:\Windows\SendTo folder, as we discussed back in Chapter 1.

For our purposes in this chapter, we only care about having a tool that makes it easy to type the *<OBJECT>*, *<PARAM>*, and *</OBJECT>* tags needed to place an ActiveX control in a web page. That aspect of the ActiveX Control Pad is certainly simple to use. When you first start the ActiveX Control Pad, it opens and displays a web page with only the bare essential HTML tags already in it, as shown in Figure 12-12.

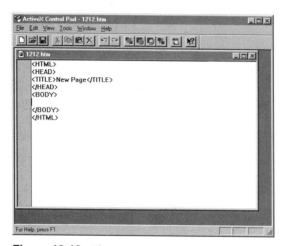

Figure 12-12. *The ActiveX Control Pad showing a new, blank web page.*

If you don't want to start with a new blank page, you can choose Open from the File menu in the ActiveX Control Pad to open any HTML document on your system. If you do start with a new blank page in the Control Pad, it might be a good idea to save the page you're about to create by choosing Save from the File menu. Save the page into the same folder as your other web pages. That way, any references to other objects within the page are more likely to contain the correct relative references for publishing on the Web.

To insert an ActiveX control using the Control Pad, follow these basic steps:

1. Move the cursor to about where you want to place the ActiveX control (between the *<BODY>...</BODY>* tags is fine if you're creating a new page).

2. Choose Insert ActiveX Control from the Edit menu.

3. In the dialog box that appears, select a control and then click OK. In Figure 12-13 on the next page, I selected a control named Label Object.

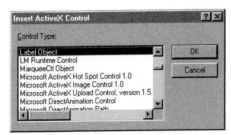

Figure 12-13. *The Label Object control is selected for insertion.*

4. This displays the Edit ActiveX Control grid and Properties sheet, as discussed earlier. There you can specify parameters for the control.

I specified the following values in the Properties sheet:

Angle = 45
Caption = ActiveX
FontBold = -1 - True
FontSize = 24
ID = axLabel

In the grid, I dragged down the lower-right sizing handle so that the control is large enough to display the full text, as shown in Figure 12-14.

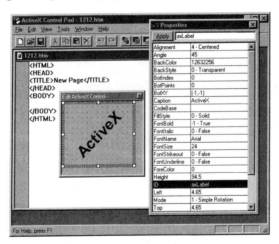

Figure 12-14. *The Label Object properties are set, and the control is sized.*

After specifying parameters and sizing the control, I closed the Properties sheet and the Edit ActiveX Control grid by clicking the Close button in the upper-right corner of each. The appropriate tags for displaying the ActiveX control are inserted into the page, as shown in Figure 12-15.

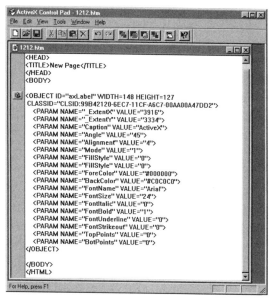

Figure 12-15. *The* <OBJECT> *and* <PARAM> *tags are inserted by the ActiveX Control Pad.*

At this point, if you need to make changes to the tags, you can type them manually into the document source. Or if you want to get back to the Edit ActiveX Control grid and Properties sheet, click the little cube button just to the left of the opening *<OBJECT>* tag that defines the control you want to edit. To actually view the finished page, you must close and save it. Then open the page with Internet Explorer. For example, Figure 12-16 on the next page shows how the sample page I just developed looks when opened in Internet Explorer 4. It shows the word *ActiveX* tilted at a 45-degree angle. (The ActiveX Label Object control just displays text, but it can do so at any angle.)

So the bottom line is that you can type the *<OBJECT>* and *<PARAM>* tags needed to display an ActiveX control directly in a web page. Or you can use FrontPage or the ActiveX Control Pad to help you type those tags. It doesn't matter which tool you use because in the end the result is the same: The page contains the new *<OBJECT>* and *<PARAM>* tags.

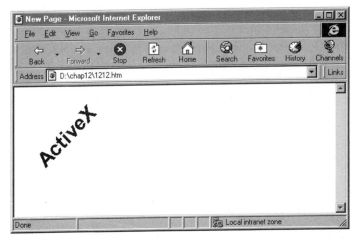

Figure 12-16. *A page containing an ActiveX Label Object control as viewed in Internet Explorer 4.*

MANIPULATING ACTIVEX CONTROLS

Once you insert an ActiveX control in a web page, your knowledge of manipulating objects still applies. Let me show you a couple of examples.

Positioning ActiveX Controls

ActiveX controls can be positioned, just like any other object, using the CSS attributes. For example, in Figure 12-17 I positioned the object named *axLabel* absolutely on the page, 100 pixels from the left edge of the page and 50 pixels down from the top edge, by adding a *STYLE="position:absolute; left:100; top:50"* attribute to the *<OBJECT>* tag that defines the ActiveX control.

Scripting ActiveX Controls

Scripting ActiveX controls is virtually identical to scripting built-in objects. The syntax to change a parameter (property) is:

```
objectName.parameterName = newValue
```

Figure 12-17. *An HTML document containing a positioned ActiveX control.*

objectName is any valid name to identify the ActiveX control such as the name specified with the *ID* attribute in the *<OBJECT>* tag. *parameterName* is any valid parameter for the control. *newValue* is a new value to assign to the parameter.

Here's a simple example using our sample *axLabel* control. Clicking the button changes the angle of the text in the control from 45 to 135:

```
<BUTTON ID="myButton">Click Me</BUTTON>
<SCRIPT FOR="myButton" EVENT="onclick" LANGUAGE="VBScript">
   axLabel.angle = 135
</SCRIPT>
```

Figure 12-18 shows the entire document source with all the tags in place, and Figure 12-19 shows how the page looks in Internet Explorer after the button has been clicked.

```
1218.htm - WordPad
File  Edit  View  Insert  Format  Help

<HTML><HEAD>
<TITLE>VBScript and an ActiveX Label Object Control</TITLE>
</HEAD><BODY>

<OBJECT ID="axLabel" WIDTH=148 HEIGHT=127
 STYLE="position:absolute; left:100; top:50"
 CLASSID="CLSID:99B42120-6EC7-11CF-A6C7-00AA00A47DD2">
     <PARAM NAME="_ExtentX" VALUE="3916">
     <PARAM NAME="_ExtentY" VALUE="3334">
     <PARAM NAME="Caption" VALUE="ActiveX">
     <PARAM NAME="Angle" VALUE="45">
     <PARAM NAME="Alignment" VALUE="4">
     <PARAM NAME="Mode" VALUE="1">
     <PARAM NAME="FillStyle" VALUE="0">
     <PARAM NAME="FillStyle" VALUE="0">
     <PARAM NAME="ForeColor" VALUE="#000000">
     <PARAM NAME="BackColor" VALUE="#C0C0C0">
     <PARAM NAME="FontName" VALUE="Arial">
     <PARAM NAME="FontSize" VALUE="24">
     <PARAM NAME="FontItalic" VALUE="0">
     <PARAM NAME="FontBold" VALUE="1">
     <PARAM NAME="FontUnderline" VALUE="0">
     <PARAM NAME="FontStrikeout" VALUE="0">
     <PARAM NAME="TopPoints" VALUE="0">
     <PARAM NAME="BotPoints" VALUE="0">
</OBJECT>

<BUTTON ID="myButton">Click Me</BUTTON>
<SCRIPT FOR="myButton" EVENT="onclick" LANGUAGE="VBScript">
     axLabel.angle = 135
</SCRIPT>

</BODY></HTML>

For Help, press F1
```

Figure 12-18. *The document source after I added a button and a script.*

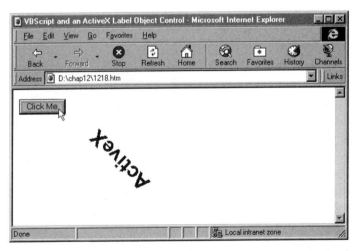

Figure 12-19. *The page whose source is shown in Figure 12-18, after the button is clicked.*

Animating a Control

As with any object, you can get an animation effect from an ActiveX control by using some kind of timer, such as the *setTimeout* or *setInterval* method, to repeatedly call a routine that changes the parameters of the ActiveX control. For example, Figure 12-20 shows a version of the sample document with a script that makes the label spin around and randomly change colors as it does so. Let's look at how the script does its thing.

The first script in the page is a sub procedure named *changeAxLabel*. This script adds 10 to the current angle of text in the *axLabel* control. An *If...Then* statement sets the angle back to 0 degrees if the angle exceeds 360. The last line in the sub procedure sets the *ForeColor* parameter of *axLabel* to a random number between 0 and 16,777,215. (Many ActiveX controls, including our sample Label Object control, allow you to specify a color as a decimal number between 0 and 16,777,215.)

```
<SCRIPT LANGUAGE = "VBScript"><!--
   Sub changeAxLabel()
      axLabel.Angle = axLabel.Angle + 10
      If axLabel.Angle > 360 Then axLabel.Angle = 0
      axLabel.ForeColor = Rnd() * 16777215
   End Sub
--></SCRIPT>
```

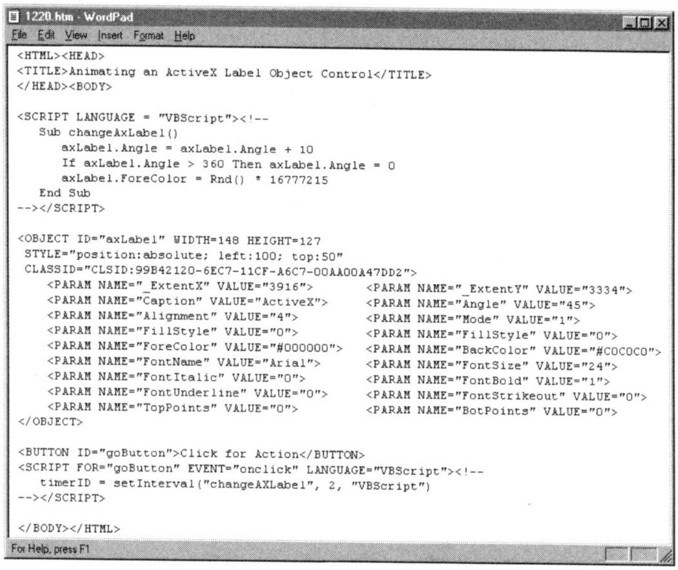

Figure 12-20. *The document source for an animated ActiveX control.*

NOTE   I doubled up the *<PARAM>* tags two to a line in Figure 12-20 to make more room for the scripts and additional tags.

The ActiveX control is defined with the tags shown below. Note the name of the object, *axLabel*, and the initial settings of the *Angle* and *ForeColor* parameters. Notice that the references to those parameters in the code, *axLabel.Angle* and *axLabel.ForeColor*, match the ID and parameter name exactly:

```
<OBJECT ID="axLabel" WIDTH=148 HEIGHT=127
 STYLE="position:absolute; left:100; top:50"
 CLASSID="CLSID:99B42120-6EC7-11CF-A6C7-00AA00A47DD2">
    <PARAM NAME="_ExtentX" VALUE="3916">
    <PARAM NAME="_ExtentY" VALUE="3334">
    <PARAM NAME="Caption" VALUE="ActiveX">
    <PARAM NAME="Angle" VALUE="45">
    <PARAM NAME="Alignment" VALUE="4">
    <PARAM NAME="Mode" VALUE="1">
    <PARAM NAME="FillStyle" VALUE="0">
    <PARAM NAME="FillStyle" VALUE="0">
    <PARAM NAME="ForeColor" VALUE="#000000">
    <PARAM NAME="BackColor" VALUE="#C0C0C0">
    <PARAM NAME="FontName" VALUE="Arial">
    <PARAM NAME="FontSize" VALUE="24">
    <PARAM NAME="FontItalic" VALUE="0">
    <PARAM NAME="FontBold" VALUE="1">
    <PARAM NAME="FontUnderline" VALUE="0">
    <PARAM NAME="FontStrikeout" VALUE="0">
    <PARAM NAME="TopPoints" VALUE="0">
    <PARAM NAME="BotPoints" VALUE="0">
</OBJECT>
```

Following the Label Object is a button and a script that kick the *changeAxLabel* sub procedure into action. Here are the tags that define the button:

```
<BUTTON ID="goButton">Click for Action</BUTTON>
```

Below is the script that's bound to the *onclick* event of that button. Notice how the script uses the *setInterval* method of the *window* object to call the *changeAxLabel* routine every two milliseconds:

```
<SCRIPT FOR="goButton" EVENT="onclick" LANGUAGE="VBScript"><!--
   timerID = setInterval("changeAxLabel", 2, "VBScript")
--></SCRIPT>

</BODY></HTML>
```

Opening the page in Internet Explorer displays the button and the tilted text. Clicking the button makes the text spin around and change colors randomly as shown in Figure 12-21.

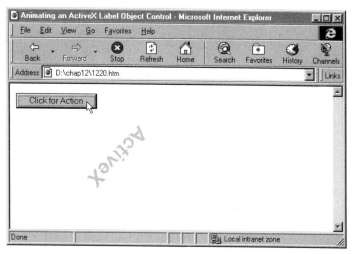

Figure 12-21. *A page showing the animated ActiveX Label Object control.*

ACTIVEX RESOURCES

At this point, you might want to cruise around the Web to get a feel for the kinds of ActiveX resources available. Here are some good sites to get you started:

- atOnce Software at www.atoncesoftware.com. The Internet section has some ActiveX controls.

- BrowserWatch ActiveX Arena at browserwatch.internet.com/ activex.html. This is a major site for information on browsers, plug-ins, and ActiveX controls.

- CNET's ActiveX.com at www.activex.com. This site lets you learn about, locate, and download ActiveX controls.

- Coolnerds' ActiveX area at www.coolnerds.com/activex/.

- CMP TechWeb's TechTools at www.techweb.com/tools/developers/. This site includes articles on ActiveX issues as well as ActiveX controls.

- Far Point Technologies' ActiveX Command Center at www.fpoint.com/ GuideA.htm. This site provides brief articles on ActiveX basics and offers ActiveX controls for sale.

- J.A.W.S. (Just Another Web Site) at www.erinet.com/cunning1/ jaws.htm.

- Microsoft's ActiveX Control Pad at http://www.microsoft.com/ workshop/author/cpad/.

- Microsoft's ActiveX FAQ at www.microsoft.com/workshop/prog/ controls/ctrlfaq.htm. This page provides answers to frequently asked questions about developing web pages with ActiveX controls.

- Microsoft's ActiveX Component Gallery at www.microsoft.com/ activex/gallery/. This page provides links to ActiveX controls and web sites.

- PartBank at www.activex.partbank.com. Here you'll find information about and links for various ActiveX controls.

- Planet FX at www.imagefx.com/planetfx/pfxhome.htm. Planet FX offers state-of-the-art special effects packaged as ActiveX controls.

- Stroud's Consummate Winsock Apps List at cws.internet.com/ 32activex.html. This site provides reviews and download locations for numerous ActiveX controls.

SUMMARY

In this chapter, we've discussed some general issues and techniques surrounding the use of ActiveX controls in web pages. The main points to keep in mind are:

- Whether Internet Explorer 4 will accept ActiveX controls while you're browsing the web is determined by its security settings, which you can get to by choosing Internet Options from the View menu and then clicking on the Security tab.

- Many ActiveX controls for web pages come in two "flavors," a run-time version that is supplied to viewers of a site and a developer's version for web authors.

- If you want to use an ActiveX control in your own web site, you'll probably need to buy the developer's version of the control and follow the control manufacturer's instructions for using the control correctly.

- In a web page's document source, every ActiveX control is repre-sented by a pair of *<OBJECT>...</OBJECT>* tags, typically with *<PARAM>* tags in between.

- The *<PARAM>* tags initialize the parameters (or properties) of the ActiveX control.

- The Insert menu in FrontPage (including FrontPage Express) offers commands for inserting ActiveX controls into a web page.

- Another handy tool for inserting ActiveX controls into a web page is the ActiveX Control Pad.

- Since an ActiveX control is represented by the HTML *<OBJECT>...</OBJECT>* and *<PARAM>* tags, you can also insert an ActiveX control into a page by typing the correct tags into the document source of the web page.

- You modify and script an ActiveX control just as you do any other built-in object.

In the next chapter, we'll start working directly with some of the ActiveX controls that come with Internet Explorer 4.

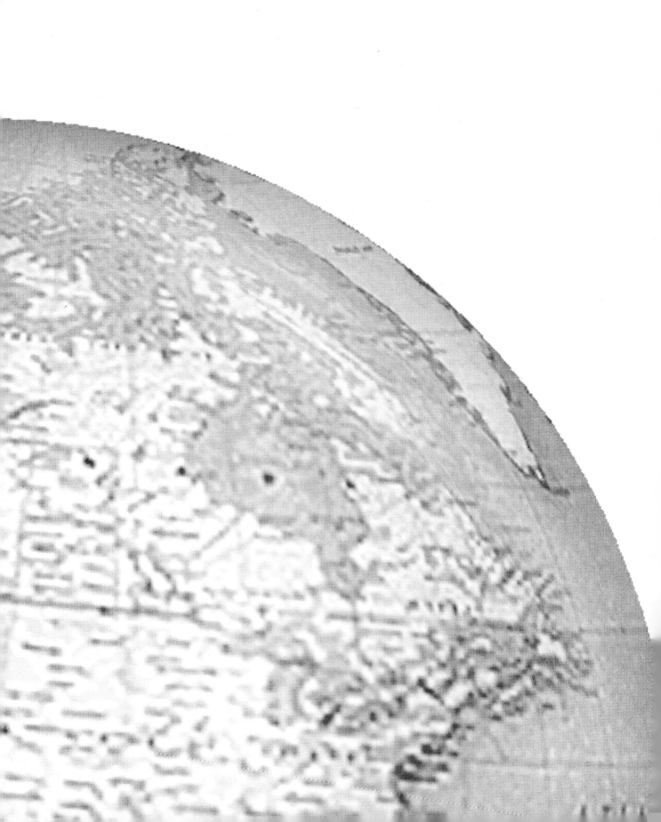

Chapter 13

ActiveX for
Sound and Video

In this chapter, I'll introduce you to an ActiveX control that you already own—the ActiveMovie control. I know you own it because it comes with Microsoft Internet Explorer 4. Both the run-time and developer versions of the control are automatically installed with Internet Explorer, so you can put the ActiveMovie control to work in your web page designs right away without buying any special software or license packages. The main topics we'll discuss in this chapter include:

- Adding sound to a web page

- Using the ActiveMovie control to play sounds

- Attaching sounds to virtually any object or event

- Using the ActiveMovie control to play videos

- Understanding streaming multimedia

- ActiveMovie control properties, methods, and events

We'll start with a general discussion of using sound in a web page and how the ActiveMovie control can help improve the use of sound in your page.

SOUND BASICS

Many factors determine whether your PC can play sound files and how it plays them. Many web authors have spent countless hours trying to "debug" a web page that refuses to play the sound files it's supposed to play, only to discover that the problem wasn't in the web page but rather in some basic sound card or Windows 95 setting. Here are the absolute basics required to get *any* sound out of a PC:

- A sound card.

- Sound drivers installed and properly configured.

- Speaker(s).

- Most external speakers connected to your PC must be turned on and their volume control button must be turned up high enough for you to hear the sound.

- The on-screen volume control must be turned up high enough for you to hear the sound. (On most Windows 95–based PCs, you can simply click on the little speaker icon on the taskbar to display the standard on-screen volume control or double-click on it to display the expanded on-screen volume control, as shown in Figure 13-1.)

  NOTE   If your computer plays sounds but there is no little speaker icon on your taskbar, you can get to the expanded on-screen volume control via the Windows Start menu by choosing Programs-Accessories-Multimedia-Volume Control.

- The Mute option in your on-screen volume control must be cleared.

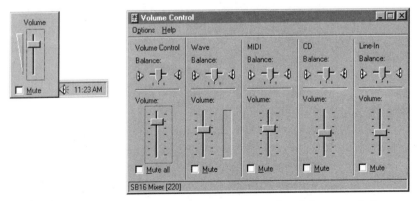

Figure 13-1. *The standard on-screen volume control and the expanded Volume Control dialog box.*

Before you start adding sound files to your web pages, first make sure that your PC will play the sounds you are adding. You can do this by double-clicking the type of sound file you're interested in. For example, one type of sound file is a WAV file. To test WAV files, on the Windows Start menu choose Find and then choose Files or Folders. In the Find dialog box, enter *wav* in the Named text box, and then click the Find Now button. Look for a file that has the .wav extension, and double-click it. If all is working well, the Sound Recorder applet (or some other sound player) will start up and you should hear the sound.

It's also a good idea to test MIDI files, which have another sound file format. Choose Find-Files or Folders from the Start menu, enter *mid* in the Named text box, and click the Find Now button. Look for a file that has the .mid extension and double-click it. If all is working well, the Media Player applet (or some other MIDI player) will start up and the MIDI file will play.

> **TIP** If you can't find any WAV or MIDI files on your PC, go to www.coolnerds.com/linkauth.htm, select the Sounds For Your Web Site link, and check out the many sites that offer free sound file downloads.

Not all sound cards can play MIDI files. If you're in doubt, check the documentation for your sound card. Some software products allow non-MIDI sound cards to play MIDI. A good place to learn about all the available options is a document called "ABCs of Using MIDI Files on the Net" at www.aitech.ac.jp/~ckelly/midi/help/index2.html. Your Windows 95 documentation can also help you configure your PC to play MIDI and other multimedia files.

Incidentally, WAV and MIDI aren't the only sound file formats. For example, AU, SND, and AIFF sound file formats are also commonly used on the Web. But chances are that if you can get .wav files to play on your PC, you'll have no problem hearing the many other sound file formats available.

WAV files and MIDI files have different characteristics. WAV, which is short for "waveform audio files," is a common sound format used in Windows. MIDI, which is short for Musical Instrument Digital Interface, is a common format used by sound synthesizers. MIDI files are more compact than WAV files, which means smaller file sizes—the smaller the file size, the faster the file will download.

Let's look at some basic techniques for incorporating sound into your web pages. We'll start with the basic HTML tags that you can use to play sound.

Background Sound

A web page can have a background sound. This is a sound that's downloaded and played as soon as the reader opens the web page. Typically, no sound player pops up on the screen when a background sound is played—the sound just plays in the background. When the reader moves to another page, the sound stops playing. For Internet Explorer or Netscape Navigator, the tag looks like this:

```
<EMBED SRC="soundfile.ext" HIDDEN="true" AUTOSTART="true">
```

With Internet Explorer, you can also use the *<BGSOUND...>* tag. Currently, Netscape Navigator ignores the *<BGSOUND...>* tag. The *<BGSOUND...>* tag looks like this:

```
<BGSOUND SRC="soundfile.ext">
```

For either tag, *soundfile.ext* is an absolute or relative reference to the sound file to be played. For example, if the sound file is in the same directory as the web page, the *SRC* attribute will look something like this:

```
SRC="mysound1.wav"
```

If the sound file is in a separate directory below the page's directory, you must precede the file name with the directory name and a forward slash. For example, if the sound file is in a directory named midfiles that's below the page's directory, the *SRC* attribute will look something like this:

```
SRC="midfiles/mysound2.mid"
```

If a visitor views a page that contains a background sound specified with the *<EMBED...>* tag in Internet Explorer, the visitor might be given the option to install the ActiveMovie control, if he or she doesn't already have it installed. One way to avoid making the visitor install the ActiveMovie control is to put both tags into your web page. When I tested this in Internet Explorer, I thought that the background sound would play twice, but it worked correctly and only played once.

Although using both tags to specify a background sound should work fine, a cleaner solution might be to add a script to your page that inserts the *<BGSOUND...>* tag if the current browser is Internet Explorer and inserts the *<EMBED...>* tag if the reader is using some other browser. Your best bet is to write this in JavaScript, since that scripting language is supported by most browsers. Figure 13-2 shows such a script. But you must substitute the reference to your background sound file in the two places where the example shows *1812over.mid*.

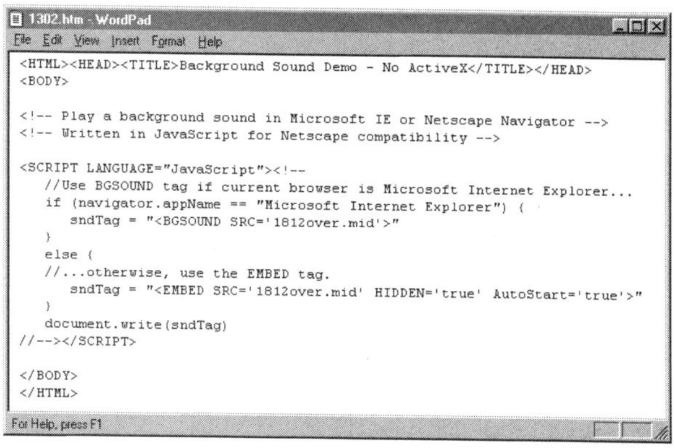

```
<HTML><HEAD><TITLE>Background Sound Demo - No ActiveX</TITLE></HEAD>
<BODY>

<!-- Play a background sound in Microsoft IE or Netscape Navigator -->
<!-- Written in JavaScript for Netscape compatibility -->

<SCRIPT LANGUAGE="JavaScript"><!--
   //Use BGSOUND tag if current browser is Microsoft Internet Explorer...
   if (navigator.appName == "Microsoft Internet Explorer") {
      sndTag = "<BGSOUND SRC='1812over.mid'>"
   }
   else {
   //...otherwise, use the EMBED tag.
      sndTag = "<EMBED SRC='1812over.mid' HIDDEN='true' AutoStart='true'>"
   }
   document.write(sndTag)
//--></SCRIPT>

</BODY>
</HTML>
```

Figure 13-2. *A JavaScript script that inserts one of two possible background sound tags based on the browser in use.*

Another point to keep in mind is that if the sound file is large, it will take some time to download. If you want to make sure the reader has something to look at while the sound file is being downloaded, place the *<BGSOUND...>* or *<EMBED...>* tag—or the entire JavaScript script shown in Figure 13-2—down near the bottom of the page, perhaps just above the closing *</BODY>* tag.

Event-Driven Sound

An event-driven sound plays when some event occurs, such as when a link is clicked. To play a sound in response to some event, "navigate" to the sound file just as you would to another HTML page. For example, suppose you want to create a hyperlink that reads *Click here for MIDI sound file* and you want the MIDI file to play when the reader clicks the link. All you need is an *<A HREF=...>* tag that points to the sound file, as in this example:

```
<!-- Click link for MIDI file. -->
<A HREF="sounds/1812over.mid">
   Click here for MIDI sound file
</A>
```

The same approach works for a WAV file, as in this example:

```
<!-- Click link for WAV file. -->
<A HREF="sounds/boing2.wav">
   Click here for WAV sound file
</A>
```

If you want the reader to click on a picture to play a sound, place the *<IMG SRC=...>* tag for the picture between the *<A HREF=...>* and *</A>* tags, as in the example below:

```
<!-- Click picture for MIDI file. -->
<A HREF="simpsons.mid">
   <IMG SRC="alanbw.gif" BORDER="0">
</A>
```

If you want to launch the sound when the reader points to a picture (no click necessary), use the *onmouseover* event in the *<IMG>* tag, as shown below:

```
<IMG SRC="alanbw.gif" BORDER="0"
onmouseover="location.href = 'simpsons.mid'">
```

The example above works only with Internet Explorer. If you want a sound to play when the reader points to a picture while browsing with either Internet Explorer or Netscape Navigator, use this syntax instead:

```
<A HREF="somepage.htm" onmouseover="location.href = 'simpsons.mid'">
   <IMG SRC="alanbw.gif" BORDER="0">
</A>
```

When writing scripts, the *location.href* property plays the same role as a hyperlink. Thus the script below plays a WAV file named whoosh.wav (from a subdirectory named sounds) as soon as the web page is opened:

```
<SCRIPT LANGUAGE="VBScript">
   location.href = "sounds/whoosh.wav"
</SCRIPT>
```

This is all pretty neat stuff. But web page sounds can have a couple of weaknesses. For example, based on the security settings, Internet Explorer might display a File Download dialog box (shown in Figure 13-3) each time a link to a sound file is clicked. To play the sound, the visitor must select the Open This File From Its Current Location option and then click OK.

Another weakness is that most browsers will pop up some kind of player to play the sound. For example, when a MIDI file is played, the ActiveMovie player might pop up, as shown in Figure 13-4. The main problem is that the web author has no control over how the visitor experiences the sound. It all depends on how the reader's browser and PC are configured to play sounds.

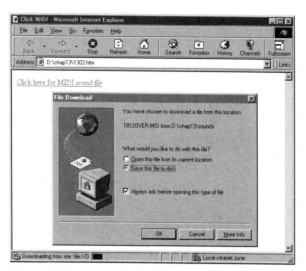

Figure 13-3. *The File Download dialog box appears when a visitor tries to play a "hyperlinked" sound.*

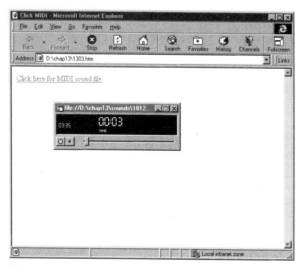

Figure 13-4. *A sound player pops up to play a "hyperlinked" sound.*

Also, many of the popup sound players don't close automatically when the sound is finished playing. When the reader clicks elsewhere on the web page, the player disappears behind the browser window. Playing another sound causes a second instance of the player to pop up on the screen. A third sound causes yet another instance of the player to pop up. It's quite possible that when the reader closes her web browser, she might find dozens of little player applets stacked up on the desktop—that is, assuming the whole thing doesn't crash first from having too many players and sound files in memory!

Enter ActiveX Sound

With so many options for playing sound, you might wonder what ActiveX has to offer. The answer, in a word (or three), is the ActiveMovie control. This ActiveX control can play the popular WAV, MIDI, AU, SND, and AIFF audio files (.wav, .mid, .midi., .au, .snd, .aif, and .aiff files). With the ActiveMovie control, sound files can be played without the visitor having to address the File Download dialog box each time. Also, rather than guessing at which player might pop up, you can ensure that the sound is played by the ActiveMovie control. You can also control the appearance and behavior of that control. For example, you can control how many times the sound plays, and you can make the player visible or invisible. If the player is visible, you can even decide which controls on the player are accessible to the visitor. (See Figure 13-5.)

WARNING   For all its great features, there is one drawback to the ActiveMovie control—only Internet Explorer can use it. Netscape Navigator doesn't support ActiveX controls.

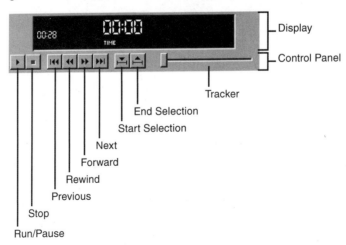

Figure 13-5. *You can give visitors any combination of user controls in the player.*

The ActiveMovie control comes with Internet Explorer 4, so you already have both the run-time version and the developer's version of that control on your PC. You can insert the control into any web page using Microsoft FrontPage or the ActiveX Control Pad.

NOTE The ActiveMovie control is also called the DirectShow ActiveMovie control because it uses the Windows DirectX technologies for improved performance.

As with all ActiveX controls, you can define default settings for these properties in the Properties sheet and in the *<PARAM>* tags. You can also write scripts that programmatically change these properties while the page is displayed in a web browser. I'll present some practical techniques and examples in the sections that follow.

Adding Small Sound Effects to Your Page

Many multimedia programs provide auditory feedback as you use them. For example, each time you click a button you hear a little click—or ding, or whoosh, or some such sound. If you have some small WAV files that make such sound effects, you can attach them to objects in your web page to give your own readers similar auditory feedback.

In this situation, you probably don't want the ActiveMovie control to appear on screen; you want it to be invisible. You also want it to play—immediately—any sound file you feed it. So to create the page, open the ActiveX Control Pad (or any other editor that allows you to insert ActiveX controls), insert the ActiveMovie control, and set the following properties. (All other properties can keep their default settings.)

AutoStart =	-1 (True)
ShowControls =	0 (False)
ShowDisplay =	0 (False)
ShowTracker =	0 (False)

You can put the control anywhere within the *<BODY>...</BODY>* tags. (Since the control will be invisible, its exact location isn't important.) Figure 13-6 on the next page shows the changes made in the Properties sheet for the ActiveMovie control in the ActiveX Control Pad. You can also see the *<OBJECT>...</OBJECT>* and *<PARAM>* tags for the control.

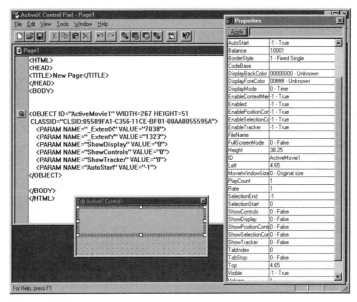

Figure 13-6. *The ActiveMovie control in the ActiveX Control Pad.*

To make sure the ActiveMovie control is entirely invisible and doesn't take up any space on the page, you can add a *STYLE="display:none"* attribute to the opening *<OBJECT>* tag. In your web page, you want the final *<OBJECT>...</OBJECT>* and *<PARAM>* tags to look like this:

```
<OBJECT ID="ActiveMovie1" WIDTH=267 HEIGHT=51
 STYLE="display:none"
 CLASSID="CLSID:05589FA1-C356-11CE-BF01-00AA0055595A">
    <PARAM NAME="_ExtentX" VALUE="7038">
    <PARAM NAME="_ExtentY" VALUE="1323">
    <PARAM NAME="ShowDisplay" VALUE="0">
    <PARAM NAME="ShowControls" VALUE="0">
    <PARAM NAME="ShowTracker" VALUE="0">
    <PARAM NAME="AutoStart" VALUE="-1">
</OBJECT>
```

Next, you can create a simple sub procedure that accepts the name of a sound file and then plays that sound file. The script just needs to set the *FileName* property of the ActiveMovie control to whatever file name is passed to it. Here is the exact script, which you can put up between the *<HEAD>...</HEAD>* tags of the same page:

```
<SCRIPT LANGUAGE="VBScript"><!--
    'playSound plays whatever sound file is passed to it.
    Sub playSound(sndFile)
       ActiveMovie1.FileName = sndFile
    End Sub
--></SCRIPT>
```

The rest is fairly easy. Just add HTML objects to the page as usual. For example, you can put in buttons, images, chunks of text, other ActiveX controls, whatever. If you want mouse contact or some other action with any of those items to make a sound, add an event using the following syntax to that object's opening HTML tag, where *onevent* is the name of the event that will trigger the sound and *soundfileRef* is a reference to the sound file.

```
onevent="playSound('soundfileRef')"
```

Let's say you have a button in your page. You also have a sound file named whoosh.wav in the same directory as the page. If you want the button to play the whoosh sound when the mouse pointer passes over the button, you set up the button's HTML tag as shown below:

```
<BUTTON onmouseover="playSound('whoosh.wav')">
I Am A Button
</BUTTON>
```

The name of the sound file must be a complete reference. For example, if the sound file is in a subdirectory named sounds under the current page's directory, the correct syntax for the opening *<BUTTON>* tag is:

```
<BUTTON onmouseover="playSound('sounds/whoosh.wav')">
I Am A Button
</BUTTON>
```

Figure 13-7 on the next page shows the document source for the completed page, including the script, the ActiveMovie control, and the *<BUTTON>* tag.

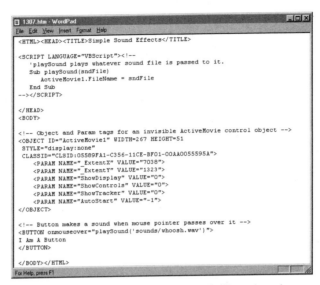

```
1.307.htm - WordPad
File  Edit  View  Insert  Format  Help
<HTML><HEAD><TITLE>Simple Sound Effects</TITLE>

<SCRIPT LANGUAGE="VBScript"><!--
    'playSound plays whatever sound file is passed to it.
    Sub playSound(sndFile)
        ActiveMovie1.FileName = sndFile
    End Sub
--></SCRIPT>

</HEAD>
<BODY>

<!-- Object and Param tags for an invisible ActiveMovie control object -->
<OBJECT ID="ActiveMovie1" WIDTH=267 HEIGHT=51
 STYLE="display:none"
 CLASSID="CLSID:05589FA1-C356-11CE-BF01-00AA0055595A">
     <PARAM NAME="_ExtentX" VALUE="7038">
     <PARAM NAME="_ExtentY" VALUE="1323">
     <PARAM NAME="ShowDisplay" VALUE="0">
     <PARAM NAME="ShowControls" VALUE="0">
     <PARAM NAME="ShowTracker" VALUE="0">
     <PARAM NAME="AutoStart" VALUE="-1">
</OBJECT>

<!-- Button makes a sound when mouse pointer passes over it -->
<BUTTON onmouseover="playSound('sounds/whoosh.wav')">
I Am A Button
</BUTTON>

</BODY></HTML>
For Help, press F1
```

Figure 13-7. *A page that plays a sound effect when the mouse pointer touches the button.*

Of course, you're not limited to button objects, the *onmouseover* event, or a single sound file. You can have as many objects in the page make as many different sound effects as you want. For example, the following tag displays a graphic image named beanyboy.gif. When the visitor clicks on the picture, the sound file named boing1.wav is played:

```
<IMG SRC="beanyboy.gif" WIDTH="100" HEIGHT="110"
onclick="playSound('boing1.wav')">
```

Here's a simple chunk of text—*Frank Zappa*—displayed in a large Comic Sans font with a DropShadow filter applied. Clicking on the text plays a sound file named alphonso.mid:

```
<SPAN STYLE="height:100px; width:300px; font:36pt Bold 'Comic Sans MS';
filter:DropShadow(Color=#C0C0C0, OffX=10, OffY=10)"
onclick="playSound('alphonso.mid')">
   Frank Zappa
</SPAN>
</P>
```

In short, once you add the *playSound* sub procedure and the ActiveMovie control as shown in Figure 13-7, you can create all kinds of sound effects by using the simple *onevent*="playSound('*soundfileRef*')" syntax.

USING THE ACTIVEMOVIE CONTROL FOR VIDEO

You might wonder why an ActiveX control that plays sound files is called the "ActiveMovie" control. Well, as it turns out, in addition to playing sound files, it also plays videos. In fact, it can play videos in the popular AVI, MPEG, and QuickTime formats (.avi, .mpg, .mpeg, .mpv, .mp2, .mpa, .mov, and .qt files). It can play AVI video with or without sound.

While there are other ways to display video, such as the *<IMG DYNSRC="videoname.ext">* tag, the ActiveMovie control offers several advantages over other approaches. For one, it offers improved interactivity. When you display a video using an *<IMG>* tag or a hyperlink, you have little control over which player will display the video on the reader's PC. Furthermore, you have little programmatic control over that player. You can't really write scripts that respond to things that the reader does while the video is playing.

In contrast, when you use an ActiveX control to display a video, you know exactly which player is showing the movie. And you have an enormous amount of programmatic control over the appearance and behavior of that player.

Streaming Video

Another advantage of the ActiveMovie control is *progressive downloading*, also called *streaming video*. This means that the person viewing the video need not wait for the entire video file to download before seeing the video. The video starts playing after only a portion of the video file has been downloaded. When the ActiveMovie control has enough of the video file to display the whole video smoothly, it starts playing the video while still downloading the rest of the video file in the background.

Streaming can help people on high-speed corporate intranets, as well as people with high-speed connections to the Internet. Unfortunately, it doesn't do a whole lot for people with dial-up connections. Let me explain why. Let's say you have a one-minute video clip that takes 15 minutes to download to someone with, say, an ISDN connection to the Internet. To play that video smoothly, the player might need to download all but about the last minute of the video. Thus, the "streaming" doesn't kick in until 14 minutes of the file have been downloaded. So the person with the ISDN connection gets to see the movie after only 14 minutes rather than 15 minutes of download time. I don't think that's quite enough difference to make that person hoot and holler with joy.

The ActiveMovie control does offer one bit of aid, though. It displays the first frame of the video pretty quickly. So, for what's it's worth, the reader can at least see a picture while the rest of the movie is downloading.

I don't like to be the bearer of bad news, but I don't want you to have unrealistic expectations about what ActiveMovie or streaming will do for the speed at which videos get to your readers. The fact is that the telephone system was designed to transmit *voice*—they weren't even *thinking* of video when they put up all those telephone poles and copper wires. There's nothing you can do in your web site to make your video files move any faster through the telephone wires.

I should also mention that you'll often hear the term *multimedia stream* as opposed to multimedia file. But the two terms refer to essentially the same thing—the file that contains the video or sound to be played.

Playing a Video on Open

Now let's say you're going to put a video in your web page, despite the slowness of telephone connections. How do you set up the ActiveMovie control to play the video? I recommend using the Microsoft ActiveX Control Pad for this one. Open an existing HTML page or create a new page and save it in the same folder where you save your other HTML pages. Saving the page is important because the ActiveMovie control can use a relative reference to find the movie file. Therefore, when you post your page and video file to a web server, you won't have to make any changes to the video file reference.

So anyway, you're in the ActiveX Control Pad, you create a new page named vidShow.htm, and you save it in a folder named myWeb. That folder also contains a video file named movie.avi. To insert an ActiveMovie control to play movie.avi at startup, you insert the ActiveMovie control object into the page. Then you define the following properties, as shown in Figure 13-8:

AutoStart =	-1 (True)
FileName =	movie.avi
ShowPositionControls =	-1 (True)
ShowSelectionControls =	-1 (True)

You'll notice that the first frame of the movie appears in the ActiveMovie control in Figure 13-8. This is handy because it gives you a sense of how large the control will be when it's in your web page. The first frame of the video will appear in the control right after you fill in the *FileName* property and click the Apply button. You should use a relative reference to specify the video file name. That's why it's so important to save the page *before* you insert the ActiveMovie control—so that the control knows which folder to start looking in for the video file. Anyway, Figure 13-9 shows the document source for the entire completed page.

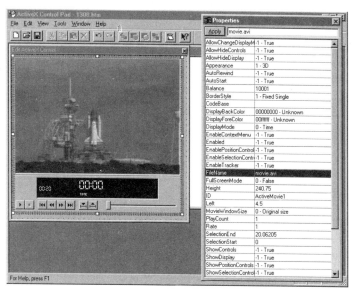

Figure 13-8. *The ActiveMovie control properties are set to play movie.avi when the page opens.*

```
<HTML>
<HEAD>
<TITLE>ActiveMovie Video Example</TITLE>
</HEAD>
<BODY>

<!-- ActiveMovie control below automatically loads and plays movie.avi -->
<OBJECT ID="ActiveMovie1" WIDTH=356 HEIGHT=321
  CLASSID="CLSID:05589FA1-C356-11CE-BF01-00AA0055595A">
    <PARAM NAME="_ExtentX" VALUE="9419">
    <PARAM NAME="_ExtentY" VALUE="8493">
    <PARAM NAME="ShowPositionControls" VALUE="-1">
    <PARAM NAME="ShowSelectionControls" VALUE="-1">
    <PARAM NAME="AutoStart" VALUE="-1">
    <PARAM NAME="FileName" VALUE="movie.avi">
</OBJECT>

</BODY>
</HTML>
```

Figure 13-9. *The document source for a web page that uses the ActiveMovie control to play a video when the page loads.*

That's really all that's required to play a video as soon as the page is opened. If I close and save the document source and then open it in Internet Explorer 4, the video starts playing as soon as it's loaded. The result looks something like Figure 13-10.

Figure 13-10. *The ActiveMovie control playing a video.*

Giving the Reader a Choice

If you're concerned about the download time for a video file, you might want to give the visitor a warning—and a choice. You can roughly estimate the download time using Table 13-1 as a guide.

Table 13-1

APPROXIMATE DOWNLOAD TIMES FOR A VIDEO FILE

Connection	100KB File	1MB File
128K ISDN	7.5 seconds	1.25 minutes
56K modem	15 seconds	2.5 minutes
28.8K modem	30 seconds	5 minutes
14.4K modem	60 seconds	10 minutes

Figure 13-11 shows a page that lets the reader decide whether to download a 1.5MB video file. (I realize that the page isn't too fancy looking, but in this book it's the underlying code that counts!) Figure 13-12 shows the document source for the page.

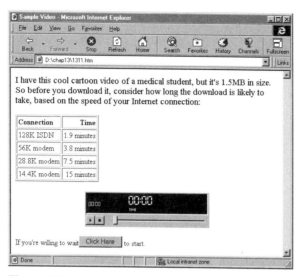

Figure 13-11. *A page that gives the reader a choice of whether to download a video file.*

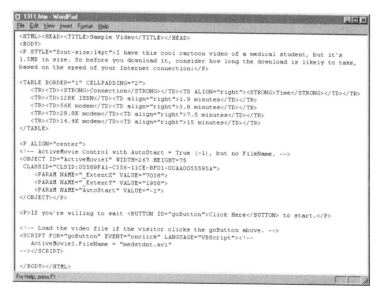

Figure 13-12. *The document source for the page shown in Figure 13-11.*

Let's step through the page to see how it all works. Within the body of the page are the text and tags that display the opening paragraph and table, as shown on the next page.

```
<BODY>
<P STYLE="font-size:14pt">I have this cool cartoon video of a medical
student, but it's 1.5MB in size. So before you download it, consider
how long the download is likely to take, based on the speed of your
Internet connection:</P>

<TABLE BORDER="1" CELLPADDING="2">
    <TR><TD><STRONG>Connection</STRONG></TD>
    <TD ALIGN="right"><STRONG>Time</STRONG></TD></TR>
    <TR><TD>128K ISDN</TD><TD align="right">1.9 minutes</TD></TR>
    <TR><TD>56K modem</TD><TD align="right">3.8 minutes</TD></TR>
    <TR><TD>28.8K modem</TD><TD align="right">7.5 minutes</TD></TR>
    <TR><TD>14.4K modem</TD><TD align="right">15 minutes</TD></TR>
</TABLE>
```

Next comes the actual ActiveMovie control. Notice that I set the *AutoStart* parameter to True (-1) so that once a video file is loaded, it will start playing automatically. However, there is no *FileName* property for this control. So initially it downloads and plays absolutely nothing:

```
<P ALIGN=Center>
<!-- ActiveMovie Control with AutoStart = True (-1), -->
<!-- but no FileName. -->
<OBJECT ID="ActiveMovie1" WIDTH=267 HEIGHT=75
 CLASSID="CLSID:05589FA1-C356-11CE-BF01-00AA0055595A">
    <PARAM NAME="_ExtentX" VALUE="7038">
    <PARAM NAME="_ExtentY" VALUE="1958">
    <PARAM NAME="AutoStart" VALUE="-1">
</OBJECT></P>
```

Next comes the sentence and button:

```
<P>If you're willing to wait <BUTTON ID="goButton">Click Here
</BUTTON> to start.</P>
```

Finally, here's the script that starts the download if the reader clicks the button. The script assigns the appropriate video file name to the *FileName* property of the ActiveMovie control. The *AutoStart* parameter in the control ensures that the movie plays once it's loaded:

```
<!-- Load the video file if the visitor clicks the -->
<!-- goButton above. -->
```

```
<SCRIPT FOR="goButton" EVENT="onclick" LANGUAGE="VBScript"><!--
   ActiveMovie1.FileName = "medstdnt.avi"
--></SCRIPT>

</BODY></HTML>
```

Even in this last example, the name of the file must be a valid absolute or relative reference to a video file. For example, let's say that you want to show an MPEG video named grill.mpeg via this page and that video is at the URL http://www.ghg.ecn.purdue.edu. To make the correct reference to the video file, you have to change the script to this:

```
<!-- Load the video file if the visitor clicks the -->
<!-- goButton above. -->
<SCRIPT FOR="goButton" EVENT="onclick" LANGUAGE="VBScript"><!--
   ActiveMovie1.FileName = "http://www.ghg.ecn.purdue.edu/grill.mpeg"
--></SCRIPT>
```

ACTIVEMOVIE CONTROL DOCUMENTATION

So far in this chapter I've introduced the ActiveMovie control mainly through examples of using it to accomplish common tasks. But you can use a whole lot of other properties and methods to control the behavior and appearance of the control. The ActiveMovie control is fully documented in the Internet Client SDK. Rather than repeat all of that information here, I'll just provide brief summaries of the ActiveMovie control's properties, methods, and events.

> **TIP** Many properties of the ActiveMovie control are accessible to the visitor who is viewing the video. In Internet Explorer, right-click on the ActiveMovie control and choose Properties from the popup menu to get to the user-controlled properties.

To get to the complete documentation, go to the starting page of the Internet Client SDK and open the "Internet Tools & Technologies" section. Select Internet Multimedia in the list of topics, and then click on DirectShow. You'll be taken to the Overview of the ActiveMovie Control page shown in Figure 13-13 on the next page. From there, you can learn all kinds of things about the ActiveMovie control.

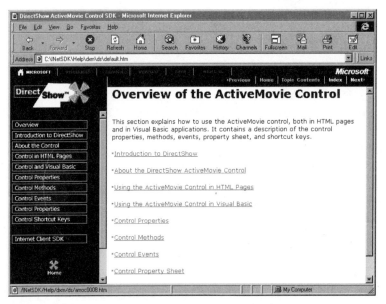

Figure 13-13. *The first page of documentation for the ActiveMovie control in the Internet Client SDK.*

ActiveMovie Control Properties

The complete set of ActiveMovie control properties is summarized in Table 13-2.

Table 13-2
ACTIVEMOVIE CONTROL PROPERTIES

Property	Description
AllowChangeDisplayMode	Specifies (using True or False) whether the reader can change the display mode from Time to Frames and vice versa.
AllowHideControls	Specifies (using True or False) whether the reader can hide the control panel.
AllowHideDisplay	Specifies (using True or False) whether the reader can hide the display.
Appearance	Specifies a flat or 3-D appearance for the control.
AutoRewind	Specifies (using True or False) whether to automatically rewind the multimedia file when it reaches the end.
AutoStart	Specifies (using True or False) whether to automatically start playing the multimedia file.

Property	Description
Balance	Specifies the stereo balance between the left and right speakers. The balance has a range of –10000 (all left channel) to 10000 (all right channel). A value of 0 is neutral balance.
BorderStyle	Specifies either a fixed single line border around the control or no border.
CurrentPosition	Specifies the current position within the multimedia stream.
CurrentState	Indicates the playback file's current state: stopped (0), paused (1), or running (2).
DisplayBackColor	Specifies the background color of the display.
DisplayForeColor	Specifies the foreground color of the display.
DisplayMode	Specifies whether the display shows the current position in Time or Frames.
EnableContextMenu	Specifies (using True or False) whether to enable the popup (right-click) menu.
Enabled	Specifies (using True or False) whether the ActiveMovie control is enabled.
EnablePositionControls	Specifies (using True or False) whether to enable the position buttons.
EnableSelectionControls	Specifies (using True or False) whether to enable the selection buttons.
EnableTracker	Specifies (using True or False) whether to enable the tracker bar.
FileName	Specifies the name of the file that contains the multimedia stream to be played.
FilterGraph	Contains the IUnknown interface pointer to the current filter graph object.
FilterGraphDispatch	Contains the IDispatch interface pointer to the current filter graph object.
FullScreenMode	Specifies whether to show the video full-screen (True) or in its original size (False).
MovieWindowSize	Specifies the size of the playback window. The values include 0 (original size), 1 (double original size), 2 ($\frac{1}{16}$ of screen), 3 ($\frac{1}{4}$ of screen), 4 ($\frac{1}{2}$ of screen).
PlayCount	Specifies the number of times to play this multimedia stream, with 0 indicating "infinite."

(continued)

ACTIVEMOVIE CONTROL PROPERTIES *continued*

Property	Description
Rate	Specifies the playback rate for the stream, with 1 indicating the original rate.
ReadyState	Indicates the ready status of the control based on how completely the source file is loaded. The values include 1 (uninitialized), 0 (loading), 3 (loaded enough data to play, but not all data has been received), and 4 (all data downloaded).
SelectionEnd	Specifies the ending position in this multimedia stream, relative to the beginning of the stream.
SelectionStart	Specifies the starting position in this multimedia stream, relative to the beginning of the stream.
ShowControls	Specifies whether the control panel is visible (True) or invisible (False).
ShowDisplay	Specifies whether the display panel is visible (True) or invisible (False).
ShowPositionControls	Specifies whether the position buttons are visible (True) or invisible (False).
ShowSelectionControls	Specifies whether the selection buttons are visible (True) or invisible (False).
ShowTracker	Specifies whether the tracker bar is visible (True) or invisible (False).
Volume	Specifies the audio volume from −10000 (no volume) to 0 (maximum volume). The default is 0.

ActiveMovie Control Methods

Methods that the ActiveMovie control supports are summarized in Table 13-3.

Table 13-3

METHODS SUPPORTED BY THE ACTIVEMOVIE CONTROL

Method	Description
AboutBox()	Displays the About Box for the ActiveMovie control.
IsSoundCardEnabled()	Indicates (using True or False) whether the sound card is enabled.
Pause()	Pauses the multimedia stream at the current position.

Method	Description
Run()	Plays the currently loaded multimedia file at the specified starting position or at the paused position.
Stop()	Stops playback of the multimedia stream and sets its position based on the *AutoRewind* and *SelectionStart* properties.

ActiveMovie Control Events

The ActiveMovie control fires many events, making it possible for you to write scripts that respond to virtually anything that happens to the control. The full set of ActiveMovie control events is summarized in Table 13-4.

Table 13-4

EVENTS SUPPORTED BY THE ACTIVEMOVIE CONTROL

Event	When It Is Triggered
Click	When the reader clicks on the control.
DblClick	When the reader double-clicks on the control.
DisplayModeChange	When the *DisplayMode* property changes.
Error	When the control generates an error, such as when it tries to load a nonexistent file.
OpenComplete	When the multimedia file has been completely loaded.
PositionChange	When the position within the file changes.
ReadyStateChange	When the *ReadyState* property changes.
StateChange	When the state (such as Stop, Pause, or Play) changes.
Timer	When the display is refreshed as the file is playing.

SUMMARY

In this chapter, we looked at the ActiveX ActiveMovie control. Both the run-time and developer's version of this control come with Internet Explorer 4, so you don't need any special files or licenses to use it in your own web pages. To summarize the main points covered in this chapter:

- The ActiveX ActiveMovie control can play sounds stored in the WAV, MIDI, AU, SND, and AIFF file formats.

- The ActiveMovie control can also play videos stored in AVI, MPEG, and QuickTime formats.

- You can use either FrontPage or the ActiveX Control Panel to insert the ActiveMovie control into any web page.

- To hide the ActiveMovie control, such as when you want to use it to play background sounds, put a *STYLE="display:none"* CSS attribute in the opening *<OBJECT>* tag for the control.

- To let the reader decide whether to download a multimedia file, leave the *FileName* property of the ActiveMovie control empty. Then add a button (or some other control) that fills in the *FileName* property if the reader decides to proceed with the download.

- Complete documentation for the ActiveMovie control is included in the Internet Client SDK, by clicking Internet Tools & Technologies-Internet Multimedia-DirectShow. You can also access the documentation by clicking Component Library-ActiveMovie Control.

The ActiveMovie control is only one of the freebie ActiveX controls that is built into Internet Explorer 4. You'll learn about some of the others in the chapters that follow.

Chapter 14

Animating with the ActiveX Path Control

In this chapter, we'll take a look at another freebie ActiveX control that you already have in your arsenal. It's called the Path control (also known as the Microsoft DirectAnimation Multimedia Path control). This control lets you animate objects by moving them around on the screen in a specific shape or pattern, at a specific speed. We'll cover these aspects of the Path control:

■   What you can do with the control

■   Its properties, methods, and events

■   How to create paths of different shapes and sizes

■   Calculating path points based on the visitor's browser size

■   Adding sound effects to a moving object

Let's start off with a general discussion of the Path control and what it has to offer us web authors.

THE PATH CONTROL

The Path control lets you define a path for an object to follow. The control itself is invisible to the visitor. The basic structure of the control, when placed in a web page, looks something like this:

```
<OBJECT ID="controlName" WIDTH=11 HEIGHT=11
 CLASSID="CLSID:D7A7D7C3-D47F-11D0-89D3-00A0C90833E6">
    <PARAM NAME="Autostart" VALUE="0">
    <PARAM NAME="Bounce" VALUE="0">
    <PARAM NAME="Direction" VALUE="0">
    <PARAM NAME="Duration" VALUE="0">
    <PARAM NAME="Repeat" VALUE="1">
    <PARAM NAME="Target" VALUE="">
    <PARAM NAME="Relative" VALUE="0">
    <PARAM NAME="TimerInterval" VALUE="0.1">
</OBJECT>
```

You can use Microsoft FrontPage or the ActiveX Control Pad to insert the Path control, just as you would any other ActiveX control. The name of the control, when viewed in the Insert ActiveX Control dialog box, is Microsoft Direct-Animation Path, as shown in Figure 14-1.

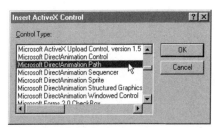

Figure 14-1. *Inserting the Path control in the ActiveX Control Pad.*

WARNING   If you try to edit an inserted Path control in the ActiveX Control Pad by clicking the cube button, an error might be displayed because the ActiveX Control Pad was created before the DirectAnimation Multimedia controls were. If you receive an error, try reinserting a new Path control (using FrontPage Express) or editing the tags manually.

Path Control Properties

The properties supported by the Path control are summarized in Table 14-1. These can be defined in the *<PARAM>* tags or set by scripting code. For example, consider the *Bounce* property, which can be set to True (-1) or False (0). If *Bounce* is set to True, the object bounces back and forth along the specified path. If *Bounce* is set to False, the object moves in one direction along its path.

In the *<PARAM>* tags, you can set the *Bounce* property to True as shown below:

```
<PARAM NAME="Bounce" VALUE="-1">
```

Or you can set it to False:

```
<PARAM NAME="Bounce" VALUE="0">
```

In VBScript code, you use the standard *objectName.property = newValue* syntax to set the property. For example, let's say the Path control object in your page is named *myPath*, via an *ID="myPath"* attribute in the control's opening *<OBJECT>* tag. The script below sets the *Bounce* property of that control to True:

```
<SCRIPT LANGUAGE="VBScript"><!--
   myPath.Bounce = True
--></SCRIPT>
```

Table 14-1

PROPERTIES OF THE PATH CONTROL

Property	Description
AutoStart	Specifies whether the Path control starts moving the object automatically when the page is loaded (–1 or True) or not until a *Play()* method is executed (0 or False). The default is 0.
Bounce	Specifies whether the object on the path should stop at the end of its path (0 or False) or reverse direction and return to the beginning (–1 or True). The default is 0.
Direction	Specifies the direction of movement of the object on the path to forward (0) or reverse (1). The default is 0.
Duration	Specifies the time for the object to move from the start to the end of the path in 0.000 (seconds.milliseconds) format.
Library	Returns the reference to the DirectAnimation Library functions. Read-only.
PlayState	Indicates the path's current playback state as 0 (stopped), 1 (playing), or 2 (paused). Read-only.
Relative	Specifies whether the Path control starts moving the object from its current position (–1 or True) or from an absolute position in the target object's coordinate space (0 or False). The default is 0.
Repeat	Specifies the number of times the object repeats its motion on the path during playback. 0 disables repeating. –1 causes infinite repetition. The default is 1.
Target	Specifies the object that the Path control will move.
Time	Indicates the elapsed playback time (in seconds.milliseconds) from the start of the path playback. Repeat count is included in returned time calculations. Read-only.
TimerInterval	Specifies the minimum number of seconds.milliseconds between path updates. The default interval is 0.100.

Path Control Methods

The Path control also has methods—things it can do. The methods are activated by scripts. Let's say the current page contains a Path control named *myPath*. The VBScript script below causes that Path control to start doing its thing:

```
<SCRIPT LANGUAGE="VBScript"><!--
   myPath.Play()
--></SCRIPT>
```

Methods supported by the Path control are summarized in Table 14-2. You'll see plenty of examples as we progress through this chapter.

Table 14-2

METHODS SUPPORTED BY THE PATH CONTROL

Method	Description
AddTimeMarker()	Sets a marker to fire an event when playback reaches the marker position.
KeyFrame()	Specifies points along the path in *x,y* coordinates and a designated time to reach each point.
Oval()	Specifies an oval path, with the starting point at top center (12 o'clock).
Pause()	Stops playback and maintains current elapsed time.
Play()	Begins playback from the current elapsed time.
Polygon()	Specifies a closed series of line segments to be used as the path.
PolyLine()	Specifies an open set of line segments to be used as the path.
Rect()	Specifies a rectangular path, with the starting point at top left.
Seek()	Sets the current elapsed time to a new specified time.
Spline()	Specifies a curve to be used as the path.
Stop()	Stops playback at the current elapsed time and returns time to 0.

Path Control Events

The Path control fires off its own events, to which you can bind scripts. You can use the any of the standard VBScript syntaxes to bind a script to an event that happens to a Path control. For example, suppose you place a Path control in your web page and name it *myPath*. You can use the syntax on the next page to set up a sub procedure that fires as soon as the control starts playing.

```
<SCRIPT LANGUAGE="VBScript"><!--
   Sub myPath_onplay()
       code...
   End Sub
--></SCRIPT>
```

Table 14-3 summarizes the events supported by the Path control.

Table 14-3

EVENTS FIRED BY THE PATH CONTROL

Event	Description
OnMarker	Fires when a time marker has been reached either during path playback or when stopped.
OnPause	Fires when path playback is paused.
OnPlay	Fires when path playback is played.
OnPlayMarker	Fires when a time marker is reached during path playback.
OnSeek	Fires when a seek call has been completed.
OnStop	Fires when path playback is stopped.

You can get more information about the Path control from the Internet Client SDK. From the starting page, choose Internet Tools & Technologies, and then choose Internet Multimedia, DirectAnimation, Controls, and Path Control. The first page of the Path control's documentation looks something like Figure 14-2.

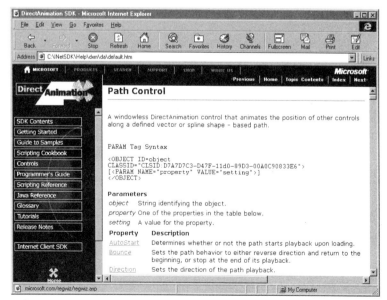

Figure 14-2. *Complete documentation for the Path control is in the Internet Client SDK.*

As usual, I won't bother to repeat all the online documentation. I'd rather show you some practical examples of putting the Path control to work.

PATH CONTROL EXAMPLES

The basic idea behind the Path control is that you set up a shape, or a series of points, that creates a path for some object to follow. Exactly how you define the shape or points depends on what you're trying to do, as we'll discuss in a moment. But to illustrate the basic idea, let me show you an example. To define an oval path, you use this basic syntax:

```
Oval(left, top, width, height)
```

left defines the leftmost point of the oval in pixels. *top* defines the topmost point of the oval in pixels. *width* and *height* define how wide and how tall the oval should be in pixels. So let's say I set up the following Path control:

```
<OBJECT ID="myPath" WIDTH=11 HEIGHT=11
 CLASSID="CLSID:D7A7D7C3-D47F-11D0-89D3-00A0C90833E6">
    <PARAM NAME="AutoStart" VALUE="-1">
    <PARAM NAME="Bounce" VALUE="0">
    <PARAM NAME="Direction" VALUE="0">
    <PARAM NAME="Duration" VALUE="5">
    <PARAM NAME="Repeat" VALUE="-1">
    <PARAM NAME="Target" VALUE="myImg">
    <PARAM NAME="Relative" VALUE="0">
    <PARAM NAME="Shape" VALUE="Oval(100, 20, 400, 300)">
    <PARAM NAME="TimerInterval" VALUE="0.1">
</OBJECT>
```

The path defined by this control creates an oval whose leftmost point is 100 pixels from the left edge of the page and whose topmost point is 20 pixels down from the top of the page. The oval is 400 pixels wide and 300 pixels tall. If you could actually *see* the path on the screen, it would look something like Figure 14-3. (The graph-paper background, originally discussed back in Chapter 8, is there simply to give you some perspective.) Even though you can't see the path itself, you can certainly see any object moving along that path. So if the image of the eight ball in Figure 14-3 moves along that path, its top-left corner will always be touching the invisible oval as it moves around and around on the page.

The source code for a page that moves an eight ball image around an oval path is shown in Figure 14-4. Near the top of the body of the document, the following tag displays the eight ball image and gives that image the object name *myImg*.

```
<BODY>

<!-- The myImg object is a picture, defined by <IMG> tag below -->
<IMG ID="myImg" SRC="eightbal.gif"
STYLE="position:absolute; left:300; top:20; zindex:2">
```

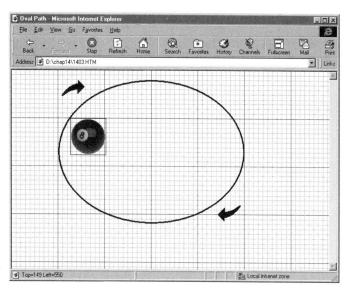

Figure 14-3. *The (normally invisible) large oval is a path defined as*
Oval(100, 20, 400, 300).

```
<HTML><HEAD>
<TITLE>Microsoft DirectAnimation Multimedia Path Control Demo</TITLE>
</HEAD>
<BODY>

<!-- The myImg object is a picture, defined by the <IMG> tag below -->
<IMG ID="myImg" SRC="eightbal.gif"
STYLE="position:absolute; left:300; top:20; zindex:2">

<!-- Here's the Path control object, with a few parameters pre-defined -->
<OBJECT ID="myPath" WIDTH=11 HEIGHT=11
 CLASSID="CLSID:D7A7D7C3-D47F-11D0-89D3-00A0C90833E6">
    <PARAM NAME="Autostart" VALUE="-1">
    <PARAM NAME="Bounce" VALUE="0">
    <PARAM NAME="Direction" VALUE="0">
    <PARAM NAME="Duration" VALUE="5">
    <PARAM NAME="Repeat" VALUE="-1">
    <PARAM NAME="Target" VALUE="myImg">
    <PARAM NAME="Relative" VALUE="0">
    <PARAM NAME="Shape" VALUE="Oval(100, 20, 400, 300)">
    <PARAM NAME="TimerInterval" VALUE="0.1">
</OBJECT>
</BODY></HTML>
```

Figure 14-4. *An HTML document containing an image object and a*
Path control.

Then comes the Path control itself. No scripting code is required in this page because the Path control is set to kick in automatically as soon as the web page is opened. (*AutoStart* is set to –1, or True.) Note the use of the *Shape* parameter to define an oval path, and notice the *Target* parameter that defines the object that will move along that path—the *myImg* object in this example:

```
<!-- Here's the Path control object... -->
<OBJECT ID="myPath" WIDTH=11 HEIGHT=11
 CLASSID="CLSID:D7A7D7C3-D47F-11D0-89D3-00A0C90833E6">
    <PARAM NAME="AutoStart" VALUE="-1">
    <PARAM NAME="Bounce" VALUE="0">
    <PARAM NAME="Direction" VALUE="0">
    <PARAM NAME="Duration" VALUE="5">
    <PARAM NAME="Repeat" VALUE="-1">
    <PARAM NAME="Target" VALUE="myImg">
    <PARAM NAME="Relative" VALUE="0">
    <PARAM NAME="Shape" VALUE="Oval(100, 20, 400, 300)">
    <PARAM NAME="TimerInterval" VALUE="0.1">
</OBJECT>
</BODY>
```

I'm sure it seems a bit strange at first glance—you have to try it out yourself to get the hang of it. To help out, I'll show you some techniques for setting up different kinds of paths for objects to follow. To see some of these in action, open the page named 1405.htm from the Chapter 14 examples on the companion CD or at my web site. That page will look like Figure 14-5 when you first open it. To see a path in action, click any button along the bottom of the page.

There's also a Path control object in the page, shown below. Its name is *pathControl*. Its initial parameters do not activate its autostart capability, so initially nothing moves on this page. Similarly, no *Shape* parameter is defined. As you'll see, the buttons and scripts that come later in the document source define a path for the object to follow and then get the Path control to do its thing.

```
<!-- Path control object, with a few parameters predefined -->
<OBJECT ID="pathControl"
CLASSID="CLSID:D7A7D7C3-D47F-11D0-89D3-00A0C90833E6">
    <PARAM NAME="AutoStart" VALUE="0">
    <PARAM NAME="Repeat" VALUE="-1">
    <PARAM NAME="Bounce" VALUE="0">
    <PARAM NAME="Duration" VALUE="0">
    <PARAM NAME="Shape" VALUE="">
    <PARAM NAME="Target" VALUE="myImg">
</OBJECT>
```

In the code on the next page, you can see the object named *myImg*, which is just a graphic image. Figure 14-6 shows part of the document source for the sample page.

```
<IMG ID="myImg" SRC="eightbal.gif"
STYLE="position:absolute; top:100; left:200; height:75; width:75:
zindex:1">
```

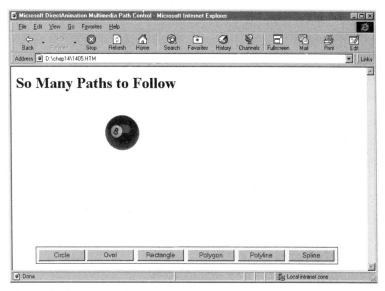

Figure 14-5. *A page showing an object that can move along many different defined paths.*

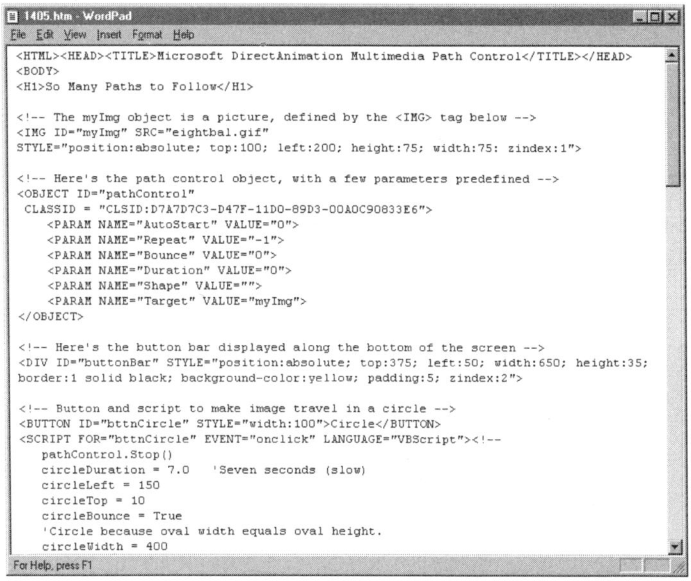

Figure 14-6. *Part of the document source for the page shown in Figure 14-5.*

Moving in an Oval or Circle

As you saw in the previous section, you can use the Oval shape to move an object along an oval or circular path. The syntax for defining an oval within a Path control's *<OBJECT>...</OBJECT>* tags is as follows:

```
<PARAM NAME="Shape" VALUE="Oval(left, top, width, height)">
```

With VBScript code, the syntax is:

```
controlName.Oval left, top, width, height
```

controlName is the name of the Path control. *left* is the leftmost point of the oval in pixels from the left edge of the page. *top* is the topmost point of the oval in pixels from the top of the page. *width* is how wide the oval is, in pixels. *height* is how tall the oval is, in pixels.

So to make the image travel in a circle that's 400 pixels in diameter using a button and VBScript code, you add these tags and code to the page:

```
<!-- Button and script to make image travel in a circle -->
<BUTTON ID="bttnCircle" STYLE="width:100">Circle</BUTTON>
<SCRIPT FOR="bttnCircle" EVENT="onclick" LANGUAGE="VBScript"><!--
    pathControl.Stop()
    circleDuration = 7.0    'Seven seconds (slow)
    circleLeft = 80
    circleTop = 10
    circleBounce = True
    'Circle because oval width equals oval height.
    circleWidth = 400
    circleHeight = 400
    pathControl.Duration = circleDuration
    pathControl.Bounce = circleBounce
    pathControl.Oval circleLeft, circleTop, circleWidth, circleHeight
    pathControl.Play()
--></SCRIPT>
```

Notice that in the above example I defined more than just the position and size of the path. I also defined a duration of 7 seconds to complete the circle. Furthermore, in this example the object switches direction each time it completes a circle because I set the *Bounce* parameter to True.

On the next page is a sample button and script that make the object travel in an oval shape 550 pixels wide and 250 pixels tall. It takes only 2.5 seconds to complete the oval—the object moves pretty quickly. The object travels in only one direction because the *Bounce* property is turned off.

```
<!-- Button and script to make image travel in an oval -->
<BUTTON ID="bttnOval" STYLE="width:100">Oval</BUTTON>
<SCRIPT FOR="bttnOval" EVENT="onclick" LANGUAGE="VBScript"><!--
   pathControl.Stop()
   ovalDuration = 2.5 'Two and a half seconds (fast)
   ovalLeft = 50
   ovalTop = 10
   ovalWidth = 550
   ovalHeight = 250
   ovalBounce = False
   pathControl.Duration = ovalDuration
   pathControl.Bounce = ovalBounce
   pathControl.Oval ovalLeft, ovalTop, ovalWidth, ovalHeight
   pathControl.Play()
--></SCRIPT>
```

Moving in a Rectangle

To define a rectangular or square path, use this syntax in the Path control's
<OBJECT>...</OBJECT> tags:

```
<PARAM NAME="Shape" VALUE="Rect(left, top, width, height)">
```

Here's a Path control that moves an object named *myImg* in a rectangular
path. The rectangle starts 100 pixels from the left edge of the page and 10 pixels
down from the top of the page. The rectangle is 500 pixels wide and 200 pixels tall.

```
<OBJECT ID="pathControl"
CLASSID="CLSID:D7A7D7C3-D47F-11D0-89D3-00A0C90833E6">
    <PARAM NAME="AutoStart" VALUE="-1">
    <PARAM NAME="Repeat" VALUE="-1">
    <PARAM NAME="Bounce" VALUE="0">
    <PARAM NAME="Duration" VALUE="5">
    <PARAM NAME="Shape" VALUE="Rect(100, 10, 500, 200)">
    <PARAM NAME="Target" VALUE="myImg">
</OBJECT>
```

With VBScript code, you use this syntax to define a rectangular path:

```
controlName.Rect left, top, width, height
```

Here's a more complete example, using the Rectangle button shown in
Figure 14-5:

```
<!-- Button and script to make image travel in a rectangle -->
<BUTTON ID="bttnRectangle" STYLE="width:100">Rectangle</BUTTON>
<SCRIPT FOR="bttnRectangle" EVENT="onclick" LANGUAGE="VBScript"><!--
   pathControl.Stop()
   rectDuration = 2    'Two seconds
   rectBounce = False
```

(continued)

```
        rectLeft = 10
        rectTop = 10
        rectWidth = 600
        rectHeight = 290
        pathControl.Duration = rectDuration
        pathControl.Bounce = rectBounce
        pathControl.Rect rectLeft, rectTop, rectWidth, rectHeight
        pathControl.Play()
    --></SCRIPT>
```

Moving in a Polygon or Polyline

A polygon is any closed shape that has corners. For example, a square, triangle, and star shape are all polygons. A polyline is a series of points that doesn't close. Straight lines and jagged lines are both examples of a polyline. To define a polygon path or a polyline path, you must tell the Path control how many points are in the path and the exact location of each of those points. Each point is defined by two numbers, x and y, where x is the number of pixels from the left edge of the page and y is the number of pixels from the top of the page.

In the Path control's *<OBJECT>...</OBJECT>* tags, you use this syntax to define a polygon shape:

```
<PARAM NAME="Shape" VALUE="Polygon(n, x1,y1, ... xN,yN)">
```

n is the number of points used to define the polygon. x is the distance from the left edge of the page for one point and y is the distance from the top edge of the page for one point.

For example, this tag defines a triangular polygon with three (3) points:

```
<PARAM NAME="Shape" VALUE="Polygon(3, 300,10, 400,300, 200,300)">
```

The first point is at position 300,10, the second point is at position 400,300, and the third point is at position 200,300. The object follows the path defined by the three pairs of points and then returns to the first pair of points 300,10 to close the polygon.

The polyline path uses a similar syntax. However, the path isn't closed after the last position is listed. For example, here's a *<PARAM>* tag that defines a kind of jagged-line path:

```
<PARAM NAME="Shape" VALUE="PolyLine(3, 10,10, 50,50, 20,70)">
```

The VBScript syntax for defining a polygon or polyline is a little different because you must explicitly define an array of path points. The syntax for defining a polygon looks like this:

```
nPoints = n
ptArray = Array(x1,y1, ... xN,yN)
controlName.Polygon nPoints, ptArray
```

The same basic syntax is used to define a polyline path in VBScript:

```
nPoints = n
ptArray = Array(x1,y1, ... xN,yN)
controlName.PolyLine nPoints, ptArray
```

nPoints is the number of points, *ptArray* is an array containing all of the points, *x* and *y* are the left and top pixel positions for one point, and *controlName* is the name of the Path control.

Referring back to Figure 14-5, here are the tags and script that define the Polygon button and the path along which the image moves. The path has eight points.

```
<!-- Button and script to make image travel in a polygon -->
<BUTTON ID="bttnPolygon" STYLE="width:100">Polygon</BUTTON>
<SCRIPT FOR="bttnPolygon" EVENT="onclick" LANGUAGE="VBScript"><!--
    pathControl.Stop()
    polygonDuration = 5    'Five seconds
    polygonBounce = True
    polygonNpoints = 8
    polygonArray = Array(0,0, 350,200, 700,0, 350,200, 700,400, _
        350,200, 0,400, 350,200)
    pathControl.Duration = polygonDuration
    pathControl.Bounce = polygonBounce
    pathControl.Polygon polygonNpoints, polygonArray
    pathControl.Play()
--></SCRIPT>
```

Here are the tags and script for the Polyline button. The polyline has four points.

```
<!-- Button and script to make image travel in a polyline -->
<BUTTON ID="bttnPolyLine" STYLE="width:100">Polyline</BUTTON>
<SCRIPT FOR="bttnPolyLine" EVENT="onclick" LANGUAGE="VBScript"><!--
    pathControl.Stop()
    polyLineDuration = 15    'Fifteen seconds
    polyLineBounce = True
    polyLineNpoints = 4
    polyLineArray = Array(0,0, 600,100, 0,200, 600,300)
    pathControl.Duration = polyLineDuration
    pathControl.Bounce = polyLineBounce
    pathControl.PolyLine polyLineNpoints, polyLineArray
    pathControl.Play()
--></SCRIPT>
```

Moving in a Spline (Curve)

The Path control also lets you define a curved path—called a *spline*—from a series of points. The points can define a jagged line; the *Spline* method automatically calculates a smooth curve for that set of points. The syntax for defining a spline in the Path control's *<OBJECT>...</OBJECT>* tags is similar to the syntax used to define a polyline:

```
<PARAM NAME="Shape" VALUE="Spline(n, x1,y1, x2,y2, ...)">
```

n is the number of points in the curve, each point being defined by the usual *x,y* coordinates. To define a spline, you must specify at least 4 points.

For example, here's a Path control with a spline defined with 4 points. The first point in the curve is at 0,0, the next point is at 200,200, the next point is at 400,500, and the last point is at 600,100:

```
<OBJECT ID="pathControl"
 CLASSID="CLSID:D7A7D7C3-D47F-11D0-89D3-00A0C90833E6">
    <PARAM NAME="AutoStart" VALUE="-1">
    <PARAM NAME="Repeat" VALUE="1">
    <PARAM NAME="Bounce" VALUE="0">
    <PARAM NAME="Duration" VALUE="4">
    <PARAM NAME="Shape"
       VALUE="Spline(4, 0,0, 200,200, 400,500, 600,100)">
    <PARAM NAME="Target" VALUE="myImg">
</OBJECT>
```

In VBScript code, the syntax for defining a spline looks more like this:

```
splineNpoints = n
splineArray = Array(x1,y1, ... xN,yN)
pathControl.Spline splineNpoints, splineArray
```

Below is the Spline button from Figure 14-5 and the code that makes the image move along the curve defined by the points in the *splineArray* variable:

```
<!-- Button and script to make image travel along -->
<!-- a spline (curve) -->
<BUTTON ID="bttnSpline" STYLE="width:100">Spline</BUTTON>
<SCRIPT FOR="bttnSpline" EVENT="onclick" LANGUAGE="VBScript"><!--
    pathControl.Stop()
    splineDuration = 4    'Four seconds
    splineBounce = True
    splineNpoints = 4
    splineArray = Array(0,300, 200,-40, 400,-40, 600,300)
    pathControl.Duration = splineDuration
    pathControl.Bounce = splineBounce
    pathControl.Spline splineNpoints, splineArray
    pathControl.Play()
--></SCRIPT>
```

Keep in mind that the examples I've presented so far are just examples. Your best bet to really get a feel for the Path control is to play around with it. Try different settings for the *Bounce, Direction, Duration,* and *Repeat* parameters. Play around with the various shapes—Oval, Rect, Polygon, PolyLine, and Spline. Keep in mind that the *AutoStart* parameter must be set to -1 in the parameters list if you want the motion to start automatically when the page opens. Otherwise, you can use the *Play()* method in a script to start the motion and use the *Stop()* method in a script to stop the motion.

CALCULATING PATHS AND POINTS

One problem with publishing on the Internet or an intranet is that visitors will have their browser windows sized differently. For example, some people like having their browser window maximized and some like having it smaller. Also, some people set their displays at 640 x 480 resolution, some prefer 800 x 600, and some prefer 1024 x 768 or higher. In code, you can use the *clientWidth* and *clientHeight* properties of the *body* object to get the visitor's current document window size. Then you can calculate points or sizes for a path based on that information.

For example, suppose your page contains an image named *myImg*, like the image in our previous examples. You also put the Path control into that page, as shown below. Note that *AutoStart* is turned off so motion won't start automatically. The *Shape* parameter is undefined.

```
<IMG ID="myImg" SRC="eightbal.gif"
STYLE="position:absolute; left:80; top:10; zindex:2">

<OBJECT ID="pathControl"
 CLASSID="CLSID:D7A7D7C3-D47F-11D0-89D3-00A0C90833E6">
    <PARAM NAME="AutoStart" VALUE="0">
    <PARAM NAME="Repeat" VALUE="-1">
    <PARAM NAME="Bounce" VALUE="0">
    <PARAM NAME="Duration" VALUE="4">
    <PARAM NAME="Shape" VALUE="">
    <PARAM NAME="Target" VALUE="myImg">
</OBJECT>
```

Now suppose you want to make the *myImg* object travel along an oval whose top is 25 percent of the distance across the document window and 10 percent of the distance down the document window. You also want the width and height of the oval to be such that the *myImg* object is always within the document window no matter what its size. The following script will calculate all the right measurements and define the oval accordingly by using the *clientWidth* and *clientHeight* properties.

```
<SCRIPT LANGUAGE="VBScript"><!--
    'Calculate the top, left, height, and width of oval
    'based on current document window size.
    Sub computeOval()
        'Compute document window width and height.
        bodyWidth = document.body.clientWidth
        bodyHeight = document.body.clientHeight
        'Calculate 25% of distance across the document window.
        ovalLeft = (0.25 * bodyWidth)
        'Calculate 10% down from top of the document window.
        ovalTop = (0.10 * bodyHeight)
        'Calculate oval width and height so that it keeps the myImg
        'within the document window.
        ovalWidth = bodyWidth - (ovalLeft + myImg.width)
        ovalHeight = bodyHeight - (ovalTop + myImg.height)
        pathControl.Oval ovalLeft, ovalTop, ovalWidth, ovalHeight
    End Sub
```

Now a script is needed to call *computeOval* and start moving the *myImg* object along the oval path. The following procedure does just that when the page loads:

```
'When page is loaded, compute oval and start moving
'object along oval path.
Sub window_onload()
    computeOval()
    pathControl.Play()
End Sub
```

Now suppose that while the image is moving along the oval path, you resize the browser window. The image might move outside the visible window area. To prevent this, you can recompute the oval measurements when the window is resized, like this:

```
'If browser is sized, stop motion, recalculate oval
'measurements, and start motion again.
Sub window_onresize()
    pathControl.Stop()
    computeOval()
    pathControl.Play()
End Sub
--></SCRIPT>
```

Now the *myImg* object will stay within the visible boundaries of the document window for any window size. Figure 14-7 shows a sample of how this page looks.

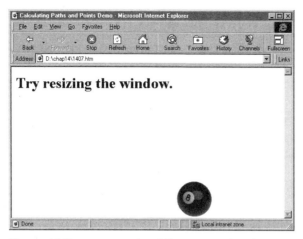

Figure 14-7. *An image that follows an oval path and always stays within the document window, even if the window is resized.*

ADDING SOUND EFFECTS TO A PATH

You can get some extra mileage out of an animation path by adding some sound effects. For example, you might have a ball traveling around the page, and each time it bounces off the edge of the document window, it plays a "boing" sound. Suppose I want the eight ball image to travel from one point to the next in Figure 14-8. Each time it hits one of the points and heads for the next point, it makes a sound—as if it's bouncing off the edge of the window.

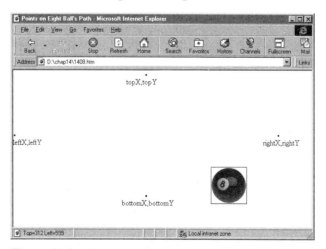

Figure 14-8. *The eight ball image and the four points of its path.*

While you're looking at Figure 14-8, notice that the eight ball image has a border around it. As I've mentioned, it's always the top-left corner of the traveling object that touches the various points in the path. Each of the points in the figure is calculated so that the edge of the ball that's nearest the edge of the document window just touches that edge. This adds to the illusion that the ball is bouncing off the sides of the window as it travels along the path.

To actually see and hear this example in action, open 1409.htm from the Chapter 14 examples on the companion CD or at my web site. At first, the screen will look something like Figure 14-9. To get the ball rolling, click the Do Motion & Sound button.

Now we need to look behind the scenes at the ActiveX controls, HTML, and scripting code required to make the eight ball travel to those points and play its sounds. In this example, I'll use the *KeyFrame()* method of the Path control because it allows you to define the exact point that the object will travel to and how long it will take to get from one point to the next. I'll also use the *AddTime-Marker()* method to set up events that will trigger for the sound to be played.

The document source for the page starts off with the usual *<HTML>*, *<HEAD>*, and other tags. However, I did add a *SCROLL="no"* attribute to the opening *<BODY>* tag. This removes the vertical scroll bar from the browser. This attribute is not required, but since the scroll bar isn't necessary for this example and the eight ball will bounce off the right window edge, I decided to include it.

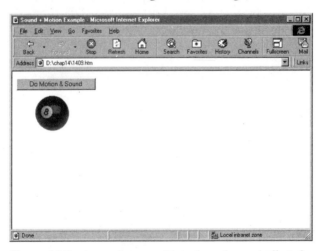

Figure 14-9. *A sample page with path and sound effects from the visitor's perspective.*

Next comes the Path control, which you can insert with the ActiveX Control Pad or FrontPage Express. When defining the parameters of the Path control, set the *AutoStart*, *Bounce*, and *Direction* parameters to 0. Set the *Repeat* parameter to -1 (True). Finally, set the *Target* property to the name of the object that the control will move. In this example, that object is *myImg*. So for starters, the document source looks like this:

```
<HTML><HEAD><TITLE>Sound + Motion Example</TITLE></HEAD>
<BODY SCROLL="no">
<!-- Embed Path control with target set to myImg object -->
<OBJECT ID="pathControl" WIDTH=11 HEIGHT=11
 CLASSID="CLSID:D7A7D7C3-D47F-11D0-89D3-00A0C90833E6">
    <PARAM NAME="AutoStart" VALUE="0">
    <PARAM NAME="Bounce" VALUE="0">
    <PARAM NAME="Direction" VALUE="0">
    <PARAM NAME="Repeat" VALUE="-1">
    <PARAM NAME="Target" VALUE="myImg">
    <PARAM NAME="Relative" VALUE="0">
    <PARAM NAME="TimerInterval" VALUE="0.1">
</OBJECT>
```

Next, we need some means of playing sound effects. The ActiveMovie control will come in handy here. Insert it using the ActiveX Control Pad or FrontPage Express, and set its parameters so that everything is invisible. Make the *FileName* a relative reference to the sound file that you want the control to play. (I'm using boing.wav in this example.) Once the *<OBJECT>...</OBJECT>* tags are in the page, add a *STYLE="display:none"* attribute to the opening *<OBJECT>* tag to ensure that the ActiveMovie control is entirely invisible. When you're done, the *<OBJECT>* tags for the ActiveMovie control should look something like this:

```
<!-- Embed ActiveMovie control with boing.wav sound ready to play -->
<OBJECT ID="activeMovieControl" WIDTH=267 HEIGHT=51
 STYLE="display:none"
 CLASSID="CLSID:05589FA1-C356-11CE-BF01-00AA0055595A">
    <PARAM NAME="_ExtentX" VALUE="7064">
    <PARAM NAME="_ExtentY" VALUE="1349">
    <PARAM NAME="ShowDisplay" VALUE="0">
    <PARAM NAME="ShowControls" VALUE="0">
    <PARAM NAME="ShowTracker" VALUE="0">
    <PARAM NAME="FileName" VALUE="boing.wav">
</OBJECT>
```

> **WARNING** Make sure the *FileName* property is an accurate relative or absolute reference to the sound file on the web server. Otherwise, the sound won't play.

Now that we have a control to provide motion and another to provide sound, we need some kind of object to show the reader on the page. We also need a button or something similar to get the action going. For this example, I'm using a simple graphic image named eightbal.gif as the object to be moved. I named this object *myImg* in the *<IMG>* tag that places the ball on the page. I also added a button named *goButton* to this page, as you can see below:

```
<!-- The myImg object is a picture, defined by <IMG> tag below -->
<IMG ID="myImg" SRC="eightbal.gif" STYLE="position:absolute;
top:50px; left:50px; height:75px; width:75px: zindex:1">

<!-- Button to get things going -->
<BUTTON ID="goButton">Do Motion &amp; Sound</BUTTON>
```

So that's it for ActiveX controls and HTML tags. Now we need VBScript code to do the rest. First comes a sub procedure that handles the *goButton* click and a second sub procedure that defines the path, event points, and so forth, and it also gets the ball moving. Here are both procedures. I'll discuss specific lines in more detail as we go along.

```
<SCRIPT LANGUAGE="VBScript"><!--
    'Bounce object when button is clicked.
    Sub goButton_onclick()
        bounceEightBall()
    End Sub

    Sub bounceEightBall()
        'Stop the object if it's moving.
        pathControl.Stop()
        'Calculate bounce points based on document window size.
        computeBouncePoints topX,topY, rightX,rightY, _
            bottomX,bottomY, leftX,leftY
        'Number of points in the path.
        nPoints = 5
        'Store bounce points in an array.
        KeyFrameArray = Array(topX,topY, rightX,rightY, _
            bottomX,bottomY, leftX,leftY, topX,topY)
        'It will take 1.5 seconds for the ball to traverse each leg.
        TimeFrameArray = Array(1.5, 1.5, 1.5, 1.5)
        'Set up the Path control.
        pathControl.KeyFrame nPoints, KeyFrameArray, TimeFrameArray
        'Add Time Markers
        pathControl.AddTimeMarker 1.5, "bounce1", False
        pathControl.AddTimeMarker 3.0, "bounce2", False
        pathControl.AddTimeMarker 4.5, "bounce3", False
        pathControl.AddTimeMarker 6.0, "bounce4", False
```

```
'Now get the object moving.
pathControl.Play()
End Sub
```

The first sub procedure simply calls the *bounceEightBall* sub procedure when the *goButton* is clicked:

```
'Bounce object when button is clicked.
Sub goButton_onclick()
    bounceEightBall()
End Sub
```

The first statement in the *bounceEightBall* sub procedure, shown below, just stops the path control in case it happens to be moving already:

```
Sub bounceEightBall()
    'Stop the object if it's moving.
    pathControl.Stop()
```

The next statement calls the *computeBouncePoints* sub procedure to calculate the bounce points, as shown earlier in Figure 14-8, based on the document window size. I'll discuss more about *computeBouncePoints* a little later.

```
'Calculate bounce points based on document window size.
computeBouncePoints topX,topY, rightX,rightY, _
    bottomX,bottomY, leftX,leftY
```

To set up a *KeyFrame*, we must tell the Path control how many points will be in the path, the *x, y* coordinates of each point, and how long it will take to traverse each leg. Here we define the number of points (*nPoints*) as 5:

```
'Number of points in the path.
nPoints = 5
```

The *computeBouncePoints* procedure calculated the following bounce points for our moving object: *topX,topY, rightX,rightY, bottomX,bottomY,* and *leftX,leftY*. The following statement stores those points in an array named *KeyFrameArray*:

```
'Store bounce points in an array.
KeyFrameArray = Array(topX,topY, rightX,rightY, _
    bottomX,bottomY, leftX,leftY, topX,topY)
```

The *KeyFrame* method needs to know how long it will take to traverse each leg. In this example, we'll say each leg takes exactly 1.5 seconds to traverse. We can set up this information in an array as well, and in this case the array is named *TimeFrameArray*:

```
'It will take 1.5 seconds for the ball to traverse each leg.
TimeFrameArray = Array(1.5, 1.5, 1.5, 1.5)
```

You might notice that *TimeFrameArray* only has four elements in it, while *KeyFrame* contains five elements (five pixel coordinates). *TimeFrameArray* always has one fewer element than *KeyFrame* because there are fewer legs than travel points. In this example, the first time setting determines the time required to get from *topX,topY* to *rightX,rightY* and the second time setting determines how long it takes to get from *rightX,rightY* to *bottomX,bottomY*. The third time setting determines how long it takes to get from *bottomX,bottomY* to *leftX,leftY*, and the fourth time setting determines how long it takes to get from *leftX,leftY* back to *topX,topY*. That last leg completes the journey around the path.

So far, we've only defined and stored all these values in VBScript variables. To apply them all to the Path control, we need to pass all the information to the control using this line of code:

```
'Set up the Path control.
pathControl.KeyFrame nPoints, KeyFrameArray, TimeFrameArray
```

Next, we need to figure out how to get the sound to play each time the ball bounces off a wall. This is pretty easy because we determined that each leg takes 1.5 seconds to complete. So if we set up events that fire every 1.5 seconds and we play the sound in response to those events, we'll get exactly the effect we want. You use the *AddTimeMarker()* method of the Path control to set up these timed events. In the code below, I set a time marker at 1.5 seconds, another at 3.0 seconds, another at 4.5 seconds, and another at 6.0 seconds. I named these markers *bounce1*, *bounce2*, *bounce3*, and *bounce4*:

```
'Add Time Markers.
pathControl.AddTimeMarker 1.5, "bounce1", False
pathControl.AddTimeMarker 3.0, "bounce2", False
pathControl.AddTimeMarker 4.5, "bounce3", False
pathControl.AddTimeMarker 6.0, "bounce4", False
```

With all those parameters set up, we can now get the ball moving. Here's the last statement in the *bounceEightBall* procedure, which does just that:

```
'Now get the object moving.
pathControl.Play()
End Sub
```

Now we need some code that plays the sound file each time the traveling ball reaches a bounce point:

```
'Each Sub procedure below plays boing.wav when ball bounces.
Sub pathControl_onplaymarker(bounce1)
activeMovieControl.Run()
End Sub
```

```
Sub pathControl_onplaymarker(bounce2)
   activeMovieControl.Run()
End Sub
Sub pathControl_onplaymarker(bounce3)
   activeMovieControl.Run()
End Sub
Sub pathControl_onplaymarker(bounce4)
   activeMovieControl.Run()
End Sub
```

Note that each procedure is bound to one of the timer markers. I used the following line of code in the *bounceEightBall* procedure to define a time marker named *bounce1* that fires every time the object is 1.5 seconds into its journey around the path:

```
pathControl.AddTimeMarker 1.5, "bounce1", False
```

The sub procedure below is bound to that event simply because of the way it's named. Since the ActiveMovie control already has the boing.wav sound file loaded into it, the sub procedure just has to play that sound:

```
Sub pathControl_onplaymarker(bounce1)
   activeMovieControl.Run()
End Sub
```

The next procedure calculates the bounce points *topX, topY*, *rightX, rightY*, *bottomX, bottomY*, and *leftX, leftY* based on the current document window size. Since an object moves along a path based on its upper-left corner, the size of the *myImg* object is also taken into account in the calculations:

```
'Compute the bounce points based on current document window size.
Sub computeBouncePoints(topX,topY, rightX,rightY, _
bottomX,bottomY, leftX,leftY)
   'Get document window width and height.
   bodyWidth = document.body.clientWidth
   bodyHeight = document.body.clientHeight
   'Calculate one-half the width and one-half the height
   'of the myImg object.
   halfImageWidth = myImg.Width / 2
   halfImageHeight = myImg.Height / 2
   topX = 0.5 * bodyWidth - halfImageWidth
   topY = 0
   rightX = bodyWidth - myImg.width
   rightY = 0.5 * bodyHeight - halfImageHeight
   bottomX = topX
   bottomY = bodyHeight - myImg.height
   leftX = 0
   leftY = rightY
End Sub
```

The last sub procedure, *window_onresize*, is executed whenever the browser window is resized. When the window is resized, the *bounceEightBall* procedure is called, which updates the bounce points and defines a new path for the new window size. The *window_onresize* sub procedure and the remaining code is shown here:

```
'If window is resized, update calculations for new window size.
Sub window_onresize()
    bounceEightBall()
End Sub
--></SCRIPT>

</BODY></HTML>
```

That, in a nutshell, is how the whole thing works. To summarize: You need to use the *KeyFrame()* method of the Path control to set up a path of multiple points and the time required to traverse from one point to the next. You use the *AddTimeMarker()* method of the Path control to define some "moments" when the path control will fire events. Then you create procedures that are bound to those events so they play at specific time intervals. You can use the *clientWidth* and *clientHeight* properties of the body object to compute the path points based on the current document window size. The *resize* event of the window object fires whenever the visitor resizes the browser window. You can bind this event to a script that will update calculations for the new window size.

SUMMARY

Well, I think we've covered the ActiveX Path control pretty well. Remember that you can get more information and details on the Path control (and all the other ActiveX controls discussed in this book) from the Internet Client SDK. The Path control is lumped together with similar DirectAnimation Multimedia controls under the general heading "Internet Multimedia." Now let's review the main points covered in this chapter:

- The Path control (also called the Microsoft DirectAnimation Multimedia Path control) allows you to define a path of points that an object will travel along.

- The Path control also provides methods to start and stop the movement of the object along the path.

- Various predefined paths are available, including Oval, Rectangle, Polygon, PolyLine, and Spline (curve).

- You can use the *KeyFrame()* method of the Path control to define a specific set of path points and the time it will take for the object to traverse each leg of the path.

- You can use the *AddTimeMarker()* method to set up events that fire at specific time intervals as the object moves along the path. Those events can then execute scripts, such as a script to play a sound file.

But wait, there's more. As you'll learn in the next chapter, paths are not the only special effect that ActiveX controls have to offer.

Chapter 15

More Freebie ActiveX Controls

In this chapter, we'll look at three more ActiveX controls that come with Internet Explorer 4. These controls are all part of Microsoft's DirectAnimation technology, which, in a nutshell, is all about giving programmers and web authors better tools for creating better animations. We'll cover:

- The Structured Graphics control, which can display text and graphics that can be scaled, rotated, and translated in three dimensions

- The Sequencer control, which acts as a sophisticated timer

- The Sprite control, which lets you turn a series of images into an animation

DirectAnimation is a big topic, and not all of it is relevant to web authors. My goal is to introduce you to the three main DirectAnimation ActiveX controls in this chapter and show you examples of using them effectively in your web pages.

THE STRUCTURED GRAPHICS CONTROL

The Structured Graphics control offers an entirely new way to display graphics and text in a web page. The Structured Graphics control lets you display *vector images*, which are different from bitmap images such as GIF and JPEG that you are familiar with. Vector images are composed of a series of instructions written in text that define lines and curves called vectors. Bitmap images, on the other hand, are composed of pixels. Vector images are generally smaller in file size than bitmap images, and as a result, they download more quickly. But the real advantage of the Structured Graphics control and vector images is that you can programmatically scale, rotate, and translate an image to produce even more interesting visual effects in your web pages.

You can insert the Structured Graphics control into a web page using Microsoft FrontPage or FrontPage Express. The syntax of the control's *<OBJECT>...</OBJECT>* tags looks something like this, where *objectName* is any name you want to assign to this control:

```
<OBJECT ID="objectName"
 CLASSID="CLSID:369303C2-D7AC-11D0-89D5-00A0C90833E6">
</OBJECT>
```

I'll cover the basics of using the Structured Graphics control in this chapter—in particular, the properties and methods that are most important to web authors. For more detailed information on this control, see the Internet Client SDK. The Structured Graphics control is covered under Internet Tools & Technologies-Internet Multimedia-DirectAnimation-Controls-Structured Graphics Control.

Structured Graphics Control Properties

Let's look at the properties you can set using *<PARAM>* tags within the Structured Graphics control's *<OBJECT>* tag. As with most ActiveX controls, you can set properties for the Structured Graphics control using this syntax:

```
<PARAM NAME="propertyName" VALUE="propertyValue">
```

propertyName is any property listed in the left column of Table 15-1, and *propertyValue* is any valid value for that property.

Table 15-1

PROPERTIES SUPPORTED BY THE
STRUCTURED GRAPHICS CONTROL

Property	Description
CoordinateSystem	Sets the control's coordinate system. A value of 0 specifies Windows coordinates where y values start at the top of the page and progress downwards; 1 (or nonzero) specifies a Cartesian system where y values start at the bottom of the page and progress upward. The default is the Windows coordinates.
DrawingSurface	Sets or returns the drawing surface—the visible rendering of the control's contents. (For scripts only.)
ExtentHeight, *ExtentWidth*, *ExtentLeft*, *ExtentTop*	Set the height, width, left, and top values of the structured graphic in pixels.
HighQuality	Turns anti-aliasing (line-smoothing) on or off. True (−1 or nonzero) activates anti-aliasing, and False (0) disables anti-aliasing. The default is False.
Image	Fills the structured graphic shape with a DirectAnimation image (*IDAImage*). (For scripts only.)
Library	Returns a reference to the DirectAnimation Library. (For scripts only.)
MouseEventsEnabled	Determines whether mouse events will be processed against the Structured Graphics object. Possible values are 0 (False) and True (−1 or nonzero). The default is False.
PreserveAspectRatio	Gets or sets a value indicating whether the object should retain its aspect ratio when *Extent* properties are changed. Possible values are False (0) and True (−1 or nonzero).
SourceURL	Specifies an absolute or relative reference to a text file that contains *<PARAM>* tags that define an image.
Transform	Transforms the object using one of the predefined DirectAnimation Transform behaviors. (For scripts only.)

Choosing a Coordinate System

I don't want to bog you down with too much detail on all the Structured Graphics control properties here, but one property is important to understand right off the bat—the *CoordinateSystem* property.

The Structured Graphics control is a three-dimensional artist's canvas—sometimes called a *world*—on which you can draw using code. Where objects appear on this canvas depends on a set of coordinates unlike what you've seen before. The x,y coordinates are laid out so that 0,0 is the dead center of the drawing canvas. On most drawing and positioning surfaces, 0,0 is in the upper-left corner.

You also have two coordinate systems to choose from. One is the default Windows-based system in which y values decrease as you progress upward. Say we create a Structured Graphics control that's 200 pixels wide and 200 pixels tall, using the default Windows scheme. The x,y coordinates of that control are positioned as shown in Figure 15-1.

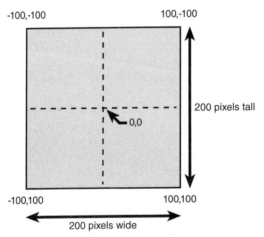

Figure 15-1. *How* x,y *coordinates are positioned in a Windows-based coordinate system.*

NOTE   The Structured Graphics control is completely invisible when empty—you don't see the border and lines shown in Figure 15-1. I added those for the purposes of illustration.

If you want to use the Windows-based coordinate system, you can either eliminate the *<PARAM NAME="CoordinateSystem"...>* tag from the control's definition or explicitly set that property to 0. For example, the tag below creates a Structured Graphics control that's 200 pixels wide and 200 pixels tall and uses the Windows-based coordinate system:

```
<!-- Structured Graphics control, Windows coordinates -->
<OBJECT ID="whatever" WIDTH="200" HEIGHT="200"
```

```
CLASSID="CLSID:369303C2-D7AC-11D0-89D5-00A0C90833E6">
    <PARAM NAME="CoordinateSystem" VALUE="0">
</OBJECT>
```

The other coordinate system, the Cartesian system, organizes *x,y* coordinates so that *y* values increase as you progress upward. To use the Cartesian system in a Structured Graphics control, you must set the *CoordinateSystem* parameter to 1 or a nonzero value, as shown below:

```
<!-- Structured Graphics control, Cartesian coordinates -->
<OBJECT ID="whatever" WIDTH="200" HEIGHT="200"
 CLASSID="CLSID:369303C2-D7AC-11D0-89D5-00A0C90833E6">
    <PARAM NAME="CoordinateSystem" VALUE="1">
</OBJECT>
```

The tag above also creates a Structured Graphics control that's 200 pixels wide and 200 pixels tall. As in our previous example, the 0,0 coordinates stand for dead center of the drawing area. But the *y*-axis numbering direction is reversed so that *x,y* coordinates are positioned as shown in Figure 15-2.

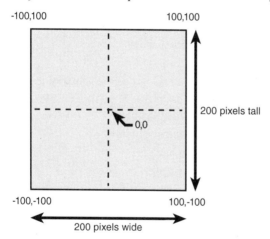

Figure 15-2. *How* x,y *coordinates are laid out in the Cartesian coordinate system.*

Of course, you can use whichever system you prefer. I'll stick with the default Windows-based system in this chapter—to me, it's a little easier because small *x,y* values are in the upper-left corner and large *x,y* values are in the lower-right corner (just as with other drawing and positioning tools you saw in earlier chapters). In the Windows-based system, the upper-left corner is −1 times half of the object width and −1 times half of the object height. For example, in a drawing object that's 500 pixels wide and 200 pixels tall, the upper-left corner is at −250,−100. The 0,0 coordinates are always dead center.

Structured Graphics Control Methods

The Structured Graphics control supports several methods. The syntax for defining methods in the *<OBJECT>* tag is a little different than the syntax for assigning properties because each line is numbered using this syntax:

```
<PARAM NAME="Linennnn" VALUE="method(params)">
```

nnnn is a four-digit number that specifies the order in which the methods are executed. *nnnn* must start at 0001 and must be incremented by one for each method. If any numbers are skipped, execution will stop. *method* is the name of any valid method from Table 15-2, and *params* are any valid parameters for the specified method.

Table 15-2
METHODS SUPPORTED BY THE
STRUCTURED GRAPHICS CONTROL

Method	Description
Arc()	Draws a single circular or elliptical arc
FillSpline()	Draws a filled spline
Oval()	Draws an oval or a circle
Pie()	Draws an arc closed at the center of the bounding rectangle to form a wedge (pie) shape
Polygon()	Draws a closed polygon
PolyLine()	Draws a segmented line
PolySpline()	Draws a spline
Rect()	Draws a rectangle or square
RoundRect()	Draws a rounded rectangle or square
SetFillColor()	Sets the foreground and background colors for graphic fills
SetFillStyle()	Sets the type of fill
SetFont()	Sets the font for any text displayed by the control
SetGradientFill()	Specifies the start point, end point, and strength for a gradient fill
SetGradientShape()	Sets the shape of a gradient to be an outline of a polygon shape
SetHatchFill()	Specifies whether the hatch fill is transparent
SetLineColor()	Sets the line color
SetLineStyle()	Sets the line style
SetTextureFill()	Sets the texture source to be used to fill a shape
Text()	Creates a string with the current font and color

The Structured Graphics control also supports a few methods that can *only* be called from scripting code. The syntax for calling these methods is:

```
objectName.methodName(methodParameters)
```

objectName is the name of the Structured Graphics control to which you want to apply the method, *methodName* is any method name listed in the left column of Table 15-3, and *methodParameters* is any valid value for the selected method.

Table 15-3

SCRIPTABLE-ONLY STRUCTURED GRAPHICS CONTROL METHODS

Method	*Description*
Clear()	Clears the control of its contents
Rotate()	Rotates the graphic
Scale()	Scales the graphic
SetIdentity()	Returns the object to its original state
Transform4x4()	Sets scaling, rotating, and translation information all at once, using a transform matrix
Translate()	Moves the graphic

Next I want to discuss the various *Set* methods. These never actually draw anything—they just define the tools to be used for drawing. More specifically, the *Set* methods let you specify line width, colors, fonts, and more.

Choosing a Line Style and Color

The size and color of lines drawn by the Structured Graphics control are determined by two methods, *SetLineStyle()* and *SetLineColor()*. The *SetLineStyle()* method specifies the style and width of any line drawn. The syntax for this method in the *<PARAM>* tags is:

```
<PARAM NAME="Linennnn" VALUE="SetLineStyle(style, lineWidth)">
```

style is a value between 0 and 2 indicating the style of line to draw; 0 = Null (invisible), 1 = solid, and 2 = dashed. *lineWidth* is the width of the line to draw, in pixels. For example, the following *<PARAM>* tag sets up the Structured Graphics control to draw a solid line 2 pixels wide:

```
<PARAM NAME="Line0001" VALUE="SetLineStyle(1, 2)">
```

The *SetLineColor()* method specifies the color of the lines. The syntax for this method is:

```
<PARAM NAME="Linennnn" VALUE="SetLineColor(red, green, blue)">
```

red, *green*, and *blue* are values between 0 and 255 that indicate the strength of each color. For example, the following *<PARAM>* tag defines purple (lots of red and blue, no green) as the color for the lines:

```
<PARAM NAME="Line0002" VALUE="SetLineColor(255,0,255)">
```

Take a look at the document source for a web page that contains a Structured Graphics control named SGControl1. I used the *SetLineStyle()* method to define a solid line style that's four pixels wide (*SetLineStyle(1, 4)*). I also set the line color to black (*SetLineColor(0,0,0)*). The control draws an oval using that information. The resulting oval is shown in Figure 15-3. (It's not the most exciting page in the world, but bear with me here.)

```
<HTML><HEAD>
<TITLE>Structured Graphics Pen and Ink</TITLE>
</HEAD>
<BODY>

<!-- Structured Graphics Control -->
<OBJECT ID="SGControl1" WIDTH="400" HEIGHT="200"
 CLASSID="CLSID:369303C2-D7AC-11D0-89D5-00A0C90833E6"
 STYLE="Border:solid 2 gray">
    <PARAM NAME="CoordinateSystem" VALUE="0">
    <PARAM NAME="HighQuality" VALUE="0">
    <!-- Set 'pen' to solid line 4 pixels wide. -->
    <PARAM NAME="Line0001" VALUE="SetLineStyle(1, 4)">
    <!-- Set 'ink' color to black. -->
    <PARAM NAME="Line0002" VALUE="SetLineColor(0,0,0)">
    <!-- Draw an oval. -->
    <PARAM NAME="Line0003" VALUE="Oval(-190,-90, 380,180, 0)">
</OBJECT>

</BODY></HTML>
```

NOTE   If you have trouble getting the same results that I did in this chapter, try changing your computer's display settings. I've found that setting your display color palette to High Color (16 bit) or a higher value produces the best results.

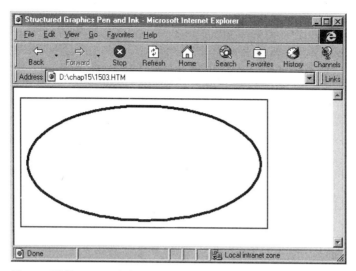

Figure 15-3. *An oval drawn with a black line that's four pixels wide.*

Choosing a Fill Style and Color

The Structured Graphics control can color in any closed shapes that you draw. To have the control color things in, you have to define a fill color and a fill style using the *SetFillColor()* and *SetFillStyle()* methods. The basic syntax of the *SetFillColor()* method is:

```
<PARAM NAME="Linennnn" VALUE="SetFillColor(rForeColor, gForeColor,
bForeColor)">
```

or

```
<PARAM NAME="Linennnn" VALUE="SetFillColor(rForeColor, gForeColor,
bForeColor, rBackColor, gBackColor, bBackColor)">
```

The fill color or foreground color is expressed as an RGB triplet— *rForeColor*, *gForeColor*, and *bForeColor*—where each color component—red (*r*), green (*g*), and blue (*b*)—is a value between 0 and 255. The optional background color— *rBackColor*, *gBackColor*, and *bBackColor*—is useful only when you use certain fill styles, as I'll discuss in a moment. For solid fills, the background color is ignored.

The syntax for the *SetFillStyle()* method is shown below, where *type* is a number between 0 and 14 representing a fill style from Table 15-4 on the next page.

```
<PARAM NAME="Linennnn" VALUE="SetFillStyle(type)">
```

Table 15-4

**VALUES FOR THE *TYPE* PROPERTY
OF THE *SETFILLSTYLE()* METHOD**

type	Description
0	Null (no fill)
1	Solid
3	Hatch horizontal
4	Hatch vertical
5	Hatch forward diagonal
6	Hatch backward diagonal
7	Hatch cross
8	Hatch diagonal cross
9	Horizontal gradient
10	Vertical gradient
11	Radial gradient
12	Line gradient
13	Rectangular gradient
14	Shaped gradient

Going back to our first sample web page, suppose I add a couple of <PARAM> tags to the Structured Graphics control to set the fill style to solid and the fill color to gray, like this:

```
<HTML><HEAD>
<TITLE>Structured Graphics Demos</TITLE>
</HEAD><BODY>

<!-- Structured Graphics Control -->
<OBJECT ID="SGControl1" WIDTH="400" HEIGHT="200"
 CLASSID="CLSID:369303C2-D7AC-11D0-89D5-00A0C90833E6"
 STYLE="Border:solid 2 gray">
    <PARAM NAME="CoordinateSystem" VALUE="0">
    <PARAM NAME="HighQuality" VALUE="1">
    <!-- Set 'pen' to solid line 4 pixels wide. -->
    <PARAM NAME="Line0001" VALUE="SetLineStyle(1, 4)">
    <!-- Set 'ink' color to black. -->
    <PARAM NAME="Line0002" VALUE="SetLineColor(0,0,0)">
```

```
      <!-- Set fill color to gray. -->
      <PARAM NAME="Line0003" VALUE="SetFillColor(128,128,128)">
      <!-- Set fill style to Solid Fill (1). -->
      <PARAM NAME="Line0004" VALUE="SetFillStyle(1)">
      <!-- Draw an oval. -->
      <PARAM NAME="Line0005" VALUE="Oval(-190,-90, 380,180, 0)">
</OBJECT>

</BODY></HTML>
```

The result, when viewed in Internet Explorer, is that the Structured Graphics control draws its oval with a black line that's four pixels wide, just as in the preceding example. However, this time the oval is filled in with gray, as shown in Figure 15-4.

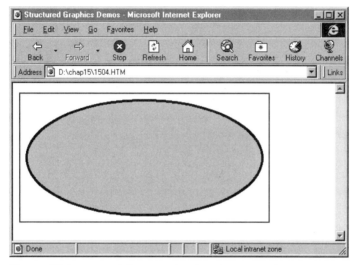

Figure 15-4. *An oval drawn with a black line and filled in with gray.*

If you look at Table 15-4, you'll notice that several of the fill styles support hatching (types 3–8). Others (types 9–14) support gradient fills. If you want to use a hatch fill, you have to decide whether to make the hatch fill transparent or not. You can do this by using the *SetHatchFill()* method with this syntax, where *isTransparent* is either 0 (False) to make the hatch fill not transparent or −1 or nonzero (True) to make it transparent:

```
<PARAM NAME="Linennnn" VALUE="SetHatchFill(isTransparent)">
```

Suppose you define a foreground color of red and a background color of blue, like this:

```
<PARAM NAME="Line0003" VALUE="SetFillColor(128,0,0, 0,0,128)">
```

If you then set the hatch fill to transparent, like this:

```
<!-- Set hatch fill to transparent. -->
<PARAM NAME="Line0004" VALUE=SetHatchFill(-1)">
```

and select a hatch style like this:

```
<!-- Set fill style to hatch cross (7). -->
<PARAM NAME="Line0005" VALUE="SetFillStyle(7)">
```

any shape you draw will be filled with a crosshatch grid, the lines of which are the foreground color (red in this example). The back of the grid is the background color (blue in this example).

If, on the other hand, you set the hatch fill to not transparent, as shown below, the background color, if any, is ignored.

```
<!-- Set hatch fill to not transparent. -->
<PARAM NAME="Line0004" VALUE="SetHatchFill(0)">
```

Here's an example using a transparent hatch background and a crosshatch:

```
<HTML><HEAD><TITLE>Structured Graphics Demos</TITLE>
</HEAD><BODY>

<!-- Structured Graphics Control -->
<OBJECT ID="SGControl1" WIDTH="400" HEIGHT="200"
 CLASSID="CLSID:369303C2-D7AC-11D0-89D5-00A0C90833E6"
 STYLE="Border:solid 2 gray">
    <PARAM NAME="CoordinateSystem" VALUE="0">
    <PARAM NAME="HighQuality" VALUE="1">
    <!-- Set 'pen' to solid line 4 pixels wide. -->
    <PARAM NAME="Line0001" VALUE="SetLineStyle(1, 4)">
    <!-- Set 'ink' color to black. -->
    <PARAM NAME="Line0002" VALUE="SetLineColor(0,0,0)">
    <!-- Set foreground to red, background to gray. -->
    <PARAM NAME="Line0003"
       VALUE="SetFillColor(128,0,0, 128,128,128)">
    <!-- Set hatch fill transparent. -->
    <PARAM NAME="Line0004" VALUE="SetHatchFill(-1)">
    <!-- Set fill style to hatch cross (7). -->
    <PARAM NAME="Line0005" VALUE="SetFillStyle(7)">
```

```
    <!-- Draw an oval. -->
    <PARAM NAME="Line0006" VALUE="Oval(-190,-90, 380,180, 0)">
</OBJECT>

</BODY></HTML>
```

The resulting oval is shown in Figure 15-5. You can't tell in the book, but the hatch lines inside the oval are red. Since I set the hatch fill to transparent, the background color behind those hatch lines is gray.

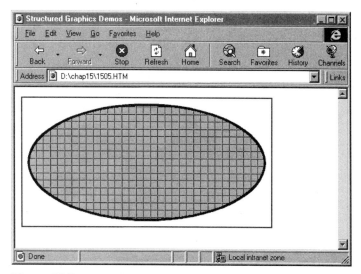

Figure 15-5. *An oval with a transparent crosshatch fill.*

You can also fill closed shapes with a color gradient. To do a gradient fill, you must define both a foreground color and background color using the *SetFillColor()* method. Then you have to use a *SetGradientFill()* method to define the size and strength of the gradient. And finally, you have to set the fill style to one of the gradient options (types 9–14 in Table 15-4).

Let's take a closer look at the *SetGradientFill()* method. It's syntax is:

```
<PARAM NAME="Linennnn" VALUE="SetGradientFill(startX, startY,
finishX, finishY, strength)">
```

startX,startY are the *x* and *y* coordinates where the gradient begins. *finishX,finishY* are the *x* and *y* coordinates where the gradient ends. *strength* is a value between 0 and 100 indicating the intensity of the gradient effect; the higher the number, the stronger the effect.

Here's an example that's similar to our previous examples but uses a gradient fill that goes from blue (0,0,255 in RGB triplet notation) to a very light blue (128,255,255 in RGB triplet notation). The gradient fill extends from the center of the object 0,0 to the edges 200,100, which is half the width and half the height of the entire drawing object. The fill style used is radial gradient (11).

```
<HTML><HEAD><TITLE>Structured Graphics Demos</TITLE>
</HEAD><BODY>

<!-- Structured Graphics Control -->
<OBJECT ID="SGControl1" WIDTH="400" HEIGHT="200"
 CLASSID="CLSID:369303C2-D7AC-11D0-89D5-00A0C90833E6"
 STYLE="Border:solid 2 gray">
    <PARAM NAME="CoordinateSystem" VALUE="0">
    <PARAM NAME="HighQuality" VALUE="1">
    <!-- Set 'pen' to solid line 4 pixels wide. -->
    <PARAM NAME="Line0001" VALUE="SetLineStyle(1, 4)">
    <!-- Set 'ink' color to black. -->
    <PARAM NAME="Line0002" VALUE="SetLineColor(0,0,0)">
    <!-- Set foreground color to blue, background to light blue. -->
    <PARAM NAME="Line0003"
       VALUE="SetFillColor(0,0,128, 128,255,255)">
    <!-- Make gradient fill extend from center 0,0 outward. -->
    <PARAM NAME="Line0004"
       VALUE="SetGradientFill(0,0, 200,100, 90)">
    <!-- Set fill style to radial gradient (11). -->
    <PARAM NAME="Line0005" VALUE="SetFillStyle(11)">
    <!-- Draw an oval. -->
    <PARAM NAME="Line0006" VALUE="Oval(-190,-90, 380,180, 0)">
</OBJECT>

</BODY></HTML>
```

The result of opening this page in Internet Explorer is shown in Figure 15-6. You can't see the blue, but you can tell from the shading that the oval is indeed filled with a radial gradient that goes from dark in the center to lighter near the edges.

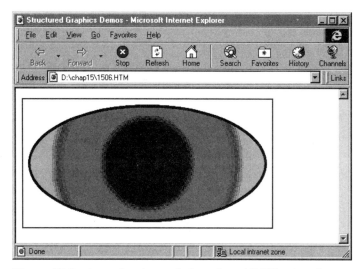

Figure 15-6. *An oval with a radial gradient fill (fill style 11).*

Structured Graphics Control Shapes

The *Set* methods we've looked at specify settings such as size and the color used to draw within the Structured Graphics control; the other methods, such as *Oval()*, do the actual drawing. The drawing methods used by the Structured Graphics control are sometimes called *primitives* because they can't draw anything fancy like a face or a jet plane. They can draw only simple, primitive shapes such as lines, ovals, and rectangles. But you can build more complex images out of those primitives, as you'll see.

The methods of the Structured Graphics control that draw shapes are listed below, along with the syntax required to draw each type of shape:

```
Arc(x, y, width, height, startAngle, arcAngle, rotation)
FillSpline(nPoints, action1, x1, y1, ... actionn, xn, yn, rotation)
Oval(x, y, width, height, rotation)
Pie(x, y, width, height, startAngle, arcAngle, rotation)
Polygon(nPoints, x1, y1, ... xn, yn, rotation)
PolyLine(nPoints, x1, y1, ... xn, yn, rotation)
PolySpline(nPoints, action1, x1, y1, ... actionn, xn, yn, rotation)
Rect(x, y, width, height, rotation)
RoundRect(x, y, width, height, arcWidth, arcHeight, rotation)
```

x determines the distance, in pixels, from dead center of the object to the left edge of the shape being drawn. *y* determines the distance, in pixels, from dead center of the object to the top edge of the shape. *nPoints* is the number of points used to draw the shape. *width* is the width of the object in pixels. *height* is the height of the object in pixels. *rotation* is the amount of rotation in degrees (from 0).

startAngle is the beginning angle of an arc or pie. *arcAngle* is the angle of the arc relative to *startAngle*, in degrees. *actionn* is what the spline does at the specified point—for example, move to the specified point, draw a line to the specified point from the previous point, or close the shape. *arcWidth* is the horizontal diameter of the arc at the rectangle's four corners. *arcHeight* is the vertical diameter of the arc at the rectangle's four corners.

Figure 15-7 shows examples of the methods used to draw shapes. Each shape is drawn using a Structured Graphics control whose tags look something like this, where *varies* is any of the methods shown to the right of the shapes in the figure:

```
<OBJECT ID="SGControln" WIDTH="100" HEIGHT="100"
 CLASSID="CLSID:369303C2-D7AC-11D0-89D5-00A0C90833E6"
 STYLE="border:solid 1 black">
    <PARAM NAME="Line0001" VALUE="SetLineStyle(1, 4)">
    <PARAM NAME="Line0002" VALUE="SetLineColor(0,0,0)">
    <PARAM NAME="Line0003" VALUE="SetFillColor(128,128,128)">
    <PARAM NAME="Line0004" VALUE="SetFillStyle(1)">
    <PARAM NAME="Line0005" VALUE="varies">
</OBJECT>
```

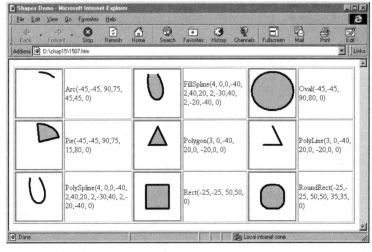

Figure 15-7. *Shapes drawn using Structured Graphics control methods.*

For example, the triangular polygon is drawn with this control:

```
<OBJECT ID="SGControl5" WIDTH="100" HEIGHT="100"
 CLASSID="CLSID:369303C2-D7AC-11D0-89D5-00A0C90833E6"
 STYLE="border:solid 1 black">
    <PARAM NAME="Line0001" VALUE="SetLineStyle(1, 4)">
    <PARAM NAME="Line0002" VALUE="SetLineColor(0,0,0)">
    <PARAM NAME="Line0003" VALUE="SetFillColor(128,128,128)">
    <PARAM NAME="Line0004" VALUE="SetFillStyle(1)">
    <PARAM NAME="Line0005"
       VALUE="Polygon(3, 0,-40, 20,0, -20,0, 0)">
</OBJECT>
```

You might wonder how anybody can draw anything "meaningful" using these primitive shapes. Well, I suspect that some graphic artists out there who are familiar with vector graphics can do pretty fancy things with primitives. For the rest of us though, trying to draw a picture using a bunch of primitives is probably close to impossible. Fortunately, there are ways around that problem, as we'll discuss next.

Converting WMF Images to Structured Graphics

The Internet Client SDK comes with a program named WMF Converter that can translate any Windows Meta File (WMF) graphic image into a series of *<PARAM>* tags that the Structured Graphics control can use to display the image.

You can find a fair amount of predrawn WMF images in clip art collections. If you have Microsoft Office or Microsoft Publisher, for example, you probably already have a number of .wmf images stored on your hard disk. To go searching, use Find on the Windows Start menu to search your hard disk for files with that extension.

If you are a registered owner of Office 97, Publisher 97, FrontPage 98, or Microsoft Works 4.5, you can download WMF clip art images from Microsoft's web site at www.microsoft.com/clipgallerylive/. You should learn about the Microsoft Clip Art Gallery, which comes with those products, to fully take advantage of the download site.

You can also create your own WMF graphic images. In fact, many 3-D rendering programs let you create 3-D objects and save them in WMF format. Figure 15-8 on the next page shows an example of a 3-D object—the word *Hey!*—in a program named AddDepth by Fractal Design Corporation. (Visit www.fractal.com for more information.) AddDepth allows me to save this image in WMF format. I can then convert that image to *<PARAM>* tags using the WMF Converter and then display it in a web page using the Structured Graphics control.

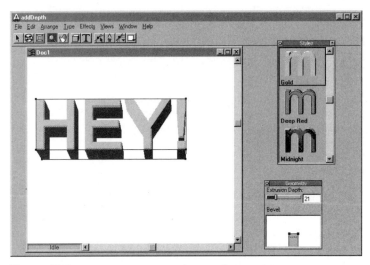

Figure 15-8. *This 3-D image can be saved as a WMF image.*

The WMF Converter is stored in the \BIN folder of the Internet Client SDK. The program is named wmfcnv.exe, and its readme file is named wmfcnv.txt. You can copy both files to a new folder on your hard disk, such as C:\Wmfconvert. You don't need to install the WMF Converter, though—there's no fancy setup program or anything. You just double-click the wmfcnv.exe program icon to start the program.

Once you start the program, choose Open from the File menu and open a WMF graphic image. After the image is loaded, it's squeezed into the available window (possibly distorted), as shown in Figure 15-9.

Figure 15-9. *A graphic named hey.wmf loaded into the WMF Converter.*

To convert the loaded image to Structured Graphics primitives, choose Options from the File menu and then set the Height and Width options to the size (in pixels) you want to make the converted image. For example, in Figure 15-10, I set the width to 300 and the height to 150. You must also select HTML <PARAM> Tags as the output format, as I did. The rest of the options are entirely optional. Click OK after making your selections.

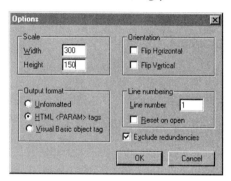

Figure 15-10. *Options for converting a WMF image to <PARAM> tag primitives.*

TIP   If you're not sure of the original size of a WMF image, you can open it in Paint Shop Pro. Rest the mouse pointer on the image. Its width x height x color depth will appear near the lower-right corner of the Paint Shop Pro window. Do not save the image after viewing it in Paint Shop Pro—just exit without saving.

Finally, you must choose Save from the File menu to save the WMF image as a file of *<PARAM>* tags. When you do, you'll see a typical Save As dialog box. Browse to the folder where you want to store the *<PARAM>* tags (probably the same folder as the rest of your web page materials). Give the file a name (I named mine hey.txt), and then click OK.

If you then open the resulting text file (hey.txt) using Notepad or Wordpad, you'll see that the file does, indeed, contain a whole bunch of *<PARAM>* tags— the exact tags needed to draw the translated picture using a Structured Graphics control. Figure 15-11 on the next page shows a portion of my hey.txt file in Notepad. The entire hey.txt file actually contains 251 lines (251 *<PARAM>* tags).

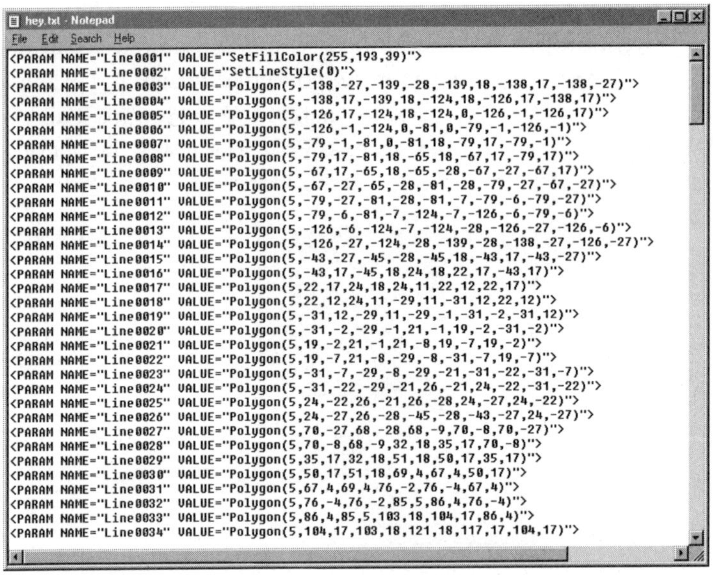

Figure 15-11. *The result of converting a WMF image to <PARAM> tags.*

After you create a text file containing *<PARAM>* tags, you can use that information with the Structured Graphics control. At first, I tried to add a reference to the text file using the *SourceURL* property of the Structured Graphics control. For example, I used this code to add a relative reference to the hey.txt file:

```
<OBJECT ID="SGControl1" WIDTH="325" HEIGHT="325"
 CLASSID="CLSID:369303C2-D7AC-11D0-89D5-00A0C90833E6">
    <PARAM NAME="SourceURL" VALUE="hey.txt">
    <PARAM NAME="CoordinateSystem" VALUE="1">
    <PARAM NAME="HighQuality" VALUE="0">
</OBJECT>
```

Unfortunately, I wasn't able to get this approach to display the *Hey!* image when I viewed the page in Internet Explorer. So instead, I copied and pasted all the *<PARAM>* tags from the text file right into the document source. For example, in Figure 15-12, you can see where I pasted the lines from the hey.txt file right into the *<OBJECT>* tag for a Structured Graphics control in an HTML document. (You can't see all the *<PARAM>* tags because there are 251 of them, most of them scrolled off the bottom of the document.)

> **TIP** If an image is displayed upside down by the Structured Graphics control, change the coordinate system by changing the *<PARAM NAME="CoordinateSystem"...>* tag inside the *<OBJECT>* tag. For example, if you use *<PARAM NAME="CoordinateSystem" VALUE="0">* and the image appears upside down, change the tag to *<PARAM NAME="CoordinateSystem" VALUE="1">*.

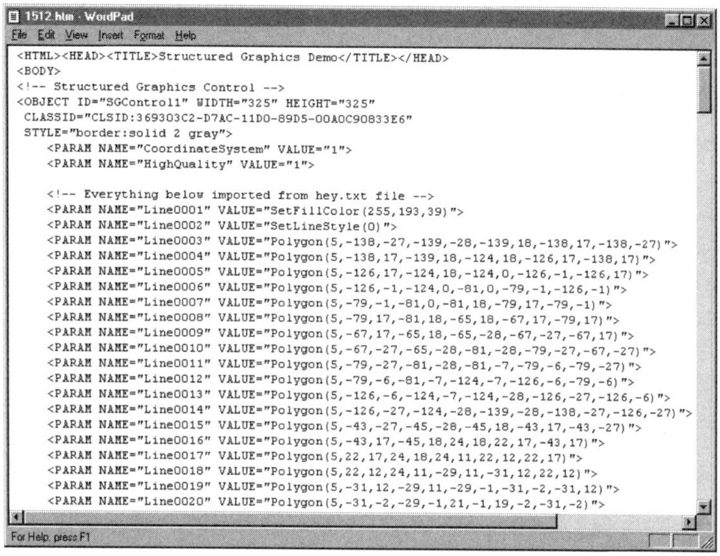

Figure 15-12. <PARAM> *tags generated by the WMF Converter are pasted into a Structured Graphics control's* <OBJECT> *tags.*

Displaying Text with the Structured Graphics Control

In addition to displaying shapes, the Structured Graphics control can display text. Text is displayed as a vector image, not as regular text; it can thus be scaled and rotated, as we'll discuss in a moment. The two main methods used to display text are *SetFont()*, which specifies the font, and *Text()*, which actually draws the text.

The syntax of the *SetFont()* method is:

```
<PARAM NAME="Linennnn" VALUE="SetFont(name, height, weight, isItalic,
isUnderline, isStrikethrough)">
```

name is the font name. *height* is the size of the font, in points. If the font height is set as a negative value, the font will be drawn upside down and backward. *weight* is the weight of the font expressed as an integer in the range 0 to 700, where 300 is normal weight and 700 is heavy bold. *isItalic*, *isUnderline*, and *isStrikethrough* are values specifying whether the font is italic, underlined, or strikethrough. If True (−1 or nonzero), the font has the corresponding attribute; if False (0), the font does not.

For example, this *<PARAM>* tag sets the font to 72-point Verdana, normal weight (300), no italic, no underline, and no strikethrough:

```
PARAM NAME="Line0001" VALUE="SetFont('Verdana', 72, 300, 0, 0, 0)">
```

The *Text()* method actually draws the text. Its syntax is:

```
<PARAM NAME="Linennnn" VALUE="Text('str', x, y, rotation)">
```

str is the text string to be displayed. *x,y* are the coordinates of the baseline position of the first character in pixels. *rotation* is the number of degrees of rotation.

Let's look at a complete example. Figure 15-13 shows an HTML document that uses a Structured Graphics control to display the word *Yowsa*. The text will be displayed in 72-point Comic Sans MS font at double the normal weight (600 instead of 300), without italics, underline, or strikethrough, because of the tag *<PARAM NAME="Line0001" VALUE="SetFont('Comic Sans MS', 72, 600, 0, 0, 0)">*.

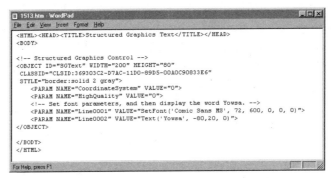

```
1513.htm - WordPad
File  Edit  View  Insert  Format  Help

<HTML><HEAD><TITLE>Structured Graphics Text</TITLE></HEAD>
<BODY>

<!-- Structured Graphics Control -->
<OBJECT ID="SGText" WIDTH="200" HEIGHT="80"
 CLASSID="CLSID:369303C2-D7AC-11D0-89D5-00A0C90833E6"
 STYLE="border:solid 2 gray">
     <PARAM NAME="CoordinateSystem" VALUE="0">
     <PARAM NAME="HighQuality" VALUE="0">
     <!-- Set font parameters, and then display the word Yowsa. -->
     <PARAM NAME="Line0001" VALUE="SetFont('Comic Sans MS', 72, 600, 0, 0, 0)">
     <PARAM NAME="Line0002" VALUE="Text('Yowsa', -80,20, 0)">
</OBJECT>

</BODY>
</HTML>

For Help, press F1
```

Figure 15-13. *The source code for a page that displays text by using a Structured Graphics control.*

The text—the word *Yowsa*—will start 80 pixels to the left of the center (–80) and 20 pixels below the center (20) of the control, with no rotation, because of this tag: *<PARAM NAME="Line0002" VALUE="Text('Yowsa', –80,20, 0)">*. Figure 15-14 shows how the page looks when opened in Internet Explorer.

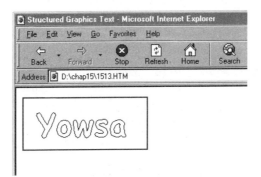

Figure 15-14. Yowsa *is displayed by a Structured Graphics control.*

The Text() method pays attention to any settings you specified using the *Set* methods. For example, suppose I set the line style to solid, two points wide (*SetLineStyle(1, 2)*); the line color to black (*SetLineColor(0,0,0)*); the fill color to gray (*SetFillColor(128,128,128)*); and the fill style to solid (*SetFillStyle(1)*), as shown below:

```
<!-- Structured Graphics Control -->
<OBJECT ID="SGText" WIDTH="200" HEIGHT="80"
 CLASSID="CLSID:369303C2-D7AC-11D0-89D5-00A0C90833E6"
 STYLE="border:solid 2 gray">
    <PARAM NAME="CoordinateSystem" VALUE="0">
    <PARAM NAME="HighQuality" VALUE="-1">
    <PARAM NAME="Line0001" VALUE="SetLineStyle(1, 2)">
    <PARAM NAME="Line0002" VALUE="SetLineColor(0,0,0)">
    <PARAM NAME="Line0003" VALUE="SetFillColor(128,128,128)">
    <PARAM NAME="Line0004" VALUE="SetFillStyle(1)">
    <PARAM NAME="Line0005"
       VALUE="SetFont('Comic Sans MS', 72, 600, 0, 0, 0)">
    <PARAM NAME="Line0006" VALUE="Text('Yowsa', -80,20, 0)">
</OBJECT>
```

The result is that the word *Yowsa* is drawn with a two-point wide black line and filled in with gray, as shown in Figure 15-15.

You can use hatch fills and gradient fills to color in letters as well. You can also rotate text on an angle by using that last parameter of the *Text()* tag. Figure 15-16 on the next page shows the document source for a page that adds gradient fill and rotation settings to display the *Yowsa* text.

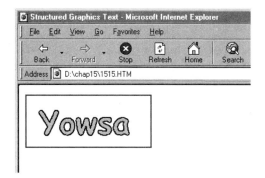

Figure 15-15. *The text displayed by a Structured Graphics control with attributes specified using the* Set *methods.*

```
1516.htm - WordPad
File  Edit  View  Insert  Format  Help

<HTML><HEAD><TITLE>Structured Graphics Text</TITLE></HEAD>
<BODY>

<!-- Structured Graphics Control -->
<OBJECT ID="SGText" WIDTH="200" HEIGHT="80"
 CLASSID="CLSID:369303C2-D7AC-11D0-89D5-00A0C90833E6"
 STYLE="Border:solid 2 gray">
    <PARAM NAME="CoordinateSystem" VALUE="0">
    <PARAM NAME="HighQuality" VALUE="-1">
    <PARAM NAME="Line0001" VALUE="SetLineStyle(1, 2)">
    <PARAM NAME="Line0002" VALUE="SetLineColor(0,0,0)">

    <!-- Set up colors, intensity, and fill style for gradient. -->
    <PARAM NAME="Line0003" VALUE="SetFillColor(0,128,0, 0,255,128)">
    <PARAM NAME="Line0004" VALUE="SetGradientFill(-100,-40, 100,40, 100)">
    <PARAM NAME="Line0005" VALUE="SetFillStyle(9)">

    <!-- Set font -->
    <PARAM NAME="Line0006" VALUE="SetFont('Comic Sans MS', 72, 600, 0, 0, 0)">

    <!-- Tilt the text 15 degrees -->
    <PARAM NAME="Line0007" VALUE="Text('Yowsa', -80,0, 15)">
</OBJECT>

</BODY></HTML>

For Help, press F1
```

Figure 15-16. *The document source for a page in which gradient and rotation settings have been added.*

The resulting text, viewed in Internet Explorer, is tilted down about 15 degrees, as shown in Figure 15-17. You can't really tell from the figure, but the word *Yowsa* is filled in with a color gradient that goes from a medium green to a light green.

It might seem that the Structured Graphics control makes you jump through a lot of hoops just to show some text and pictures. But the beauty of this control is that you can then use code to rotate, resize, and move the text or image, producing some interesting special effects. We'll take a look at some examples in the next section.

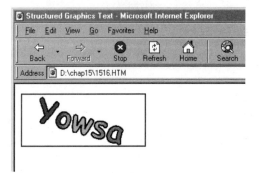

Figure 15-17. *A color gradient and tilt are added to the text.*

Animating the Structured Graphics Control

Like all ActiveX controls, the Structured Graphics control can be manipulated with scripting code. Perhaps the most interesting thing you can do is rotate the object using the *Rotate()* method and this syntax:

```
<SCRIPT LANGUAGE="VBScript"><!--
   call objectName.Rotate(x, y, z)
--></SCRIPT>
```

objectName is the name of the Structured Graphics control, as defined by the *ID* attribute of the opening *<OBJECT>* tag. The *x*, *y*, and *z* parameters are all numbers in the range of 0 to 360, indicating how far to rotate the object along the respective axis.

As Figure 15-18 illustrates, rotating an object on the *x*-axis makes it spin sort of like the big paddlewheel on a riverboat, as viewed from behind. The *y*-axis rotation spins the object like a top, as viewed from the side. And the *z*-axis rotation moves the object around like a wheel viewed from the side. The direction of the movement depends on whether you increase or decrease the rotation degrees.

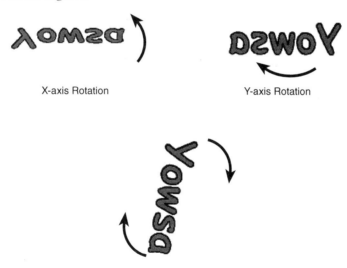

X-axis Rotation

Y-axis Rotation

Z-axis Rotation

Figure 15-18. *X-axis, y-axis, and z-axis rotations.*

473

You can achieve interesting animations and special effects by creating a simple VBScript sub procedure that rotates an object slightly. You can then create a second procedure that calls the first procedure repeatedly. If you want the animation to start automatically as the page is opened, name the second sub procedure *window_onload*, as in this example:

```
<SCRIPT LANGUAGE="VBScript"><!--
   Sub spinIt()
      'Rotate the objectName object a little.
      call objectName.Rotate(-1,1,2)
   End Sub

   Sub window_onload()
      'Call spinIt() sub to animate the rotation.
      intervalID = window.setInterval("spinIt()", 1, "VBScript")
   End Sub
--></SCRIPT>
```

The *spinIt* sub procedure slightly rotates, on all three axes, a Structured Graphics control object named *objectName*. The *window_onload* sub procedure, which starts executing as soon as the page opens, launches an interval timer that repeatedly calls that *spinIt* sub procedure.

Figure 15-19 shows the code in the context of a complete HTML document. The object to be spun is a Structured Graphics control named *SGImg* that displays the 3-D *Hey!* image.

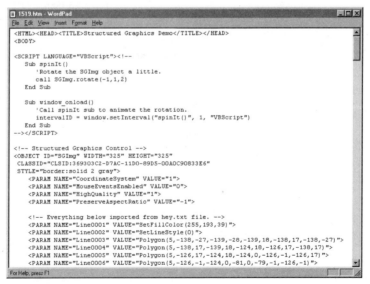

Figure 15-19. *An HTML document that automatically spins a structured graphic object.*

Opening that page displays the 3-D object and gets it spinning. Although you (obviously) can't see the motion here, Figure 15-20 gives you some idea of how the resulting page looks to a visitor.

Figure 15-20. *The document from Figure 15-19 as viewed in Internet Explorer.*

Figure 15-21 shows another example, in which the person viewing the page can control the direction of spin simply by clicking a button.

Figure 15-21. *The visitor controls the direction of spin by using buttons.*

TIP To view these animated examples live, open 1519.htm and 1521.htm from the Chapter 15 samples on the companion CD or at my web site (www.coolnerds.com).

Figure 15-22 shows the top portion of the document source for the page shown in Figure 15-21. That part of the document essentially shows the tags needed to insert a Structured Graphics control named *SGImg* and, in this example, to display the 3-D word *Hey!*

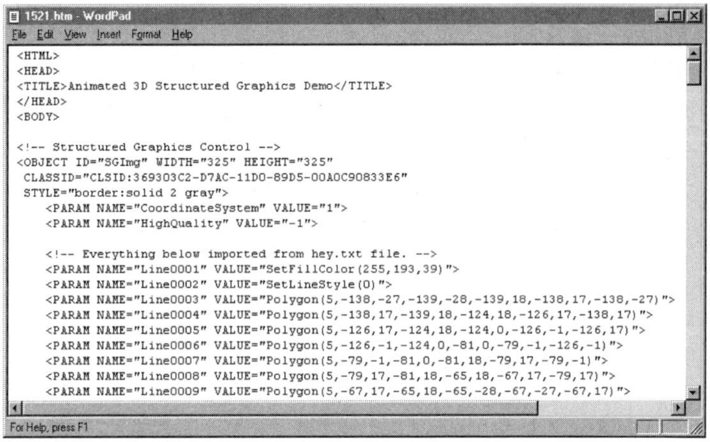


```
<HTML>
<HEAD>
<TITLE>Animated 3D Structured Graphics Demo</TITLE>
</HEAD>
<BODY>

<!-- Structured Graphics Control -->
<OBJECT ID="SGImg" WIDTH="325" HEIGHT="325"
 CLASSID="CLSID:369303C2-D7AC-11D0-89D5-00A0C90833E6"
 STYLE="border:solid 2 gray">
    <PARAM NAME="CoordinateSystem" VALUE="1">
    <PARAM NAME="HighQuality" VALUE="-1">

    <!-- Everything below imported from hey.txt file. -->
    <PARAM NAME="Line0001" VALUE="SetFillColor(255,193,39)">
    <PARAM NAME="Line0002" VALUE="SetLineStyle(0)">
    <PARAM NAME="Line0003" VALUE="Polygon(5,-138,-27,-139,-28,-139,18,-138,17,-138,-27)">
    <PARAM NAME="Line0004" VALUE="Polygon(5,-138,17,-139,18,-124,18,-126,17,-138,17)">
    <PARAM NAME="Line0005" VALUE="Polygon(5,-126,17,-124,18,-124,0,-126,-1,-126,17)">
    <PARAM NAME="Line0006" VALUE="Polygon(5,-126,-1,-124,0,-81,0,-79,-1,-126,-1)">
    <PARAM NAME="Line0007" VALUE="Polygon(5,-79,-1,-81,0,-81,18,-79,17,-79,-1)">
    <PARAM NAME="Line0008" VALUE="Polygon(5,-79,17,-81,18,-65,18,-67,17,-79,17)">
    <PARAM NAME="Line0009" VALUE="Polygon(5,-67,17,-65,18,-65,-28,-67,-27,-67,17)">
```

Figure 15-22. *The top portion of the document source for the page shown in Figure 15-21.*

Figure 15-23 shows the bottom portion of the document source for the page shown in Figure 15-21. You can see the tags for the four buttons and the VBScript code that makes all the activity happen on the page.

Let's take a moment to look at the scripting code. The first two lines, shown below, are executed as soon as the page opens:

```
<SCRIPT LANGUAGE="VBScript"><!--
   Public intervalID
   intervalID = 0
```

These lines create a public variable named *intervalID* and give it an initial value of 0. This means that all sub procedures in this page will have access to the variable named *intervalID*.

The first actual procedure in the page looks like this:

```
   Sub stopButton_onclick()
      'Stop interval timer.
      clearInterval(intervalID)
      'Return object to original appearance.
      SGImg.SetIdentity()
   End Sub
```

```
🗎 1521.htm - WordPad                                                    _ ☐ ✕
File  Edit  View  Insert  Format  Help
<!-- Buttons -->
<BUTTON ID="rotateXbutton">Rotate X</BUTTON> 
<BUTTON ID="rotateYbutton">Rotate Y</BUTTON> 
<BUTTON ID="rotateZbutton">Rotate Z</BUTTON> 
<BUTTON ID="stopButton">Stop Rotation</BUTTON>

<!-- Scripting Code -->
<SCRIPT LANGUAGE="VBScript"><!--
    'Public variable used for interval timer.
    Public intervalID
    intervalID = 0
    Sub stopButton_onclick()
        clearInterval(intervalID)      'Stop interval timer.
        SGImg.SetIdentity()            'Return object to original appearance.
    End Sub
    Sub rotateXbutton_onclick()
        call stopButton_onclick()
        'Rotate 10 degrees along the x-axis, repeatedly.
        intervalID = setInterval("call SGImg.Rotate(10,0,0)", 1, "VBScript")
    End Sub
    Sub rotateYbutton_onclick()
        call stopButton_onclick()
        'Rotate 10 degrees along the y-axis, repeatedly.
        intervalID = setInterval("call SGImg.Rotate(0,10,0)", 1, "VBScript")
    End Sub
    Sub rotateZbutton_onclick()
        call stopButton_onclick()
        'Rotate 10 degrees along the z-axis, repeatedly.
        intervalID = setInterval("call SGImg.Rotate(0,0,10)", 1, "VBScript")
    End Sub
--></SCRIPT>
</BODY></HTML>

For Help, press F1
```

Figure 15-23. *The bottom portion of document source for the page shown in Figure 15-21.*

As you can probably guess from the name, this procedure is executed when the visitor clicks on the button named *stopButton*. The procedure stops the *intervalID* timer by calling the *clearInterval()* method of the *window* object. It also sets the *SGImg* object back to its original appearance by calling the *SetIdentity()* method of the Structured Graphics control.

The rest of the scripting code is sub procedures that are bound to the *onclick* events of the buttons that let the visitor rotate the text. Each sub procedure contains two statements. The first statement stops the timer and sets the object back to its original appearance. It does this by calling the procedure named *stopButton_onclick()*. Then it sets up an interval timer that repeatedly executes the VBScript statement *"call SGImg.Rotate(…)"*. For *rotateXbutton*, the sub procedure looks like this:

```
Sub rotateXbutton_onclick()
    call stopButton_onclick()
    'Rotate 10 degrees along the x-axis, repeatedly.
    intervalID = setInterval("call SGImg.Rotate(10,0,0)", 1, _
        "VBScript")
End Sub
```

The VBScript statement *call SGImg.Rotate(10,0,0)* rotates the *SGImg* object 10 degrees on its *x*-axis. That statement is executed repeatedly (once every millisecond), giving the appearance that the *SGImg* object is moving.

The sub procedure attached to *rotateYbutton* does the same thing. However, it rotates the *SGImg* object 10 degrees along its *y*-axis (*call SGImg.Rotate(0,10,0)*), rather than its *x*-axis:

```
Sub rotateYbutton_onclick()
   call stopButton_onclick()
   'Rotate 10 degrees along the y-axis, repeatedly.
   intervalID = setInterval("call SGImg.Rotate(0,10,0)", 1, _
      "VBScript")
End Sub
```

The button that's bound to the *onclick* event of *rotateZbutton* follows suit. But it rotates the *SGImg* object 10 degrees along its *z*-axis (*call SGImg.Rotate(0,0,10)*):

```
Sub rotateZbutton_onclick()
   call stopButton_onclick()
   'Rotate 10 degrees along the z-axis, repeatedly.
   intervalID = setInterval("call SGImg.Rotate(0,0,10)", 1, _
      "VBScript")
End Sub
--></SCRIPT>
```

Structured Graphics Control Events

The Structured Graphics control also supports its own events. Note, however, that these work only if the *MouseEventsEnabled* property is set to True. The events for the Structured Graphics control are summarized in Table 15-5.

Table 15-5

EVENTS SUPPORTED BY THE STRUCTURED GRAPHICS CONTROL

Event	*When It Fires*
onclick	When the visitor clicks on the control
ondblclick	When the visitor double-clicks on the control
onmousedown	When the visitor points to the control and presses the left mouse button
onmousemove	When the mouse pointer moves over the control
onmouseout	When the mouse pointer leaves the control
onmouseover	When the mouse pointer first enters the control
onmouseup	When the mouse pointer is over the element and the left mouse button has just been released

NOTE   Some of the events that I tested for the Structured Graphics control (and also some of the events for the Sequencer and Sprite controls) did not appear to fire. If you need to use a particular event for one of these controls, be sure to test it to verify that it is working properly.

You'll see more examples of the Structured Graphics control as we explore other ActiveX controls in the rest of this chapter. Next I'll introduce you to another ActiveX control that comes with Internet Explorer 4, the Sequencer control.

THE SEQUENCER CONTROL

The DirectAnimation Sequencer control is a timer, like the built-in *setTimer()* and *setInterval()* methods. However, unlike the built-in methods, it can run several activities at a time. You can also prioritize those activities so that if two events try to happen at the same time, one of them goes first. You can add a Sequencer control to a web page using the ActiveX Control Pad or FrontPage. Once inserted, the control looks something like this:

```
<OBJECT ID="objectName" WIDTH="x" HEIGHT="y"
 CLASSID="CLSID:B0A6BAE2-AAF0-11D0-A152-00A0C908DB96">
</OBJECT>
```

objectName is a name you give to the control, and *x* and *y* are pixel measurements defining the size of the control.

Typically, there's no reason to even display the Sequencer control on the screen because there's nothing to see. You're just using it as a timer. So you can make sure it doesn't occupy any space on a page by setting its CSS *display* attribute to *none*. Here's a Sequencer control named *seqControl* that's embedded in a page and completely invisible:

```
<OBJECT ID="seqControl" WIDTH="0" HEIGHT="0" STYLE="display:none"
 CLASSID="CLSID:B0A6BAE2-AAF0-11D0-A152-00A0C908DB96">
</OBJECT>
```

Sequencer Control Methods

The Sequencer control offers several methods that can be accessed through VBScript code. These methods let you define *action sets*—timing events for multiple activities. They also let you start, stop, and pause the timer. The VBScript syntax is:

```
call objectName("actionSetName").methodName
```

objectName is the name of the Sequencer control; *actionSetName* is either the name of an action set that's about to be defined using an *At()* method or it's the name of an action set that's already been defined. *methodName* is one of the methods summarized in Table 15-6 on the next page.

Table 15-6

METHODS SUPPORTED BY THE SEQUENCER CONTROL

Method	Description
At()	Defines a new action set.
Pause()	Stops the action set at the current position. Keeps the time pointer and queue.
Play()	Starts the action set (if it's stopped). Resumes playback if the sequencer is paused. Does nothing if the sequencer is already playing.
Seek()	Changes the current playback position of the action set to a new specified time.
Stop()	Stops the action set playback and resets its position to the beginning.

Defining an Action Set

The main trick to using the Sequencer control is knowing how to define an action set. The syntax for doing so is:

```
call objectName("actionSetName").At(initialDelay, "procedure" [, loop,
loopInterval, tieOrder, dropThreshold])
```

objectName is the name of the Sequencer control as defined by the *ID* attribute of the sequencer's *<OBJECT>* tag. *actionSetName* is the name you're giving to the action set. Action sets are typically named *ActionSet1*, *ActionSet2*, *ActionSet3*, and so forth. *initialDelay* sets the start time in *seconds.milliseconds* format. For example, if *initialDelay* is set to 5.0, the procedure specified by the *procedure* parameter will be called five seconds after the action set is called upon to play. *procedure* is the name of a VBScript procedure to call.

loop (optional) specifies how many times to call the specified procedure. If *loop* is omitted, the procedure is called just once. If it is set to −1, the procedure is called repeatedly until the action set is stopped. If it is set to some other positive number, the procedure is called exactly that many times. If it is set to 0 or a negative number other than −1, the procedure is never called. *loopInterval* (optional) is the time delay, in *seconds.milliseconds* format, between executions of the *loop*.

In the event of a tie (two actions attempting to occur at exactly the same moment), the (optional) *tieOrder* value determines which one goes first. The lower the *tieOrder* number, the higher the priority. 0 has the highest priority. For example, in the event of a tie, an action with a priority of 0 will occur before an action with a priority of 1. An action with a priority of −1 is the lowest priority so its action takes place last, but it cannot be dropped altogether. The default, if *tieOrder* is omitted, is −1.

dropThreshold (optional) also helps settle ties. Expressed in *seconds.milliseconds* format, it sets a limit on how long an action can wait to be executed before being dropped from consideration. The default is –1.000, which means the action will never be dropped.

To really understand the *tieOrder* and *dropThreshold* settings, you have to understand a bit about how the Sequencer control works. When the Sequencer control is called upon to perform some action, it attempts to carry out that action immediately. If it can't do so because it is busy carrying out some other action, it puts the requested action into a queue. The sequencer might process queued actions some time after the action was actually scheduled to occur.

If events are being requested more quickly than the sequencer can process them, the queue can become quite long. This can cause the sequencer to behave strangely—slowing down and speeding up as it attempts to deal with the backlog. The sequencer might continue to run for a while after the visitor stops it so that it can empty its backlog.

The *dropThreshold* setting can help smooth things out by preventing the backlog from growing too large. In a sense, the *dropThreshold* setting says, "If you can't make this action happen within *x* seconds of when I want it to happen, forget it (drop it from the queue)."

Often, you can just omit the *tieOrder* and *dropThreshold* settings from the *At()* method altogether. But if you have a lot of activity happening on the page and the timing seems to be getting weird, you can tweak the *tieOrder* and *dropThreshold* settings to try and smooth things out.

Let's take a look at some examples of action sets. Suppose we have a Sequencer control named *seq*, which is embedded in a web page:

```
<OBJECT ID="seq" WIDTH="0" HEIGHT="0" STYLE="display:none"
 CLASSID="CLSID:B0A6BAE2-AAF0-11D0-A152-00A0C908DB96">
</OBJECT>
```

The following script creates an action set named *ActionSet1*. When called by a *Play()* method, this action set starts immediately (with a 0.000 initial delay). It calls a sub procedure named *rotateIt* repeatedly and indefinitely (–1 for the loop value). It pauses a half second (.050) between calls to *rotateIt*. I opted not to give the action a *tieOrder* setting or a *dropThreshold* setting and thus have omitted those settings:

```
<SCRIPT LANGUAGE="VBScript"><!--
   call seq("ActionSet1").At(0.000, "rotateIt", -1, 0.50)
   call seq("ActionSet1").Play()
--></SCRIPT>
```

Here's an example in which we're creating a new action set named *ActionSet2* that calls a procedure named *grandChange* just once, 10 seconds (10.000) after the *Play()* method is executed. There is no looping or tie prioritization, so the *grandChange* procedure just gets played once:

```
<SCRIPT LANGUAGE="VBScript"><!--
    call seq("ActionSet2").At(10.000, "grandChange")
    call seq("ActionSet2").Play()
--></SCRIPT>
```

Here's an example in which the action set immediately (with a 0.000 initial delay) calls a procedure named *scaleDown* when it is activated by the *Play()* method. It calls that procedure five times, once every quarter of a second (0.25). This action is high priority (0) but can be dropped if it doesn't occur within one second (1.00):

```
<SCRIPT LANGUAGE="VBScript"><!--
    call seq("ActionSet3").At(0.000, "scaleDown", 5, 0.25, 0, 1.00)
    call seq("ActionSet3").Play()
--></SCRIPT>
```

Here's an example in which the sequencer has to wait one second (1.000) and then calls a procedure named *flipIt*. Once the sequencer starts, it has to call *flipIt* 100 times, with a 0.125-second delay between calls. In the event of a conflict, this call gets executed last but it cannot be dropped from the queue (−1):

```
<SCRIPT LANGUAGE="VBScript"><!--
    call seq("ActionSet2").At(1.000, "flipIt", 100, 0.125, -1)
    call seq("ActionSet2").Play()
--></SCRIPT>
```

Now, before I show you more practical examples of the Sequencer control, I'd like to introduce you to the events that the Sequencer control supports.

Sequencer Control Events

The Sequencer control supports several events, as summarized in Table 15-7. The events let you launch scripts in response to things that the Sequencer control does. The *onInit* event is especially important because it fires when the sequencer is fully loaded into memory and is ready for action. I'll show you an example of how to use the *onInit* event in a moment.

Table 15-7

EVENTS SUPPORTED BY THE SEQUENCER CONTROL

Event	When It Fires
onInit	When the sequencer is first completely loaded into memory.
onPause	When the action set playback has been paused.
onPlay	When the action set has started playback from a stopped or paused state. It does not fire when a currently playing action set loops back to the beginning to repeat playback.
onSeek	After the *Seek* method call has been completed.
onStop	When the action set playback ends or is stopped.

Sequencer Example 1

Let's start with a really simple example—a web page that shows the following sentence, where *x* increases by one every second:

```
Sequencer control has been running for x seconds.
```

The document source for this page is shown in Figure 15-24 on the next page. Note that the Sequencer control, though invisible to the visitor, is defined by *<OBJECT>* tags near the bottom of the page. I named the control *seqControl* in this example:

```
<!-- Sequencer Control (not visible on screen) -->
<OBJECT ID="seqControl" WIDTH="0" HEIGHT="0" STYLE="display:none"
 CLASSID="CLSID:B0A6BAE2-AAF0-11D0-A152-00A0C908DB96">
</OBJECT>
```

Up near the top of the screen, VBScript declares a public variable named *secondsCounter* and gives it an initial value of 0. Since *secondsCounter* is a public variable, any script in the same page can access its contents:

```
<SCRIPT LANGUAGE="VBScript"><!--
   'This public variable, secondsCounter, will keep track of time.
   Public secondsCounter
   secondsCounter = 0
```

Here's a sub procedure that adds 1 to the current value of the *secondsCounter* variable and then displays that new value on the screen:

```
   'This sub procedure adds 1 to secondsCounter and displays the
   'new value on the screen.
   Sub upCounter()
      secondsCounter = secondsCounter + 1
      showSeconds.innerText = secondsCounter
   End Sub
```

483

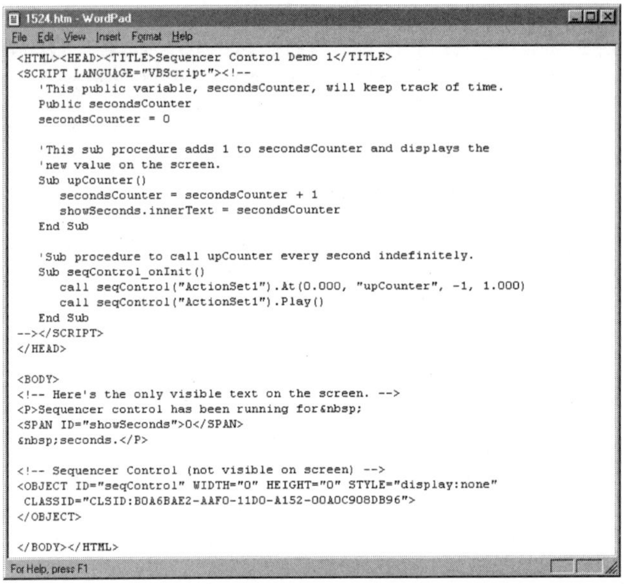

```
[1524.htm - WordPad]                                        _ □ ×
File  Edit  View  Insert  Format  Help

<HTML><HEAD><TITLE>Sequencer Control Demo 1</TITLE>
<SCRIPT LANGUAGE="VBScript"><!--
    'This public variable, secondsCounter, will keep track of time.
    Public secondsCounter
    secondsCounter = 0

    'This sub procedure adds 1 to secondsCounter and displays the
    'new value on the screen.
    Sub upCounter()
        secondsCounter = secondsCounter + 1
        showSeconds.innerText = secondsCounter
    End Sub

    'Sub procedure to call upCounter every second indefinitely.
    Sub seqControl_onInit()
        call seqControl("ActionSet1").At(0.000, "upCounter", -1, 1.000)
        call seqControl("ActionSet1").Play()
    End Sub
--></SCRIPT>
</HEAD>

<BODY>
<!-- Here's the only visible text on the screen. -->
<P>Sequencer control has been running for 
<SPAN ID="showSeconds">0</SPAN>
 seconds.</P>

<!-- Sequencer Control (not visible on screen) -->
<OBJECT ID="seqControl" WIDTH="0" HEIGHT="0" STYLE="display:none"
 CLASSID="CLSID:B0A6BAE2-AAF0-11D0-A152-00A0C908DB96">
</OBJECT>

</BODY></HTML>

For Help, press F1
```

Figure 15-24. *The document source for a web page that counts and shows the elapsed seconds.*

You might wonder what *showSeconds.innerText* refers to. Well, if you look at Figure 15-24, you'll see a little object named *showSeconds*—enclosed in *<SPAN>* tags—that's part of the sentence displayed in the web page:

```
<BODY>
<!-- Here's the only visible text on the screen. -->
<P>Sequencer control has been running for 
<SPAN ID="showSeconds">0</SPAN>
 seconds.</P>
```

So now the question is how to get the Sequencer control to call the *upCounter* procedure indefinitely, every second. The answer is in this sub procedure:

```
'Sub procedure to call upCounter every second indefinitely.
Sub seqControl_onInit()
  call seqControl("ActionSet1").At(0.000, "upCounter", -1, 1.000)
  call seqControl("ActionSet1").Play()
End Sub
```

Notice that the entire sub procedure doesn't get called until the Sequencer control is loaded and ready for action (*Sub seqControl_onInit( )*). Once called, it defines an action set named *ActionSet1* that has no initial delay (0.000). It calls the *upCounter* procedure indefinitely (−1) every one second (1.000). Right after the action set is defined, the next statement puts it into action using the *Play( )* method.

We don't need to worry about priorities or backlogs in this example because it takes less than one second to execute the *upCounter* procedure (because it's such a simple, tiny little procedure). Therefore, it's very unlikely that two actions will try to be executed at the same time. This page will probably run smoothly on any PC.

Running Multiple Sequences

Let's complicate the above example by adding some more actions to the sequencer's responsibilities. We'll create a page that does three things:

- Every 1 second, increases the seconds counter on the screen
- Every 5 seconds, changes the background color
- Every 10 seconds, plays a little sound file

Here we know that conflicts will arise. Every 5 seconds, the sequencer must increase the seconds counter *and* change the background color. Every 10 seconds, the sequencer must increase the counter *and* change the background color *and* play the sound file. We can prioritize the actions so the counter gets updated first (priority 0), the screen color gets changed second (priority 1), and the sound file plays last (priority 2). We won't, however, allow the page to drop any action. (By omitting the last optional parameter, *dropThreshold*, we cause the default, -1, to be instantiated, which means the action cannot be dropped from the queue).

Let's take a look at the document source for this page. First, we need a sub procedure for each activity. Those sub procedures, named *upCounter*, *changeColor*, and *makeNoise*, are visible in the *<HEAD>* section of Figure 15-25 on the next page.

Cut off near the bottom of Figure 15-25 is the procedure that defines, and launches, the action sets that make all these events happen. Here's that complete procedure:

```
'Define all action sets and get them rolling.
Sub seqControl_onInit()
   call seqControl("ActionSet1").At(0.000, "upCounter", -1, 1.000, 0)
   call seqControl("ActionSet2").At(0.000, "changeColor", -1, 5.000, 1)
   call seqControl("ActionSet3").At(0.000, "makeNoise", -1, 10.000, 2)
   call seqControl("ActionSet1").Play()
   call seqControl("ActionSet2").Play()
   call seqControl("ActionSet3").Play()
End Sub
```

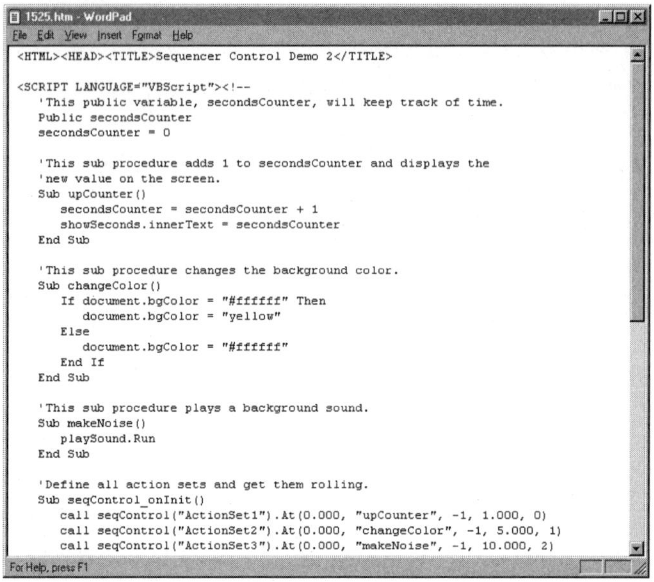

Figure 15-25. *Three sub procedures*—upCounter, changeColor, *and* makeNoise.

Notice that *ActionSet1* is set up to call the *upCounter* procedure, indefinitely, every 1.000 seconds. It has high priority (0) in the event of a tie. *ActionSet2* is set up to call the *changeColor* procedure repeatedly and indefinitely, every 5.000 seconds. Its priority, in the event of a tie, is 1—that is, it will be executed after the *upCounter* procedure.

The third action set calls the *makeNoise* procedure, indefinitely, every 10.000 seconds. Its priority is pretty low (2); in the event of a tie with the *upCounter* and *changeColor* procedures, it will be played last. Note that only one Sequencer control (the one I named *seqControl*) is used to run all three action sets.

> **TIP** When designing your own pages, keep in mind that it's always more efficient to use one Sequencer control with multiple action sets than it is to use multiple Sequencer controls, each with one action set.

So where is the Sequencer control named *seqControl* in this example? And what about that *makeNoise* procedure that plays a sound using *playSound.Run*? Where are these objects? They're defined down in the body of that same page, shown in Figure 15-26.

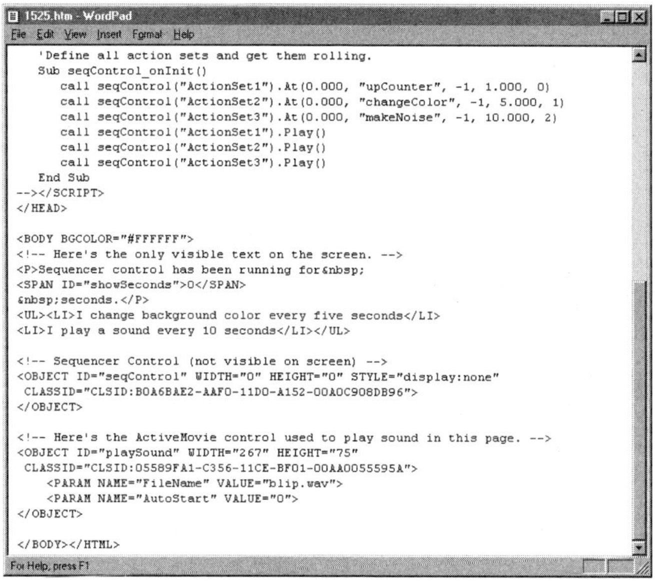

Figure 15-26. *The rest of the document source for the document shown in Figure 15-25.*

Though it's hard to tell by looking at the *<OBJECT>* tags, rest assured that the object named *seqControl* is the Sequencer control. The control named *playSound* is an ActiveMovie control with a sound file named blip.wav already loaded into it. The type in Figure 15-26 is kind of small, so let me show you what the tags for those two objects look like up close:

```
<!-- Sequencer Control (not visible on screen) -->
<OBJECT ID="seqControl" WIDTH="0" HEIGHT="0" STYLE="display:none"
 CLASSID="CLSID:B0A6BAE2-AAF0-11D0-A152-00A0C908DB96">
</OBJECT>

<!-- Here's the ActiveMovie control used to play sound in -->
<!-- this page. -->
<OBJECT ID="playSound" WIDTH="267" HEIGHT="75"
 CLASSID="CLSID:05589FA1-C356-11CE-BF01-00AA0055595A">
    <PARAM NAME="FileName" VALUE="blip.wav">
    <PARAM NAME="AutoStart" VALUE="0">
</OBJECT>
```

Figure 15-27 on the next page shows how this page looks in Internet Explorer.

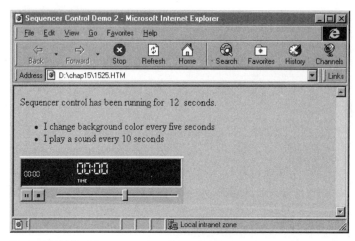

Figure 15-27. *The* upCounter, changeColor, makeNoise *sample in Internet Explorer.*

A Visitor-Controlled Animation Sequence

Next let's look at how we can use the Sequencer control to help with an animation. Also, we'll add a button to the sample page that allows the visitor to start and stop the animation. Figure 15-28 shows the page. At the moment, the animation is paused. But clicking the Play button makes the text spin around. While the text is spinning, the label on the button changes to Pause; the visitor can click that button to stop the animation.

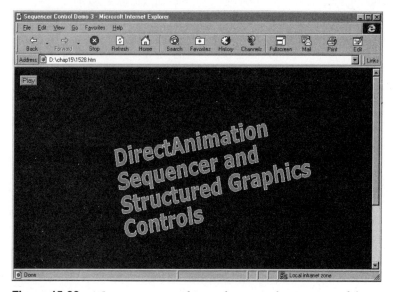

Figure 15-28. *A Sequencer control is used to control animation of the text.*

Figure 15-29 shows the top half of the document source for the page shown in Figure 15-28.

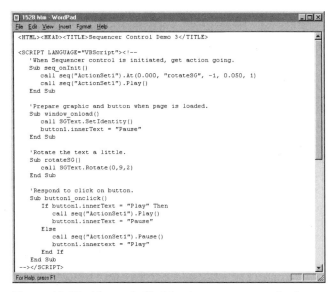

Figure 15-29. *The top half of the document source for the page shown in Figure 15-28.*

Let's discuss its VBScript procedures first. The procedure named *seq_onInit* is executed when the sequencer has been loaded and is ready for action. *seq_onInit* defines an action set that calls a procedure named *rotateSG* repeatedly, every 0.050 seconds:

```
<HTML><HEAD><TITLE>Sequencer Control Demo 3</TITLE>

<SCRIPT LANGUAGE="VBScript"><!--
   'When Sequencer control is initiated, get action going.
   Sub seq_onInit()
      call seq("ActionSet1").At(0.000, "rotateSG", -1, 0.050, 1)
      call seq("ActionSet1").Play()
   End Sub
```

The next procedure, *window_onload*, is executed when the page is fully loaded into the web browser. It makes sure that the structured graphic is in its original position, *call SGText.SetIdentity()*, and it sets the label of the button to the word *Pause*. (We know that the timer is running when the page is loaded because *seq_onInit* defines and plays the action set as soon as the sequencer itself is loaded.)

```
'Prepare graphic and button when page is loaded.
Sub window_onload()
   call SGText.SetIdentity()
   button1.innerText = "Pause"
End Sub
```

Here's the *rotateSG* procedure that the action set calls. It slightly rotates the object named *SGText*—0 degrees on its *x*-axis, 9 degrees on its *y*-axis, and 2 degrees on its *z*-axis:

```
'Rotate the text a little.
Sub rotateSG()
   call SGText.Rotate(0,9,2)
End Sub
```

You'll recall that this page has a button that can start and stop the sequencer. When the sequencer is paused, the button is labeled *Play* and clicking that button makes the sequencer start again. When the sequencer is playing, the button is labeled *Pause* and clicking it pauses the sequencer. Here's the sub procedure that makes all that happen when the visitor clicks the button named *button1*:

```
'Respond to click on button.
Sub button1_onclick()
   If button1.innerText = "Play" Then
      call seq("ActionSet1").Play()
      button1.innerText = "Pause"
   Else
      call seq("ActionSet1").Pause()
      button1.innertext = "Play"
   End If
End Sub
--></SCRIPT>
```

That's it for scripts in this page. Figure 15-30 shows the rest of the document source for the page shown in Figure 15-28 on page 488. As you can see, the body of the page contains the three objects referred to by the procedures: the *button1* object (a button), the sequencer object named *seq*, and the Structured Graphics control named *SGText*, which displays the text that you see on the screen.

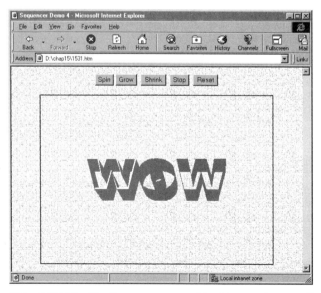

```
1528.htm - WordPad
File  Edit  View  Insert  Format  Help

--></SCRIPT>

</HEAD>

<BODY BGCOLOR="black">
<BUTTON ID="button1"></BUTTON>

<!-- Sequencer Control (named seq) -->
<OBJECT ID="seq"
 CLASSID="CLSID:B0A6BAE2-AAF0-11D0-A152-00A0C908DB96">
</OBJECT>

<!-- Strucured Graphics Control (named SGText) -->
<OBJECT ID="SGText"
 CLASSID="CLSID:369303C2-D7AC-11D0-89D5-00A0C90833E6"
 STYLE="position:absolute; height:500; width:700; top:100; left:60">
    <PARAM NAME="Line0001" VALUE="SetLineColor(255,255,255)">
    <PARAM NAME="Line0002" VALUE="SetFillColor(0,0,255)">
    <PARAM NAME="Line0003" VALUE="SetFillSTYLE(1)">
    <PARAM NAME="Line0004" VALUE="SetLineSTYLE(1)">
    <PARAM NAME="Line0005" VALUE="SetFont('Verdana', 60, 650, 0, 0, 0)">
    <PARAM NAME="Line0006" VALUE="Text('DirectAnimation', -220,-180, 0)">
    <PARAM NAME="Line0007" VALUE="Text('Sequencer and', -220,-130, 0)">
    <PARAM NAME="Line0008" VALUE="Text('Structured Graphics', -220,-80, 0)">
    <PARAM NAME="Line0009" VALUE="Text('Controls', -220,-30, 0)">
</OBJECT>

</BODY></HTML>

For Help, press F1
```

Figure 15-30. *The rest of the document source for the page shown in Figure 15-28.*

Spinning and Sizing with a Sequencer Control

I'd like to show you one more example of using the Sequencer control to animate a Structured Graphics control. The page I'll be discussing is shown, from the visitor's perspective, in Figure 15-31. The word *WOW* is actually a structured graphic displayed by a Structured Graphics control. The frame around *WOW* is the border of the control.

Figure 15-31. *The Sequencer control in this page is controlled by the buttons.*

The Spin button, when clicked, gets the word *WOW* spinning in clockwise motion. The word keeps spinning until the reader clicks the Stop button. The Grow button scales up the word so it appears to rush toward the reader. The Shrink button scales down the word so it appears to rush away from the reader. The Reset button sets the word *WOW* back to its original magnification.

Let's look behind the scenes at this page's document source to see what makes it tick. Figure 15-32 shows the top portion of that page's source. The first few procedures are all attached to buttons. We'll discuss those first.

The button named *spinButton*, when clicked, calls a procedure that defines an action set named *ActionSet3*. That action set calls a procedure named *spinText* repeatedly (−1) every 0.02 seconds. This action has a priority level of 2, but it can never be dropped from the queue (−1):

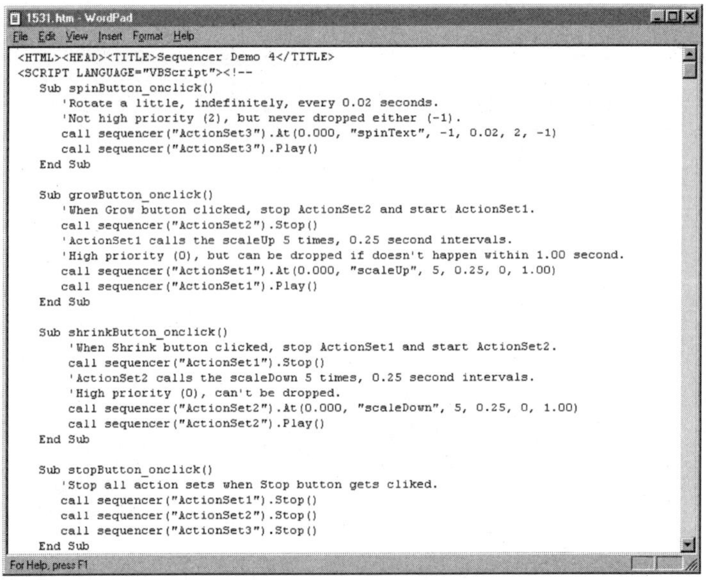

```
<HTML><HEAD><TITLE>Sequencer Demo 4</TITLE>
<SCRIPT LANGUAGE="VBScript"><!--
    Sub spinButton_onclick()
        'Rotate a little, indefinitely, every 0.02 seconds.
        'Not high priority (2), but never dropped either (-1).
        call sequencer("ActionSet3").At(0.00, "spinText", -1, 0.02, _
            2, -1)
        call sequencer("ActionSet3").Play()
    End Sub
```

Figure 15-32. *The top portion of the document source for the page shown in Figure 15-31.*

The script that's bound to the *growButton* object sets up a new action set named *ActionSet2* and gets it playing. However, since the object can't grow and shrink at the same time, this procedure actually stops the shrinkage first. It does so by stopping *ActionSet2* (which you haven't seen defined yet) before creating and playing its own action set, named *ActionSet1*. As you can see, *ActionSet2* calls a procedure named *scaleUp* five times, once every 0.25 seconds. This action gets high priority in the event of a tie (0). However, if it can't be executed in 1.00 seconds, it gets dropped from the queue:

```
Sub growButton_onclick()
    'When Grow button clicked, stop ActionSet2, start ActionSet1.
    call sequencer("ActionSet2").Stop()
    'ActionSet1 calls scaleUp 5 times at 0.25 second intervals.
    'High priority (0), but can be dropped if doesn't happen
    'within 1.00 second.
    call sequencer("ActionSet1").AT(0.000, "scaleUp", 5, 0.25, _
        0, 1.00)
    call sequencer("ActionSet1").Play()
End Sub
```

The script that's bound to *shrinkButton* is similar to the script above. If the object is growing when this button is clicked, that action is stopped by calling an end to *ActionSet1*. Then this procedure creates an action set named *ActionSet2*, which in turn calls a procedure named *ScaleDown* five times, once every 0.25 seconds. This action also gets high priority (0), but it can be dropped from the queue if it is not executed within three seconds of when it was supposed to be executed:

```
Sub shrinkButton_onclick()
    'When Shrink button clicked, stop ActionSet1, start ActionSet2.
    call sequencer("ActionSet1").Stop()
    'ActionSet2 calls scaleDown 5 times at 0.25 second intervals.
    'High priority (0), drop if not executed in 3 seconds.
    call sequencer("ActionSet2").At(0.00, "scaleDown", 5, 0.25, _
        0, 3.00)
    call sequencer("ActionSet2").Play()
End Sub
```

The Stop button stops all motion—spinning, growth, and shrinkage—by stopping all three action sets dead in their tracks:

```
Sub stopButton_onclick()
    'Stop all action sets when Stop button gets clicked.
    call sequencer("ActionSet1").Stop()
    call sequencer("ActionSet2").Stop()
    call sequencer("ActionSet3").Stop()
End Sub
```

Figure 15-33 shows the next portion of the document source for the example shown in Figure 15-31 on page 491. This part of the document contains more scripts, which we'll discuss below.

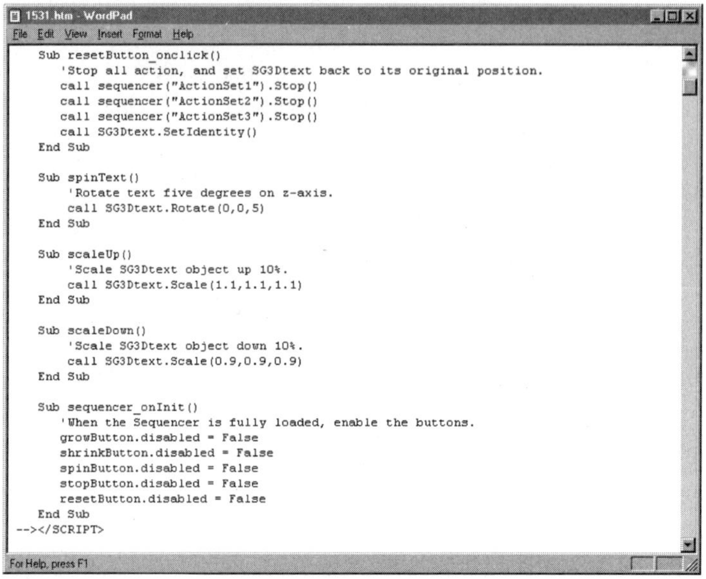

Figure 15-33. *The next portion of the document source for the page shown in Figure 15-31.*

The procedure that's bound to the Reset button stops all action sets and sets the word *WOW* back to its original appearance.

```
Sub resetButton_onclick()
    'Stop all action, and set SG3Dtext back to its original
    'position.
    call sequencer("ActionSet1").Stop()
    call sequencer("ActionSet2").Stop()
    call sequencer("ActionSet3").Stop()
    call SG3Dtext.SetIdentity()
End Sub
```

That's it for procedures that are attached to buttons. Here's the *spinText* sub procedure that's called repeatedly to make the object spin on its *z*-axis. It uses the *Rotate()* method of the Structured Graphics control to do the spinning:

```
Sub spinText()
    'Rotate text five degrees on z-axis.
    call SG3Dtext.Rotate(0,0,5)
End Sub
```

The *scaleUp* procedure increases the size of the Structured Graphics object by about 10 percent by scaling the image to 1.1 times its current size. It uses the *Scale()* method of the Structured Graphics control to accomplish this:

```
Sub scaleUp()
    'Scale SG3Dtext object up 10%.
    call SG3Dtext.Scale(1.1,1.1,1.1)
End Sub
```

The *scaleDown* procedure uses the *Scale()* method of the Structured Graphics control to shrink the object by about 10 percent, by scaling it to 0.9 times its current size:

```
Sub scaleDown()
    'Scale SG3Dtext object down 10%.
    call SG3Dtext.Scale(0.9,0.9,0.9)
End Sub
```

This page initially poses a little problem. The buttons on the page are visible and look ready for action before the Structured Graphics and Sequencer controls are fully loaded and ready for action. To fix that problem, the page initially shows the buttons as disabled (grayed out). The buttons stay disabled until the sequencer is fully loaded. Once the sequencer is ready for action, it sends out an *onInit* event, which in turn triggers this next procedure:

```
Sub sequencer_onInit()
    'When the Sequencer is fully loaded, enable the buttons.
    growButton.disabled = False
    shrinkButton.disabled = False
    spinButton.disabled = False
    stopButton.disabled = False
    resetButton.disabled = False
End Sub
--></SCRIPT>
```

As you can see, the *sequencer_onInit* procedure sets the *disabled* property of all the buttons to False, which returns them to their normal enabled state.

The rest of the page is the body of the document, in which all the objects discussed above —*spinButton, growButton, sequencer, SG3Dtext,* and so forth— are defined. You can see that portion of the page in Figure 15-34 on the next page. Notice that each button is initially disabled—its *DISABLED* property is set to True:

```
<!-- Here are the buttons. -->
<P ALIGN="center">
<BUTTON ID="spinButton" DISABLED="True">Spin</BUTTON> 
<BUTTON ID="growButton" DISABLED="True">Grow</BUTTON> 
<BUTTON ID="shrinkButton" DISABLED="True">Shrink</BUTTON> 
<BUTTON ID="stopButton" DISABLED="True">Stop</BUTTON> 
<BUTTON ID="resetButton" DISABLED="True">Reset</BUTTON>
</P>
```

Figure 15-34. *The next portion of the document source for the page shown in Figure 15-31.*

The *sequencer* object is a Sequencer control. The *SG3Dtext* object is a Structured Graphics control, and it is centered on the page by a pair of *<CENTER>...</CENTER>* tags. The remaining portion of the document contains 827 *<PARAM...>* tags that define the *WOW* text.

THE SPRITE CONTROL

The DirectAnimation Sprite control lets you put a *sprite* into a web page. A sprite is usually some small animation, like an animated GIF. The Sprite control lets you place these little animations in your web page and control them through VBScript.

The sprite control needs a source—a set of images to work with. The images can be in .png, .gif, .jpg, or .wmf format. They can all be stored together in a single file if each image is exactly the same size in both height and width.

Let me show you an example. In real life, an animator would probably draw each picture for the sprite. But I have to settle for less because I can't draw worth beans. Using my trusty low-budget coolnerds logo (which I created from clip art), the Paint Shop Pro program, and Kai's Power Tools (KPT), I can create five different versions of my little logo, as shown in Figure 15-35.

TIP Paint Shop Pro is made by JASC (www.jasc.com). KPT is made by MetaTools (www.metatools.com).

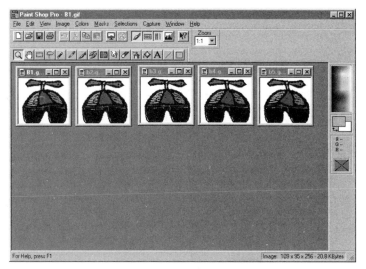

Figure 15-35. *The small logo graphic copied and distorted with a KPT Twist filter.*

To make a sprite source, I have to combine the five images into one graphic image, sort of like a filmstrip. I know that each of these images is 109 pixels wide and 95 pixels tall (because Paint Shop Pro's status bar tells me that when I point to the picture). To put all of these pictures side by side in one image, I need an image that's 5 × 109, or 545, pixels wide. The height has to be 95 pixels. So by choosing New from the File menu in Paint Shop Pro, I create a new empty image that's 545 pixels wide and 95 pixels tall.

I then cut-and-paste a copy of each image into the new empty image, making sure each one is *exactly* 109 pixels wide and 95 pixels tall. The resulting image is shown in Figure 15-36 on the next page, under the original five images. The new, long image is our sprite source. I save that file as wigglbny.gif (for wiggle beanie) in the same folder that I keep the rest of my web site files.

Now that I have a sprite source—the wigglbny.gif file—the Sprite control can be of some use to me. With the Sprite control, I can show the images in a video format, creating the illusion that the beanie is twisting back and forth. You can use the ActiveX Control Pad or FrontPage to insert the Sprite control into any web page.

The Sprite control's *<OBJECT>* tag looks like this:

```
<OBJECT ID="objectName"
 CLASSID="CLSID:FD179533-D86E-11D0-89D6-00A0C90833E6">
    <PARAM NAME="property" VALUE="setting">
</OBJECT>
```

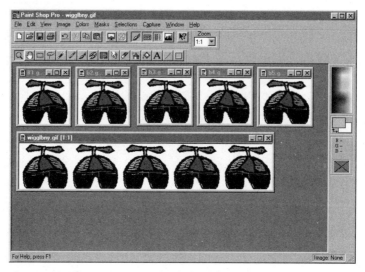

Figure 15-36. *A new image made from the other five makes a good sprite source.*

objectName is a name you give the control, *property* is any property listed in Table 15-8, and *setting* is any valid setting for the selected property. As you'll see, this control exposes lots of properties. But I think they'll make sense to you after you understand what a frame is.

Table 15-8

PROPERTIES SUPPORTED BY THE SPRITE CONTROL

Property	Description
AutoStart	Determines whether the sprite starts playback upon loading. Possible settings are 0 (False) and −1 (True).
ColorKey	Defines a single color in the format *r,g,b* that will be transparent in the sprite source. For example, a *ColorKey* value of 0,0,0 sets the transparency color to black. This property works only if the *UseColorKey* property is set to −1 (True).
FinalFrame	Sets the sprite to display a designated frame when playback is stopped.
Frame	Returns the sprite image frame currently displayed (read-only).
FrameMap	Sets the order in which sprite frames play back and the length of time that each frame is displayed.
Image	Sets or returns a DirectAnimation image from the Sprite control.

Property	Description
InitialFrame	Sets or returns the frame number that the sprite displays when it first becomes visible.
Library	Returns the DirectAnimation Library reference.
MaximumRate	Sets or returns the maximum rendering speed of the sprite (the number of times the control will render per second). The default, 30, is a widely used standard.
MouseEventsEnabled	Sets or returns whether the sprite responds to mouse events (−1) or ignores mouse events (0).
NumFrames	Describes the number of frames in the sprite source.
NumFramesAcross	Describes the width, in frames, of the sprite source.
NumFramesDown	Describes the height, in frames, of the sprite source.
PlayRate	Sets or returns the playback speed of the sprite. Possible values are as follows: 1 for normal speed (the default); a value of 0 disables playback; positive values play the sprite forward; and negative numbers play the sprite backward.
PlayState	Returns the playback state of the sprite—stopped (0), playing (1), or paused (2). Read-only.
Repeat	Sets or returns the number of times the sprite will loop during playback. A value of −1 means "infinite."
SourceURL	Describes the location of the sprite source as an absolute or relative reference.
Time	Returns the elapsed playback time for the sprite, including looping. Read-only.
TimerInterval	The default length of time between frames (in milliseconds) for the sprite's rendering. The default value, if the property is omitted, is 0.10 (10 frames per second).
UseColorKey	Sets or returns whether to use the transparency information defined by the *ColorKey* property.

Recall that our sprite source consisted of five frames (images). If we mentally number those frames from left to right, as in Figure 15-37 on the next page, we can easily refer to any single frame by number:

1—beanie twisted 10 degrees left

2—beanie twisted 5 degrees left

3—untwisted beanie

4—beanie twisted 5 degrees right

5—beanie twisted 10 degrees right

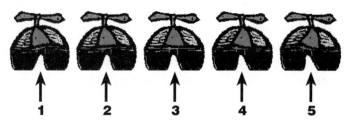

Figure 15-37. *How frames are numbered in our sprite source.*

Since we can refer to each frame as a simple number, we can give the Sprite control all kinds of instructions on how to handle the frames. For example, suppose we want the sprite to initially show the untwisted beanie on the screen. We simply tell it to show frame number 3. Suppose we want the sprite to play frames in rapid succession to give the illusion of the beanie twisting left and right. If the motion starts from the center (untwisted beanie), the following series of frames give the illusion of the beanie twisting to the far right, twisting to the far left, and then coming back to the middle:

Frame number order: 4, 5, 4, 3, 2, 1, 2, 3

Playing that sequence over and over gives the illusion of the beanie dancing—sort of. Anyway, let me show you the *<OBJECT>* tag that turns my little filmstrip—er, I mean sprite source—into a dancing beanie. Figure 15-38 shows the document source for the complete web page. What really does the trick, though, is the Sprite control, defined by those *<OBJECT>* tags, shown below:

```
<!-- Sprite Control -->
<OBJECT ID="spriteControl" WIDTH="150" HEIGHT="200"
 STYLE="border:solid 2 black; visibility:visible"
 CLASSID="CLSID:FD179533-D86E-11D0-89D6-00A0C90833E6">
    <PARAM NAME="SourceURL" VALUE="wigglbny.gif">
    <PARAM NAME="AutoStart" VALUE="-1">
    <PARAM NAME="InitialFrame" VALUE="3">
    <PARAM NAME="FinalFrame" VALUE="3">
    <PARAM NAME="Repeat" VALUE="-1">
    <PARAM NAME="TimerInterval" VALUE="0.25">
    <PARAM NAME="PlayRate" VALUE="1">
    <PARAM NAME="MaximumRate" VALUE="30">
    <PARAM NAME="NumFrames" VALUE="5">
    <PARAM NAME="NumFramesAcross" VALUE="5">
    <PARAM NAME="NumFramesDown" VALUE="1">
    <PARAM NAME="ColorKey" VALUE="255,255,255">
    <PARAM NAME="UseColorKey" VALUE="-1">
    <PARAM NAME="MouseEventsEnabled" VALUE="0">
    <PARAM NAME="FrameMap" VALUE="4,0.25; 5,0.25; 4,0.25; 3,0.25;
        2,0.25; 1,0.25; 2,0.25; 3,0.25">
</OBJECT>
```

```
┌─────────────────────────────────────────────────────────────┐
│ ▣ 1538.htm - WordPad                                 _ □ ✕   │
├─────────────────────────────────────────────────────────────┤
│ File  Edit  View  Insert  Format  Help                        │
├─────────────────────────────────────────────────────────────┤
│ <HTML>                                                        │
│ <HEAD>                                                        │
│ <TITLE>Sprite Control Demo - Dancing Beanie</TITLE>           │
│ </HEAD>                                                       │
│ <BODY>                                                        │
│                                                               │
│ <!-- Sprite Control -->                                       │
│ <OBJECT ID="spriteControl" WIDTH="150" HEIGHT="200"           │
│  STYLE="border:solid 2 black; visibility:visible"             │
│  CLASSID="CLSID:FD179533-D86E-11D0-89D6-00A0C90833E6">        │
│     <PARAM NAME="SourceURL" VALUE="wigglbny.gif">             │
│     <PARAM NAME="AutoStart" VALUE="-1">                       │
│     <PARAM NAME="InitialFrame" VALUE="3">                     │
│     <PARAM NAME="FinalFrame" VALUE="3">                       │
│     <PARAM NAME="Repeat" VALUE="-1">                          │
│     <PARAM NAME="TimerInterval" VALUE="0.25">                 │
│     <PARAM NAME="PlayRate" VALUE="1">                         │
│     <PARAM NAME="MaximumRate" VALUE="30">                     │
│     <PARAM NAME="NumFrames" VALUE="5">                        │
│     <PARAM NAME="NumFramesAcross" VALUE="5">                  │
│     <PARAM NAME="NumFramesDown" VALUE="1">                    │
│     <PARAM NAME="ColorKey" VALUE="255,255,255">               │
│     <PARAM NAME="UseColorKey" VALUE="-1">                     │
│     <PARAM NAME="MouseEventsEnabled" VALUE="0">               │
│     <PARAM NAME="FrameMap" VALUE="4,0.25; 5,0.25; 4,0.25; 3,0.25; │
│         2,0.25; 1,0.25; 2,0.25; 3,0.25">                      │
│ </OBJECT>                                                     │
│                                                               │
│ </BODY>                                                       │
│ </HTML>                                                       │
├─────────────────────────────────────────────────────────────┤
│ For Help, press F1                                            │
└─────────────────────────────────────────────────────────────┘
```

Figure 15-38. *The document source for the page that displays the dancing beanie.*

Notice that there is no scripting code—just the *<OBJECT>…</OBJECT>* tags for the Sprite control. Fortunately, that's all we need because we can set up its properties to make it do exactly what we want. Let's take a look at these, as an example, and see why it all works.

The first parameter tells the Sprite control that the sprite source is in a file named wigglbny.gif in the same directory as this page:

```
<PARAM NAME="SourceURL" VALUE="wigglbny.gif">
```

The next parameter tells the Sprite control to start doing its thing as soon as the page and the control are loaded into a web browser:

```
<PARAM NAME="AutoStart" VALUE="-1">
```

These next two parameters tell the Sprite control which frame to show when the sprite isn't moving. *InitialFrame* is the one that appears before any motion starts. *FinalFrame* is the frame to be shown after motion stops. I'll use my untwisted beanie, frame 3, for both of those still frames:

```
<PARAM NAME="InitialFrame" VALUE="3">
<PARAM NAME="FinalFrame" VALUE="3">
```

I want this sprite to repeat indefinitely—as long as the visitor is viewing the page. Hence I set the *Repeat* parameter to infinity (−1):

```
<PARAM NAME="Repeat" VALUE="-1">
```

The *TimerInterval* property sets a "tolerance" that says how "late" a frame can be without being dropped out of the picture. Setting this property to a low value such as 0.25 or 0.20 causes frames that are even a little late to be dropped from the queue. But this is good because it prevents the sprite from building up a huge backlog, which can make it run slowly or unevenly.

```
<PARAM NAME="TimerInterval" VALUE="0.25">
```

The *PlayRate* property defines a default play rate. The default value, 1, means a normal rate. A value greater than 1 speeds up the frame rate. A value less than 1 but greater than 0 slows down the frame rate. A 0 value disables all playback, and a negative value plays the sprite backward. For our current example, I stuck with the default value of 1:

```
<PARAM NAME="PlayRate" VALUE="1">
```

The *MaximumRate* property sets a cap on how fast the sprite can play back. The default value of 30 fps (frames per second) is a widely used standard and is sufficient for the current sample page:

```
<PARAM NAME="MaximumRate" VALUE="30">
```

The next three parameters are important because they tell the Sprite control how frames are arranged in your sprite source file. Mine has five frames, so I need to set the *NumFrames* property to 5:

```
<PARAM NAME="NumFrames" VALUE="5">
```

My five frames are side by side, so the correct value for the number-of-frames-across property (*NumFramesAcross*) is 5:

```
<PARAM NAME="NumFramesAcross" VALUE="5">
```

My sprite source has only one row across. So the correct value for the number-of-frames-down property (*NumFramesDown*) is 1:

```
<PARAM NAME="NumFramesDown" VALUE="1">
```

My sprite source has a white background. Since I did not save my sprite with any transparency information, I can make white the transparent color to give the sprite a transparent background. The next two tags take care of that little job. If I had saved my sprite with a transparent color, the following tags would have no effect:

```
<PARAM NAME="ColorKey" VALUE="255,255,255">
<PARAM NAME="UseColorKey" VALUE="-1">
```

I really don't care about mouse events in this example, so I'll just turn them off:

```
<PARAM NAME="MouseEventsEnabled" VALUE="0">
```

The next tag, the *FrameMap* property, is perhaps the most important because it tells the Sprite control exactly which frame to show and how long to show it. The syntax looks something like this:

```
<PARAM NAME="FrameMap" VALUE="frame1, howLong1; ... framen, howLongn">
```

Each *framen* parameter is actually a frame number to show. It's followed by a comma and then the *howLongn* parameter, which describes how long to show the frame in 0.000 (*seconds.milliseconds*) format. Notice that a semicolon separates each *framen, howLongn;* pair of numbers. I decided earlier in this section to show the frames in the order 4, 5, 4, 3, 2, 1, 2, 3 to get a smooth, twisting, back-and-forth effect. I suppose I can try it with each frame being displayed for 0.25 seconds. If that's too fast or too slow, I can always try a larger (slower) or smaller (faster) show time.

Anyway, to show each frame for 0.25 seconds in the order I want, I need a long *FrameMap* tag that looks like this:

```
<PARAM NAME="FrameMap" VALUE="4,0.25; 5,0.25; 4,0.25; 3,0.25;
   2,0.25; 1,0.25; 2,0.25; 3,0.25">
```

That's how it all works—it's pretty simple, really. You create a little "filmstrip" of equal-sized images, and then you tell the Sprite control how to display them.

As with all ActiveX controls, you can manipulate the Sprite control using VBScript code. You can change or set any property (except read-only properties) using this standard syntax:

```
objectName.property = newValue
```

objectName is the Sprite control's name (*ID*), *property* is some valid property for that control (as listed earlier in Table 15-8), and *newValue* is the new value to assign to the property.

Sprite Control Methods

The Sprite control offers several methods to give you more control over the behavior of the sprite. The methods are all called from code using this syntax:

```
<SCRIPT LANGUAGE="VBScript"><!--
   objectName.method(parameters)
--></SCRIPT>
```

objectName is the name of the Sprite control, as determined by the *ID* attribute of the control's *<OBJECT>* tag. *method* is one of the methods summarized in Table 15-9, and *parameters* are values for the parameters that the method accepts. Many methods don't require parameters. For example,

```
myVideo.Stop()
```

or even

```
myVideo.Stop
```

in VBScript is sufficient to stop a Sprite control named *myVideo* from playing.

Table 15-9

METHODS SUPPORTED BY THE SPRITE CONTROL

Method	*Description*
AddFrameMarker()	Sets a marker to fire an event when playback reaches the designated frame.
AddTimeMarker()	Sets a marker to fire an event when playback reaches the designated time.
FrameSeek()	Sets the sprite playback to a specific frame.
Pause()	Stops playback at the current frame and maintains the current frame position.
Play()	Begins playback from the current frame.
Seek()	Sets the sprite playback to a specific elapsed time.
Stop()	Stops playback and resets frame position to the beginning.

Let's use a couple of methods in a sample page that presents the sprite as motionless initially and displays a Go button that, when clicked, starts the sprite playing. There's a Stop button, too, that stops the sprite dead in its tracks, as you can see in Figure 15-39.

Figure 15-40 shows the top portion of the document source for the button-controlled sprite in Figure 15-39. The *<OBJECT>* tag for this page is identical to the *<OBJECT>* tag for the first example —in fact, it's the same wigglbny.gif sprite. However, in this page you might want to change the *AutoStart* property from True (−1) to False (0), as shown below:

```
<PARAM NAME="AutoStart" VALUE="0">
```

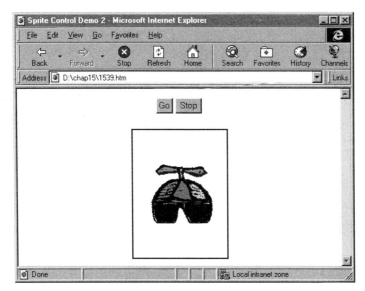

Figure 15-39. *The sprite is controlled by two buttons.*

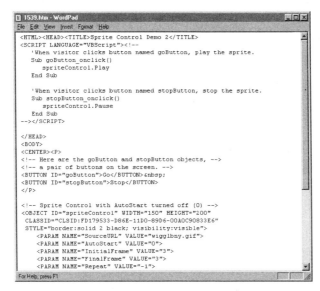

Figure 15-40. *The top portion of the document source for the page shown in Figure 15-39.*

Doing so makes the sprite appear stationary at first. The reader has to click the Play button to start the sprite. This is just an option—a little variation.

The two buttons that the visitor clicks to control the motion are courtesy of these two tags, which create the buttons named *goButton* and *stopButton*:

```
<BODY>
<CENTER><P>
<!-- Here are the goButton and stopButton objects, -->
<!-- a pair of buttons on the screen. -->
<BUTTON ID="goButton">Go</BUTTON> 
<BUTTON ID="stopButton">Stop</BUTTON>
</P>
```

The sub procedures that breathe life into those buttons are up in the *<HEAD>* section. The one named *goButton_onclick* is, of course, bound to the Go button. When clicked, the Go button calls the *Play()* method of the Sprite control named *spriteControl*, thereby making it play its frames. Clicking the Stop button calls the *stopButton_onclick* procedure, which calls the *Pause()* method of the Sprite control to stop the playback immediately:

```
<SCRIPT LANGUAGE="VBScript"><!--
    'When visitor clicks button named goButton, play the sprite.
    Sub goButton_onclick()
        spriteControl.Play
    End Sub

    'When visitor clicks button named stopButton, stop the sprite.
    Sub stopButton_onclick()
        spriteControl.Pause
    End Sub
--></SCRIPT>
```

Sprite Control Events

Last but not least, the Sprite control can trigger events of its own. They're summarized in Table 15-10.

To illustrate a couple of sub procedures that are bound to a couple of these events, let's change the rules on our last sprite example. Rather than having to click a button to start the sprite, the visitor only has to point to it. And rather than clicking a Stop button to stop the sprite, the visitor only has to move the mouse pointer off the sprite.

Table 15-10

EVENTS SUPPORTED BY THE SPRITE CONTROL

Event	When It Fires
onclick	When the user clicks on the sprite once
ondblclick	When the user double-clicks on the sprite
onframeseek	After the *FrameSeek* method has been called
onmarker	When a frame marker or a time marker has been reached either during sprite playback or when the sprite is stopped
onmedialoaded	When a piece of sprite media is completely downloaded
onmousedown	When the user presses the mouse button over a sprite
onmousemove	When the user moves the mouse across the non-transparent area of the sprite
onmouseout	When the cursor leaves the nontransparent area of the sprite
onmouseover	When the cursor enters a nontransparent area of the sprite
onmouseup	When the user releases the mouse button over a sprite
onpause	When sprite playback is paused
onplay	When the sprite begins playback
onplaymarker	When a frame marker or a time marker is reached during sprite playback
onseek	After the *Seek* method is called
onstop	When the sprite stops playback

A few changes from our two-button example are required. Within the actual *<OBJECT>* tag, the *MouseEventsEnabled* parameter must be set to True, as shown below, so the sprite will support its own events:

```
<PARAM NAME="MouseEventsEnabled" VALUE="-1">
```

I also got rid of the visible border by removing the *border:solid 2 black* attribute from the *STYLE* attribute of the opening *<OBJECT>* tag. I did so because in a sprite like this, which has transparent pixels, only the nontransparent pixels pick up mouse events. Leaving the border visible might make the visitor think it's sufficient to point anywhere within the frame to get the hat dancing, when in fact the beanie don't boogie until the mouse pointer touches some visible part of the sprite.

Another point: You can remove the buttons from the page entirely. The two sub procedures previously named *goButton_onclick* and *stopButton_onclick* won't do any good without any objects named *goButton* and *stopButton*. So those sub procedures have to be renamed to respond to events that happen to the sprite itself.

The sub procedure shown below, named *spriteControl_onmouseover*, makes the sprite start playing when the mouse pointer hovers over the sprite:

```
<SCRIPT LANGUAGE="VBScript"><!--
    'Play the sprite when visitor points to it.
    Sub spriteControl_onmouseover()
        spriteControl.Play
    End Sub
```

The next sub procedure pauses the sprite as soon as the mouse pointer moves off the sprite:

```
    'Pause sprite when visitor moves mouse pointer off the sprite.
    Sub spriteControl_onmouseout()
        spriteControl.Pause
    End Sub
--></SCRIPT>
```

Figure 15-41 shows the scripts and other changes made to our previous example to make it work in response to mouse pointing. Be sure the *MouseEventsEnabled* property is set to −1 (True) in the *MouseEventsEnabled* <*PARAM*> tag.

Figure 15-41. *The document source for a page in which the sprite responds to* onmouseover *and* onmouseout *events.*

Drop Shadows on Sprites

You can use visual filters (discussed in Chapter 11) on sprites. For instance, if you have a transparent-background sprite like our wiggle beanie, you can put a drop shadow behind it, as in Figure 15-42. When the mouse pointer touches the beanie, the twist dance begins and the shadow follows the movement, just like a real shadow does.

Figure 15-42. *The dancing beanie has a drop shadow behind it.*

To make the drop-shadow version of wiggle beanie, I had to make the control itself a little larger to allow room for the drop shadow. I set the size attributes in the opening object tag to *WIDTH="200" HEIGHT="250"*— a little larger than the 150-by-200 dimensions used in previous examples:

```
<!-- Sprite Control... -->
<OBJECT ID="spriteControl" WIDTH="200" HEIGHT="250"
 CLASSID="CLSID:FD179533-D86E-11D0-89D6-00A0C90833E6"
 STYLE="float:left;
 filter:DropShadow(Color:#C0C0C0, OffX:-35, OffY:-35, Positive:1)">
    <PARAM NAME="SourceURL" VALUE="wigglbny.gif">
       ...
<OBJECT>
```

In addition to changing the size, I radically altered the *STYLE* attribute. But the one attribute that makes the drop shadow work is this one:

```
filter:DropShadow(Color:#C0C0C0, OffX:-35, OffY:-35, Positive:1)
```

Just a quick review of what the parameters mean: *#C0C0C0* is a silver or light gray drop shadow. The offsets of −35 move the shadow up and to the left. In real life, a smaller offset, perhaps −20 or even smaller, would look best. The last parameter, *Positive:1*, says that only nontransparent (visible) pixels within the source will cast a shadow.

> **NOTE** The *float* CSS attribute makes the object float next to neighboring text—just as an *<IMG>* tag's *ALIGN* attribute does. The *float:left* attribute says that the object will float to the left of any neighboring text. This is the same as *ALIGN="left"* in an *<IMG>* tag.

We've covered the basics of the DirectAnimation Structured Graphics, Sequencer, and Sprite controls. I hope that these skills, techniques, and examples will get you started using those controls in your own web designs. You can get more information about these controls from the *Internet Multimedia* section of the Internet Client SDK.

SUMMARY

That about wraps it up for the DirectAnimation ActiveX controls. Let's review what you've learned about the Structured Graphics, Sequencer, and Sprite controls in this chapter before we move on to a new topic:

■ The Structured Graphics control can display vector graphics that you can scale, rotate, and translate on three axes.

■ The WMF Converter, a freebie program that comes with the Internet Client SDK, lets you convert existing WMF graphics to *<PARAM>* tags for use in a Structured Graphics control.

■ The Structured Graphics control can also display text, and that text can be scaled, rotated, and translated on three axes.

■ The Sequencer control offers an alternative to the relatively simple *setTimeout()* and *setInterval()* methods.

■ When designing complex pages with lots of action, your best bet is to use one Sequencer control with multiple action sets.

■ The Sprite control lets you display a series of images from a sprite source in rapid succession, creating an animation.

■ More information on the Structured Graphics, Sequencer, and Sprite controls is available in the Internet Client SDK by choosing Internet Tools & Technologies-Internet Multimedia-DirectAnimation-Controls.

In the next chapter, we'll look at one more ActiveX control—the Tabular Data control. It doesn't have anything to do with animation or special effects, but it's pretty handy if you have a collection of database data that you want to present to visitors of your web site.

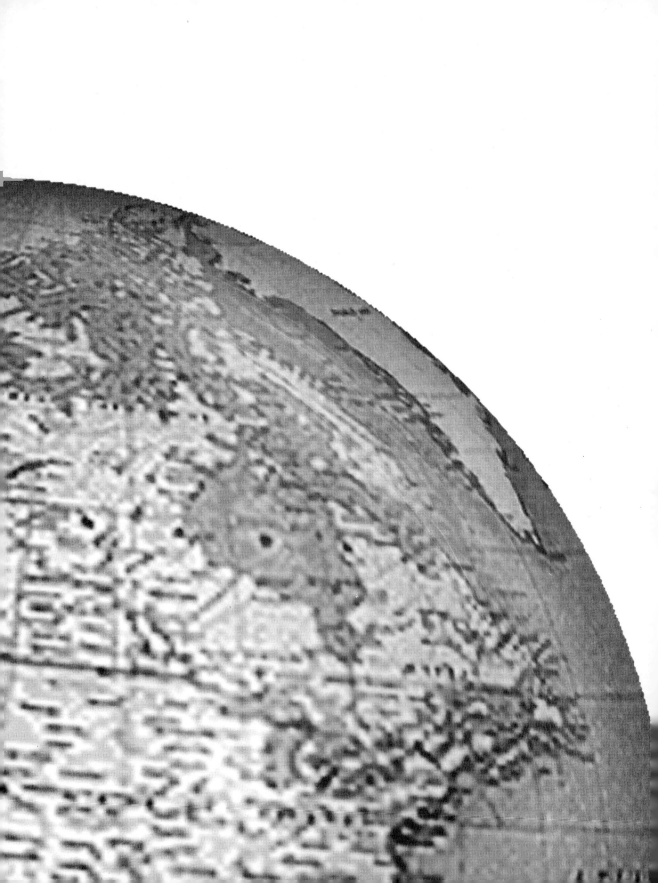

PART IV

POTPOURRI

In this last part of the book, I'll cover more new technologies offered by Microsoft Internet Explorer 4. The first is data binding, which allows a web page to show data from a separate data file. The web page can contain options that allow the visitor to sort and alphabetize data in the data file. Data binding is handled by an ActiveX control called the Tabular Data control, as well as by some special attributes that you can use in HTML tags when the Tabular Data control is active.

We'll also look at subscriptions and channels, two new (and still emerging) content delivery mechanisms that provide new ways to reach your audience. We'll look at subscriptions and channels from the visitor's perspective so you can get a feel for how your audience will experience those new technologies, and then I'll show you how to convert an existing web site into a channel.

Chapter 16

Data Binding with the Tabular Data Control

In this chapter, we'll look at a web authoring technique that you'll find useful if you want your web pages to display information exported from a database. The technique is called *data binding,* and it allows you to create a page that can display raw data from a simple text file. The primary tool you'll use is an ActiveX control named the Tabular Data control. In this chapter, you'll learn:

- What data binding is all about

- How to create a comma-delimited text file data source

- How to bind a data source to a web page using the Tabular Data control

- How to display and format data using HTML tags along with the new *DATASRC* and *DATAFLD* attributes

- How to offer database-like sorting and filtering capabilities to visitors

Unfortunately, we won't talk about live, interactive database connections here. That kind of database connectivity involves all kinds of special server hardware and software that goes beyond the scope of this book. However, those of you who rent web server space from an Internet Service Provider will be happy to know that the techniques described here will work with virtually any web server on the planet!

WHAT IS TABULAR DATA?

As you can probably guess, the Tabular Data control has something to do with *tabular data*. So what the heck is tabular data? Basically, it's information that's neatly organized into a table of rows and columns. The whole concept of tables comes from the world of database management, which you might already be familiar with. In the database world, *data* (information) is stored in tables. Each table is a neat collection of *records* (rows) and *fields* (columns) of information.

Figure 16-1 shows an example of a database table and illustrates the meanings of the words *table, record,* and *field*. Note that each field also has its own unique *field name* appearing at the top of each column, like a column heading. In this example, the field names are *LastName, FirstName,* and *Phone.*

> TIP Here's a gimmick for remembering database jargon. Remember that *rows rest* across a table, and the words *row, record,* and *rest* all start with *r*. Fields, also called columns, are like the columns in front of a building.

You can use database tables to keep track of and manage all kinds of information, including names and addresses, product inventory, and transaction histories, just to name a few examples.

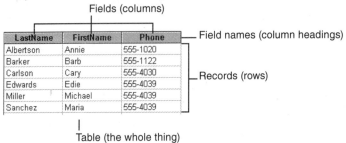

Figure 16-1. *A table that shows records (rows), fields (columns), and field names (column headings).*

What the Tabular Data Control Offers

The Tabular Data control lets you display tabular data in a web page and give visitors options for *sorting* and *filtering* the data. To see what I mean, take a look at the slightly larger table shown in Figure 16-2. That table contains data about people in a league. Each record in the table stores a player's name, a team name, a shirt number, and a phone number. (Actually, there are 27 records in that sample table—some are scrolled off the bottom of the screen.)

With the Tabular Data control, I can show visitors a copy of that information and let them sort and filter it according to their own needs. For example, the web page in Figure 16-3 on the next page shows league data. In this example, the visitor has just clicked the Alphabetize By Name button near the top of the page, so all of the players are *sorted* (alphabetized) by last name in that page (Adams, Baker, Carlos, Dixson, and so forth).

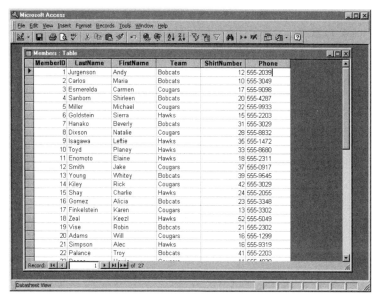

Figure 16-2. *Sample tabular data that hasn't yet been put in a web page.*

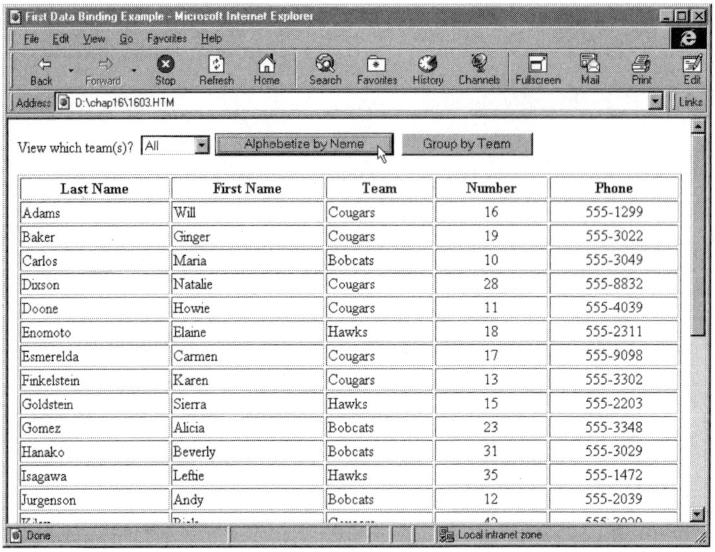

Figure 16-3. *The league members' names listed in alphabetical order.*

If the visitor wants to see who's on what team, she can click the Group By Team button to alphabetize by team name—all of the Bobcats will appear first, followed by all the Cougars, and so forth, as shown in Figure 16-4.

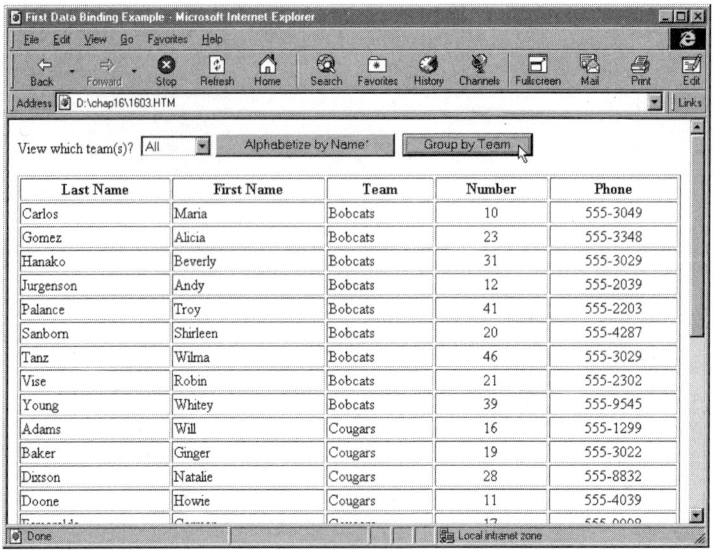

Figure 16-4. *The league members listed by team name.*

The filtering capability allows the visitor to isolate a particular type or category of information. For example, suppose our visitor is interested only in the team called the Hawks. Selecting Hawks from the drop-down list hides all other team members and displays only players for the Hawks, as shown in Figure 16-5.

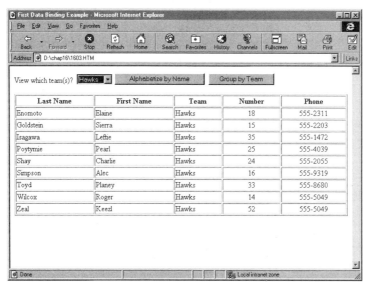

Figure 16-5. *The table is filtered to display only Hawks team members.*

That, in a nutshell, is what the Tabular Data control is all about. It lets you display tabular data on a web page, and it lets you give visitors options for sorting and filtering that tabular data. Now, before I explain any more about the Tabular Data control, let's take a moment to discuss what the Tabular Data control *isn't*.

What the Tabular Data Control *Doesn't* Do

As I already mentioned, the Tabular Data control is mainly for web authors who don't have their own web servers and don't have any way to hook a "live" database to the web. It allows visitors to *read* data from a table but not to add, change, or delete data.

Furthermore, the data displayed by the Tabular Data control generally isn't in a database at all. Instead, the data is usually a *copy* of the data from a database that has been *exported* to a text file and uploaded to the web server. If the data in your database changes and you want to post the new data to the web site, you have to manually copy data from your local database to your web site.

> **NOTE** A couple of other buzzwords you might run across are *static data*
> and *live data*. The Tabular Data control displays static data—data
> exported from a database that is no longer directly connected to the
> original database source. The Tabular Data control does not display live
> data—data that's still in the original database.

You might think that it would be easier to just hook the "real" database to
the web page and let visitors see that data as it stands at any given moment. But
in truth, that's not so easy. For one thing, connecting a live database to a web
page can be a complex and expensive undertaking. Typically you need your own
web server, a full-time T1 connection to the Internet, and a whole lot of specialized server and database software, not to mention expertise. Furthermore, putting your real database on the web page exposes that database to millions of
total strangers. Hence, security becomes a big issue as well.

So now that you know that tabular data is information neatly organized
into records (rows) and columns (fields), let me show you a little more about
how the Tabular Data control works.

PUTTING LIVE DATA ON THE WEB

Connecting live data to a web page is a topic that goes beyond the scope
of this book, because it takes a lot of extra work on the server side. I'm
going to focus only on the kinds of things that those who rent web server
space can do. If you want to learn about posting live data on a web page,
check out the many books dedicated solely to that topic. If you're interested in seeing what products Microsoft offers in this area, take a look at
Microsoft Site Server (www.microsoft.com/siteserver/), Microsoft Windows NT Server (www.microsoft.com/ntserver/), and Microsoft SQL
Server (www.microsoft.com/sql/).

If you plan to do business on the Web, you'll also have to imple-
ment some kind of payment strategy. Microsoft has strategies and tools
to help with that. Visit Microsoft's Internet Commerce Strategy site at
www.microsoft.com/commerce/ for starters.

HOW IT ALL WORKS

One of the beauties of the Tabular Data control is that it lets you store your web page and your data source in two separate files, as shown in Figure 16-6. I realize that the figure is a little small, but you can probably tell that the web page and the data source each contain two different types of things. The data source contains only the actual data—no HTML, scripting code, or ActiveX controls. The web page contains the Tabular Data control, HTML, and scripting code to define the appearance of the data on the screen, but it doesn't contain any actual data.

Splitting the web page and data source into two separate files offers a couple of advantages. For one thing, both pages are fairly small. The data source contains just the raw data—no HTML tags or anything else. The web page contains just enough information to define how the data will look on the screen—no actual data. Keeping both pages small helps decrease download time, so the information gets to visitors faster.

Figure 16-6. *In tabular data binding, data and HTML are stored in two separate files.*

Another advantage is that when the contents of the database change, only a new data source file needs to be uploaded to the server to reflect those changes. The web page that displays the data need not be changed at all.

It makes sense to always create the data source first, because the web page has to be written to accommodate the structure of the data source. Let's take a moment to discuss how one might go about creating a data source.

CREATING A DATA SOURCE

The data source for a Tabular Data control is generally a *comma-delimited text file* (also called a CSV file, where CSV stands for *comma-separated values*.) This file contains only table data. Each record (row) of data appears on its own line. Fields within each record are separated (delimited) by commas. The table might contain one special record at the top, sometimes called a *header* or *header row,* which contains field names. Figure 16-7 shows a data source created from our table of league members.

Notice that the header row—the first row across the table—defines the name of each field in the records that follow it: *MemberID, LastName, FirstName, Team, ShirtNumber*, and *Phone*. The actual data records begin below the header row. Each record is stored on its own line. Each record is also divided into fields, and the fields are separated by commas. As a general rule, numbers (such as *MemberID* and *ShirtNumber*) are not enclosed in quotation marks. Strings (text), such as people's names, are enclosed in quotation marks.

Figure 16-7. *A data source stored in a comma-delimited text file.*

A comma-delimited text file is a simple text file, like a web page. Technically, you can manually type such a file using a simple text editor like Notepad. However, most people will probably use a database management program (such as Microsoft Access, Microsoft FoxPro, Paradox, or dBASE) to create a comma-delimited text file. Virtually all database programs support exporting to comma-delimited text files, and that's the main reason that the Tabular Data control is written to handle data stored in that format.

Exactly *how* you go about exporting data from a database to a comma-delimited text file depends on the database management system in use. I can't give you exact step-by-step instructions for exporting data from every database management program in the world. But I'll present an example using Access 97, just so you can get a feel for how it's done.

Let's say I'm involved with a kid's sports league. I keep track of league members' names, addresses, team names, shirt numbers, and phone numbers in the table I showed you back in Figure 16-2. I'd like to export a copy of the table data from Access 97 to a comma-delimited text file that the Tabular Data control can use. In Access, I select the table I want to export, and I choose Save As/Export from the File menu. In the Save As dialog box, I select To An External File Or Database and then click OK. In the Save Table dialog box, I browse to the folder where I keep the rest of my web materials (AlansWeb, in this example). I select Text Files as the type of file to export to, and I give the exported data a file name, such as league.txt, as I've done in Figure 16-8 on the next page.

PHONE NUMBERS AND ZIP CODES AREN'T NUMBERS

In the computer world, a true number can contain only numeric characters (0 through 9), perhaps one decimal point (as in 123.45), and perhaps a leading hyphen for negation (as in −123.45). What we call "numbers" in common parlance don't always fit that computer definition of a number.

For instance, phone numbers can contain parentheses and embedded hyphens, as in (619)555-1234, so they are not true numbers. Zip codes can contain hyphens as well, as in 92067-0630. Some countries even put letters in their postal codes, as in HC1 4LB. So zip codes and postal codes aren't really numbers, either. And Social Security numbers, which can contain two hyphens, as in 123-45-6789, also don't qualify as true numbers. In the computer world, phone numbers, zip codes, and social security numbers should be stored and treated as strings rather than as numbers. That's why the phone numbers in Figure 16-7 are all enclosed in quotation marks.

TIP If you have a database program but don't know how to export data to text files, check the program's documentation or help files for the following buzzwords: export, comma-delimited, comma-separated values (or CSV), text file, ASCII text file, and delimited text file.

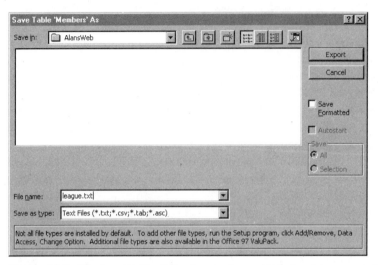

Figure 16-8. *The Save Table dialog box in Access 97 before I export a table to a text file named league.txt in my AlansWeb folder.*

I click the Export button, which takes me to a wizard that asks me how I want to format the exported data. I select Delimited, as shown in Figure 16-9, and then I click the Next button.

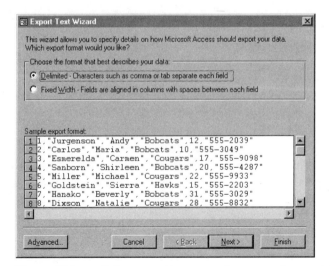

Figure 16-9. *I tell the Export Text Wizard to export data in delimited format.*

In the next wizard screen, I specify that I want to separate fields with commas, include field names on the first row, and use double quotation marks as the text delimiter, because this is the format that the Tabular Data control prefers. Figure 16-10 shows how that wizard screen looks when filled out.

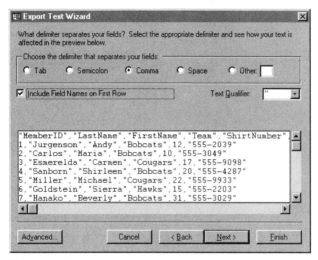

Figure 16-10. *I specify commas as delimiters and quotation marks as text qualifiers, and I opt to include field names in the first row.*

I click the Finish button to create the comma-delimited text file, and then I close Access and focus on the exported data. If I open the exported file, league.txt, in a simple text editor such as Notepad, I can see that the exported data is, in-deed, in comma-delimited format, with field names across the top row, as shown in Figure 16-11.

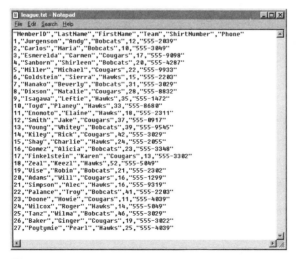

Figure 16-11. *How the exported league.txt file looks in Notepad.*

With the data source file, league.txt, created and safely stored on disk, I can turn my attention to the other half of the equation—the web page and the Tabular Data control.

CREATING THE WEB PAGE

The web page that displays data from the data source must contain, among other things, a Tabular Data control to bind the data source to the web page. The Tabular Data control is a Microsoft ActiveX control that comes with Internet Explorer 4. You can insert it into a web page using Microsoft FrontPage or Microsoft FrontPage Express. Like all other ActiveX controls, the Tabular Data control is represented by a pair of *<OBJECT>...</OBJECT>* tags with *<PARAM>* tags in between. Here's a general example of the tag's syntax:

```
<OBJECT ID="anyName"
 CLASSID="clsid:333C7BC4-460F-11D0-BC04-0080C7055A83">
    <PARAM NAME="DataURL" VALUE="filename.txt">
    <PARAM NAME="UseHeader" VALUE="Boolean">
</OBJECT>
```

anyName is a name you assign to the control, and *filename.txt* is a reference to the data source file. The Boolean value is either True (if the first row of the data source contains field names) or False (if the first row does not contain field names). The parameters shown in the example, *DataURL* and *UseHeader*, are often the only two parameters required if the data source is in the standard comma-delimited format we've seen so far.

HTML Data Binding Attributes

In addition to containing the Tabular Data control's object tags, the web page that displays the data also has to include HTML tags that describe how to display the external data on the page. Internet Explorer 4's version of Dynamic HTML provides several attributes that help you bind tags to items of data in a data source. At a glance, those attributes are:

- *DATASRC*—specifies the data source object (the name of the Tabular Data control) from which subsequent *DATAFLD* attributes get their data

- *DATAFLD*—specifies the field from the data source to bind to a particular HTML tag

- *DATAFORMATAS*—determines whether the external data should be treated as text (the default) or as HTML

- *DATAPAGESIZE*—when displaying multiple records in a table, determines the maximum number of records that can be displayed on the screen at a time

The following HTML tags support the *DATASRC* attribute: *<A>*, *<APPLET>*, *<BUTTON>*, *<DIV>*, *<FRAME>*, *<IFRAME>*, *<IMG>*, *<LABEL>*, *<MARQUEE>*, *<OBJECT>*, *<PARAM>*, *<SELECT>*, *<SPAN>*, *<TABLE>*, and *<TEXTAREA>*.

The following HTML tags support the *DATAFLD* attribute: *<A>*, *<APPLET>*, *<BUTTON>*, *<DIV>*, *<FRAME>*, *<IFRAME>*, *<IMG>*, *<LABEL>*, *<MARQUEE>*, *<OBJECT>*, *<PARAM>*, *<SELECT>*, *<SPAN>*, and *<TEXTAREA>*.

The following HTML tags support the *DATAFORMATAS* attribute: *<BUTTON>*, *<DIV>*, *<LABEL>*, *<MARQUEE>*, *<PARAM>*, and *<SPAN>*.

Only the *<TABLE>* HTML tag supports the *DATAPAGESIZE* attribute.

A Live Example

Probably the best way to get your feet wet at this point is to look at a live example of using the Tabular Data control and various *DATA* attributes to display data from a table. We'll try to keep this first example simple. Our data source will be the league.txt data file described earlier. Our goal will be to display all data from league.txt in a table in a web page, as shown in Figure 16-12.

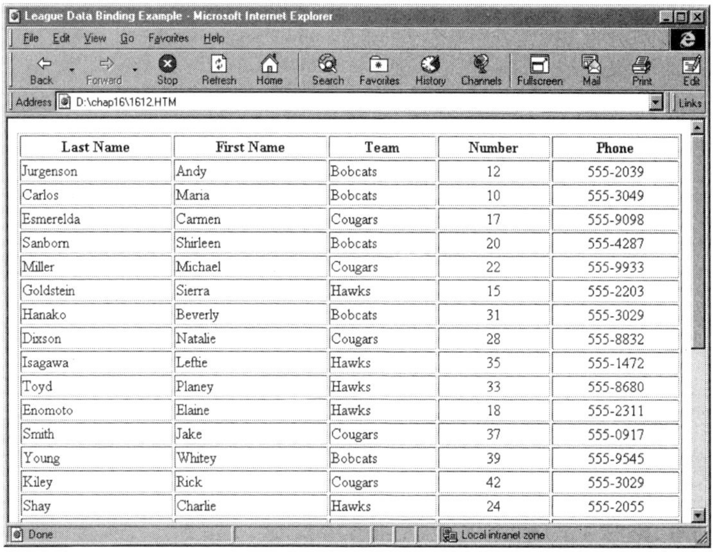

Last Name	First Name	Team	Number	Phone
Jurgenson	Andy	Bobcats	12	555-2039
Carlos	Maria	Bobcats	10	555-3049
Esmerelda	Carmen	Cougars	17	555-9098
Sanborn	Shirleen	Bobcats	20	555-4287
Miller	Michael	Cougars	22	555-9933
Goldstein	Sierra	Hawks	15	555-2203
Hanako	Beverly	Bobcats	31	555-3029
Dixson	Natalie	Cougars	28	555-8832
Isagawa	Leftie	Hawks	35	555-1472
Toyd	Planey	Hawks	33	555-8680
Enomoto	Elaine	Hawks	18	555-2311
Smith	Jake	Cougars	37	555-0917
Young	Whitey	Bobcats	39	555-9545
Kiley	Rick	Cougars	42	555-3029
Shay	Charlie	Hawks	24	555-2055

Figure 16-12. *Data from league.txt displayed in a table in a web page.*

As you might guess, the data in the web page is actually displayed by an HTML table. When used to display data from a data source, the various HTML *<TABLE>* tags play pretty much their usual roles. However, the *<TBODY>* tags, which mark the table body, automatically display a table row for every record in the data source. For that reason, this approach to showing data from a data source is called the *repeated table approach*.

Here's a quick summary of the HTML table tags and the role each plays when used with a Tabular Data control and *DATA* attributes:

- *<TABLE>*...*</TABLE>* marks the beginning and end of a table.

- *<THEAD>*...*</THEAD>* marks the start and end of the table header rows. The header row appears only once at the top of the table.

- *<TBODY>*...*</TBODY>* marks the start and end of the table body. Each row in the table body is automatically repeated once for every record in the data source.

- *<TR>*...*</TR>* marks the start and end of one row in the table.

- *<TD>*...*</TD>* marks the start and end of one table data cell.

Figure 16-13 shows the complete document source for the web page shown in Figure 16-12. Let's discuss how and why that page works.

Figure 16-13. *The document source for the page shown in Figure 16-12.*

The page starts with the usual opening *<HTML>* and heading tags, followed by a Tabular Data control named *leagueData* that binds the data source named league.txt to the page. Recall that league.txt has field names listed across the top row. To use those names, we have to set the *UseHeader* parameter to True in the ActiveX control:

```
<HTML><HEAD><TITLE>League Data Binding Example</TITLE>
<!-- This Tabular Data control binds a comma-delimited text -->
<!-- file named league.txt to this page.-->
<!-- league.txt already has field names across the top row. -->
<OBJECT ID="leagueData"
 CLASSID="clsid:333C7BC4-460F-11D0-BC04-0080C7055A83">
    <PARAM NAME="DataURL" VALUE="league.txt">
    <PARAM NAME="UseHeader" VALUE="True">
</OBJECT>
</HEAD>
```

Next we move to the body of the page, where we start a table using the *<TABLE>* tag. Note the use of the *DATASRC* attribute to bind the Tabular Data control, which is named *leagueData*, to the table. Also notice that the # character is added before the name in the *DATASRC* attribute. This character is always required with the *DATASRC* attribute.

```
<BODY>
<!-- Bind data source to table. -->
<TABLE BORDER="1" WIDTH="100%" DATASRC="#leagueData">
```

To create the row of column headings across the top of the table, we define a table header row for the table. We use the *<THEAD>...</THEAD>* tags to enclose the header row, which in turn is defined by the usual *<TR>...</TR>* and *<TD>...</TD>* tags. To center and boldface the column headings in this example, we also create a little style for the table header row:

```
<!-- Header row appears once across first row of table -->
<STYLE> THEAD {text-align:center; font-weight:bold} </STYLE>
<THEAD><TR>
    <TD>Last Name</TD><TD>First Name</TD>
    <TD>Team</TD><TD>Number</TD><TD>Phone</TD>
</TR></THEAD>
```

The body of the table is where we bind individual fields from the data source to elements on this web page. In this case, we'll bind each field to a cell in the table. Recall that in league.txt, the field names listed across the top of the page are *MemberID*, *LastName*, *FirstName*, *Team*, *ShirtNumber*, and *Phone*. We won't bother to show the *MemberID* field in the web page—it's really just a record number that Access assigns to each record automatically in this example (an *AutoNumber* field, for those of you in the know about Access). Each of the remaining fields, however, is bound to a cell by the *<SPAN DATAFLD="fieldName">...</SPAN>* tags within one cell (where *<TD>* marks the start of a cell and *</TD>* marks the end of a cell):

```
<!-- Body automatically repeats for each record in data source. -->
<TBODY><TR>
    <!-- Field names below MUST match data source header names -->
    <TD><SPAN DATAFLD="LastName"></SPAN></TD>
    <TD><SPAN DATAFLD="FirstName"></SPAN></TD>
    <TD><SPAN DATAFLD="Team"></SPAN></TD>
    <TD ALIGN="center"><SPAN DATAFLD="ShirtNumber"></SPAN></TD>
    <TD ALIGN="center"><SPAN DATAFLD="Phone"></SPAN></TD>
</TR></TBODY>

</TABLE>
</BODY></HTML>
```

That's all there is to the entire page. To summarize how it all works:

■ The Tabular Data control named *leagueData* binds the data source, league.txt, to the web page.

■ The *DATASRC="#leagueData"* attribute in the *<TABLE>* tag binds the table to the Tabular Data control named *leagueData* in this page.

■ The *DATAFLD="fieldName"* attributes mark the exact place where each field from the data source will appear.

In this example, the *DATAFLD* attributes are enclosed in *<TD>...</TD>* tags, which puts each field in a table cell. The *<TD>...</TD>* tags are, in turn, inside the *<TBODY>...</TBODY>* tags. The *<TBODY>...</TBODY>* tags, in turn, are inside the table that has a *DATASRC* attribute in its opening *<TABLE>* tag. All of these facts combined are what make the table in the page automatically generate and display a table row for each record in the data source. (Whew!)

Adding a Sort Capability

Let's add a couple of buttons to our sample page so the reader can choose between an alphabetical sort by name and an alphabetical sort by team name, where team members are grouped together and names are alphabetized within each team, as in Figure 16-14.

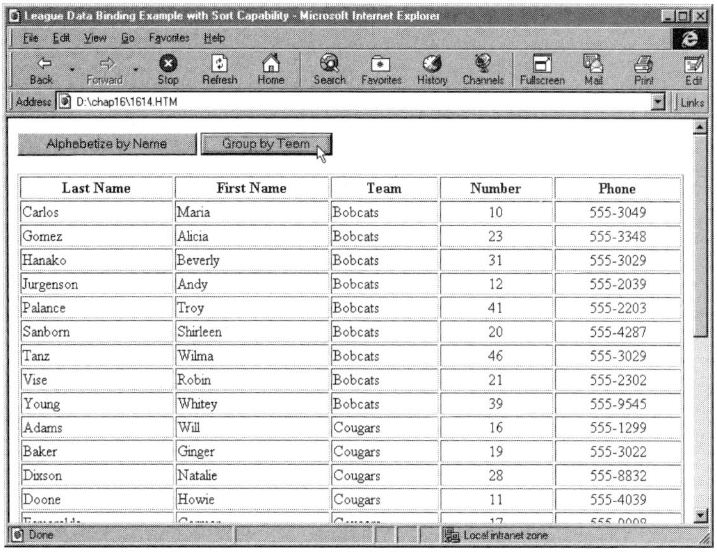

Last Name	First Name	Team	Number	Phone
Carlos	Maria	Bobcats	10	555-3049
Gomez	Alicia	Bobcats	23	555-3348
Hanako	Beverly	Bobcats	31	555-3029
Jurgenson	Andy	Bobcats	12	555-2039
Palance	Troy	Bobcats	41	555-2203
Sanborn	Shirleen	Bobcats	20	555-4287
Tanz	Wilma	Bobcats	46	555-3029
Vise	Robin	Bobcats	21	555-2302
Young	Whitey	Bobcats	39	555-9545
Adams	Will	Cougars	16	555-1299
Baker	Ginger	Cougars	19	555-3022
Dixson	Natalie	Cougars	28	555-8832
Doone	Howie	Cougars	11	555-4039

Figure 16-14. *Two sorting options added to our sample page.*

To make that happen, we have to use the *Sort* property of the Tabular Data control. The syntax for using this property in VBScript is:

```
<SCRIPT LANGUAGE="VBScript"><!--
   objectName.Sort = "fieldName1 [; fieldNamen]"
--></SCRIPT>
```

objectName is the name of the Tabular Data control (as defined by its *ID* attribute), and *fieldName1* is the name of the field to use for sorting purposes. If you list multiple field names separated by semicolons, the later fields become tiebreakers for the earlier fields. In this example, the VBScript script *doesn't* list multiple field names for the sort:

```
<SCRIPT LANGUAGE="VBScript"><!--
   leagueData.Sort = "LastName"
   leagueData.Reset
--></SCRIPT>
```

The script will indeed alphabetize data by the *LastName* field, but since there is no tiebreaker field, records with the same *LastName* value will be in random order. For instance, if the table contains the names Mary Smith, Zeke Smith, and Adam Smith, those names might be listed in this order:

```
Smith, Mary
Smith, Zeke
Smith, Adam
```

If you add the *FirstName* field as a tiebreaker, as shown below, any records with identical *LastName* values will be alphabetized by the next field, *FirstName*.

```
<SCRIPT LANGUAGE="VBScript"><!--
    leagueData.Sort = "LastName; FirstName"
    leagueData.Reset
--></SCRIPT>
```

The resulting sort is more like the way the telephone directory does it, with records sorted by first name within common last names, like this:

```
Smith, Adam
Smith, Mary
Smith, Zeke
```

The *Reset* method used in the sample script is necessary to rewrite the data with the new sort order. I'll talk about the *Reset* method in just a moment.

If you want to sort a column in descending order (Z to A rather than A to Z), precede the field name with a hyphen. For example, this little script sorts names into descending alphabetical order:

```
<SCRIPT LANGUAGE="VBScript"><!--
    leagueData.Sort = "-LastName; -FirstName"
    leagueData.Reset
--></SCRIPT>
```

In our sample web page, we want to offer our visitors two sort orders:

- Alphabetize By Name—records listed in *LastName; FirstName* sort order

- Group By Team—records listed by *Team; LastName; FirstName* to group team members together

We want to use a couple of buttons to present these options. We can place the tags for the buttons right under the opening *<BODY>* tag, as shown below, so they appear at the top of the open web page:

```
<BODY>
<P><!-- Buttons for selecting sort order. -->
<BUTTON ID="nameSort">Alphabetize by Name</BUTTON>
 <BUTTON ID="teamSort">Group by Team</BUTTON>
</P>
```

Now we need to create a sub procedure for each button. Here is the appropriate code, which you can put anywhere between the *<HEAD>...</HEAD>* tags in the sample page:

```
<SCRIPT LANGUAGE="VBScript"><!--
    'Alphabetize list by people's names.
    Sub nameSort_onclick()
        leagueData.SortColumn = "LastName; FirstName"
        leagueData.Reset()
    End Sub

    'Group by team, alphabetize within each team.
    Sub teamSort_onclick()
        leagueData.SortColumn = "Team; LastName; FirstName"
        leagueData.Reset()
    End Sub
--></SCRIPT>
```

Figure 16-15 shows exactly where I placed the new code and HTML into the original web page—VBScript code in the head section, buttons just under the opening *<BODY>* tag.

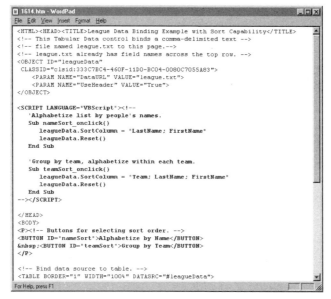

Figure 16-15. *Tags and script for the Sort buttons added to the previous example.*

Adding a Filter Capability

Since we're being magnanimous about providing sort options, maybe we should throw in a filtering option as well. For example, we could let the visitor select a particular team to view—or all teams—from a drop-down list, as shown in Figure 16-16. Selecting a team hides all records except those that belong to the selected team. For example, if you look at the records behind the drop-down list in Figure 16-16, you'll see that the records have been filtered to show only Hawks team members:

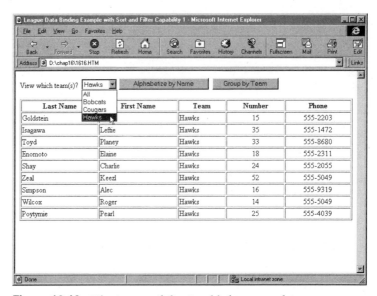

Figure 16-16. *Filtering capability is added to our web page.*

To add this capability to our page, we first have to put in the drop-down list. We use the *<SELECT>* tag to do that. In this example, I inserted a brief instruction—*View which team(s)?*—along with the SELECT tags and some non-breaking spaces (* *) near the top of the body of the page so that the instruction and select box appear to the left of the sorting buttons. Here is the exact HTML:

```
<BODY>
<P><!-- Select Box for selecting a team for filtering. -->
View which team(s)? 
<SELECT NAME="filterChoice" SIZE="1">
   <OPTION SELECTED>All</OPTION>
   <OPTION>Bobcats</OPTION>
   <OPTION>Cougars</OPTION>
   <OPTION>Hawks</OPTION>
</SELECT> 
```

Next we need a script that applies a filter after the reader selects from the drop-down list. The Tabular Data control properties we need to apply a filter are:

■ *FilterColumn*—specifies the field in the data source on which to perform the search

■ *FilterCriterion*—specifies the comparison operator used to perform the search

■ *FilterValue*—specifies the value to look for in the search

The syntax for expressing and executing a filter criterion in VBScript code is:

```
<SCRIPT LANGUAGE="VBScript"><!--
    objectName.FilterColumn ="fieldName"
    objectName.FilterCriterion ="operator"
    objectName.FilterValue = "value"
    objectName.Reset()
--></SCRIPT>
```

fieldName refers to one of the fields in the data source, *operator* is one of the comparison operators listed in Table 16-1, and *value* is the value to search for. The *Reset* method carries out the filtering operation so that only the requested records are displayed.

Table 16-1

OPERATORS FOR BUILDING SEARCH CRITERION EXPRESSIONS

Operator	Meaning
=	Equals
<>	Does not equal
>	Greater than
<	Less than
>=	Greater than or equal to
<=	Less than or equal to

Let's look at a couple of quick examples. This script displays only those records from the data source in which the *LastName* field equals *Smith*:

```
<SCRIPT LANGUAGE="VBScript"><!--
    leagueData.FilterColumn = "LastName"
    leagueData.FilterCriterion = "="
    leagueData.FilterValue = "Smith"
    leagueData.Reset()
--></SCRIPT>
```

For our current example, we need to set up a sub procedure that isolates records with a specific name in the *Team* field. We'll also allow an All option, which displays all team members. We want this procedure to be executed whenever the visitor makes a selection from the drop-down list. As you might recall, I named that drop-down list *filterChoice* in the *ID* attribute of the *<SELECT>* tag. The sub procedure we need is shown below:

```
'When select box data changes, use its data to apply filter.
Sub filterChoice_onchange()
    showTeam = filterChoice.options(filterChoice.selectedIndex).text
    If showTeam = "All" Then
    'Selecting All teams puts in a null ("") filter criterion.
        leagueData.FilterColumn = ""
        leagueData.FilterCriterion = ""
        leagueData.FilterValue = ""
        leagueData.Reset()
    Else
        'Selecting a single team sets filter to that team name.
        leagueData.FilterColumn = "Team"
        leagueData.FilterCriterion = "="
        leagueData.FilterValue = showTeam
        leagueData.Reset()
    End If
End Sub
```

In our page, this sub procedure can be tucked in with the existing sub procedures. Figure 16-17 shows the new tags and script (in boldface) tucked into the page we've been working on.

I'll take a moment now to describe how the sub procedure works. The name of the procedure, shown below, binds the procedure to the *onchange* event of the drop-down list. So any time the visitor selects from that drop-down list, this sub procedure is called into action.

```
'When select box data changes, use its data to apply filter.
Sub filterChoice_onchange()
```

The first statement takes whatever word is currently displayed within the drop-down list (for example, All, Bobcats, Cougars, or Hawks) and stores that word in a variable named *showTeam*:

```
showTeam = filterChoice.options(filterChoice.selectedIndex).text
```

An *If...Then* statement then decides what to do based on the current contents of the *showTeam* variable. If *showTeam* equals *All*, the filter properties are all set to null ("") which, in essence, means "no filter." The *Reset* method then executes the filter, displaying all records in the underlying data source:

```
If showTeam = "All" Then
    'Selecting All teams puts in a null ("") filter criterion.
    leagueData.FilterColumn = ""
    leagueData.FilterCriterion = ""
    leagueData.FilterValue = ""
    leagueData.Reset()
```

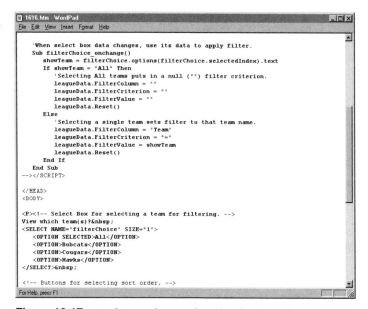

Figure 16-17. *A sub procedure and a select box have been added near the* <BODY> *tag of our page.*

If, however, the *showTeam* variable does not equal *All*, it must contain one of the team names. The sub procedure must then filter the table based on that team name. Here's the code that does that job:

```
Else
    'Selecting a single team sets filter to that team name.
    leagueData.FilterColumn = "Team"
    leagueData.FilterCriterion = "="
    leagueData.FilterValue = showTeam
    leagueData.Reset()
    End If
End Sub
```

That, in a nutshell, is how the Tabular Data control works. You create a data source, and then you create a web page containing a Tabular Data control that links the data source to the page. Then you use the *DATASRC* and *DATAFLD* attributes to bind HTML tags to specific fields in the underlying data source. You can also use the *Sort, FilterColumn, FilterCriterion,* and *FilterValue* properties and the *Reset* method of the Tabular Data control to set up scripts that allow visitors to sort and filter the data to their liking.

Incidentally, one teeny-tiny cosmetic embellishment I might add to this page centers around the Group By Team button. That button makes sense only when all teams are displayed. When only one team is displayed, that button doesn't do anything. Therefore, it probably behooves us to disable (gray out) that button when only one team's records are displayed. To add that embellishment, we have to add a couple of statements to the *filterChoice_onchange* sub procedure, as shown below:

```
Sub filterChoice_onchange()
    showTeam = filterChoice.Options(filterChoice.selectedIndex).text
    If showTeam = "All" Then
        'Selecting All teams puts in a null ("") filter criterion.
        leagueData.FilterColumn = ""
        leagueData.FilterCriterion = ""
        leagueData.FilterValue = ""
        leagueData.Reset()
        'Make Group by Team button work.
        teamSort.disabled = False
    Else
        'Selecting a single team sets filter to that team name.
        leagueData.FilterColumn = "Team"
        leagueData.FilterCriterion = "="
        leagueData.FilterValue = showTeam
        leagueData.Reset()
        'Disable the Group by Team button.
        teamSort.disabled = True
    End If
End Sub
```

SHOWING ONE RECORD AT A TIME

As an alternative to showing a big list of records to the reader, you can set up a little form that simply displays one record at a time to the reader. That approach is called the *current record approach*. It's especially handy when you want to show table data that's too wide to fit across the screen in single rows. For example, Figure 16-18 shows a sample data source in which each record contains information about a shareware product. Even from that WordPad view of the data source, you can see that each record is very wide and scrolls right off the edge of the window.

Figure 16-18. *A data source that contains some lengthy fields.*

To give you an idea of how much information is in each record of that data source, here are the field names and contents of just the first record:

Category	"Business and Professional"
ProgramName	"Accounts Payable - Medlin's MWAP"
Description	"MWAP for Windows is a fast easy accounts payable and check writing program for small and medium businesses. MWAP exports paid invoices (checks) to Medlin Windows General Ledger."
Company	"Medlin Accounting Shareware"
URL	"<A HREF='http://www.medlin.com/~medlinsw'> http://www.medlin.com/~medlinsw</A>"

In this example, I also did something a little tricky. That last field, named *URL*, is actually complete HTML tags *<A HREF=…>…</A>* that show the URL on the screen, in case the visitor just wants to print the page for future reference. But the URL is also "hot"—clicking on it takes the visitor right to that site.

Since each record has so much data, it probably makes sense to show the visitor just one record at a time and then provide a means of scrolling through the records. We can design the page to look something like Figure 16-19 on the next page, in which the visitor can select a shareware category from a drop-down list and then navigate through those records using buttons. The navigation buttons I used in this example are marked with the symbols listed below:

<<   Go to first record

<   Go to previous record

>   Go to next record

>>   Go to last record

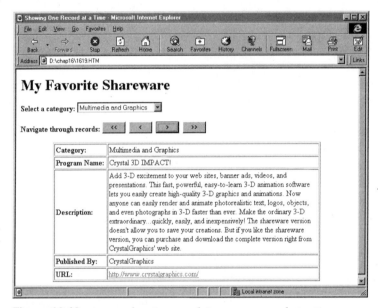

Figure 16-19. *A page showing one data source record at a time.*

The main trick to showing one record at a time is to *not* bind the entire data source to the table. Instead, put the *DATASRC* attribute right next to the *DATAFLD* attribute that displays field contents. For example, the opening *<TABLE>* tag for the example shown in Figure 16-19 looks like this:

```
<TABLE BORDER="1" ALIGN="center" CELLSPACING="2" CELLPADDING="2"
WIDTH="80%">
```

The individual table cells that show the contents of one field in one record in the data source each contain the following *<SPAN>…</SPAN>* tags, where *fieldName* is the name of a field in the data source:

```
<SPAN DATASRC="#sharewareData" DATAFLD="fieldName"></SPAN>
```

Of course, there's more to it than that. I'll take you through the entire document source for the page shown in Figure 16-19 to show you what makes it tick. As you might have guessed, the page contains a Tabular Data control that binds the data source—that big file named sharewar.txt I showed you earlier in Figure 16-18—to the page. I put the Tabular Data control in the head section of the page, as you can see in Figure 16-20.

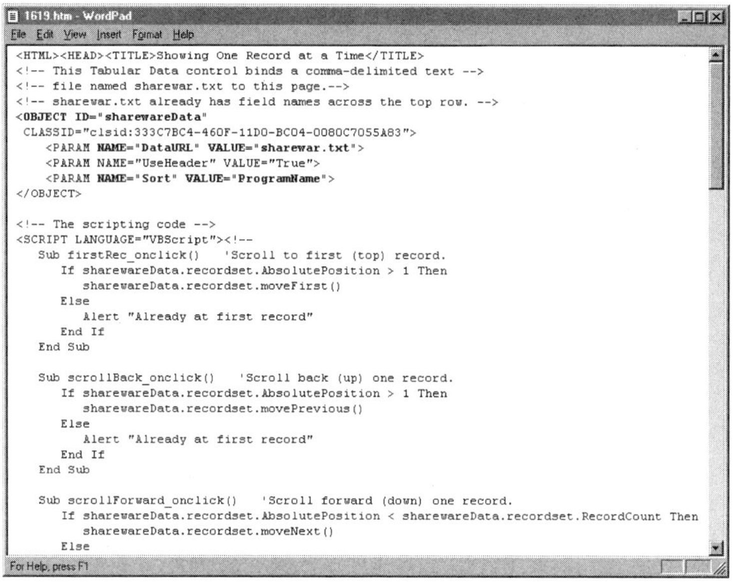

Figure 16-20. *The Tabular Data control is defined by* <OBJECT>...</OBJECT> *tags.*

I named the control *sharewareData* and specified sharewar.txt (in the same directory) as the data source to bind. In this example, I want to always show program names in alphabetical order, so I added a <*PARAM*> tag that sets the *Sort* property to the *ProgramName* field, as you can see here:

```
<OBJECT ID="sharewareData"
    CLASSID="clsid:333C7BC4-460F-11D0-BC04-0080C7055A83">
    <PARAM NAME="DataURL" VALUE="sharewar.txt">
    <PARAM NAME="UseHeader" VALUE="True">
    <PARAM NAME="Sort" VALUE="ProgramName">
</OBJECT>
```

Before I discuss the scripts used in this page, let me show you how the body of the page is set up to display the drop-down list, buttons, and data source record. Figure 16-21 on the next page shows the document source, just under the *<BODY>* tag, in which the drop-down list and buttons are defined. Note the names of those objects (in boldface) to which we'll later bind some scripts.

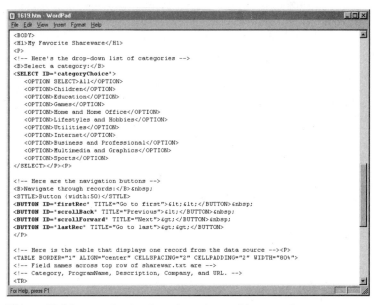

Figure 16-21. *Tags for the drop-down list and buttons shown in Figure 16-19.*

These tags display the main heading (*My Favorite Shareware*) and the drop-down list, which is named *categoryChoice*:

```
<H1>My Favorite Shareware</H1>
<P>
<!-- Here's the drop-down list of categories -->
<B>Select a category:</B>
<SELECT ID="categoryChoice">
    <OPTION SELECT>All</OPTION>
    <OPTION>Children</OPTION>
    <OPTION>Education</OPTION>
    <OPTION>Games</OPTION>
    <OPTION>Home and Home Office</OPTION>
    <OPTION>Lifestyles and Hobbies</OPTION>
    <OPTION>Utilities</OPTION>
    <OPTION>Internet</OPTION>
    <OPTION>Business and Professional</OPTION>
    <OPTION>Multimedia and Graphics</OPTION>
    <OPTION>Sports</OPTION>
</SELECT></P><P>
```

The following tags display the buttons. I made each button the same width by creating a little style that applies to all buttons. But that's just for cosmetic reasons—it has nothing to do with the data binding.

```
<!-- Here are the navigation buttons -->
<B>Navigate through records:</B> 
<STYLE>Button {width:50}</STYLE>
<BUTTON ID="firstRec" TITLE="Go to first">&lt;&lt;</BUTTON> 
<BUTTON ID="scrollBack" TITLE="Previous">&lt;</BUTTON> 
<BUTTON ID="scrollForward" TITLE="Next">&gt;</BUTTON> 
<BUTTON ID="lastRec" TITLE="Go to last">&gt;&gt;</BUTTON>
</P>
```

> **NOTE** The *<* and *>* codes in the button labels are just the HTML codes for displaying less-than (<) and greater-than (>) characters on the button labels. They have nothing to do with data binding or the Tabular Data control.

Current Record Table

Figure 16-22 shows the *<TABLE>...</TABLE>* tags that actually show the data—one record at a time—from the data source. Since we *don't* want to show multiple records in this page, the opening *<TABLE>* tag doesn't contain a *DATASRC* attribute:

```
<TABLE BORDER="1" ALIGN="center" CELLSPACING="2" CELLPADDING="2"
WIDTH="80%">
```

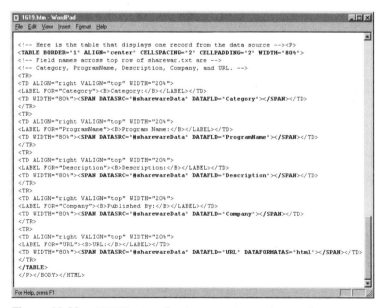

Figure 16-22. <TABLE> *tags for the current record example.*

Instead, each row in the table contains a cell that shows a field name label followed by another cell that shows the actual contents of that field using both the *DATASRC* and *DATAFLD* attributes. Here are the tags that show the label *Category:*

as well as the contents of the *Category* field of the current record. (I broke things up a bit to fit on this page—but the same tags shown in Figure 16-22 are also shown below.)

```
<!-- Field names across top row of sharewar.txt are -->
<!-- Category, ProgramName, Description, Company, and URL. -->
<TR>
<TD ALIGN="right" VALIGN="top" WIDTH="20%">
<LABEL FOR="Category"><B>Category:</B></LABEL>
</TD>

<TD WIDTH="80%">
<SPAN DATASRC="#sharewareData" DATAFLD="Category"></SPAN>
</TD>
</TR>
```

Each row in the table follows that same basic structure. Here is the row that shows the label *Program Name:* as well as the contents of the *ProgramName* field from the current record:

```
<TR>
<TD ALIGN="right" VALIGN="top" WIDTH="20%">
<LABEL FOR="ProgramName"><B>Program Name:</B></LABEL>
</TD>

<TD WIDTH="80%">
<SPAN DATASRC="#sharewareData" DATAFLD="ProgramName"></SPAN>
</TD>
</TR>
```

The last table cell, which shows the publisher's URL as an active hyperlink, requires a little special handling. Recall that in the data source, the URL field contains a complete *<A HREF=...>* tag, as in this hypothetical example:

```
"<A HREF='http://www.coolnerds.com'>http://www.coolnerds.com</A>"
```

To make Internet Explorer treat that as an HTML tag rather than a chunk of text, we need to add a *DATAFORMATAS="html"* attribute to that field's *<SPAN>...</SPAN>* tags, as shown below:

```
<TR>
<TD ALIGN="right" VALIGN="top" WIDTH="20%">
<LABEL FOR="URL"><B>URL:</B></LABEL>
</TD>
<TD WIDTH="80%">
<SPAN DATASRC="#sharewareData" DATAFLD="URL" DATAFORMATAS="html">
</SPAN>
</TD>
</TR>
```

Current Record Scripts

The scripts attached to the various navigation buttons in this example use some properties and methods we haven't discussed yet. These are all part of the Tabular Data control. The properties are:

- *objectName.recordset.AbsolutePosition*—returns the current position in the data source, where 1 equals the first (topmost) record

- *objectName.recordset.RecordCount*—returns the total number of records in the data source

The methods are summarized below:

- *objectName.recordset.moveFirst()*—moves to the first (topmost) record in the data source

- *objectName.recordset.moveNext()*—moves to the next record in the data source

- *objectName.recordset.moveLast()*—moves to the last (bottommost) record in the data source

- *objectName.recordset.movePrevious()*—moves to the previous record in the data source

In each instance, *objectName* refers to the name of the Tabular Data control as defined by the *ID* attribute in the control's opening *<OBJECT>* tag. Figure 16-23 on the next page shows the navigational sub procedures used in our example.

The first sub procedure, which is bound to the *firstRec* button, moves the visitor to the first record in the data source. The sub procedure first checks to see if the visitor is already at the topmost record using the If statement *If sharewareData.recordset.AbsolutePosition > 1 Then*. If the visitor is not at record 1, the statement *sharewareData.recordset.moveFirst()* moves the visitor to that record. If the visitor is already at record one, an Alert message appears on the screen instead:

```
Sub firstRec_onclick()    'Scroll to first (top) record.
   If sharewareData.recordset.AbsolutePosition > 1 Then
      sharewareData.recordset.moveFirst()
   Else
      Alert "Already at first record"
   End If
End Sub
```

```
□ 1619.htm - WordPad                                                    _□×
File  Edit  View  Insert  Format  Help
<!-- The scripting code -->
<SCRIPT LANGUAGE="VBScript"><!--
    Sub firstRec_onclick()    'Scroll to first (top) record.
        If sharewareData.recordset.AbsolutePosition > 1 Then
            sharewareData.recordset.moveFirst()
        Else
            Alert "Already at first record"
        End If
    End Sub

    Sub scrollBack_onclick()    'Scroll back (up) one record.
        If sharewareData.recordset.AbsolutePosition > 1 Then
            sharewareData.recordset.movePrevious()
        Else
            Alert "Already at first record"
        End If
    End Sub

    Sub scrollForward_onclick()    'Scroll forward (down) one record.
        If sharewareData.recordset.AbsolutePosition < sharewareData.recordset.RecordCount Then
            sharewareData.recordset.moveNext()
        Else
            Alert "Already at last record"
        End If
    End Sub

    Sub lastRec_onclick()    'Scroll to last (bottommost) record.
        If sharewareData.recordset.AbsolutePosition < sharewareData.recordset.RecordCount Then
            sharewareData.recordset.moveLast()
        Else
            Alert "Already at last record"
        End If
    End Sub
For Help, press F1
```

Figure 16-23. *Sub procedures used for record navigation.*

Each of the remaining procedures works the same way. The sub procedure that scrolls to the previous record also checks to see if the visitor is already at the first record. If not, the procedure moves the visitor back one record using the *sharewareData.recordset.movePrevious()* method:

```
Sub scrollBack_onclick()    'Scroll back (up) one record.
   If sharewareData.recordset.AbsolutePosition > 1 Then
      sharewareData.recordset.movePrevious()
   Else
      Alert "Already at first record"
   End If
End Sub
```

The sub procedure to move the visitor down to the next record first checks to make sure that the visitor isn't already at the last record. The *If* condition compares the current record position (*AbsolutePosition*) to the total number of records in the table (*RecordCount*) to determine whether the visitor is at the last record. If the visitor isn't at the last record, the statement *sharewareData.recordset.moveNext()* moves the visitor down to the next record. If there are no records below the current record to scroll down to, an Alert message appears on the screen instead:

```
Sub scrollForward_onclick()   'Scroll forward (down) one record.
   If sharewareData.recordset.AbsolutePosition < _
   sharewareData.recordset.RecordCount Then
      sharewareData.recordset.moveNext()
   Else
      Alert "Already at last record"
   End If
End Sub
```

The sub procedure for the *lastRec* button works on the same principle. If the visitor isn't already at the last record, you take her there using a *sharewareData.recordset.moveLast()* statement. Otherwise, you display an Alert message:

```
Sub lastRec_onclick()   'Scroll to last (bottommost) record.
   If sharewareData.recordset.AbsolutePosition < _
   sharewareData.recordset.RecordCount Then
      sharewareData.recordset.moveLast()
   Else
      Alert "Already at last record"
   End If
End Sub
```

The procedure that filters the records in response to a selection from the drop-down list is shown below. It's virtually identical to the script used for the league example drop-down list. The names have been changed to jibe with the object names used in this particular example. Figure 16-24 on the next page shows the *categoryChoice_onchange* sub procedure in the actual document source.

```
'When select box data changes, use its data to apply filter.
Sub categoryChoice_onchange()
   showCategory = categoryChoice.options _
      (categoryChoice.selectedIndex).text
   If showCategory = "All" Then
      'Selecting All categories puts nulls ("") into filter
      'criteria.
      sharewareData.FilterColumn = ""
      sharewareData.FilterCriterion = ""
      sharewareData.FilterValue = ""
      sharewareData.Reset()
```

(continued)

```
    Else
        'Selecting a single category sets filter to that team name.
        sharewareData.FilterColumn = "Category"
        sharewareData.FilterCriterion = "="
        sharewareData.FilterValue = showCategory
        sharewareData.Reset()
    End If
End Sub
```

> **NOTE**   Some statements in the *scrollForward_onclick*, *lastRec_onclick*,
> and *categoryChoice_onchange* sub procedures are broken into two lines
> to fit into this book. If you need to break a VBScript statement into two or
> more lines, you must break it in an appropriate spot and you must add a
> space and a line continuation character (underscore).

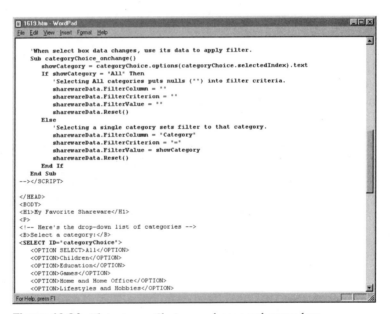

Figure 16-24.   *The* categoryChoice_onchange *sub procedure.*

YET ANOTHER WAY TO VIEW RECORDS

I don't want you to get the impression that the current record approach to showing table data is the only way to show large records. You can use the repeated
table approach as well. But rather than positioning all the fields side-by-side, you
can display multiple table rows per record. For example, Figure 16-25 on the next
page shows my sample shareware data displayed using the repeated table approach. But each record displays much more information than could fit across
the screen in a single row.

It's all in how you set up the *<TABLE>* tags. Figure 16-26 shows the document source for the *<TABLE>...</TABLE>* portion of the page shown in Figure 16-25. Let me walk you through it.

Figure 16-25. *The repeated table approach with multiple table rows per record.*

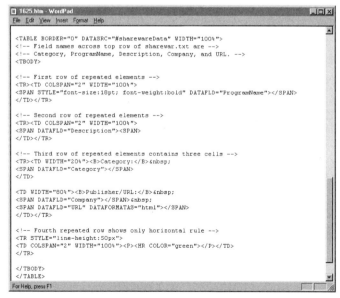

Figure 16-26. *The <TABLE>...</TABLE> tags for the page shown in Figure 16-25.*

The *DATASRC* attribute for the binding is included in the opening *<TABLE>* tag in this example, which sets us up for the repeated table approach. (The *#sharewareData* name comes from a Tabular Data control that binds the page to the sharewar.txt data source, just as in our current record example.)

```
<TABLE BORDER="0" DATASRC="#sharewareData" WIDTH="100%">
```

The *<TBODY>* tag starts the body of the table. Remember that rows in the table body are automatically repeated for every record in the underlying data source:

```
<!-- Field names across top row of sharewar.txt are -->
<!-- Category, ProgramName, Description, Company, and URL. -->
<TBODY>
```

The data cell in the first row of data spans two columns and occupies the full width of the table. This cell shows the program name in large, dark letters (18-point boldface):

```
 <!-- First row of repeated elements -->
<TR><TD COLSPAN="2" WIDTH="100%">
<SPAN STYLE="font-size:18pt; font-weight:bold"
DATAFLD="ProgramName"></SPAN>
</TD></TR>
```

The second row also consists of one data cell that spans two columns and extends the full width of the table. This cell shows the lengthy *Description* field:

```
<!-- Second row of repeated elements -->
<TR><TD COLSPAN="2" WIDTH="100%">
<SPAN DATAFLD="Description"><SPAN>
</TD></TR>
```

The third row is divided into two cells. This row is the reason that *COLSPAN="2"* was required in the two preceding rows. The first cell in this row shows the text *Category:* in boldface, followed by a blank space and the contents of the *Category* field from the current record:

```
<!-- Third row of repeated elements contains three cells -->
<TR><TD WIDTH="20%"><B>Category:</B> 
<SPAN DATAFLD="Category"></SPAN>
</TD>
```

The second cell in this row displays the text *Publisher/URL:* in boldface, followed by the contents of the *Company* field and the *URL* field:

```
<TD WIDTH="80%"><B>Publisher/URL:</B> 
<SPAN DATAFLD="Company"></SPAN> 
<SPAN DATAFLD="URL" DATAFORMATAS="html"></SPAN>
</TD></TR>
```

The fourth row displays the green horizontal rule that separates each record on the screen—and that's the end of the table:

```
<!-- Fourth repeated row shows only horizontal rule -->
<TR STYLE="line-height:50px">
<TD COLSPAN="2" WIDTH="100%"><P><HR COLOR="green"></P></TD>
</TR>

</TBODY>
</TABLE>
```

All of the web pages I've shown you are merely examples of how you can format data in a web page. As I mentioned earlier, the *DATASRC* and *DATAFLD* attributes are supported by a wide range of HTML tags, leaving you lots of room for creativity. To explore those attributes in the Internet SDK, click on the Dynamic HTML-DHTML References-Document Object Model References-Properties links in the SDK's opening page. The various data attributes are listed, in alphabetical order, with lots of other properties, as you can see in Figure 16-27.

Figure 16-27. *The Internet Client SDK references* DATA *attributes as HTML properties.*

The Tabular Data control itself also offers a few more properties that can help you bind a web page to data sources that don't exactly fit the comma-delimited format we relied on here. To learn more about the Tabular Data control, open up the *Component Library* section of the SDK, where you'll find references for the Tabular Data control.

Finally, if you plan to export data from a database program, be sure you learn about that database program's exporting capability. The only place to get that information is from the documentation or online help for that particular database program.

SORTING NUMBERS AND DATES

Here's a little "gotcha" that could drive you crazy if I don't warn you about it. By default, the Tabular Data control assumes that all fields in a file are strings. Hence, it always sorts records using a lexical approach—sort of like a dictionary. This can lead to some surprising results when you try to sort numbers and dates. Simply stated, sorting doesn't work right on those fields—unless you take a few extra steps to identify the data types of the fields in the data source.

If your data source file includes numbers and dates and you want to allow visitors to sort on those fields, you must tell the Tabular Data control which fields are numbers and which fields are dates. You can do so right in the data source by adding a data type to each field name. The data types that the Tabular Data control accepts are summarized in Table 16-2.

Table 16-2

DATA TYPES THAT THE TABULAR DATA CONTROL CAN SORT PROPERLY

Data Type	Description
String	Any text or pseudo-numbers such as zip codes, phone numbers, and social security numbers.
Int	Integers (whole numbers) such as 1, 15, 26, and 123.
Float	Decimal numbers such as 123.45, 1,234.56, 0.50, and 2.1.
Date	Dates that express the day, month, and year in any order and separated by some separation character. For example, *mm/dd/yy*.
Boolean	True/False, Yes/No, 0/nonzero values.

Let's look at an example. Suppose you have a table similar to the one in Figure 16-28. Exporting that data to a comma-delimited text file, with fields names in the first record, produces the text file shown in Figure 16-29.

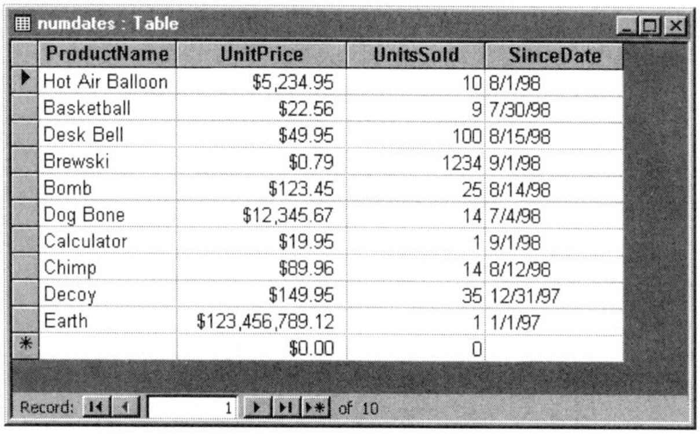

numdates : Table

ProductName	UnitPrice	UnitsSold	SinceDate
Hot Air Balloon	$5,234.95	10	8/1/98
Basketball	$22.56	9	7/30/98
Desk Bell	$49.95	100	8/15/98
Brewski	$0.79	1234	9/1/98
Bomb	$123.45	25	8/14/98
Dog Bone	$12,345.67	14	7/4/98
Calculator	$19.95	1	9/1/98
Chimp	$89.96	14	8/12/98
Decoy	$149.95	35	12/31/97
Earth	$123,456,789.12	1	1/1/97
*	$0.00	0	

Record: 1 of 10

Figure 16-28. *A sample table containing numbers and dates.*

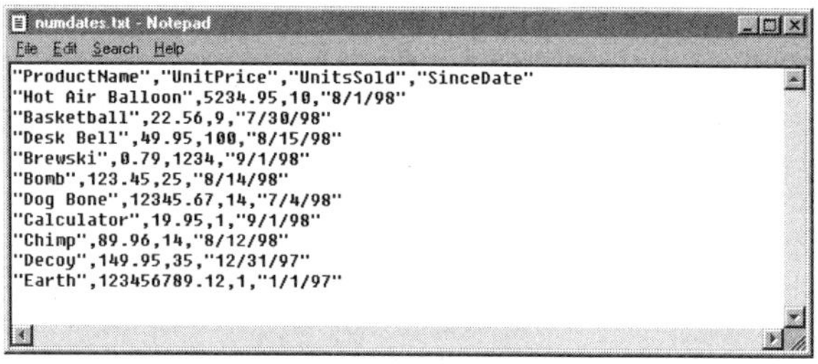

numdates.txt - Notepad

File Edit Search Help

```
"ProductName","UnitPrice","UnitsSold","SinceDate"
"Hot Air Balloon",5234.95,10,"8/1/98"
"Basketball",22.56,9,"7/30/98"
"Desk Bell",49.95,100,"8/15/98"
"Brewski",0.79,1234,"9/1/98"
"Bomb",123.45,25,"8/14/98"
"Dog Bone",12345.67,14,"7/4/98"
"Calculator",19.95,1,"9/1/98"
"Chimp",89.96,14,"8/12/98"
"Decoy",149.95,35,"12/31/97"
"Earth",123456789.12,1,"1/1/97"
```

Figure 16-29. *A comma-delimited text file from the table shown in Figure 16-28.*

You could use the data source as is. But if you give the visitor the option to sort on the *UnitPrice*, *UnitsSold*, or *SinceDate* fields, the sorts on those fields won't work correctly.

If you open up the data source and add field types after each field name, the sorts should work fine. The syntax to use is:

```
"fieldName1:type1","fieldName2:type2"...
```

fieldName is the name you want to give to the field, and *type* is one of the words listed in the first column of Table 16-2.

So, to get the dates and numbers in our data source to work correctly, I have to change the first line in that file from this:

```
"ProductName","UnitPrice","UnitsSold","SinceDate"
```

to this:

```
"ProductName:string","UnitPrice:float","UnitsSold:int","SinceDate:date"
```

Figure 16-30 shows the changes in place. The web page itself doesn't require any special handling because once the Tabular Data control "sees" the data types in the data source file, it "knows" how to sort those fields correctly.

Figure 16-30. *Field types added to field names in the data source.*

SUMMARY

In this chapter, you've learned the basics of using the Tabular Data control to bind a data source that contains information to a web page. To summarize the main points:

- Tabular data is any information that's neatly organized into records (rows); each record is broken into an identical set of fields (columns).

- To bind tabular data to a web page, you first have to create a comma-delimited text file version of the database data.

- The collection of data that a web page will show is called the data source.

- You use the Tabular Data control to bind a data source to a web page.

- Within a web page, you use the *DATASRC* and *DATAFLD* attributes in HTML tags to display data from the data source.

- To display multiple records from a data source in a single web page, you need to set up a table that has a *DATSRC* attribute in its opening *<TABLE>* tag.

■ To display only one record at a time in a web page, place the *DATASRC* attribute in some tag other than the opening *<TABLE>* tag.

■ If your data source file contains dates and/or numbers and you want to be able to sort on those fields, you must define the data type of each field in your table in the top row of that data source file.

■ More information on the Tabular Data control is available in the *Component Library* section of the Internet Client SDK.

In the next chapter, we'll look at an entirely new way to present your web pages to the public.

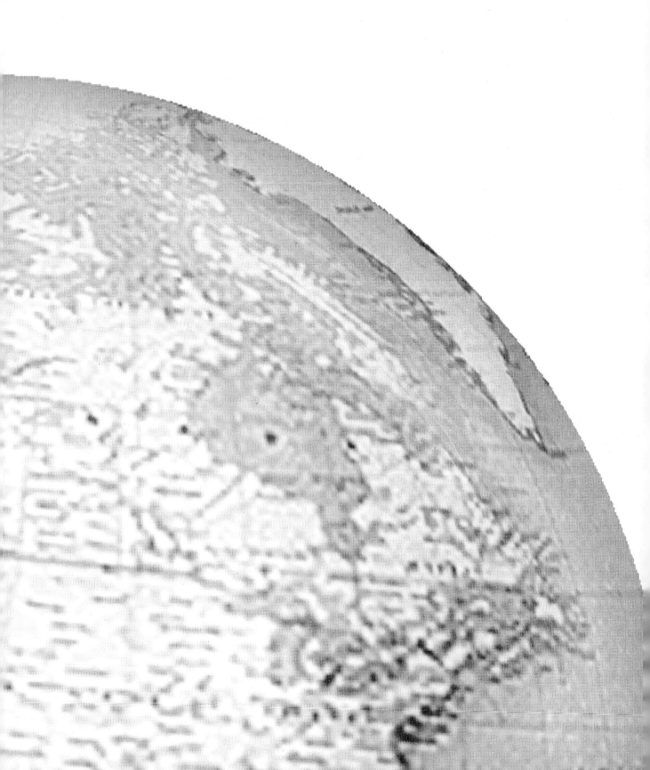

Chapter 17

Channels, Subscriptions, and Webcasting

In this chapter, I'll introduce you to some new opportunities for presenting your web site to the public. The overall technology is called *webcasting,* and it will have a big impact on how we all experience the World Wide Web. Microsoft Internet Explorer 4 makes webcasting possible today. I'll introduce you to the two webcasting techniques that Internet Explorer 4 offers: *channels* and *subscriptions.* Specifically, you'll learn:

■ What webcasting is

■ What channels are and how to subscribe to them

■ What subscriptions are and how to subscribe to regular (nonchannel) web sites

■ What advantages channels offer web publishers

If you're interested in turning your web site into a channel after you read this chapter, move on to Chapter 18. Everything you need to know is right there.

WHAT IS WEBCASTING?

Webcasting helps address those two common complaints about the Web:

- It's too slow.

- It's hard to keep up-to-date with new information in web sites without wasting a lot of time revisiting old information.

Webcasting helps by offering Web users automatic delivery of new and relevant information from their favorite web sites. They can receive notification when new information is made available at a designated site. They can even have the new pages downloaded while they're away from the computer.

Internet Explorer offers two options for webcasting. One requires no effort from you, the publisher. The other requires a little effort—no changes to your web site, but the addition of a small Channel Definition Format (CDF) file.

But before we get into that, it's important that you be aware of how visitors experience webcasting. Therefore, for the rest of this chapter, I'd like you to stop thinking of yourself as a web author or publisher. Instead, just be a consumer who's learning about webcasting from the consumer point of view and who has just discovered a couple of peculiar new things in Internet Explorer 4—channels and subscriptions.

A channel offers push-button access to specific web sites from a remote control–like Channel Bar. It also offers notification of, and optionally the automatic downloading of, new material from these web sites. A subscription is similar, but it doesn't have a Channel Bar and some other goodies.

First we'll walk through the process of subscribing to a channel as a consumer. We'll look at subscriptions a little later in this chapter.

CHANNELS

Channels provide easy access to designated web sites and automatic notification of new information at those sites. A channel can even download new material to the Internet Cache on your local hard disk while you're sleeping. You don't have to wait for any dreadful downloads, and you can even review the material off line—say, on a laptop computer in a subway train.

When it comes to channels, the main point of focus is the Channel Bar. The Channel Bar is like a TV remote control, but it floats around on your computer's screen. Instead of channel numbers, it has little logos and names.

The Channel Bar

When the Channel Bar is open on the desktop, it's pretty hard to miss, as you can see in Figure 17-1. You can size the Channel Bar by dragging any edge, and you can position it by dragging its title bar. If the Channel Bar isn't already visible on your desktop, how you bring it into view depends on whether you installed the Windows Desktop Update component with Internet Explorer.

If you installed Internet Explorer with the standard Windows desktop, you can bring the Channel Bar into view by choosing Programs from the Start menu, choosing Internet Explorer, and then choosing Channel Bar. Figure 17-1 shows how the Channel Bar looks on the standard Windows desktop.

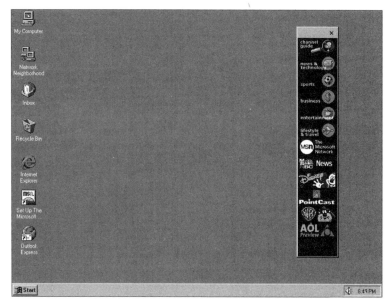

Figure 17-1. *The Channel Bar on the standard Windows desktop.*

If you installed Internet Explorer with the Windows Desktop Update component, which offers the Active Desktop interface, you can bring the Channel Bar into view using the following steps:

1. Right-click on the desktop, and then choose Properties.

2. Click on the Web tab, and then make sure the View My Active Desktop As A Web Page check box in the middle of the dialog box is selected.

3. Make sure the Internet Explorer Channel Bar check box is selected, as shown in Figure 17-2 on the next page.

4. Click the OK button.

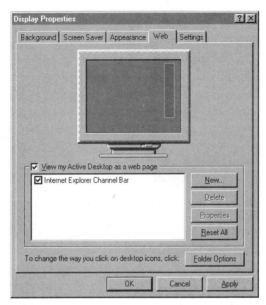

Figure 17-2. *The Channel Bar is selected in the Display Properties dialog box.*

Figure 17-3 shows how the Channel Bar looks on the Windows Active Desktop.

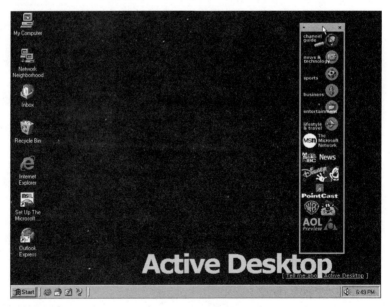

Figure 17-3. *The Channel Bar on the Windows Active Desktop.*

Accessing Channels in Internet Explorer

The channels in the Channel Bar can also appear along the left edge of Internet Explorer's window, in either the standard browser view or the full-screen view. To toggle between the standard browser view and the full-screen view, click the Fullscreen button on Internet Explorer's toolbar. In the standard browser view, the channels appear in a bar called the Explorer Bar, as shown in Figure 17-4. You can control the appearance of channels in the Explorer Bar in the following ways:

- To show or hide channels in the Explorer Bar, click the Channels button on Internet Explorer's toolbar.

- To show channels in the Explorer Bar, choose Explorer Bar from the View menu and then choose Channels from the submenu.

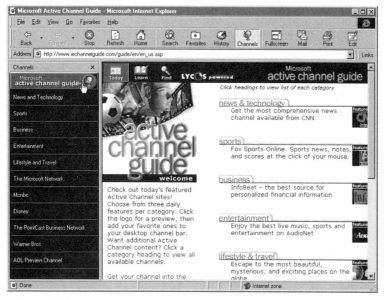

Figure 17-4. *Channels in the Explorer Bar in the standard browser view.*

In full-screen view, the channels appear in the Channel pane, as shown in Figure 17-5 on the next page. The Channel pane slides out of view when the mouse pointer isn't touching it, just like an AutoHide taskbar. You can control the appearance of the Channel pane in the following ways:

- To show or hide the Channel pane, click the Channels button on Internet Explorer's toolbar.

- If the Channels button is pressed in and the Channel pane is not visible, touch the mouse pointer to the left edge of the screen. This will bring the Channel pane out of hiding.

- To make the Channel pane stay open, click the little pushpin icon at the top of the pane.

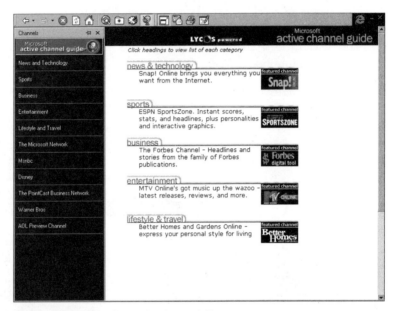

Figure 17-5. *The Channel pane in full-screen view.*

TIP   Channels are not the only items that can appear on the left edge of Internet Explorer. For example, you can also view various search engines, your favorites list, or a history of previously visited pages. To view these, click the Search, Favorites, or History toolbar button.

So What Is a Channel?

The Channel Bar, channels in the Explorer Bar, and the Channel pane are virtually identical in function. So let's refer to them using one term—Channel Bar. OK? At first glance, the Channel Bar shows two types of buttons. One type links to actual channels such as The Microsoft Network (MSN), MSNBC News, Disney, PointCast, Warner Brothers (WB), and AOL Preview, as shown earlier in Figures 17-1 and 17-3. Clicking a channel takes you to the web site to which the channel refers.

NOTE   A channel really is just a web site, and as you'll learn in the next chapter, you can probably convert your existing web site to a channel quite easily.

The other type of button is for channel categories such as News and Technology, Sports, Business, Entertainment, and Lifestyle and Travel. Clicking one of those buttons doesn't take you directly to a web site but rather to a list of channels within that category. The list of channels appears directly under the category button in Internet Explorer. The page to the right of the channel list also shows an icon for each channel in that category.

For example, in Figure 17-6, I opened the Business channel category in full-screen view. You can see several channels listed below that button (The Quicken.com Channel, The Wall Street Journal Interactive Edition, Companies Online Channel, and so forth). The page on the right shows icons for each of these channels. You can get to a business channel either from the buttons on the bar or from the icons on the page on the right.

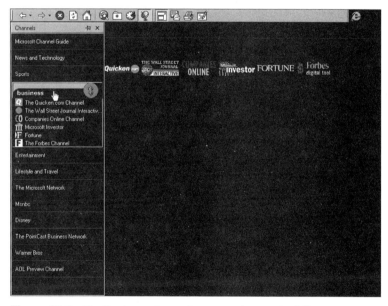

Figure 17-6. *The Business channel category is open in full-screen view.*

The Channel Guide

One of the buttons on the Channel Bar is named Microsoft Channel Guide. Clicking that button takes you directly to Microsoft's Channel Guide, where you can preview channels, learn more about channels, and subscribe to channels. For example, in Figure 17-7 on the next page, I chose to preview channels in the News and Technology category. Several channel options appear down the left side of the screen; instructions for previewing a channel appear to the right of those options.

Figure 17-7. *A page from Microsoft's Channel Guide.*

If you create a channel and it has wide audience appeal, you might be able to get it into the Channel Guide for free. Lots of exposure there! For more information, swing by the Site Builder Network at www.microsoft.com/sitebuilder/. (Last time I checked, the exact URL was www.microsoft.com/sitebuilder/sbnmember/channels/default.asp.)

Why Subscribe to a Channel?

So why would someone want to download channel content? Well, suppose you have a slow modem connection and hate waiting around for pages to arrive. Or maybe you like to review web content on your portable computer, off line, while taking the subway to work. In either case, it might be worthwhile to have the channel content downloaded at night so that it's all in your Internet cache when you get up the next morning. You can browse through all the new material quickly—on line or off line—because all the new material has already been downloaded to your PC.

In view of that, why would someone *not* want to subscribe? Well, for starters, if you don't subscribe you'll still be notified when new material is available at the channel. That material just won't be downloaded to your computer. If you have a high-speed, full-time connection to the Internet through a company LAN, this might be the best approach, especially if other people use your computer while you're not there. They might not enjoy trying to work while the computer is downloading megs of information for you. Besides, if you have a high-speed connection, you probably don't have the long waits that modem users endure anyway.

Subscribing to a Channel

The channels that appear in the default Channel Bar are just examples and suggestions. The Channel Bar allows visitors to create their own channels that are readily accessible from the Channel Bar. Not all web sites can be subscribed to as channels. Those that can be subscribed to as channels offer some kind of link or button that starts the subscription process. A couple of sample buttons are shown in Figure 17-8.

Clicking the button to subscribe to a web site as a channel brings up the Modify Channel Usage dialog box if the channel has already been added to the Channel Bar. If the site is not already listed on the Channel Bar, clicking the button to subscribe to a channel brings up the Add Active Channel(TM) Content dialog box shown in Figure 17-9. Here I just clicked the Add Active Channel button in the CMPnet site.

Figure 17-8. *Buttons a visitor might click to subscribe to a channel.*

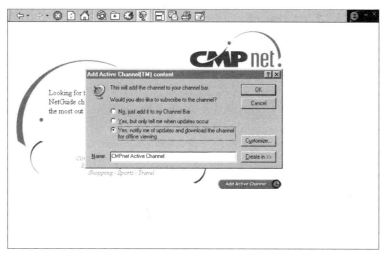

Figure 17-9. *The Add Active Channel(TM) Content dialog box is displayed after the Add Active Channel button is clicked.*

In the Add Active Channel(TM) Content dialog box, you have three options. You can select the first option to add the channel to your Channel Bar only. You can select the second option if you want to be notified when new material is available at the channel. You can select the third option if you want to be notified when new material is available at the channel and also have channel content automatically downloaded to your PC.

Selecting the second option enables the Customize button. If you click the Customize button, the Subscription Wizard starts. This wizard has only one screen, shown in Figure 17-10, which asks how you want to be notified when new material is available. Keep in mind that you'll be notified whether or not you choose to download content. The default method of notifying you when new content is available is a little red gleam—like the one shown in the dialog box—in the upper-left corner of the channel button or on the small icon for the channel.

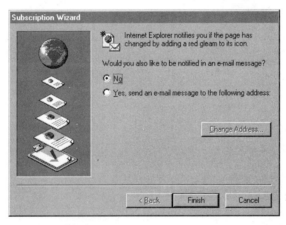

Figure 17-10. *Specifying whether to add e-mail notification to the default red gleam notification.*

In addition to the gleam, you can have an e-mail notification message sent to you. If you want to receive e-mail notification, you must provide an e-mail address, such as someone@somewhere.com, as well as an SMTP (mail) server address, such as smtp.cts.com.

Selecting the third option in the Add Active Channel(TM) Content dialog box also enables the Customize button. Clicking the Customize button starts the Subscription Wizard, but this time the wizard has three screens. Figure 17-11 shows the first screen, which allows you specify which content to download. You can specify the channel home page only or content specified by the channel publisher.

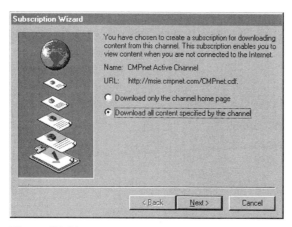

Figure 17-11. *Specifying which channel content to download.*

In the second screen, you can add e-mail notification to the default red gleam notification. This is the same screen that was shown in Figure 17-10.

The third screen, shown in Figure 17-12, asks how you want to schedule these let's-see-what's-new forays to the channel. You can have a scheduled download that occurs daily, weekly, monthly, or according to the publisher's recommended schedule. In this screen, you can indicate whether you are connecting through a modem. You can also specify manual downloading of content.

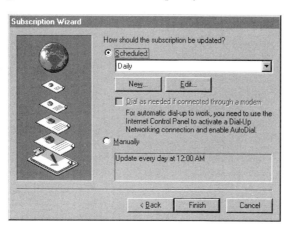

Figure 17-12. *Specifying scheduling options.*

WARNING Unattended dial-up will work only if your modem is capable of autodialing.

If these default scheduling options aren't appropriate for you, you can create a new schedule by using the New button. Or you can edit the currently selected schedule by clicking the Edit button. If you decide to create or alter a schedule, you'll see the Custom Schedule dialog box (shown in Figure 17-13), where you can be very specific about when your computer connects to the Internet and checks the channel. You select a schedule or create a new schedule near the top of the dialog box. Then you specify how often, and at what time, you want the update to happen, using the Days and Time areas of the dialog box. In Figure 17-13, I changed my Weekly schedule so that it happens every Wednesday at 1:00 in the morning (that is, if I remember to leave the computer turned on that night—a big "if").

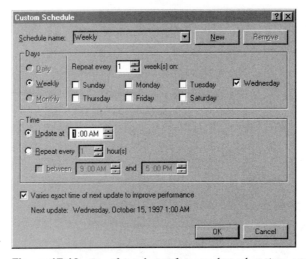

Figure 17-13. *Specifying how often, and at what time, updates occur.*

After you complete the last wizard screen and click the Finish button, the Add Active Channel(TM) Content dialog box appears again. If the channel supports channel screen savers, clicking OK in the dialog box displays the Channel Screen Saver dialog box, shown in Figure 17-14. Channel publishers can easily create custom screen savers (presumably of the promotional kind) and give them away to subscribers.

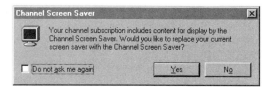

Figure 17-14. *Specifying whether to accept screen savers offered by the channel publisher.*

Clicking Yes or No in the Channel Screen Saver dialog box finishes the job and adds the channel to your Channel Bar. Figure 17-15 shows CMPnet added to the bottom of my Channel Bar. The mouse pointer is resting on the new button. That little message next to the mouse pointer is a tooltip. When you, the web author/publisher, turn your own web site into a channel, you can define the button, the tooltip, and a whole lot more.

Figure 17-15. *The CMPnet channel is added to the bottom of my Channel Bar.*

Changing or Unsubscribing from a Channel

To change something about or to unsubscribe from a channel you have subscribed to, follow these steps:

1. On the Channel Bar, right-click the button that represents the channel you want to change or unsubscribe from.

2. Choose Properties from the popup menu. The Properties dialog box appears.

3. To unsubscribe from the channel, click the Unsubscribe button on the Subscription tab, as shown in Figure 17-16 on the next page. If you want to change something, look around on the various tabs, especially the Subscription, Receiving, and Schedule tabs.

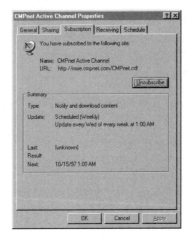

Figure 17-16. *The Subscription tab of the Properties dialog box.*

4. Click OK after making your selections.

TIP If you want to delete a channel, right-click the button that represents the channel and choose Delete from the popup menu. In the Confirm Delete dialog box that appears, click the Yes button. This will move the channel contents to the Recycle Bin and remove the button from the Channel Bar.

Specifying a Login Name and a Password

If a channel requires a login name and a password, you can click the Login button at the bottom of the Receiving tab of the Properties dialog box. You'll see the simple dialog box shown in Figure 17-17. There you can type in your user name and password so you don't have to retype it every time you visit the site.

That pretty much covers channels from a user's perspective. Microsoft has certainly made channels easy and intuitive to use. Next, let's talk about subscriptions—an alternative way to receive notification of new material from the Web.

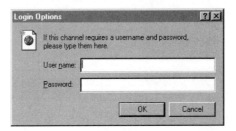

Figure 17-17. *Login options for channels that require a user name and a password.*

SUBSCRIPTIONS

Subscriptions are similar to channels in that you receive notification when a web site has new material and you can also specify that new material be automatically downloaded. But unlike channels, subscriptions can be made to any web site—not just sites offering an Add Active Channel option. Another difference between a subscription and a channel is that a subscription doesn't have a Channel Bar; it is simply listed as one of your browser favorites. Let's see what the visitor experiences when subscribing to a web site.

Subscribing to a Web Site

To subscribe to a site, you begin by opening the site in Internet Explorer and choosing Add To Favorites from the Favorites menu. This displays the Add Favorite dialog box, shown in Figure 17-18. As you can see, this dialog box is similar to the Add Active Channel(TM) Content dialog box shown in Figure 17-9 on page 565. (In fact, the process for subscribing to a web site is very similar to the process we discussed earlier for subscribing to a channel.)

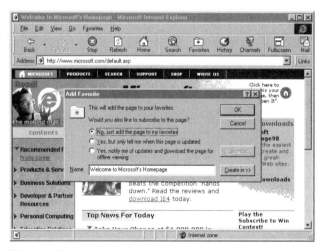

Figure 17-18. *The Add Favorite dialog box.*

In the Add Favorite dialog box, if you select the second option, you will be notified only when the web page changes. If you select the third option, you will be notified when changes have occurred at the web site; you can specify how many linked pages deep to check for changed or new pages, and you can have the changed or new pages automatically downloaded to your PC.

Selecting the second option enables the Customize button. If you click the Customize button, the Subscription Wizard starts. This time, the Subscription Wizard has two screens, both shown in Figure 17-19 on the next page.

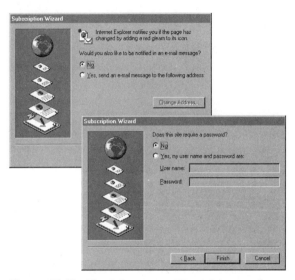

Figure 17-19. *The Subscription Wizard screens that are displayed when you subscribe to a web page with notification only.*

When changes occur to a subscribed web page, a red gleam is added to the web page's icon in the favorites list. In the first screen of the wizard, you can specify whether to also be notified by e-mail and you can enter your e-mail address and e-mail server name.

Some sites require a login. In the second screen of the wizard, you can specify the user name and password.

Selecting the third option in the Add Favorite dialog box enables the Customize button. If you click the Customize button, the Subscription Wizard starts.

In the first screen, you specify which pages to download. You can specify only the current page you are viewing or you can specify the current page plus pages linked to it. If you select the Download This Page And Pages Linked To It option and click the Next button, the next screen lets you specify how many linked pages deep to check for changed and new pages to download. Figure 17-20 shows these two screens. The next screen is the same screen shown in Figure 17-19; it lets you specify whether you want to be notified by e-mail if changes occur.

In the next screen, you specify when you want to download the changed or new pages. This screen has the same download options that you saw in Figure 17-12 on page 567. In the last screen of the wizard, you specify login options. Figure 17-21 shows these last three wizard screens.

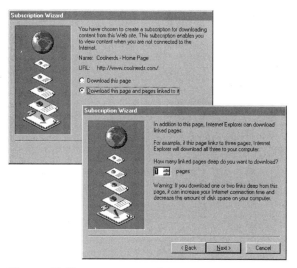

Figure 17-20. *Two screens of the Subscription Wizard when you subscribe to a web site with notification and downloading.*

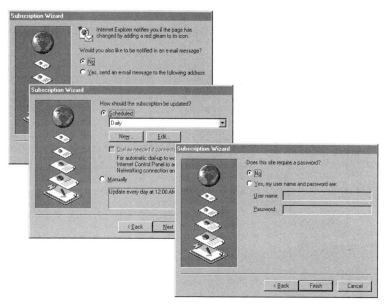

Figure 17-21. *The last three screens of the wizard when you subscribe to a web site with notification and downloading.*

Changing, Updating, or Deleting a Subscription

Once you subscribe to a web site, you can change, update, and delete the subscription in the Subscriptions window, as shown in Figure 17-22. You open the Subscriptions window by choosing Manage Subscriptions from Internet Explorer's Favorites menu.

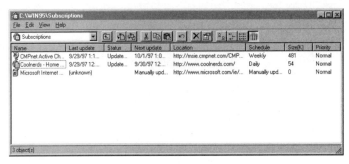

Figure 17-22. *In the Subscriptions window, you can change, update, and delete subscriptions.*

To modify a subscription, you right-click on it in the Subscriptions window and choose Properties from the popup menu. This displays the Properties dialog box, as shown in Figure 17-23. On the Subscription tab, you can delete (unsubscribe from) a subscription by clicking the Unsubscribe button. The Receiving and Schedule tabs allow you to modify subscription options and update the subscription.

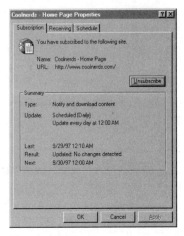

Figure 17-23. *The Properties dialog box for a subscription.*

TIP   The Subscriptions window also lists your channel subscriptions, so you can modify your channel subscriptions simply by right-clicking on them in the Subscriptions window and choosing Properties from the popup menu.

SO WHAT'S THE DIFFERENCE?

From the consumer's perspective, the main difference between a channel and a subscription is that a channel has a Channel Bar. But from a web publisher's perspective, there's a much greater difference.

When you provide a channel subscription to your web site, your logo gets some actual exposure right on the visitor's screen, even when that person isn't visiting your site. But more importantly (and not as obviously), you get a lot more control over exactly what gets delivered to your subscribers, when it gets delivered, and how it's presented. As you'll learn in the next chapter, it's all in a fairly simple file called a Channel Definition Format (CDF) file.

But the future holds even greater potential. Microsoft recently announced that its Broadcast Architecture for Windows initiative will allow PC users to receive web channel content over existing broadcast media such as analog and cable TV, as well as from future broadcast networks such as high-bandwidth direct broadcast satellites. (In case you haven't heard, Microsoft now owns WebTV.) This will allow even casual home users to be kept updated constantly from your server. In addition, Microsoft's relationship with AirMedia promises to make channel content available to home users everywhere via the airwaves, which makes for a mighty large potential audience.

PUSH AND PULL

You might have heard the terms *push technology* and *pull technology* in your wanderings around the Web and wondered what they're about. Well, the subscription approach to webcasting is a pull technology. The client PC is scheduled to go out and "pull" information off the Web according to some predetermined schedule. It simply compares the dates of pages on the local PC to the dates of the equivalent pages in the local PC's Internet cache. If the copy on the Web is newer than the copy in the local Internet cache, the site's icon is marked with the red gleam. The newer copy is also downloaded to the subscriber's Internet cache if the subscriber requested automatic downloading.

The channel approach is more of a push technology. While you can't force content onto everyone's PC (that would be a bit *too* pushy), you do have more control over how often information on your subscribers' PCs gets updated. You can also define what constitutes "new material." And, because you push a CDF file onto the subscriber's PC (with the subscriber's permission), you have a lot more control over how the subscriber experiences the information you send.

If you're interested in making your web site into a channel, move on to Chapter 18. I think you'll be pleasantly surprised by how easy it is to take your current web site and whip it into a channel. If you're content to offer plain subscription services, you don't have to do anything to your site. Subscriptions are handled entirely on the client's PC.

SUMMARY

In this chapter, we talked about webcasting, channels, and subscriptions, mainly from a user's perspective. As a web publisher, you might want to subscribe to some channels just to get your feet wet and get some ideas on how you'd like to present your own site as a channel. Here's a quick recap of the main points covered in this chapter:

- Webcasting is a new way for users to pull information from the Web and for web publishers to push information to subscribers.

- A subscription is a relatively simple pull technology that scours selected web sites for more recent pages according to a predetermined schedule.

- A channel subscription is more of a push technology because the publisher has more control over what gets downloaded, when it gets downloaded, and how it's presented when it gets there.

- Anybody with Internet Explorer 4 can subscribe to any site on the Web. As a web publisher, you don't have to do anything to make your site "subscribable."

- Only certain sites can be subscribed to as channels. Those sites have CDF files that define the channel.

- If you want people to subscribe to your site as a channel, you must create a CDF file for that site.

Now on to CDF files, for those of you willing to venture forth into channelized hyperspace.

Chapter 18

Becoming a Channel

You can make any of your web sites into a channel. You probably don't even need to change an existing site much—you can just add a few new files to it. In this chapter, you'll learn exactly what you need to do to offer a channel. You'll learn how to:

■ Select or create web pages for your channel

■ Create the Channel Bar button logo

■ Create a small icon for the Channel Bar

■ Create the CDF file that defines the channel

■ Upload and test your channel files

In the previous chapter, we looked at channels from a visitor's perspective. In this chapter, we're back to the web author and web publisher's perspective.

ON BECOMING A CHANNEL

To allow visitors to subscribe to your web site as a channel, you need to add three things to your site:

- A **main web page** that subscribers see when they click your Channel button. This can be your existing home page or a new web page that you create just for subscribers. Since only Microsoft Internet Explorer 4 users can subscribe, you can use all the fancy Internet Explorer 4 goodies (such as Dynamic HTML, CSS, and even ActiveX controls and Java applets) to add pizzazz to your pages.

  NOTE   Remember that some subscribers will download your channel content and read it off line. Therefore, avoid using Java applets and ActiveX controls that won't work if the reader is off line. You can test your pages for off line use after you create your channel pages.

- **Two graphic images**—a GIF image (exactly 80 pixels wide by 32 pixels tall) that will act as the channel's button in the Channel Bar and a tiny icon (.ico) file (16 by 16 pixels) that will appear on the smaller Channel and Favorites submenus.

- A **CDF file** that describes the organization and scheduling of the channel. This file is similar to an HTML file but uses XML (Extensible Markup Language) tags rather than HTML tags. XML is an abbreviated version of SGML (Standard Generalized Markup Language) and is used to define document types. The Site Builder Network Channel Wizard, discussed later in this chapter, can simplify the process of creating the CDF file.

To show you how all these things look to a channel subscriber, Figure 18-1 shows an example of Wired's channel materials. The Wired button, near the mouse pointer, is the 80-by-32-pixel logo (the GIF image). That button is "open," and subpages within that channel (LiveWired, WiredNews, and so forth) are shown under the channel button. The tiny logo next to the subpage titles is the tiny icon you need to create.

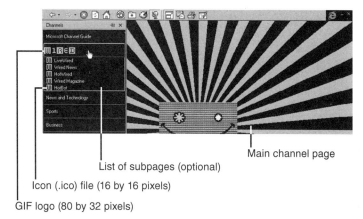

Main channel page

List of subpages (optional)

Icon (.ico) file (16 by 16 pixels)

GIF logo (80 by 32 pixels)

Figure 18-1. *A sample channel button logo, subpages list with icons, and main page.*

The page to the right of the channel pane is the main page—the first page a visitor sees after clicking the channel button. This can be the site's original home page or a new page you create. The titles of the subpages are listed below the Wired button on the channel pane. The aforementioned CDF file contains the information needed to define the title and URL of the main page and the subpages. However, those subpages are entirely optional. In fact, many channels don't list subpages at all. Clicking the channel button on such a site takes you straight to the site's opening page without displaying the list of subpages.

CREATING THE MAIN PAGE

The main page, or home page, for your channel can be any normal HTML page or a page containing Dynamic HTML, CSS, and other features offered by Internet Explorer 4. You can use your existing home page, or you can create a special entry page for channel subscribers.

For example, suppose I create a web page named chstart.htm that looks like Figure 18-2 on the next page. I want that page to be the first page that channel subscribers see when they click my channel button, so it's important that I put that chstart.htm page on my server. Later, it'll be important for me to remember the exact URL, including the file name, of this page.

Figure 18-2. *A channel main page named chstart.htm.*

There's nothing special about the document source behind the chstart.htm page. It's just a standard HTML page, as you can see in Figure 18-3.

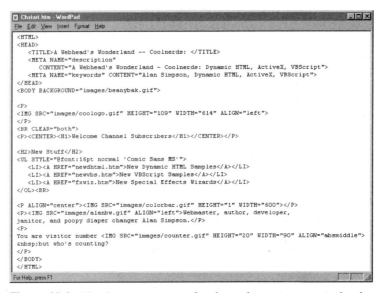

Figure 18-3. *The document source for chstart.htm—just a typical web page.*

CREATING THE LOGO IMAGE

To create the logo image that acts as your channel button, you can use any graphics program that supports the GIF format. Paint Shop Pro (www.jasc.com), Microsoft Image Composer (www.microsoft.com/imagecomposer/), and a host of other programs let you create GIF files. If, like me, you can't draw worth beans, you might want to hire a professional artist to create the logo for you.

For our purposes, I created a simple logo for my Coolnerds web site (soon to be the Coolnerds channel). Figure 18-4 shows the logo image in Paint Shop Pro. The image is exactly 80 pixels wide and 32 pixels tall, as is required to fit the space allotted for channel buttons. (To create it, I made a little WordArt image in Microsoft Word 97, cut-and-pasted the image into Paint Shop Pro, and sized it to 80 by 32 pixels. I then saved the image as chlogo.gif.)

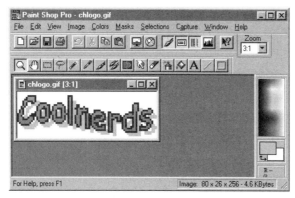

Figure 18-4. *Chlogo.gif, my 80-by-32-pixel GIF image logo for my channel button.*

In case you're wondering, the image in Figure 18-4 looks larger than 80 by 32 pixels because it's magnified three times. The actual image is pretty small and is smoother than the jagged magnified version.

CREATING THE ICON

Next I need to create an icon that is 16 pixels wide and 16 pixels tall and is saved in the .ico format. Not a whole lot of graphics programs can save in that format. However, the Windows 95 Resource Kit contains the Microsoft Image Editor, which allows you to create and edit icons. You can also download a good shareware program called IconEdit Pro, from pcwww.uibk.ac.at/subz/c40551/. Figure 18-5 on the next page shows a sample icon that I created in IconEdit Pro for the Coolnerds channel. I named this file chicon.ico.

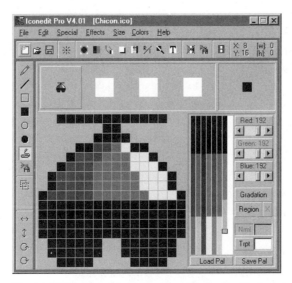

Figure 18-5. *The chicon.ico icon file for the Coolnerds channel.*

CREATING THE CDF FILE

The next step is to create the Channel Definition Format (CDF) file. I'll use a wizard that mainly asks questions about the names and locations of the files I've created so far. So I might want to make a list of the names of the files I've created, the name of the CDF file I'm about to create, and the URL where I plan to put all those files. For future reference, Table 18-1 shows the files for the Coolnerds channel.

In this step, you might want to think about how often you plan to make updates and how often you want to alert subscribers to those changes. A site that thrives on news and updates might make announcements daily or even several times a day. Most sites will probably use a less hectic schedule, such as weekly. For the Coolnerds channel, I'll make it weekly.

Table 18-1

FILES FOR THE COOLNERDS CHANNEL

Item	File Name
Channel main page	chstart.htm
80-by-32 GIF image	chlogo.gif
16-by-16 icon file	chicon.ico
CDF file (not yet created)	coolnerd.cdf

Creating an Empty CDF File

To create a new blank text file that will become your CDF file, follow these steps:

1. Using Windows My Computer or Windows Explorer, open the folder in which you normally keep web pages that get uploaded to your sever.

2. Right-click on a neutral area in that folder. Choose New, and then choose Text Document from the popup menu. A new text file named New Text Document.txt appears in the folder.

3. Press the F2 key and type in a name for the CDF file. Be sure to add the .cdf extension to the file name. In my example, I'll rename the New Text Document.txt file to coolnerd.cdf.

4. Press Enter or click anywhere outside the new icon to save it with the new name.

    NOTE   After you complete step 4, you'll probably see a message saying that it's not always smart to change the extension of an existing file. In this case, however, since we know what we're doing, you can ignore the warning by choosing Yes.

    When I want to open the coolnerd.cdf file for editing, I can just right-click on it and choose Notepad or WordPad from the Send To menu.

Using a CDF File Wizard

I know of a few tools that can help you create a CDF file in a wizardlike manner rather than from scratch. These tools include:

- Microsoft FrontPage 98.

- Microsoft CDF Generator (cdfgen.exe), which was code-named Liburnia and which comes with the Internet Client SDK. It is described in the SDK at help\cdfgen\cdfgen.htm and also at www.microsoft.com/msdn/sdk/inetsdk/help/liburnia/liburnia.htm.

- The Site Builder Network's Channel Wizard at www.microsoft.com/workshop/prog/ie4/cdfwiz/.

For our current example, I'll walk you through the Site Builder Network's Channel Wizard. It's easy to use and is well suited to current CDF capabilities. When you go to www.microsoft.com/workshop/prog/ie4/cdfwiz/, you'll see a brief explanation of the wizard. At the bottom of the opening page is a link that starts the wizard. Click that link to go to the opening wizard screen, shown in Figure 18-6.

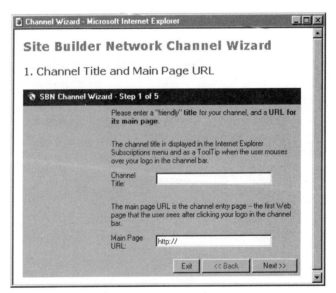

Figure 18-6. *The first screen of the Channel Wizard.*

In this screen, you enter the channel title, which is just the casual name of the web site (not the URL). For example, I used *Coolnerds* as the channel title. Below that you enter the complete URL of the page. For my example, it is the http://www.coolnerds.com/chstart.htm page that I created earlier in this chapter as the channel's main web page. Click the Next button to move to the second Channel Wizard screen, shown in Figure 18-7.

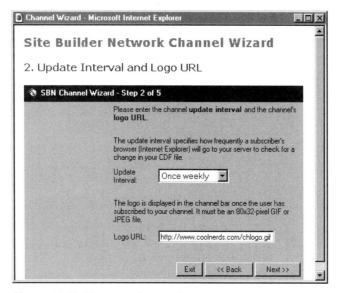

Figure 18-7. *The second wizard screen.*

In the second screen, you specify the update interval, such as Once Weekly. You also type in the exact URL to the channel logo file (the 80-by-32 GIF image, described earlier, that will appear on the channel button). In my example, that file is named chlogo.gif, so I typed in the URL *http://www.coolnerds.com/ chlogo.gif.*

Click Next to move to the third wizard screen, shown in Figure 18-8 on the next page. This screen shows the tags required in your CDF file. To copy those tags to your CDF file, right-click on the tags and choose Select All from the popup menu. Then press Ctrl+C to copy the selected tags to the Clipboard.

Figure 18-8. *The third wizard screen showing the created XML tags.*

Using Notepad or WordPad, open the empty CDF file you created earlier (the one I named coolnerd.cdf in my example). Position the cursor within the document, and press Ctrl+V to paste the code into the current document. Initially the text might be spread along one line with funny rectangular characters appearing where lines should end. You can delete the strange characters and put in line breaks after closing tags (>) to make the file more intelligible, as in the example in Figure 18-9. Close and save that text file because you won't be needing it again right away.

When you get back to the wizard, click the Next button to go to the fourth wizard screen, shown in Figure 18-10. In this screen, you specify the URL for the CDF file. In this example, I'm putting that CDF file in with the rest of my main web pages. So I enter *http://www.coolnerds.com/coolnerd.cdf.*

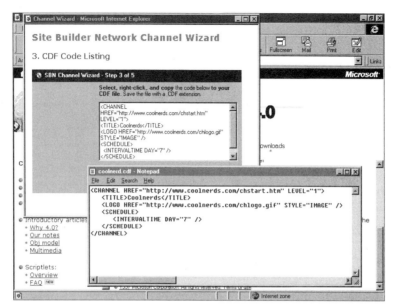

Figure 18-9. *Wizard-generated tags pasted into coolnerd.cdf.*

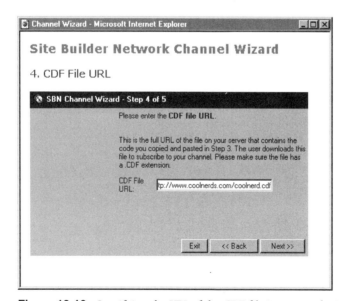

Figure 18-10. *Specifying the URL of the CDF file in your web site.*

Click Next to move to step 5 of the wizard, shown in Figure 18-11. This screen contains a small <*A HREF=...*> tag that you can paste into any page and that will offer visitors the option to subscribe to your channel. To copy the tag, right-click on it and choose Select All from the popup menu. Then press Ctrl+C to copy the selection to the Clipboard.

In Notepad or WordPad, open any HTML file from which you'll offer subscriptions. Paste the copied <*A HREF=...*> tag into the document source at the point where you want the link to appear. Remember that this link can be used in any web page in your site. For testing and experimentation, you can add this link to a new web page that only you can access on the server. For example, I created a little web page named testcdf.htm, shown in Figure 18-12, so I can test my channel later.

Close and save the file into which you pasted the <*A HREF=...*> tag, and return to the wizard. Click the More button to move to the final wizard screen, which provides some references for learning more about channels, as shown in Figure 18-13. Feel free to close the wizard, if you want, by clicking its Close button.

Next I'd like to discuss some ways that you can embellish the CDF file.

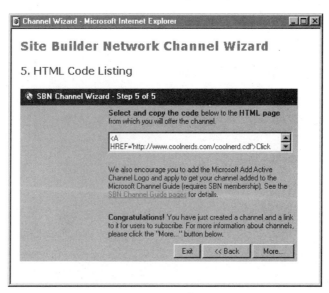

Figure 18-11. *A link generated by the wizard to help visitors subscribe.*

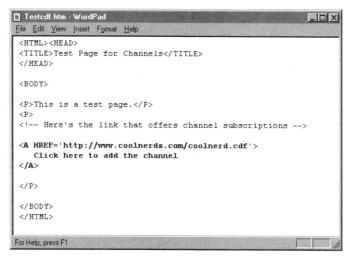

Figure 18-12. *Code from Figure 18-11 pasted into the testcdf.htm web page.*

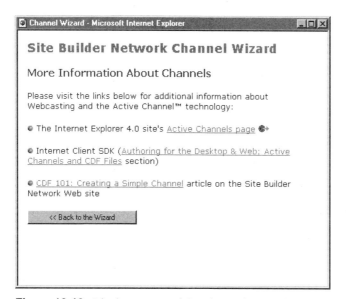

Figure 18-13. *The last screen of the Channel Wizard.*

EMBELLISHING THE CDF FILE

The CDF file created by the Channel Wizard is about as plain-vanilla as you can get. But you can change it and add to it as you would any other text file. Just open the file in Notepad or WordPad to edit it.

Adding the *<XML>* Tag

For reasons that elude me, the Channel Wizard leaves out an important opening tag that defines the content of the CDF file as being written in Extensible Markup Language (XML). That tag should look like this:

```
<?XML VERSION="1.0" ENCODING="UTF-8"?>
```

This should be the first tag in the CDF file. Go ahead and type that into the top of your CDF file, as I did in my sample coolnerd.cdf file in Figure 18-14.

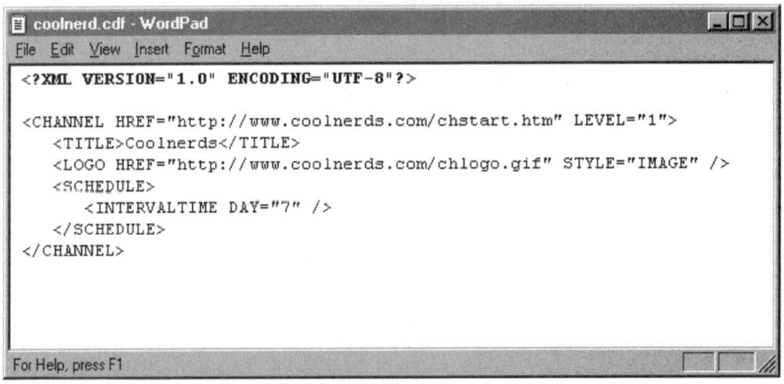

Figure 18-14. *The odd <?XML...> tag added to the top of coolnerd.cdf.*

The *<CHANNEL>* Tag

The opening *<CHANNEL>* tag in the CDF file is important because it specifies where a subscriber will be sent after clicking the channel button. For our example, the opening *<CHANNEL>* tag (shown below) tells the browser that when the reader clicks the channel button, he or she should be sent to the page at http://www.coolnerds.com/chstart.htm:

```
<CHANNEL HREF="http://www.coolnerds.com/chstart.htm" LEVEL="1">
```

The *LEVEL* attribute in the channel tag defines how many levels deep the channel button should "site crawl" into your web site to identify new or current information. A setting of 0 means that only the channel startup page, chstart.htm in this example, will be checked and downloaded to the subscriber's PC (if the subscriber has requested downloads).

A setting of 1 checks and optionally downloads the start page, as well as any pages that have links inside that start page. A setting of 2 checks the start page, all the pages linked to by the start page, and all the pages linked to by those subpages. Pages within frames are considered to be at the same level. Links that can be "crawled" are restricted to URLs within the same domain as the startup page (for example, links only within www.coolnerds.com). Currently, the maximum number of levels you can specify is three. For our example, I'll just leave the *LEVEL* setting at 1.

The *<TITLE>* Tag

The *<TITLE>* tag defines the casual name of the channel—Coolnerds in my example. If you do not have the Windows Desktop Update component installed, Internet Explorer will display this title as a tooltip when the mouse pointer touches the button on the Channel Bar. For this example, the following simple tag is sufficient:

```
<TITLE>Coolnerds</TITLE>
```

The *<ABSTRACT>* Tag

The Channel Wizard doesn't ask for or insert an *<ABSTRACT>* tag in your CDF file. However, it can be a useful tag for writing messages to subscribers. The syntax of the *<ABSTRACT>* tag is as follows, where *Your text here* is any message you want to present:

```
<ABSTRACT>Your text here</ABSTRACT>
```

If you have the Windows Desktop Update component installed, buttons on the Channel Bar will display the abstract as a tooltip. For example, that king-sized tooltip you see under the Microsoft Network button in Figure 18-15 is an abstract.

Figure 18-15. *An abstract appearing as a giant tooltip for a channel button.*

> **TIP**   To peek around in other people's CDF files, right-click any channel button on the Channel Bar and choose View Source. The CDF file that goes along with that button appears in a text editor. The CDF files (as well as the icons and logos) of many channels are stored in your C:\Windows\Web folder. The files for channels that you subscribe to might be stored in this same folder or in C:\Windows\Temporary Internet Files.

If I want to add a similar abstract to the coolnerd.cdf file, I can do so by manually typing the tags and the message, as in the example in Figure 18-16.

```
coolnerd.cdf - WordPad                                              _ □ ×
File  Edit  View  Insert  Format  Help

<?XML VERSION="1.0" ENCODING="UTF-8"?>

<!-- Defines my chstart.htm file as the opening page for subscribers -->
<CHANNEL HREF="http://www.coolnerds.com/chstart.htm" LEVEL="1">

    <!-- Tooltip title -->
    <TITLE>Coolnerds</TITLE>

    <!-- Abstract appears as a giant tooltip to channel button -->
    <ABSTRACT>If you're into Dynamic HTML, CSS, VBScript, ActiveX,
        JavaScript, or any other cutting-edge web-authoring tools,
        be sure to stop by Coolnerds for lots of good tips, tricks,
        free code, and even some handy wizards!
    </ABSTRACT>

    <LOGO HREF="http://www.coolnerds.com/chlogo.gif" STYLE="IMAGE" />
    <SCHEDULE>
        <INTERVALTIME DAY="7" />
    </SCHEDULE>
</CHANNEL>

For Help, press F1
```

Figure 18-16. *New <ABSTRACT>...</ABSTRACT> tags added to coolnerd.cdf.*

The *<LOGO>* Tag

The *<LOGO>* tag specifies the URL of the channel logo button—that 80-by-32-pixel GIF image used for the face of the channel button. The syntax is as follows, where *urlToImage* is an absolute reference to the .gif file that contains the channel logo:

```
<LOGO HREF="urlToImage" STYLE="IMAGE" />
```

The Channel Wizard correctly created a *<LOGO>* tag for my coolnerd.cdf file, which you can see below:

```
<LOGO HREF="http://www.coolnerds.com/chlogo.gif" STYLE="IMAGE" />
```

The Channel Wizard doesn't ask for the URL of the icon file, but you can manually type one in if you like. The syntax is as follows, where *urlToIcon* is an absolute reference to the channel icon (.ico) file:

```
<LOGO HREF="urlToIcon" STYLE="ICON" />
```

I did create an icon for my Coolnerds channel. So I can add the tag shown below to my coolnerd.cdf file, as shown in Figure 18-17.

```
<LOGO HREF="http://www.coolnerds.com/chicon.ico" STYLE="ICON" />
```

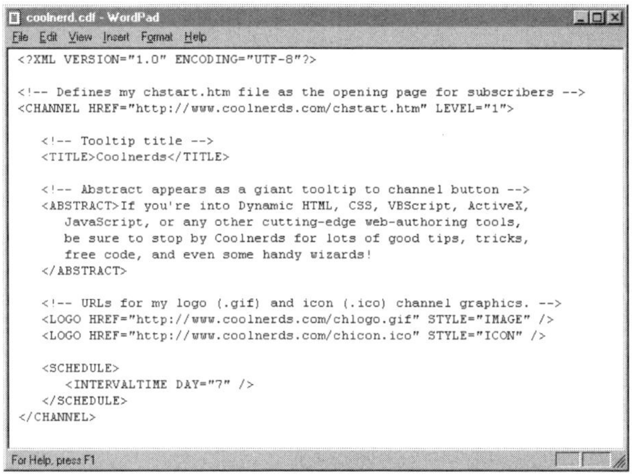

Figure 18-17. *A* <LOGO> *tag for my channel icon added to coolnerd.cdf.*

The *<SCHEDULE>* Tag

You can't force subscribers to check your channel at specific intervals—they are free to set their own schedules. However, you can suggest an update interval by adding <SCHEDULE>...</SCHEDULE> tags to your CDF file. Whatever you suggest as a schedule will be presented to visitors as the "Publisher's recommended schedule" when they subscribe. Quite a few subscribers will probably go along with your suggestion.

To define a suggested update schedule for your channel, use the <INTERVALTIME> tag between a pair of <SCHEDULE>...</SCHEDULE> tags. The syntax for the <INTERVALTIME> tag is:

```
<INTERVALTIME DAY="d" HOUR="h" MIN="m" />
```

d represents the number of days between updates; for instance, 1 represents daily updates and 7 represents weekly updates. *h* represents how often updating occurs in hours. *m* represents how often updating occurs in minutes.

Let's look at a few examples. Here's the pair of schedule tags in coolnerd.cdf that suggests weekly updates (every seven days):

```
<SCHEDULE>
   <INTERVALTIME DAY="7" />
<SCHEDULE>
```

This next schedule recommends daily updates:

```
<SCHEDULE>
   <INTERVALTIME DAY="1" />
<SCHEDULE>
```

And this one recommends updating pages twice a day (every 12 hours):

```
<SCHEDULE>
    <INTERVALTIME HOUR="12" />
<SCHEDULE>
```

This pair of schedule tags suggests updating every 30 minutes:

```
<SCHEDULE>
    <INTERVALTIME MIN="30" />
<SCHEDULE>
```

For most web sites, a weekly or daily schedule is probably sufficient.

You can use the *<EARLIESTTIME>* and *<LATESTTIME>* tags within the schedule tags to further refine when updates occur. For example, if you want updates to occur between midnight and 6:00 A.M. weekly, you can embellish the weekly schedule as shown in Figure 18-18.

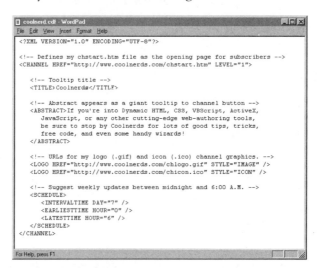

Figure 18-18. *Coolnerd.cdf suggests weekly updates at night.*

WARNING Don't forget that the tags used in CDF files are XML tags, not HTML tags. Some XML tags close with /> characters rather than with the more familiar > character. The XML tags used in CDF files are referenced under "CDF Reference" in the *Delivering Content to the Web* section of the Internet Client SDK, not in the *Dynamic HTML* section.

POSTING THE CHANNEL FILES

When the CDF file is finished, it's time to upload all your channel materials—the logo files, the CDF file, any new pages created for the channel (such as my chstart.htm page), and any pages that you modified or created to test the channel (such as my testcdf.htm file). You can use the same techniques that you use to upload other files to your server. Just be sure to put them in the correct directory—the directory you specified in any URLs that point to those files. For my example, I'll post all my Coolnerds channel files right in the home directory for that site, http://www.coolnerds.com.

TESTING THE CHANNEL

With all your channel materials created and uploaded to the server, you can test your channel. In my example, I'll open up my web browser and navigate to the page where I put the subscription link, http://www.coolnerds.com/testcdf.htm. When I get to that page I can click the link, which starts the subscription process, as shown in Figure 18-19.

Figure 18-19. *Testing my channel subscription.*

Like any subscriber, you can click the OK button to accept the suggested channel settings. Clicking OK downloads the CDF file, the logo (button image), and the icon to the C:\Windows\Temporary Internet Files folder on the client machine. The channel button is automatically added to the Channel Bar. Pointing to that button shows the abstract (or the title, if you don't have the Windows Desktop Update component installed), as shown in Figure 18-20.

Figure 18-20. *The Coolnerds button added to my Channel Bar. I've subscribed!*

Clicking the Channel Bar button takes you to whatever page you specified that the button should take subscribers to. In my example, clicking the Channel button takes the subscriber to http://www.coolnerds.com/chstart.htm because of this tag in the CDF file:

```
<CHANNEL HREF="http://www.coolnerds.com/chstart.htm" LEVEL="1">
```

To test for automatic downloading, you can wait for the next scheduled download. Or, better yet, you can force an update by right-clicking the channel button and choosing Update Now from the popup menu. Remember, however, that only pages that have changed since your last update will be downloaded to your PC.

TIP Remember that you can always take a quick peek at the current contents of your CDF file by right-clicking your channel button and choosing View Source.

If you'd like to test downloading from scratch, you can clear out your local Internet cache by choosing Internet Options from the View menu in Internet Explorer. On the General tab, under Temporary Internet Files, click the Delete Files button. In the next dialog box that appears, select the Delete All Subscription Content check box, as in Figure 18-21, and then click OK. This action will remove downloaded channel content from your hard disk. When you reconnect to a channel, Internet Explorer will have to download a new set of your channel materials.

Figure 18-21. *You can clear out your local Internet cache to better test your own channel.*

When you test a channel, you'll probably want to remove the channel button so you can test your site from the perspective of a first-time user. On the Channel Bar, right-click the channel button and choose Delete from the popup menu. In the Confirm Delete dialog box, click Yes. This deletes the channel subscription and removes the channel button.

ADDING PAGES TO A CHANNEL

After you get your basic channel working, you might want to add some subpages to your channel button. As you might recall, those subpages appear in a menu below the channel button when the reader clicks the channel button. Figure 18-22 shows subpages listed below the channel button for Wired.

Figure 18-22. *Subpages available under Wired's channel button.*

Use the *<ITEM>...</ITEM>* tags, along with the *<TITLE>*, *<ABSTRACT>*, and *<LOGO>* tags, to define each subpage. The syntax for each referenced subpage in your CDF file is:

```
<ITEM HREF="urlToSubpage">
    <TITLE>subpageTitle</TITLE>
    <ABSTRACT>subpageAbstract</ABSTRACT>
    <LOGO HREF="urlToIcon" STYLE="ICON" />
</ITEM>
```

597

urlToSubpage is a complete URL to the exact page that the link should open. *subpageTitle* is the text to display for this subpage. *subPageAbstract* is the tooltip abstract for the current page. *urlToIcon* is a complete URL to an icon (.ico) file.

Suppose I want to make a direct link a "New Dynamic HTML Stuff" page, named newdhtml.htm, within my web site. And let's say that newdhtml.htm is stored in the same directory as the rest of my main web pages. Also, I want to use the Coolnerds icon I created earlier as the subpage icon. The tags I need to add to my CDF file are shown below. Figure 18-23 shows this new set of tags added to my complete coolnerd.cdf file.

```
<ITEM HREF="http://www.coolnerds.com/newdhtml.htm">
   <TITLE>New Dynamic HTML Stuff</TITLE>
   <ABSTRACT>Come see what's new this week in my
      Dynamic HTML samples</ABSTRACT>
   <LOGO HREF="http://www.coolnerds.com/chicon.ico" STYLE="ICON" />
</ITEM>
```

Figure 18-24 shows how the Coolnerds channel looks with the subpage added, the icon file added, and the abstract tooltip displayed.

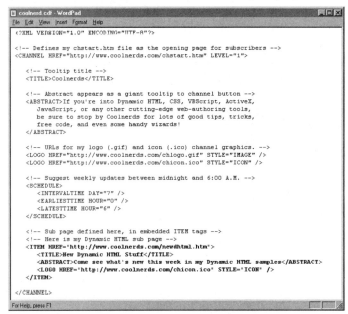

Figure 18-23. *Tags for a subpage added to my coolnerd.cdf file.*

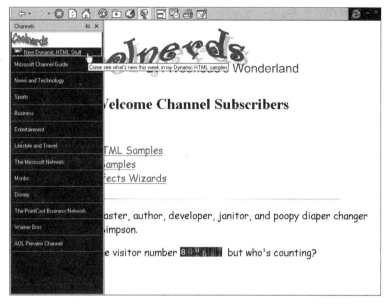

Figure 18-24. *A subpage added under the Coolnerds channel button.*

MAKING IT OFFICIAL

When you're satisfied that your channel is working properly, you can add the "official" Add Active Channel button to your web pages. However, you need to read the rules first at www.microsoft.com/sbnmember/ielogo/default.asp. After you read the license agreement and jump through all the hoops, you'll see a page where you can copy the Add Active Channel button to your own PC. From there, you can upload the image to your web server and copy scripts provided by Microsoft.

If your channel has wide audience appeal and uses Microsoft's Dynamic HTML, you might also be able to get your channel into Microsoft's Channel Guide. Doing so will bring extra exposure to your channel. For more information on the Channel Guide, click the Channel Guide button on your Channel Bar.

MORE ON CHANNELS

Channels are still an evolving technology, and standards are few and far between. The information presented in this chapter should get you started in creating your first channel, but when no standards exist, there's no telling what will change or when. For more information on channels and to keep up-to-date with new developments as they occur, see the resources below. I'll also try to post important changes and new features in my own web site at www.coolnerds.com.

- The Internet Client SDK (described in Appendix A). See "Active Channels," "Creating Active Channels," and "CDF Reference" under the *Delivering Content to the Web* section.
- Microsoft's Internet Explorer 4 site at www.microsoft.com/ie/ie40/.
- The Site Builder Network at www.microsoft.com/sitebuilder/.

SUMMARY

In this chapter, you've learned how to turn an ordinary web site into a channel. Do keep in mind that as I wrote this chapter, channel technology was still in its infancy and was not standardized. Things might change. But as it stands now, here are the hoops you need to jump through to turn an existing web site into a channel:

- Create a main page, or choose an existing page as your main page, that the channel button will send subscribers to.
- Create an 80-by-32-pixel GIF logo file to be used as the button graphic on the Channel Bar.
- Create a 16-by-16-pixel icon (.ico) file to be used as an icon on smaller Channel Bar submenus.
- Create a CDF file that links subscribers to your main page. You can also define a tooltip title, a tooltip abstract, and a suggested updating schedule in your CDF file.

■ Add hyperlinks to your web pages that allow visitors to subscribe. Those hyperlinks should take the visitor to the CDF file on your web server.

■ Be sure to upload to your web server the CDF file, logo image file, icon file, and any special pages that you created for the channel.

■ To obtain the official channel logo button for your site and possibly get your channel into Microsoft's Channel Guide, stop by www.microsoft.com/sbnmember/ielogo/default.asp.

And that, my friends, marks the end of the book. I hope you've learned a lot about all the exciting new web authoring features that Internet Explorer has to offer, and I hope you'll stop by my web site at www.coolnerds.com to check for new stuff related to this book. Thanks for reading.

PART V

APPENDIXES

Appendix A

Using the Internet Client SDK

The Internet Client Software Development Kit (also called the Internet Client SDK and the Internet Explorer 4.0 Author's Toolkit) is an important resource for anyone who authors web pages for Microsoft Internet Explorer 4.

The CD that comes with this book includes the Internet Client SDK. The SDK is available on the CD in two forms. First, it comes preinstalled, which means you can access information in the SDK directly from the CD. This helps save on hard drive space. The SDK is also included on the CD as a setup program so you can install it on your hard drive. You can also access the SDK from Microsoft's web site. In this appendix, I'll discuss the ways to access the SDK and how to get the most out of it.

USING THE SDK FROM THE CD

To use the SDK off line and without copying any files to your hard drive, follow these steps:

1. Put the CD in your CD-ROM drive.

2. In My Computer, double-click on the icon that represents your CD-ROM drive.

3. Open the BrowseMe.htm file.

4. Click the Internet Client SDK link.

5. Click the link to access the preinstalled Internet Client SDK from the CD.

If you want to put a shortcut icon to the Internet Client SDK right on your Microsoft Windows 95 (or Windows 98) desktop, follow these steps:

1. Put the CD in your CD-ROM drive.

2. In My Computer, double-click on the icon that represents your CD-ROM drive.

3. Open the INetSDK folder.

4. Open the Installed folder, and then open the Help folder.

5. Locate the file named default.htm, and use your right mouse button to drag the file to anywhere on your Windows desktop.

6. Release the mouse button, and choose Create Shortcut(s) Here from the popup menu.

7. To give the shortcut a better name, right-click on the new shortcut icon and choose Rename. Type in a new name, such as Internet SDK, and then click anywhere outside the icon to save the new name.

From this point on, you can fire up the SDK by putting the CD into your CD-ROM drive and clicking on the Internet SDK shortcut icon on your desktop.

INSTALLING THE SDK FROM THE CD

If you want, you can install the entire Internet Client SDK (about 150 MB) or portions of it to your hard drive. By default, it is installed in C:\INetSDK. This gives you quick access to the SDK. To install the SDK, you must be running Internet Explorer 4. Here are the steps:

1. Put the CD in your CD-ROM drive.

2. In My Computer, double-click on the icon that represents your CD-ROM drive.

3. Open the BrowseMe.htm file in Internet Explorer 4.

4. Click the Internet Client SDK link.

5. Click the link to install the Internet Client SDK.

6. Follow the instructions to install the entire SDK or portions of the SDK.

After you install the SDK, you can access it from your Start menu by choosing Programs-Internet Client SDK-Internet Client SDK.

UNINSTALLING THE SDK

If you want to uninstall the SDK from your computer, follow these steps:

1. From the Start menu, choose Settings-Control Panel.

2. In the Control Panel window, double-click Add/Remove Programs.

3. On the Install/Uninstall tab of the Add/Remove Programs Properties dialog box, select Internet Client SDK 4.0 from the list.

4. Click the Add/Remove button.

5. In the dialog box that asks whether you want to remove the SDK, click OK.

6. Click OK to close the Add/Remove Programs Properties dialog box.

7. Close the Control Panel window.

USING THE SDK ON LINE

You can use the Internet Client SDK on line by pointing Internet Explorer 4 to www.microsoft.com/msdn/sdk/inetsdk/help/default.htm. You might want to create a Favorites shortcut to that URL since it's such a long one to type in.

You can also subscribe to the online SDK as a channel. Locate and click the Add To Channels or Add Active Channel button, and follow the instructions on the screen. For more information on subscribing to channels, see Chapter 17 of this book.

INSIDE THE SDK

Regardless of how you access the SDK, it will look something like Figure A-1 when you first open it. To explore a major section of the SDK, such as *Dynamic HTML*, click that entry in the left-hand column. The entry will expand to show subtopics within, as in Figure A-2.

Figure A-1. *The opening page of the Internet Client SDK.*

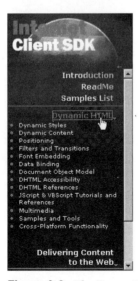

Figure A-2. *The Dynamic HTML section expanded to show subtopics.*

Many topics have several levels that you can drill down to. For example, clicking the DHTML References topic expands that list to show a lot of topics relevant to this book, such as Document Object Model References, HTML References, CSS Attributes Reference, and more, as shown in Figure A-3.

Figure A-3. *Drilling down further in the Internet SDK.*

You can also view the Internet Client SDK Index by clicking the Index link near the upper-right corner of the browser window. (See Figure A-4.)

Figure A-4. *You can use the Index link to search the SDK's index.*

Major SDK Topics

The SDK contains articles, tutorials, and references on many topics. Most of the reference sections are very large. I didn't attempt to repeat *everything* that's in those references in this book. (If I had, you'd need a wheelbarrow just to tote the book around!) The main goal of this book is to teach, through tutorial and example, the basic concepts and skills necessary to really apply the new tools and techniques that Microsoft Internet Explorer 4 offers.

When you need a detailed reference to a major topic or technology, you can find it in the Internet Client SDK. To save you time, Table A-1 lists all the major references that are relevant to this book. To use the table, look up the major topic in the left column. Then, in the Internet SDK opening page, select from the topics listed in the right-hand column. For example, to find information on HTML tags, select Dynamic HTML in the left-hand column of the opening page, select DHTML References, select HTML References, and then select HTML Elements.

Table A-1

MAJOR TOPICS IN THE INTERNET CLIENT SDK

Topic	*SDK Section*
ActiveMovie control	Component Library - ActiveMovie Control
ActiveX DirectAnimation Controls	Internet Tools & Technologies - Internet Multimedia - DirectAnimation - Controls
Cascading Style Sheets	Dynamic HTML - DHTML References - CSS Attributes Reference - CSS Attributes
Channels and CDF	Delivering Content To The Web - CDF Reference
Collections	Dynamic HTML - DHTML References - Document Object Model References - Collections
Dynamic HTML Object Model	Dynamic HTML - Document Object Model
Filter effects and transitions	Dynamic HTML - Filters And Transitions - Visual And Transition Filters Reference
HTML tags	Dynamic HTML - DHTML References - HTML References - HTML Elements
Methods	Dynamic HTML - DHTML References - Document Object Model References - Methods
Objects	Dynamic HTML - DHTML References - Document Object Model References - Objects
Properties	Dynamic HTML - DHTML References - Document Object Model References - Properties
Tabular Data control	Component Library - Tabular Data Control (TDC)
VBScript	Dynamic HTML - JScript & VBScript Tutorials And References

Special Characters

You can represent special characters and characters that have meaning in HTML using the symbols listed in the table below. For example, to display the characters ®,©, ¥, <, >, and & separated by nonbreaking spaces in a web page, you would type the following into the body of the document:

®   ©   ¥   <   >   &

You can find more information on character sets in the Internet Client SDK. In the left-hand column of the SDK, select Dynamic HTML, select DHTML References, select HTML References, and then select HTML Character Sets.

Character Name	*Appearance*	*HTML Symbol*
Acute accent	´	&acute;
Ampersand	&	&amp;
Broken vertical bar	¦	¦ or &brkbar;
Capital A, acute accent	Á	&Aacute;
Capital A, circumflex	Â	&Acirc;
Capital A, diæresis/umlaut	Ä	&Auml;
Capital A, grave accent	À	&Agrave;
Capital A, ring	Å	&Aring;
Capital A, tilde	Ã	&Atilde;
Capital AE ligature	Æ	&AElig;
Capital C, cedilla	Ç	&Ccedil;
Capital E, acute accent	É	&Eacute;

(continued)

continued

Character Name	Appearance	HTML Symbol
Capital E, circumflex	Ê	&Ecirc;
Capital E, diæresis/umlaut	Ë	&Euml;
Capital E, grave accent	È	&Egrave;
Capital Eth, Icelandic	Ð	&ETH;
Capital I, acute accent	Í	&Iacute;
Capital I, circumflex	Î	&Icirc;
Capital I, diæresis/umlaut	Ï	&Iuml;
Capital I, grave accent	Ì	&Igrave;
Capital N, tilde	Ñ	&Ntilde;
Capital O, acute accent	Ó	&Oacute;
Capital O, circumflex	Ô	&Ocirc;
Capital O, diæresis/umlaut	Ö	&Ouml;
Capital O, grave accent	Ò	&Ograve;
Capital O, slash	Ø	&Oslash;
Capital O, tilde	Õ	&Otilde;
Capital Thorn, Icelandic	Þ	&THORN;
Capital U, acute accent	Ú	&Uacute;
Capital U, circumflex	Û	&Ucirc;
Capital U, diæresis/umlaut	Ü	&Uuml;
Capital U, grave accent	Ù	&Ugrave;
Capital Y, acute accent	Ý	&Yacute;
Cedilla	¸	&cedil;
Cent sign	¢	&cent;
Copyright	©	&copy;
Degree sign	°	&deg;
Diæresis/umlaut	¨	¨ or ¨
Division sign	÷	&divide;
Feminine ordinal	ª	&ordf;
Fraction one-fourth	¼	&frac14;
Fraction one-half	½	&frac12;
Fraction three-fourths	¾	&frac34;
General currency sign	¤	&curren;
Greater than	>	&gt;
Inverted exclamation	¡	&iexcl;

Character Name	*Appearance*	*HTML Symbol*
Inverted question mark	¿	&iquest;
Left angle quote, guillemot left	«	&laquo;
Less than	<	&lt;
Macron accent	¯	¯ or &hibar;
Masculine ordinal	º	&ordm;
Micro sign	µ	&micro;
Middle dot	·	&middot;
Multiply sign	×	&times;
Nonbreaking space		
Plus or minus	±	&plusmn;
Pound sterling	£	&pound;
Quotation mark	"	&quot;
Registered trademark	®	&reg;
Right angle quote, guillemot right	»	&raquo;
Section sign	§	&sect;
Small a, acute accent	á	&aacute;
Small a, circumflex	â	&acirc;
Small a, diæresis/umlaut	ä	&auml;
Small a, grave accent	à	&agrave;
Small a, ring	å	&aring;
Small a, tilde	ã	&atilde;
Small ae ligature	æ	&aelig;
Small c, cedilla	ç	&ccedil;
Small e, acute accent	é	&eacute;
Small e, circumflex	ê	&ecirc;
Small e, diæresis/umlaut	ë	&euml;
Small e, grave accent	è	&egrave;
Small eth, Icelandic	ð	&eth;
Small i, acute accent	í	&iacute;
Small i, circumflex	î	&icirc;
Small i, diæresis/umlaut	ï	&iuml;
Small i, grave accent	ì	&igrave;
Small n, tilde	ñ	&ntilde;
Small o, acute accent	ó	&oacute;

(continued)

continued

Character Name	Appearance	HTML Symbol
Small o, circumflex	ô	&ocirc;
Small o, diæresis/umlaut	ö	&ouml;
Small o, grave accent	ò	&ograve;
Small o, slash	ø	&oslash;
Small o, tilde	õ	&otilde;
Small sharp s, German sz	ß	&szlig;
Small thorn, Icelandic	þ	&thorn;
Small u, acute accent	ú	&uacute;
Small u, circumflex	û	&ucirc;
Small u, diæresis/umlaut	ü	&uuml;
Small u, grave accent	ù	&ugrave;
Small y, acute accent	ý	&yacute;
Small y, diæresis/umlaut	ÿ	&yuml;
Soft hyphen	-	&shy;
Superscript one	1	&sup1;
Superscript three	3	&sup3;
Superscript two	2	&sup2;
Yen sign	¥	&yen;

Appendix C

Colors

This appendix lists color names, their RGB triplets, and their decimal equivalents. While you can use color names in HTML tags, not all browsers interpret colors in the same way. Therefore it's best to use the RGB triplet rather than the color name. For example, to set the background color of a page to Antiquewhite, you use this tag:

```
<BODY BGCOLOR="#FAEBD7">
```

In the table beginning on the next page, the decimal values in the third column apply only to ActiveX controls and to Java applets that require colors to be specified as decimal numbers.

To actually see the colors or to create your own colors, open the colors web page on the CD that comes with this book. Or visit my web site at www.coolnerds.com.

Color Name	RGB Triplet	Decimal Value	Color Name	RGB Triplet	Decimal Value
Aliceblue	#F0F8FF	15792383	Darkred	#8B0000	9109504
Antiquewhite	#FAEBD7	16444375	Darksalmon	#E9967A	15308410
Aqua	#00FFFF	65535	Darkseagreen	#8FBC8B	9419915
Aquamarine	#7FFFD4	8388564	Darkslateblue	#483D8B	4734347
Azure	#F0FFFF	15794175	Darkslategray	#2F4F4F	3100495
Beige	#F5F5DC	16119260	Darkturquoise	#00CED1	52945
Bisque	#FFE4C4	16770244	Darkviolet	#9400D3	9699539
Black	#000000	0	Deeppink	#FF1493	16716947
Blanchedalmond	#FFEBCD	16772045	Deepskyblue	#00BFFF	49151
Blue	#0000FF	255	Dimgray	#696969	6908265
Blueviolet	#8A2BE2	9055202	Dodgerblue	#1E90FF	2003199
Brown	#A52A2A	10824234	Firebrick	#B22222	11674146
Burlywood	#DEB887	14596231	Floralwhite	#FFFAF0	16775920
Cadetblue	#5F9EA0	6266528	Forestgreen	#228B22	2263842
Chartreuse	#7FFF00	8388352	Fuchia	#FF00FF	16711935
Chocolate	#D2691E	13789470	Gainsboro	#DCDCDC	14474460
Coral	#FF7F50	16744272	Ghostwhite	#F8F8FF	16316671
Cornflower	#6495ED	6591981	Gold	#FFD700	16766720
Cornsilk	#FFF8DC	16775388	Goldenrod	#DAA520	14329120
Crimson	#DC143C	14423100	Gray	#808080	8421504
Cyan	#00FFFF	65535	Green	#008000	32768
Darkblue	#00008B	139	Greenyellow	#ADFF2F	11403055
Darkcyan	#008B8B	35723	Honeydew	#F0FFF0	15794160
Darkgoldenrod	#B8860B	12092939	Hotpink	#FF69B4	16738740
Darkgray	#A9A9A9	11119017	Indianred	#CD5C5C	13458524
Darkgreen	#006400	25600	Indigo	#4B0082	4915330
Darkkhaki	#BDB76B	12433259	Ivory	#FFFFF0	16777200
Darkmagenta	#8B008B	9109643	Khaki	#F0E68C	15787660
Darkolive-green	#556B2F	5597999	Lavender	#E6E6FA	15132410
Darkorange	#FF8C00	16747520	Lavender-blush	#FFF0F5	16773365
Darkorchid	#9932CC	10040012	Lawngreen	#7CFC00	8190976

Color Name	RGB Triplet	Decimal Value	Color Name	RGB Triplet	Decimal Value
Lemonchiffon	#FFFACD	16775885	Mistyrose	#FFE4E1	16770273
Lightblue	#ADD8E6	11393254	Moccasin	#FFE4B5	16770229
Lightcoral	#F08080	15761536	Navajowhite	#FFDEAD	16768685
Lightcyan	#E0FFFF	14745599	Navy	#000080	128
Lightgoldenrod-yellow	#FAFAD2	16448210	Oldlace	#FDF5E6	16643558
			Olive	#808000	8421376
Lightgreen	#90EE90	9498256	Olivedrab	#6B8E23	7048739
Lightgrey	#D3D3D3	13882323	Orange	#FFA500	16753920
Lightpink	#FFB6C1	16758465	Orangered	#FF4500	16729344
Lightsalmon	#FFA07A	16752762	Orchid	#DA70D6	14315734
Lightseagreen	#20B2AA	2142890	Palegoldenrod	#EEE8AA	15657130
Lightskyblue	#87CEFA	8900346	Palegreen	#98FB98	10025880
Lightslategray	#778899	7833753	Paleturquoise	#AFEEEE	11529966
Lightsteelblue	#B0C4DE	11584734	Palevioletred	#DB7093	14381203
Lightyellow	#FFFFE0	16777184	Papayawhip	#FFEFD5	16773077
Lime	#00FF00	65280	Peachpuff	#FFDAB9	16767673
Limegreen	#32CD32	3329330	Peru	#CD853F	13468991
Linen	#FAF0E6	16445670	Pink	#FFC0CB	16761035
Magenta	#FF00FF	16711935	Plum	#DDA0DD	14524637
Maroon	#800000	8388608	Powderblue	#B0E0E6	11591910
Mediumaqua-marine	#66CDAA	6737322	Purple	#800080	8388736
			Red	#FF0000	16711680
Mediumblue	#0000CD	205	Rosybrown	#BC8F8F	12357519
Mediumorchid	#BA55D3	12211667	Royalblue	#4169E1	4286945
Mediumpurple	#9370DB	9662683	Saddlebrown	#8B4513	9127187
Mediumseagreen	#3CB371	3978097	Salmon	#FA8072	16416882
Mediumslateblue	#7B68EE	8087790	Sandybrown	#F4A460	16032864
Mediumspring-green	#00FA9A	64154	Seagreen	#2E8B57	3050327
Mediumturquoise	#48D1CC	4772300	Seashell	#FFF5EE	16774638
Mediumvioletred	#C71585	13047173	Sienna	#A0522D	10506797
Midnightblue	#191970	1644912	Silver	#C0C0C0	12632256
Mintcream	#F5FFFA	16121850	Skyblue	#87CEEB	8900331

(continued)

continued

Color Name	RGB Triplet	Decimal Value
Slateblue	#6A5ACD	6970061
Slategray	#708090	7372944
Snow	#FFFAFA	16775930
Springgreen	#00FF7F	65407
Steelblue	#4682B4	4620980
Tan	#D2B48C	13808780
Teal	#008080	32896
Thistle	#D8BFD8	14204888
Tomato	#FF6347	16737095
Turquoise	#40E0D0	4251856
Violet	#EE82EE	15631086
Wheat	#F5DEB3	16113331
White	#FFFFFF	16777215
Whitesmoke	#F5F5F5	16119285
Yellow	#FFFF00	16776960
Yellowgreen	#9ACD32	10145074

Appendix D

Using the CD

The CD that accompanies this book contains a number of helpful items. The CD contents are organized like a web site for easy one-click access.

First, it contains an installer for Microsoft Internet Explorer 4. (This saves you from having to download Internet Explorer from Microsoft's web site.) This is a full version of Internet Explorer, which includes the browser, Microsoft FrontPage Express, Microsoft Outlook Express, and many other accessories. If you want, you can install these accessories when you install Internet Explorer.

The CD also contains the Internet Client SDK, a must-have online reference for all serious web authors. The SDK is a complete electronic reference for all the main authoring techniques discussed in this book, including Dynamic HTML, Cascading Style Sheets, VBScript, and ActiveX controls. See Appendix A for more information on using the SDK. The SDK is available on the CD in two forms. It comes preinstalled, which means you can access information in the SDK directly from the CD. This helps save on hard drive space. It also comes as a setup program so you can install the SDK on your hard drive.

The CD also includes copies of all the sample web pages and scripts presented in this book. Feel free to explore, use, abuse, tweak, borrow, and swipe the material to your heart's content.

Finally, the CD contains an HTML version of the book, along with a couple of handy references for electronic resources, colors, and special characters.

HOW TO START THE CD

There's not much to "starting" the CD:

1.   Put the CD in your CD-ROM drive.

2.   Open My Computer, and then double-click on the icon for your CD-ROM drive.

3.   Double-click on the HTML page named BrowseMe.htm. You'll see the opening screen, as shown in Figure D-1.

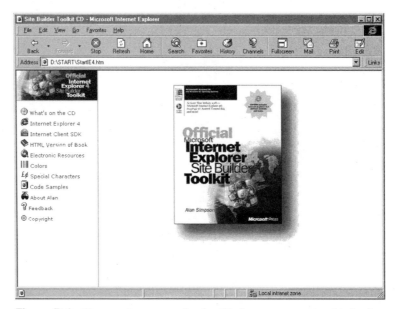

Figure D-1. *The opening screen for the CD that accompanies this book.*

As with any web site, you can click on whatever topic interests you. Here's a quick rundown of the main topics available from the opening screen:

■   *Internet Explorer 4*—takes you to a page that explains how to install Internet Explorer 4.

■   *Internet Client SDK*—takes you to a page that explains how to install the Internet Client SDK on your computer and how to access the preinstalled version on the CD. (See also Appendix A.)

■   *HTML Version Of Book*—takes you to a page that explains how to open and read an online version of the book.

■   *Electronic Resources*—gives you quick, one-click access to additional resources on the Internet.

■ *Colors*—shows you how to create your own colors and find the RGB triplet or decimal value to express any of 140-plus colors. (See also Appendix C.)

■ *Special Characters*—a list of the codes for showing special characters such as © and ® and ¥. (See also Appendix B.)

■ *Code Samples*—takes you to a list of the sample web pages in the book.

Because the entire CD is essentially a web site, you should have no problem getting around and finding things. Just be sure to open the BrowseMe.htm page with Internet Explorer 4 to get the full benefit of all that the CD has to offer.

Index

ALAN SIMPSON

Alan Simpson has written more than 60 books dealing with computers and the Internet. His books are published throughout the world in over a dozen languages and have sold millions of copies. Prior to writing books full time, Alan was a teacher and software consultant. He lives in San Diego, California, with his wife and their two young children.

The manuscript for this book was prepared using Microsoft Word 97. Pages were composed by Microsoft Press, with text in Garamond and display type in Helvetica Black. Composed pages were delivered to the printer as electronic prepress files.

Cover Graphic Designer

Gregory J. Erickson

Cover Illustrator

Robin Bartholick

Interior Graphic Designer

Kim Eggleston

Interior Graphic Artist

Joel Panchot

Principal Compositors

Abby Hall, Steven Hopster

Principal Proofreader / Copy Editor

Devon Musgrave

Indexer

Hugh Maddocks

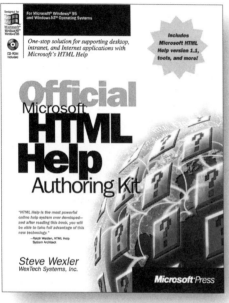

Discover *in a* *flash* how to publish on your **intranet** or the **World Wide Web!**

U.S.A. **$24.99**
U.K. £22.99
Canada $34.99
ISBN 1-57231-629-2

The OFFICIAL MICROSOFT® FRONTPAGE® 98 BOOK gives you all the information you need to use Microsoft FrontPage 98 quickly and effectively. Packed with creative insights, this book is the ideal guide to follow as you build great Web pages.

The OFFICIAL MICROSOFT FRONTPAGE 98 BOOK shows you how to:

- Employ wizards, templates, page editing, graphics, themes, forms, and FrontPage components to create awesome-looking Web pages

- Populate Web sites with Microsoft Office–based documents and files

- Create and edit frames-based sites using the WYSIWYG interface FrontPage Editor

- Take advantage of FrontPage's advanced features: ActiveX™ controls, Java applets, plug-ins, PowerPoint® animations, VBScript, JavaScript, your own HTML code, and more

- Manage your Web site

- Use Personal Web Server and the server administrator

Microsoft®*Press*

When you have
questions about
Microsoft®
FrontPage® 98,
here's the answer book.

One-Stop Reference

Covers Microsoft FrontPage 98 for Windows® 95
and Windows NT® 4.0

In-Depth
Reference
and Inside
Tips from
the Software
Experts

Running
Microsoft®
FrontPage 98

Jim Buyens

Microsoft Press

U.S.A.	**$39.99**
U.K.	£37.49 [V.A.T. included]
Canada	$55.99
ISBN 1-57231-645-4	

It's packed with everything from quick, clear instructions for new users to comprehensive answers for power users. And it's complete in one volume. With RUNNING MICROSOFT FRONTPAGE 98, you'll learn to:

- Create your own Web pages and sites the easy way—unique tools such as FrontPage components make it simple even for beginners.

- Start fast with simple pages and quickly move up to building full-fledged sites.

- Use Microsoft FrontPage 98 to streamline and automate site management chores—especially helpful if you're a Webmaster.

- Spare yourself the usual Web server problems—this is the one book that covers crucial server connection issues.

RUNNING MICROSOFT FRONTPAGE 98 makes information easy to find and understand. The enclosed CD is full of must-have extras, including a searchable version of the book. Get RUNNING MICROSOFT FRONTPAGE 98. And get the authoritative handbook you'll keep by your computer and use every day.

Microsoft *Press*

To really **understand** Dynamic HTML,
go to the source.

U.S.A.	**$39.99**
U.K.	£37.49 [V.A.T. included]
Canada	$55.99
ISBN	1-57231-686-1

Web sites developed for Microsoft® Internet Explorer 4 can offer the most advanced, most exciting interactive features, thanks to Dynamic HTML—a technology that author Scott Isaacs helped create. Now he's written the programmer's bible on this important subject. Part technical manifesto, part application sourcebook, INSIDE DYNAMIC HTML starts by laying out core concepts and tools—HTML, cascading style sheets, and scripting fundamentals. Subsequent chapters explain the object model and element collections.

But beyond presenting the technical blueprint to Dynamic HTML, this book delivers what you need most—provocative, reusable techniques that demonstrate key benefits of the new object model. What's more, the companion CD-ROM supplies you with a copy of Microsoft Internet Explorer 4.0, the Internet Client Software Development Kit (SDK), sample scripts, and more. INSIDE DYNAMIC HTML is for Web developers, sophisticated content providers, users of JavaScript and other scripting tools, and anyone else who wants the lowdown on this widely embraced approach to a livelier Web. Give your pages the power of dynamic content. Get INSIDE DYNAMIC HTML.

Microsoft *Press*

IMPORTANT—READ CAREFULLY BEFORE OPENING SOFTWARE PACKET(S). By opening the sealed packet(s) containing the software, you indicate your acceptance of the following Microsoft License Agreement.

MICROSOFT LICENSE AGREEMENT
(Book Companion CD)

This is a legal agreement between you (either an individual or an entity) and Microsoft Corporation. By opening the sealed software packet(s) you are agreeing to be bound by the terms of this agreement. If you do not agree to the terms of this agreement, promptly return the unopened software packet(s) and any accompanying written materials to the place you obtained them for a full refund.

MICROSOFT SOFTWARE LICENSE

1. GRANT OF LICENSE. Microsoft grants to you the right to use one copy of the Microsoft software program included with this book (the "SOFTWARE") on a single terminal connected to a single computer. The SOFTWARE is in "use" on a computer when it is loaded into the temporary memory (i.e., RAM) or installed into the permanent memory (e.g., hard disk, CD-ROM, or other storage device) of that computer. You may not network the SOFTWARE or otherwise use it on more than one computer or computer terminal at the same time.

2. COPYRIGHT. The SOFTWARE is owned by Microsoft or its suppliers and is protected by United States copyright laws and international treaty provisions. Therefore, you must treat the SOFTWARE like any other copyrighted material (e.g., a book or musical recording) except that you may either (a) make one copy of the SOFTWARE solely for backup or archival purposes, or (b) transfer the SOFTWARE to a single hard disk provided you keep the original solely for backup or archival purposes. You may not copy the written materials accompanying the SOFTWARE.

3. OTHER RESTRICTIONS. You may not rent or lease the SOFTWARE, but you may transfer the SOFTWARE and accompanying written materials on a permanent basis provided you retain no copies and the recipient agrees to the terms of this Agreement. You may not reverse engineer, decompile, or disassemble the SOFTWARE. If the SOFTWARE is an update or has been updated, any transfer must include the most recent update and all prior versions.

4. DUAL MEDIA SOFTWARE. If the SOFTWARE package contains more than one kind of disk (3.5", 5.25", and CD-ROM), then you may use only the disks appropriate for your single-user computer. You may not use the other disks on another computer or loan, rent, lease, or transfer them to another user except as part of the permanent transfer (as provided above) of all SOFTWARE and written materials.

5. SAMPLE CODE. If the SOFTWARE includes Sample Code, then Microsoft grants you a royalty-free right to reproduce and distribute the sample code of the SOFTWARE provided that you: (a) distribute the sample code only in conjunction with and as a part of your software product; (b) do not use Microsoft's or its authors' names, logos, or trademarks to market your software product; (c) include the copyright notice that appears on the SOFTWARE on your product label and as a part of the sign-on message for your software product; and (d) agree to indemnify, hold harmless, and defend Microsoft and its authors from and against any claims or lawsuits, including attorneys' fees, that arise or result from the use or distribution of your software product.

DISCLAIMER OF WARRANTY

The SOFTWARE (including instructions for its use) is provided "AS IS" WITHOUT WARRANTY OF ANY KIND. MICROSOFT FURTHER DISCLAIMS ALL IMPLIED WARRANTIES INCLUDING WITHOUT LIMITATION ANY IMPLIED WARRANTIES OF MERCHANTABILITY OR OF FITNESS FOR A PARTICULAR PURPOSE. THE ENTIRE RISK ARISING OUT OF THE USE OR PERFORMANCE OF THE SOFTWARE AND DOCUMENTATION REMAINS WITH YOU.

IN NO EVENT SHALL MICROSOFT, ITS AUTHORS, OR ANYONE ELSE INVOLVED IN THE CREATION, PRODUCTION, OR DELIVERY OF THE SOFTWARE BE LIABLE FOR ANY DAMAGES WHATSOEVER (INCLUDING, WITHOUT LIMITATION, DAMAGES FOR LOSS OF BUSINESS PROFITS, BUSINESS INTERRUPTION, LOSS OF BUSINESS INFORMATION, OR OTHER PECUNIARY LOSS) ARISING OUT OF THE USE OF OR INABILITY TO USE THE SOFTWARE OR DOCUMENTATION, EVEN IF MICROSOFT HAS BEEN ADVISED OF THE POSSIBILITY OF SUCH DAMAGES. BECAUSE SOME STATES/COUNTRIES DO NOT ALLOW THE EXCLUSION OR LIMITATION OF LIABILITY FOR CONSEQUENTIAL OR INCIDENTAL DAMAGES, THE ABOVE LIMITATION MAY NOT APPLY TO YOU.

U.S. GOVERNMENT RESTRICTED RIGHTS

The SOFTWARE and documentation are provided with RESTRICTED RIGHTS. Use, duplication, or disclosure by the Government is subject to restrictions as set forth in subparagraph (c)(1)(ii) of The Rights in Technical Data and Computer Software clause at DFARS 252.227-7013 or subparagraphs (c)(1) and (2) of the Commercial Computer Software — Restricted Rights 48 CFR 52.227-19, as applicable. Manufacturer is Microsoft Corporation, One Microsoft Way, Redmond, WA 98052-6399.

If you acquired this product in the United States, this Agreement is governed by the laws of the State of Washington.

Should you have any questions concerning this Agreement, or if you desire to contact Microsoft Press for any reason, please write: Microsoft Press, One Microsoft Way, Redmond, WA 98052-6399.

Register Today!

Return this
*Official Microsoft® Internet Explorer 4
Site Builder Toolkit*
registration card for
a Microsoft Press® catalog

U.S. and Canada addresses only. Fill in information below and mail postage-free. Please mail only the bottom half of this page.

1-57231-572-5A   *OFFICIAL MICROSOFT® INTERNET*   *Owner Registration Card*
                            EXPLORER 4 SITE BUILDER TOOLKIT

NAME

INSTITUTION OR COMPANY NAME

ADDRESS

CITY   STATE   ZIP

Microsoft Press
Quality Computer Books

For a free catalog of
Microsoft Press® products, call
1-800-MSPRESS